Shipping

code of federal regulations

46

PARTS 156 TO 165

Revised as of October 1, 1997

CONTAINING
A CODIFICATION OF DOCUMENTS
OF GENERAL APPLICABILITY
AND FUTURE EFFECT

AS OF OCTOBER 1, 1997

With Ancillaries

Published by
the Office of the Federal Register
National Archives and Records
Administration

as a Special Edition of
the Federal Register

U.S. GOVERNMENT PRINTING OFFICE
WASHINGTON : 1997

For sale by U.S. Government Printing Office
Superintendent of Documents, Mail Stop: SSOP, Washington, DC 20402-9328

Table of Contents

Cite this Code: **CFR**

To cite the regulations in this volume use title, part and section number. Thus, **46 CFR** **159.001–1** *refers to title 46, part 159, section 001–1.*

Explanation

The Code of Federal Regulations is a codification of the general and permanent rules published in the Federal Register by the Executive departments and agencies of the Federal Government. The Code is divided into 50 titles which represent broad areas subject to Federal regulation. Each title is divided into chapters which usually bear the name of the issuing agency. Each chapter is further subdivided into parts covering specific regulatory areas.

Each volume of the Code is revised at least once each calendar year and issued on a quarterly basis approximately as follows:

Title 1 through Title 16..as of January 1
Title 17 through Title 27 ....as of April 1
Title 28 through Title 41 ....as of July 1
Title 42 through Title 50..as of October 1

The appropriate revision date is printed on the cover of each volume.

LEGAL STATUS

The contents of the Federal Register are required to be judicially noticed (44 U.S.C. 1507). The Code of Federal Regulations is prima facie evidence of the text of the original documents (44 U.S.C. 1510).

HOW TO USE THE CODE OF FEDERAL REGULATIONS

The Code of Federal Regulations is kept up to date by the individual issues of the Federal Register. These two publications must be used together to determine the latest version of any given rule.

To determine whether a Code volume has been amended since its revision date (in this case, October 1, 1997), consult the "List of CFR Sections Affected (LSA)," which is issued monthly, and the "Cumulative List of Parts Affected," which appears in the Reader Aids section of the daily Federal Register. These two lists will identify the Federal Register page number of the latest amendment of any given rule.

EFFECTIVE AND EXPIRATION DATES

Each volume of the Code contains amendments published in the Federal Register since the last revision of that volume of the Code. Source citations for the regulations are referred to by volume number and page number of the Federal Register and date of publication. Publication dates and effective dates are usually not the same and care must be exercised by the user in determining the actual effective date. In instances where the effective date is beyond the cut-off date for the Code a note has been inserted to reflect the future effective date. In those instances where a regulation published in the Federal Register states a date certain for expiration, an appropriate note will be inserted following the text.

OMB CONTROL NUMBERS

The Paperwork Reduction Act of 1980 (Pub. L. 96-511) requires Federal agencies to display an OMB control number with their information collection request.

Many agencies have begun publishing numerous OMB control numbers as amendments to existing regulations in the CFR. These OMB numbers are placed as close as possible to the applicable recordkeeping or reporting requirements.

OBSOLETE PROVISIONS

Provisions that become obsolete before the revision date stated on the cover of each volume are not carried. Code users may find the text of provisions in effect on a given date in the past by using the appropriate numerical list of sections affected. For the period before January 1, 1986, consult either the List of CFR Sections Affected, 1949–1963, 1964–1972, or 1973–1985, published in seven separate volumes. For the period beginning January 1, 1986, a "List of CFR Sections Affected" is published at the end of each CFR volume.

INCORPORATION BY REFERENCE

What is incorporation by reference? Incorporation by reference was established by statute and allows Federal agencies to meet the requirement to publish regulations in the Federal Register by referring to materials already published elsewhere. For an incorporation to be valid, the Director of the Federal Register must approve it. The legal effect of incorporation by reference is that the material is treated as if it were published in full in the Federal Register (5 U.S.C. 552(a)). This material, like any other properly issued regulation, has the force of law.

What is a proper incorporation by reference? The Director of the Federal Register will approve an incorporation by reference only when the requirements of 1 CFR part 51 are met. Some of the elements on which approval is based are:

(a) The incorporation will substantially reduce the volume of material published in the Federal Register.

(b) The matter incorporated is in fact available to the extent necessary to afford fairness and uniformity in the administrative process.

(c) The incorporating document is drafted and submitted for publication in accordance with 1 CFR part 51.

Properly approved incorporations by reference in this volume are listed in the Finding Aids at the end of this volume.

What if the material incorporated by reference cannot be found? If you have any problem locating or obtaining a copy of material listed in the Finding Aids of this volume as an approved incorporation by reference, please contact the agency that issued the regulation containing that incorporation. If, after contacting the agency, you find the material is not available, please notify the Director of the Federal Register, National Archives and Records Administration, Washington DC 20408, or call (202) 523–4534.

CFR INDEXES AND TABULAR GUIDES

A subject index to the Code of Federal Regulations is contained in a separate volume, revised annually as of January 1, entitled CFR INDEX AND FINDING AIDS. This volume contains the Parallel Table of Statutory Authorities and Agency Rules (Table I), and Acts Requiring Publication in the Federal Register (Table II). A list of CFR titles, chapters, and parts and an alphabetical list of agencies publishing in the CFR are also included in this volume.

An index to the text of "Title 3—The President" is carried within that volume.

The Federal Register Index is issued monthly in cumulative form. This index is based on a consolidation of the "Contents" entries in the daily Federal Register.

A List of CFR Sections Affected (LSA) is published monthly, keyed to the revision dates of the 50 CFR titles.

REPUBLICATION OF MATERIAL

There are no restrictions on the republication of material appearing in the Code of Federal Regulations.

INQUIRIES

For a legal interpretation or explanation of any regulation in this volume, contact the issuing agency. The issuing agency's name appears at the top of odd-numbered pages.

For inquiries concerning CFR reference assistance, call 202-523-5227 or write to the Director, Office of the Federal Register, National Archives and Records Administration, Washington, DC 20408.

SALES

The Government Printing Office (GPO) processes all sales and distribution of the CFR. For payment by credit card, call 202-512-1800, M-F, 8 a.m. to 4 p.m. e.s.t. or fax your order to 202-512-2233, 24 hours a day. For payment by check, write to the Superintendent of Documents, Attn: New Orders, P.O. Box 371954, Pittsburgh, PA 15250-7954. For GPO Customer Service call 202-512-1803.

RAYMOND A. MOSLEY,
Director,
Office of the Federal Register.

October 1, 1997.

THIS TITLE

Title 46—SHIPPING is composed of nine volumes. The parts in these volumes are arranged in the following order: Parts 1–40, 41–69, 70–89, 90–139, 140–155, 156–165, 166–199, 200–499 and 500 to End. The first seven volumes containing parts 1–199 comprise chapter I—Coast Guard, Department of Transportation. The eighth volume, containing parts 200 to 499, includes chapter II—Maritime Administration, DOT. The ninth volume, containing part 500 to End, includes chapter IV—Federal Maritime Commission. The contents of these volumes represent all current regulations codified under this title of the CFR as of October 1, 1997.

Subject indexes appear for subchapter B—Merchant Marine Officers and Seamen, subchapter C—Uninspected Vessels, and subchapter D—Tank Vessels following the subchapters in parts 1–40; for subchapter F—Marine Engineering following the subchapter in parts 41–69; for subchapter H—Passenger Vessels following the subchapter in parts 70–89; for subchapter I—Cargo and Miscellaneous Vessels, subchapter I–A—Mobile Offshore Drilling Units, subchapter J—Electrical Engineering, subchapter K—Small Passenger Vessels Carrying More Than 150 Passengers or With Overnight Accommodations for More Than 49 Passengers, and subchapter L—Offshore Supply Vessels following the subchapters in parts 90–139 for subchapter S—Subdivision and Stability, subchapter T—Small Passenger Vessels (Under 100 Gross Tons), and subchapter W—Lifesaving Appliances and Arrangements following the subchapters in parts 166–199.

For this volume, Kenneth R. Payne was Chief Editor. The Code of Federal Regulations publication program is under the direction of Frances D. McDonald, assisted by Alomha S. Morris.

Would you like to know...

if any changes have been made to the *Code of Federal Regulations* or what documents have been published in the *Federal Register* without reading the *Federal Register* every day? If so, you may wish to subscribe to the *LSA* (List of CFR Sections Affected), the *Federal Register Index,* or both.

LSA

The *LSA* (List of CFR Sections Affected) is designed to lead users of the *Code of Federal Regulations* to amendatory actions published in the *Federal Register*. The *LSA* is issued monthly in cumulative form. Entries indicate the nature of the changes—such as revised, removed, or corrected. **$27 per year.**

Federal Register Index

The index, covering the contents of the daily *Federal Register,* is issued monthly in cumulative form. Entries are carried primarily under the names of the issuing agencies. Significant subjects are carried as cross-references. **$25 per year.**

A finding aid is included in each publication which lists *Federal Register* page numbers with the date of publication in the *Federal Register.*

Superintendent of Documents Subscription Order Form

Order Processing Code:
*5421

❑ **YES,** send me the following indicated subscriptions for one year:

____ **LSA (List of CFR Sections Affected),** (LCS) for $27 per year.

____ **Federal Register Index** (FRSU) $25 per year.

The total cost of my order is $ _____
Price is subject to change. International customers please add 25%.

_____
Company or personal name

_____
Street address

_____
City, State, ZIP code

_____
Daytime phone with area code

_____
Purchase order No.   (optional)

(Includes regular shipping and handling.)

For privacy check box below:

❑ Do not make my name available to other mailers

Check method of payment:

❑ Check payable to Superintendent of Documents

❑ GPO Deposit Account ⬚⬚⬚⬚⬚⬚⬚—⬚

❑ VISA ❑ MasterCard ⬚⬚⬚⬚ (expiration date)

_____
Credit card No.   (must be 20 digits)

Thank you for your order!

_____
Authorizing signature   1/97

Mail To: Superintendent of Documents
PO Box 371954
Pittsburgh PA 15250-7954

Fax your orders (202) 512–2250

Phone your orders (202) 512–1800

Title 46—Shipping

(This book contains parts 156 to 165)

1

Chapter I—Coast Guard, Department of Transportation—Continued

SUBCHAPTER P—MANNING OF VESSELS [RESERVED]

SUBCHAPTER Q—EQUIPMENT, CONSTRUCTION, AND MATERIALS: SPECIFICATIONS AND APPROVAL

SUBCHAPTER P—MANNING OF VESSELS [RESERVED]
SUBCHAPTER Q—EQUIPMENT, CONSTRUCTION, AND MATERIALS: SPECIFICATIONS AND APPROVAL

PART 159—APPROVAL OF EQUIPMENT AND MATERIALS

Subpart 159.001—General

AUTHORITY: 46 U.S.C. 3306, 3703; 49 CFR 1.45, 1.46; Section 159.001-9 also issued under the authority of 44 U.S.C. 3507.

SOURCE: 44 FR 73043, Dec. 17, 1979, unless otherwise noted.

Subpart 159.001—General

§ 159.001-1 Purpose.

(a) This part contains the procedures for the approval of equipment and materials when that equipment or material is inspected or tested by an independent laboratory or by the manufacturer of the equipment or material.

(b) [Reserved]

§ 159.001-2 Right of appeal.

Any person directly affected by a decision or action taken under this subchapter, by or on behalf of the Coast Guard, may appeal to the Chief, Marine Safety and Environmental Protection (Commandant (G-M)) as provided in § 1.03-15 of this chapter.

[CGD 93-055, 61 FR 13927, Mar. 28, 1996, as amended by CGD 96-041, 61 FR 50733, Sept. 27, 1996]

§ 159.001-3 Definitions.

As used in this part:

Classification society means an organization involved in the inspection of ships and ship equipment, and which, as determined by the Commandant, meets the standards in IMO Resolution A.739(18).

Independent laboratory means an organization which meets the standards for acceptance in § 159.010-3 of this part, and which is accepted by the Coast

5

Guard for performing certain tests and inspections. In addition to commercial testing laboratories, the Commandant may also accept classification societies and agencies of governments that are involved in the inspection and testing of marine safety equipment that meet the requirements of § 159.010–3.

Memorandum of Understanding (MOU) is an agreement between the Coast Guard and a laboratory that specifies the approval functions a recognized independent laboratory performs for the Coast Guard and the recognized independent laboratory's working arrangements with the Coast Guard.

Recognized independent laboratory means an independent laboratory which meets the standards of § 159.010–3, and is accepted by the Coast Guard to perform certain equipment approval functions on behalf of the Coast Guard, as described in a Memorandum of Understanding signed by the laboratory and the Coast Guard in accordance with § 159.010–7(b).

[CGD 93–055, 61 FR 13927, Mar. 28, 1996]

§ 159.001-4 Incorporation by reference.

(a) Certain materials is incorporated by reference into this part with the approval of the Director of the Federal Register under 5 U.S.C. 552(a) and 1 CFR part 51. To enforce any edition other than that specified in paragraph (b) of this section, the Coast Guard must publish notice of change in the FEDERAL REGISTER; and the material must be available to the public. All approved material is available for inspection at the Office of the Federal Register, 800 North Capitol Street NW, suite 700, Washington, DC, and at the U.S. Coast Guard, Lifesaving and Fire Safety Standards Division (G–MSE–4), 2100 Second Street SW, Washington, DC 20593–0001, and is available from the sources indicated in paragraph (b) of this section.

(b) The material approved for incorporation by reference in this part (subchapter) and the sections affected are as follows:

INTERNATIONAL MARITIME ORGANIZATION (IMO)
Publications Section, 4 Albert Embankment, London SE1 7SR, United Kingdom
Resolution A.739(18), Guidelines for the Authorization of Organizations Acting on Be-

half of the Administration, November 22, 1993: 159.001-3

[CGD 93–055, 61 FR 13928, Mar. 28, 1996, as amended by CGD 96–041, 61 FR 50733, Sept. 27, 1996; CGD 97–057, 62 FR 51048, Sept. 30, 1997]

§ 159.001-5 Correspondence and applications.

Unless otherwise specified, all correspondence and applications in connection with approval and testing of equipment and materials must be addressed to: Commandant (G–MSE–4), U.S. Coast Guard, 2100 Second Street SW, Washington, DC 20593–0001, Telephone: (202) 267–1444, Facsimile: (202) 267–1069, Electronic mail: MVI–3/G–M@cgsmtp.uscg.mil.

[CGD 93–055, 61 FR 13928, Mar. 28, 1996, as amended by CGD 96–041, 61 FR 50733, Sept. 27, 1996]

§ 159.001-7 Substituted procedures.

(a) The Commandant may substitute the procedures in this part for the procedures in any other part of this subchapter. Each person known to be affected by the substitution shall be informed that the procedures in this part apply.

(b) [Reserved]

§ 159.001-9 OMB Control Numbers assigned pursuant to the Paperwork Reduction Act.

(a) *Purpose.* This section collects and displays the control numbers assigned to information collection and record-keeping requirements in this subchapter by the Office of Management and Budget (OMB) pursuant to the Paperwork Reduction Act of 1980, (44 U.S.C. 3501 et seq.). The Coast Guard intends that this section comply with the requirements of 44 U.S.C. 3507(f) which requires that agencies display a current control number assigned by the Director of the OMB for each approved agency information collection requirement.

(b) *Display.*

46 CFR part or section where identified or described	Current OMB control No.
§ 159.007–11.13	2115–0090
§ 160.002–5	2115–0090
§ 160.047–5	2115–0090
§ 160.048–5	2115–0090
§ 160.050–5	2115–0090
§ 160.052–7	2115–0090

46 CFR part or section where identified or described	Current OMB control No.
§ 160.053–4	2115–0090
§ 160.055–4	2115–0090
§ 160.064–6	2115–0090
§§ 161.001 through 161.010	2115–0121
§ 161.171–15	2115–0141
§ 161.171–23	2115–0141
§§ 162.001 through 161.018	2115–0525
§ 162.041	2115–0525
§ 162.043	2115–0525
§ 164.012–13	2115–0121
§ 164.019–5	2115–0141
§ 164.019–7	2115–0141
§ 164.019–9	2115–0141
§ 164.019–13	2115–0141
§ 164.019–15	2115–0141
§ 164.023–15	2115–0141

[49 FR 38121, Sept. 27, 1984, as amended by CGD 86–057, 51 FR 35220, Oct. 2, 1986; CGD 84–068, 58 FR 29492, May 20, 1993]

Subpart 159.005—Approval Procedures

§ 159.005–1 Purpose.

(a) This subpart contains the procedures by which the Coast Guard approves equipment and materials under other subparts of this subchapter that require—

(1) Preapproval inspections and tests by an independent laboratory;

(2) Preapproval inspections and tests by the manufacturer; or

(3) No preapproval inspections or tests.

(b) [Reserved]

§ 159.005–3 Application for preapproval review.

(a) Each manufacturer of equipment or material who seeks Coast Guard approval under an applicable subpart must submit an application that meets § 159.005–5 to the Commandant unless—

(1) The subpart contains a list of independent laboratories;

(2) The subpart does not require Coast Guard review prior to testing; and

(3) The manufacturer meets the requirements of paragraph (b) of this section.

(b) If the applicable subpart contains a list of independent laboratories and does not specifically require preapproval review by the Coast Guard, the manufacturer may have the tests performed by a listed laboratory and submit the report required by § 159.005–11 to the Commandant.

§ 159.005–5 Preapproval review: Contents of application.

(a) Each application must contain the following:

(1) The name and address of the manufacturer and the factory where the finished equipment or material is produced.

(2) One or more of the following as required by the applicable subpart:

(i) Two sets of general plans of the equipment or material.

(ii) Two sets of specifications of the equipment or material.

(iii) A sample of the equipment or material accompanied by a written description of its components.

(3) A statement signed by the manufacturer or the manufacturer's representative, that an official representative of the Coast Guard is allowed access to the place of manufacture and to the place of test to verify the information submitted in the application or to witness tests.

(4) If the material submitted under paragraph (a)(2) of this section contains confidential commercial information that could cause substantial competitive harm if released to the public, a statement to the effect that the material is considered privileged and confidential under exemption (b)(4) of the Freedom of Information Act (5 U.S.C. 552), and that it should not be released to anyone other than the original submitter.

(b) If the equipment or material is required by the subpart to be inspected and tested by an independent laboratory, the application must contain the following additional information:

(1) The name and address of a laboratory that meets § 159.010–3(a) and that is selected by the manufacturer to perform or supervise the inspections and tests.

(2) If the laboratory has not been accepted previously for inspecting and testing the manufacturer's equipment or material under the applicable subpart, the completed application under § 159.010–5(a).

[44 FR 73043, Dec. 17, 1979, as amended by CGD 85–205, 62 FR 25545, May 9, 1997]

§ 159.005-7 Preapproval review: Coast Guard action.

(a) If approval inspections and tests are required under the applicable subpart, the Commandant takes the following action:

(1) If the Commandant determines from the application that the equipment or material appears to meet the design requirements of an applicable subpart or appears to have equivalent performance characteristics, and that the laboratory meets § 159.010-3(a), the Commandant informs the manufacturer that the required approval inspections and tests may be conducted.

(2) If the Commandant determines from the application for approval that the equipment or material does not appear to meet the design requirements of an applicable subpart or does not appear to have equivalent performance characteristics, or that the laboratory does not meet § 159.010-3(a), the Commandant informs the manufacturer of the reason why the equipment or material is not acceptable for approval inspections and tests or why the laboratory is not accepted.

(b) If no approval inspections or tests are required under the applicable subpart, the Commandant—

(1) Takes action in accordance with § 159.005-13; or

(2) Informs the manufacturer of additional information required before action under § 159.005-13 can be taken.

(c) An item of equipment or material that does not meet all of the requirements of this subchapter for design or performance may be approved by the Commandant if it has equivalent performance characteristics. The item has equivalent performance characteristics if the application and any approval tests prescribed by the Commandant, in place of or in addition to the approval tests required by this subchapter, demonstrate to the satisfaction of the Commandant that the item is at least as effective as one that meets the requirements of this subchapter.

[44 FR 73043, Dec. 17, 1979, as amended by CGD 85-205, 62 FR 25545, May 9, 1997]

§ 159.005-9 Approval inspections and tests.

(a) Each manufacturer of equipment or material that is required to be subjected to approval inspections and tests must—

(1) If the applicable subpart requires the equipment or material to be inspected or tested, have the approval inspections or tests performed;

(2) If the applicable subpart requires the equipment or material to be inspected or tested by an independent laboratory, insure that a laboratory accepted by the Commandant performs or supervises the approval inspections or tests;

(3) Bear all costs of the approval inspections and tests;

(4) If requested, advise the Commandant of the time, date, and place of each approval inspection or test, or both, before the inspection or test is performed; and

(5) After completion of the approval inspections and tests, submit to the Commandant—

(i) A test report that meets § 159.005-11;

(ii) At least two sets of specifications of the materisl as inspected or tested or at least two sets of plans of the equipment as inspected or tested that meet § 159.005-12; and

(iii) A description of the quality control procedures that will be in effect during the production of the equipment or material.

(b) [Reserved]

§ 159.005-11 Approval inspection or test report: Contents.

(a) Each approval inspection or test report must contain the following:

(1) The name of the manufacturer.

(2) If the inspections or tests are performed or supervised by an independent laboratory, the name and address of the laboratory.

(3) The trade name, product designation (such as model numbers), and a brief description of the equipment or material inspected or tested.

(4) The time, date, and place of each approval inspection and test.

(5) The name and title of each person performing, supervising, and witnessing the approval inspections or tests.

(6) The performance data for each test required in the applicable subpart, including a description of each failure.

(7) A description or photographs of the procedures and apparatus used in the inspections or tests, or a reference to another document that contains an appropriate description or photographs.

(8) At least one photograph that shows an overall view of the equipment or material submitted for approval and other photographs that show—

(i) Design details; and

(ii) Each occurrence of damage or deformation to the equipment or material that occurred during the approval tests.

(b) Each inspection or test report must bear an attestation that the inspections or tests were conducted as required by the applicable subpart and that the report contains no known errors, omissions, or false statements. The attestation must be signed by:

(1) The manufacturer or manufacturer's representative, if the inspection or tests are conducted by the manufacturer; or

(2) The chief officer of the laboratory, or the chief officer's representative, if the inspection or tests were conducted by an independent laboratory.

NOTE: A false representation on a report is a ground for suspension or withdrawal of approval of the equipment or material. A false representation is also punishable as a crime under 18 U.S.C. 1001.

§159.005–12 Plans.

(a) Each set of plans under §159.005–9(a)(5)(ii) for equipment must include the following:

(1) An assembly drawing or general arrangement drawing.

(2) A description of each component of the equipment that includes the name, the manufacturer, and the part identification of each component in—

(i) A detail drawing;

(ii) A bill of material or parts list; or

(iii) A specification for that component.

(3) A list of the drawings and specifications in the set of plans, including each revision, and the date of that list.

(4) If a manufacturer's instructions or manual is required in the applicable subpart, a copy of the instructions or manual.

(b) [Reserved]

§159.005–13 Equipment or material: Approval.

(a) If from analysis of the material and data required to be submitted under this subpart, the Commandant determines that the equipment or material meets the applicable subpart or has equivalent performance characteristics in accordance with §159.005–7(c), the Commandant—

(1) Approves the equipment or material;

(2) Issues a certificate of approval to the manufacturer under §2.75–5 of this chapter;

(3) Retains one set of approved plans and returns all others to the manufacturer; and

(4) Publishes a record of the approval in "Equipment Lists." The most recent edition of "Equipment Lists" U.S. Coast Guard Publication M16714.3 (series) is available from the Superintendent of Documents, U.S. Government Printing Office, P.O. Box 371954, Pittsburgh, PA 15250–7954.

(b) If from analysis of the material and data submitted the Commandant determines that the equipment or material does not meet the applicable subpart, the Commandant informs the manufacturer of the reason why that equipment or material does not meet the subpart.

(c) If an independent laboratory performs the approval inspections or tests, the Commandant will notify the laboratory of the actions taken under paragraph (a) or (b) of this section, unless the manufacturer specifically requests that the laboratory not be notified.

[44 FR 73043, Dec. 17, 1979, as amended by CGD 93–055, 61 FR 13928, Mar. 28, 1996; CGD 85–205, 62 FR 25545, May 9, 1997]

§159.005–15 Approval of equipment or material: Suspensions, withdrawals, and terminations.

(a) The Commandant suspends an approval issued under this subchapter in accordance with §2.75–40 of this chapter, withdraws an approval issued under this subchapter in accordance with §2.75–50(a) of this chapter, and terminates an approval issued under this subchapter in accordance with § 2.75–50(b) of this chapter.

(b) [Reserved]

Subpart 159.007—Production Inspection and Tests of Approved Equipment and Materials

§ 159.007-1 Purpose.

(a) This subpart contains the procedures under which production inspections and tests of approved equipment or materials are to be performed under this subchapter.

(b) [Reserved]

§ 159.007-3 Production inspections and tests: Independent laboratory's procedures.

(a) The manufacturer may follow an independent laboratory's procedures for production inspections and tests if those procedures—

(1) Meet or exceed the production inspection and test requirements of the applicable subpart or are equivalent to those inspections and tests;

(2) Include labeling or marking the equipment or material when the equipment or material meets the inspection and test procedures of the laboratory; and

(3) Are accepted by the Commandant under § 159.007-7(b).

(b) [Reserved]

§ 159.007-5 Production inspections and tests: Application for acceptance.

(a) If the applicable subpart requires production inspections and tests by an independent laboratory, the manufacturer must select a laboratory and submit an application for acceptance that meets § 159.010-5(a) unless the laboratory—

(1) Is listed in the subpart; or

(2) Is accepted by the Commandant for approval inspections and tests of the equipment or material under § 159.005-7(a)(1).

(b) If the manufacturer wants to follow the laboratory's procedures for production inspections and tests instead of meeting the Coast Guard procedures under this subchapter, the application must contain a description of those procedures.

§ 159.007-7 Application for acceptance for production inspections and tests: Coast Guard action.

(a) From the information submitted with the application, the Commandant determines whether or not the laboratory is accepted for production inspections and tests. The Commandant informs the manufacturer of the results of this determination, if the Commandant does not accept a laboratory, the reason for the disapproval will be given.

(b) From the description of the laboratory's procedures for production inspections and tests, the Commandant determines whether or not those procedures are accepted. The Commandant informs the manufacturer of the results of this determination. If the Commandant does not accept the laboratory's procedures, the reasons why they are not accepted will be given.

§ 159.007-9 Production inspections and tests.

(a) If the applicable subpart requires the production inspections and tests to be performed or supervised by an independent laboratory, the manufacturer shall insure that all required production inspections and tests are performed or supervised by an independent laboratory accepted by the Commandant.

(b) If the applicable subpart does not require an independent laboratory to perform the production inspections and tests, the manufacturer shall have those inspections and tests performed.

(c) Unless alternative procedures have been accepted by the Commandant under § 159.007-3 each production inspection and test must be performed or supervised in accordance with the applicable subpart.

(d) The manufacturer shall admit a Coast Guard inspector to any place where approved equipment is manufactured, for the purpose of verifying that the equipment is being manufactured in accordance with the approved plans and the requirements of this subchapter.

[44 FR 73043, Dec. 17, 1979, as amended by CGD 85-205, 62 FR 25545, May 9, 1997]

§ 159.007–11 Production inspections and tests: Yearly report.

(a) When the manufacturer uses the production inspection and test procedures in an applicable subpart he must submit a yearly report. The report is not required when inspection and test procedures approved under § 159.007–3 are used.

(b) The report must include the following:

(1) A list of all inspections and tests performed;

(2) A summary of the results of each group of inspections or tests;

(3) A detailed description of any test failures; and

(4) A statement whether or not all required tests were performed.

§ 159.007–13 Production inspections and tests: Records.

(a) The manufacturer must have a completed record with the following information for each production inspection and test:

(1) The time, date and place of each inspection and test.

(2) The name and title of each person performing, supervising and witnessing the inspections or tests.

(3) The performance data for each test required in the applicable subpart, including a description of each failure.

(4) A description or photographs of the procedures and apparatus used in the inspections or tests.

(b) The manufacturer must retain each record under this section for at least 60 months after the month in which the inspection or test was conducted.

(c) The records must be made available for examination by the Commandant upon request.

Subpart 159.010—Independent Laboratory: Acceptance, Recognition, and Termination

§ 159.010–1 Purpose.

This subpart contains the following:

(a) The standards and procedures under which the Coast Guard accepts an independent laboratory that a manufacturer proposes to use.

(b) The standards and procedures under which a laboratory is accepted as a recognized laboratory under applicable subparts.

(c) The circumstances under which the acceptance or recognition of a laboratory is terminated.

[CGD 93–055, 61 FR 13928, Mar. 28, 1996]

§ 159.010–3 Independent laboratory: Standards for acceptance.

(a) To be accepted by the Coast Guard as an independent laboratory, a laboratory must—

(1) Be engaged, as a regular part of its business, in performing inspections and tests that are the same as or similar to the inspections and tests required in the applicable subpart;

(2) Have or have access to the apparatus, facilities, personnel, and calibrated instruments that are necessary to inspect and test the equipment or material under the applicable subpart;

(3) Not be owned or controlled by—

(i) The manufacturer of the equipment or material to be inspected or tested under this subchapter or any manufacturer of similar equipment or material;

(ii) A vendor of the equipment or material to be inspected or tested under this subchapter or a vendor of similar equipment or material; or

(iii) A supplier of materials to the manufacturer;

(4) Not be dependent on Coast Guard acceptance under this subchapter to remain in business; and

(5) Not advertise or promote the manufacturer's equipment or material that the laboratory inspects and tests under this subchapter.

(b) [Reserved]

§ 159.010–5 Independent laboratory: application for acceptance.

(a) Each application for acceptance of an organization as an independent laboratory must contain the following:

(1) The name and address of the organization.

(2) A list of the equipment or material that the organization would inspect, or test, or both, under this subchapter.

(3) A description of the organization's experience and its qualifications for conducting the inspections and tests required in the applicable subpart.

11

(4) A description of the apparatus and facilities available to the organization for conducting those inspections and tests.

(5) If instruments are used in the required tests and inspections, a description of the instrument calibration program applying to those instruments.

(6) The position titles of personnel who are to perform, supervise, or witness those inspections or tests, along with the training and experience required for personnel in those positions.

(7) A statement signed by the chief officer of the organization or the chief officer's representative, that an official representative of the Coast Guard is allowed access upon request to the place where tests and inspections take place, to verify the information submitted in the application, or to witness tests and inspections.

(b) Each application for acceptance as an independent laboratory that is not submitted by an agency of a state or another national government, or by a classification society, must also contain the following:

(1) The name and address of each subsidiary and division of the organization, or a statement that none are involved in the testing or manufacturing of equipment approved under this subchapter.

(2) The name, title, address, and principal business activity of each of the organization's officers and directors, and the name, address, and principal business activity of each person, company, or corporation that owns at least three-percent interest in the organization or in a company or corporation that controls the organization.

[CGD 93–055, 61 FR 13928, Mar. 28, 1996]

§ 159.010-7 Recognized independent laboratory: Memorandum of Understanding.

(a) Only laboratories that have entered into an MOU with the Coast Guard may perform the functions of a recognized laboratory under this chapter.

(b) An independent laboratory seeking to become a recognized independent laboratory must submit a signed MOU to the Commandant that includes—

(1) A statement of purpose;

(2) An identification and description of the parties involved;

(3) A description of the problem resolution and appeals processes;

(4) A description of the process for measuring effectiveness and efficiency of the program under the MOU;

(5) The effective date of the MOU and terms for its termination;

(6) A statement to the effect that the MOU is not an exclusive agreement between the recognized independent laboratory and the Coast Guard;

(7) An agreement to conduct comparison testing with other recognized laboratories as directed by the Coast Guard, no more often than twice each year, with the laboratory bearing the cost of sample acquisition and testing;

(8) A statement as to how the costs of implementing the MOU will be borne; and

(9) A description of each party's responsibilities for—

(i) Equipment review and approval;

(ii) Coast Guard oversight of the recognized independent laboratory's procedures and processes;

(iii) Coordination between the parties;

(iv) Developing and maintaining regulations and standards;

(v) Handling review and approval of new and novel items not anticipated by existing regulations and standards;

(vi) Testing and inspection facilities and procedures;

(vii) Production quality control; and

(viii) Maintenance of records.

(c) The signature on the MOU required by paragraph (b) of this section must be that of the chief officer of the independent laboratory or the chief officer's representative. The Commandant or an authorized representative of the Commandant will review the MOU to ensure that it contains the information required by paragraph (b) of this section, and that the substantive provisions submitted in compliance with that paragraph are equivalent to those contained in other MOUs signed by the Commandant. If the Commandant determines that the MOU is acceptable and the independent laboratory is capable of carrying out the equipment approval functions identified in the MOU in accordance with all appropriate requirements, the Commandant or authorized representative may at his discretion sign the MOU. Where qualitative tests or determinations are required for approval or follow-up, provision must be made for conducting comparison tests with other recognized laboratories.

(d) Copies of MOUs signed by the Commandant in accordance with this part and of lists of independent laboratories which have been accepted as recognized laboratories but which have not yet been added to the lists included in this subchapter may be obtained at the address listed in §159.001–5.

[CGD 93–055, 61 FR 13928, Mar. 28, 1996; 61 FR 15868, Apr. 9, 1996]

§159.010–11 Changes in the laboratory's qualifications.

(a) If any of the information submitted under §159.010–5(a) changes, the laboratory shall notify the Commandant in writing of each change within 30 days after the change has occurred.

(b) If any change in the independent laboratory occurs which affects its performance under the MOU required under §159.010–7, the laboratory shall notify the Commandant in writing within 30 days after the change occurs. The Commandant may terminate the MOU, or may require amendments or revisions.

[CGD 93–055, 61 FR 13929, Mar. 28, 1996]

§159.010–15 Contracting inspections and tests or transferrals to another laboratory or person.

(a) No independent laboratory may contract or transfer to another person or laboratory the performance or supervision of inspections or tests, or both, required under an applicable subpart for which it is accepted or listed unless—

(1) A request in writing regarding the contract or transfer is submitted to the Commandant before the contract is executed or the transfer is completed; and

(2) The Commandant notifies the laboratory in writing that the contract or the transfer is allowed.

(b) [Reserved]

§159.010–17 Termination of acceptance or recognition of an independent laboratory.

The acceptance or recognition of a laboratory terminates if the laboratory—

(a) Requests termination;

(b) Is no longer in business;

(c) Knowingly fails to perform or supervise an inspection or test, or both, as required in an applicable subpart;

(d) Knowingly attests to the lack of errors, omissions, or false statement of an approval test report that contains errors omissions, or false statements;

(e) Does not meet the requirements of §159.010–3(a);

(f) Does not comply with §159.010–11;

(g) Contracts or transfers the performance or supervision of required inspections or tests to another laboratory or person without the approval of the Commandant; or

(h) Fails to, or in the opinion of the Commandant is unable to, carry out its responsibilities under an MOU required by §159.010–7.

[CGD 93–055, 61 FR 13929, Mar. 28, 1996]

§159.010–19 Termination of acceptance or recognition: Procedure.

(a) If the Coast Guard receives evidence of grounds for termination of acceptance or recognition of an independent laboratory under §159.010–17, the Commandant will notify the laboratory that termination is under consideration. The laboratory may submit written comments to the Commandant within 21 days of receipt of the notification. The Commandant will take all timely written comments into account before taking final action in the matter, and in no case will the Commandant take final action until at least 30 days after the laboratory has received the notification. Any final action taken by the Commandant is final agency action on the matter.

(b) If a deficiency could materially affect the validity of an approval issued under an applicable subpart, the Commandant may temporarily suspend the acceptance of the laboratory and may direct the holder of the certificate of approval to cease claiming that the items tested or inspected by the laboratory are Coast Guard approved, pending a final decision in the matter.

[CGD 93–055, 61 FR 13929, Mar. 28, 1996]

PART 160—LIFESAVING EQUIPMENT

Subpart 160.023—Hand Combination Flare and Smoke Distress Signals

160.023-1 Incorporations by reference.
160.023-2 Type.
160.023-3 Materials, workmanship, construction and performance requirements.
160.023-4 Approval and production tests.
160.023-5 Labeling and marking.
160.023-6 Container.
160.023-7 Procedure for approval.

Subpart 160.024—Pistol-Projected Parachute Red Flare Distress Signals

160.024-1 Incorporations by reference.
160.024-2 Type.
160.024-3 Materials, workmanship, construction, and performance requirements.
160.024-4 Approval and production tests.
160.024-5 Marking.
160.024-7 Procedure for approval.

Subpart 160.026—Water, Emergency Drinking (in Hermetically Sealed Containers), for Merchant Vessels

160.026-1 Applicable specifications and standards.
160.026-2 Type.
160.026-3 Container.
160.026-4 Water.
160.026-5 Marking.
160.026-6 Sampling, inspection, and tests of production lots.
160.026-7 Procedure for approval.

Subpart 160.027—Life Floats for Merchant Vessels

160.027-2 Type.
160.027-3 Additional requirements for life floats.
160.027-7 Pre-approval tests for alternate platform designs.

Subpart 160.028—Signal Pistols for Red Flare Distress Signals

160.028-2 Type.
160.028-3 Materials, workmanship, construction, and performance requirements.
160.028-4 Approval and production tests.
160.028-5 Marking.
160.028-6 Container.
160.028-7 Procedure for approval.

Subpart 160.031—Line-Throwing Appliance, Shoulder Gun Type (and Equipment)

160.031-1 Incorporation by reference.
160.031-2 Type and size.
160.031-3 Materials, construction, workmanship, and performance requirements.
160.031-4 Equipment for shoulder gun type line-throwing appliance.
160.031-5 Approval and production tests.

160.031-6 Marking.
160.031-7 Procedure for approval.

Subpart 160.032—Davits for Merchant Vessel

160.032-1 Applicable specifications.
160.032-2 General requirements for davits.
160.032-3 Construction of davits.
160.032-4 Capacity of davits.
160.032-5 Inspection and testing of davits.
160.032-6 Procedure for approval of davits.

Subpart 160.033—Mechanical Disengaging Apparatus, Lifeboat, for Merchant Vessels

160.033-1 Applicable specifications.
160.033-2 General requirements for mechanical disengaging apparatus.
160.033-3 Construction of mechanical disengaging apparatus.
160.033-4 Inspection and testing of mechanical disengaging apparatus.
160.033-5 Procedure for approval of mechanical disengaging apparatus.

Subpart 160.035—Lifeboats for Merchant Vessels

160.035-1 Applicable specifications.
160.035-2 General requirements for lifeboats.
160.035-3 Construction of steel oar-propelled lifeboats.
160.035-5 Construction of steel motor-propelled lifeboats with and without radio cabin.
160.035-6 Construction of aluminum oar-, hand-, and motor-propelled lifeboats.
160.035-8 Construction of fibrous glass reinforced plastic (F.R.P.) oar-, hand-, and motor-propelled lifeboats.
160.035-9 Cubic capacity of lifeboats.
160.035-10 Number of persons allowed in lifeboats.
160.035-11 Inspection and testing of lifeboats.
160.035-12 Additional preapproval tests required for F.R.P. lifeboats.
160.035-13 Testing and inspection after approval.
160.035-14 Procedure for approval of lifeboats.

Subpart 160.036—Hand-Held Rocket-Propelled Parachute Red Flare Distress Signals

160.036-1 Incorporation by reference.
160.036-2 Type.
160.036-3 Materials, workmanship, construction and performance requirements.
160.036-4 Approval and production tests.
160.036-5 Marking.
160.036-6 Container.
160.036-7 Procedure for approval.

17

AUTHORITY: 46 U.S.C. 2103, 3306, 3703 and 4302; E.O. 12234, 45 FR 58801, 3 CFR, 1980 Comp., p. 277; 49 CFR 1.46.

EDITORIAL NOTE: At 62 FR 51209–51216, Sept. 30, 1997, §§160.006–1, 160.006–4, 160.006–5, 160.013–4, 160.013–6, 160.016–3, 160.024–6, 160.035–4, 160.035–7, 160.041–7, 160.043–7, 160.044–6, 160.056–5, 160.058–6, 160.061–6, and 160.061–7 were removed and part 160 was amended, effective Oct. 30, 1997. The superseded text consisting of the removed, revised, and amended sections remaining in effect until Oct. 30, 1997, appears in the October 1, 1996, revision of title 46 parts 156–165.

Subpart 160.001—Life Preservers, General

§ 160.001-1 Scope.

(a) This subpart contains the general:

(1) Characteristics of life preservers (Type I personal flotation devices (PFDs));

(2) Approval procedures for life preservers; and

(3) Production oversight requirements for life preservers.

(b) Other subparts in this part specify the detailed requirements for standard type life preservers and may supplement the requirements in this subpart.

[CGD 95–028, 62 FR 51209, Sept. 30, 1997]

EFFECTIVE DATE NOTE: At 62 FR 51209, Sept. 30, 1997, § 160.001–1 was revised, effective Oct. 30, 1997.

§ 160.001-2 General characteristics of life preservers.

(a) A life preserver must be of such construction, material and workmanship that it can perform its intended function in all weathers and at all temperatures which may be expected in the normal usage of the life preserver. All components used in the construction of a life preserver must meet the applicable requirements of subpart 164.019 of the chapter.

(b) A life preserver must be capable of supporting a minimum of 22 pounds in fresh water for 48 hours.

(c) Life preservers which depend upon loose or granulated material for buoyancy are prohibited.

(d) A life preserver must be:

(1) Simple in design;

(2) Capable of being:

(i) Worn inside-out,

(ii) worn clearly in only one way, or

(iii) Donned correctly without demonstration, instructions, or assistance by at least 75 percent of persons unfamiliar with the design; and

(3) Capable of being quickly adjusted for a secure fit to the body of wearers for which it is intended.

(e) A life preserver shall support the wearer in the water in an upright or slightly backward position, and shall provide support to the head so that the face of an unconscious or exhausted person is held above the water.

(f) A life preserver shall be capable of turning the wearer, upon entering the water, to a safe flotation position as described in paragraph (e) of this section.

(g) A life preserver shall not be appreciably deteriorated or rendered unable to perform its intended function by common oils or oil products.

(h) A life preserver shall be of a highly visible color, such as Indian Orange, International Orange, or Scarlet Munsell Red.

(i) A life preserver shall be of such construction, materials, and workmanship as to be at least equivalent to a standard type life preserver described in detail by other subparts in this part.

(j) Each thread in a life preserver regulated under subparts 160.002, 160.005 and 160.055 of this part must meet the requirements of a Federal or military specification in table 164.023-5(a) of this chapter. Only one kind of thread may be used in each seam.

[CGFR 66–33, 31 FR 15297, Dec. 6, 1966, as amended by CGD 78–012, 43 FR 27152, June 22, 1978; CGD 78–174b, 54 FR 50320, Dec. 5, 1989; CGD 84–068, 58 FR 29493, May 20, 1993; CGD 95–028, 62 FR 51209, Sept. 30, 1997]

EFFECTIVE DATE NOTE: At 62 FR 51209, Sept. 30, 1997, § 160.001-2 was amended by revising paragraphs (b) and (d), effective Oct. 30, 1997.

§ 160.001-3 Procedure for approval.

(a) *General.* Designs of life preservers are approved only by the Commandant, U.S. Coast Guard. Manufacturers seeking approval of a life preserver design shall follow the procedures of this section and subpart 159.005 of this chapter.

(b) Each application for approval of a life preserver must contain the information specified in § 159.005-5 of this chapter. The application and, except as provided in paragraphs (c) and (d)(2) of this section, a prototype life preserver must be submitted to the Commandant for preapproval review. If a similar design has already been approved, the Commandant may waive the preapproval review under §§ 159.005-5 and 159.005-7 of this chapter.

(c) If the life preserver is of a standard design, as described by subpart 160.002, 160.005, or 160.055, the application:

(1) Must include the following: A statement of any exceptions to the standard plans and specifications, including drawings, product description, construction specifications, and/or bill of materials.

(2) Need not include: The information specified in § 159.005-5(a)(2).

(d) If the life preserver is of a nonstandard design, the application must include the following:

(1) Plans and specifications containing the information required by § 159.005-12 of this chapter, including drawings, product description, construction specifications, and bill of materials.

(2) The information specified in § 159.005-5(a)(2) (i) through (iii) of this chapter, except that, if preapproval review has been waived, the manufacturer is not required to send a prototype PFD sample to the Commandant.

(3) Performance testing results of the design performed by an independent laboratory, that has a Memorandum of Understanding with the Coast Guard under § 159.010-7 of this subchapter covering the in-water testing of personal flotation devices, showing equivalence to the standard design's performance in all material respects.

(4) The Approval Type sought (Type I or Type V).

(5) Any special purpose(s) for which the life preserver is designed and the vessel(s) or vessel type(s) on which its use is intended.

(6) Buoyancy and other relevant tolerances to be complied with during production.

(7) The text of any optional marking to be included on the life preserver in

addition to the markings required by the applicable approval subpart.

(8) For any conditionally approved life preserver, the intended approval condition(s).

(e) The description of quality control procedures required by § 159.005–9 of this chapter may be omitted if the manufacturer's planned quality control procedures meet the requirements of those accepted by the Commandant for the independent laboratory performing production inspections and tests.

(f) *Waiver of tests.* A manufacturer may request that the Commandant waive any test prescribed for approval under the applicable subpart. To request a waiver, the manufacturer must submit to the Commandant and the laboratory described in § 159.010, one of the following:

(1) Satisfactory test results on a PFD of sufficiently similar design as determined by the Commandant.

(2) Engineering analysis demonstrating that the test for which a waiver is requested is not appropriate for the particular design submitted for approval or that, because of its design or construction, it is not possible for the PFD to fail that test.

[CGD 95–028, 62 FR 51209, Sept. 30, 1997]

EFFECTIVE DATE NOTE: At 62 FR 51209, Sept. 30, 1997, § 160.001–3 was revised, effective Oct. 30, 1997.

§ 160.001–5 **Production oversight.**

(a) *General.* Production tests and inspections must be conducted in accordance with this section, subpart 159.007 of this chapter, and if conducted by an independent laboratory, the independent laboratory's procedures for production inspections and tests as accepted by the Commandant. The Commandant may prescribe additional production tests and inspections necessary to maintain quality control and to monitor compliance with the requirements of this subchapter.

(b) *Oversight.* In addition to responsibilities set out in part 159 of this chapter and the accepted laboratory procedures for production inspections and tests, each manufacturer of a life preserver and each laboratory inspector shall comply with the following, as applicable:

(1) *Manufacturer.* Each manufacturer must—

(i) Perform all tests and examinations necessary to show compliance with this subpart and subpart under which the life preserver is approved on each lot before any inspector's tests and inspection of the lot;

(ii) Follow established procedures for maintaining quality control of the materials used, manufacturing operations, and the finished product; and

(iii) Allow an inspector to take samples of completed units or of component materials for tests required by this subpart and for tests relating to the safety of the design.

(2) *Laboratory.* An inspector from the accepted laboratory shall oversee production in accordance with the laboratory's procedures for production inspections and tests accepted by the Commandant. During production oversight, the inspector shall not perform or supervise any production test or inspection unless—

(i) The manufacturer has a valid approval certificate; and

(ii) The inspector has first observed the manufacturer's production methods and any revisions to those methods.

(3) At least quarterly, the inspector shall check the manufacturer's compliance with the company's quality control procedures, examine the manufacturer's required records, and observe the manufacturer perform each of the required production tests.

(c) *Test facilities.* The manufacturer shall provide a suitable place and apparatus for conducting the tests and inspections necessary to determine compliance of life preservers with this subpart. The manufacturer shall provide means to secure any test that is not continuously observed, such as the 48 hour buoyancy test. The manufacturer must have the calibration of all test equipment checked in accordance with the test equipment manufacturer's recommendation and interval but not less than at least once every year.

(d) *Lots.* A lot may not consist of more than 1000 life preservers. A lot number must be assigned to each group of life preservers produced. Lots must be numbered serially. A new lot must be started whenever any change in materials or a revision to a production method is made, and whenever any substantial discontinuity in the production process occurs. The lot number assigned, along with the approval number, must enable the PFD manufacturer to determine the supplier's identifying information for the component lot.

(e) *Samples.* (1) From each lot of life preservers, manufacturers shall randomly select a number of samples from completed units at least equal to the applicable number required by table 160.001-5(e) for buoyancy testing. Additional samples must be selected for any tests, examinations, and inspections required by the laboratory's production inspections and tests procedures.

TABLE 160.001-5(e)—SAMPLING FOR BUOYANCY TESTS

Lot size	Number of life preservers in sample
100 and under	1
101 to 200	2
201 to 300	3
301 to 500	4
501 to 750	6
751 to 1000	8

(2) For a lot next succeeding one from which any sample life preserver failed the buoyancy test, the sample shall consist of not less than ten specimen life preservers to be tested for buoyancy in accordance with paragraph (f) of this section.

(f) *Buoyancy test.* The buoyancy of the life preservers must be determined by measuring the upward force exerted by the individual submerged unit. The buoyancy measurement must be made at the end of the 24 or 48 hours of submersion, as specified in the applicable approval subpart, during which period the pad inserts must not be disturbed.

(g) *Buoyancy required.* The buoyancy must meet the requirements of the applicable approval subpart.

(h) *Lot inspection.* On each lot, the laboratory inspector shall perform a final lot inspection to be satisfied that the life preservers meet this subpart. Each lot must demonstrate—

(1) First quality workmanship;

(2) That the general arrangement and attachment of all components, such as body straps, closures, tie tapes, and drawstrings, are as specified in the approved plans and specifications;

(3) Compliance with the marking requirements in the applicable approval subpart; and

(4) The information pamphlet specified in 33 CFR part 181 subpart G, if required, is securely attached to the device, with the PFD selection information visible and accessible prior to purchase.

(i) *Lot acceptance.* When the independent laboratory has determined that the life preservers in the lot are of a type officially approved in the name of the company, and that such life preservers meet the requirements of this subpart, they shall be plainly marked in waterproof ink with the independent laboratory's name or identifying mark.

(j) *Lot rejection.* Each nonconforming unit must be rejected. If three or more nonconforming units are rejected for the same kind of defect, lot inspection must be discontinued and the lot rejected. The inspector must discontinue lot inspection and reject the lot if examination of individual units or the records for the lot shows noncompliance with either this subchapter or the laboratory's or the manufacturer's quality control procedures. A rejected unit or lot may be resubmitted for testing and inspection if the manufacturer first removes and destroys each defective unit or, if authorized by the laboratory, reworks the unit or lot to correct the defect. A rejected lot or rejected unit may not be sold or offered for sale under the representation that it meets this subpart or that it is Coast Guard-approved.

[CGD 95-028, 62 FR 51210, Sept. 30, 1997]

EFFECTIVE DATE NOTE: At 62 FR 51210, Sept. 30, 1997, § 160.001-5 was added, effective Oct. 30, 1997.

Subpart 160.002—Life Preservers, Kapok, Adult and Child (Jacket Type), Models 3 and 5

§ 160.002-1 Incorporation by reference.

(a) *Specifications and standards.* This subpart makes reference to the following documents:

(1) Military Specifications:

MIL–W–530—Webbing, Textile, Cotton. General Purpose, Natural or in Colors.

(2) Federal Specification:

L–P–375—Plastic Film, Flexible, Vinyl Chloride.

(3) Federal Standards:

No. 191—Textile Test Methods.
No. 751A—Stitches, Seams, and Stitchings.

(4) Coast Guard specifications:

164.003—Kapok, Processed.

(b) *Plans.* The following plans, of the issue in effect on the date life preservers are manufactured, form a part of this specification:

Dwg. No. F–49–6–1:
  (Sheet 1) Cutting Pattern and General Arrangement (adult).
  (Sheet 1A) Alternate stitching of tapes and webbing (adult and child).
  (Sheet 2) Pad Detail (adult).
Dwg. No. F–49–6–5:
  (Sheet 1) Cutting Pattern and General Arrangement (child).
  (Sheet 2) Pad Detail (child).

(c) *Copies on file.* Copies of the specifications and plans referred to in this section shall be kept on file by the manufacturer, together with the certificate of approval. They shall be kept for a period consisting of the duration of approval and 6 months after termination of approval. The Coast Guard specifications and plans may be obtained upon request from the Commandant (G–MSE), U.S. Coast Guard, Washington, DC, 20593–0001. The Federal specifications and standards may be purchased from the Business Service Center, General Services Administration, Washington, DC, 20407. The Military specifications may be obtained from the Commanding Officer, Naval Supply Depot, 5801 Tabor Avenue, Philadelphia, Pa., 19120.

(d) [Reserved]

[CGFR 53–25, 18 FR 7855, Dec. 5, 1953, as amended by CGFR 65–16, 30 FR 10897, Aug. 21, 1965; CGD 78–012, 43 FR 27153, 27154, June 22, 1978; CGD 88–070, 53 FR 34535, Sept. 7, 1988; CGD 95–072, 60 FR 50467, Sept. 29, 1995; CGD 96–041, 61 FR 50733, Sept. 27, 1996]

§ 160.002–2 Size and models.

Each life preserver specified in this subpart is to be a:

(a) Model 3, adult, 24 ounces kapok; or

(b) Model 5, child, 16 ounces kapok.

[CGD 72–163R, 38 FR 8118, Mar. 28, 1973]

§ 160.002–3 Materials.

All components used in the construction of the life preserver must meet the applicable requirements of subpart 164.019 of this chapter and the following requirements apply to individual components;

(a) *Kapok.* The kapok shall be all new material complying with subpart 164.003 of this subchapter and shall be properly processed.

(b) *Envelope.* The life preserver envelope, or cover, shall be made of cotton drill. The color shall be Indian Orange, Cable No. 70072, Standard Color Card of America, issued by the Textile Color Association of the United States, Inc., 200 Madison Avenue, New York, N.Y., or Scarlet Munsell 7.5 Red 6/10. The drill shall be evenly dyed, and the fastness of the color to laundering, water, crocking, and light shall be rated "good" when tested in accordance with Federal Test Method Standard No. 191, Methods 5610, 5630, 5650, and 5660. After dyeing, the drill shall be treated with a mildew-inhibitor of the type specified in paragraph (j) of this section. The finished goods shall contain not more than 2 percent residual sizing or other non-fibrous material, shall weigh not less than 6.5 ounces per square yard, shall have a thread count of not less than 72 in the warp and 54 in the filling, and shall have a breaking strength (grab method) of not less than 105 pounds in the warp and 70 pounds in the filling. If it is proposed to treat the fabric with a fire-retardant substance, full details shall be submitted to the Commandant for determination as to what samples will be needed for testing.

(c) *Tunnel strip.* The tunnel strip shall be made of cotton drill conforming to the requirements for the envelope cover.

(d) *Pad covering.* The covering for the kapok pad inserts shall be flexible vinyl film not less than 0.006 inch in thickness meeting the requirements of specification L–P–375 for Type I film Type II, Class 1 film not less than 0.008 inch in thickness will also be acceptable.

(e) *Tie tapes and drawstrings.* The tie tapes at the neck and the lower drawstrings shall be made of 1¼-inch cotton tape weighing not less than 0.3 ounce per linear yard, and having a minimum breaking strength of 200 pounds. The tie tapes and drawstrings shall be treated with a mildew-inhibitor of the type specified in paragraph (j) of this section.

(f) *Body strap.* The body strap shall be made of one-inch cotton webbing having a minimum breaking strength of 400 pounds. One-inch cotton webbing meeting the requirements of specification MIL-W-530 for Type IIb webbing is acceptable. The complete body strap assembly shall have a minimum breaking strength of 360 pounds. The body strap shall be treated with a mildew-inhibitor of the type specified in paragraph (j) of this section.

(g) *Dee rings and snap hook.* The dee rings and snap hook shall be of brass, bronze, or stainless steel, and of the approximate size indicated by Dwg. F-49-6-1, Sheet 1. The snap hook spring shall be phosphor bronze or other suitable corrosion-resistant material. Dee ring ends shall be welded to form a continuous ring. The webbing opening of the snap hook shall be a continuous ring.

(h) *Reinforcing tape.* The reinforcing tape shall be made of ¾-inch cotton tape weighing not less than 0.18 ounce per linear yard and having a minimum breaking strength of 120 pounds, and shall be treated with a mildew-inhibitor of the type specified in paragraph (j) of this section.

(i) *Thread.* Each thread must meet the requirements of subpart 164.023 of this chapter. Only one kind of thread may be used in each seam.

(j) *Mildew-inhibitor.* The mildew-inhibitor shall be dihydroxydichlorodiphenylmethane, known commercially as Compound G-4, applied by the aqueous method. The amount of inhibitor deposited shall be not more than 1.50 percent and not less than 1.00 percent of the dry weight of the finished goods.

[CGFR 58-23, 23 FR 4627, June 25, 1958, as amended by CGFR 65-16, 30 FR 10897, Aug. 21, 1965; CGD 78-012, 43 FR 27153, 27154; June 22, 1978; CGD 84-068, 58 FR 29493, May 20, 1993]

§ 160.002-4 Construction.

(a) *General.* This specification covers life preservers which essentially consist of a vest-cut envelope containing pockets in which are enclosed pads of buoyant material, the life preserver being fitted with tapes and webbing to provide complete reversibility, proper adjustment for close fit to the bodies of various size wearers, and proper flotation characteristics to hold the wearer in an upright backward position with head and face out of water.

(b) *Envelope.* The envelope shall be of not more than two pieces, one piece for either side, cut to the pattern shown on Dwg. No. F-49-6-1, Sheet 1, for adult size, and Dwg. F-49-6-5, Sheet 1, for child size, joined by seams and stitching as shown on the drawing. A drawstring tunnel shall be formed by stitching a strip of the tunnel strip material as shown on the drawing. The ends of the tunnel strip shall be tucked under the reinforcing tape stitched around the end openings so there is no direct access to the pads from the outside. Three pockets shall be formed for insertion of the kapok pads. The two front pads shall be removable from the envelope when portions of the lower longitudinal seam are opened, and the back pad shall be removable when a portion of one armhole seam is opened.

(c) *Pad inserts*—(1) *Forming, sealing, and distribution of kapok.* The buoyant pad inserts shall be formed from two pieces of film cut to the patterns shown by Dwg. No. F-49-6-1, Sheet 2, for adult size, and Dwg. No. F-49-6-5, Sheet 2, for child size, which shall be heat-sealed tight. The heat-sealed pad seams shall show an adhesion of not less than 8 pounds when one inch strips cut across and perpendicular to the seams are pulled apart at a rate of separation of the clamping jaws of the test machine of 12 inches per minute. The pad inserts shall be filled with kapok distributed as follows:

TABLE 160.002-4 (C)(1)—DISTRIBUTION OF KAPOK IN PAD INSERTS

	Model 3 (minimum)	Model 5 (minimum)
Front pad (2):		
Lower section	5.25 oz. each	3.50 oz. each.

TABLE 160.002–4 (C)(1)—DISTRIBUTION OF KAPOK IN PAD INSERTS—Continued

	Model 3 (minimum)	Model 5 (minimum)
Upper section	3.75 oz. each	2.50 oz. each.
Back Pad	6.00 oz.	4.00 oz.
Total	24.00 oz.	16.00 oz.

(2) *Displacement of pad inserts.* The volume of the finished individual heat-sealed buoyant pad inserts shall be such as to provide buoyancy as set forth in the following table when tested in accordance with the method set forth in § 160.002–5(d), except that the period of submergence shall be only long enough to determine the displacement of the pads:

TABLE 160.002–4(C)(2)—VOLUME DISPLACEMENT OF SEALED PADS

	Model 3	Model 5
Front pads	12½ lbs. each±¾ lb ..	6½ lbs. each±½ lb.
Back pads	8 lbs. each±½ lb	4½ lbs. each±½ lb.

(d) *Tie tapes.* The tie tapes at the neck shall extend not less than 14 inches from the edge of the adult life preserver and not less than 12 inches from the edge of the child life preserver. They shall be stitched through both thicknesses of the envelope as shown by Dwg. No. F–49–6–1, Sheet 1, for adult size, and Dwg. No. F–49–6–5, Sheet 1, for child size, or by the alternate stitching shown on Sheet 1A. The free ends shall be doubled over and stitched in accordance with section G–G of Sheet 1.

(e) *Drawstrings.* The drawstrings at the waist shall extend not less than 8 inches from the edge of the life preserver and shall be secured in the drawstring tunnel as shown by Dwg. No. F–49–6–1, Sheet 1, for adult size, and Dwg. No. F–49–6–5, Sheet 1, for child size, or by the alternate stitching shown on Sheet 1A. The free ends shall be doubled over and stitched in accordance with section G–G of Sheet 1.

(f) *Body strap.* The body strap shall be fitted with a single Dee ring on one end with the arrangement of a snap hook and pre-threaded double Dee rings as shown on Dwg. No. F–49–6–1, Sheet 1, on the other. The body strap shall be stitched as shown on the drawings, and the edge of the single Dee ring shall be 20 inches from the center line for adult size and 15 inches for child size.

(g) *Reinforcing tape.* Binding tape shall be stitched approximately 15 inches for adult jackets and 12 inches for child jackets around the back of the neck, and also around the openings of the drawstring tunnel and around the bottom of the armholes, as indicated by the drawings.

(h) *Stitching.* All stitching shall be a short lock stitch conforming to Stitch Type 301 of Federal standard No. 751 and there shall be not less than 7, nor more than 9 stitches to the inch.

(i) *Workmanship.* Life preservers shall be of first-class workmanship and shall be free from any defects materially affecting their appearance or serviceability.

[CGFR 53–25, 18 FR 7856, Dec. 5, 1953, as amended by CGFR 58–23, 23 FR 4627, June 25, 1958; CGFR 65–16, 30 FR 10897, Aug. 21, 1965]

§ 160.002–5 **Sampling, tests, and inspections.**

(a) Production tests and inspections must be conducted by the manufacturer of a life preserver and the accepted laboratory inspector in accordance with this section and § 160.001–5.

(b) *Buoyancy test.* The buoyancy of the pad inserts from the life preserver shall be determined according to § 160.001–5(f) of this part with each compartment of the buoyant pad insert covers slit so as not to entrap air. The period of submersion must be at least 48 hours.

(c) *Buoyancy required.* The buoyant pad inserts from Model 3 adult life preservers shall provide not less than 25 pounds buoyancy in fresh water, and the pads from Model 5 child life preservers shall provide not less than 16.5 pounds buoyancy.

[CGD 95–028, 62 FR 51211, Sept. 30, 1997]

EFFECTIVE DATE NOTE: At 62 FR 51211, Sept. 30, 1997, § 160.002–5 was revised, effective Oct. 30, 1997.

§ 160.002–6 **Marking.**

Each life preserver must have the following clearly marked in waterproof ink on a front section:

(a) In letters three-quarters of an inch or more in height:

(1) Adult (for persons weighing over 90 pounds); or

(2) Child (for persons weighing less than 90 pounds).

(b) In letters that can be read at a distance of 2 feet:

Type I Personal Flotation Device.
Inspected and tested in accordance with U.S. Coast Guard regulations.
Kapok buoyant material provides a minimum buoyant force of (25 lb. or 16½ lb.).
Do not snag or puncture inner plastic cover.
Approved for use on all vessels by persons weighing (90 lb. or more, or less than 90 lb.).
U.S. Coast Guard Approval No. 160.002/(assigned manufacturer's No.)/(Revision No.); (Model No.).
(Name and address of manufacturer or distributor.).
(Lot No.).

[CGD 72–163R, 38 FR 8118, Mar. 28, 1973, as amended by CGD 75–008, 43 FR 9770, Mar. 9, 1978]

§ 160.002-7 Procedure for approval.

General. Manufacturers seeking approval of a life preserver design shall follow the procedures of subpart 159.005 of this chapter, as explained in § 160.001–3 of this part.

[CGD 95–028, 62 FR 51211, Sept. 30, 1997]

EFFECTIVE DATE NOTE: At 62 FR 51211, Sept. 30, 1997, § 160.002–7 was revised, effective Oct. 30, 1997.

Subpart 160.005—Life Preservers, Fibrous Glass, Adult and Child (Jacket Type), Models 52 and 56

§ 160.005-1 Incorporation by reference.

(a) *Specifications and Standards.* This subpart makes reference to the following documents:

(1) Federal Specification:

L-P-375C—Plastic Film, Flexible, Vinyl Chloride.

(2) Federal Standards:

No. 191—Textile Test Methods.
No. 751A—Stitches, Seams, and Stitchings.

(3) Military Specification:

MIL-W-530F—Webbing, Textiles, Cotton, General Purpose, Natural and in colors.
MIL-R-2766B—Batt, Fibrous Glass, Lifesaving Equipment.

(b) *Plans.* The following plans, of the issue in effect on the date life preservers are manufactured, form a part of this subpart:

Dwg. No. 160.005–1:
    (Sheet 1) Cutting Pattern and General Arrangement (Adult).
    (Sheet 2) Alternate Stitching of Tapes and Webbing (Adult and Child).
    (Sheet 3) Pad Detail (Adult).
    (Sheet 4) Cutting Pattern and General Arrangement (Child).
    (Sheet 5) Pad Detail (Child).

(c) *Copies on file.* Copies of the specifications and plans referred to in this section shall be kept on file by the manufacturer, together with the certificate of approval. They shall be kept for a period consisting of the duration of approval and 6 months after termination of approval. The Coast Guard plans may be obtained upon request from the Commandant, U.S. Coast Guard. The Federal specifications and standards may be purchased from the Business Service Center, General Services Administration, Washington, DC 20407. The Military specifications may be obtained from the Commanding Officer, Naval Supply Depot, 5801 Tabor Avenue, Philadelphia, Pa. 19120.

[CGFR 53–25, 18 FR 7862, Dec. 5, 1953, as amended by CGFR 65–16, 30 FR 10897, Aug. 21, 1965; CGD 78–012, 43 FR 27153, 27154, June 22, 1978; CGD 88–070, 53 FR 34535, Sept. 7, 1988]

§ 160.005-2 Size and model.

Each life preserver specified in this subpart is a:

(a) Model 52, adult, 46 ounces fibrous glass; or

(b) Model 56, child, 30 ounces fibrous glass.

[CGD 72–163R, 38 FR 8118, Mar. 28, 1973]

§ 160.005-3 Materials.

All components used in the construction of a life preserver must meet the applicable requirements of subpart 164.019 of this chapter and the following requirements apply to individual components:

(a) *Fibrous glass.* The fibrous glass shall be all new material complying with the requirements of Specification MIL-B-2766.

(b) *Envelope.* The life preserver envelope, or cover, shall be made of cotton drill. The color shall be Indian Orange, Cable No. 70072, Standard Color Card of America, issued by the Textile Color

Association of the United States, Inc., 200 Madison Avenue, New York, N.Y., or Scarlet Munsell 7.5 Red 6/10. The drill shall be evenly dyed, and the fastness of the color to laundering, water, crocking, and light shall be rated "good" when tested in accordance with Federal Test Method Standard No. 191, Methods 5610, 5630, 5650, and 5660. After dyeing, the drill shall be treated with a mildew-inhibitor of the type specified in paragraph (j) of this section. The finished goods shall contain not more than 2 percent residual sizing or other nonfibrous material, shall weigh not less than 6.5 ounces per square yard, shall have a thread count of not less than 72 in the warp and 54 in the filling, and shall have a breaking strength (grab method) of not less than 105 pounds in the warp and 70 pounds in the filling. If it is proposed to treat the fabric with a fire-retardant substance, full details shall be submitted to the Commandant for determination as to what samples will be needed for testing.

(c) *Tunnel strip.* The tunnel strip shall be made of cotton drill conforming to the requirements for the envelope cover.

(d) *Pad covering.* The covering for the fibrous glass pad inserts shall be flexible vinyl film not less than 0.006 inch in thickness meeting the requirements of specification L–P–375 for Type I film. Type II, Class 1 film not less than 0.008 inch in thickness will also be acceptable.

(e) *Tie tapes and drawstrings.* The tie tapes at the neck and the lower drawstrings shall be made of 1¼-inch cotton tape weighing not less than 0.3 ounce per linear yard, and having a minimum breaking strength of 200 pounds. The tie tapes and drawstrings shall be treated with a mildew-inhibitor of the type specified in paragraph (j) of this section.

(f) *Body strap.* The body strap shall be made of one-inch cotton webbing having a minimum breaking strength of 400 pounds. One-inch cotton webbing meeting the requirements of specification MIL–W–530 for Type IIb webbing is acceptable. The complete body strap assembly shall have a minimum breaking strength of 360 pounds. The body strap shall be treated with a mildew-in-hibitor of the type specified in paragraph (j) of this section.

(g) *Dee rings and snap hook.* The dee rings and snap hook shall be brass, bronze, or stainless steel, and of the approximate size indicated by Dwg. No. 160.005–1, Sheet 1. The snap hook spring shall be phosphor bronze or other suitable corrosion-resistant material. Dee ring ends shall be welded to form a continuous ring. The webbing opening of the snap hook shall be a continuous ring.

(h) *Reinforcing tape.* The reinforcing tape shall be made of ¾-inch cotton tape weighing not less than 0.18 ounce per linear yard and having a minimum breaking strength of 120 pounds, and shall be treated with a mildew-inhibitor of the type specified in paragraph (j) of this section.

(i) *Thread.* Each thread must meet the requirements of subpart 164.023 of this chapter. Only one kind of thread may be used in each seam.

(j) *Mildew-inhibitor.* The mildew-inhibitor shall be dihydroxydichlorodiphenylmethane, known commercially as Compound G–4, applied by the aqueous method. The amount of inhibitor deposited shall be not more than 1.50 percent and not less than 1.00 percent of the dry weight of the finished goods.

[CGFR 58–23, 23 FR 4628, June 25, 1958, as amended by CGFR 65–16, 30 FR 10898, Aug. 21, 1965; CGD 78–012, 43 FR 27153, 27154, June 22, 1978; CGD 84–068, 58 FR 29493, May 20, 1993]

§ 160.005–4 Construction.

(a) *General.* This specification covers life preservers which essentially consist of a vest-cut envelope containing pockets in which are enclosed pads of buoyant material, the life preserver being fitted with tapes and webbing to provide complete reversibility, proper adjustment for close fit to the bodies of various size wearers, and proper flotation characteristics to hold the wearer in an upright backward position with head and face out of water.

(b) *Envelope.* The envelope shall be of not more than two pieces, one piece for either side, cut to the pattern shown on Dwg. No. 160.005–1, Sheet 1, for adult size, and Sheet 4, for child size, joined by seams and stitching as shown on the drawing. A drawstring tunnel shall be formed by stitching a strip of the tunnel strip material as shown by the drawing. The ends of the tunnel strip shall be tucked under the reinforcing tape stitched around the end openings so there is no direct access to the pads from the outside. Three pockets shall be formed for insertion of the pads. The two front pads shall be removable from the envelope when portions of the lower longitudinal seam are opened, and the back pad shall be removable when a portion of one armhole seam is opened.

(c) *Pad inserts*—(1) *Forming, sealing, and distribution of fibrous glass.* The buoyant pad inserts shall be formed from two pieces of film cut to the patterns shown by Dwg. No. 160.005–1, Sheet 3, for adult size, and Sheet 5, for child size, which shall be heat-sealed tight. The heat-sealed pad seams shall show an adhesion of not less than 8 pounds when 1-inch strips cut across and perpendicular to the seams are pulled apart at a rate of separation of the clamping jaws of the test machine of 12 inches per minute. The pad inserts shall be filled with fibrous glass distributed as follows:

TABLE 160.005–4(C)(1)—DISTRIBUTION OF FIBROUS GLASS IN PAD INSERTS

	Model 52 (minimum)	Model 56 (minimum)
Front pad (2):		
Lower section	10.00 oz. each ...	6.50 oz. each.
Upper section	7.25 oz. each	4.75 oz. each.
Back pad	11.50 oz.	7.50 oz.
Total	46.00 oz.	30.00 oz.

(2) *Displacement of pad inserts.* The volume of the finished individual heat-sealed buoyant pad inserts shall be such as to provide buoyancy as set forth in the following table when tested in accordance with the method set forth in § 160.005–5(d), except that the period of submergence shall be only long enough to determine the displacement of the pads:

TABLE 160.005–4(C)(2)—VOLUME DISPLACEMENT OF SEALED PADS

	Model 52	Model 56
Front pads	12½ lbs. each ±¾ lb.	6½ lbs. each ±½ lbs.
Back pads	8 lbs. each ±½ lb.	4½ lbs. each ±½ lb.

(d) *Tie tapes.* The tie tapes at the neck shall extend not less than 14 inches from the edge of the adult life preserver and not less than 12 inches from the edge of the child life preserver. They shall be stitched through both thicknesses of the envelope as shown by Dwg. No. 160.005–1, Sheet 1, for adult size, and Sheet 4, for child size, or by the alternate stitching shown on Sheet 2. The free ends shall be doubled over and stitched in accordance with section E–E of Sheet 1.

(e) *Drawstrings.* The drawstrings at the waist shall extend not less than 8 inches from the edge of the life preserver and shall be secured in the drawstring tunnel as shown by Dwg. No. 160.005–1, Sheet 1, for adult size, and Sheet 4, for child size, or by the alternate stitching shown on Sheet 2. The free ends shall be doubled over and stitched in accordance with section E–E of Sheet 1.

(f) *Body strap.* The body strap shall be fitted with a single dee ring on one end and with the arrangement of a snap hook and prethreaded double dee rings as shown on Dwg. No. 160.005–1, Sheet 1, on the other. The body strap shall be stitched as shown on the drawings, and the edge of the single dee ring shall be 20 inches from the center line for adult size and 15 inches for child size.

(g) *Reinforcing tape.* Binding tape shall be stitched approximately 15 inches for adult life preservers and 12 inches for child life preservers around the back of the neck, and also around the openings of the drawstring tunnel and around the bottom of the arm holes as indicated by the drawings.

(h) *Stitching.* All stitching shall be a short lock stitch conforming to Stitch Type 301 of Federal Standard No. 751, and there shall be not less than 7, nor more than 9 stitches to the inch.

(i) *Workmanship.* Life preservers shall be of first-class workmanship and shall be free from any defects materially affecting their appearance or serviceability.

[CGFR 53–25, 18 FR 7863, Dec. 5, 1953, as amended by CGFR 58–23, 23 FR 4628, June 25, 1958; CGFR 65–16, 30 FR 10898, Aug. 21, 1965]

§ 160.005–5 Sampling, tests, and inspections.

(a) Production tests and inspections must be conducted by the manufacturer of a life preserver and the accepted laboratory inspector in accordance with this section and § 160.001–5.

(b) *Buoyancy test.* The buoyancy of the pad inserts from the life preserver shall be determined according to § 160.001–5(f) of this part with each compartment of the buoyant pad insert covers slit so as not to entrap air. The period of submersion must be at least 48 hours.

(c) *Buoyancy required.* The buoyant pad inserts from Model 3 adult life preservers shall provide not less than 25 pounds buoyancy in fresh water, and the pads from Model 5 child life preservers shall provide not less than 16.5 pounds buoyancy.

[CGD 95–028, 62 FR 51211, Sept. 30, 1997]

EFFECTIVE DATE NOTE: At 62 FR 51211, Sept. 30, 1997, § 160.005–5 was revised, effective Oct. 30, 1997.

§ 160.005–6 Marking.

Each life preserver must have the following clearly marked in waterproof lettering on a front section:

(a) In letters three-fourths inch or more in height:

(1) Adult (for persons weighing over 90 pounds); or

(2) Child (for persons weighing less than 90 pounds).

(b) In letters capable of being read at a distance of 2 feet:

Type I—Personal Flotation Device.
Inspected and tested in accordance with U.S. Coast Guard regulations.
Fibrous glass buoyant material provides a minimum buoyant force of (25 lb. or 16½ lb.).
Approved for use on all vessels by persons weighing (90 lb. or more, or less than 90 lb).
U.S. Coast Guard Approval No. 160.005/ (assigned manufacturer's No.)/(Revision No.).
(Model No.);
(Name and address of manufacturer or distributor.).
(Lot No.).

[CGD 163R, 38 FR 8118, Mar. 28, 1973, as amended by CGD 75–008, 43 FR 9770, Mar. 9, 1978]

§ 160.005–7 Procedure for approval.

General. Manufacturers seeking approval of a life preserver design shall follow the procedures of subpart 159.005 of this chapter, as explained in § 160.001–3 of this part.

[CGD 95–028, 62 FR 51211, Sept. 30, 1997]

EFFECTIVE DATE NOTE: At 62 FR 51211, Sept. 30, 1997, § 160.005–7 was revised, effective Oct. 30, 1997.

Subpart 160.006—Life Preservers: Repairing

SOURCE: 11 FR 187, Jan. 3, 1946; 11 FR 561, Jan. 12, 1946, unless otherwise noted.

§ 160.006–2 Repairing.

(a) *General.* No repairs, except in emergency, shall be made to an approved life preserver without advance notice to the Officer in Charge, Marine Inspection, of the district in which such repairs are to be made. Emergency repairs shall be reported as soon as practicable to the Officer in Charge, Marine Inspection.

(b) *Kind of repairs.* Except in emergency, tapes or straps may not be repaired, but may be renewed, and small holes, tears, or rips in the envelope cover fabric may be repaired, at the discretion of the Officer in Charge, Marine Inspection.

Subpart 160.010—Buoyant Apparatus for Merchant Vessels

SOURCE: CGD 79–167, 47 FR 41372, Sept. 20, 1982, unless otherwise noted.

§ 160.010–1 Incorporations by reference.

(a) Certain materials are incorporated by reference into this subpart with the approval of the Director of the Federal Register. The Office of the Federal Register publishes a table, "Material Approved for Incorporation by Reference," which appears in the Finding Aids section of this volume. In that table is found the date of the edition approved, citations to the particular sections of this part where the material is incorporated, addresses where the material is available, and the date of the approval by the Director of the

Federal Register. To enforce any edition other than the one listed in the table, notice of change must be published in the FEDERAL REGISTER and the material made available. All approved material is on file at the Office of the Federal Register, Washington, DC 20408, and at the U.S. Coast Guard, Lifesaving and Fire Safety Division (G–MSE–4), Washington, DC 20593.

(b) The materials approved for incorporation by reference in this subpart are:

NATIONAL BUREAU OF STANDARDS (NBS)
"The Universal Color Language" and "The Color Names Dictionary" in *Color: Universal Language and Dictionary of Names*, National Bureau of Standards Special Publication 440.

MILITARY SPECIFICATIONS
MIL–P–19644 C—Plastic Molding Material (Polystyrene Foam, Expanded Bead).
MIL–R–21607 C—Resins, Polyester, Low Pressure Laminating, Fire Retardant.
MIL–P–21929 B—Plastic Material, Cellular Polyurethane, Foam-In-Place, Rigid (2 and 4 Pounds per Cubic Foot).
MIL–P–40619 A—Plastic Material, Cellular, Polystyrene (For Buoyancy Applications).

[CGD 79–167, 47 FR 41372, Sept. 20, 1982, as amended by CGD 95–072, 60 FR 50467, Sept. 29, 1995; CGD 96–041, 61 FR 50733, Sept. 27, 1996]

§ 160.010-2 Definitions.

Buoyant apparatus. Buoyant apparatus is flotation equipment (other than lifeboats, liferafts, and personal flotation devices) designed to support a specified number of persons in the water, and of such construction that it retains its shape and properties and requires no adjustment or preparation for use. The types of buoyant apparatus generally in use are the box-float type and the peripheral-body type defined in paragraphs (b) and (c) of this section.

Box-float. Box-float is buoyant apparatus of a box-like shape.

Commandant (G–MSE–4). Commandant (G–MSE–4) is the Chief of the Lifesaving and Fire Safety Standards Division, Marine Safety and Environmental Protection.

Peripheral-body. Peripheral body is buoyant apparatus with a continuous body in the shape of either an ellipse or rectangle with a circular, elliptical, or rectangular body cross-section.

Inflatable buoyant apparatus. An inflatable buoyant apparatus is flotation equipment that depends on inflated compartments for buoyancy and is designed to support a specified number of persons completely out of the water.

[CGD 79–167, 47 FR 41372, Sept. 20, 1982, as amended by CGD 95–072, 60 FR 50466, Sept. 29, 1995; CGD 96–041, 61 FR 50733, Sept. 27, 1996; CGD 85–205, 62 FR 25545, May 9, 1997]

§ 160.010-3 Inflatable buoyant apparatus.

(a) *Design and performance.* To obtain Coast Guard approval, an inflatable buoyant apparatus must comply with subpart 160.151, with the following exceptions:

(1) *Canopy requirements (SOLAS Chapter III, regulation 38, paragraph 1.5 (III/38.1.5)).* It does not need a canopy.

(2) *Capacity (Regulation III/38.2.1).* The carrying capacity must be not less than four persons.

(3) *Floor insulation (Regulation III/39.2.2).* The floor may be uninsulated.

(4) *Stability (Regulation III/39.5.1).* It does not need stability pockets.

(5) *Righting (Regulation III/39.5.2).* A reversible one does not need arrangements for righting.

(6) One with a capacity of 13 or more persons must be reversible, with the floor arranged between the buoyancy chambers so that the apparatus can, floating either side up, accommodate the number of persons for which it is approved. One with a capacity of 12 or fewer persons must either be reversible in the same manner, or be designed so that it can be readily righted by one person.

(7) One with a capacity of 25 or more persons must be provided with self-bailing floor drains. If the floor of a reversible one includes one or more drains, each drain must be arranged to completely drain the floor of water when the device is fully loaded, and must prevent water from flowing back onto the floor.

(8) If the buoyancy tubes are not vivid reddish orange, vivid yellow, or a fluorescent color of a similar hue, panels of such hue must be secured to the buoyancy chambers so that a minimum of 1 m² (11 ft²) is visible from above the apparatus when it is floating either side up.

(9) *Boarding ramp (Regulation III/39.4.1)*. Boarding ramps are not required if the combined cross-section diameter of the buoyancy chambers is 500 millimeters (mm) (19.5 in.) or less. An apparatus with a combined cross-section diameter greater than 500 mm (19.5 in.) requires boarding ramps as follows:

(i) For an apparatus with a capacity of less than 25 persons, at least one ramp must be provided;

(ii) For an apparatus with a capacity of 25 or more persons, at least two ramps must be provided; and

(iii) The boarding ramps required by this paragraph must allow persons to board with either side of a reversible apparatus floating up, or the full number of ramps required must be installed on each side.

(10) *Boarding ladder (Regulation III/39.4.2)*. Boarding ladders must be provided on each inflatable buoyant apparatus as follows:

(i) One ladder must be provided on each apparatus with a capacity of less than 25 persons, except that, for an apparatus with a capacity of 13 or more persons that is not equipped with a boarding ramp, two ladders must be provided.

(ii) Two ladders must be provided on each apparatus with a capacity of 25 or more persons.

(iii) The ladders required by this paragraph must allow persons to board with either side of a reversible apparatus floating up, or the full number of ladders required must be installed on each side.

(11) One or more exterior canopy lamps meeting the requirements of § 160.151-15(n) of this subchapter must be provided such that—

(i) On a non-reversible inflatable buoyant apparatus, one lamp is mounted so that it is on the uppermost surface of the floating apparatus; and

(ii) On a reversible apparatus, two lamps are mounted so that one lamp is on the uppermost surface of the apparatus, whichever side is floating up.

(12) *Equipment (Regulation III/38.5.1)*. All equipment required by this paragraph must be either packed in a container accessible to the occupants, or otherwise secured to the apparatus. Duplicate equipment must be provided, for each side of a reversible

inflatable buoyant apparatus, if the equipment is not accessible from both sides. In lieu of the equipment specified in § 160.151-7(b) and Regulation III/38.5.1, each apparatus must be provided with—

(i) *Rescue quoit and heaving line.* One rescue quoit and a heaving line as described in § 160.151-21(a) on each apparatus with a capacity of less than 25 persons; or two on each apparatus for a capacity of 25 or more persons. The heaving line(s) must be mounted adjacent to a boarding ramp (or boarding ladder, if no ramps are installed), and ready for immediate use;

(ii) *Knives.* Two buoyant safety knives ready for use near the painter attachment;

(iii) *Bailer.* One bailer as described in § 160.151-21(c) on each apparatus with a capacity of less than 25 persons; or two bailers on each apparatus with a capacity of 25 or more persons, except that no bailers are necessary if both sides of the floor of a reversible apparatus are equipped with drains;

(iv) *Sponge.* One sponge as described in § 160.151-21(d) on each apparatus with a capacity of less than 25 persons, or two sponges on each apparatus with a capacity of 25 or more persons;

(v) *Paddles.* Two paddles as described in § 160.151-21(f) on each apparatus with a capacity of less than 25 persons, or four paddles on each apparatus with a capacity of 25 or more persons;

(vi) *Flashlight.* One flashlight with spare batteries as described in § 160.151-21(m);

(vii) *Signaling mirror.* One signaling mirror as described in § 160.151-21(o);

(viii) *Repair outfit.* One set of sealing clamps or plugs as described in § 160.151-21(y)(1);

(ix) *Pump or bellows.* One pump or bellows as described in § 160.151-21(z); and

(x) *Sea anchor.* One sea anchor as described in § 160.151-21(e), attached so as to be readily deployable when the apparatus inflates.

(13) *Marking and labeling (Regulations III/39.7.3.4, III/39.7.3.5, and III/39.8.6)*. Marking and labeling of inflatable buoyant apparatus must be in accordance with the requirements of § 160.151-33, except that the device must be identified as an "INFLATABLE BUOYANT APPARATUS", and no "SOLAS"

markings shall be placed on the container of the apparatus. The capacity marking specified in regulation III/39.8.6 must be applied to the top of each buoyancy tube.

(14) *Drop test.* The drop test required under paragraph 1/5.1 of IMO Resolution A.689(17) and § 160.151–27(a) may be from a lesser height, if that height is the maximum height of stowage marked on the container.

(15) *Loading and seating test.* For the loading and seating test required under paragraph 1/5.7 of IMO Resolution A.689(17) and § 160.151–27(a), the loaded freeboard of the apparatus must be not less than 200 mm (8 in.).

(16) *Cold-inflation test.* The cold-inflation test required under paragraph 1/5.17.3.3.2 of IMO Resolution A.689(17) and § 160.151–27(a) must be conducted at a test temperature of –18 °C (0 °F).

(b) *Production inspections and tests.* Production inspections and tests for inflatable buoyant apparatus must be performed in accordance with the applicable requirements of § 160.151–31.

(c) *Servicing.* Inflatable buoyant apparatus must be serviced periodically at approved servicing facilities in accordance with the applicable requirements of §§ 160.151–35 through 160.151–57.

(d) *Instruction placard.* An instruction placard meeting the requirements of § 160.151–59(c), giving simple procedures and illustrations for inflating, launching, and boarding the inflatable buoyant apparatus, must be made available to the operator or master of each vessel on which the apparatus is to be carried.

(e) *Requirements for "open reversible liferafts" under the IMO International Code of Safety for High-Speed Craft (HSC Code).* To be approved as meeting the requirements for open reversible liferafts in Annex 10 to the HSC Code, an inflatable buoyant apparatus must meet all of the requirements in paragraphs (a) through (d) of this section, with the following exceptions:

(1) The apparatus must be reversible regardless of size.

(2) The surface of the buoyancy tubes must be of a non-slip material. At least 25 percent of the surface of the buoyancy tubes must meet the color requirements of § 160.151–15(e).

(3) The length of the painter should be such that the apparatus inflates automatically upon reaching the water.

(4) An additional bowsing-in line must be fitted to an apparatus with a capacity of more than 30 persons.

(5) The apparatus must be fitted with boarding ramps regardless of size.

(6) An apparatus with a capacity of 30 or fewer persons must be fitted with at least one floor drain.

(7) In addition to the equipment specified in § 160.010–3(a)(12), the apparatus must be provided with—

(i) *Sponge.* One additional sponge as described in § 160.151–21(d) on each apparatus with a capacity of less than 25 persons;

(ii) *First-aid kit.* A first-aid kit approved by the Commandant under approval series 160.054;

(iii) *Whistle.* A ball-type or multitone whistle of corrosion-resistant construction;

(iv) *Hand flares.* Two hand flares approved by the Commandant under approval series 160.121.

(8) Marking and labeling of the apparatus must be in accordance with § 160.151–33, except that the device must be identified as a "NON-SOLAS REVERSIBLE", and the equipment pack must be identified as an "HSC Pack".

[CGD 85–205, 62 FR 25545, May 9, 1997]

§ 160.010–4 General requirements for buoyant apparatus.

(a) Each buoyant apparatus must be capable of passing the tests in § 160.010–7.

(b) Materials not covered in this subpart must be of good quality and suitable for the purpose intended.

(c) Buoyant apparatus must be effective and stable, floating either side up.

(d) Each buoyant apparatus must be of such size and strength that it can be handled without the use of mechanical appliances, and its weight must not exceed 185 kg (400 lb.).

(e) The buoyant material must be as near as possible to the sides of the apparatus.

(f) Each buoyant apparatus must have a life line securely attached around the outside, festooned in bights no longer than 1 m (3 ft.), with a seine float in each bight, unless the line is of an inherently buoyant material and absorbs little or no water. The life line must be at least 10 mm (⅜ in.) diameter and have a breaking strength of at least 5400 N (1215 lb.).

(g) Pendants must be fitted approximately 450 mm (18 in.) apart around the outside of each buoyant apparatus. Each pendant must be at least 6 mm (¼ in.) diameter, at least 3.5 m (12 ft.) long, secured in the middle, and have a breaking strength of at least 2400 N (540 lb.). Each pendant must be made up in a hank, and the hank secured by not more than two turns of light twine.

(h) Each peripheral body type buoyant apparatus without a net or plat-form on the inside must also have a life line and pendants around the inside.

(i) Synthetic line or webbing must not be used unless it is of a type represented by its manufacturer as ultraviolet light resistant, or it is pigmented in a dark color. A typical method of securing lifelines and pendants to straps of webbing is shown in Figure 160.010-3(i). If webbing is used to secure life lines and pendants, it must be at least 50 mm (2 in.) wide and must have a breaking strength of at least 3.4 kN (750 lb.) for apparatus of under 25 persons capacity, and 6.7 kN (1,500 lb.) for apparatus of 25 persons capacity and higher.

33

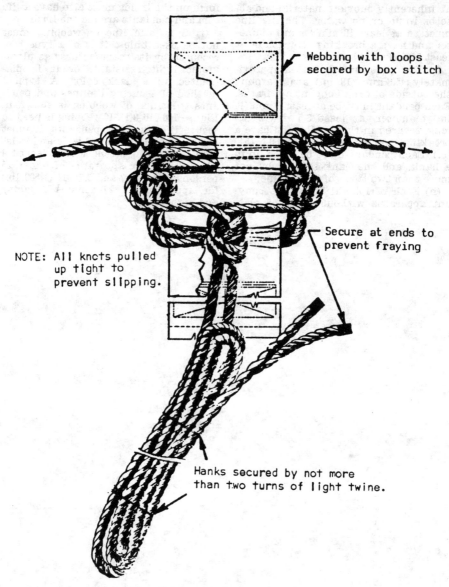

Webbing with loops
secured by box stitch

Secure at ends to
prevent fraying

NOTE: All knots pulled
up tight to
prevent slipping.

Hanks secured by not more
than two turns of light twine.

Figure 160.010-3(i)-Acceptable method of rigging a pendant.

(j) Buoyant apparatus must have a fitting with an inside diameter of at least 50 mm (2 in.) for the attachment of a painter.

(k) Each edge and exposed corner must be well rounded. Buoyant apparatus with a rectangular cross-section must have corners rounded to a radius of at least 75 mm (3 in.).

(1) Buoyant apparatus must not have any evident defects in workmanship.

(m) Each metal part of a buoyant apparatus must be—

(1) 410 stainless steel or have salt water and salt air corrosion characteristics equal or superior to 410 stainless steel; and

(2) Galvanically compatible with each other metal part in contact with it.

(n) The color of the buoyant apparatus must be primarily vivid reddish orange as defined by sections 13 and 14 of the "Color Names Dictionary."

(o) When fibrous-glass-reinforced plastic is used in the construction of a buoyant apparatus, each cut edge of laminate must be protected from entry of moisture by resin putty or an equivalent method.

(p) Each buoyant apparatus must have Type II retroreflective material meeting subpart 164.018 of this chapter on each side and end. The material must be in strips at least 50 mm (2 in.) wide extending from top to bottom over the side or end and continuing over the top and bottom surfaces of the apparatus. For peripheral body apparatus, each strip must extend completely over the top and bottom surface of the body. For box type apparatus, the strip must extend at least 300 mm (12 in.) inboard from the edge over the top and bottom surface. Each strip must be positioned near the center of the side or end, but so that it is not obscured by any strap. A typical arrangement is shown in Figure 160.010-3(p).

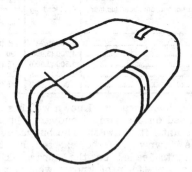

[CGD 79-167, 47 FR 41372, Sept. 20, 1982. Redesignated by CGD 85-205, 62 FR 25545, May 9, 1997]

§ 160.010-5 Buoyant apparatus with plastic foam buoyancy.

(a) Buoyant apparatus with plastic foam buoyancy must have a plastic foam body with an external protective covering. The body may be reinforced as necessary to meet the tests in § 160.010-7.

(b) Plastic foam used in the construction of buoyant apparatus must be a unicellular type accepted by the Commandant (G-MSE) as meeting one of the following:

(1) Subpart 164.015 of this chapter.

(2) MIL-P-19644.

(3) MIL-P-21929.

(4) MIL-P-40619.

(c) The external protective covering must be—

(1) Fibrous-glass-reinforced plastic, constructed of a polyester resin listed on the current Qualified Products List for MIL-P-21607, or accepted by the Commandant (G-MSE) as meeting MIL-P-21607;

(2) Elastomeric vinyl accepted by the Commandant (G-MSE) as meeting § 160.055-3(j) of this chapter; or

(3) Any other material accepted by the Commandant (G-MSE) as providing equivalent protection for the body of the apparatus.

[CGD 79-167, 47 FR 41372, Sept. 20, 1982, as amended by CGD 95-072, 60 FR 50466, Sept. 29, 1995; CGD 96-041, 61 FR 50733, Sept. 27, 1996. Redesignated by CGD 85-205, 62 FR 25545, May 9, 1997]

§ 160.010-6 Capacity of buoyant apparatus.

(a) The number of persons for which a buoyant apparatus is approved must be the lowest number determined by the following methods:

(1) Final buoyancy of the buoyant apparatus in Newtons after the watertight integrity test as described in § 160.010-7 (e) and (f), divided by 145 (divided by 32 if buoyancy is measured in pounds). The divisor must be changed to 180 (40 if buoyancy is measured in pounds) if the apparatus is designed so that persons supported are only partially immersed or where facilities are provided for climbing on top of the apparatus.

(2) Number of 300 mm (1 ft.) increments in the outside perimeter of the buoyant apparatus. The inside edge of

peripheral-body type buoyant apparatus is not considered in determining the capacity.

(b) [Reserved]

§ 160.010-7 Methods of sampling, inspections and tests.

(a) *General.* Production tests must be conducted under the procedures in subpart 159.007 of this chapter. An inspector from the independent laboratory must inspect the place of manufacture, observe the various operations involved in the construction process and determine that buoyant apparatus are made in accordance with this subpart and of materials and parts conforming strictly with the plans and specifications submitted by the manufacturer and approved by the Commandant (G–MSE).

(b) *Sampling of production lots.* A production lot must consist of not more than 300 buoyant apparatus of the same design and capacity manufactured by one factory. Samples for production tests must be selected at random from each lot. The required sample size for various lot sizes is given in Table 160.010-7(b).

TABLE 160.010-7(B)—SAMPLE SIZE FOR VARIOUS LOT SIZES

Lot size	Sample size
1 to 30	1
31 to 60	2
61 to 90	3
91 to 300	4

(c) *Testing of sample buoyant apparatus from production lots.* Each sample buoyant apparatus selected for test from a production lot must be subjected to the tests described in paragraphs (d) through (g) of this section. The stability test in paragraph (h) must be performed whenever a question of stability arises.

(d) *Strength tests.* The buoyant apparatus tested for approval must be subjected to the drop test. Buoyant apparatus tested for production lot inspections must also be subjected to the drop test except that in the case of peripheral body type apparatus, the beam loading test may be substituted.

(1) *Drop test.* Drop the complete sample buoyant apparatus into still water from a height of 18 m (60 ft.) twice,

once flat and once endwise. There must be no damage that would render the apparatus unserviceable.

(2) *Beam loading test.* The buoyant apparatus must be stood on edge on one of its longer sides. A wood block 600 mm (24 in.) long and wide enough to cover the body of the apparatus must be centered on the top edge of the apparatus. A loading beam must be set at right angles to the float at a height so that the beam is in a horizontal position with its center on the center of the wood block. The loading beam must be hinged at one end and a load applied at the other end at a uniform rate of 225 kg (500 lb.) per minute until the load at the end of the beam as shown on Table 160.010-7(d)(2) is reached. The beam is then held stationary for 10 minutes. The device used to apply the load must be a chain fall, hydraulic cylinder or other device that allows the device to unload as the strain on the buoyant apparatus relieves. At the end of the 10 minute period, the drop in the load on the device must not exceed the maximum permissible drop shown in Table 160.010-7(d)(2). If the buoyant apparatus is not one of the sizes listed in the table, the loads must be determined by linear interpolation.

NOTE: Because of the lever ratio of the beam loading apparatus described here, the actual loads applied to the apparatus are twice the loads shown in the Table.

TABLE 160.010-7(D)(2)—BEAM LOADING TEST

Size of buoyant apparatus (persons)	Test load (kg (lb.))	Maximum permissible drop (kg (lb.))
60	2,400 (5,280)	120 (264)
40	1,800 (3,960)	90 (198)
25	1,500 (3,300)	75 (165)
15	1,200 (2,640)	60 (132)
10	900 (1,980)	45 (100)

(e) *Buoyancy test.* Known weights are loaded on the sample buoyant apparatus until it is awash. The buoyancy is the downward force exerted by the weights loaded on the apparatus. A raised platform of known weight having two runners on edge spaced so as to bear on the apparatus may be used to support the weights out of water to avoid the necessity for making allowances for the displacement of submerged weights. This test is not a required production test if the manufacturer—

(1) Uses the same plastic buoyancy foam used in previous production lots,

(2) Determines that the density of each batch of foam used is within a range specified on the approved plans, and

(3) Closely controls the amount of foam used in each apparatus.

(f) *Watertight integrity test.* The buoyant apparatus is submerged for 24 hours at a depth of 3 m (10 ft.) or equivalent water pressure. The final buoyancy of the buoyant apparatus is determined in accordance with paragraph (e) of this section. The final buoyancy must be at least 145 N (32 lb.) per person capacity of the buouyant apparatus or 180 N (40 lb.) per person capacity if the apparatus is designed so that persons supported are only partially immersed or if facilities are provided for climbing on top of the apparatus. The loss of buoyancy must not exceed 5 percent of the initial buoyancy. This test is not a required production test if the manufacturer uses the plastic buoyancy foam controls permitted as an alternative to the buoyancy test in paragraph (e) of this section.

(g) *Painter attachment strength test.* The apparatus must be positioned with its painter attachment fitting at the lowest point of the apparatus, directly below the center of buoyancy. The apparatus must be suspended in this position from the highest side. A load equal to twice the buoyancy of the apparatus must be suspended from the painter attachment fitting for 10 minutes. The fitting must remain firmly attached to the buoyant apparatus and the apparatus must not sustain any visible damage.

(h) *Stability test.* With the sample buoyant apparatus floating in water, a weight of 22.5 kg of iron per meter of length (15 lb. per foot) must be suspended in the water from the life lines along one of the longer edges. The same test must be performed along one of the shorter edges. The minimum weight along any one edge must be 27 kg (60 lb.). The buoyant apparatus must neither capsize nor become partially awash under either of these tests.

(i) *Weight test.* One buoyant apparatus of the lot submitted for approval must be weighed. The weight of the complete buoyant apparatus must be within the limit required in § 160.010–3(d).

(j) *Lot acceptance or rejection.* Inability of a sample buoyant apparatus to pass any one or more of the tests required in this section causes rejection of the lot. Each buoyant apparatus in a rejected lot must be reworked by the manufacturer to correct the defects found before the lot is resubmitted for inspection and testing.

[CGD 79–167, 47 FR 41372, Sept. 20, 1982, as amended by CGD 95–072, 60 FR 50466, Sept. 29, 1995; CGD 96–041, 61 FR 50733, Sept. 27, 1996]

§ 160.010–8 Nameplate and marking.

(a) A substantial nameplate must be permanently attached to each buoyant apparatus. The nameplate must contain the name of the manufacturer, lot designation or serial number, approval number, dimensions, and number of persons capacity. Space must be provided for the date, and the identification of the independent laboratory.

(b) The nameplates of buoyant apparatus accepted must be marked with the identification of the independent laboratory and the date.

§ 160.010–9 Procedure for approval.

(a) A buoyant apparatus is approved by the Coast Guard under the procedures in subpart 159.005 of this chapter.

(b) The test required for approval are those in § 160.010–7, and must be performed on the first production lot of buoyant apparatus produced by the manufacturer.

§ 160.010–10 Independent laboratory.

(a) The approval and production tests in this subpart must be conducted by an independent laboratory accepted by the Coast Guard under subpart 159.010 of this chapter.

(b) [Reserved]

Subparts 160.011-160.012 [Reserved]

Subpart 160.013—Hatchets (Lifeboat and Liferaft) for Merchant Vessels

§ 160.013-1 Applicable specification and plan.

(a) *Specification.* The following specification, of the issue in effect on the date hatchets are manufactured, forms a part of this subpart:

(1) Federal Specification:

GGG-A-926—Axes.

(b) *Plan.* The following plan, of the issue in effect on the date hatchets are manufactured, forms a part of this subpart:

(1) Dwg. No. 160.013-1 (b)—Hatchet (Lifeboat and Life Raft).

(c) *Copy on file.* A copy of the specification and plan referred to in this section shall be kept on file by the manufacturer, together with the approved plans and certificate of approval. They shall be kept for a period consisting of the duration of approval and 6 months after termination of approval. The Federal specification may be purchased from the Business Service Center, General Services Administration, Washington, DC, 20407. The Coast Guard plan may be obtained upon request from the Commandant, U.S. Coast Guard.

[CGFR 49-43, 15 FR 116, Jan. 11, 1950, as amended by CGFR 61-23, 26 FR 5758, June 28, 1961; CGFR 65-16, 30 FR 10898, Aug. 21, 1965; CGD 88-070, 53 FR 34535, Sept. 7, 1988]

§ 160.013-2 Type and size.

(a) *Type.* Hatchets specified by this subpart shall be Type I, Class I, Design D or E, as described in Federal Specification GGG-A-926, but other hatchets equal in strength and construction will be given special consideration.

(b) *Size.* Hatchets specified by this subpart shall be of one size, and the dimensions shall be approximately in conformance with Drawing No. 160.013-1(b).

[CGFR 49-43, 15 FR 116, Jan. 11, 1950, as amended by CGFR 61-23, 26 FR 5759, June 28, 1961]

§ 160.013-3 Materials, workmanship, and construction details.

(a) *General.* All materials, workmanship, and construction details shall be in substantial compliance with the provisions of Federal Specification GGG-A-926, except as provided for in this subpart.

(b) *Handle.* A ½-inch diameter hole shall be bored in the hatchet handle in the approximate location shown on DWG No. 160.013-1(b), and the edges of the hole on both sides of the handle shall be rounded off to remove rough edges.

(c) *Lanyard.* Hatchets specified by this subpart shall be provided with a lanyard of ¼-inch diameter, 3-strand rope-laid line not less than 6 feet in length. Lanyards shall be cotton, jute, or other suitable material. The lanyard shall be attached to the hatchet by threading one end through the hole in the hatchet handle and securing the rope end by splicing or by a bowline or other suitable knot.

(d) *Sheath.* No sheaths are to be provided for hatchets specified by this subpart.

[CGFR 49-43, 15 FR 116, Jan. 11, 1950, as amended by CGFR 61-23, 26 FR 5759, June 28, 1961]

§ 160.013-5 Marking.

(a) *General.* Hatchets specified by this subpart shall be stamped or otherwise permanently marked in a legible manner on the side of the head with the manufacturer's name or with a trade mark of such known character that the source of manufacture may be readily determined, and with the manufacturer's type or size designation.

(b) [Reserved]

[CGFR 49-43, 15 FR 116, Jan. 11, 1950]

Subpart 160.015—Lifeboat Winches for Merchant Vessels

§ 160.015-1 Applicable regulations.

(a) *Regulations.* The following regulations of the issue in effect on the date lifeboat winches are manufactured, form a part of this subpart.

(1) Coast Guard regulations; Electrical Engineering Regulations, CG-259 (46 CFR (subchapter J) parts 110 to 113, inclusive of this chapter).

(2) Coast Guard regulations; Marine Engineering Regulations (46 CFR subchapter F, parts 50 to 63, inclusive in this chapter).

(b) *Copies on file.* A copy of the regulations referred to in this section shall be kept on file by the manufacturer, together with the approved plans, material affidavits, and the certificate of approval.

[CGFR 58–31, 23 FR 6883, Sept. 6, 1958, as amended by CGD 72–133R, 37 FR 17038, Aug. 24, 1972]

§ 160.015–2 General requirements for lifeboat winches.

(a) The requirements of this subpart apply to all new construction of lifeboat winches. Lifeboat winches approved and in use prior to the regulations in this subpart may be continued in service if in satisfactory condition.

(b) Lifeboat winches for use with gravity davits shall have grooved drums of such size that there will be only one wrap of wire on the drum. Lifeboat winches for use with mechanical davits need not be grooved and may be designed to take more than one wrap.

(c) Lifeboat winches shall be designed to lower under the force of gravity alone. There shall be no provisions for power lowering. A suitable hand wheel shall be attached to the winch to overhaul the falls in addition to any hand cranks provided.

(d) If the lifeboat winch is to be used in conjunction with nested lifeboats where the same falls are used for both boats, suitable means shall be provided for rapidly retrieving the falls by hand power.

(e) The installation of lifeboat winches shall be such that the fleet angle for grooved drums does not exceed 8 degrees, and for nongrooved drums does not exceed 4 degrees.

(f) Suitable hand cranks shall be provided for hoisting in addition to any other means for hoisting.

(g) Suitable fabric covers shall be provided, so fitted over exposed mechanisms that ice formations may be readily broken adrift when necessary to operate the winch.

(h) Falls shall not lead past any position that may be needed for the operation of the winch, such as hand

cranks, pay-out wheels, brake levers, etc.

(i) Where falls lead along a deck they shall be suitably covered and so arranged that the top of the cover does not exceed 12 inches above the deck.

(j) Lifeboat winches shall be so designed that when located aboard merchant vessels the operator can observe the movement of the lifeboat during the lowering operation.

(k) For the purpose of calculations and conducting tests, the working load is the maximum load in pounds applied to the winch for which approval is desired.

(k–1) The exterior of a winch shall be designed to minimize such crevices, pockets, and inaccessible areas that when corroded would require disassembly of the winch for their scaling and painting.

(k–2) [Reserved]

(l) The requirements of this subpart shall be complied with unless other arrangements in matters of construction details, design, strength, equivalent in safety and efficiency are approved by the Commandant.

[CGFR 49–18, 14 FR 5111, Aug. 17, 1949, as amended by CGFR 58–31, 23 FR 6883, Sept. 6, 1958; CGD 72–133R, 37 FR 17038, Aug. 24, 1972]

§ 160.015–3 Construction of lifeboat winches.

(a) Lifeboat winches shall be of such strength that the lifeboat may be lowered safely with its full complement of persons and equipment. Additionally, a lifeboat winch used in hoisting an emergency lifeboat of a passenger vessel shall be capable of meeting the test specified in § 160.015–5(b)(9). A minimum factor of safety of six on the ultimate strength of the material shall be maintained at all times based on the approved working load.

(b) Worm gears, spur gears, or a combination of both, may be used in the construction of lifeboat winches. All gears shall be machine cut and made of steel, bronze, or other suitable material properly keyed to shafts. The use of cast iron is not permitted for these parts.

(c) Screws, nuts, bolts, pins, keys, etc., securing moving parts shall be

39

fitted with suitable lock washers, cotter pins, or locks to prevent them from coming adrift.

(d) Drums shall be so arranged as to keep the falls separate, and to pay out the falls at the same rate. Clutches between the drums shall not be permitted unless bolted locking devices are used.

(e) The diameter of the drums shall be at least 16 times the diameter of the falls.

(f) A weighted lever hand brake shall be used to control the lowering by the lifeboat winch. It shall be of a type which is normally in the "on" position unless manually held in the "off" position, and shall return to the "on" position as soon as the brake lever is released.

(g) In addition to the hand brake, a governor type brake shall be fitted so as to control the speed of lowering of the lifeboat in accordance with § 160.015-5(b) (4) and (5).

(h) Positive means of lubrication shall be provided for all bearings. When worm gears are used the worm wheel shall operate in an oil bath. Means shall be provided so that the oil level in the gear case may be easily checked. The manufacturer shall furnish a lubrication chart for each winch together with a plate attached to the winch indicating the lubricant recommended for extremes in temperature.

(i) When lifeboat winches are fitted with power for hoisting, a suitable clutch shall be fitted to disengage the power installation during the lowering operation. In addition, the air or electric power outlet for a portable power unit shall be located adjacent to the winch where the unit is to be coupled. This power outlet shall be interconnected with and protected by the same system of safety devices as required for winches with built-in-motors.

(j) Where power-driven lifeboat winches are used, including those driven by portable power units, such as air or electric drills, positive means shall be provided for controlling the power to the lifeboat winch. This shall be so arranged that the operator must hold the master switch or controller in the "on" or "hoist" position for hoisting, and when released will immediately shut off the power.

(k) Limit switch and emergency disconnect switch requirements:

(1) A main line emergency disconnect switch shall be provided, the opening of which will disconnect all electrical potential to the lifeboat winch. This switch shall be located in a position accessible to the person in charge of the boat stowage, and for gravity davit installations, shall be in a position from which the movement of both davit arms can be observed as they approach the final stowed position.

(2) Where power driven winches are used with gravity davits, two limit switches, one for each davit arm, shall be provided to limit the travel of the davit arms as they approach the final stowed position. These switches shall be connected in series, they may be connected in either the control or the power circuit, and they shall be so arranged that the opening of either switch will disconnect all electrical potential of the circuit in which the switches are connected. These switches shall be arranged to stop the travel of the davit arms not less than 12 inches from their final stowed position and they shall remain open until the davit arms move outboard beyond the tripping position of the switches.

(3) Other arrangements equivalent in design and safety will be given special consideration.

(l) Where power driven winches are used, satisfactory means shall be provided to disconnect power to the winch before a hand crank can be engaged with the winch operating shaft, and this interruption of power shall be maintained while the hand crank is so engaged. Mechanical means for accomplishing the above, such as throw-out couplings on the sockets of the hand cranks, will be given special consideration.

(m) Motors, switches, controls, cables, etc., shall be of the waterproof type if installed on an open deck. Controls may be of the dripproof type if installed in a deck house or under deck. Installations shall be in accordance with subchapter J (Electrical Engineering) of this chapter (Electrical Engineering Regulations, CG–259).

(n) All moving parts shall have suitable guards.

(o) Welding, when employed, shall be performed by welders certified by the U. S. Coast Guard, American Bureau of Shipping, or U.S. Navy Department, and the electrodes used shall be of an approved type.

(p) Inspection openings shall be provided in the winch housing or the housing itself shall be so arranged as to permit examination of the internal working parts.

(q) Motor clutches, when used, shall be of either frictional or positive engaging type. When one motor is used for two winches, the clutch shall be so arranged that only one winch shall be engaged at any one time. The clutch operating lever shall be capable of remaining in any position when subject to vibration and shall be so arranged that when in neutral position, both lifeboats may be lowered simultaneously.

[CGFR 49–18, 14 FR 5111, Aug. 17, 1949, as amended by CGFR 51–20, 16 FR 5443, June 8, 1951; CGFR 58–31, 23 FR 6883, Sept. 6, 1958; CGFR 65–9, 30 FR 11465, Sept. 8, 1965; CGD 72–133R, 37 FR 17039, Aug. 24, 1972; CGD 73–103R, 39 FR 11273, Mar. 27, 1974]

§ 160.015–4 Capacity of lifeboat winches.

(a) A lifeboat winch shall be approved for a working load after it has been demonstrated by detailed calculations that this working load can be carried with a minimum factor of safety of six based on the ultimate strengths of the materials. It will also be necessary to conduct the tests specified in § 160.015–5.

(b) [Reserved]

[CGFR 49–18, 14 FR 5111, Aug. 17, 1949]

§ 160.015–5 Inspection and testing of lifeboat winches.

(a) *Material testing.* (1) The manufacturer shall furnish affidavits relative to the physical and chemical properties of the materials. Such affidavits shall be furnished by the foundry or mill supplying the material.

(b) *Factory test for initial approval.* (1) Lifeboat winches shall be tested for strength and operation at a place chosen by the manufacturer of the winch in the presence of an inspector. The lifeboat winch under test shall be set up similar to the intended shipboard installation. In the case of a lifeboat winch with nongrooved drums, the drums shall be built up or sufficiently filled with wire to simulate the maximum number of wraps for which the winch is to be approved. The tests to be conducted are as noted in paragraphs (b)(2) to (8) of this section. The limiting values of velocities and the 2 foot braking distance set forth in the following paragraphs of this section are the values to be actually achieved with the specific arrangement of falls contemplated for the shipboard installation. If a different arrangement of falls is used to facilitate testing, due consideration shall be given to the use of limiting velocities, braking distances, and test weights which will be equivalent to the test performed with an arrangement of falls identical to that used for the shipboard installation.

(2) A pull of 2.2 times the working load, equally divided between drums, shall be applied in a direction similar to a shipboard installation. The test weight producing this load shall be dropped through a distance of not less than 15 feet, at which time this weight shall be stopped within a distance of 2 feet by action of the counterweight alone on the hand brake.

(3) A test identical to that noted in paragraph (b)(2) of this section shall be conducted after the braking surfaces have been thoroughly wetted. The test weight shall be stopped by the action of the counterweight alone within a distance of 6 feet. The test need only be applied to lifeboat winches having external brakes.

(4) With a pull equal to the working load, it shall be determined that the governor brake will limit the speed of lowering of the test weight to a maximum of 120 feet per minute, except that, in the case of winches designed for use with emergency lifeboats aboard passenger vessels, the speed of lowering shall not exceed 160 feet per minute.

(5) With a pull equal to 0.3 times the working load, it shall be determined that the winch will lower the test weight at not less than 40 feet per minute, except that, in the case of

41

winches designed for use with emergency lifeboats aboard passenger vessels, the speed of lowering shall not be less than 60 feet per minute.

(6) With a pull equal to the working load, the test weight shall be lowered and raised a sufficient number of times so that the combined lowering distance is not less than 500 feet. This test is to determine the efficiency of the lifeboat winch for prolonged service.

(7) With a pull equal to 0.5 times the working load, it shall be demonstrated that the lifeboat winch can be hand operated by hoisting the test weight without undue effort. For gravity davits, it shall be demonstrated that this test weight can be carried easily from a point at which the traveling blocks of the falls are 1 foot below their outboard, two-blocked position, and then up and around the bend of the trackways to the stowed position of the lifeboat.

(8) Where a quick return mechanism is installed it shall be demonstrated that a weight equal to 2.2 times the weight of the empty blocks can be handily retrieved through the regular reeving of the falls at a rate of not less than 40 feet per minute at the drum by one man.

(9) The following test applies to a lifeboat winch used for hoisting an emergency lifeboat of a passenger vessel. With a weight equal to the weight of the emergency lifeboat and its full complement of persons and equipment, it shall be demonstrated that the weight can be hoisted through the regular reeving of the falls at a rate of not less than 20 feet per minute, to the embarkation position.

(10) After the tests noted in paragraphs (b)(2) to (9) of this section have been conducted, the winch shall be completely disassembled and the marine inspector shall ascertain that no undue stress or wear has been incurred.

(c) *Factory testing after approval.* (1) After a design of a lifeboat winch has been approved, subsequent winches of the same design shall be individually tested as described in paragraph (c)(2) of this section.

(2) Each lifeboat winch shall be set up in a manner similar to that described in paragraph (c)(1) of this section. With a pull equal to 1.1 times the working load, the test weight shall be dropped through a distance of not less than 15 feet, at which time the load shall be stopped by the action of the counterweight alone. This test is to demonstrate the operation of the winch, and if satisfactory, no further test need be required. However, if the inspector is not satisfied with the operation of the winch, a complete test as noted in paragraph (b) of this section may be required.

(d) *Name plate.* (1) A corrosion resistant name plate shall be affixed to each lifeboat winch on which shall be stamped the name of the manufacturer, approval number, maximum working load in pounds pull at the drums, maximum working load in pounds pull per fall type and serial number, together with the Marine Inspection Office identification letters, the date, and the letters U.S.C.G.

[CGFR 49–18, 14 FR 5112, Aug. 17, 1949, as amended by CGFR 58–31, 23 FR 6883, Sept. 6, 1958; CGFR 65–9, 30 FR 11465, Sept. 8, 1965; CGD 72–133R, 37 FR 17039, Aug. 24, 1972; CGD 75–186, 41 FR 10437, Mar. 11, 1976]

§ 160.015–6 Procedure for approval of lifeboat winches.

(a) Before action is taken on any design of lifeboat winch, detail plans covering fully the arrangement and construction of the lifeboat winch, a complete bill of material setting forth the physical properties of the materials used, and strength calculations, shall be submitted to the Commandant through the Commander of the Coast Guard District having jurisdiction over the construction of the lifeboat winch.

(b) If the drawings required in paragraph (a) of this section are satisfactory, the Commander of the Coast Guard District in which the lifeboat winch is to be built, shall be notified in writing when fabrication is to commence. An inspector will be assigned to supervise the construction in accordance with the plans and upon completion, conduct the tests required by § 160.015–5.

(c) At the time that the tests are successfully completed, the manufacturer shall present to the inspector four corrected copies of the plans noted in paragraph (a) of this section, including any corrections, changes, or additions which may have been found necessary during construction or testing. If the manufacturer desires more than one set of approved plans, additional copies shall be submitted at that time.

(d) Upon receipt of corrected drawings, material affidavits, and satisfactory test report, the Commandant will issue a certificate of approval. No change shall be made in the design or construction without first receiving permission of the Commandant via the Commander of the Coast Guard District in which the lifeboat winch is built.

[CGFR 49-18, 14 FR 5112, Aug. 17, 1949, as amended by CGFR 58-31, 23 FR 6884, Sept. 6, 1958]

Subpart 160.016—Lamps, Safety, Flame, for Merchant Vessels

SOURCE: CGFR 50-12, 15 FR 3093, May 20, 1950, unless otherwise noted.

§ 160.016-1 Applicable specification.

(a) The following specification of the issue in effect on the date flame safety lamps are manufactured forms a part of this subpart:

(1) Military specification:

MIL-L-1204, Lamps, Safety, Flame.

(b) A copy of the above specification shall be kept on file by the manufacturer together with the approved plan and certificate of approval issued by the Coast Guard.

§ 160.016-2 Requirements.

(a) Flame safety lamps for use on merchant vessels shall comply with the construction requirements of Military Specification MIL-L-1204.

(b) [Reserved]

§ 160.016-4 Marking.

(a) Flame safety lamps shall be permanently and legibly marked with the name and address of the manufacturer and the type or model designation for the lamp.

(b) [Reserved]

§ 160.016-5 Procedure for approval.

(a) General. Flame safety lamps are approved for use on merchant vessels only by the Commandant, United States Coast Guard, Washington, DC

20226. Correspondence relating to the subject matter of this specification shall be addressed to the Commander of the Coast Guard District in which such devices are manufactured.

(b) Pre-approval sample and plan. In order to apply for approval of a flame safety lamp for use on merchant vessels, submit one complete sample, together with four copies of an arrangement plan (parts drawings are not required), together with a statement that the lamp meets the construction requirements of Military Specification MIL-L-1204, as amended, to the Commander of the Coast Guard District who will forward same to the Commandant for determination as to its suitability for use on merchant vessels.

Subpart 160.017—Chain Ladder

SOURCE: CGD 74-140, 46 FR 63286, Dec. 31, 1981, unless otherwise noted.

§ 160.017-1 Scope.

(a) This subpart contains standards and approval and production tests for chain ladders used on a merchant vessel to get on and off the vessel in an emergency.

(b) The requirements in this subpart apply to a chain ladder designed for use along a vertical portion of a vessel's hull.

§ 160.017-7 Independent laboratory.

The approval and production tests in this subpart must be conducted by or under the supervision of an independent laboratory accepted by the Coast Guard under subpart 159.010 of this chapter.

§ 160.017-9 Approval procedure.

(a) General. A chain ladder is approved by the Coast Guard under the procedures in subpart 159.005 of this chapter.

(b) Approval testing. Each approval test must be conducted in accordance with § 160.017-21.

(c) Approval of alternatives. A chain ladder that does not meet the materials, construction, or performance requirements of this subpart may be approved if the application and any approval tests prescribed by the Commandant in place of or in addition to

43

the approval tests required by this subpart, show that the alternative materials, construction, or performance is at least as effective as that specified by the requirements of this subpart. The Commandant may also prescribe different production tests if the tests required by this subpart are not appropriate for the alternative ladder configuration.

§ 160.017–11 Materials.

(a) *Suspension members.* Each suspension member of a chain ladder must be a continuous length of non-kinking chain, such as single loop lock link coil chain, with a minimum breaking strength of at least 16 kN (3,560 lbs.).

(b) *Metal parts.* Each metal part of a ladder must be made of corrosion-resistant metal or of steel galvanized by the hot dip process after the part is formed. If the ends of galvanized fasteners are peened over to lock them in place, a corrosion resisting surface treatment must be applied to each peened surface.

(c) *Wooden parts.* Each wooden part of a ladder must be made of hardwood that is free of defects affecting its strength or durability.

(d) *Wood preservative.* After each wooden part is formed and finished, it must be treated with water-repellant wood preservative that is properly applied.

(e) *Lashing rings.* The inside diameter of each lashing ring must be at least 75 mm (3 in.). Each lashing ring must have a minimum breaking strength of at least 16 kN (3,560 lbs.).

§ 160.017–13 Construction.

(a) *General.* Each chain ladder must have two suspension members. Each step in the ladder must be supported at each end by a suspension member.

(b) *Suspension member.* The distance between the two suspension members must be at least 400 mm (16 in.), but not more than 480 mm (19 in.). The chain between each top lashing ring and the first step must be long enough so that the distance between the center of the lashing ring and the top of the first step is approximately 600 mm (24 in.).

(c) *Lashing rings.* A lashing ring must be securely attached to the top and bottom of each suspension member. The means of attachment must be at least as strong as the chain and the lashing ring.

(d) *Thimble or wear plate.* A thimble or wear plate must be attached to the chain where it can slide on its connections to the lashing rings.

(e) *Steps.* Each step of a ladder must have two rungs arranged to provide a suitable handhold and stepping surface. The distance between steps must be uniform. This distance must be between 300 mm (12 in.) and 380 mm (15 in.).

(f) *Rungs.* Step rungs must meet the following requirements:

(1) Each rung must be wooden, or a material of equivalent strength, durability, handhold, and step surface characteristics.

(2) In order to provide a suitable handhold and step surface, the width of each rung must be at least 40 mm (1½ in.) and the thickness must be at least 25 mm (1 in.), but not more than 40 mm (1½ in.).

(3) The distance between the rungs in each step must be uniform. This distance must be between 40 mm (1½ in.) and 65 mm (2½ in.).

(4) Each rung must be attached to a spacer ear by a method that prevents the rung from rotating and that supports it in a horizontal position when the ladder is hung vertically.

(g) *Spacer ears.* Spacer ears must meet the following requirements:

(1) All spacer ears on a ladder must be the same size and shape.

(2) The top and bottom of each spacer ear must be attached to a suspension member.

(3) The top point of attachment must be at least 100 mm (4 in.) above the top surfaces of the rungs attached to the spacer ear.

(4) Each spacer ear made of sheet metal must have features such as formed ribs, rolled flange edges, and stress relief holes at the ends of cuts, to prevent the ear from bending or tearing.

(h) *Fasteners.* Each fastening device must have a means to prevent the device from loosening.

(i) *Workmanship.* A ladder must not have splinters, burrs, sharp edges, corners, projections, or other defects that could injure a person using the ladder.

§160.017-15 Performance.

(a) Each chain ladder must be capable of being rolled up for storage.

(b) Each ladder when rolled up must be able to unroll freely and hang vertically.

§160.17-17 Strength.

(a) Each chain ladder must be designed to pass the approval tests in §160.17-21.

(b) [Reserved]

§160.017-21 Approval tests.

(a) *General.* Each approval test must be conducted on a ladder of the longest length for which approval has been requested. If a ladder fails one of the tests in this section, the cause of the failure must be identified and any needed changes made. After a test failure and any design change, the failed test, and any other previously completed tests affected by the design change, must be rerun.

(b) *Visual examination.* Before starting the tests described in this section, an assembled chain ladder is examined for evidence of noncompliance with the requirements in §§160.017.11, 160.017–13, and 160.017-15.

(c) The following approval tests must be conducted:

(1) *Strength test #1.* An assembled ladder is supported so that a static load, if placed on any of its steps, would exert a force both on the step and each suspension member. A static load of 315 kg (700 lb.) is then placed on one step for at least one minute. The load must be uniformly distributed over a contact surface that is approximately 100 mm (4 in.) wide. The center of the contact surface must be at the center of the step. This test is performed on six different steps. No step may break, crack, or incur any deformation that remains after the static load is removed. No attachment between any step and a suspension member may loosen or break during this test.

(2) *Strength test #2.* A ladder is suspended vertically to its full length from its top lashing rings. A static load

of 900 kg (2000 lbs.) is then applied to the bottom lashing rings so that it is distributed equally between the suspension members. The suspension members, lashing rings, and spacer ears must not break, incur any elongation or deformation that remains after the test load is removed, or be damaged in any other way during this test.

(3) *Strength test #3.* A rolled-up ladder is attached by its top lashing rings to anchoring fixtures in a location away from any wall or structure that would prevent it from falling freely, and where it can hang to its full length vertically. The ladder when dropped must unroll freely. When unrolling the ladder, its steps and attachments must not become cracked, broken, or loosened. Other similar damage making the ladder unsafe to use must likewise not occur.

§160.017-25 Marking.

(a) Each chain ladder step manufactured under Coast Guard approval must be branded or otherwise permanently and legibly marked on the bottom with—

(1) The name of the manufacturer;

(2) The manufacturer's brand or model designation;

(3) The lot number and date of manufacture; and

(4) The Coast Guard approval number.

(b) [Reserved]

§160.017-27 Production tests and examination.

(a) *General.* Each ladder manufactured under Coast Guard approval must be tested in accordance with this section and subpart 159.007 of this chapter. Steps that fail testing may not be marked with the Coast Guard approval number and each assembled ladder that fails testing may not be sold as Coast Guard approved.

(b) *Test #1: Steps.* Steps must be separated into lots of 100 steps or less. One step from each lot must be selected at random and tested as described in §106.017–21(c)(1), except that the step may be supported at the points where it would be attached to suspension members in an assembled ladder. If the step fails the test, ten more steps must

45

be selected at random from the lot and tested. If one or more of the ten steps fails the test, each step in the lot must be tested.

(c) *Test #2: Ladders.* Assembled ladders must be separated into lots of 20 ladders or less One ladder must be selected at random from the ladders in the lot. The ladder selected must be at least 3 m (10 ft.) long or, if each ladder in the lot is less than 3 m long, a ladder of the longest length in the lot must be selected. The ladder must be tested as prescribed in § 160.017-21(c)(2), except that only a 3 m section of the ladder need be subjected to the static load. If the ladder fails the test each other ladder in the lot must be tested.

(d) *Independent laboratory.* Each production test must be conducted or supervised by an independent laboratory. However, if a test is performed more than 4 different times per year, laboratory participation is required only 4 times per year. If the laboratory does not participate in all tests, the times of laboratory participation must be as selected by the laboratory. The times selected must provide for effective monitoring throughout the production schedule.

(e) *Visual examination.* The visual examination described in § 160.017-21(b) must be conducted as a part of each production test.

Subpart 160.021—Hand Red Flare Distress Signals

SOURCE: CGD 76-048a and 76-048b, 44 FR 73060, Dec. 17, 1979, unless otherwise noted.

§ 160.021-1 Incorporations by reference.

(a) The following is incorporated by reference into this subpart:

(1) "The Universal Color Language" and "The Color Names Dictionary" in *Color: Universal Language and Dictionary of Names,* National Bureau of Standards Special Publication 440, December 1976.

(b) NBS Special Publication 440 may be obtained by ordering from the Superintendent of Documents, U.S. Government Printing Office, Washington, DC 20402 (Order by SD Catalog No. C13.10:440).

(c) Approval to incorporate by reference the publication listed in this section was obtained from the Director of the Federal Register on November 1, 1979. The publication is on file at the Federal Register Library.

§ 160.021-2 Type.

(a) Hand red flare distress signals specified by this subpart shall be of one type which shall consist essentially of a wooden handle to which is attached a tubular casing having a sealing plug at the handle end, the casing being filled with a flare composition and having a button of ignition material at the top, with a removable cap having a friction striking material on its top which may be exposed for use by pulling a tear strip. The flare is ignited by scraping the friction striker on top of the cap against the igniter button on top of the flare. The general arrangement of the flare is shown by Figure No. 160.021-2(a). Alternate arrangements which conform to all the performance requirements of this specification (and other arrangements which conform with all performance requirements except candlepower and burning time, but provide not less than 3,000 candela-minutes with a minimum of ⅓ minute burning time) will be given special consideration.

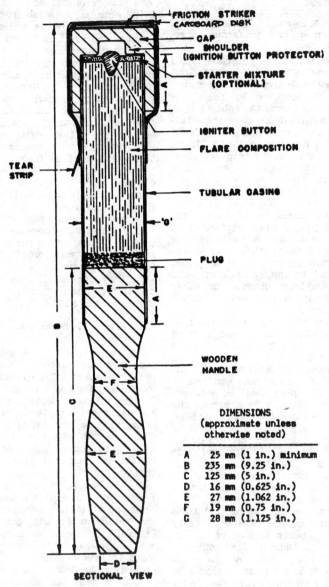

Figure 160.021-2(a). Hand Red Flare Distress Signal – General Arrangement.

DIMENSIONS
(approximate unless otherwise noted)

A	25 mm	(1 in.) minimum
B	235 mm	(9.25 in.)
C	125 mm	(5 in.)
D	16 mm	(0.625 in.)
E	27 mm	(1.062 in.)
F	19 mm	(0.75 in.)
G	28 mm	(1.125 in.)

SECTIONAL VIEW

(b) [Reserved]

§ 160.021–3 Materials, workmanship, construction and performance requirements.

(a) *Materials.* The materials shall conform strictly to the specifications and drawings submitted by the manufacturer and approved by the Commandant. The color of the tube shall be red. Flare compositions containing sulphur shall not contain more than 2.6 percent of potassium chlorate or an equivalent amount of any other chlorate. Flare compositions containing chlorates in any quantity shall not contain any ammonium salts.

(b) *Workmanship.* Hand red flare distress signals shall be of first class workmanship and shall be free from imperfections of manufacture affecting their appearance or that may affect their serviceability. Moistureproof coatings shall be applied uniformly and shall be free from pinholes or other visible defects which would impair their usefulness.

(c) *Construction.* The casing shall be fitted and secured to the handle with not less than a 25 mm (1 in.) overlap and shall be attached to the handle in such a manner that failure of the joint will not occur during tests, ignition, or operation. The plug shall be securely affixed in the casing to separate the flare composition from the wooden handle. The flare composition shall be thoroughly mixed and be uniformly compressed throughout to preclude variations of density which may adversely affect uniformity of its burning characteristics. The cap shall have a lap fit of not less than 25 mm (1 in.) over the end of the casing and flare composition to entirely and securely protect the exposed surface of the igniter button and end of flare composition and casing, and shall have an inner shoulder so constructed that it is mechanically impossible for the inner surface of the cap to come in contact with the igniter button. The cap shall be securely attached to the casing in such manner as to preclude its accidental detachment. The cap shall be provided on its top with a friction striking material which shall, by a pull of the tear strip, be entirely exposed for striking the friction igniter button.

The igniter button shall be non-water soluble or be protected from moisture by a coating of some waterproof substance, and shall be raised or exposed in such manner as to provide positive ignition by the friction striker. The igniter button shall be firmly secured in or on the top of the flare composition; the arrangement shall be such that the ignition will be transmitted to the flare composition. The assembled flare, consisting of tear strip, cap, casing, and handle, shall be sealed and treated to protect the flare from deterioration by moisture. The protective waterproof coating shall be applied so none adheres to the friction striking surface. Special consideration will be given to alternate waterproofing of the signal by means of a water-resistant coating on the signal plus packaging in a sealed plastic waterproof bag satisfactory to the Commandant.

(d) *Performance.* Signals shall meet all the inspection and test requirements contained in § 160.021–4.

§ 160.021–4 Approval and production tests.

(a) *Approval tests.* The manufacturer must produce a lot of at least 100 signals form which samples must be taken for testing for approval under § 160.021–7. The approval tests are the operational tests and technical tests in paragraphs (c) and (d) of this section. The approval tests must be conducted by an independent laboratory accepted by the Commandant under § 159.010 of this Chapter.

(b) *Production inspections and tests.* Production inspections and tests of each lot of signals produced must be conducted under the procedures in § 159.007 of this chapter. Signals from a rejected lot must not be represented as meeting this subpart or as being approved by the Coast Guard. If the manufacturer identifies the cause of the rejection of a lot of signals, the signals in the lot may be reworked by the manufacturer to correct the problem. Samples from the rejected lot must be retested in order to be accepted. Records shall be kept of the reasons for rejection, the reworking performed on the rejected lot, and the results of the second test.

(1) *Lot size.* For the purposes of sampling the production of signals, a lot must consist of not more than 30,000 signals. Lots must be numbered serially by the manufacturer. A new lot must be started with: (i) Any change in construction details, (ii) any change in sources of raw materials, or (iii) the start of production on a new production line or on a previously discontinued production line.

(2) *Inspections and tests by the manufacturer.* The manufacturer's quality control procedures must include inspection of materials entering into construction of the signals and inspection of the finished signals, to determine that signals are being produced in accordance with the approved plans. Samples from each lot must be tested in accordance with the operational tests in paragraph (c) of this section.

(3) *Inspections and tests by an independent laboratory.* An independent laboratory accepted by the Commandant under § 159.010 of this Chapter must perform or supervise the inspections and tests under paragraph (b)(2) of this section at least 4 times a year, unless the number of lots produced in year is less than four. The inspections and tests must occur at least once during each quarterly period, unless no lots are produced during that period. If less than four lots are produced, the laboratory must perform or supervise the inspection and testing of each lot. In addition, the laboratory must perform or supervise the technical tests in paragraph (d) of this section at least once for every ten lots of signals produced, except that the number of technical tests must be at least one but not more than four per year. If a lot of signals tested by the independent laboratory is rejected, the laboratory must perform or supervise the inspections and tests of the reworked lot and the next lot of signals produced. The tests of each reworked lot and the next lot produced must not be counted for the purpose of meeting the requirement for the annual number of inspections and tests performed or supervised by the independent laboratory.

(c) *Operational tests.* Each lot of signals must be sampled and tested as follows:

(1) *Sampling procedure and accept/reject criteria.* A sample of signals must be selected at random from the lot. The size of the sample must be the individual sample size in Table 160.021–4(c)(1) corresponding to the lot size. Each signal in the sample is tested as prescribed in the test procedure in paragraph (c)(2) of this section. Each signal that has a defect listed in the table of defects (Table 160.021–4(c)(2)) is assigned a score (failure percent) in accordance with that table. In the case of multiple defects, only the score having the highest numerical value is assigned to that signal. If the sum of all the failure percents (cumulative failure percent) for the number of units in the sample is less than or equal to the accept criterion, the lot is accepted. If the cumulative failure percent falls between the accept and reject criteria, another sample is selected from the production lot and the operational tests are repeated. The cumulative failure percent of each sample tested is added to that of the previous samples to obtain the cumulative failure percent for all the signals tested (cumulative sample size). Additional samples are tested and the tests repeated until either the accept or reject criterion for the cumulative sample size is met. If any signal in the sample explodes when fired or ignited in a way that could burn or otherwise injure the person firing it, the lot is rejected without further testing. (This procedure is diagrammed in figure 160.021–4(c)).

(2) *Test procedure.* Each sample signal (specimen) must be tested as follows:

(i) *Conditioning of test specimens— water resistance.* Immerse specimen horizontally with uppermost portion of the signal approximately 25 mm (1 in.) below the surface of the water for a period of 24 hours. If the signal is protected by alternate waterproofing consisting of a water-resistant coating on the signal plus packaging in a sealed plastic waterproof bag, the 24-hour water immersion conditioning will be conducted while the signal is in the sealed plastic waterproof bag and will be followed by an additional immersion of the bare signal (i.e., after removal from the bag) 25 mm (1 in.) below the surface of the water for a period of 10 minutes.

(ii) *Waterproofing of igniter button.* Remove the cap from the test specimen. Place head of specimen without cap about 25 mm (1 in.) under the surface of water for approximately 5 minutes. Remove specimen from the water and wipe dry.

(iii) *Ignition and burning characteristics.* Test specimens shall ignite and burn satisfactorily with uniform intensity when the directions on the signal are followed. Test specimens shall not ignite explosively in a manner that might be dangerous to the user or persons close by. The plug separating the flare composition from the handle shall in no case allow flame or hot gases to pass through it or between it and the casing in such manner as might burn the hand while holding the signal by the handle.

(iv) *Burning time.* The burning time of a specimen shall be obtained by stop watch measurements from the time a distinct sustained flame is emitted until it ceases. Test specimens shall burn in air not less than 2 minutes.

TABLE 160.021–4(C)(1)—ACCEPT AND REJECT CRITERIA FOR OPERATIONAL TEST LOTS.

Lot size	Individual sample size	Sample	Cumulative sample size	Accept[1]	Reject[1]
280 or less.	8	First	8	(²)	400
		Second	16	100	500
		Third	24	200	600
		Fourth ..	32	300	700
		Fifth	40	500	800
		Sixth	48	700	900
		Seventh	56	950	951
281 to 500.	13	First	13	0	400
		Second	26	100	600
		Third	39	300	800
		Fourth ..	52	500	1,000
		Fifth	65	700	1,100
		Sixth	78	1,000	1,200
		Seventh	91	1,350	1,351
501 to 1,200.	20	First	20	0	500
		Second	40	300	800
		Third	60	600	1,000
		Fourth ..	80	800	1,300
		Fifth	100	1,100	1,500
		Sixth	120	1,400	1,700
		Seventh	140	1,850	1,851
1,201 to 3,200.	32	First	32	100	700
		Second	64	400	1,000
		Third	96	800	1,300

TABLE 160.021–4(C)(1)—ACCEPT AND REJECT CRITERIA FOR OPERATIONAL TEST LOTS.—Continued

Lot size	Individual sample size	Sample	Cumulative sample size	Accept[1]	Reject[1]
		Fourth ..	128	1,200	1,700
		Fifth	160	1,700	2,000
		Sixth	192	2,100	2,300
		Seventh	224	2,550	2,551
More than 3,201.	50	First	50	200	900
		Second	100	700	1,400
		Third	150	1,300	1,900
		Fourth ..	200	1,900	2,500
		Fifth	250	2,500	2,900
		Sixth	300	3,100	3,300
		Seventh	350	3,750	3,751

[1] Cumulative failure percent.
[2] Lot may not be accepted. Next sample must be tested.

TABLE 160.021–4(C)(2)

Kind of defects	Percentage of failure
a. Failure to ignite	100
b. Ignites or burns dangerously	50
c. Nonuniform burning intensity	50
d. Burns so as to materially obscure the flame	25
e. Fire flashes down between casing and handle so as to endanger burning the hand	50
f. Burning time less than 70 pct of specified time ...	100
g. Burning time at least 70 pct but less than 80 pct of specified time	75
h. Burning time at least 80 pct but less than 90 pct of specified time	50
i. Burning time at least 90 pct but less than 100 pct of specified time	25

(d) *Technical tests.* Three signals must be subjected to each of the following tests. Two of the three signals must pass each test in order for the lot of signals to be accepted.

(1) *Underwater burning.* Condition each sample in accordance with paragraph (c)(2)(i) of this section. Ignite specimen and let it burn about 5 seconds in air. Submerge the burning signal in water in a vertical position with head down. Obtain under water burning time by stop watch measurement from time of submersion until distinct, sustained flame emission ceases. The test specimen shall burn under water not less than 5 seconds when subjected to this test.

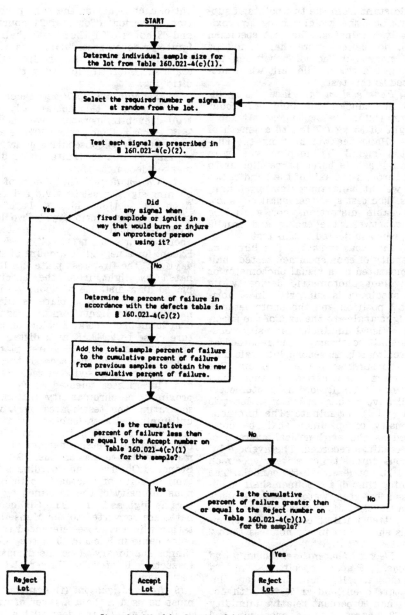

START

Determine individual sample size for
the lot from Table 160.021-4(c)(1).

Select the required number of signals
at random from the lot.

Test each signal as prescribed in
§ 160.021-4(c)(2).

Did
any signal when
fired explode or ignite in a
way that would burn or injure
an unprotected person
using it?

Yes

No

Determine the percent of failure in
accordance with the defects table in
§ 160.021-4(c)(2)

Add the total sample percent of failure
to the cumulative percent of failure
from previous samples to obtain the new
cumulative percent of failure.

Is the cumulative
percent of failure less than
or equal to the Accept number on
Table 160.021-4(c)(1)
for the sample?

No

Yes

Is the cumulative
percent of failure greater than
or equal to the Reject number on
Table 160.021-4(c)(1)
for the sample?

No

Yes

Reject
Lot

Accept
Lot

Reject
Lot

Figure 160.021-4(c).   Operational test procedure.

(2) *Bending strength.* Place the specimen on supports 15 cm (6 in.) apart. Attach a weight of 35 kg (77 lb.) to a length of wire. Hang the weight from the supported signal by looping the wire around the signal approximately

51

equidistant from the two points of support. Let the weight hang approximately 5 minutes. The test specimen shall not deflect more than 7 mm (1/4 in.), nor shall the joint between the casing and the handle fail, when subjected to this test.

(3) *Tensile strength.* Place the specimen in a chuck firmly holding it about 13 mm (1/2 in.) below the cap. Attach a weight of 35 kg (77 lb.) to a length of wire. Hang the weight from the supported signal by looping the wire through a hole bored perpendicular to and through the axis of the handle. Let the weight hang approximately 5 minutes. The test specimen shall not show noticeable distortion, nor shall the joint between the casing and handle fail, when subjected to this test.

(4) *Luminous intensity.* The luminous intensity of each specimen tested shall be measured by a visual photometer or equivalent photometric device, while the specimen is supported in a horizontal position and the photometer is at right angles to the axis of the specimen. Visual luminous intensity readings shall be observed and recorded at approximately 20 second intervals during the burning of the specimen. The minimum photometric distance shall be 3 m (10 ft.). Recording photometers shall have a chart speed of at least 25 mm (1 in.) per minute. The luminous intensity of specimen shall be computed as the arithmetical average of the readings recorded. The average luminous intensity of a test specimen shall be not less than 500 candela. The burning time of a specimen shall be obtained by stop watch measurements from the time distinct, sustained flame is emitted until it ceases. Test specimens shall burn in air not less than 2 minutes.

(5) *Elevated temperature, humidity and storage.* Place specimen in a thermostatically controlled even-temperature oven held at 75 °C. with not less than 90 percent relative humidity for 72 hours. Remove specimen and store at room temperature (20° to 25 °C.) with approximately 65 percent relative humidity for 10 days. If for any reason it is not possible to operate the oven continuously for the 72-hour period, it may be operated at the required temperature and humidity for 8 hours

out of each 24 during the 72-hour conditioning period. (Total of 24 hours on and 48 hours off.) The signal shall not ignite or decompose during this conditioning. The signal shall ignite and operate satisfactorily following this conditioning.

(6) *Spontaneous ignition.* Place the specimen in a thermostatically controlled even-temperature oven held at 75 °C. with not more than 10% relative humidity for 48 consecutive hours. The signals shall not ignite or undergo marked decomposition.

(7) *Chromaticity.* The color of the burning signal must be vivid red as defined by sections 13 and 14 of the "Color Names Dictionary." Two identical test plates of white cardboard about 30 cm × 60 cm (12″×24″) are used. Except for a negligible amount of stray daylight, the first test plate is illuminated by light from the specimen placed at a distance of about 1.5 m (5 ft.). The second test plate is illuminated only by light from an incandescent lamp operated at a color temperature close to 2,848 °K at a distance of about 30 cm (1 ft.). The first plate is viewed directly, the second through combinations of Lovibond red, yellow, and blue glasses selected so as to approximate a chromaticity match. By separating the test plates by a wide unilluminated area (subtending at the observer about 45°), it is possible to make accurate determinations of chromaticity in terms of the 1931 CIE Standard Observer and Coordinate System, in spite of fluctuations in luminous intensity of the specimen by factors as high as 2 or 3. The CIE coordinates are converted to the Munsell notation which is cross-referenced to the color name in Section 13 of the "Color Names Dictionary" (see the discussion in section 10 of "The Universal Color Language").

(8) *Heptane ignition.* (i) A metal pan must be used to hold a layer of water at least 12mm (½ in.) deep with a layer of technical grade heptane on top of the water. The pan must be at least 1 m (39 in.) square with sides extending between 175 mm (7 in.) and 200 mm (8 in.) above the surface of the water. The amount of heptane used to form the layer must be 2.0 liters per square

meter of pan area (6.25 fluid ounces per square foot).

(ii) The test must be conducted in a draft-free location. The ambient temperature, the temperature of the water, and the temperature of the heptane must all be between 20 °C (68 °F) and 25 °C (77 °F) at the time of the test.

(iii) The signal under test must be held with the flame end pointing upward at an angle of approximately 45°, 1.2 m (4 ft.) directly above the center of the pan. The signal must be ignited as soon as the heptane is observed to spread out over the water in continuous layer. The signal must be allowed to burn completely, and must remain in position until is has cooled.

(iv) The heptane must not be ignited by the flare or by material from the flare.

CAUTION: Heptane ignites rapidly and burns vigorously. The flare should be remotely ignited and all personnel should stay clear of the test pan while the flare is burning and while any part of it remains hot.

[CGD 76–048a and 76–048b, 44 FR 73060, Dec. 17, 1979, as amended by CGD 80–021, 45 FR 45280, July 3, 1980]

§ 160.021–5 Labeling and marking.

(a) *Labeling.* Each hand red flare distress signal shall bear a label securely affixed thereto, showing in clear, indelible black lettering on a red background, the following wording and information:

(Company brand or style designation)

Hand Red Flare Distress Signal

500 Candela—2 Minutes Burning Time

USE ONLY WHEN AIRCRAFT OR VESSEL IS SIGHTED

DIRECTIONS: Pull tape over top of cap. Remove cap and ignite flare by rubbing scratch surface on top of cap sharply across igniter button on head of signal.

CAUTION: Stand with back to wind and point away from body when igniting or flare is burning.

Service Life Expiration Date (Month and year to be inserted by manufacturer) (Month and year manufactured) (Lot No.___). Manufactured by (Name and address of manufacturer). U.S. Coast Guard Approval No.___

(b) *Marking of expiration date.* The expiration date must be not more than 42 months from the date of manufacture.

(c) *Other marking.* (1) There shall be die-stamped, in the side of the wooden handle in figures not less than 3 mm (C⅛ in.) high, numbers indicating the month and year of manufacture, thus: "6–54" indicating June, 1954.

(2) In addition to any other marking placed on the smallest packing carton or box containing hand red flare distress signals, such cartons or boxes shall be plainly and permanently marked to show the service life expiration date, date of manufacture, and lot number.

(3) The largest carton or box in which the manufacturer ships signals must be marked with the following or equivalent words: "Keep under cover in a dry place."

NOTE: Compliance with the labeling requirements of this section does not relieve the manufacturer of the responsibility of complying with the label requirements of 15 U.S.C. 1263, the Federal Hazardous Substances Act.

§ 160.021–6 Container.

(a) *General.* Containers for stowage of hand red flare distress signals in lifeboats and life rafts on merchant vessels are not required to have specific approval or to be of special design, but they shall meet the following test for watertightness when closed, and shall be capable of being opened and reclosed hand-tight to meet the same watertightness test. The materials shall be copper, brass, bronze, or equally corrosion-resistant to salt water and spray. The type container illustrated by Figure Number 160.021–6(a) is recommended for most purposes.

(b) *Watertightness test for containers.* Whenever a question arises as to the watertightness of a container, the following test may be made to determine whether it is satisfactory in this respect. Open the container, remove the contents, insert colored blotting paper as a lining, re-close container as tightly as possible by hand (no wrenches or special tools permitted), submerge container with top about 30 cm (1 ft.) below the surface of the water for two hours, remove container from water, wipe off excess moisture on outside, then open the container and examine the blotting paper and entire interior for evidence of moisture penetration. If any moisture or water is evidenced, the container is not satisfactory.

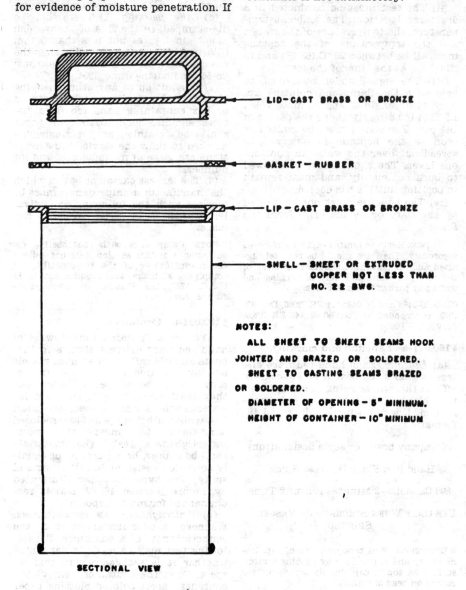

LID-CAST BRASS OR BRONZE

GASKET-RUBBER

LIP-CAST BRASS OR BRONZE

SHELL-SHEET OR EXTRUDED COPPER NOT LESS THAN NO. 22 BWG.

NOTES:

ALL SHEET TO SHEET SEAMS HOOK JOINTED AND BRAZED OR SOLDERED.

SHEET TO CASTING SEAMS BRAZED OR SOLDERED.

DIAMETER OF OPENING – 5" MINIMUM.

HEIGHT OF CONTAINER – 10" MINIMUM

SECTIONAL VIEW

Figure 160.021-6(a). Watertight Container for Hand Red Flare Distress Signals.

(c) *Marking of container.* Containers shall be embossed or bear a brass or equivalent corrosion-resistant nameplate, or otherwise be suitably and permanently marked, to plainly show in letters not less than 13 mm (½ in.) high the following wording: "HAND RED FLARE DISTRESS SIGNALS". No additional marking which might cause confusion as to the contents shall be permitted. The vessel's name ordinarily is painted or branded on equipment such as this container, and nothing in this subpart shall be construed as prohibiting same.

§ 160.021-7 **Procedure for approval.**

(a) Signals are approved by the Coast Guard under the procedures in subpart 159.005 of this chapter.

(b) [Reserved]

Subpart 160.022—Floating Orange Smoke Distress Signals (5 Minutes)

SOURCE: CGD 76–048a and 76–048b, 44 FR 73067, Dec. 17, 1979, unless otherwise noted.

§ 160.022-1 **Incorporations by reference.**

(a) The following are incorporated by reference into this subpart:

(1) "The Color Names Dictionary" in *Color: Universal Language and Dictionary of Names*, National Bureau of Standards Special Publication 440, December 1976.

(2) "Development of a Laboratory Test for Evaluation of the Effectiveness of Smoke Signals," National Bureau of Standards Report 4792, July 1956.

(b) NBS Special Publication 440 may be obtained by ordering from the Superintendent of Documents, U.S. Government Printing Office, Washington, DC 20402 (Order by SD Catalog No. C13.10:440).

(c) NBS Report 4792 may be obtained from the Commandant (G–MSE), U.S. Coast Guard, Washington, DC 20593-0001.

(d) Approval to incorporate by reference the materials listed in this section was obtained from the Director of the Federal Register on November 1

and 29, 1979. The materials are on file in the Federal Register Library.

[CGD 76–048a and 76–048b, 44 FR 73067, Dec. 17, 1979, as amended by CGD 82–063b, 48 FR 4782, Feb. 3, 1983; CGD 88–070, 53 FR 34535, Sept. 7, 1988; CGD 95–072, 60 FR 50467, Sept. 29, 1995; CGD 96–041, 61 FR 50733, Sept. 27, 1996]

§ 160.022-2 **Type.**

(a) Floating orange smoke distress signals, specified by this subpart shall be of one type which shall consist essentially of an outer container, ballast, an air chamber, an inner container, the smoke producing composition, and an igniter mechanism. Alternate arrangements which conform to the performance requirements of this specification will be given special consideration.

(b) [Reserved]

§ 160.022-3 **Materials, workmanship, construction, and performance requirements.**

(a) *Materials.* The materials shall conform strictly to the specifications and drawings submitted by the manufacturer and approved by the Commandant. Metal for containers shall be not less than 0.5 mm (0.020 in.) in thickness. Other dimensions or materials may be considered upon special request when presented with supporting data. Igniter systems shall be corrosion-resistant metal. The combustible material shall be of such nature that it will not deteriorate during long storage, nor when subjected to frigid or tropical climates, or both.

(b) *Workmanship.* Floating orange smoke distress signals shall be of first class workmanship and shall be free from imperfections of manufacture affecting their appearance or that may affect their serviceability.

(c) *Construction.* The outer container shall be of a size suitable for its intended use. All sheet metal seams should be hook-jointed and soldered. The whole container shall be covered with two coats of waterproof paint or equivalent protection system. The igniter mechanism shall be simple to operate and provide ignition in most unfavorable weather. The mechanism shall be protected with a watertight cover having a finish which is corrosion-resistant to salt water and spray. The cover shall be easily and quickly

55

removable by hand without the use of tools. If attachment of the cover is by formed screw threads, it shall be of such construction or material to prevent rusting or corrosion and will not back off and loosen under shipboard vibration.

(d) *Performance.* Signals shall meet all the inspection and test requirements contained in § 160.022-4.

§ 160.022-4 **Approval and production tests.**

(a) *Approval tests.* The manufacturer must produce a lot of at least 100 signals from which samples must be taken for testing for approval under § 160.022-7. The approval tests are the operational tests and technical tests in paragraphs (c) and (d) of this section. The approval tests must be conducted by an independent laboratory accepted by the Commandant under § 159.010 of this chapter.

(b) *Production inspections and tests.* Production inspections and tests of each lot of signals produced must be conducted under the procedures in § 159.007 of this chapter. Signals from a rejected lot must not be represented as meeting this subpart or as being approved by the Coast Guard. If the manufacturer identifies the cause of the rejection of a lot of signals, the signals in the lot may be reworked by the manufacturer to correct the problem. Samples from the rejected lot must be retested in order to be accepted. Records shall be kept of the reasons for rejection, the reworking performed on the rejected lot, and the results of the second test.

(1) *Lot size.* For the purposes of sampling the production of signals, a lot must consist of not more than 30,000 signals. Lots must be numbered serially by the manufacturer. A new lot must be started with:

(i) Any change in construction details,

(ii) Any change in sources of raw materials, or

(iii) The start of production on a new production line or on a previously discontinued production line.

(2) *Inspections and tests by the manufacturer.* The manufacturer's quality control procedures must include inspection of materials entering into construction of the signals and inspection of the finished signals, to determine that signals are being produced in accordance with the approved plans. Samples from each lot must be tested in accordance with the operational tests in paragraph (c) of this section.

(3) *Inspections and tests by an independent laboratory.* An independent laboratory accepted by the Commandant under § 159.010 of this chapter must perform or supervise the inspections and tests under paragraph (b)(2) of this section at least 4 times a year, unless the number of lots produced in a year is less than four. The inspections and tests must occur at least once during each quarterly period, unless no lots are produced during that period. If less than four lots are produced, the laboratory must perform or supervise the inspection and testing of each lot. In addition, the laboratory must perform or supervise the technical tests in paragraph (d) of this section at least once for every ten lots of signals produced, except that the number of technical tests must be at least one but not more than four per year. If a lot of signals tested by the independent laboratory is rejected, the laboratory must perform or supervise the inspections and tests of the reworked lot and the next lot of signals produced. The tests of each reworked lot and the next lot of signals must not be counted for the purpose of meeting the requirement for the annual number of inspections and tests performed or supervised by the independent laboratory.

(c) *Operational tests.* Each lot of signals must be sampled and tested as follows:

(1) *Sampling procedure and accept/reject criteria.* A sample of signals must be selected at random from the lot. The size of the sample must be the individual sample size in Table 160.022-4(c)(1) corresponding to the lot size. Each signal in the sample is tested as prescribed in the test procedure in paragraph (c)(2) of this section. Each signal that has a defect listed in the table of defects (Table 160.022-4(c)(2)) is assigned a score (failure percent) in accordance with that table. In the case of multiple defects, only the score having the highest numerical value is assigned

to that signal. If the sum of all the failure percents (cumulative failure percent) for the number of units in the sample is less than or equal to the accept criterion, the lot is accepted. If this sum is equal to or more than the reject criterion the lot is rejected. If the cumulative failure percent falls between the accept and reject criteria, another sample is selected from the production lot and the operational tests are repeated. The cumulative failure percent of each sample tested is added to that of the previous samples to obtain the cumulative failure percent for all the signals tested (cumulative sample size). Additional samples are tested and the tests repeated until either the accept or reject criterion for the cumulative sample size is met. If any signal in the sample explodes when fired or ignited in a way that could burn or otherwise injure the person firing it, the lot is rejected without further testing. (This procedure is diagrammed in figure 160.022–4(c).)

(2) *Test Procedure.* Each sample signal (specimen) must be tested as follows:

(i) *Conditioning of test specimens—water-resistance.* Immerse specimens horizontally with uppermost portion of the signal approximately 25 mm (1 in.) below the surface of the water for a period of 24 hours.

(ii) *Smoke emitting time.* Ignite specimen according to the directions printed on the signal and place signal in tub or barrel of water. The smoke emitting time of a specimen shall be obtained by stop watch measurements from the time of distinct, sustained smoke emission until it ceases. The watch shall be stopped during periods of flame emission. The smoke emitting time for a specimen shall be not less than 4 minutes.

(iii) *Ignition and smoke emitting characteristics.* Test specimens shall ignite and emit smoke properly when the directions on the signal are followed. Test specimens shall not ignite explosively in a manner that might be dangerous to the user or persons close by. Test specimens shall emit smoke at a uniform rate while floating in calm to rough water. Signals should be so constructed that water submerging the

signal in moderately heavy seas will not cause it to become inoperative.

TABLE 160.022–4(C)(1)—ACCEPT AND REJECT CRITERIA FOR OPERATIONAL TEST LOTS.

Lot size	Individual sample size	Sample	Cumulative sample size	Accept[1]	Reject[1]
280 or less.	8	First	8	(2)	400
		Second	16	100	500
		Third	24	200	600
		Fourth ..	32	300	700
		Fifth	40	500	800
		Sixth	48	700	900
		Seventh	56	950	951
281 to 500.	13	First	13	0	400
		Second	26	100	600
		Third	39	300	800
		Fourth ..	52	500	1,000
		Fifth	65	700	1,100
		Sixth	78	1,000	1,200
		Seventh	91	1,350	1,351
501 to 1,200.	20	First	20	0	500
		Second	40	300	800
		Third	60	600	1,000
		Fourth ..	80	800	1,300
		Fifth	100	1,100	1,500
		Sixth	120	1,400	1,700
		Seventh	140	1,850	1,851
1,201 to 3,200.	32	First	32	100	700
		Second	64	400	1,000
		Third	96	800	1,300
		Fourth ..	128	1,200	1,700
		Fifth	160	1,700	2,000
		Sixth	192	2,100	2,300
		Seventh	224	2,550	2,551
More than 3,201.	50	First	50	200	900
		Second	100	700	1,400
		Third	150	1,300	1,900
		Fourth ..	200	1,900	2,500
		Fifth	250	2,500	2,900
		Sixth	300	3,100	3,300
		Seventh	350	3,750	3,751

[1] Cumulative failure percent.
[2] Lot may not be accepted. Next sample must be tested.

TABLE 160.022–4(C)(2)

Kind of defects	Percentage of failure
a. Failure to ignite	100
b. Ignites or burns dangerously	50
c. Nonuniform smoke emitting rate	50
d. Smoke-emitting time less than 70 pct of specified time	100
e. Smoke-emitting time at least 70 pct but less than 30 pct of specified time	75
f. Smoke-emitting time at least 80 pct but less than 90 pct of specified time	50
g. Smoke-emitting time at least 90 pct but less than 100 pct of specified time	25

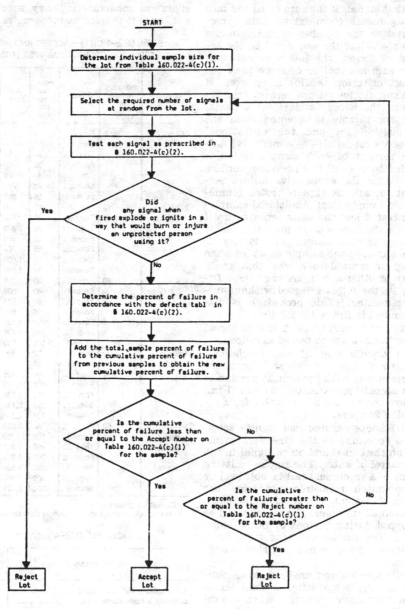

START

Determine individual sample size for the lot from Table 160.022-4(c)(1).

Select the required number of signals at random from the lot.

Test each signal as prescribed in § 160.022-4(c)(2).

Did any signal when fired explode or ignite in a way that would burn or injure an unprotected person using it?

Yes

No

Determine the percent of failure in accordance with the defects tabl in § 160.022-4(c)(2).

Add the total sample percent of failure to the cumulative percent of failure from previous samples to obtain the new cumulative percent of failure.

Is the cumulative percent of failure less than or equal to the Accept number on Table 160.022-4(c)(1) for the sample?

No

Yes

Is the cumulative percent of failure greater than or equal to the Reject number on Table 160.022-4(c)(1) for the sample?

No

Yes

Reject Lot

Accept Lot

Reject Lot

Figure 160.022-4(c). Operational test procedure.

(d) *Technical tests.* Three signals must be subjected to each of the following tests. Two of the three signals must pass the test in order for the lot of signals to be accepted.

58

(1) *Smoke emission in waves.* The signal shall be ignited and thrown overboard under conditions where the waves are at least 30 cm (1 ft.) high. The smoke emitting time must be at least 4 minutes and the signal shall float in such a manner that the signal shall function properly during this test. Failure to pass this test shall be cause for the lot to be rejected.

(2) *Underwater smoke emission.* Condition each sample in accordance with paragraph (c)(2)(i) of this section. Ignite specimen and let it burn about 15 seconds in air. Submerge the burning signal in water in a vertical position with head down. Obtain underwater smoke emission time by stop watch measurements from time of submersion until distinct, sustained smoke emission ceases. The test specimen shall emit smoke underwater not less than 15 seconds when subjected to this test.

(3) *Elevated temperature, humidity, and storage.* Place specimen in a thermostatically controlled even-temperature oven held at 75 °C. with not less than 90 percent relative humidity for 72 hours. Remove specimen and store at room temperature (20° to 25 °C.) with approximately 65 percent relative humidity for ten days. If for any reason it is not possible to operate the oven continuously for the 72-hour period, it may be operated at the required temperature and humidity for 8 hours out of each 24 during 72-hour conditioning period. (Total of 24 hours on and 48 hours off.) The signal shall not ignite or decompose during this conditioning. The signal shall ignite and operate satisfactorily following this conditioning.

(4) *Spontaneous ignition.* Place the specimen in a thermostatically controlled even-temperature oven held at 75 °C. with not more than 10% relative humidity for 48 consecutive hours. The signal shall not ignite or undergo marked decomposition.

(5) *Susceptibility to explosion.* Remove smoke composition from signal and punch a small hole in the composition. Insert a No. 6 commercial blasting cap. Ignite the cap. The test specimen shall not explode or ignite.

(6) *Corrosion resistance.* Expose the complete specimen with cover secured hand-tight to a finely divided spray of 20 percent by weight sodium chloride solution at a temperature between 32 °C and 38 °C (90 °F and 100 °F) for 100 hours. The container and cap must not be corroded in any fashion that would impair their proper functioning.

(7) *Color of smoke.* Ignite specimen in the open air in daytime according to the directions printed on the signal, and determine the smoke color by direct visual comparison of the unshadowed portions of the smoke with a color chart held so as to receive the same daylight illumination as the unshadowed portions of the smoke. The color of the smoke must be orange as defined by Sections 13 and 14 of the "Color Names Dictionary" (colors 34–39 and 48–54).

(8) *Volume and density of smoke.* The test specimen shall show less than 20 percent transmission for not less than 3 minutes when measured with apparatus having a light path of 19 cm (7½ in.), an optical system aperture of +3.7 degrees, and an entrance air flow of 18.4m³ per minute (650 cu. ft. per minute), such apparatus to be as described in National Bureau of Standards Report No. 4792.

§ 160.022–5 Marking.

(a) *Directions for use.* Each floating orange smoke distress signal shall be plainly and indelibly marked in black lettering not less than 3 mm (⅛ in.) high "Approved for daytime use only", and in black lettering not less than 5 mm (³⁄₁₆ in.) high with the word "Directions". Immediately below shall be similarly marked in black lettering not less than 3 mm (⅛ in.) high: "1. Use Only When Aircraft or Vessel Is Sighted". Then in numbered paragraphs, in similar lettering, there shall follow in simply and easily understood wording, instructions to be followed to make the device operative. Pasted-on labels are not acceptable.

(b) *Other markings.* (1) There shall be embossed or die-stamped, in the outer container in figures not less than 5 mm (³⁄₁₆ in.) high, numbers, indicating the month and year of manufacture, thus: "6–54" indicating June 1954. The outer container shall also be plainly and indelibly marked with the commercial designation of the signal, the words

"Floating Orange Smoke Distress Signal", name and address of the manufacturer, the Coast Guard Approval No., the service life expiration date (month and year to be entered by the manufacturer), the month and year of manufacture and the lot number.

(2) In addition to any other marking placed on the smallest packing carton or box containing floating orange smoke distress signals, such cartons or boxes shall be plainly and indelibly marked to show the service life expiration date, the month and year of manufacture, and the lot number.

(3) The largest carton or box in which the manufacturer ships signals must be marked with the following or equivalent words: "Keep under cover in a dry place."

(c) *Marking of expiration date.* The expiration date must be not more than 42 months from the date of manufacture.

NOTE: Compliance with the labeling requirements of this section does not relieve the manufacturer of the responsibility of complying with the label requirements of 15 U.S.C. 1263, the Federal Hazardous Substances Act.

§ 160.022–7 **Procedure for approval.**

(a) Signals are approved by the Coast Guard under the procedures in subpart 159.005 of this chapter.

(b) [Reserved]

Subpart 160.023—Hand Combination Flare and Smoke Distress Signals

SOURCE: CGD 76–048a and 76–048b, 44 FR 73070, Dec. 17, 1979, unless otherwise noted.

§ 160.023–1 **Incorporations by reference.**

(a) The following are incorporated by reference into this subpart:

(1) Military specifications MIL–S–18655 C, 3 May 1971—Signal, Smoke and Illumination, Marine, Mark 13, Mod 0.

(b) The military specification may be obtained from Customer Service, Naval Publications and Forms Center, 5801 Tabor Avenue, Philadelphia, PA. 19120 (tel: (215)697–2000). This specification is also on file in the Federal Register library.

(c) Approval to incorporate by reference the materials listed in this section was obtained from the Director of the Federal Register on November 1, 1979.

§ 160.023–2 **Type.**

(a) Hand combination flare and smoke distress signals specified by this subpart shall be of the type described in specification MIL–S–18655.

(b) [Reserved]

§ 160.023–3 **Materials, workmanship, construction, and performance requirements.**

(a) The materials, construction, workmanship, general and detail requirements shall conform to the requirements of specification MIL–S–18655, except as otherwise specifically provided by this subpart.

(b) [Reserved]

§ 160.023–4 **Approval and production tests.**

(a) *Approval tests.* The approval tests are those tests prescribed for the preproduction sample in MIL–S–18655. The approval tests must be conducted by an independent laboratory accepted by the Commandant under § 159.010 of this chapter.

(b) *Production inspections and tests.* Production inspections and tests of each lot of signals produced must be conducted under the procedures in § 159.007 of this chapter. Signals from a rejected lot must not be represented as meeting this subpart or as being approved by the Coast Guard. If the manufacturer identifies the cause of the rejection of a lot of signals, the signals in the lot may be reworked by the manufacturer to correct the problem. Samples from the rejected lot must be retested in order to be accepted. Records shall be kept of the reasons for rejection, the reworking performed on the rejected lot, and the results of the second test.

(1) *Inspections and tests by the manufacturer.* The manufacturer's quality control procedures must include inspection of materials entering into construction of the signals and inspection of the finished signals, to determine that signals are being produced in accordance with the approved plans.

The manufacturer must select samples from each lot and test them as specified in the production lot procedures in MIL–S–18655.

(2) *Inspections and tests by an independent laboratory.* An independent laboratory accepted by the Commandant under § 159.010 of this chapter must perform or supervise the inspections and tests under paragraph (b)(1) of this section at least 4 times a year, unless the number of lots is less than four. The inspections and tests must occur at least once during each quarterly period, unless no lots are produced during this period. If less than four lots are produced, the laboratory must perform or supervise the inspection and testing of each lot. If a lot of signals tested by the independent laboratory is rejected, the laboratory must perform or supervise the inspections and tests of the reworked lot and the next lot of signals produced. The tests of each reworked lot and the next lot produced must not be counted for the purpose of meeting the requirement for the annual number of inspections and tests performed or supervised by the independent laboratory.

§ 160.023-5   Labeling and marking.

(a) *Labeling.* A label showing firing instructions in accordance with specification MIL–S–18655, and to include the commercial designation of the signal, the lot number, Coast Guard approval number, the service life expiration date (month and year to be inserted by the manufacturer), and month and year of manufacture, shall be applied in a neat, workmanlike manner after the paint has become thoroughly dry. The label shall be attached to the signal and then protected by a transparent moisture impervious coating.

(b) *Marking of expiration date.* The expiration date must be not more than 42 months from the date of manufacture.

(c) *Other marking.* (1) In addition to any other marking placed on the smallest packing carton or box containing signals, such cartons or boxes shall be plainly and indelibly marked to show the service life expiration date, the date of manufacture, and the lot number.

(2) The largest carton or box in which the manufacturer ships signals must be marked with the following or equivalent words: "Keep under cover in a dry place."

NOTE: Compliance with the labeling requirements of this section does not relieve the manufacturer of the responsibility of complying with the label requirements of 15 U.S.C. 1263, the Federal Hazardous Substances Act.

§ 160.023-6   Container.

(a) *General.* The container for storing the signals on lifeboats and liferafts is not required to be of a special design or be approved by the Coast Guard. The container must meet the requirements in Subpart 160.021 (§ 160.021–6) except that the wording on the container must be: "HAND COMBINATION FLARE AND SMOKE DISTRESS SIGNALS."

(b) [Reserved]

§ 160.023-7   Procedure for approval.

(a) Signals are approved by the Coast Guard under the procedures in subpart 159.005 of this chapter.

(b) [Reserved]

Subpart 160.024—Pistol–Projected Parachute Red Flare Distress Signals

SOURCE: CGD 76–048a and 76–048b, 44 FR 73071, Dec. 17, 1979, unless otherwise noted.

§ 160.024-1   Incorporations by reference.

(a) The following is incorporated by reference into this subpart:

(1) "The Universal Color Language" and "The Color Names Dictionary" in *Color: Universal Language and Dictionary of Names,* National Bureau of Standards Special Publication 440, Dictionary 1976.

(b) NBS Special Publication 440 may be obtained by ordering from the Superintendent of Documents, U.S. Government Printing Office, Washington, DC 20402 (Order by SD Catalog No. C13.10:440).

(c) Approval to incorporate by reference the publication listed in this section was obtained from the Director of the Federal Register on November 1,

1979. The publication is on file at the Federal Register Library.

§ 160.024-2 Type.

(a) Pistol-projected parachute red flare distress signals specified by this subpart shall be of one type which shall consist essentially of a cartridge having centered primer, propelling charge, and projectile consisting of a case, delay element, expelling charge, and pyrotechnic candle attached to a parachute by shroud lines; the cartridge to be of such dimensions that it can be fitted into and fired from a signal pistol with chamber and bore dimensions within the limits provided by Figure 160.028-2(a) of subpart 160.028 of this chapter.

(b) [Reserved]

§ 160.024-3 Materials, workmanship, construction, and performance requirements.

(a) *Materials.* The materials used in pistol-projected parachute red flare distress signals shall conform strictly to the specifications and drawings submitted by the manufacturer and approved by the Commandant. In general, all metallic parts shall be corrosion-resistant or properly protected against corrosion.

(b) *Workmanship.* Pistol-projected parachute red flare distress signals shall be of first class workmanship and shall be free from imperfections of manufacture affecting their appearance or that may affect their serviceability.

(c) *Construction.* The exterior case of the cartridge shall be made of suitable metal and shall protect against the entrance of moisture. The projectile case and delay element shall be so constructed as to prevent any possibility of the propelling charge blowing by and causing premature ejection of the projectile contents. The shoulder of the base of the cartridge shall be between 2.29 mm (0.090 in.) and 2.67 mm (0.015 in.) in thickness. The centered primer shall be set below the surface of the base between 0.25 mm (0.010 in.) and 0.50 mm (0.020 in.).

(d) *Performance.* Signals shall meet all of the inspection and test requirements contained in § 160.024-4.

§ 160.024-4 Approval and production tests.

(a) *Approval tests.* The manufacturer must produce a lot of at least 100 signals from which samples must be taken for testing for approval under § 160.024-7. The approval tests are the operational tests and technical tests in paragraphs (c) and (d) of this section. The approval tests must be conducted by an independent laboratory accepted by the Commandant under § 159.010 of this chapter.

(b) *Production inspections and tests.* Production inspections and tests of each lot of signals produced must be conducted under the procedures in § 159.007 of this chapter. Signals from a rejected lot must not be represented as meeting this subpart or as being approved by the Coast Guard. If the manufacturer identifies the cause of the rejection of a lot of signals, the signals in the lot may be reworked by the manufacturer to correct the problem. Samples from the rejected lot must be retested in order to be accepted. Records shall be kept of the reasons for rejection, the reworking performed on the rejected lot, and the results of the second test.

(1) *Lot size.* For the purposes of sampling the production of signals, a lot must consist of not more than 30,000 signals. Lots must be numbered serially by the manufacturer. A new lot must be started with: (i) Any change in construction details, (ii) any change in sources of raw materials, or (iii) the start of production on a new production line or on a previously discontinued production line.

(2) *Inspections and tests by the manufacturer.* The manufacturer's quality control procedures must include inspection of materials entering into construction of the signals and inspection of the finished signals, to determine that signals are being produced in accordance with the approved plans. Samples from each lot must be tested in accordance with the operational tests in paragraph (c) of this section.

(3) *Inspections and tests by an independent laboratory.* An independent laboratory accepted by the Commandant under § 159.010 of this chapter must perform or supervise the inspections and

tests under paragraph (b)(2) of this section at least 4 times a year, unless the number of lots produced in a year is less than four. The inspections and tests must occur at least once during each quarterly period, unless no lots are produced during this period. If less than four lots are produced, the laboratory must perform or supervise the inspection and testing of each lot. In addition, the laboratory must perform or supervise the technical tests in paragraph (d) of this section at least once for every ten lots of signals produced, except that the number of technical tests must be at least one but not more than four per year. If a lot of signals tested by the independent laboratory is rejected, the laboratory must perform or supervise the inspections and tests of the reworked lot and the next lot of signals produced. The tests of each reworked lot and the next lot produced must not be counted for the purpose of meeting the requirement for the annual number of inspections and tests performed or supervised by the independent laboratory.

(c) *Operational tests.* Each lot of signals must be sampled and tested as follows:

(1) *Sampling procedure and accept/reject criteria.* A sample of signals must be selected at random from the lot. The size of the sample must be the individual sample size in Table 160.024-4(c)(1) corresponding to the lot size. Each signal in the sample is tested as prescribed in the test procedure in paragraph (c)(2) of this section. Each signal that has a defect listed in the table of defects. (Table 160.024-4(c)(2)) is assigned a score (failure percent) in accordance with the table. In the case of multiple defects, only the score having the highest numerical value is assigned to that signal. If the sum of all the failure percents (cumulative failure percent) for the number of units in the sample is less than or equal to the accept criterion, the lot is accepted. If this sum is equal to or more than the reject criterion the lot is rejected. If the cumulative failure percent falls between the accept and reject criteria, another sample is selected from the production lot and the operational tests are repeated. The cumulative failure percent of each sample tested is

added to that of the previous samples to obtain the cumulative failure percent for all the signals tested (cumulative sample size). Additional samples are tested and the tests repeated until either the accept or reject criterion for the cumulative sample size is met. If any signal in the sample explodes when fired or ignites in a way that could burn or otherwise injure the person firing it, the lot is rejected without further testing. (This procedure is diagrammed in figure 160.024-4(c).)

(2) *Test procedure.* Each sample signal (specimen) must be tested as follows:

(i) *Conditioning of test specimens— water resistance.* Immerse specimen horizontally with uppermost portion of the signal approximately 25 mm (1 in.) below the surface of the water for a period of 24 hours.

(ii) *Firing and operating characteristics.* Signals shall fire and operate satisfactorily when shot from a pistol of the type described in subpart 160.028. The parachute and pyrotechnic candle shall be ejected at approximately the maximum altitude reached by the projectile case. The parachute shall open and properly suspend the pyrotechnic candle without fouling. The pyrotechnic candle shall burn with uniform intensity and without damaging the parachute, shrouds, or leader line.

(iii) *Altitude.* The altitude reached by a signal is considered to be the height at which the parachute and pyrotechnic candle are ejected from the projectile case, as determined by visual observation against an object of known height, such as a tower or ballon, or by triangulation from two or more points of observation, or by other method satisfactory to the Commandant. The altitude reached shall be not less than 45 m (150 ft.).

(iv) *Rate of descent.* The rate of descent of a signal is considered to be the calculated average rate obtained by dividing the altitude by the time of descent to the surface. The rate of descent shall not exceed 1.8 m (6 ft.) per second.

(v) *Burning time.* The burning time of the pyrotechnic candle shall be obtained by stop watch measurement from the time distinct, sustained flame is emitted until it ceases. The burning time shall be not less than 30 seconds.

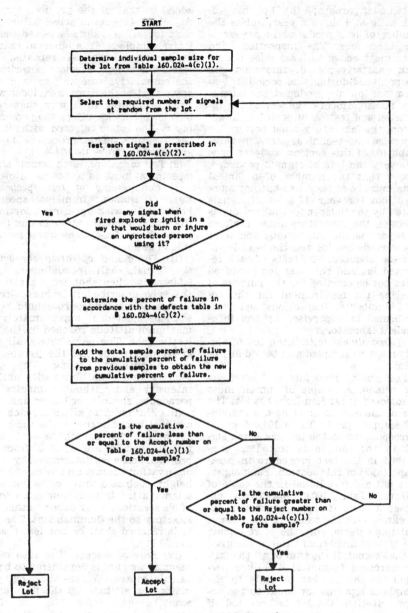

Figure 160.024-4(c). Operational test procedure.

TABLE 160.024-4(C)(1)—ACCEPT AND REJECT CRITERIA FOR OPERATIONAL TEST LOTS.

Lot size	Individual sample size	Sample	Cumulative sample size	Accept[1]	Reject[1]
280 or less.	8	First	8	[2]	400
		Second	16	100	500
		Third	24	200	600
		Fourth	32	300	700
		Fifth	40	500	800
		Sixth	48	700	900
		Seventh	56	950	951
281 to 500.	13	First	13	0	400
		Second	26	100	600
		Third	39	300	800
		Fourth	52	500	1,000
		Fifth	65	700	1,100
		Sixth	78	1,000	1,200
		Seventh	91	1,350	1,351
501 to 1,200.	20	First	20	0	500
		Second	40	300	800
		Third	60	600	1,000
		Fourth	80	800	1,300
		Fifth	100	1,100	1,500
		Sixth	120	1,400	1,700
		Seventh	140	1,850	1,851
1,201 to 3,200.	32	First	32	100	700
		Second	64	400	1,000
		Third	96	800	1,300
		Fourth	128	1,200	1,700
		Fifth	160	1,700	2,000
		Sixth	192	2,100	2,300
		Seventh	224	2,550	2,551
More than 3,201.	50	First	50	200	900
		Second	100	700	1,400
		Third	150	1,300	1,900
		Fourth	200	1,900	2,500
		Fifth	250	2,500	2,900
		Sixth	300	3,100	3,300
		Seventh	350	3,750	3,751

[1] Cumulative failure percent.
[2] Lot may not be accepted. Next sample must be tested.

TABLE 160.024-4(C)(2)

Kind of defect	Percentage of failure
a. Failure to fire (when attributable to the primer and not to the malfunction of the pistol) ...	100
b. Failure to eject projectile contents	100
c. Failure to ignite pyrotechnic candle	75
d. Failure of parachute to open completely	75
e. Complete carrying away or destruction of parachute	75
f. Altitude less than 70 pct of that required	100
g. Altitude at least 70 pct but less than 80 pct of that required	75
h. Altitude at least 80 pct but less than 90 pct of that required	50
i. Altitude at least 90 pct but less than 100 pct of that required	25
j. Average rate of descent greater than 4 times maximum permitted	100
k. Average rate of descent less than 4 but greater than 3 times maximum permitted	75
l. Average rate of descent less than 3 but greater than 2 times maximum permitted	50
m. Average rate of descent less than twice but greater than maximum permitted	25
n. Burning time less than 70 pct of that required	100

TABLE 160.024-4(C)(2)—Continued

Kind of defect	Percentage of failure
o. Burning time at least 70 pct but less than 80 pct of that required	75
p. Burning time at least 80 pct but less than 90 pct of that required	50
q. Burning time at least 90 pct but less than 100 pct of that required	25

(d) *Technical tests.* Three signals must be subjected to each of the following tests. Two of the three signals must pass each test in order for the lot of signals to be accepted.

(1) *Luminous intensity.* The luminous intensity of each pyrotechnic candle tested shall be measured by a visual photometer or equivalent photometric device while the specimen is supported in a horizontal position and the photometer is at right angles to the axis of the specimen. Visual luminous intensity readings shall be observed and recorded at approximately 5-second intervals during the burning of the specimen. The minimum photometric distance shall be 3 m (10 ft.). Recording photometers shall have a chart speed of at least 10 cm (4 in.) per minute. The luminous intensity of the specimen shall be computed as the arithmetical average of the readings recorded. The average luminous intensity of a specimen shall be not less than 20,000 candela.

(2) *Elevated temperature, humidity, and storage.* Place specimen in a thermostatically controlled even-temperature oven held at 75 °C. with not less than 90 percent relative humidity for 72 hours. Remove specimen and store at room temperature (20° to 25 °C.) with approximately 65 percent relative humidity for 10 days. If for any reason it is not possible to operate the oven continuously for the 72-hour period, it may be operated at the required temperature and humidity for 8 hours out of each 24 during the 72-hour conditioning period. (Total of 24 hours on and 48 hours off.) The signal shall not ignite or decompose during this conditioning. The signal shall fire and operate satisfactorily following this conditioning.

(3) *Spontaneous ignition.* Place the specimen in a thermostatically controlled even-temperature oven held at 75 °C. with not more than 10% relative

humidity for 48 consecutive hours. The signal shall not ignite or undergo marked decomposition.

(4) *Chromaticity.* The color of the burning signal must be vivid red as defined by Sections 13 and 14 of the "Color Names Dictionary." Two identical test plates of white cardboard about 30 cm × 60 cm (12″ × 24″) are used. Except for a negligible amount of stray daylight, the first test plate is illuminated by light from the specimen placed at a distance of about 1.5 cm (5 ft.). The second test plate is illuminated only by light from an incandescent lamp operated at a color temperature close to 2,848° K at a distance of about 30 cm (1 ft.). The first plate is viewed directly, the second through combinations of lovibond red, yellow, and blue glasses selected so as to approximate a chromaticity match. By separating the test plates by a wide unilluminated area (subtending at the observer about 45°), it is possible to make accurate determinations of chromaticity in terms of the 1931 CIE Standard Observer and Coordinate System, in spite of fluctuations in luminous intensity of the specimen by factors as high as 2 or 3. The CIE coordinates are converted to the Munsell notation which is cross-referenced to the color name in Section 13 of the "Color Names Dictionary" (see the discussion in section 10 of "the Universal Color Language").

§ 160.024–5 **Marking.**

(a) *Cartridge.* Each pistol-projected parachute red flare distress signal shall be legibly marked as follows:

PISTOL-PROJECTED PARACHUTE RED FLARE DISTRESS SIGNAL

20,000 candela—30 seconds burning time

USE ONLY WHEN AIRCRAFT OR VESSEL IS SIGHTED DIRECTIONS— Fire upward from signal pistol Service Life Expiration Date (date to be inserted by manufacturer) (Month and year manufactured) Lot No.____

Manufactured by (Name and address of manufacturer)

U.S. COAST GUARD APPROVAL NO.____.

(b) *Marking of expiration date.* The expiration date must be not more than 42 months from the date of manufacture.

(c) *Other marking.* (1) On each pistol-projected parachute red flare distress signal there shall be die-stamped, in figures not less than 3mm (⅛ in.) high, on the cartridge, numbers indicating the month and year of manufacture, thus: "6–54" indicating June 1954.

(2) The pyrotechnic candle shall be legibly marked with the month and year of manufacture.

(3) In addition to any other marking placed on the smallest packing carton or box containing cartridges, each carton or box shall be plainly and permanently marked to show the service life expiration date, the date of manufacture, and the lot number.

(4) The largest carton or box in which the manufacturer ships signals must be marked with the following or equivalent words: "Keep under cover in a dry place."

NOTE: Compliance with the labeling requirements of this section does not relieve the manufacturer of the responsibility of complying with the label requirements of 15 U.S.C. 1263, the Federal Hazardous Substances Act.

§ 160.024–7 **Procedure for approval.**

(a) Signals are approved by the Coast Guard under the procedures in subpart 159.005 of this chapter.

(b) [Reserved]

Subpart 160.026—Water, Emergency Drinking (In Hermetically Sealed Containers), for Merchant Vessels

§ 160.026–1 **Applicable specifications and standard.**

(a) *General.* The following specifications and standard, of the issue in effect on the date emergency drinking water is packed, form a part of this subpart:

(1) Military specifications:

MIL–L–7178—Lacquer; cellulose nitrate, gloss for aircraft use.

MIL–E–15090—Enamel, equipment, light-gray (Formula No. 111).

MIL–W–15117—Water, drinking, canned, emergency.

(2) U.S. Public Health Service:

Drinking Water Standards (Publication No. 956).

(b) *Copies on file.* Copies of the specifications referred to in this section shall be kept on file by the packer, together with the approved plans and certificate of approval issued by the Coast Guard. The military specifications may be obtained from the Commanding Officer, Naval Supply Depot, 5801 Tabor Avenue, Philadelphia, Pa., 19120. The "Drinking Water Standards" may be obtained from the U.S. Department of Health and Human Services, Public Health Service, Washington, DC, 20201.

[CGFR 65–9, 30 FR 11466, Sept. 8, 1965, as amended by CGD 84–064, 49 FR 34004, Aug. 28, 1984]

§ 160.026–2 Type.

(a) Emergency drinking water for lifeboats and life rafts and its hermetically sealed container shall be as specified herein, but alternate containers will be given special consideration.

(b) [Reserved]

[CGFR 53–25, 18 FR 7865, Dec. 5, 1953]

§ 160.026–3 Container.

(a) *General.* The emergency drinking water container shall be a sanitary type can, approximately $2^{11}/_{16}$ in diameter by $4^7/_8''$ in height. The top and bottom of the can shall be double-seamed and compound-lined. The side seam shall be of a locked type, soldered on the outside. The can shall be made of 1.25-pound coating coke tin-plate throughout, with not less than 100-pound plate for the body and 85-pound plate for the ends.

(b) *Interior and exterior coatings.* The interior of the container shall be uncoated, except for the tin-plating required by paragraph (a) of this section. In addition to the tin-plating, the exterior surfaces of the container, including the ends, but excluding the side seam, shall be lithographed a gray enamel conforming to Type I or II, Class 2 of Specification MIL–E–15090, with the marking as provided by § 160.026–5 lithographed in black print. After filling, sealing, autoclaving, and marking, the container shall be dip-coated with one coat of clear base lacquer conforming to Specification MIL–L–7178.

(c) *Plant sanitation, sterilizing and filling.* The plant and equipment in which the water is canned shall be maintained in a clean and sanitary condition at all times, and standard aseptic procedures shall be followed throughout in filling the cans. The container shall be free from all foreign materials, and shall be filled with approximately $10^2/_3$ oz. of water meeting the requirements of § 160.026–4. After filling, it shall be hermetically sealed under vacuum, and after sealing, it shall be autoclaved at a temperature of not less than 250 °F. for not less than 15 minutes.

[CGFR 53–25, 18 FR 7865, Dec. 5, 1953]

§ 160.026–4 Water.

(a) Only water meeting the U.S. Public Health Service "Drinking Water Standards" which has been suitably inhibited to protect the container against corrosion shall be used. After treatment and packing the water shall be free from organic matter, sediment and odor. It shall have a pH between 7.0 and 9.0 as determined by means of a standard pH meter using glass electrodes.

(b) [Reserved]

[CGFR 65–9, 30 FR 11466, Sept. 8, 1965]

§ 160.026–5 Marking.

(a) *General.* The month and year of packing and the lot number shall be embossed on the top of the container. The container shall also be lithographed on one side in accordance with § 160.026–3(b) with the following:

"U. S. Coast Guard

Approval No. ____"

(Not less than ³⁄₂₂″ in height)

"Contents

Approx. 10⅝ oz."

(Not less than ³⁄₃₂″ in height)

"EMERGENCY

DRINKING

WATER"

(Not less than ⅔″ in height)

(Name and address of packer)

(Not less than ⅛″ in height)

(b) *Other marking.* In addition to any other marking placed on the smallest packing carton or box in which emergency drinking water containers are placed prior to shipment, each carton or box shall be plainly and permanently marked with the name and address of the packer, the month and year of packing, and the lot number.

[CGFR 53-25, 18 FR 7865, Dec. 5, 1953]

§ 160.026-6 Sampling, inspection, and tests of production lots.

(a) *General.* Containers of emergency drinking water must be tested in accordance with the provisions of this section by an independent laboratory accepted by the Coast Guard under 46 CFR 159.010.

(b) *Lots.* For purposes of sampling the production of approved emergency drinking water for lifeboats and life rafts, a lot shall consist of all cans of water to be offered for inspection at one time. Lots shall be numbered serially by the packer, and a new lot shall be started with any change or modification in materials or production methods.

(c) *Visual inspection of containers.* The independent laboratory inspector shall select at random from each lot the number of sample filled containers indicated in table 160.026-6(c), which shall be examined visually for compliance with the requirements of this subpart. If the number of defective cans exceeds the acceptance number shown in the table for the samples selected, the lot shall be rejected.

TABLE 160.026-6(C)—SAMPLING FOR VISUAL INSPECTION OF CONTAINERS

Lot size	No. of cans in sample	Acceptance number
800 and under	35	0
801 to 1,300	50	1
1,301 to 3,200	75	2
3,201 to 8,000	110	3
8,001 and over	150	4

(d) *Laboratory tests of containers and water.* The manufacturer shall select at random from each lot the number of sets of 11 filled sample containers indicated in Table 160.026-6(d1), which shall be forwarded to an independent laboratory accepted by the Coast Guard under 46 CFR 159.010. The independent laboratory shall perform the tests outlined in Table 160.026-6(d2). If any sample is found to be non-conforming in any of these tests, the lot shall be rejected.

TABLE 160.026-6(D1)—SAMPLING FOR LABORATORY TESTS

Lot size	Number of sets of samples to be selected
3,200 and under	1 set of 11 containers each.
3,201 and over	2 sets of 11 containers each.

TABLE 160.026-6(D)(2)—DESCRIPTION OF LABORATORY TESTS

Number of containers per set of samples to be tested	Type of test	Reference specification for test procedure to be followed
2	Internal corrosion and vacuum	MIL-W-15117.
9	Bacteriological limits and salt content	MIL-W-15117 and U.S. Public Health "Drinking Water Standards."

(e) *Lot acceptance.* When the independent laboratory is satisfied that the emergency drinking water meets the requirements of this subpart, the lot shall be accepted. When permitted by the independent laboratory, rejected lots may be resubmitted for official inspection, provided all containers in the lot have been reworked by the packer, and all defective units removed. Emergency drinking water from rejected lots may not, unless subsequently accepted, be sold or offered for sale under representation as being in compliance with this subpart or as being approved for use on merchant vessels.

[CGFR 53–25, 18 FR 7865, Dec. 5, 1953, as amended by CGFR 65–9, 30 FR 11466, Sept. 8, 1965; CGD 75–186, 41 FR 10437, Mar. 11, 1976; CGD 95–028, 62 FR 51211, Sept. 30, 1997]

EFFECTIVE DATE NOTE: At 62 FR 51211, Sept. 30, 1997, § 160.026–6 was amended by removing paragraphs (f) and (g) and revising paragraphs (a) and (e) and the texts of paragraphs (c) and (d), effective Oct. 30, 1997.

§ 160.026–7 **Procedure for approval.**

(a) *General.* Emergency drinking water for lifeboats and liferafts on merchant vessels is approved only by the Commandant, U.S. Coast Guard.

(b) *Pre-approval samples and plans.* Packers who desire to pack approved emergency drinking water shall have the required tests in accordance with § 160.026–5 performed by an independent laboratory accepted by the Coast Guard under 46 CFR 159.010. A copy of the independent laboratory's report will be forwarded to the Commandant for examination, and, if satisfactory, an official approval number will be assigned to the manufacturer for the emergency drinking water.

[CGD 95–028, 62 FR 51211, Sept. 30, 1997]

EFFECTIVE DATE NOTE: At 62 FR 51211, Sept. 30, 1997, § 160.026–7 was revised, effective Oct. 30, 1997.

Subpart 160.027—Life Floats for Merchant Vessels

SOURCE: CGD 79–167, 47 FR 41376, Sept. 20, 1982, unless otherwise noted.

§ 160.027–2 **Type.**

(a) Each life float must meet the requirements in subpart 160.010 of this chapter for a peripheral body type buoyant apparatus designed so that persons supported are only partially immersed (180 N (40 lb.) of buoyancy per person required).

(b) [Reserved]

§ 160.027–3 **Additional requirements for life floats.**

(a) Each life float must have a platform designed to drop through the center of the float, whichever way the life float is floating. A typical arrangement is shown in Figure 160.027–3(a).

(b) The platform must meet the requirements of one of the following paragraphs:

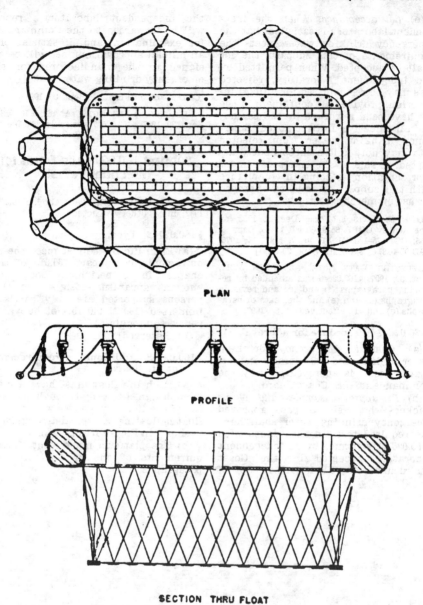

PLAN

PROFILE

SECTION THRU FLOAT

Figure 160.027-3(a) - Typical Life Float.

(1) A lattice type platform must be of western red cedar, port orford cedar, sitka spruce, northern white pine, or southern cypress slats constructed on an oak frame. The slats must have nominal cross-section dimensions not less than 90 mm (3⅝ in.) by 9.5 mm (⅜ in.). The frame members must have

nominal cross-section dimensions not less than 100 mm (4 in.) by 12.5 mm (½ in.). The space between adjacent slats must not exceed the width of the slats. The space between each frame member and the adjacent slat must not exceed twice the width of the slats. The platform must be riveted together at each intersection of—

(i) Frame members,

(ii) Slats, and

(iii) Frame members and slats.

(2) A plywood platform must be made of exterior or marine type plywood with surfaces that are either "A" or "B" grade as commonly designated in the plywood industry. Holes 35 mm (1⅜ in.) to 50 mm (2 in.) in diameter must be drilled through the platform. The number of holes must be at least the number equal to (L–25) (W–25)/225, where L is the length of the platform in cm and W is the width of the platform in cm. (The formula is (L–10)(W–10)/36 where L and W are measured in inches.) The thickness of the plywood must be at least—

(i) 12.5 mm (½ in.) for life floats of 10 persons capacity and under,

(ii) 16 mm (⅝ in.) for life floats between 11 and 25 persons capacity inclusive, and

(iii) 19 mm (¾ in.) for life floats of 26 persons capacity and over.

(3) A platform of construction differing from that described in either (1) or (2) of this paragraph will be approved if it has holes to permit the passage of water and if it passes the tests in § 160.027-7. The number of holes must be the same as required for a plywood platform. If the platform is netting on a frame, the netting must be constructed of cordage with a breaking strength of at least 1600 N (355 lb.). The netting must be constructed on not more than 5 cm (2 in.) centers and must be knotted together at each point where the lines intersect.

(c) Each platform must be of a material that is resistant to deterioration by exposure to weather or must have a surface that protects it from deterioration by exposure to weather. For a wood platform, this surface must be at least two coats of water resistant spar varnish, or two coats of marine paint.

(d) Each part of the platform, including surfaces, edges, and rivets must be smooth and must not have cutting edges, points, or splinters which would be dangerous for bare feet.

(e) The platform must be arranged so that under normal stowed conditions, it can be retained in the center of the float and can be readily released from this position for use.

(f) The platform must be suspended from the body of the float by a net or an equivalent arrangement, which when fully extended, holds the top of the platform approximately 900 mm (36 in.) below the center of the float body.

(1) The net must be constructed of cordage with a minimum breaking strength of 1600 N (355 lb.). The net must be attached to the platform through holes on centers that do not exceed 165 mm (6½ in.).

(2) If the platform is suspended from the body of the float by an arrangement other than a net as described in paragraph (c)(1) of this section, the arrangement must be of equivalent to the net in terms of strength, resistance to tangling, and allowing the platform to freely pass through the center of the life float body.

§ 160.027-7 Pre-approval tests for alternate platform designs.

(a) The tests in this section are for life float platforms that do not meet the requirements of either § 160.027-3(b) (1) or (2).

(b) The float body must be supported so that the platform is suspended in the air by the net or equivalent supporting arrangement. The platform must be loaded evenly with a weight equal to 60 percent of the weight of the total number of persons for which the float is to be rated, assuming a weight of 75 kg (165 lb.) per person. The weight must be allowed to remain on the platform for ten minutes after which it is removed. The supporting arrangement and platform must not show any evidence of damage or permanent deformation as a result of this test.

(c) The float body must be supported so that the platform is suspended in the air by the net or equivalent supporting arrangement. A bag of sand, shot or similar granular material weighing 90 kg (200 lb.) must be dropped onto the center of the platform from a height of 3 m (10 ft.). The supporting arrangement and platform must not show any damage that would affect the serviceability of the float or platform.

(d) As part of the buoyancy test required in § 160.010-7(e) of this chapter, the platform must be loaded with weights equal to ½ the rated capacity of the float. There must be no damage to the supporting arrangement or platform as a result of this test.

NOTE: Since the weights on the platform will be submerged during this test, allowance must be made for the displacement of the submerged weights. The weight required is calculated by the formula $W=(18d)/(d-4895)$, where W is the required submerged weight per person (in kg) and d is the density of the material (in kg/m³). (In customary U.S. units, the formula is $W=40d)/(d-63)$ where W is in lb. and d is in lb./ft.³).

Subpart 160.028—Signal Pistols for Red Flare Distress Signals

SOURCE: CGD 76-048a and 76-048b, 44 FR 73078, Dec. 17, 1979, unless otherwise noted.

§ 160.028-2 Type.

(a) Each signal pistol for launching a parachute distress signal that meets subpart 160.024 of this part must be of the center-firing type having chamber and bore dimensions within the limits indicated by Figure No. 160.028-2(a).

(b) A signal pistol for launching an aerial flare not under paragraph (a) of this section may have any chamber and bore dimensions if they are not the dimensions for a conventional round of ammunition.

§ 160.028-3 Materials, workmanship, construction, and performance requirements.

(a) *Materials.* The materials used in signal pistols shall conform strictly to the specifications and drawings submitted by the manufacturer and approved by the Commandant. In general, all parts shall be corrosion-resistant or properly protected against corrosion. The ejection mechanism shall be of material possessing excellent wearing qualities.

(b) *Workmanship.* Signal pistols shall be of first class workmanship and shall be free from imperfections of manufac-

ture affecting their serviceability or appearance.

(c) *Construction and performance requirements. (Pistols intended for signals meeting Subpart 160.024).* Signal pistols shall be of rugged construction and shall operate satisfactorily in firing and ejecting pistol-projected parachute red flare distress signals of the type covered by Subpart 160.024. The ejection mechanism shall be of sturdy design capable of withstanding rough and repeated usage. The overall size and weight of signal pistols should be kept to a minimum consistent with adequate strength and safety. When the pistol is cocked and the trigger is pulled, the firing pin shall project between 1.52 mm and 2.54 mm (0.060 in. and 0.100 in.) beyond the face plate of the frame. When the barrel is locked in the firing position, the barrel chamber shall be not more than 0.25 mm (0.010 in.) from the face plate of the frame.

§ 160.028-4 Approval and production tests.

(a) *Approval test.* An independent laboratory accepted by the Commandant under § 159.010 of this chapter must test three pistols in accordance with the operational test in paragraph (c) of this section.

(b) *Production inspections and tests.* Production inspections and tests of each pistol must be conducted under the procedures in § 159.007 of this chapter. Each pistol which passes the production inspections and tests must be stamped with the letters "P.T." Each pistol which fails the test must not be represented as meeting this subpart or as being approved by the Coast Guard.

(1) *Inspections and tests by the manufacturer.* The manufacturer's quality control procedures must include the inspection of the pistols during production, and inspection of the finished pistols, to determine that the pistols are being produced in accordance with the approved plans. Each pistol must be tested in accordance with the operational test in paragraph (c) of this section, except that checking of the chamber and bore dimensions is not required.

(2) *Inspections and tests by an independent laboratory.* An independent laboratory accepted by the Commandant

under §159.010 of this Chapter must inspect and test three pistols at least one each year. The inspection must determine that the pistols are being produced in accordance with the approved plans. The test must be in accordance with paragraph (c) of this section.

(c) *Operational test.* The operational test must be conducted as follows:

(1) Check the chamber and bore dimensions of the pistol.

(2) Fire a dummy cartridge simulating a normal signal in size and weight, but with a charge double the normal charge.

(3) Fire a normal signal.

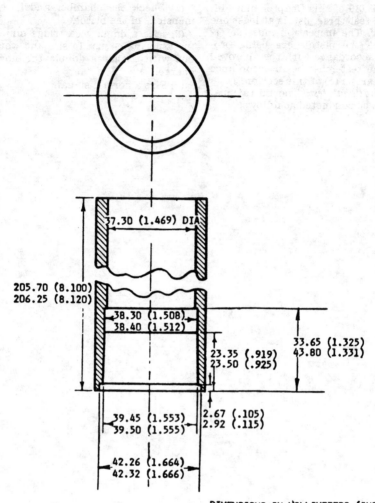

37.30 (1.469) DIA

205.70 (8.100)
206.25 (8.120)

38.30 (1.508)
38.40 (1.512)

23.35 (.919)
23.50 (.925)

33.65 (1.325)
43.80 (1.331)

39.45 (1.553)
39.50 (1.555)

2.67 (.105)
2.92 (.115)

42.26 (1.664)
42.32 (1.666)

DIMENSIONS IN MILLIMETERS (INCHES)

Figure 160.028-2(a). Signal Pistol - Chamber and Bore
Dimensions.

(4) Recheck the chamber and bore dimensions.

(5) The pistol must fire the signal properly, must not have any visible deformation or damage as a result of the test, and must not have any change in the chamber and bore dimensions.

§ 160.028–5 Marking.

(a) *General.* Each signal pistol shall be permanently and legibly marked with its serial number, Coast Guard approval number, and the name and address of the manufacturer.

(b) [Reserved]

§ 160.028–6 Container.

(a) *General.* Containers for the stowage of signal pistols and pistol projected parachute red flare distress signals in lifeboats and life rafts on merchant vessels are not required to have specific approval or to be of specific design except for certain material, marking, and test requirements, which requirements are contained in § 160.024–6 of subpart 160.024.

(b) [Reserved]

§ 160.028–7 Procedure for approval.

(a) Signals are approved by the Coast Guard under the procedures in subpart 159.005 of this chapter.

(b) [Reserved]

Subpart 160.031—Line-Throwing Appliance, Shoulder Gun Type (and Equipment)

SOURCE: CGD 76–048a and 76–048b, 44 FR 73080, Dec. 17, 1979, unless otherwise noted.

§ 160.031–1 Incorporation by reference.

(a) The following Federal specification is incorporated by reference into this subpart:

(1) T–R–605 b, December 13, 1963 and Amendment 3, April 17, 1973—Rope, Manila, and Sisal.

(b) The Federal specification may be obtained from Customer Service, Naval Publications and Forms Center, 5801 Tabor Avenue, Philadelphia, PA. 19120 (tel: (215)697–2000). This specification is also on file in the Federal Register library.

(c) Approval to incorporate by reference the material listed in this section was obtained from the Director of the Federal Register on September 24, 1979.

§ 160.031–2 Type and size.

(a) The shoulder gun type line-throwing appliance shall be breech-loading for the cartridge and muzzle-loading for the projectile, of not more than 13 mm (0.50 in.) caliber, chambered for blank rifle cartridges, smooth bored, and properly stocked, with shot line canister attached in a position below the barrel.

(b) [Reserved]

§ 160.031–3 Materials, construction, workmanship, and performance requirements.

(a) All materials used in the construction of shoulder gun type line-throwing appliances and equipment shall be of good quality, suitable for the purpose intended, and shall conform to the requirements of this specification. The choice of materials shall be such that resistance to corrosion by salt water or spray, shock, temperature change, and wear will be obtained. The use of dissimilar metals in combination shall be avoided wherever possible, but when such contacts are necessary, provision shall be made to prevent such deleterious effects as galvanic corrosion, freezing or buckling of moving parts, and loosening or tightening of joints due to difference in coefficients of thermal expansion.

(b) The design and construction shall be proper and substantial for effective and safe operation aboard ship.

(c) The workmanship shall be first class and free from any imperfections of manufacture affecting appearance or serviceability of the gun.

(d) The gun, when loaded and fired in accordance with the manufacturer's instructions, shall be capable of propelling through relatively still air, the service projectile with service line attached, for a distance of not less than 75 m (250 ft.) with deviation from the target not to exceed 4.5 m (15 ft.) either side.

§ 160.031–4 Equipment for shoulder gun type line-throwing appliance.

(a) Ten service projectiles, each machined from steel or bronze, weighing about 225 g (8 oz.), and having a shank of sufficient length to project slightly beyond the muzzle, with an eye at the upper end for securing the service line.

(b) Four service lines, each not less than 180 m (600 ft.) in length, of 1.5 mm (1⁄16-in.) or more in diameter, woven or braided nylon, very flexible, and having

75

a breaking strength of not less than 625 N (140 lb.), or equivalent. Each line shall be one continuous length without splice, knot, or other weakening features and shall be made up or coiled in such way as to render it ready at all times for immediate use. The end of the line intended to be attached to projectile shall have securely attached thereto a substantial tag bearing a permanent legend indicating its purpose, and the other end of the line shall be tagged in the same manner to prevent delay in securing proper and immediate action with the equipment. The line shall be coiled or reeled in such manner that when all the line leaves the canister it automatically becomes unattached and free from the canister and the gun. The line canister shall be secured by clamps or brackets below the barrel of the gun.

(c) One auxiliary line consisting of at least 150 m (500 ft.) of 7.5 mm (3 in.) circumference manila complying with federal specification T–R–605.

(d) Twenty-five cartridges of the caliber and loading specified in the instructions furnished by the manufacturer of the gun. The cartridges shall be blank with waterproof paper wad.

(e) One cleaning rod with brush.

(f) One can of oil suitable for cleaning the gun and preserving the finish of the metal parts.

(g) Twelve wiping patches of a size suitable for cleaning the bore.

(h) One set of instructions including a list of the equipment furnished with the gun, the proper caliber and loading of the cartridges to be used in firing the gun, information as to the proper maintenance of the gun and equipment, and directions for loading and firing in service use shall be permanently engraved in plastic and mounted conspicuously in the case or box required by § 160.031–4(i).

(i) A suitable case or box, properly compartmented for stowage of the appliance and auxiliary equipment, is required for stowage on merchant vessels. The auxiliary line need not be stowed in the case.

§ 160.031–5 Approval and production tests.

(a) *Approval test.* An independent laboratory accepted by the Commandant under § 159.010 of this chapter must test an appliance in accordance with the operational test in paragraph (c) of this section.

(b) *Production inspections and tests.* Production inspections and tests of each appliance must be conducted under the procedures in § 159.007 of this chapter. Each appliance which fails the inspections and tests must not be represented as meeting this Subpart or as being approved by the Coast Guard.

(1) *Inspections and tests by the manufacturer.* The manufacturer's quality control procedures must include the inspection of appliances during production as well as inspection of finished appliances to determine that the appliances are being produced in accordance with the approved plans. Each appliance must be tested in accordance with paragraph (c) of this section except that the projectile may be fired without a service line attached, and the distance and deviation do not have to be measured.

(2) *Inspections and test by an independent laboratory.* An independent laboratory accepted by the Commandant under § 159.010 of this chapter must inspect and test one appliance at least once each year. The inspection must determine that the appliances are being produced in accordance with the approved plans. The test must be in accordance with paragraph (c) of this section.

(c) *Operational test.* The operational test must be conducted as follows:

(1) Three rounds must be fired by the gun, at least one of which must be with a service line attached to a projectile.

(2) The projectile must be fired first by aiming it down an open course, and measuring the distance and deviation of the projectile.

(3) After the projectile is fired, the other two rounds must be fired.

(4) The distance and deviation of the projectile must be in accordance with § 160.031–3(d) the gun must fire each round properly and the gun must not be fractured or damaged by the test.

§ 160.031–6 Marking.

(a) *Gun.* The gun shall be permanently and legibly marked on the barrel with the manufacturer's model or type designation of the gun, the serial number for the gun, the official Coast Guard approval number, and the name of the manufacturer. The gun stock shall have recessed in it a brass or other corrosion-restistant plate showing legible maintenance instructions for the care of the gun and its parts to prevent corrosion. After the proof test, the gun barrel shall be marked with the letters "P.T." and the name or mark of the company.

(b) *Projectile.* Projectiles shall be permanently and legibly marked with the name of the manufacturer.

(c) *Line and container.* The end of a service line intended to be attached to the projectile shall have securely attached thereto a substantial tag bearing a permanent legend indicating its purpose, and the other end of the line shall be tagged in the same manner to prevent delay in securing proper and immediate action with the equipment. The container of new service lines shall bear the name of the manufacturer, date of manufacture, and a statement to the effect that in all respects the line meets the requirements of this subpart for service lines. Line canisters and reels shall bear the name of the manufacturer.

§160.031-7 Procedure for approval.

(a) Shoulder gun line throwing appliances are approved by the Coast Guard under the procedures in subpart 159.005 of this chapter.

(b) [Reserved]

Subpart 160.032—Davits for Merchant Vessels

§160.032-1 Applicable specifications.

(a) *Specifications.* The following specifications of the issue in effect on the date the davits are manufactured form a part of this subpart:

(1) A.S.T.M. standards:

A7, Specification for Steel for Bridges and Buildings.
A27, Specification for Mild to Medium Strength Carbon Steel Castings for General Application.
A216, Specification for Carbon-Steel Castings Suitable for Fusion Welding for High Temperature Service.

(b) *Copies on file.* Copies of the specification standards referred to in this section shall be kept on file by the manufacturer, together with the approved plans and certificate of approval. The A.S.T.M. Standards may be purchased from the American Society for Testing Materials, 1916 Race Street, Philadelphia, Pa., 19103.

[CGFR 65-9, 30 FR 11466, Sept. 8, 1965]

§160.032-2 General requirements for davits.

(a) The requirements of this section apply to all new construction. Davits approved and in use prior to the regulations in this subpart may be continued in service if in satisfactory condition.

(b) Davits may be either of the mechanical or gravity types.

(1) Mechanical davits shall be designed to be swung out by screws, gears, or other means, using manual power for operation. Radial type davits with mechanical means for operating are not acceptable under this category.

(2) Gravity davits shall be designed to be swung out without the use of manual, electric, steam, or other power supplied by the vessel.

(3) Other types of davits will be given special consideration.

(c) Davits shall be so designed that it will not be necessary to take up or slack the falls in order to crank out the davits.

(d) For the purpose of calculations and conducting tests, the weight of the persons shall be taken at 165 pounds each.

(e) The requirements of this subpart shall be complied with unless other arrangements in matters of construction details, design, strength, equivalent in safety and efficiency are approved by the Commandant.

[CGFR 49-18, 14 FR 5112, Aug. 17, 1949]

§160.032-3 Construction of davits.

(a) *Strength required.* Davits shall be of such strength that the lifeboat may be lowered safely with its full complement of persons and equipment, it being assumed that the vessel is heeled 15 degrees in either direction and with a 10-degree trim. A minimum factor of safety of 6 on the ultimate strength of the materials shall be maintained at all times based on the approved working load.

(b) *Turning out.* (1) Mechanical davits shall be designed so that they may be operated from the full inboard to the full outboard position when the lifeboat is fully equipped, but not loaded with persons, it being assumed that the vessel is heeled 15 degrees in either direction and with a 10-degree trim.

(2) Gravity davits shall be designed so that they may be operated automatically from the full inboard to the full outboard position when the lifeboat is fully equipped, but not loaded with persons, it being assumed that the vessel is heeled 15 degrees in either direction and with a 10-degree trim. This operation shall be accomplished by merely releasing the brake of the lifeboat winch.

(c) *Materials.* (1) Structural steel made by the open-hearth or electric furnace process shall be in accordance with A.S.T.M. Standard Specification A7.

(2) Steel castings not intended for fusion welding shall be in accordance with A.S.T.M. Standard Specification A27, Grades U-60-30, 60-30, 65-30, 65-35, and 70-36.

(3) Steel castings intended to be fabricated by fusion welding shall be in accordance with A.S.T.M. Standard Specification A216, Grades WCA and WCB.

(4) Cast iron shall not be used in the construction of davits.

(5) Special consideration shall be given to the use of other materials. Proper affidavits concerning these materials will be required.

(d) *Bearings.* Bearings of davits shall be of non-ferrous metal, or shall be of the roller or ball-bearing type. Positive means of retaining the bearings in position and of lubricating same shall be provided except that self-lubricated bearings in sheaves of manila rope blocks will be acceptable. The manufacturer shall furnish a lubrication chart for each davit together with a plate attached to the davit indicating the lubricants recommended for extremes in temperature.

(e) *Guards.* All moving parts shall have suitable guards.

(f) *Welding.* Welding, when employed, shall be performed by welders certified by the U.S. Coast Guard, American Bureau of Shipping, or U.S. Navy Department, and the electrodes used shall be of an approved type.

[CGFR 49-18, 14 FR 5112, Aug. 17, 1949, as amended by CGFR 65-16, 30 FR 10898, Aug. 21, 1965; CGFR 65-9, 30 FR 11466, Sept. 8, 1965]

§ 160.032-4 Capacity of davits.

(a) Davits shall be approved for a working load after it has been demonstrated by detailed calculations that this working load can be carried with a minimum factor of safety of six based on the ultimate strength of the materials. It will also be necessary to conduct the tests specified in § 160.032-5.

(b) [Reserved]

[CGFR 49-18, 14 FR 5113, Aug. 17, 1949]

§ 160.032-5 Inspection and testing of davits.

(a) *Material testing.* (1) Where davit arms and frames are fabricated of steel castings, an inspector shall be present at the foundry where such castings are made to witness the tests prescribed by the applicable specification. The manufacturer shall furnish an affidavit stating that the material complies with the requirement of the specification noted in § 160.032-3(c) (2) or (3). The inspector shall stamp the casting with the letters U.S.C.G., the Marine Inspection Office identification letters, the letters F.T., and the date of inspection.

(2) The manufacturer shall furnish an affidavit stating that the structural steel complies with the requirements of the specification noted in § 160.032-3(c)(1).

(3) The affidavits referred to above shall be obtained from the foundry or mill supplying the material.

(b) *Factory tests for initial approval.* (1) Mechanical davits shall be tested for strength and operation at the place of manufacture in the presence of an inspector. The davits shall be completely assembled. The tests to be conducted are as noted in paragraphs (b) (2) through (4) of this section.

(2) A weight equal to 2.2 times the working load shall be suspended from the eye or end of the davit arm. With this load suspended from the davit it shall be operated from the full inboard to the full outboard position using the same operating crank or device used in actual practice aboard ship. The load

shall then be swung in a fore and aft direction through an arc of approximately 10 degrees, each side of the vertical. The davit arm and frame shall show no permanent set or undue stress from this test. While this test is being conducted, the frame and arm, if of cast material, shall be subject to a test by being hammered to satisfy the inspector that the castings are sound and without flaws.

(3) A weight equal to 0.5 times the normal working load shall be suspended from the eye or end of the davit arm. This load shall be moved from the full inboard to the full outboard position using the actual handles supplied with the davit. The time required for this operation shall not exceed 90 seconds. The above test shall also be conducted with the davits set up to simulate a 15-degree inboard list with a 10-degree trim to determine that the davits may be satisfactorily operated in that condition. The above test shall also be conducted with the davits set up to simulate a 15-degree outboard list with a 10-degree trim. This test shall determine that the davit arms will not run out under the weight of the light boat.

(4) A load of 1.1 times the normal working load shall be moved from the full outboard to the full inboard position to demonstrate the strength of operation of the return mechanism.

(5) Gravity davits shall be tested for strength and operation at the place of manufacture in the presence of an inspector. The davit arms, tracks, frames, attachments, etc., shall be set up in a manner similar to an actual shipboard installation. This installation shall include a lifeboat winch suitable for gravity davits and the falls shall be reeved in the normal manner. The tests to be conducted are as noted in paragraphs (b)(6) to (8) of this paragraph.

(6) A weight equal to 1.1 times the working load shall be run from the full inboard to the full outboard position with the davit assembly in the normal upright condition. The davit arm, trackways, etc., shall show no permanent set or undue stress from this test.

(7) A weight equal to 2.2 times the working load shall be attached to the falls and suspended from the davit arm when in the full outboard position. The load shall be swung in a fore and aft direction through an arc of approximately 10 degrees each side of the vertical. The davit arm and trackways shall show no permanent set or undue stress from this test.

(8) The entire davit assembly shall then be heeled inboard 15 degrees and with a 10-degree trim. In this condition a weight equal to 0.5 times the working load shall be suspended from the falls and shall be operated from the full inboard to the full outboard position. This test shall demonstrate that the load is sufficient to turn out the davit by merely releasing the brake on the winch. Stops shall be made at intervals between the inboard and outboard positions to assure that the davit will start from any position.

(c) *Factory testing after approval.* (1) After the design of a mechanical davit has been approved, subsequent davits of the same design shall be individually tested as described in paragraph (b)(2) of this section.

(2) After the design of a gravity davit has been approved, subsequent davit arms of the same design shall be individually tested as described in paragraph (b)(7) of this section, except that the swing test may be eliminated if not practicable.

(d) *Name plate.* (1) A corrosion resistant name plate shall be affixed to each davit arm and frame on which shall be stamped the name of the manufacturer, approval number, type and serial number of the davit, maximum working load in pounds per arm together with the Marine Inspection Office identification letters, the date, and the letters "U.S.C.G."

[CGFR 49–18, 14 FR 5113, Aug. 17, 1949, as amended by CGFR 65–9, 30 FR 11467, Sept. 8, 1965; CGD 75–186, 41 FR 10437, Mar. 11, 1976]

§ 160.032–6 Procedure for approval of davits.

(a) Before action is taken on any design of davit, detailed plans covering fully the arrangement and construction of the davit together with stress diagrams and calculations relative to the strength of the davit, and a complete bill of material setting forth the physical properties of all materials used shall be submitted to the Commandant through the Commander of the Coast Guard District having jurisdiction over the construction of the davit.

(b) If the drawings required in paragraph (a) of this section are satisfactory the Commander of the Coast Guard District in which the davits are to be built shall be notified in writing when fabrication is to commence. An inspector will be assigned to supervise the construction in accordance with the plans and upon completion conduct the tests required by § 160.032–5.

(c) At the time that the tests are successfully completed, the manufacturer shall present to the inspector four corrected copies of the plans noted in paragraph (a) of this section, including any corrections, changes, or additions which may have been found necessary during construction or testing. If the manufacturer desires more than one set of approved plans, additional copies shall be submitted at that time.

(d) Upon receipt of corrected drawings and satisfactory test report, the Commandant will issue a certificate of approval. No change shall be made in the design or construction without first receiving permission of the Commandant via the Commander of the Coast Guard District in which the davits are built.

[CGFR 49–18, 14 FR 5113, Aug. 17, 1949]

Subpart 160.033—Mechanical Disengaging Apparatus, Lifeboat, for Merchant Vessels

§ 160.033–1 Applicable specifications.

(a) *Specifications.* The following specifications of the issue in effect on the date mechanical disengaging apparatus is manufactured form a part of this subpart.

(1) Coast Guard specifications:

160.035, Specification for Lifeboats for Merchant Vessels.

(b) *Copies on file.* A copy of the specification regulations referred to in this section shall be kept on file by the manufacturer, together with the approved plans and certificate of approval. They shall be kept for a period consisting of the duration of approval and 6 months after termination of ap-

proval. The specification may be obtained from the Commandant (G–MSE), U.S. Coast Guard, Washington, DC 20593–0001.

[CGFR 49–18, 14 FR 5113, Aug. 17, 1949, as amended by CGFR 65–16, 30 FR 10899, Aug. 21, 1965; CGD 88–070, 53 FR 34535, Sept. 7, 1988; CGD 95–072, 60 FR 50467, Sept. 29, 1995; CGD 96–041, 61 FR 50733, Sept. 27, 1996]

§ 160.033–2 General requirements for mechanical disengaging apparatus.

(a) The requirements of this subpart apply to all new construction. Mechanical disengaging apparatus approved and in use prior to the regulations in this subpart may be continued in service if in satisfactory condition.

(b) Mechanical disengaging apparatus installed in approved lifeboats shall be designed to release both ends of the lifeboat simultaneously under tension.

(c) Other types of mechanical disengaging apparatus will be considered for lifeboats fitted on vessels operating on waters other than ocean, coastwise or Great Lakes, or for vessels of 3,000 gross tons and under operating in ocean, coastwise or Great Lakes service.

[CGFR 49–18, 14 FR 5113, Aug. 17, 1949, as amended by CGFR 60–36, 25 FR 10637, Nov. 5, 1960]

§ 160.033–3 Construction of mechanical disengaging apparatus.

(a) Mechanical disengaging apparatus shall be of such strength that the lifeboat in which installed may be safely lowered with its full complement of persons and equipment. A minimum factor of safety of six on the ultimate strength of the materials used shall be maintained at all times based on the approved working load per hook.

(b) Mechanical disengaging apparatus shall be designed to release both ends of the lifeboat simultaneously under tension, which shall be effected by partially rotating a shaft which shall be continuous and extend from point of contact with the hooks. The control effecting the rotation of the shaft shall be painted bright red and shall have thereon in raised letters the words "DANGER—LEVER DROPS BOAT". The control shall be readily accessible, secured to a permanent part of the lifeboat structure, and so installed as not to interfere with the inspection of any removable parts of the lifeboat or its equipment.

(c) If closed type hooks are used, arrangements shall be made to effect the release of the falls in the event that the gear is inoperable.

(d) Positive means of lubrication shall be provided for all bearings.

(e) Welding, when employed, shall be performed by welders certified by the U. S. Coast Guard, American Bureau of Shipping, or U. S. Navy Department, and the electrodes used shall be of an approved type.

(f) The manufacturer shall furnish mill or foundry affidavits relative to the physical and chemical properties of the materials used.

[CGFR 49–18, 14 FR 5113, Aug. 17, 1949, as amended by CGFR 52–10, 17 FR 2365, Mar. 19, 1952; CGFR 57–27, 22 FR 4021, June 7, 1957]

§ 160.033–4 Inspection and testing of mechanical disengaging apparatus.

(a) *Inspection.* Mechanical disengaging apparatus shall be inspected during the course of construction to determine that the arrangement and materials entering into the construction are in accordance with the approved plans.

(b) *Factory tests for initial approval.* (1) Mechanical disengaging apparatus shall be tested to destruction in a jig built in accordance with the drawing required in § 160.033–5(a). This test shall be conducted in the presence of an inspector.

(2) Universal connections used to transmit the release power from the throw lever to the hook release shall be set up in a jig with the angles of leads set at 0.30, and 60 degrees, respectively. A load of 200 pounds shall be applied at the end of a lever arm 24 inches long. This load shall be applied with the connecting rod secured beyond the universal and with the lever arm in the horizontal position. This test shall demonstrate that the universals have strength adequate for the purpose intended. There shall be no permanent set, or undue stress as a result of this test. Consideration will be given to arrangements other than universals submitted for this transmission of power.

(c) *Installation test prior to passing first unit installed.* (1) Each new type or arrangement of mechanical disengaging apparatus shall be tested by suspending a lifeboat loaded with deadweight equivalent to the number of persons allowed in the lifeboat (165 pounds per person) together with the weight of the equipment, plus 10 percent of the total load. The release lever shall then be thrown over with this load suspended until the lifeboat is released. This test shall demonstrate the efficiency of the installation in an actual lifeboat. (This test may be conducted ashore by suspending the lifeboat just clear of the ground.)

(d) *Factory testing after approval.* (1) In general, no factory tests after approval are required. However, each lifeboat in which mechanical disengaging apparatus is fitted shall be tested in accordance with § 160.035–13(a) of subpart 160.035.

(e) *Name plate.* A corrosion resistant name plate shall be attached to each hook assembly giving the manufacturer's name, approval number, and approved working load (as installed).

[CGFR 49–18, 14 FR 5113, Aug. 17, 1949, as amended by CGFR 52–10, 17 FR 2365, Mar. 19, 1952; CGFR 65–9, 30 FR 11467, Sept. 8, 1965]

§ 160.033–5 Procedure for approval of mechanical disengaging apparatus.

(a) Before action is taken on any design of mechanical disengaging apparatus, detailed plans covering fully the arrangement and construction of the apparatus, together with stress diagrams and calculations relative to the strength, proposed test jig to be used in the test prescribed in § 160.033–4(b)(1), and a complete bill of material setting forth the physical and chemical properties of all the materials used shall be submitted to the Commandant through the Commander of the Coast Guard District having jurisdiction over the construction of the mechanical disengaging apparatus.

(b) If the drawings required in paragraph (a) of this section are satisfactory, the Commander of the Coast Guard District in which the mechanical disengaging apparatus is to be built, shall be notified in writing when fabrication is to commence. An inspector will be assigned to supervise the construction in accordance with the plans and upon completion, conduct the tests required by § 160.033–4.

(c) At the time that the tests are successfully completed, the manufacturer shall present to the inspector four corrected copies of the plans noted in paragraph (a) of this section, including any corrections, changes, or additions which may have been found necessary during construction or testing. If the manufacturer desires more than one set of approved plans, additional copies shall be submitted at that time.

(d) Upon receipt of corrected drawings and satisfactory test report, the Commandant will issue a certificate of approval. No change shall be made in the design or construction without first receiving permission of the Commandant via the Commander of the Coast Guard District in which the mechanical disengaging apparatus is built.

[CGFR 49–18, 14 FR 5113, Aug. 17, 1949]

Subpart 160.035—Lifeboats for Merchant Vessels

SOURCE: CGFR 65–9, 30 FR 11467, Sept. 8, 1965, unless otherwise noted.

§ 160.035–1 Applicable specifications.

(a) *Specifications.* The following specifications, of the issue in effect on the date lifeboats are manufactured form a part of this subpart.

(1) A.S.T.M. standards:

A 525—Specification for Delivery of Zinc-Coated (Galvanized) Iron or Steel Sheets, Coils, and Cut Lengths Coated by Hot Dip Method.

A 36—Specification for Structural Steel

(2) Military specifications:

MIL-P-18066—Plywood, Ship and Boat Construction.

MIL-Y-1140—Yarn, Cord, Sleeving, Cloth and Tape—Glass.

MIL-M-15617—Mats, Fibrous Glass, For Reinforcing Plastics.

MIL-R-7575—Resin, Polyester, Low-Pressure Laminating.

MIL-P-40619—Plastic Material, Cellular Polystyrene.

MIL-P-17549—Plastic Laminates, Fibrous Glass Reinforced, Marine Structural.

MIL-P-19644—Plastic Foam, Molded Polystyrene (Expanded Bead Type).

MIL-C-19663—Cloth, Glass, Woven Roving For Plastic Laminate.

MIL-R-21607—Resins, Polyester, Low Pressure Laminating, Fire Retardant.

MIL-P-21929—Plastic Material, Cellular Polyurethane, Rigid, Foam-In-Place, Low Density.

(3) Federal specifications:

TT-P-59—Paint, Ready-Mixed, International Orange.

(4) Federal test method standard:

406—Plastics: Method of Testing.

(5) Federal Communications Commission:

47 CFR part 83, Rules Governing Stations on Shipboard in the Maritime Service.

(6) Coast Guard specifications:

160.033—Mechanical Disengaging Apparatus (For Lifeboats).
160.034—Hand Propelling Gear (For Lifeboats).
161.006—Searchlights, Motor Lifeboat.

(b) *Copies on file.* Copies of the specifications and rules referred to in this section shall be kept on file by the manufacturer, together with the approved plans and certificate of approval. The Coast Guard Specifications may be obtained upon request from the Commandant. United States Coast Guard Headquarters, Washington, DC 20226. The A.S.T.M. Standards may be purchased from the American Society for Testing Materials, 1916 Race Street, Philadelphia, Pa. 19103. The Military Specifications may be obtained from the Commanding Officer, Naval Supply Depot, 5801 Tabor Avenue, Philadelphia, Pa. 19120. The Federal Communications Commission's Rules and Regulations may be obtained from the Federal Communications Commission, Washington, DC 20554. Federal Specifications and Standards may be obtained from the General Services Administration, Business Service Center, Washington, DC 20407.

[CGFR 65–9, 30 FR 11467, Sept. 8, 1965, as amended by CGD 72–133R, 37 FR 17039, Aug. 24, 1972]

§ 160.035–2 General requirements for lifeboats.

(a) The requirements of this subpart apply to all new construction. Lifeboats approved and in use prior to the regulations in this subpart may be continued in service if in satisfactory condition.

(b) All lifeboats must be properly constructed and shall be of such form and proportions that they shall be readily maneuverable, have ample stability in a seaway, and sufficient freeboard when fully loaded with their full complement of persons and equipment. All lifeboats shall be capable of maintaining positive stability when open to the sea and loaded with their full complement of persons and equipment. All lifeboats must be open boats with rigid sides having internal buoyancy only. Lifeboats with a rigid shelter may be approved, provided that it may be readily opened from both inside and outside, and does not impede rapid embarkation and disembarkation or the launching and handling of the lifeboat.

(c) Lifeboats may be constructed of steel, aluminum, fibrous glass reinforced plastic (FRP), or other materials receiving specific approval: *Provided,* That, the weight of the fully equipped and loaded lifeboat shall not exceed 44,800 pounds, and the carrying capacity calculated in accordance with §160.035–9 of this specification shall not exceed 150 persons.

(1) The thwarts, side benches and footings of lifeboats shall be painted or otherwise colored international orange in accordance with Federal Specification TT–P–59. The area in way of the red mechanical disengaging gear control lever, from the keel to the side bench, shall be painted or otherwise colored white, to provide a contrasting background for the lever. This band of white should be approximately 12 inches wide depending on the internal arrangements of the lifeboat.

(d) For the purpose of calculations and conducting tests, the weight of the persons shall be taken at 165 pounds each.

[CGFR 65–9, 30 FR 11467, Sept. 8, 1965, as amended by CGD 95–028, 62 FR 51211, Sept. 30, 1997]

EFFECTIVE DATE NOTE: At 62 FR 51211, Sept. 30, 1997, §160.035–2 was amended by removing paragraph (e), effective Oct. 30, 1997.

§160.035–3 Construction of steel oar-propelled lifeboats.

(a) *Type.* Lifeboats shall have rigid sides and be fitted with internal buoyancy so arranged that the boats will float in the flooded condition when fully loaded with persons and equipment. The capacity of an oar-propelled lifeboat is limited to a maximum of 59 persons. Lifeboats designed to carry 60, but not more than 100, persons shall be either hand-propelled or motor-propelled. Lifeboats designed to carry more than 100 persons shall be motor-propelled, except that a lifeboat designed to carry more than 100 persons may be hand-propelled if it is a replacement for a previously approved hand-propelled lifeboat.

(b) *Materials.* (1) Plating for shell, floors, air tanks, etc., shall be made by the open-hearth or electric furnace process in accordance with ASTM Standards A–525 Class 1.25 Commercial. The bend tests required by these specifications shall be made after the galvanizing or other anticorrosive treatment has been applied.

(2) Rivets and rolled or extruded shapes such as keel, stem, sternpost, gunwales, etc., shall be made by the open-hearth or electric furnace process in accordance with ASTM Standard Specification A–36. Consideration will be given to the use of other steels having equivalent strength where longitudinal cold forming is necessary.

(c) *Riveting.* (1) Riveting of the shell plating to the keel, stem, and sternpost shall be button head rivets, staggered with not less than 12 rivets to the foot. The distance from the edge of the plate to the centers of the rivets in the nearest row shall be not less than ½ inch nor more than ¾ inch. Rivets connecting the shell to the gunwale shall be spaced not more than 3 inches on centers. The size of the rivets for connecting the shell plating to the keel, stem, sternpost, and gunwale shall be ¼-inch diameter for boats 28 feet and under and ⁵⁄₁₆-inch diameter for boats over 28 feet.

(2) The connection of the floors to the shell shall be a single row of rivets not less than ³⁄₁₆ inch in diameter and spaced not more than 3 inches on centers.

(d) *Welding.* Welding may be substituted for riveting in any location. It shall be performed by welders qualified by the U.S. Coast Guard, American Bureau of Shipping, or U.S. Navy Department, and only approved electrodes shall be used. Details of the joints shall be indicated on the construction drawings submitted for approval.

(e) *Gunwale braces.* (1) The gunwale braces shall be bolted to the thwarts with at least two carriage bolts of a size not less than that noted in table 160.035-3(e)(1) and riveted or welded to the gunwales. Where riveted to the gunwale, at least two rivets of a size not less than that noted in table 160.035-3(e)(1) shall be used.

TABLE 160.035–3(E)(1)

Length of lifeboat	Brace size (inches)	Bolts and rivets diameter (inch)
22 feet and under	3×¼	⁵⁄₁₆
Over 22 feet and not over 28.	3×⁵⁄₁₆	³⁄₈
Over 28 feet	3×³⁄₈	⁷⁄₁₆

(2) Bracket type gunwale braces will be given special consideration.

(f) *Seats.* (1) The thwarts, side benches, and end benches shall be of fir, yellow pine, fibrous glass reinforced plastic (FRP), or approved equivalent.

(2) The edges of all thwarts, side, and end benches shall be well rounded.

(3) Suitable foot rests shall be furnished at a distance of between 17 and 20 inches below the thwarts and side benches. This may be accomplished by raising the footings from the bottom of the boat.

(4) The leading edge of the thwart or end bench shall be located a minimum of 3 inches and a maximum of 6 inches distance from the Rottmer release gear.

(g) *Stretchers.* Stretchers of sufficient size and strength shall be fitted in suitable positions for rowing.

(h) *Disengaging apparatus.* (1) Connections for the disengaging apparatus shall have a minimum factor of safety of six.

(2) For construction and capacity of disengaging apparatus, see subpart 160.033.

(i) *Plugs.* Each lifeboat shall be fitted with an automatic plug so designed and installed as to insure complete drainage at all times when the boat is out of the water. The automatic plug shall be provided with a cap attached to the lifeboat by a suitable chain. The location of drain plug is to be marked on the vertical surface in the vicinity of the plug below the side bench with the word "plug" in 3-inch white letters and with an arrow pointing in the direction of the drain plug.

(j) *Protection against corrosion.* (1) All steel or iron entering into the construction of lifeboats shall be galvanized by the hot dipped process. All fabricated pieces or sections are to be galvanized after fabrication. Other methods of corrosion prevention will be given special consideration.

(2) Where welded construction is employed, the material shall be galvanized after welding unless impractical to do so in which case consideration will be given to equivalent protection.

(3) Provisions shall be made to obtain a satisfactory bond between the metal and the paint.

(k) *Rudders.* (1) Each lifeboat shall be fitted with a rudder and tiller. The rudder shall be fitted with a ½-inch diameter manila lanyard of such length as to permit the rudder to be shipped without untying the lanyard.

(2) A suitable hinged or pivoted tiller shall be provided.

(3) Rudder stops shall be provided to limit the rudder angle to approximately 45 degrees each side of the centerline.

(l) *Buoyancy tanks.* (1) All lifeboats shall have inherent buoyancy, or shall be fitted with buoyancy tanks or other equivalent noncorrodible buoyancy units, which shall not be adversely affected by oil or oil products, sufficient to float the boat and its equipment when the boat is flooded and open to the sea. An additional volume of buoyancy, or buoyancy units, equal to at least one-tenth the cubic capacity of the lifeboat shall be provided.

(2) At least 50 percent of the buoyancy shall be located along the sides of the boat and shall be so located that the boat will be on even keel when flooded.

(3) The tops of the buoyancy tanks or buoyancy units shall be protected by the side benches or other suitable means. The construction shall be such that water will not collect on the tops of the tanks.

(4) *Built-in buoyancy tanks.* Each built-in buoyancy tank shall be filled with buoyancy material. The amount

of material required shall be determined by the flooding test in accordance with § 160.035–11(b)(2). The buoyancy materials used shall meet the requirements set forth for core materials as follows:

Core .... Poly- MIL–P–
　　　　　　 styrene. 40619
　　　　　　　　　　 MIL–P–
　　　　　　　　　　 19644
　　　　　 Polyuthane MIL–P–
　　　　　　　　　　 21929

(m) *Equipment stowage.* (1) Provision lockers, water tanks, and special equipment lockers shall be watertight and so designed and located as to fit under the side benches, end benches, or footings without projecting into the accommodation spaces of the lifeboat. In special cases, stowage under the thwarts will be permitted. Standard ¼ inch pipe size testing nipples shall be fitted to all such lockers or tanks.

(2) Water tanks shall be constructed of at least 18 USSG material. An opening with a dogged type cover shall be provided for removal of water cans. This opening shall be at least 7 inches in diameter, but in any case shall be of sufficient size that all water cans can be removed. In addition, built-in water tanks shall have an opening at least 13 inches in diameter with a bolted cover for the purpose of inspection and maintenance. A 2-inch diameter fill cap shall be installed for the purpose of storing rain water. A standard ¼-inch pipe size drainage nipple with hexagonal cap shall be fitted in the bottom of the tank in an accessible location and may be used for air testing the water tank.

(n) *Grab rails.* Grab rails shall be substantially attached to each lifeboat below the turn of the bilge and extend approximately one-half of the length of the lifeboat on each side. The ends of the grab rails shall be faired to prevent fouling and all connections of the rails to the lifeboat shall be made by riveting the palms of the brackets to a small plate and riveting the plate to the shell. To prevent rupture of the shell if the grab rail is carried away, more rivets shall be used in attaching the plate to the shell than in fastening the bracket to the plate. The clearance between the grab rail pipe and the hull

shall be at least 1½ inches. The connections of the rails to a fibrous glass reinforced plastic lifeboat hull will be given special consideration.

(o) *Hand rails.* All lifeboats intended for use in ocean and coastwise service shall be fitted with hand rails approximately 18 inches in length, constructed and attached to the lifeboat in the same manner as the grab rails required by paragraph (n) of this section. The clearance between the hand rail pipe and the hull shall be at least 1½ inches. The hand rails shall be located approximately parallel to and at both ends of the grab rails and spaced midway between the grab rail and the gunwale and midway between the grab rail and the keel on both sides of the lifeboat provided that, when the distance from grab rail to gunwale or to the keel exceeds 4 feet, two hand rails shall be fitted so as to provide equal spacing. In no case shall the hand rails project beyond the widest part of the boat. Recessed hand rails or other alternate arrangements will be given consideration.

[CGD 95–028, 62 FR 51211, Sept. 30, 1997]

EFFECTIVE DATE NOTE: At 62 FR 51211, Sept. 30, 1997, § 160.035–3 was revised, effective Oct. 30, 1997.

§ 160.035–5 Construction of steel motor-propelled lifeboats with and without radio cabin.

(a) *General provisions applicable to all motor-propelled lifeboats.* (1) A motor-propelled lifeboat, carried as part of the lifesaving equipment of a vessel, whether required or not, shall comply with all the requirements for an oar-propelled lifeboat, and in addition, shall have sufficient additional buoyancy to compensate for the weight of the engine and other equipment.

(2) The engine shall be enclosed in a suitable engine box which shall be watertight with the exception of the top which may be weathertight. If the engine box is made of material other than steel or aluminum, such as fibrous glass reinforced plastic, it shall be made of fire retardant material. The top of the engine box shall be fitted with a screwdown mushroom vent. The

engine box shall be fitted with a suitable drain. An engine starting instruction plate shall be permanently attached to the engine box. There shall be ample space between the engine and the engine box to permit proper maintenance and removal of engine accessories when necessary. If the internal arrangements of the engine in the engine box do not permit this, then suitable watertight hand-hole plates shall be installed in the vicinity of these accessories. The location of these plates and the accessibility to the accessories shall be to the satisfaction of the marine inspector. The marine inspector may require the removal of any accessory through these hand-hole plates that he may deem necessary to establish that it is of proper size and location.

(3) Fuel tanks must be constructed of steel, fibrous glass reinforced plastic or other approved equivalent. Fuel tanks must be adequately supported and securely fastened inside the lifeboat to prevent any movement. Fuel tanks must have no openings in the bottom, sides or ends. Openings for fill, vent and feed pipes must be on the top surface of the tanks. The vent size for tanks of 50 gallons or less must not be less than ¼-inch O.D. tubing. Vents for larger tanks will be given special consideration. The access openings in the thwarts for the fill tank cap must have a flush cover or the top of the cap must be flush with the top of the thwart. Fuel feed pipes must be provided with a shutoff valve at the tank, where it is readily accessible and its location marked. Tanks must be tested by a static head above the tank top of ten feet of water without showing leakage or permanent deformation. A graduated measure stick or other means must be provided to determine the amount of the fuel in the tank.

(i) Steel diesel oil fuel tanks shall have a thickness of not less than 12 USSG and shall not be galvanized on the inside; however, the outside of such tanks shall be so treated as to to obtain a corrosion resistance approximately equivalent to hot-dip galvanizing. Swash plates shall be fitted in tanks over 30 inches in length.

(ii) Fibrous glass reinforced plastic diesel oil fuel tanks shall have a thickness of not less than 0.187 inch. The resins used shall be of a fire retardant type and shall qualify under military specification MIL–R–21607. The mechanical properties of the tank shall not be less than Grade No. 4 of military specification MIL–P–17549. Mat, woven roving and 1000th cloth shall be used. Tank laminates shall not be constructed exclusively with fibrous glass fabrics. An increment of random oriented, chopped fibrous glass reinforcement is deemed necessary to prevent porosity. An ounce and a half per square foot is considered minimum. Inclusion of fabrics in low pressure laminates are recommended to impart satisfactory containment, strength, and rigidity. For maximum strength, tank surfaces should be cambered and curved wherein practical. Fittings shall be made of nonferrous metal and securely bonded to the tank with epoxy resin. A fibrous glass reinforced plate or boss of the same thickness as the tank proper and 1½ times the outside dimensions of the fitting shall be used to strengthen the openings for fuel, fill and vent lines. Tanks shall be constructed of a minimum possible number of sections. Where two parts are joined there shall be a minimum of 2-inch overlap. Tanks exceeding 18 inches in any horizontal dimension shall be fitted with vertical baffle plates at intervals not exceeding 18 inches. Baffle plate flanges shall be integral and shall be of the same strength and stiffness as the tank wall. Flanges shall be bonded in place with mat and fabric. A suitable striking plate shall be installed at the bottom of the fuel measurement and fill pipe line. The laminate may be increased in thickness, in the way of the fill pipe. The cover of the fuel tank shall be through bolted as well as bonded. All fuel tanks shall bear legible, permanent labels, conveniently located for visual inspection, signifying full compliance with these specifications and including the following:

(a) Manufacturer's name and address.

(b) Date of construction and the inspector's initials.

(c) Wall thickness (in decimals of one inch) and capacity U.S. gallons.

(d) Material of construction: Polyester—Glass.

(4) Propeller shafting shall be of bronze or other suitable corrosion resistant materials. Fittings, pipes, connections, etc., shall be of high standard and good workmanship, and installed in accordance with good marine practice. The exhaust manifold shall be suitably insulated.

(5) All engines shall be permanently installed and shall be equipped with an efficient cranking system. This system shall be one that can be operated by hand, such as a hand cranking, hydraulic cranking, or inertia cranking system, acceptable to the Commandant. If an electric cranking system consisting of an electric starter motor, generator and batteries are fitted, it shall be in addition to the required acceptable cranking system, the battery or batteries shall be installed within the watertight engine box. The battery box shall be so constructed as to retain the battery in position when the lifeboat is in a seaway. The battery box shall be 1 inch longer and 1 inch wider than the battery and shall be lined with 4-pound lead flashed up 3 inches on the sides and ends. The battery box may be made of fibrous glass reinforced plastic using a fire-retardant epoxy resin. This type of battery box will not be required to be lead lined.

(i) *Engines.* The engine shall be a reliable, marine, compression-ignition type and shall be capable of propelling the fully equipped and loaded lifeboat at a sustained speed of not less than 6 knots through smooth water over a measured course. Provision shall be made for going astern. Sufficient fuel for 24 hours continuous operation at 6 knots shall be provided. The engine used in approved lifeboats shall be capable of being started without the use of starting aids at a temperature of 20 °F., by the use of an acceptable cranking system. If water cooled, the engine shall be equipped with a closed fresh water cooling system. This system shall be cooled by a secondary medium, such as a water cooled heat exchanger.

(ii) The hydraulic cranking system shall be a self-contained system which will provide the required cranking forces and engine r.p.m. as recommended by the engine manufacturer. The capacity of the hydraulic cranking system shall provide not less

than six cranking cycles. Each cranking cycle shall provide the necessary number of revolutions at the required r.p.m. to the engine to meet the requirements of carrying its full rated load within twenty seconds after cranking is initiated with intake air and hydraulic cranking system at 20 °F. Capacity of the hydraulic cranking system sufficient for three cranking cycles under the above conditions, shall be held in reserve and arranged so that the operation of a single control by one person will isolate the discharged or initially used part of the system and permit the reserve capacity to be employed. The installation of an engine-driven pump is recommended but is not required. The hydraulic cranking shall meet the requirements prescribed in 46 CFR 58.30 and 46 CFR 61.10–5 of Subchapter F, Marine Engineering Regulations. The hydraulic system when used in lifeboats as engine cranking systems shall be leak-tested at its operating pressure after installation.

(6) The following tools to perform emergency repairs and ordinary servicing shall be provided:

One 12-ounce ball peen hammer.
One screwdriver with 6-inch blade.
One pair of 8-inch slip-joint pliers.
One 8-inch adjustable end wrench.
One 12-inch adjustable end wrench.
One Phillips or cross-head screwdriver with a 6-inch blade.

(b) *Steel motor-propelled lifeboats without radio cabin or searchlight (Class 1).* (1) The engine shall be a reliable marine type and shall be in accordance with paragraph (a)(5)(i) of this section. If a starting battery is supplied, the engine shall be fitted with a marine type generator or alternator insulated as required by AIEE rules for marine service capable of charging the starting batteries. The battery box shall be in accordance with paragraph (a)(5) of this section.

(c) *Steel motor-propelled lifeboats without radio cabin but with searchlight (Class 2).* (1) The engine shall be of a reliable marine type and shall be in accordance with paragraph (a)(5)(i) of this section. The lifeboat shall be equipped with a searchlight constructed in accordance with subpart

87

161.006 of this subchapter Q (Specifications). The engine shall be fitted with a marine type generator or alternator insulated as required by AIEE rules for marine service capable of charging the batteries used for the searchlight as well as the starting batteries, if fitted. The battery box shall be in accordance with paragraph (a)(5) of this section.

(d) *Steel motor-propelled lifeboats with radio cabin and searchlight (Class 3).* (1) The engine shall be a reliable, marine type and shall be in accordance with paragraph (a)(5)(i) of this section. The engine shall be fitted with a marine type generator or alternator insulated as required by AIEE rules for marine service, capable of charging the batteries used for the radio and searchlight as well as the starting battery, if fitted.

(2) The radio and source of power for the radio and the searchlight shall be housed and protected from the elements by a suitable radio cabin. The entire installation shall comply with the requirements of the Federal Communications Commission, Rules Governing Stations on Shipboard in the Maritime Services. The radio cabin shall be of a size to contain the radio and source of power for the radio and searchlight, and the operator of the equipment. The top and sides of the radio cabin shall be watertight with the exception of the door which need not be watertight but shall be at least weathertight. The installation of the radio cabin shall take into consideration the concentration of weight in this area.

(3) The searchlight shall be of an approved type constructed in accordance with specification Subpart 161.006 of this subchapter and shall be securely mounted on top of the radio cabin.

(4) The batteries shall be installed in a box securely fastened inside the radio cabin. The battery box shall be in accordance with paragraph (a)(5) of this section.

[CGFR 65–9, 30 FR 11467, Sept. 8, 1965, as amended by CGD 72–133R, 37 FR 17039, Aug. 24, 1972; CGD 73–116R, 39 FR 12747, Apr. 8, 1974]

§ 160.035–6 Construction of aluminum oar-, hand-, and motor-propelled lifeboats.

(a) *General.* Aluminum lifeboats shall comply with the general requirements for the construction and arrangement of steel lifeboats unless otherwise specified.

TABLE 160.035–6—ALUMINUM LIFEBOATS

Length of boat not over (feet)	Bar keel, stem and sternpost (inches)	Gunwales [1]		Shell plating (Brown and Sharpe gage) [2]											
				Independent air tanks				Built-in-air tanks							
	5086–H112/6061–T6	Angle bar (inches) 5086–H112/6061–T6	Flanged flat bar (inches) 5086–H112/6061–T6	5052–H32		6061–T6		5052–H32				6061–T6			
				Side	Bottom	Side	Bottom	Side	Bottom	Inner shell	Bulk-heads	Side	Bottom	Inner shell	Bulk-heads
12.0	2¾x¾	2¼x2 5/16	4x5/16	14	14	14	14	14	14	14	14	14	14	15	15
14.0	2¾x¾	2¼x2 5/16	4x5/16	14	14	14	14	14	14	14	14	14	14	15	15
16.0	2¾x¾	2½x2¼x5/16	4½x5/16	14	14	14	14	14	14	14	14	14	14	15	15
18.0	3x¾	2½x2¼x5/16	4½x5/16	14	14	14	14	14	14	14	14	14	14	15	15
20.0	3x1	2¾x2½x5/16	5x5/16	13	13	13	13	13	13	14	14	13	13	14	14
22.0	3x1	2¾x2½x5/16	5x5/16	12	12	12	12	13	12	14	14	13	13	14	14
24.0	3¼x1	2¾x2½x⅜	5x⅜	11	11	11	11	11	11	13	13	12	12	14	14
26.0	3½x1	2¾x2½x⅜	5x⅜	10	9	11	10	11	10	12	12	11	11	13	13
28.0	3¾x1	2¾x2½x⅜	5x⅜	9	8	10	9	10	9	12	12	11	10	13	13
30.0	4x1	3x2¾x⅜	5½x⅜	9	8	9	8	9	8	11	11	10	9	12	12
32.0	4x1	3x2¾x⅜	5½x⅜	8	7	9	8	9	8	11	11	10	9	12	12
34.0	4x1	3x2¾x⅜	5½x⅜	8	7	8	7	8	7	10	10	9	8	11	11
36.0	4x1	3x2¾x⅜	5½x⅜	7	6	8	7	8	7	10	10	9	8	11	11

[1] Extruded shapes having substantially the scantlings of the angle bar gunwale are permitted. Where extruded shapes are used, a nosing as per § 160.035–3(j) is not required provided the extruded shape has at its heel a generously rounded curve.

[2] Brown and Sharpe gage decimal values: 15 gage equals 0.05707, 14 gage equals 0.06408; 13 gage equals 0.07196; 12 gage equals 0.08081; 11 gage equals 0.09074, 10 gage equals 0.1019; 9 gage equals 0.1144; 8 gage equals 0.1285; 7 gage equals 0.1443, and 6 gage equals 0.1620.

(b) *Materials.* (1) Plating for shell, air tanks, etc., shall be as shown in Table 160.035–6.

(c) *Welding.* (1) Welding may be substituted for riveting in the following locations: Hoist plate to keel, disengaging gear grace plate to stem and sternpost, rudder attachment fitting to the sternpost, and the propeller shaft stern tube to the sternpost. When using 6061–T6 aluminum, the welded area is to be heat-treated and checked by X-ray to assure a satisfactory weld. When using 5086–H 112 aluminum, the welded area is to be checked by a non-destructive test method such as X-ray, ultrasonic waves or fluorescent materials, to assure a satisfactory weld. Other methods of checking aluminum welds will be given separate consideration. The welding shall be performed by a welder qualified by the U.S. Coast Guard, American Bureau of Shipping, or U.S. Navy Department, and only suitable electrodes shall be used. Details of the joints shall be indicated on the construction drawings submitted for approval.

(d) *Dissimilar metals.* (1) Where in the construction of aluminum lifeboats the use of dissimilar metals are employed such as, the installation of the mechanical disengaging gear, hand propelling gear, or engine, suitable insulation between the aluminum and these metals shall be used. Porous or absorbent materials shall not be used as insulating materials. Only non-porous materials such as plastics, rubber or neoprene base compounds, or micarta shall be used. Other suitable material will be given separate consideration. Fasteners used in joining dissimilar metals together shall be of the type that will minimize corrosion.

[CGFR 65–9, 30 FR 11467, Sept. 8, 1965, as amended by CGD 95–028, 62 FR 51213, Sept. 30, 1997]

EFFECTIVE DATE NOTE: At 62 FR 51213, Sept. 30, 1997, § 160.035–6 was amended by removing the text of paragraphs (b), (d), (f), (g), and (h) and redesignating paragraphs (c), (e), and (i) as paragraphs (b), (c), and (d), respectively, and by removing table 160.035–6(d)(1), effective Oct. 30, 1997.

§ 160.035–8 **Construction of fibrous glass reinforced plastic (F.R.P.), oar-, hand-, and motor-propelled lifeboats.**

(a) *General requirements.* (1) Plastic lifeboats shall comply with the general requirements for the construction and arrangement of steel lifeboats, except that unless otherwise specified, materials, scantlings, methods of construction, fastenings, methods of attachment of component parts, and other specific construction details may be varied by the builder in order to produce a structurally sound boat meeting in every respect recognized standards of first class construction and one which will satisfactorily meet the performance requirements set forth in this subpart.

(2) Fibrous glass reinforced plastic lifeboats may be of the following categories of hull construction:

A—Single piece, outer hull construction.
B—Two piece, outer hull construction.
C—Single piece, inner hull construction.
D—Two piece, inner hull construction.
E—Multi-piece, inner hull construction.

(b) *Specific requirements*—(1) *Resin.* The resin used shall be of the fire retardant, nonair inhibited-type conforming to Class A of Military Specification MIL–R–21607 and Grade A, Class O of Military Specification MIL–R–7575, including tests after 1 year's weathering. In addition, the test panels shall be tested for continued conformance with Military Specification MIL–R–21607. All tests, including weathering of samples, shall be accomplished by an independent laboratory. Complete certification by the independent laboratory with test data shall be submitted to Coast Guard (G–MSE) for acceptance. Class A resin shall be fire retardant without additives. Class B resins will be given consideration upon request. Class B resin shall be fire retardant with additives and shall meet the same test requirements as that for Class A resins. When Class B resin is used for the prototype lifeboat, additives for fire retardancy shall not be used in order to obtain a translucent laminate for inspection purposes. This prototype test lifeboat will not be stamped approved, nor will it be acceptable for merchant vessels. Whichever class of resin the manufacturer decides to use for his prototype lifeboat, shall be used in his production lifeboats. A note to this effect shall be included in his specifications and drawings for this particular size and type lifeboat.

(2) *Glass reinforcement.* The glass reinforcement used shall have good laminated wet strength retention and shall meet the appropriate military specification stated in this paragraph. Glass cloth shall meet Military Specification MIL–Y–1140, Class C, form 4, No. 1000–150. Woven roving shall conform to Military Specification MIL–C–19663, Style 605–308 or Style 605–604. Other glass materials equivalent in strength, design, wet out, and efficiency will be given consideration upon request.

(3) *Laminate.* All exposed surfaces of the finished laminate shall present a smooth finish, and there shall be no protruding surface fibers, open voids, pits, cracks, bubbles or blisters. The laminate shall be essentially free from resin-starved or overimpregnated areas, and no foreign matter shall remain in the finished laminate. The entire laminate shall be fully cured and free of tackiness, and shall show no tendency to delaminate, peel, or craze in any overlay. The laminate shall not be released from the mold until a Barcol hardness reading of not less than 40–55 is obtained from at least 10 places on the nongel coated surface, including all interior inner and outer hull surfaces and built-in lockers. The mechanical properties of the laminate shall meet the requirements for a Grade 3 laminate as specified in Table I of Military Specification MIL–P–17549. Other grades will be given consideration on specific request. For the prototype boat of each design made by each manufacturer, the layup shall be made of unpigmented clear resins so that all details of construction will be visible for inspection and test panels representative of each prototype layup shall be tested in accordance with MIL–P–17549.

(4) *Weights of F.R.P. lifeboats.* (i) The variations in weight between the fibrous glass reinforced plastic in the prototype F.R.P. lifeboat and the fibrous glass reinforced plastic in the production F.R.P. lifeboat shall be within 5 percent. This weight shall be for the F.R.P. sections only and shall not include the weight of any hardware or equipment.

(ii) When assembling two similar sections as indicated by categories B and D of paragraph (a)(2) of this section, the weights of the matching F.R.P. pieces shall be within 5 percent of each other.

(iii) The recorded weights of the items indicated in paragraphs (b)(4) (i) and (ii) of this section shall be kept by the manufacturer, with each boat listed by size, type, and serial number.

[CGFR 65–9, 30 FR 11467, Sept. 8, 1965, as amended by CGD 72–133R, 37 FR 17039, Aug. 24, 1972; CGD 82–063b, 48 FR 4782, Feb. 3, 1983; CGD 95–072, 60 FR 50467, Sept. 29, 1995; CGD 96–041, 61 FR 50733, Sept. 27, 1996]

§ 160.035–9 **Cubic capacity of lifeboats.**

(a) *Definitions.* The following definitions apply to the measurement of a lifeboat to determine its cubic capacity.

(1) *Length* (*L*). The length is the distance in feet from the inside of the plating or planking at the stem to the corresponding position at the stern. In the case of a boat with a square stern, the after terminus is the inside of the transom.

(2) *Breadth* (*B*). The breadth is the distance in feet over the plating or planking at the point where the breadth of the boat is greatest.

(3) *Depth* (*D*). The depth is the distance in feet amidships inside the plating from the top of the keel to the level of the gunwale. The depth used for calculating purposes shall not exceed 45 percent of the breadth.

(4) *Sheer.* Lifeboats shall have a sheer at each end at least equal to 4 percent of the length, and a sheer at the quarter points of at least 1 percent of the length. If less sheer is provided, the depth used to determine the cubic capacity shall be assumed to be reduced so as to achieve this minimum sheer.

(b) *Formula.* The cubic capacity shall be determined by the following formula:

$$L \times B \times D \times 0.64$$

In the case of lifeboats with unusual proportions, the Commandant may require that the cubic capacity be calculated by exact measurements from which the exact seating capacity may be determined.

(c) *Motor-propelled lifeboat.* The cubic capacity of a motor-propelled lifeboat shall be determined in the same manner as an oar-propelled lifeboat and then deducting from the gross volume, a volume equal to the engine box and accessories, and when carried, the radio cabin, searchlight, and their accessories. The volume of such equipment extending above the sheer line need not be deducted.

[CGFR 65–9, 30 FR 11467, Sept. 8, 1965, as amended by CGD 95–028, 62 FR 51213, Sept. 30, 1997]

EFFECTIVE DATE NOTE: At 62 FR 51213, Sept. 30, 1997, § 160.035–9 was amended by removing paragraph (c) and redesignating paragraph (d) as (c), effective Oct. 30, 1997.

§ 160.035–10 Number of persons allowed in lifeboats.

(a) The maximum number of persons for which the lifeboat may be rated is determined as noted in paragraphs (a) (1), (2), and (3) of this section. The smallest number obtained is the number to be used.

(1) The number of persons which a lifeboat shall be permitted to accommodate shall be equal to the greatest whole number obtained by dividing the capacity in cubic feet by the factor shown in Table 160.035–10(a). The net cubic capacity shall be determined by § 160.035–9(b).

TABLE 160.035–10(A)

Length in feet—		Factor
Of—	But less than—	
	18	14
18	20	13
20	22	12
22	24	11
24	Or over	10

(2) The number of persons permitted in the lifeboat shall not exceed the number for which seating space is provided as determined by drawing figures to scale of a size as noted in Figure 160.035–10(a)(2) on an arrangement plan of the lifeboat.

(3) The number of persons permitted in the lifeboat shall not exceed the number of persons wearing life preservers which can be seated in the lifeboat without interfering with the use of the oars or the operation of other propulsion equipment.

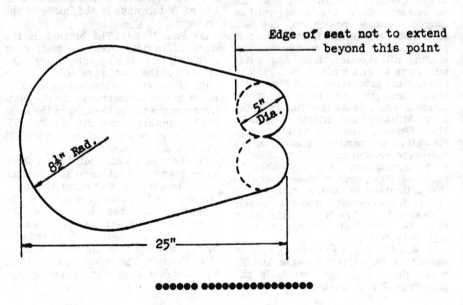

Edge of seat not to extend beyond this point

(b) [Reserved]

§ 160.035–11 Inspection and testing of lifeboats.

(a) *General.* Coast Guard marine inspectors shall be admitted to any place in the builder's factory where work is done on these lifeboats or component materials or parts. Lifeboats shall be inspected during the course of construction to determine that the arrangements and materials entering into the construction are in accordance with approved plans, and to insure that the workmanship is of good quality. Samples of materials entering into construction may be taken by the marine inspectors for such tests as may be deemed necessary at any time there is any question as to suitability or adequacy of any material or arrangement.

(b) *Preapproval tests.* Before approval is granted to any design of lifeboat, the following tests shall be made by a marine inspector:

(1) *Strength test.* The light lifeboat shall be suspended by shackles at the bow and stern, or by means of the releasing gear, and the length, beam, and depth shall be measured. Weights shall then be added to equal the weight of the equipment, food, water, etc., and persons for which the boat is to be approved, and the length, beam, and depth measured. Additional weight shall then be added so that the suspended load is 25 percent greater than the weight of the fully equipped and loaded lifeboat and the measurements repeated. All weights shall then be removed and the measurements rechecked. There shall be no appreciable set as a result of this test.

(2) *Flooding test.* Lifeboats shall be flooded while open to the sea to determine the amount of buoyancy necessary to float the complete boat including releasing gear but with no equipment, provision lockers, water tanks, or fuel tanks aboard. If provision lockers, water tanks, and fuel tanks cannot be removed, they should be flooded or filled to the final waterline. Lifeboats fitted with watertight stowage compartments to accommodate individual drinking water containers shall have these individual containers aboard and placed in the stowage compartments which shall be sealed watertight during the flooding test. Ballast of equivalent weight and density should be substituted for the motor, shaft, propeller, radio battery, searchlight, etc., if they are to be installed.

(i) *Boats with independent buoyancy tanks or buoyancy units.* The estimated amount of buoyancy to just float the boat in this condition should be fitted symmetrically aboard the lifeboat, and then the boat flooded. If the tops of the gunwales at their lowest point do not clear the surface of the water, the buoyancy shall be increased as necessary. An additional volume of buoyancy, or buoyancy units, equal to at least one-tenth the cubic capacity of the lifeboat shall be provided.

(ii) *Boats with built-in buoyancy compartments.* When flood testing lifeboats with built-in buoyancy compartments weights shall be placed in the bottom of the lifeboat to counteract the buoyancy provided for the persons to be carried. The amount of weight required per person carried shall be as follows:

Materials	Weight per person (pounds)
Iron or steel	72
Lead	69
Concrete	110

Other impervious material may be used if more convenient. The weight per person required is determined from the formula

$$W = 63d \div d - 63$$

where *d* is the density of material in pounds per cubic foot (Sandbags should not be used for this purpose inasmuch as their weight under water is not readily predictable.) If the lifeboat weighted as above does not float with the gunwale at the lowest point just clear of the surface of the water, unit air tanks should be slipped beneath the thwarts until the gunwales do clear the surface of the water. The additional air tankage required shall be incorporated in the design of the lifeboat.

(3) *Seating capacity test.* The lifeboat shall be fully loaded with equipment, and in this condition the number of persons for which the lifeboat is to be approved shall be seated, in accordance

with the seating plan required in § 160.035-14(a). All persons shall wear an approved life preserver and it shall be demonstrated by actual test that there is sufficient room to row the boat without interference.

(4) *Freeboard test.* Freeboards shall be measured to the low point of the sheer with the lifeboat in light condition with neither equipment nor persons aboard, and in the loaded condition with full equipment and persons aboard.

(5) *Stability test.* Upon the conclusion of the seating test, all persons on one side of the centerline shall disembark. The remaining people should sit upright and not move from their original positions. (Not less than one-half in total number of persons should remain in the lifeboat.) Freeboard to the low point of sheer shall then be measured. This freeboard should, in general, be not less than 10 percent of the depth of the lifeboat.

(c) Motor-propelled lifeboats must pass the tests as required for an oar-propelled lifeboat in § 160.035-3. In addition, speed tests over a measured course and fuel consumption tests on a time basis shall be made to determine that the fully loaded motor-propelled lifeboats can maintain a speed of 6 knots for all classes of motor-propelled lifeboats, and that for each class of motor-propelled lifeboat its fuel tanks carry sufficient fuel for at least 24 hours at 6 knots. A 4-hour endurance trial shall be conducted with the fully loaded lifeboat at the RPM attained in the speed test in order to insure that there is no overheating, undue vibration, or other condition which would warrant the belief that the lifeboat could not maintain its proper speed for 24 hours. The time consumed in conducting the speed and fuel consumption tests may be counted toward the 4-hour endurance test. It shall be demonstrated that all engines installed in motor lifeboats can be started by the acceptable cranking system installed with no previous warming up period.

(d) Hand-propelled lifeboats shall be subjected to the same tests as required for an oar-propelled lifeboat. In addition, a test shall be made to assure that the lifeboat can be satisfactorily maneuvered with the hand-propelling gear. A speed of at least three knots shall be achieved in both light and load condition over a measured course of not less than 1,000 feet.

[CGFR 65-9, 30 FR 11467, Sept. 8, 1965, as amended by CGD 72-133R, 37 FR 17040, Aug. 24, 1972]

§ 160.035-12 Additional preapproval tests required for F.R.P. lifeboats.

(a) *General.* These tests are required in addition to the preapproval tests required for steel lifeboats in § 160.035-11. The prototype boat of each size or design submitted will be required to perform satisfactorily in the following tests which will be made in the presence of a marine inspector.

(b) *Strength test.* The following tests described in this paragraph are in lieu of the strength test in § 160.035-11(b)(1):

(1) *Suspension tests.* The light lifeboat shall be suspended freely from the releasing gear and the length, beam, and depth measured. Weights shall then be added to equal the weight of the equipment, food, water, and persons to be carried (see § 160.035-11(b)(2)(ii)), and the length, beam, and depth measured. Additional weights shall then be added so that the suspended load is 25, 50, 75, and 100 percent greater than the weight of the fully equipped and loaded lifeboat and the measurements taken at each 25 percent increments. (Water may be used for all or any portion of the weight if desired.) All weights shall then be removed and final measurements taken. There shall be no fractures or other signs of excessive stress and no appreciable set as a result of this test.

(2) *Chock test.* The light lifeboat shall be placed on blocks located under the keel at the quarter points and measurements of length, beam, and depth taken. The boat shall be flooded with water equal to the weight of all equipment, food, water, and persons to be carried and measurements of length, beam, and depth taken again. Additional measurements of 25, 50, 75, and 100 percent of the weight of the fully equipped and loaded lifeboat shall be added and the measurements taken at 25 percent increments. If the boat becomes full of water before 100 percent overload is reached, no additional

weight need be added, and the last deflection measurements with the boat under load shall be taken at this point. The boat shall be drained and final measurements taken. There shall be no fractures or other signs of excessive stress and no appreciable set as a result of this test.

(3) *Swing test.* The boat shall be loaded with weights equal to the weight of all equipment, food, water and persons to be carried. It shall then be suspended by the releasing gear with falls 20 feet in length so arranged that when hanging freely the gunwale on one side of the boat is approximately 2 inches from a stationary concrete or steel wall or other structure of similar construction and rigidity. The boat shall then be hauled outboard a horizontal distance of 8 feet from its original position. From this point, the boat shall be allowed to freely swing inboard and strike the wall along one side. There shall be no damage which would render the boat unserviceable.

(4) *Drop test.* The boat shall be loaded with weights equal to the full weight of all equipment, food, water and persons to be carried. The boat shall then be suspended freely from the releasing gear and shall be dropped in a free fall into the water from a height of 10 feet. There shall be no damage which would render the boat unserviceable.

(5) *Thwart test.* A 200-pound sand bag shall be dropped from a height of 6 feet on the center of each thwart span. The thwarts shall not fracture or otherwise be rendered unserviceable.

(6) *Towing test.* With a towline rigged around the forward thwart in the same manner as the sea painter is normally rigged, the fully loaded lifeboat shall be towed at least 1,000 yards at a speed of not less than 5 knots. The boat shall exhibit satisfactory towing characteristics and there shall be no appreciable damage to the thwart.

(7) *Tanks and lockers.* Equipment tanks and watertight lockers shall be tested with not less than 1.0 p.s.i. of air pressure both before and after the tests described in paragraphs (b)(1) through (6) of this section.

§ 160.035–13 Testing and inspection after approval.

(a) *General.* After the design of a lifeboat has been approved, subsequent lifeboats of the same design shall be individually inspected and tested as noted in § 160.035–11(a) for metal lifeboats and paragraph (b) of this section for FRP. lifeboats. In addition, motors and band-propelling gear when installed shall be operated in the "ahead", "neutral", and "astern" positions. If mechanical disengaging apparatus is fitted, it shall be tested by suspending the lifeboat loaded with deadweight equivalent to the number of persons allowed in the lifeboat (165 pounds per person) together with the weight of the equipment, plus 10 percent of the total load, including the weight of the lifeboat. The release lever shall then be thrown over with this load suspended until the lifeboat is released. The apparatus shall be capable of being operated freely by one man, without the use of aids or undue force to the satisfaction of the marine inspector. (This test may be conducted ashore by suspending the lifeboat just clear of the ground.)

(b) *Additional production inspection and tests for FRP. lifeboats*—(1) *Inspection requirements.* Each production model fibrous glass reinforced plastic lifeboat shall as a condition to its being accepted as Coast Guard approved equipment, be examined by a marine inspector at the following stages in its manufacture:

(i) When the major, individual components of the shell and inner hull or buoyancy casing are completed but before they are assembled together. At this stage the marine inspector shall satisfy himself that these components comply with the approved plans and specifications by visual inspection, thickness measurements and comparison of the weights of the components with the weights recorded for the same components in the prototype.

(ii) At the time the internal buoyancy is installed. If block plastic foam is used, it shall be inspected after it has been cut to size and shaped but before it is inserted and covered. The installation shall be completed in the presence of the marine inspector and he shall verify that the required amount is used by weighing the material. If foamed-in-place plastic foam is used, the marine inspector shall be present during the foaming operation. A sample of the foam shall be retained outside the boat and when it sets it shall be used to make a density determination of the material.

(iii) When the boat is completed. At this stage the marine inspector shall check the scantlings of the minor components and the overall compliance with the plans. The manufacturer shall certify that the materials used are in accordance with the approved bill of materials.

(2) *Test requirements.* After the inspections listed in paragraph (b)(1) of this section are completed, the following tests are to be carried out to the satisfaction of the marine inspector:

(i) The boat shall be suspended freely from the releasing gear and the length, breadth and depth measured. The boat shall then be flooded with water equal to 1½ times the weight of the boat, persons, equipment, and provisions and fuel (if motor driven) less the weight of the boat. This is represented by the following formula:

Water added = 1.5 × (empty boat + equipment + provisions + fuel + people) − empty boat

The length, breadth and depth shall be measured in this loaded condition and, again, after the load has been removed. The loaded deflections and the permanent deformations shall not significantly exceed those recorded for the prototype in the pre-approval tests. Also, while flooded, the exterior of the hull shall be examined for leaks or other defects. After the boat is drained, the attachment of the release gear shall be carefully examined.

(ii) All provision tanks shall be tested by a static head above the tank top of 2 feet of water without showing leakage or permanent deformation.

(iii) The plastic fuel tanks shall be tested by a static head above the tank top of 10 feet of water without showing leakage or permanent deformation.

(c) *Marking.* (1) A corrosion resistant nameplate shall be affixed at the bow of each lifeboat on which is stamped the name of the manufacturer, serial number, approval number, dimensions of the lifeboat, cubic capacity, buoyancy capacity, net weight of the boat in Condition A and Condition B, the number of persons for which the lifeboat is approved, together with the Marine Inspection Office identification letters, the date, and the letters U.S.C.G. *Condition A* includes buoyancy and water tanks and provision stowage compartments but no equipment, provisions, water or persons. *Condition B* includes full required provisions and equipment, persons allowed at 10 cubic feet or by seating test whichever is less at 165 pounds and 3 quarts of water (6.25 pounds)—per person.

[CGFR 65-9, 30 FR 11467, Sept. 8, 1965, as amended by CGD 72-133R, 37 FR 17040, Aug. 24, 1972; CGD 75-186, 41 FR 10437, Mar. 11, 1976]

§ 160.035-14 Procedure for approval of lifeboats.

(a) Before action is taken on any design of lifeboat, plans covering fully the arrangement and construction of the lifeboat, material specifications, together with a lines drawing, stowage arrangement, seating arrangement, and other details shall be submitted to the Commandant through the Commander of the Coast Guard District in which the lifeboat is built. The plans for approval must be detailed to a degree that the lifeboat can be constructed from the plans submitted.

(b) If the drawings required in paragraph (a) of this section are satisfactory, the manufacturer shall notify the Commander of the Coast Guard District in which the lifeboat is built in writing when fabrication is to commence. A marine inspector will be assigned to witness the construction procedure in accordance with the plans, verify the tests required by § 160.035-11 for metal lifeboats and § 160.035-12 for additional tests required for F.R.P. lifeboats. Also, the manufacturer shall provide the necessary tools and facilities required to conduct the tests. The Coast Guard shall have the right to require such other additional tests as reasonably may be deemed necessary, either with the completed boat or component parts, depending upon the particular construction methods and materials used by the builder, or any unusual conditions or circumstances which may arise during the construction or testing.

(c) At the time that the tests are successfully completed, the manufacturer shall present to the marine inspector four corrected copies of the plans noted in paragraph (a) of this section, including any corrections, changes, or additions which may have been found necessary during construction or testing. If the manufacturer desires more than one set of approved plans, additional copies shall be submitted at that time.

(d) Upon receipt of corrected drawings and satisfactory test reports, the Commandant will issue a certificate of approval. No change shall be made in the design or construction without first receiving permission of the Commandant via the Commander of the Coast Guard District in which the lifeboat is built.

Subpart 160.036—Hand-Held Rocket-Propelled Parachute Red Flare Distress Signals

SOURCE: CGD 76–048a and 76–048b, 44 FR 73081, Dec. 17, 1979, unless otherwise noted.

§ 160.036–1 Incorporation by reference.

(a) The following is incorporated by reference into this subpart:

(1) "The Universal Color Language" and "The Color Names Dictionary" in *Color: Universal Language and Dictionary of Names*, National Bureau of Standards Special Publication 440, December 1976.

(b) NBS Special Publication 440 may be obtained by ordering from the Superintendent of Documents, U.S. Government Printing Office, Washington, DC 20402 (Order by SD Catalog No. C13.10:440).

(c) Approval to incorporate by reference the material listed in this section was obtained from the director of the Federal Register on November 1, 1979. The material is on file in the Federal Register library.

§ 160.036–2 Type.

(a) Handheld rocket-propelled parachute red flare distress signals specified by this subpart shall be of one type which shall consist essentially of a completely self-contained device which can be fired from the hand to provide a rocket-propelled parachute red flare distress signal.

(b) [Reserved]

§ 160.036–3 Materials, workmanship, construction and performance requirements.

(a) *Materials.* The materials used in handheld rocket-propelled parachute red flare distress signals shall conform strictly to the specifications and drawings submitted by the manufacturer and approved by the Commandant. In general, all exposed parts shall be corrosion-resistant or properly protected against corrosion.

(b) *Workmanship.* Handheld rocket-propelled parachute red flare distress signals shall be of first class workmanship and shall be free from imperfections of manufacture affecting their appearance or that may affect their serviceability.

(c) *Construction.* The exterior case of the cartridge shall be made of a suitable metal and shall protect against the entrance of moisture. The construction shall be such that the parachute and pyrotechnic candle will be expelled at approximately the maximum altitude reached.

(d) *Performance.* Signals shall meet all of the inspection and test requirements contained in § 160.036–4.

§ 160.036–4 Approval and production tests.

(a) *Approval tests.* The manufacturer must produce a lot of at least 100 signals from which samples must be taken for testing for approval under § 160.036–7. The approval tests are the operational tests and technical tests in paragraphs (c) and (d) of this section. The approval tests must be conducted by an independent laboratory accepted by the Commandant under § 159.010 of this chapter.

(b) *Production inspections and tests.* Production inspections and tests of each lot of signals produced must be conducted under the procedures in § 159.007 of this chapter. Signals from a rejected lot must not be represented as meeting this Subpart or as being approved by the Coast Guard. If the manufacturer identifies the cause of the rejection of a lot of signals, the signals in the lot may be reworked by the manufacturer to correct the problem. Samples from the rejected lot must be retested in order to be accepted. Records shall be kept of the reasons for rejection, the reworking performed on the rejected lot, and the results of the second test.

(1) *Lot size.* For the purposes of sampling the production of signals, a lot must consist of not more than 30,000 signals. Lots must be numbered serially by the manufacturer. A new lot must be started with:

(i) Any change in construction details,

(ii) Any changes in sources of raw materials, or

(iii) The start of production on a new production line or on a previously discontinued production line.

(2) *Inspections and tests by the manufacturer.* The manufacturer's quality control procedures must include inspection of materials entering into construction of the signals and inspection of the finished signals, to determine that signals are being produced in accordance with the approved plans. Samples from each lot must be tested in accordance with the operational tests in paragraph (c) of this section.

(3) *Inspections and test by an independent laboratory.* An independent laboratory accepted by the Commandant under § 159.010 of this chapter must perform or supervise the inspections and tests under paragraph (b)(2) of this section at least 4 times a year, unless the number of lots produced in a year is less than four. The inspections and tests must occur at least once during each quarterly period, unless no lots are produced during this period. If less than four lots are produced, the laboratory must perform or supervise the inspection and testing of each lot. In addition, the laboratory must perform or supervise the technical tests in paragraph (d) of this section at least once for every ten lots of signals produced, except that the number of technical tests must be at least one but not more than four per year. If a lot of signals tested by the independent laboratory is rejected, the laboratory must perform or supervise the inspections and tests of the reworked lot and the next lot of signals produced. The tests of each reworked lot and the next lot produced must not be counted for the purpose of meeting the requirement for the annual number of inspections and tests performed or supervised by the independent laboratory.

(c) *Operational tests.* Each lot of signals must be sampled and tested as follows:

(1) *Sampling procedure and accept/reject criteria.* A sample of signals must be selected at random from the lot. The size of the sample must be the individual sample size in Table 160.036-4(c)(1) corresponding to the lot size. Each signal in the sample is tested as prescribed in the test procedure in paragraph (c)(2) of this section. Each signal that has a defect listed in the table of defects (Table 160.036-4(c)(2)) is assigned a score (failure percent) in accordance with that table. In the case of multiple defects, only the score having the highest numerical value is assigned to that signal. If the sum of all the failure percents (cumulative failure percent) for the number of units in the sample is less than or equal to the accept criterion, the lot is accepted. If this sum is equal to or more than the reject criterion the lot is rejected. If the cumulative failure percent falls between the accept and reject criteria, another sample is selected from the production lot and the operational tests are repeated. The cumulative failure percent of each sample tested is added to that of the previous samples to obtain the cumulative failure percent for all the signals tested (cumulative sample size). Additional samples are tested and the tests repeated until either the accept or reject criterion for the cumulative sample size is met. If any signal in the sample explodes when fired or ignites in a way that could burn or otherwise injure the person firing it, the lot is rejected without further testing. (This procedure is diagrammed in figure 160.036-4(c)).

(2) *Test procedure.* Each sample signal (specimen) must be tested as follows:

(i) *Conditioning of test specimens—water resistence.* Immerse specimen horizontally with uppermost portion of the signal approximately 25 mm (1 in.) below the surface of the water for a period of 24 hours.

(ii) *Firing and operating characteristics.* Signals shall fire and operate satisfactorily when the manufacturer's directions are followed. The parachute and pyrotechnic candle shall be ejected at approximately the maximum altitude reached by the projectile case. The parachute shall open and properly suspend the pyrotechnic candle without fouling. The pyrotechnic candle shall burn with uniform intensity and without damaging the parachute, shrouds, or leader line.

(iii) *Altitude.* The altitude reached by a signal is considered to be the height at which the parachute and pyrotechnic candle are ejected from the projectile case, as determined by visual observation against an object of known height, such as a tower or balloon, or by triangulation from two or more points of observation, or by other method satisfactory to the Commandant. The altitude reached shall be not less than 150 m (500 ft.).

(iv) *Rate of descent.* The rate of descent of a signal is considered to be the calculated average rate obtained by dividing the altitude by the time of descent to the surface. The rate of descent shall not exceed 4.5 m (15 ft.) per second.

(v) *Burning time.* The burning time of the pyrotechnic candle shall be obtained by stop watch measurement from the time a distinct, sustained flame is emitted until it ceases. The burning time shall be not less than 30 seconds.

TABLE 160.036–4(C)(1)—ACCEPT AND REJECT CRITERIA FOR OPERATIONAL TEST LOTS

Lot size	Individual sample size	Sample	Cumulative sample size	Accept[1]	Reject[1]
280 or less.	8	First	8	(2)	400
		Second	16	100	500
		Third	24	200	600
		Fourth ..	32	300	700
		Fifth	40	500	800
		Sixth	48	700	900
		Seventh	56	950	951
281 to 500.	13	First	13	0	400
		Second	26	100	600
		Third	39	300	800
		Fourth ..	52	500	1,000
		Fifth	65	700	1,100
		Sixth	78	1,000	1,200
		Seventh	91	1,350	1,351

TABLE 160.036–4(C)(1)—ACCEPT AND REJECT CRITERIA FOR OPERATIONAL TEST LOTS—Continued

Lot size	Individual sample size	Sample	Cumulative sample size	Accept[1]	Reject[1]
501 to 1,200.	20	First	20	0	500
		Second	40	300	800
		Third	60	600	1,000
		Fourth ..	80	800	1,300
		Fifth	100	1,100	1,500
		Sixth	120	1,400	1,700
		Seventh	140	1,850	1,851
1,201 to 3,200.	32	First	32	100	700
		Second	64	400	1,000
		Third	96	800	1,300
		Fourth ..	128	1,200	1,700
		Fifth	160	1,700	2,000
		Sixth	192	2,100	2,300
		Seventh	224	2,550	2,551
More than 3,201.	50	First	50	200	900
		Second	100	700	1,400
		Third	150	1,300	1,900
		Fourth ..	200	1,900	2,500
		Fifth	250	2,500	2,900
		Sixth	300	3,100	3,300
		Seventh	350	3,750	3,751

[1] Cumulative failure percent.
[2] Lot may not be accepted. Next sample must be tested.

TABLE 160.036–4(C)(2)

Kind of defect	Percentage of failure
a. Failure to fire	100
b. Failure to eject projectile contents	100
c. Failure to ignite pyrotechnic candle	100
d. Failure of parachute to open completely	75
e. Complete carrying away or destruction of parachute	75
f. Altitude less than 70 pct of that required	100
g. Altitude less than 70 pct but less than 80 pct of that required	75
h. Altitude at least 80 pct but less than 90 pct of that required	50
i. Altitude at least 90 pct but less than 100 pct of that required	25
j. Average rate of descent greater than four times maximum permitted	100
k. Average rate of descent less than 4 but greater than 3 times maximum permitted	75
l. Average rate of descent less than 3 but greater than 2 times maximum permitted	50
m. Average rate of descent less than twice but greater than maximum permitted	25
n. Burning time less than 70 pct of that required	100
o. Burning time at least 70 pct but less than 80 pct of that required	75
p. Burning time at least 80 pct but less than 90 pct of that required	50
q. Burning time at least 90 pct but less than 100 pct of that required	25

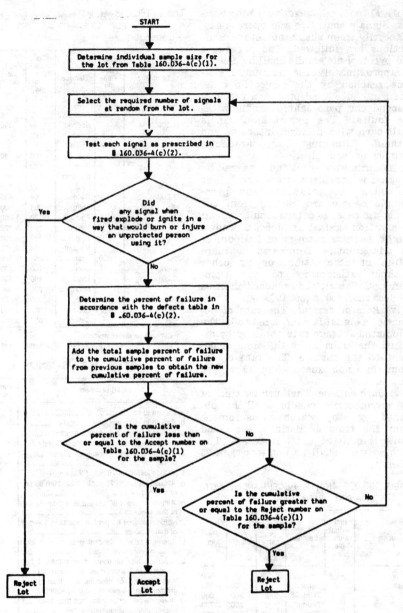

Figure 160.036-4(c).   Operational test procedure.

(d) *Technical tests.* Three signals must be subjected to each of the following tests. Two of the three signals must pass each test in order for the lot of signals to be accepted.

(1) *Luminous intensity.* The luminous intensity of each pyrotechnic candle

tested shall be measured by a visual photometer or equivalent photometric device while the specimen is supported in a horizontal position and the photometer is at right angles to the axis of the specimen. Visual luminous intensity readings shall be observed and recorded at approximately 5-second intervals during the burning of the specimen. The minimum photometric distance shall be 3 m (10 ft.). Recording photometers shall have a chart speed of at least 10 cm (4 in.) per minute. The luminous intensity of the specimen shall be computed as the arithmetical average of the readings recorded. The average luminous intensity of a specimen shall be not less than 20,000 candela.

(2) *Elevated temperature, humidity, and storage.* Place specimen in a thermostatically controlled even-temperature oven held at 75 °C. with not less than 90 percent relative humidity for 72 hours. Remove specimen and store at room temperature (20° to 25 °C.) with approximately 65 percent relative humidity for ten days. If for any reason it is not possible to operate the oven continuously for the 72-hour period, it may be operated at the required temperature and humidity for 8 hours out of each 24 during the 72-hour conditioning period. (Total of 24 hours on and 48 hours off.) The signal shall not ignite or decompose during this conditioning. The signal shall fire and operate satisfactorily following this conditioning.

(3) *Spontaneous ignition.* Place the specimen in a thermostatically controlled even-temperature oven held at 75 °C. with not more than 10% relative humidity for 48 consecutive hours. The signal shall not ignite or undergo marked decomposition.

(4) *Chromaticity.* The color of the burning signal must be vivid red as defined by Sections 13 and 14 of the "Color Names Dictionary." Two identical test plates of white cardboard about 30 cm × 60 cm (12″×24″) are used. Except for a negligible amount of stray daylight, the first test plate is illuminated by light from the specimen placed at a distance of about 1.5 m (5 ft.). The second test plate is illuminated only by light from an incandescent lamp operated at a color tempera-

ture close to 2,848° K at a distance of about 30 cm (1 ft.). The first plate is viewed directly, the second through combinations of Lovibond red, yellow, and blue glasses selected so as to approximate a chromaticity match. By separating the test plates by a wide unilluminated area (subtending at the observer about 45°), it is possible to make accurate determinations of chromaticity in terms of the 1931 CIE Standard Observer and Coordinate System, in spite of fluctuations in luminous intensity of the specimen by factors as high as 2 or 3. The CIE coordinates are converted to the Munsell notation which is cross-referenced to the color name in Section 13 of the "Color Names Dictionary" (see the discussion in Section 10 of "The Universal Color Language").

§ 160.036–5 Marking.

(a) *General.* Each hand-held rocket-propelled parachute red flare distress signal shall be legibly marked or labeled as follows:

(Company brand or style designation) HAND-HELD ROCKET-PROPELLED PARACHUTE RED FLARE DISTRESS SIGNAL—20,000 candela—30 seconds burning time. USE ONLY WHEN AIRCRAFT OR VESSEL IS SIGHTED. DIRECTIONS—(In numbered paragraphs, simply worded instructions for firing the device). Service Life Expiration Date (date to be inserted by manufacturer) (Month and year manufactured) (Lot No. ___) Manufactured by (Name and address of manufacturer) U.S. Coast Guard Approval No. ___.

(b) *Marking of expiration date.* The expiration date must be not more than 42 months from the date of manufacture.

(c) *Other marking.* (1) On each hand-held rocket propelled parachute red flare distress signal there shall be die-stamped in figures not less than 3 mm (⅛ in.) high, on the signal, numbers indicating the month and year of manufacture, thus: "6–54" indicating June, 1954.

(2) The pyrotechnic candle shall be legibly marked with the month and year of manufacture.

(3) In addition to any other marking place on the smallest packing carton or box containing signals, each carton or box shall be plainly and permanently

marked to show the service life expiration date, date of manufacture, and lot number.

(4) The largest carton or box in which the manufacturer ships signals must be marked with the following or equivalent words: "Keep under cover in a dry place."

NOTE: Compliance with the labeling requirements of this section does not relieve the manufacturer of the responsibility of complying with the label requirements of 15 U.S.C. 1263, the Federal Hazardous Substances Act.

§ 160.036-6   Container.

(a) *General.* The container for storing the signals on lifeboats and liferafts is not required to be of a special design or be approved by the Coast Guard. The container must meet the requirements in Subpart 160.021 (§ 160.021-6) except that the wording on the container must be:

HAND-HELD ROCKET-PROPELLED PARACHUTE
RED FLARE DISTRESS SIGNALS

(b) [Reserved]

§ 160.036-7   Procedure for approval.

(a) Signals are approved by the Coast Guard under the procedures in subpart 159.005 of this chapter.

(b) [Reserved]

Subpart 160.037—Hand Orange Smoke Distress Signals

SOURCE: CGD 76-048a and 76-048b, 44 FR 73085, Dec. 17, 1979, unless otherwise noted.

§ 160.037-1   Incorporations by reference.

(a) The following are incorporated by reference into this subpart:

(1) "The Color Names Dictionary" in *Color: Universal Language and Dictionary of Names,* National Bureau of Standards Special Publication 440, December 1976.

(2) "Development of a Laboratory Test for Evaluation of the Effectiveness of Smoke Signals," National Bureau of Standards Report 4792, July 1956.

(b) NBS Special Publication 440 may be obtained by ordering from the Superintendent of Documents, U.S. Government Printing Office, Washington, DC 20402 (Order by SD Catalog No. C13.10:440).

(c) NBS Report 4792 may be obtained from the Commandant (G-MSE), U.S. Coast Guard, Washington, DC 20593-0001.

(d) Approval to incorporate by reference the materials listed in this section was obtained from the Director of the Federal Register on November 1 and 29, 1979. The materials are on file in the Federal Register library.

[CGD 76-048a and 76-048b, 44 FR 73085, Dec. 17, 1979, as amended by CGD 82-063b, 48 FR 4782, Feb. 3, 1983; CGD 88-070, 53 FR 34535, Sept. 7, 1988; CGD 95-072, 60 FR 50467, Sept. 29, 1995; CGD 96-041, 61 FR 50733, Sept. 27, 1996]

§ 160.037-2   Type.

(a) Hand orange smoke distress signals specified by this subpart shall be one type which shall consist essentially of a wooden handle to which is attached a tubular casing having a sealing plug at the handle end, the casing being filled with a smoke producing composition and fuse with button of ignition material at the top, and a removable cap having a friction striking material on its top which may be exposed for use by pulling a tear strip. The signal is ignited by scraping the friction striker on top of the cap against the igniter button on top of the body of the signal. Alternate arrangements which conform to the performance requirements of this specification will be given special consideration.

(b) [Reserved]

§ 160.037-3   Materials, workmanship, construction, and performance requirements.

(a) *Materials.* The materials shall conform strictly to the specifications and drawings submitted by the manufacturer and approved by the Commandant. The color of the tube shall be orange. The combustible materials shall be of such nature as will not deteriorate during long storage, nor when subjected to frigid or tropical climates, or both.

(b) *Workmanship.* Hand orange smoke distress signals shall be of first class workmanship and shall be free from imperfections of manufacture affecting their appearance or that may affect their serviceability. Moisture proof coatings shall be applied uniformly and shall be free from pinholes or other visible defects which would impair their usefulness.

(c) *Construction.* The casing shall be fitted and secured to the handle with not less than a 25 mm (1 in.) overlap and shall be attached to the handle in such a manner that failure of the joint will not occur during tests, ignition, or operation. The plug shall be securely affixed in the casing to separate the smoke composition from the wooden handle. The smoke composition shall be thoroughly mixed and be uniformly compresssed throughout to preclude variations of density which may adversely affect uniformity of its smoke emitting characteristics. The cap shall have a lap fit of not less than 25 mm (1 in.) over the end of the casing and smoke composition to entirely and securely protect the exposed surface of the igniter button and end of smoke composition and casing, and shall have an inner shoulder so constructed that it is mechanically impossible for the inner surface of the cap to come in contact with the igniter button. The cap shall be securely attached to the casing in such manner as to preclude its accidental detachment. The cap shall be provided on its top with a friction striking material which shall, by a pull of the tear strip, be entirely exposed for striking the friction igniter button. The igniter button shall be non-water soluble or be protected from moisture by a coating of some waterproof substance, and shall be raised or exposed in such manner as to provide positive ignition by the friction striker. The igniter button shall be firmly secured in or on the top of the smoke composition; the arrangement shall be such that the ignition will be transmitted to the smoke producing composition. The assembled signal, consisting of tear strip, cap, casing, and handle, shall be sealed and treated to protect the signal from deterioration by moisture. The protective waterproof coating shall be applied so none adheres to the friction striking surface. Special consideration will be given to alternate waterproofing of the signal by means of a water-resistant coating on the signal plus packaging in a sealed plastic water-proof bag satisfactory to the Commandant.

(d) *Performance.* Signals shall meet all the inspection and test requirements contained in § 160.037–4.

§ 160.037–4 Approval and production tests.

(a) *Approval tests.* The manufacturer must produce a lot of at least 100 signals from which samples must be taken for testing for approval under § 160.037–7. The approval tests are the operational tests and technical tests in paragraphs (c) and (d) of this section. The approval tests must be conducted by an independent laboratory accepted by the Commandant under § 159.010 of this chapter.

(b) *Production inspections and tests.* Production inspections and tests of each lot of signals produced must be conducted under the procedures in § 159.007 of this chapter. Signals from a rejected lot must not be represented as meeting this subpart or as being approved by the Coast Guard. If the manufacturer identifies the cause of the rejection of a lot of signals, the signals in the lot may be reworked by the manufacturer to correct the problem. Samples from the rejected lot must be retested in order to be accepted. Records shall be kept of the reasons for rejection, the reworking performed on the rejected lot, and the results of the second test.

(1) *Lot size.* For the purposes of sampling the production of signals, a lot must consist of not more than 30,000 signals. Lots must be numbered serially by the manufacturer. A new lot must be started with:

(i) Any change in construction details,

(ii) Any change in sources of raw materials, or

(iii) The start of production on a new production line or on a previously discontinued production line.

(2) *Inspections and tests by the manufacturer.* The manufacturer's quality control procedures must include inspection of materials entering into construction of the signals and inspection of the finished signals, to determine that signals are being produced in accordance with the approved plans. Samples from each lot must be tested

in accordance with the operational tests in paragraph (c) of this section.

(3) *Inspections and tests by an independent laboratory.* An independent laboratory accepted by the Commandant under § 159.010 of this Chapter must perform or supervise the inspections and tests under paragraph (b)(2) of this section at least 4 times a year, unless the number of lots produced in a year is less than four. The inspections and tests must occur at least once during each quarterly period, unless no lots are produced during this period. If less than four lots are produced, the laboratory must perform or supervise the inspection and testing of each lot. In addition, the laboratory must perform or supervise the technical tests in paragraph (d) of this section at least once for every ten lots of signals produced, except that the number of technical tests must be at least one but not more than four per year. If a lot of signals tested by the independent laboratory is rejected, the laboratory must perform or supervise the inspections and tests of the reworked lot and the next lot of signals produced. The tests of each reworked lot and the next lot produced must not be counted for the purpose of meeting the requirement for the annual number of inspections and tests performed or supervised by the independent laboratory.

(c) *Operational tests.* Each lot of signals must be sampled and tested as follows:

(1) *Sampling procedure and accept/reject criteria.* A sample of signals must be selected at random from the lot. The size of the sample must be the individual sample size in Table 160.037-4(c)(1) corresponding to the lot size. Each signal in the sample is tested as prescribed in the test procedure in paragraph (c)(2) of this section. Each signal that has a defect listed in the table of defeats (Table 160.037-4(c)(2)) is assigned a score (failure percent) in accordance with that table. In the case of multiple defects, only the score having the highest numerical value is assigned to that signal. If the sum of all the failure percents (cumulative failure percent) for the number of units in the sample is less than or equal to the accept criterion, the lot is accepted. If the sum is equal to or more than the

reject criterion the lot is rejected. If the cumulative failure percent falls between the accept and reject criteria, another sample is selected from the production lot and the operational tests are repeated. The cumulative failure percent of each sample tested is added to that of the previous samples to obtain the cumulative failure percent for all the signals tested (cumulative sample size). Additional samples are tested and the tests repeated until either the accept or reject criterion for the cumulative sample size is met. If any signal in the sample explodes when fired, or ignites in a way that could burn or otherwise injure the person firing it, the lot is rejected without further testing. (This procedure is diagrammed in figure 160.037-4(c)).

(2) *Test procedure.* Each sample signal (specimen) must be tested as follows:

(i) *Conditioning of test specimens—water resistance.* Immerse specimen horizontally with uppermost portion of the signal approximately 25 mm (1 in.) below the surface of the water for a period of 24 hours. If the signal is protected by alternate waterproofing consisting of a water-resistant coating on the signal plus packaging in a sealed plastic waterproof bag, the 24-hour water immersion conditioning will be conducted while the signal is in the sealed plastic waterproof bag and will be followed by an additional immersion of the bare signal (i.e., after removal from the bag) 25 mm (1 in.) below the surface of the water for a period of 10 minutes.

(ii) *Waterproofing of igniter button.* Remove the cap from the test specimen. Place head of specimen without cap about 25 mm (1 in.) under the surface of water for approximately 5 minutes. Remove specimen from the water and wipe dry.

(iii) *Smoke emitting time.* Ignite specimen according to directions printed on the signal. The smoke emitting time of a specimen shall be obtained by stop watch measurements from the time of distinct, sustained smoke emission until it ceases. The watch shall be stopped during periods of flame emission. The smoke emitting time for a specimen shall be not less than 50 seconds.

(iv) *Ignition and smoke emitting characteristics.* Test specimens shall ignite and emit smoke properly when the directions on the signal are followed. Test specimens shall not ignite explosively in a manner that might be dangerous to the user or persons close by. The plug separating the smoke producing composition from the handle shall in no case allow flame or hot gases to pass through it or between it and the casing in such manner as might burn the hand while holding the signal by the handle.

TABLE 160.037–4(C)(1)—ACCEPT AND REJECT CRITERIA FOR OPERATIONAL TEST LOTS

Lot size	Individual sample size	Sample	Cumulative sample size	Accept[1]	Reject[1]
280 or less.	8	First	8	([2])	400
		Second	16	100	500
		Third	24	200	600
		Fourth ..	32	300	700
		Fifth	40	500	800
		Sixth	48	700	900
		Seventh	56	950	951
281 to 500.	13	First	13	0	400
		Second	26	100	600
		Third	39	300	800
		Fourth ..	52	500	1,000
		Fifth	65	700	1,100
		Sixth	78	1,000	1,200
		Seventh	91	1,350	1,351
501 to 1,200.	20	First	20	0	500
		Second	40	300	800
		Third	60	600	1,000
		Fourth ..	80	800	1,300
		Fifth	100	1,100	1,500

TABLE 160.037–4(C)(1)—ACCEPT AND REJECT CRITERIA FOR OPERATIONAL TEST LOTS—Continued

Lot size	Individual sample size	Sample	Cumulative sample size	Accept[1]	Reject[1]
		Sixth	120	1,400	1,700
		Seventh	140	1,850	1,851
1,201 to 3,200.	32	First	32	100	700
		Second	64	400	1,000
		Third	96	800	1,300
		Fourth ..	128	1,200	1,700
		Fifth	160	1,700	2,000
		Sixth	192	2,100	2,300
		Seventh	224	2,550	2,551
More than 3,201.	50	First	50	200	900
		Second	100	700	1,400
		Third	150	1,300	1,900
		Fourth ..	200	1,900	2,500
		Fifth	250	2,500	2,900
		Sixth	300	3,100	3,300
		Seventh	350	3,750	3,751

[1] Cumulative failure percent.
[2] Lot may not be accepted. Next sample must be tested.

TABLE 160.037–4(C)(2)

Kind of defects	Percentage of failure
a. Failure to ignite	100
b. Ignites or burns dangerously	50
c. Non-uniform smoke-emitting rate	50
d. Smoke-emitting time less than 70 pct of specified time.	100
e. Smoke-emitting time at least 70 pct but less than 80 pct of specified time.	75
f. Smoke-emitting time at least 80 pct but less than 90 pct of specified time.	50
g. Smoke-emitting time at least 90 pct but less than 100 pct of specified time.	25

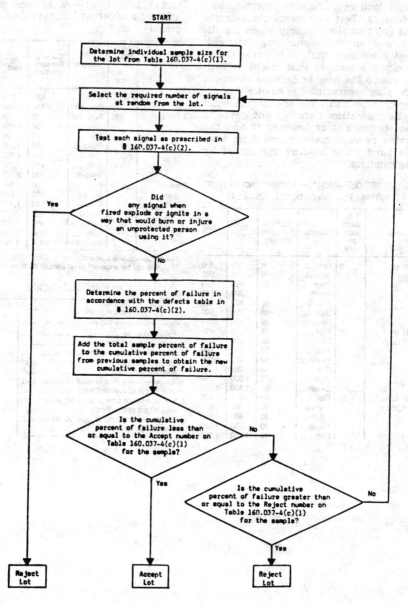

Figure 160.037–4(c). Operational test procedure.

(d) *Technical tests.* Three signals must be subjected to each of the following tests. Two of the three signals must pass each test in order for the lot of signals to be accepted.

(1) *Underwater smoke emission.* Condition each sample in accordance with

paragraph (c)(2)(i) of this section. Ignite specimen and let it burn about 15 seconds in air. Submerge the burning signal in water in a vertical position with head down. Obtain underwater smoke emission time by stop watch measurements from time of submersion until smoke emission ceases. The test specimen shall burn underwater not less than 10 seconds when subjected to this test.

(2) *Bending strength.* Place the specimen on supports 15 cm (6 in.) apart. Attach a weight of 35 kg (77 lb.) to a length of wire. Hang the weight from the supported signal by looping the wire around the signal approximately equidistant from the two points of support. Let the weight hang approximately 5 minutes. The test specimen shall not deflect more than 7 mm (¼ in.), nor shall the joint between the casing and the handle fail when subjected to this test.

(3) *Tensile strength.* Place the specimen in a chuck firmly holding it about 13 mm (½ in.) below the cap. Attach a weight of 35 kg (77 lb.) to a length of wire. Hang the weight from the supported signal by looping the wire through a hole bored perpendicular to and through the axis of the handle. Let the weight hang approximately 5 minutes. The test specimen shall not show noticeable distortion, nor shall the joint between the casing and handle fail, when subjected to this test.

(4) *Elevated temperature, humidity and storage.* Place specimen in a thermostatically controlled even-temperature oven held at 75 °C. with not less than 90 percent relative humidity for 72 hours. Remove specimen and store at room temperature (20° to 25 °C.) with approximately 65 percent relative humidity for 10 days. If for any reason it is not possible to operate the oven continuously for the 72-hour period, it may be operated at the required temperature and humidity for 8 hours out of each 24 during the 72-hour conditioning period. (Total of 24 hours on and 48 hours off.) The signal shall not ignite or decompose during this conditioning. The signal shall ignite and operate satisfactorily following this conditioning.

(5) *Spontaneous ignition.* Place the specimen in a thermostatically controlled even-temperature oven held at 75 °C. with not more than 10% relative humidity for 48 consecutive hours. The signal shall not ignite or undergo marked decomposition.

(6) *Susceptibility to explosion.* Remove smoke composition from signal and punch a small hole in the composition. Insert a No. 6 commercial blasting cap. Ignite the cap. The test specimen shall not explode or ignite.

(7) *Color of smoke.* Ignite specimen in the open air in daytime according to the directions printed on the signal, and determine the smoke color by direct visual comparison of the unshadowed portions of the smoke with a color chart held so as to receive the same daylight illumination as the unshadowed portions of the smoke. The color of the smoke must be orange as defined by Sections 13 and 14 of the "Color Names Dictionary" (colors 34–39 and 48–54).

(8) *Volume and density of smoke.* The test specimen shall show less than 70 percent transmission for not less than 30 seconds when measured with apparatus having a light path of 19 cm (7½ in.), an optical system aperture of +3.7 degrees, and an entrance air flow of 18.4m³ per minute (650 cu. ft. per minute), such apparatus to be as described in National Bureau of Standards Report No. 4792.

§160.037-5 Labeling and marking.

(a) *Labeling.* Each hand orange smoke distress signal shall bear a label securely affixed thereto, showing in clear, indelible black lettering on an orange background, the following wording and information:

(Company brand or style designation)

HAND ORANGE SMOKE DISTRESS SIGNAL

For daytime use—50 seconds burning time

USE ONLY WHEN AIRCRAFT OR VESSEL IS SIGHTED

DIRECTIONS: Pull tape over top of cap. Remove cap and ignite flare by rubbing scratch surface on top of cap sharply across igniter button on head of signal.

CAUTION: Stand with back to wind and point away from body when igniting or signal is burning.

Service Life Expiration Date (Month and year to be inserted by manufacturer) (Month and year manufactured) (Lot No. _____). Manufactured by (Name and address of manufacturer). U.S. Coast Guard Approval No. _____.

(b) *Marking of expiration date.* The expiration date must not be more than 42 months from the date of manufacture.

(c) *Other marking.* (1) There shall be die-stamped, in the side of the wooden handle in figures not less than 3 mm (1/8 in.) high, numbers indicating the month and year of manufacture, thus: "6-54" indicating June, 1954.

(2) In addition to any other marking place on the smallest packing carton or box containing hand orange smoke distress signals such cartons or boxes shall be plainly and permanently marked to show the service life expiration date, date of manufacture, and lot number.

(3) The largest carton or box in which the manufacturer ships signals must be marked with the following or equivalent words: "Keep under cover in a dry place."

NOTE: Compliance with the labeling requirements of this section does not relieve the manufacturer of the responsibility of complying with the label requirements of 15 U.S.C. 1263, the Federal Hazardous Substances Act.

§ 160.037-6 Container.

(a) *General.* The container for storing the signals on lifeboats and liferafts is not required to be of a special design or be approved by the Coast Guard. The container must meet the requirements in subpart 160.021 (§ 160.021-6) except that the wording on the container must be: "Hand Orange Smoke Distress Signals."

(b) [Reserved]

§ 160.037-7 Procedure for approval.

(a) Signals are approved by the Coast Guard under the procedures in subpart 159.005 of this chapter.

(b) [Reserved]

Subpart 160.038—Magazine Chests, Portable, for Merchant Vessels

SOURCE: CGFR 49-43, 15 FR 122 Jan. 11, 1950, unless otherwise noted.

§ 160.038-1 Applicable specifications.

(a) There are no other specifications applicable to this subpart.

(b) [Reserved]

§ 160.038-2 Type.

(a) Portable magazine chests shall be of a type suitable for stowage of pyrotechnic distress signals, rockets, or powder for line-throwing guns, and shall be of a size not less than 6 nor more than 40 cubic feet capacity. Alternate types of construction to that specified below will be given special consideration.

(b) [Reserved]

§ 160.038-3 Materials, workmanship, and construction.

(a) Portable magazine chests shall be constructed of metal and lined with wood.

(b) The lining shall be so fitted and finished as to form a smooth surface within the interior of the chest. Fastenings shall be recessed below the surface to avoid projections within the interior. Construction shall be such as to separate all containers of explosives or pyrotechnics from contact with metal surfaces.

(c) The metal shall be 1/8 inch thick and free from crimps, buckles, and rough edges. All metal surfaces shall be wire brushed and all oil, grease, rust, loose scale, and other extraneous matter, removed before application of any primer. All surfaces of the metal chest and fittings shall be given a heavy coat of quick drying red lead, zinc chromate, or other suitable primer before painting. The finish shall consist of two coats of paint. The interior shall be lined with wood sheathing of a minimum thickness of 3/4 inch. Securing means shall be countersunk below the surface of the sheathing. Securing means for the cover and 4 lashing rings shall be provided. The lashing rings shall be 3" I.D. × 3/8" wire permanently attached to the magazine chest. Two runners, not less than 2 inches high shall be permanently attached to the bottom of the chest.

§ 160.038-4 Inspections and tests.

(a) Portable magazine chests specified by this subpart are not ordinarily subject to regularly s scheduled factory inspections.

(b) [Reserved]

§ 160.038-5 Marking.

(a) Portable magazine chests used for the stowage of pyrotechnic signals, rockets, and powder for line-throwing guns shall be marked, in letters at least 3 inches high, with the following legend: "Portable Magazine Chest, Inflammable—Keep Lights and Fire Away."

(b) [Reserved]

§ 160.038-6 Procedure for approval.

(a) Portable magazine chests are not subject to formal approval, but will be accepted by the inspector on the basis of this subpart at annual inspections and reinspections of vessels.

(b) [Reserved]

Subpart 160.039 [Reserved]

Subpart 160.040—Line-Throwing Appliance, Impluse-Projected Rocket Type (and Equipment)

SOURCE: CGD 76-048a and 76-048b, 44 FR 73089, Dec. 17, 1979, unless otherwise noted.

§ 160.040-1 Incorporations by reference.

(a) The following military specifications are incorporated by reference into this subpart:

(1) MIL–R–23139 B, 16 August 1965—Rocket Motors, Surface Launched, Development and Qualification Requirements for.

(2) MIL–R–45505 A, 2 April 1971—Line Throwing Apparatuses, Rocket and Projectile Units.

(b) The military specifications may be obtained from Customer Service, Naval Publications and Forms Center, 5801 Tabor Avenue, Philadelphia, PA 19120 (tel: (215) 697-2000). These specifications are also on file in the Federal Register library.

(c) Approval to incorporate by reference the materials listed in this section was obtained from the Director of the Federal Register on September 24, 1979.

§ 160.040-2 Type and size.

(a) Impulse-projected rocket type line-throwing appliances required by this subpart shall be of a type consisting essentially of a pistol or launcher, which can be hand held and hand directed, or suitably supported and hand directed.

(b) Impulse-projected rocket type line-throwing appliances shall weigh (complete with one rocket, bridle, and leader) not to exceed 16 kg (35 lb.) and shall be of a size easily manageable by one person.

(c) Alternate arrangements which meet the performance requirements of this subpart will be given special consideration. Line-throwing appliances meeting the requirements of MIL–L–45505 Type I will be considered as meeting the requirements of this subpart subject to approval of the Commandant.

§ 160.040-3 Materials, construction, workmanship, and performance requirements.

(a) *Materials.* All materials used in the construction of impulse-projected rocket type line-throwing appliances and equipment shall be of good quality suitable for the purpose intended, and shall conform ot this subpart and to the specifications submitted by the manufacturer and approved by the Commandant. The choice of materials, when there is no specific requirement, shall be such that maximum safety to operating personnel will be maintained, and that resistance to corrosion by salt water or spray, shock, temperature change, and wear will be obtained. The use of dissimilar materials in combination shall be avoided wherever possible, but when such contacts are necessary, provision shall be made to prevent such deleterious effects as galvanic corrosion, freezing or buckling of moving parts, and loosening or tightening of joints due to differences in coefficients of thermal expansion.

(b) *Construction.* The design and construction shall be such as to obtain effective and safe operation aboard vessels at sea.

(c) *Workmanship.* Impulse-projected rocket type line-throwing appliances shall be of first class workmanship and shall be free from imperfections of manufacture affecting their appearance or that may affect their serviceability.

(d) *Performance.* When the rocket is fired from the appliance in accordance with the manufacturer's instructions, it shall be capable of passing the tests specified by § 160.040-5(c).

§ 160.040-4 Equipment for impulse-projected rocket type line-throwing appliance.

(a) Four rocket projectiles, each complete with bridle and leader of fire-resistant materials. Two of the projectiles shall be of the buoyant type.

(b) Not less than 4 primer-ejector cartridges which fit the chamber of the pistol, gun, or launcher.

(c) Four service lines, each 4 mm (5/32 in.) minimum diameter with a minimum breaking strenght of at least 2,250 N (500 lb.), and in one continual length not less than that specified in the approval of the appliance carried, without splice, knot, or other retarding or weaking features. The length of each service line will be assigned in the approval of the appliance as a round number approximately one-third in excess of the average distance the line is carried in the tests required by § 160.040-7(c). The line shall be of either natural or synthetic fibers suitable for marine usage. The end of the line intended to be attached to the projectile shall have securely attached thereto a substantial tag bearing a permanent legend indicating its purpose, and the other end of the line shall be tagged in the same manner to prevent delay in securing proper and immediate action with the equipment. Each line shall be coiled, faked, or reeled in its own faking box or reel in such manner that when all the line leaves the container, it shall automatically become unattached and free from the container. The faking box or reel shall be big enough for the line. The reel type container shall consist of a reel upon which the line may be readily coiled and a canister or container into which the line may be placed that affords a fair lead through which the line may pay out. The reel must be so designed as to permit easy withdrawal after the line has been coiled. Containers of new lines shall bear the name of the manufacturer, date of manufacture, and a statement to the effect that in all respects the line meets the requirements of this specification.

(d) [Reserved]

(e) One cleaning rod with wire brush of non-ferrous metal, prongs arranged in a spiral of sufficient rigidity and size to clean the bore.

(f) One can of oil suitable for cleaning and preserving the appliance.

(g) Twelve flannel wiping patches of sufficient size to cover the brush and suitable for wiping the bore clean.

(h) One set of instructions including a list of the equipment furnished with the appliance, information as to the proper maintenance of the appliance and equipment, and directions for loading and firing the appliance in service use shall be permanently engraved in plastic and mounted conspicuously in the case or box required by paragraph (i) of this section.

(i) A suitable case or box, properly compartmented for stowage of the appliance and auxiliary equipment, is required for stowage on merchant vessels. The service line and auxiliary line need not be stowed in the case.

§ 160.040-5 Approval and production tests.

(a) *Approval tests.* An independent laboratory accepted by the Commandant under § 159.010 of this chapter must perform or supervise the performance tests in paragraph (c) of this section.

(b) *Production inspections and tests.* Production inspections and tests must be conducted under the procedures in § 159.007 of this chapter. Each appliance or lot of rockets which fails the inspections and tests must not be represented as meeting this subpart or as being approved by the Coast Guard.

(1) *Inspections and tests by the manufacturer.* The manufacturer's quality control procedures must include the inspection of appliances during production as well as inspection of finished appliances, to determine that the appliances are being produced in accordance with the approved plans. The performance tests in paragraph (c) of this section must be performed by the manufacturer.

(2) *Inspections and tests by an independent laboratory.* An independent laboratory accepted by the Commandant under §159.010 of this chapter must inspect and test appliances and rockets at least once each year. The inspection must determine that the appliances and rockets are being produced in accordance with the appropriate plans. The tests must be in accordance with paragraph (c) of this section.

(c) *Performance tests—(1) Appliances.* Each appliance shall be tested by firing three rounds. These rounds may be regular rockets or buoyant type rockets carrying regular service lines, as provided in paragraph (c)(2) of this paragraph or may be dummy projectiles, of the same size and weight as the regular rocket projectile, expelled into an earthen bank or other resisting medium from a reasonable distance. At least one of the rounds shall be fired using a primer-ejector cartridge loaded with a charge double the normal charge; the other rounds may be fired using regular primer-ejector cartridges. After the firing tests have been completed, each appliance shall be fired twice using the regular primer-ejector cartridges only, for the purposes of demonstrating that the appliance is still in operating condition. The entire assembly of the appliance shall then be examined. Results of the test firing and the physical examination shall show none of the following: Failure to eject cartridge, failure to close breech, trigger malfunction, safety lock failure to function, breech catch malfunction, broken spring, broken handgrips, cracked barrel or discharge chamber, firing pin or plunger broken, distorted or excessively worn or loose breech. A single misfire is acceptable if a second cartridge fires on repeated test. Misfire of both shall be cause for rejection of the appliance. More than one loose screw shall be cause for rejection. If an appliance exhibits a single loose screw, it may be retightened.

(2) *Rockets.* The rocket shall utilize a solid fuel propellant which shall function in accordance with all applicable requirements of MIL–R–23139. The use of black powder for the rocket motor is not acceptable. The ignition of the rocket motor shall occur at such a distance from the appliance so as not to spew flame, hot gaseous exhaust, or hot particles of propellant in such a manner as to create a hazard to personnel or the vessel. The rocket shall have a service line carrier assembly permanently attached and made of material, or suitably protected, to withstand the heat from the rocket motor's exhaust. From each 200 rockets manufactured, not less than three must be selected to be tested by firing with service line attached. The rockets selected will, over a period of time, include representative samples of both the regular and buoyant type rockets, except that the approval test must include both types. The line shall be carried, under conditions of reasonably still atmosphere, a minimum of 230 m (750 ft.), without breaking or fouling the line, and the rocket shall alight not more than 15 m (50 ft.) from either side of the target line. In no case shall a test rocket be fired without a line attached. After a buoyant type rocket is fired, it shall demonstrate its ability to float in water for not less than 2 hours. Failure to meet any of the test requirements, nose cone cracks, rupture in flight, erratic flight, or unusual burning rate, shall be cause for rejection of rockets produced until suitable correction has been made. If rockets selected from this lot are used for the tests required in paragraph (c)(1) of this section this may be accepted as meeting the requirements of this paragraph.

(3) *Primer-ejector cartridges.* Inasmuch as primer-ejector cartridges are used for the tests required by paragraphs (c)(1) and (2) of this paragraph, additional tests of primer-ejector cartridges will be made only when deemed advisable by the independent laboratory. Misfiring or failure of any kind shall be cause for rejection of cartridges produced until suitable correction has been made.

§160.040-6 **Marking and labeling.**

(a) The appliance shall be permanently and legibly marked by die-stamping or raised letters with the model designation of the appliance, the manufacturer's serial number for the appliance, the official Coast Guard approval number, and the name of the manufacturer. The rocket-projectiles shall be legibly marked with the name of the manufacturer, the model designation, the official Coast Guard approval number, and month and year manufactured. Primer-ejector cartridges shall be permanently and legibly marked with the name of the manufacturer, and the model designation, the official Coast Guard approval number, and the month and year manufactured.

(b) The containers of new service lines shall bear the name of the manufacturer, date of manufacture, and a statement to the effect that in all respects the line meets the requirements of this subpart for service lines. Line faking boxes and reels shall bear the name of the manufacturer.

NOTE: Compliance with the labeling requirements of this section does not relieve the manufacturer of the responsibility of complying with the label requirements of 15 U.S.C 1263, the Federal Hazardous Substances Act.

§ 160.040–7 Procedure for approval.

(a) Rocket type line-throwing appliances are approved by the Coast Guard under the procedures in subpart 159.005 of this chapter.

(b) [Reserved]

Subpart 160.041—Kits, First-Aid, for Merchant Vessels

SOURCE: CGFR 50–12, 15 FR 3093, May 20, 1950, unless otherwise noted.

§ 160.041–1 Applicable specification and publication.

(a) *Specification.* The following specification, of the issue in effect on the date first-aid kits are manufactured, forms a part of this subpart:

(1) Federal specification:

GG–K–391, Kits (Empty), First Aid, Burn Treatment, and Snake Bite; and Kit Contents.

(b) *Publication.* The following publication, of the issue in effect on the date first-aid kits are manufactured, forms a part of this subpart:

(1) National Bureau of Standards Simplified Practice Recommendation:

No. R178–41, Packaging of First-aid Unit Dressings and Treatments.

(c) Copies of the specification and publication referred to in this section shall be kept on file by the manufacturer, together with the approved plans and certificate of approval. They shall be kept for a period consisting of the duration of approval and 6 months after termination of approval. The Federal specification may be purchased from the Business Service Center, General Services Administration, Washington, DC 20407. The Naval Bureau of Standards publication may be purchased from the Superintendent of Documents, U.S. Government Printing Office, Washington, DC 20402.

[CGFR 50–12, 15 FR 3093, May 20, 1950, as amended by CGFR 65–16, 30 FR 10899, Aug. 21, 1965]

§ 160.041–2 Type and size.

(a) *Type.* First-aid kits covered by this specification shall be of the watertight cabinet carrying type designated as Type II, Grade A, class B by Federal Specification GG–K–391. Alternate arrangements of materials meeting the performance requirements of this specification will be given special consideration.

(b) *Size.* First-aid kits shall be of a size (approximately 9″×9″×2½″ inside) adequate for packing 24 standard single cartons (defined by National Bureau of Standards Simplified Practice Recommendations for Packaging of First-aid Unit Dressings and Treatments), or equivalent combinations of single, double, or triple cartons, the arrangement of the cartons to be such as to permit ready access to each item contained in the kit.

§ 160.041–3 Construction and workmanship.

(a) *Construction.* The container shall be of substantial and rugged construction, with the body, handle, and all fittings of a corrosion-resistant material or suitably protected against corrosion. All ferrous metal employed shall be protected by hot dip galvanizing, or other equally effective means. The thickness of metal in the container shall be at least equal to 20 USSG and all seams and joints shall be welded or brazed. Either the body or the cover shall contain a gasket of molded rubber or other material which will give a suitable watertight seal, and the mating piece shall be flanged or turned to form an effective bearing surface. The cover shall be fastened to the body by two positive closed type pull-down snap fasteners on one edge, which together with two positive open type pull-down snap fasteners at the opposite edge, and one positive open type pull-down snap fastener at each of the other two edges, shall effectively hold the bearing surfaces together to provide the required watertight closure. The container shall be capable of being opened and reclosed watertight.

(b) *Handle*. A suitable carrying handle, approximately 3″×1¼″, of 0.125″ diameter steel wire, shall be securely mounted on the side or end of the body of the container, and be so arranged that when laid flat against the container it will not project beyond either the upper or lower edge, and shall provide ample finger clearance for carrying.

(c) *Cover fasteners*. The cover fasteners shall be of the pull-down, draw bolt type or equivalent and of sufficient size and strength for the purpose. The fasteners shall be so constructed as not to jar loose by vibration, but to permit easy and quick opening with one hand. There may be no sharp edges and all parts shall be adequately protected against corrosion.

§ 160.041-4 Contents.

(a) *Individual cartons*. Cartons shall be of the standard commercial unit type referred to by Simplified Practice Recommendation R178-41, properly labeled to designate the name, size of contents, and method of use, and shall contain all information required by Federal and State laws. Each package shall be inclosed in a jacket of tough, transparent material, properly sealed, which shall meet the watertight requirements of § 160.041-5(f). Each carton and the contents therein shall conform to the applicable requirements of Federal Specification GG-K-391. Medicinal products shall conform to the latest revision of the U.S. Pharmacopoeia. Vials for tablets shall not be made of glass.

(b) *Items*. The items contained in first-aid kit shall be as listed in Table 160.041-4(b).

TABLE 160.041-4(B)—ITEMS FOR FIRST-AID KIT

Item	Number per package	Size of package	No. of packages
Bandage compress—4″	1	Single	5
Bandage compress—2″	4	do	2
Waterproof adhesive compress—1″	16	do	2
Triangular bandage—40″	1	do	3
Eye dressing packet, ⅛ ounce Opthalmic ointment, adhesive strips, cotton pads.	3	do	1
Bandage, gauze, compressed, 2 inches by 6 yards	2	do	1
Tourniquet, forceps, scissors, 12 safety pins	1, 1, 1, and 12, respectively.	Double	1
Wire splint	1	Single	1
Ammonia inhalants	10	do	1
Iodine applicators (½ ml swab type)	10	do	1
Aspirin, phenacetin and caffeine compound, 6½ gr tablets, vials of 20	5	Double	1
Sterile petrolatum gauze, 3″×18″	4	Single	3

(c) *Instructions*. Instructions for the use of the contents of the first-aid kit shall be printed in legible type on a durable surface and shall be securely attached to the inside of the cover. The instructions for the use of the contents are as follows:

DIRECTIONS FOR THE USE OF THE FIRST-AID KIT

Item title	Remarks
Ammonia inhalants	Break one and inhale for faintness, fainting, or collapse.
Aspirin, phenacetin, caffeine tablets	Chew up and swallow 2 tablets every three hours for headache, colds, minor aches, pains, and fever. Maximum of 8 in twenty-four hours.
Bandage compress, 4″ and 2″	Apply as a dressing over wound. DON'T touch part that comes in contact with wound.
Bandage, gauze, compressed, 2″	For securing splints, dressings, etc.
Bandage, triangular, compressed	Use as arm sling, tourniquet, or for retaining splints or dressings in place.

113

DIRECTIONS FOR THE USE OF THE FIRST-AID KIT—Continued

Item title	Remarks
Burn dressing	The petrolatum gauze bandage is applied in at least two layers over the burned surface and an area extending 2″ beyond it. The first dressing should be allowed to remain in place, changing only the outer, dry bandage as needed, for at least 10 days unless signs of infection develop after several days, in which case the dressing should be removed and the burn treated as an infected wound. Watch for blueness or coldness of the skin beyond the dressing and loosen the dressing if they appear.
Compress, adhesive, 1″	Apply as dressing over small wounds. DON'T touch part that comes in contact with wound.
Eye patch	Apply as dressing over inflamed or injured eye.
Forceps	Use to remove splinters or foreign bodies. Don't dig.
Ophthalmic ointment	Apply in space formed by pulling lower eyelid down, once daily for inflamed or injured eyes. Don't touch eyeball with tube.
Splint, wire	Pad with gauze and mold to member to immobilize broken bones. Hold in place with bandage. Do not attempt to set the bone.
Tincture of iodine, mild	Remove protective sleeve, crush tube and apply swab end. DON'T use in or around eyes.
Tourniquet	For control of hemorrhage. Loosen for a few seconds every 15 minutes.

§ 160.041-5 Inspections and tests.

(a) *Accelerated weathering.* The container without contents shall be exposed to ultra violet light and subjected to a spray of water for about 30 seconds every 20 minutes for 100 hours at 120 °F. As an alternate to this test the container may be exposed to an ultra violet light for 100 hours at 130 °F. without the water spray. There shall be no evidence of warping or deterioration as a result of this test.

(b) *Salt spray.* The container shall be exposed to a spray of 20% by weight of reagent grade sodium chloride at about 95 °F. for 100 hours. There shall be no evidence of corrosion or disintegration of the material as a result of this test.

(c) *Temperature change.* The container shall be exposed to a temperature of 150 °F. for one hour and then to a temperature of 30 °F. below zero for one hour. There shall be no warping or deterioration of the gasket material as a result of this test.

(d) *Container watertightness.* After the completion of all other container tests, a closed empty container, lined with colored blotting paper, with the cover in a horizontal position and uppermost shall be submerged under a head of one foot of water for a period of two hours. At the end of this period the container shall be removed, opened, and examined for the presence of moisture. No seepage shall be allowed.

(e) *Carton watertightness.* Four cartons from each container tested shall be submerged under a head of one foot of water for a period of two hours. Upon opening the sealed wrappers there shall be no evidence of leakage of water.

[CGFR 65–9, 30 FR 11467, Sept. 8, 1965, as amended by CGD 95–028, 62 FR 51213, Sept. 30, 1997]

EFFECTIVE DATE NOTE: At 62 FR 51213, Sept. 30, 1997, § 160.041–5 was amended by removing paragraph (a) and redesignating paragraphs (b) through (f) as paragraphs (a) through (e), effective Oct. 30, 1997.

§ 160.041-6 Marking.

(a) Each approved first-aid kit shall be permanently marked with the following information: name of manufacturer, trade name symbol, model number, or other identification used by the manufacturer, the Coast Guard Approval Number, and the words "FIRST-AID KIT." This information may be embossed on the container or may be applied by silk screen process, using a suitable paint and protected as necessary to withstand the required tests, or by other means shown to be acceptable.

(b) [Reserved]

Subpart 160.042—Skids, Liferaft, for Merchant Vessels

SOURCE: CGFR 50–12, 15 FR 3095, May 20, 1950, unless otherwise noted.

§ 160.042-1 Applicable specification.

(a) The following specification, of the issue in effect on the date life raft skids are manufactured, forms a part of this subpart:

(1) Coast Guard specification:

160.018, Life Rafts.

(b) [Reserved]

§ 160.042-2 General requirements.

(a) The requirements of this subpart provide for a standard life raft skid for use on ocean and coastwise vessels in conjunction with the stowage of Type A rafts which may be used on such vessels.

(b) Life raft skids shall be constructed and arranged so as to properly support a Type A life raft in the stowed position and permit the launching of the life raft directly into the water without the application of any force other than that necessary to release the gripping arrangement and operate the release mechanism.

(c) Arrangements other than those specified by this subpart will be given special consideration.

§ 160.042-3 Construction.

(a) The trackways of the skids shall be constructed of 6″×3½″×½″ structural angles, or of material of approved shape and equivalent strength, inclined approximately 60 degrees from the horizontal. The trackways shall be spaced 8′-4″ from the inside of the 3½″ vertical leg of one trackway angle to the inside of the 3½″ vertical leg of the other trackway angle. The inside of the 6″ leg of the trackway angles shall form the skid surface for the life raft. The trackways shall be supported by a substantial structure suitable for stowing a Type A life raft at a 60-degree angle without having the raft project over the side of the vessel.

(b) The lower end of the life raft shall be supported by a base plate so arranged as to permit launching of the raft by a quick release assembly.

(c) All bearing surfaces of the quick release mechanism shall be constructed of non-corrosive metal. Alemite fittings shall be provided to insure positive lubrication of all bearing surfaces.

§ 160.042-4 Inspection.

(a) Life raft skids covered by this subpart are not subject to inspection at the place of manufacture, but are inspected on the basis of this specification during the annual or other inspection of the vessel upon which they are placed.

(b) [Reserved]

§ 160.042-5 Procedure for approval.

(a) Life raft skids are not subject to formal approval by the Commandant, but for each merchant vessel on which Type A life rafts are to be installed, plans showing the construction and arrangement of the life raft stowage and launching device on the vessel are required to be submitted for approval to the Commandant through the Commander of the Coast Guard District prior to the actual installation. Life raft skids should comply with the requirements of this specification in order to be acceptable for use in such installations.

(b) Correspondence pertaining to the subject matter of this specification should be addressed to the Commander of the Coast Guard District in which the skids are to be installed.

Subpart 160.043—Jackknife (With Can Opener) for Merchant Vessels

Source: CGFR 50-12, 15 FR 3095, May 20, 1950, unless otherwise noted.

§ 160.043-1 Applicable specification and plan.

(a) *Specification.* The following specification, of the issue in effect on the date jackknives are manufactured, forms a part of this subpart:

(1) Federal specification:

QQ-M-151, Metals; General Specification for Inspection of.

(b) *Plan.* The following plan, of the issue in effect on the date jackknives are manufactured, forms a part of this subpart:

(1) Coast Guard:

Dwg. No. 160.043-1(b), Jackknife (With Can Opener).

(c) *Copies on file.* A copy of the above specification and reference plan shall be kept on file by the manufacturer, together with the approved plans and certificate of approval.

§ 160.043-2 Type.

(a) The jackknife specified by this subpart shall be of a type as illustrated by Drawing No. 160.043-1(b), which consists of a one-bladed knife fitted with a can opener and a shackle to which a lanyard is attached, all made from materials as specified in this subpart. Alternate arrangements will be given special consideration.

(b) [Reserved]

§ 160.043-3 Materials.

(a) *Blade, can opener, and springs.* The blade shall be made of AISI Type 440B stainless steel, heat treated to show a Rockwell hardness of C55 to C59. The can opener shall be made of AISI Type 420 stainless steel, heat treated to show a Rockwell hardness of C50 to C54. The springs shall be made of AISI Type 420 stainless steel, heat treated to show a Rockwell hardness of C44 to C48.

(b) *Linings and center.* The linings and center shall be hard brass.

(c) *Bolsters and shackle.* The bolsters and shackle shall be 18 percent nickel-silver.

(d) *Handles.* The handles shall be good quality, thermosetting, high impact plastic.

(e) *Rivets and pins.* The rivets and pins shall be either hard brass or 18 percent nickel-silver as specified in this subpart.

(f) *Lanyard.* The lanyard shall be cotton rope, ⅛ inch nominal diameter.

§ 160.043-4 Construction and workmanship.

(a) *Blade.* The blade shall be not less than 0.095 inch thick at the tang. Shall have a triangular section and sheeps foot point. It shall have a cutting edge approximately 3⅛ inches in length and shall be approximately ¹³⁄₁₆ inch in height at the point. The blade shall be uniformly ground and finished on both sides and sharpened to a uniform and keen edge, and it shall have a common nail nick on one side. Before assembling, the sides of the tang shall be uniformly polished.

(b) *Can opener.* The can opener shall be not less than 0.072 inch thick at the

tang, and 1¹¹⁄₁₆ to 1¹⁵⁄₁₆ inches long overall. It shall be so designed that the cutting action turns the ragged edge down into the can, and shall be mounted at the same end of the knife as the blade and in such a manner that both rectangular and circular cans may be opened with a minimum of effort when the knife is held in the right hand and operated in a clockwise direction around the can. The cutting edge shall be suitably formed to obtain a smooth cutting action. It shall have a common nail nick on one side, and the extreme distal end shall be pointed. It shall be polished on both sides, and before assembling, the side of the tang shall be polished.

(c) *Springs.* Each spring shall be of a thickness corresponding to the blade it operates, and the back edge and that section of the front edge coming in contact with the end of the tang of the blade shall be polished.

(d) *Linings and center.* Linings and center shall be not less than 0.022 inch in thickness and shall be polished before assembly.

(e) *Bolsters.* The bolsters shall be approximately ⁹⁄₁₆ inch long by 0.100 inch thick measured at the center line.

(f) *Shackle.* The shackle shall be of conventional design, not less than 0.120 inch in diameter, and shall extend not less than ¾ inch from the end of the knife. The shackle shall be attached to the knife by a solid nickel-silver pin not less than 0.080 inch in diameter which shall pass through the shackle and be securely fastened.

(g) *Handles.* The handles shall be approximately 3¾ inches long. They shall be well fitted at the bolsters and fastened to the linings by two solid rivets countersunk on the inside of the linings and smoothly rounded on the outside.

(h) *Rivets and pins.* Pins holding the handles to the linings shall be of hard brass, not less than 0.048 inch in diameter. Middle and end pins shall be of hard brass not less than 0.095 inch in diameter. The bolster rivet shall be 18 percent nickel-silver not less than 0.095 inch in diameter. All rivets and pins shall have carefully spun heads.

(i) *Lanyard.* A lanyard 6 feet in length shall be secured to the shackle.

(j) *Polishing and oiling.* After assembly all outside surfaces shall be buffed, and the metal parts polished uniformly. The working parts shall be cleaned and oiled with a good grade of joint oil.

(k) *Workmanship.* Workmanship shall be first class in all respects, and jackknives shall be free from defects which may affect their serviceability.

§160.043–5 Inspections and tests.

(a) *General.* Jackknives are not ordinarily subjected to regularly scheduled factory inspections, but the Commander of the Coast Guard District in which they are manufactured may detail an inspector at any time to places where jackknives are manufactured to check materials and construction methods, and to conduct such tests as may be required to satisfy himself that jackknives are being manufactured in compliance with the requirements of this specification and the manufacturer's plans and specifications as approved by the Commandant. The manufacturer shall admit the inspector to his plant and shall provide a suitable place and the necessary apparatus for use of the inspector in conducting tests at the place of manufacture.

(b) *Hardness test.* Hardness of the blade, can opener, and spring metal shall be determined in accordance with the Rockwell method as described in Federal Specification QQ–M–151. Hardness impressions shall be made at locations representing the cutting edges and surfaces subject to wear, and they shall fall within the ranges set forth in §160.043–3(a).

(c) *Bending and drop tests.* With all of the blade of the knife except the tang clamped in vertical jaws so that the handle is in a horizontal position, a downward load of 15 pounds shall be suspended from the lanyard and allowed to hang for a period of 5 minutes. The knife shall then be turned over, and the test repeated with the can opener in the jaws. The knife shall then be dropped on its side from a height of 8 feet onto a concrete floor. Both the blade and the can opener shall open and close properly, and the knife shall show no other evidence of failure at the conclusion of these tests.

(d) *Cutting test.* The knife shall be used to cut various nonmetallic objects, including at least 10 shavings from a strip of oak or other hardwood, and to open various rectangular and circular cans, and shall show no noticeable loss in cutting ability.

§160.043–6 Marking and packing.

(a) *General.* Jackknives specified by this subpart shall be stamped or otherwise permanently and legibly marked on the tang of the blade with the manufacturer's name or with a trade mark of such known character that the source of manufacture may be readily determined, and with the manufacturer's type or size designation.

(b) *Instructions for can opener.* With each jackknife the manufacturer shall supply instructions, complete with an illustration, indicating the proper method for using the can opener.

(c) *Packing.* Each jackknife, complete with lanyard attached, shall be packed in a heat-sealed bag of waterproof vinyl resin or polyethylene film not less than 0.004 inch in thickness. The bag shall be marked in a clear and legible manner with the Coast Guard approval number, the name and address of the manufacturer, and in letters not less than ¼ inch in height with the words. "JACKKNIFE (WITH CAN OPENER)". The instructions for use of the can opener as required by paragraph (b) of this section may also be printed on the bag.

Subpart 160.044—Pumps, Bilge, Lifeboat, for Merchant Vessels

SOURCE: CGFR 50–30, 16 FR 1085, Feb. 6, 1951, unless otherwise noted.

§160.044–1 Applicable specifications.

(a) There are no other specifications applicable to this subpart.

(b) [Reserved]

§160.044–2 Types and sizes.

(a) *Type.* Bilge pumps covered by this subpart shall be manually operated, either oscillating, wing type, or full rotary type, with mountings so arranged as to permit attachment to a thwart or other part of the lifeboat structure without interference with the seating arrangement. Alternate types, arrangements or materials, which meet the performance requirements of this subpart will be given special consideration.

(b) *Sizes.* Bilge pumps covered by this subpart shall be of three sizes, having capacities as follows:

(1) *Size No. 1.* 5 gallons per minute at 65 double strokes,[1] for lifeboats up to 330 cubic feet capacity.[2]

(2) *Size No. 2.* 6 gallons per minute at 50 double strokes, for lifeboats from 330 cubic feet up to 700 cubic feet capacity.

(3) *Size No. 3.* 15 gallons per minute at 50 double strokes, for lifeboats of 700 cubic feet or more capacity.

§ 160.044-3 General requirements.

(a) Bilge pumps shall be of rugged construction, of first class workmanship in every respect, and free from any defects affecting serviceability. Where a choice of materials is permitted, the materials used shall be of good quality and suitable for the purpose intended, and shall be corrosion-resistant or protected against corrosion by acceptable means, except that parts subject to wear shall not depend upon coatings for corrosion resistance.

(b) Bilge pumps covered by this subpart shall be capable of operating against a head pressure of 20 pounds per square inch when tested in accordance with § 160.044-4(c).

(c) The bilge pump body shall be of bronze and shall be provided with a cover plate or plates, attached by means of wing nuts at least 1¼ inches long, on not more than 6 studs, or by means of a suitable bayonet type joint, so as to be readily removable for inspection or cleaning.

(d) The operating lever shall have a steel or bronze core through its entire length, but for comfort may have a gripping surface of wood or other suitable material. The lever shall be removable and shall be attached to the pump shaft which is to be square

ended, by means of a set screw with 1¼-inch wings, and further shall be connected to the pump body or shaft end by a retaining chain to prevent loss.

(e) The suction line shall be fitted with an intake check valve and a suitable strainer. The strainer shall be removable for cleaning without the use of tools. The suction line shall contain no hose or fittings subject to collapsing when the pump is in service.

(f) Suction and discharge outlets shall be not less than 1 inch inside diameter for pump sizes Nos. 1 and 2, and not less than 1¼ inches inside diameter for pump size No. 3. Discharge outlets shall be provided with a tee of cast bronze or other corrosion-resistant material, with a removable plug at the top for priming, the plug to have a wing arrangement for removal by hand, and be secured to the tee by a retaining chain. The bottom of the tee shall have pipe threads to fit the discharge outlet of the pump, and the discharge portion of the tee shall be a plain clamp type male hose connection, with inside diameter not less than that of the pump discharge opening.

§ 160.044-4 Inspection and tests.

(a) *Capacity.* The bilge pump being tested shall be set up over a source of water for operation with all the required fittings and connections, the set-up to simulate an installation in a lifeboat. The bilge pump shall be operated at the standard speed specified for its size, and the flow of water measured. The amount of water discharged shall not be less than that required by § 160.044-2(b).

(b) *Head pressure.* After the successful completion of the test outlined in paragraph (b) of this section, a pressure gage capable of registering 20 pounds per square inch, and a variable restriction, such as a nozzle, valve, etc., shall be fitted in the discharge line. The pump shall be put in operation with the discharge line open, and then the restriction shall be gradually closed until the pressure builds up to at least 20 pounds per square inch. This pressure shall be maintained for at least 15 seconds, after which the pump shall be

[1] A double stroke is a complete cycle from one extreme to the other and back again to the original starting point, or, for rotary type, one complete revolution.

[2] The capacity of a lifeboat for determining the size of the bilge pump shall be 0.6 times the product of the length, breadth, and depth of the lifeboat, in feet.

disassembled and inspected. No destruction or deformation of parts sufficient to affect the serviceability of the pump shall be permitted as a result of this test.

(c) *Operating lever.* With the pump firmly secured in such a position that both the shaft and operating lever are in a horizontal position, apply a downward load of 200 pounds for a period of 5 minutes at the free end of the operating lever and perpendicular to its axis and the axis of the shaft. There shall be no slippage of the lever around the shaft, nor any evidence of permanent set or undue stress in any part of the pump. In cases where the design of the pump is such that this test may not be applicable to the complete pump, the pump shall be disassembled and the 200-pound load applied to the shaft and operating lever while the free end of the shaft is held in a vise or check so that both the shaft and the operating lever are in a horizontal position.

[CGFR 65–9, 30 FR 11467, Sept. 8, 1965, as amended by CGD 95–028, 62 FR 51213, Sept. 30, 1997]

EFFECTIVE DATE NOTE: At 62 FR 51213, Sept. 30, 1997, §160.044–4 was amended by removing paragraph (a) and redesignating paragraphs (b), (c), and (d) as paragraphs (a), (b), and (c), and amending new (a), effective Oct. 30, 1997.

§ 160.044–5 Marking.

(a) Each pump shall be permanently and legibly marked, in letters not less than ¼ inch high, either cast or stamped on the body, with the name of the manufacturer, the size for which approved (USCG No. 1, 2 or 3), and the Coast Guard approval number. The tee required by § 160.044–3(f) shall be permanently and legibly marked with the word "PRIME HERE".

(b) [Reserved]

Subpart 160.047—Specification for a Buoyant Vest, Kapok or Fibrous Glass, Adult and Child

§ 160.047–1 Incorporation by reference.

(a) *Specifications and Standards.* This subpart makes reference to the following documents:

(1) Federal Specification:

L-P-375C—Plastic Film, Flexible, Vinyl Chloride.

(2) Military specifications:

MIL–W–530—Webbing, Textile, Cotton, General Purpose, Natural or in Colors.

MIL–B–2766—Batt, Fibrous Glass, Lifesaving Equipment.

(3) Federal Standards:

No. 191—Textile Test Methods.

751A—Stitches, Seams, and Stitchings.

(4) Coast Guard specification:

164.003—Kapok, Processed.

(b) *Plans.* The following plans, of the issue in effect on the date buoyant vests are manufactured, form a part of this subpart:

Dwg. No. 160.047–1:
    Sheet 1, Rev. 2—Cutting Pattern and General Arrangement, Models AK–1, and AF–1.
    Sheet 2, Rev. 2—Cutting Pattern and General Arrangement, Models CKM–1 and CFM–1.
    Sheet 3, Rev. 2—Cutting Pattern and General Arrangement, Models CKS–1 and CFS–1.
    Sheet 4, Rev. 1—Pad Patterns.

(c) *Copies on file.* The manufacturer shall keep a copy of each specification and plan required by this section on file together with the certificate of approval. Plans and specifications may be obtained as follows:

(1) The Coast Guard plans and specifications may be obtained from the Commandant (G–MSE), U.S. Coast Guard, Washington, DC 20593–0001 or a recognized laboratory listed in § 160.047–6b.

(2) The Federal Specifications and Standard may be purchased from the Business Service Center, General Services Administration, Washington, DC 20407;

(3) The military specifications may be obtained from the Commanding Officer, Naval Supply Depot, 5801 Tabor Avenue, Philadelphia, PA 19120.

[CGD 65–37, 30 FR 11581, Sept. 10, 1965, as amended by CGD 72–90R, 37 FR 10836, May 31, 1972; CGD 78–012, 43 FR 27153, 27154, June 22, 1978; CGD 82–063b, 48 FR 4782, Feb. 3, 1983; CGD 88–070, 53 FR 34535, Sept. 7, 1988; CGD 95–072, 60 FR 50467, Sept. 29, 1995; CGD 96–041, 61 FR 50733, Sept. 27, 1996]

§ 160.047–2 Model.

Each buoyant vest specified in this subpart is a:

119

(a) Model AK-1, adult, kapok (for persons weighing more than 90 pounds);

(b) Model AF-1, adult, fibrous glass (for persons weighing more than 90 pounds);

(c) Model CKM-1, child medium, kapok (for children weighing from 50 to 90 pounds);

(d) Model CFM-1, child medium, fibrous glass (for children weighing from 50 to 90 pounds);

(e) Model CKS-1, child small, kapok (for children weighing less than 50 pounds); or

(f) Model CFS-1, child small, fibrous glass (for children weighing less than 50 pounds).

[CGD 72-163R, 38 FR 8119, Mar. 23, 1973]

§ 160.047-3 Materials.

(a) *General.* All components used in the construction of buoyant vests must meet the applicable requirements of subpart 164.019 of this chapter. The requirements for materials specified in this section are minimum requirements, and consideration will be given to the use of alternate materials in lieu of those specified. Detailed technical data and samples of all proposed alternate materials must be submitted for approval before those materials are incorporated in the finished product.

(b) *Kapok.* The kapok shall be all new material complying with Subpart 164.003 of this subchapter and shall be properly processed.

(c) *Fibrous glass.* The fibrous glass shall comply with the requirements of specification MIL-B-2766.

(d) *Envelope.* The buoyant vest envelope, or cover, shall be made from 39", 2.85 cotton jeans cloth, with a thread count of approximately 96×64. The finished goods shall weigh not less than 4.2 ounces per square yard, shall have a thread count of not less than 94×60, and shall have a breaking strength of not less than 85 pounds in the warp and 50 pounds in the filling. Other cotton fabrics having a weight and breaking strength not less than the above will be acceptable. There are no restrictions as to color, but the fastness of the color to laundering, water, crocking and light shall be rated "good" when tested in accordance with Federal Test Method Standard No. 191, Methods 5610, 5630, 5650, and 5660.

(e) *Pad covering.* The covering for the buoyant pad inserts shall be flexible vinyl film not less than 0.006" in thickness meeting the requirements of Federal Specification L-P-375 for Type I or II, class 1, film.

(f) *Tie tapes and body strap loops.* The tie tapes and body strap loops for an adult or child size buoyant vest specified by this subpart must be ¾-inch cotton webbing meeting the requirements in military specification MIL-T-43566 (Class I) for Type I webbing.

(f-1) *Body straps.* The complete body strap assembly, including hardware, must have a breaking strength of 150 pounds for an adult size and 115 pounds for a child size. The specifications for the webbing are as follows:

(1) For an adult size vest, the webbing must be 1 inch.

(2) For a child size vest, the webbing must be three-fourth inch and meet the requirements of military specification MIL-W-530 for Type IIa webbing.

(f-2) *Reinforcing tape.* The reinforcing tape around the neck of a buoyant vest specified by this subpart must be ¾-inch cotton tape weighing 0.18 ounce or more per linear yard and having a minimum breaking strength of 120 pounds.

(g) [Reserved]

(h) *Thread.* Each thread must meet the requirements of subpart 164.023 of this chapter. Only one kind of thread may be used in each seam.

[CGFR 65-37, 30 FR 11581, Sept. 10, 1965, as amended by CGD 72-90R, 37 FR 10836, May 31, 1972; CGD 73-130R 39 FR 20684, June 13, 1974; CGD 78-012; 43 FR 27154, June 22, 1978; CGD 82-063b, 48 FR 4782, Feb. 3, 1983; CGD 84-068, 58 FR 29493, May 20, 1993]

§ 160.047-3a Materials—Dee ring and snap hook assemblies and other instruments of closure for buoyant vests.

(a) *Specifications.* Dee ring and snap lock assemblies and other instruments of closure for buoyant vests may have decorative platings in any thickness and must meet the following specifications:

(1) The device must be constructed of inherently corrosion resistant materials. As used in this section the term *inherently corrosion resistant materials* includes, but is not limited to, brass, bronze, and stainless steel.

(2) The size of the opening of the device must be consistent with the webbing which will pass through the opening.

(b) *Testing requirements.* Dee ring and snap hook assemblies and other instruments of closure for buoyant vests must—

(1) Be tested for weathering. The Coast Guard will determine which one or more of the following tests will be used:

(i) Application of a 20 percent sodium-chloride solution spray at a temperature of 95 °F (35 °C) for a period of 240 hours in accordance with the procedures contained in method 811 of the Federal Test Method Standard No. 151.

(ii) Exposure to a carbon-arc weather-ometer for a period of 100 hours.

(iii) Submergence for a period of 100 hours in each of the following:

(*a*) Leaded gasoline.

(*b*) Gum turpentine.

(iv) Exposure to a temperature of 0°±5 °F (—17.6±2.775 °C) for 24 hours; and

(2) Within 5 minutes of completion of the weathering test required by paragraph (b)(1) of this section, the assembly must be attached to a support and bear 150 pounds for an adult size and 115 pounds for a child size for 10 minutes at the ambient temperatures without breaking or distorting.

[CGD 73–130R, 39 FR 20684, June 13, 1974]

§ 160.047-4 Construction.

(a) *General.* This specification covers buoyant vests which essentially consist of a vest-cut envelope containing compartments in which are enclosed pads of buoyant material arranged and distributed so as to provide the proper flotation characteristics and buoyancy required to hold the wearer in an upright backward position with head and face out of water. The buoyant vests are also fitted with tapes, webbing, and hardware to provide for proper adjustment and close and comfortable fit to the bodies of various size wearers.

(b) *Envelope.* The envelope or cover shall be cut to the pattern shown on Dwg. No. 160.047-1, Sheet 1, for adult size, and Sheets 2 and 3 for child sizes, and sewed with seams and stitching as shown on the drawing. Three compartments shall be formed to hold the buoyant pad inserts, two front compartments and one back compartment, and reinforcing strips of the same material as the cover shall be stitched to the inside of the front compartments in way of the strap attachments as shown by the drawings. As alternate construction, the front and/or back cover panels may be made in two pieces, provided that the two pieces are joined by a double stitched seam from the top center of the neck hole to the top of the vest as shown in Section J–J of the drawings.

(c) *Pad inserts*—(1) *Forming and sealing.* The buoyant pad inserts shall each be formed from two pieces of film cut to the patterns shown by Dwg. No. 160.047-1, Sheet 4, which shall be heat-sealed tight. The heat-sealed pad seams shall show an adhesion of not less than 8 pounds when 1 inch strips cut across and perpendicular to the seams are pulled apart at a rate of separation of the clamping jaws of the test machine of 12 inches per minute.

(2) *Kapok-filled pads for Models AK-1, CKM-1, and CKS-1.* The buoyant pad inserts for Models AK-1, CKM-1, and CKS-1 buoyant vests shall be filled with kapok distributed as provided in Table 160.047-4(c)(2).

TABLE 160.047-4(C)(2)—DISTRIBUTION OF KAPOK IN BUOYANT PAD INSERTS

	Model AK–1 (minimum)	Model CKM–1 (minimum)	Model CKS–1 (minimum)
	Ounces	*Ounces*	*Ounces*
Front pad (2) (each)	5.75	3.75	2.50
Back pad	4.00	2.50	2.00
Total	15.50	10.00	7.00

(3) *Fibrous glass-filled pads for Models AF-1, CFM-1, and CFS-1.* The buoyant pad inserts for Models AF-1, CFM-1, and CFS-1 buoyant vests shall be filled

with fibrous glass distributed as provided in Table 160.047–4(c)(3).

TABLE 160.047–4(C)(3)—DISTRIBUTION OF FIBROUS GLASS IN BUOYANT PAD INSERTS

	Model AF–1 (minimum)	Model CFM–1 (minimum)	Model CFS–1 (minimum)
	Ounces	Ounces	Ounces
Front pad (2) (each)	10.25	6.75	4.50
Back	7.25	4.50	3.50
Total	27.75	18.00	12.50

(4) *Displacement of buoyant pad inserts.* The volume of the finished individual heat-sealed buoyant pad inserts shall be such as to provide buoyancy as set forth in Table 160.047–4(c)(4) when tested in accordance with the method set forth in § 160.047–5(e)(1), except that the pad covers shall not be slit open and the period of submergence shall be only long enough to determine the displacement of the pads.

TABLE 160.047–4(C)(4)—VOLUME DISPLACEMENT OF SEALED PADS

	Models AK–1 and AF–1	Models CKM–1 and CFM–1	Models CKS–1 and CFS–1
	Each	Each	Each
Front pads	6¼ pounds±¼ pound	4¼ pounds±¼ pound	2¾ pounds±¼ pound
Back pads	4¼ pounds±¼ pound	3¼ pounds±¼ pound	2½ pounds±¼ pound

(d) *Tie tapes.* The tie tapes at the neck shall finish not less than 12 inches in length for both adult and child size buoyant vests. They shall be arranged and attached to the envelope as shown by the drawings, and the free ends shall be doubled over and stitched in accordance with section H–H.

(e) *Body strap, hardware, and reinforcing tape.* The body strap, hardware, and reinforcing tape shall be arranged as shown on the drawings and attached to the envelope with the seams and stitching indicated.

(f) *Stitching.* All stitching shall be a short lock stitch conforming to Stitch Type 301 of Federal Standard No. 751, and there shall be not less than 7 nor more than 9 stitches to the inch. Both ends of the stitching forming the shoulder hinge seams and the top and bottom closing seams of the envelope shall be backstitched approximately ½ inch.

(g) *Workmanship.* Buoyant vests shall be of first-class workmanship and shall be free from any defects materially affecting their appearance or serviceability.

[CGFR 65–37, 30 FR 11581, Sept. 10, 1965]

§ 160.047–5 Inspections and tests.[1]

(a) *General.* Manufacturers of listed and labeled buoyant vests shall—

(1) Maintain quality control of the materials used, the manufacturing methods and the finished product to meet the requirements of this subpart by conducting sufficient inspections and tests of representative samples and components produced;

(2) Make available to the recognized laboratory inspector and to the Coast Guard inspector, upon request, records of tests conducted by the manufacturer and records of materials used during production of the device including affidavits from suppliers; and

(3) Permit any examination, inspection, and test required by the recognized laboratory or the Coast Guard for a listed and labeled device, either at the place of manufacture, or some other location.

(b) *Lot size and sampling.* (1) A lot consists of 500 buoyant vests or fewer.

[1] The manufacturer of a personal flotation device must meet 33 CFR 181.701 through 33 CFR 181.705 which require an instruction pamphlet for each device that is sold or offered for sale for use on recreational boats.

(2) A new lot begins after any change or modification in materials used or manufacturing methods employed;

(3) The manufacturer of the buoyant vests shall notify the recognized laboratory when a lot is ready for inspection;

(4) The manufacturer shall select samples in accordance with the requirements in Table 160.047–5(b)(4) from each lot of buoyant vests to be tested by the inspector in accordance with paragraph (e) of this section;

TABLE 160.047–5(B)(4)—SAMPLE FOR BUOYANCY TESTS

Lot size	Number of vests in sample
100 and under	1
101 to 200	2
201 to 300	3
301 to 500	4

(5) The recognized laboratory must assign an inspector to a plant when notified that a lot is ready for inspection, to conduct tests and inspections on samples selected in accordance with paragraph (b)(4) of this section.

(6) If a vest fails the buoyancy test, the sample from the next succeeding lot must consist of 10 specimen vests or more to be tested for buoyancy in accordance with paragraph (e) of this section.

(c) *Additional tests.* An inspector from the recognized laboratory or the Coast Guard may conduct an examination, test, and inspection of a listed and labeled buoyant device that is obtained from the manufacturer or through commercial channels to determine its conformance to the applicable requirements.

(d) *Test facilities.* The manufacturer shall admit the laboratory inspector and the Coast Guard inspector to any part of the premises at the place of manufacture of a listed and labeled device to—

(1) Examine, inspect, or test a sample of a part or a material that is included in the construction of the device; and

(2) Conduct any necessary examination, inspection, or test in a suitable place and with appropriate apparatus provided by the manufacturer.

(e) *Buoyancy*—(1) *Buoyancy test method.* Remove the buoyant pad inserts

from the vest and cut three slits each not less than 2 inches in length and not less than 2 inches apart on both sides of each pad. Securely attach the spring scale in a position directly over the test tank. Suspend the weighted wire basket from the scale in such a manner that the basket is weighed while it is completely under water. In order to measure the actual buoyancy provided by the pads, proceed as follows:

(i) Weigh the empty wire basket under water.

(ii) Place the pads inside the basket and submerge it so that the top of the basket is at least 2 inches below the surface of the water for 24 hours. The tank shall be locked or sealed during this 24-hour submergence period. It is important that after the pads have once been submerged they shall remain submerged for the duration of the test, and at no time during the course of the test shall they be removed from the tank or otherwise exposed to air.

(iii) After the 24-hour submergence period unlock or unseal the tank and weigh the weighted wire basket with the pads inside while both are still under water.

(iv) The buoyancy is computed as (i) minus (iii).

(2) *Buoyancy required.* The pad inserts from adult buoyant vests shall provide not less than 16 pounds buoyancy; the pad inserts from child medium vests shall provide not less than 11 pounds buoyancy; and the pad inserts from child small vests shall provide not less than 7¼ pounds buoyancy.

(f) *Body strap test.* The complete body strap assembly, including hardware, shall be tested for strength by attaching the dee ring to a suitable support such that the assembly hangs vertically its full length. A weight as specified in § 160.047–3(f) shall be attached to the other end on the snap hook for 10 minutes. The specified weight shall not break or excessively distort the body strap assembly.

[CGFR 65–37; 30 FR 11581, Sept. 10, 1965, as amended by CGD 72–90R, 37 FR 10836, May 31, 1972; CGD 75–008, 43 FR 9772, Mar. 9, 1978]

§ 160.047–6 Marking.

(a) Each buoyant vest must have the following information clearly marked in waterproof lettering that can be read at a distance of 2 feet:

Type II Personal Flotation Device.
Inspected and tested in accordance with U.S. Coast Guard regulations.
(Kapok or Fibrous glass) buoyant material provides a minimum buoyant force of (16 lb., 11 lb., or 7¼ lb.).
Dry out thoroughly when wet.
Do not snag or puncture inner plastic cover.
If pads become waterlogged, replace device.
Approved for use on all recreational boats and on uninspected commercial vessels less than 40 feet in length not carrying passengers for hire by persons weighing (over 90 lb., 50 to 90 lb., or less than 50 lb.).
U.S. Coast Guard Approval No. 160.047/(assigned manufacturer's No.)/(Revision No.); (Model No.).
(Name and address of manufacturer or distributor.).
(Lot No.).

(b) *Waterproof marking tags.* Marking for buoyant vests shall be sufficiently waterproof so that after 72 hours submergence in water, it will withstand vigorous rubbing by hand while wet without the printed matter becoming illegible.

[CGD 72–163R, 38 FR 8119, Mar. 28, 1973, as amended by CGD 75–008, 43 FR 9770, Mar. 9, 1978]

§ 160.047-7 Recognized laboratory

(a) A manufacturer seeking Coast Guard approval of a product under this subpart shall follow the approval procedures of subpart 159.005 of this chapter, and shall apply for approval directly to a recognized independent laboratory. The following laboratories are recognized under § 159.010–7 of this part, to perform testing and approval functions under this subpart:

Underwriters Laboratories, 12 Laboratory Drive, P.O. Box 13995, Research Triangle Park, NC 27709–3995, (919) 549–1400.

(b) Production oversight must be performed by the same laboratory that performs the approval tests unless, as determined by the Commandant, the employees of the laboratory performing production oversight receive training and support equal to that of the laboratory that performed the approval testing.

[CGD 93–055, 61 FR 13930, Mar. 28, 1996]

Subpart 160.048—Specification for a Buoyant Cushion, Fibrous Glass

§ 160.048-1 Incorporation by reference.

(a) *Specifications and Standards.* This subpart makes reference to the following documents:
(1) Military specification:

MIL–B–2766—Batt, Fibrous Glass, Lifesaving Equipment.

(2) Federal Specifications:

CCC–C–700G—Cloth, Coated, Vinyl, Coated (Artificial Leather).
CCC–C–426D—Cloth, Cotton Drill.
L–P–375C—Plastic Film, Flexible, Vinyl Chloride.

(3) Federal standard:

No. 751—Stitches, Seams, and Stitchings.

(4) Coast Guard specification:

164.003—Kapok, Processed.

(b) *Plan.* The following plan, of the issue in effect on the date kapok or fibrous glass buoyant cushions are manufactured, form a part of this subpart:
(1) Coast Guard Dwg. No. 160.048–1.
(c) *Copies on File.* Copies of the specifications and plan referred to in this section shall be kept on file by the manufacturer, together with the approved plans and certificate of approval. The Coast Guard specification and plan may be obtained upon request from the Commandant, United States Coast Guard, Washington, DC 20591, or recognized laboratory. The Federal Specifications and the Federal Standard may be purchased from the Business Service Center, General Services Administration, Washington; DC 20407. The Military Specification may be obtained from the Commanding Officer, Naval Supply Depot, 5801 Tabor Avenue, Philadelphia, PA 19120.

[CGFR 65–37, 30 FR 11583, Sept. 10, 1965, as amended by CGFR 70–143, 35 FR 19962, Dec. 30, 1970; CGD 78–012, 43 FR 27153, 27154, June 22, 1978]

§ 160.048-2 Types and sizes.

(a) *Types.* Buoyant cushions shall be of the box type, i.e., have top, bottom and gusset. Pillow type cushions without a gusset are not acceptable.
(b) *Sizes.* Buoyant cushions shall have not less than 225 square inches top surface area; widths and lengths which fall within the dimensions shown in Tables

160.048-4(c)(1)(i) and 160.048-4(c)(1)(ii); and thickness not less than 2 nor more than 3 inches, the thickness to be considered as the finished width of the gusset between seams.

[CGFR 65–37, 30 FR 11583, Sept. 10, 1965]

§160.048-3 Materials.

(a) *General.* All components used in the construction of buoyant cushions must meet the applicable requirements of subpart 164.019 of this chapter.

(b) *Kapok.* The kapok shall be all new material complying with Specification subpart 164.003 of this subchapter and shall be properly processed.

(c) *Fibrous glass.* The fibrous glass shall comply with the requirements of specification MIL–B–2766.

(d) *Cover.* Cotton fabrics and coated upholstery cloth meeting the minimum requirements set forth in paragraphs (d) (1) and (2) of this section are acceptable for use as covers for buoyant cushions, but alternate materials will be given special consideration. Pro rata widths of like construction will be acceptable.

(1) *Cotton fabrics.* Cotton fabrics shall comply with the requirements of Federal Specification CCC–C–426 for Type I, Class 3 material.

(2) *Coated upholstery cloth.* Coated upholstery cloth shall comply with the requirements of Federal Specification CCC–A–700.

(e) *Pad covering.* The covering for the buoyant pad inserts shall be flexible vinyl film not less than 0.008 inch in thickness meeting the requirements of Federal Specification L–P–375 for Type I or II, Class 1, film.

(f) *Grab straps.* The grab straps shall be of materials permitted for the cover, or approved equivalent.

(g) *Thread.* Each thread must meet the requirements of subpart 164.023 of this chapter. Only one kind of thread may be used in each seam.

(h) *Welting.* The welting where used may be any fiber or plastic material suitable for the purpose.

[CG FR 65–37, 30 FR 11583, Sept. 10, 1965, as amended by CGD 78–012, 43 FR 27154, June 22, 1978; CGD 84–068, 58 FR 29493, May 20, 1993]

§160.048-4 Construction and workmanship.

(a) *General.* This specification covers buoyant cushions of the box type filled with kapok or fibrous glass contained in heat-sealed vinyl film pad covers which are inserted in an outer cover fitted with grab straps. The primary purpose of such cushions is to provide buoyancy to aid a person in keeping afloat in the water. No hooks, snaps, or other means shall be included which might facilitate fastening the cushion to a boat. Buoyant cushions shall be of such size and volume as to provide not less than 20 pounds buoyancy when tested in the manner described in §160.048-5(e), but no cushion providing less than 225 square inches of top surface area or measuring less than 2 inches or more than 3 inches in thickness will be acceptable.

(b) *Cover.* One piece of material each for the top and bottom shall be stitched together to form the cover except that piecing of the cover material will be allowed provided it is for decorative purposes only. Gusset or boxing materials shall be of not more than two pieces. If more than one piece of material is used for the top, bottom, boxing or gusset, they shall be attached by a double row of stitching of the type shown in Federal Standard No. 751, for seam types SSw–2 or LS(b)–2. The top and bottom may be of any of the materials permitted for the cover, but the boxing or gusset shall be a cotton fabric as specified by §160.048-3(c)(1) or other equivalent material of a porous nature. Nonporous materials will not be permitted for the boxing or gusset, but coated upholstery cloth specified by §160.048-3(d)(2), perforated to permit adequate draining and drying will be acceptable.

(c) *Buoyant material.* Buoyant cushions shall be filled with the minimum amounts of kapok or fibrous glass determined as follows:

(1) Rectangular buoyant cushions 2 inches thick shall be filled with the amounts of kapok or fibrous glass indicated for the various widths and lengths of such cushions by Table 160.048-4(c)(1)(i) or 160.048-4(c)(1)(ii), as applicable. Trapezoidal buoyant cushions 2 inches thick shall be filled with the amounts of kapok or fibrous glass

indicated for the various widths and lengths of rectangular buoyant cushions by Table 160.048–4(c)(1)(i) or 160.048–4(c)(1)(ii) as applicable, on the basis that the length of a trapezoidal cushion shall be considered as its average length in each case.

TABLE 160.048–4(C)(1)(I)—WEIGHT OF KAPOK (IN OUNCES) FOR FILLING RECTANGULAR BUOYANT CUSHIONS 2 INCHES THICK

Length (inches)	Width (inches)													
	12	13	14	15	16	17	18	19	20	21	22	23	24	Over 24
15	......	......	......	20	......	......	......	......	......	......	......	......	......	......
16	......	......	......	21	23	......	......	......	......	......	......	......	......	......
17	......	......	21	23	24	26	......	......	......	......	......	......	......	......
18	......	21	22	24	26	27	29	......	......	......	......	......	......	......
19	20	22	24	25	27	29	30	32	......	......	......	......	......	......
20	21	23	25	27	28	30	32	34	36	......	......	......	......	......
21	22	24	26	28	30	32	34	35	37	39	......	......	......	......
22	23	25	27	29	31	33	35	37	39	41	43	......	......	......
23	25	27	29	31	33	35	37	39	41	43	45	47	......	......
24	26	28	30	32	34	36	38	41	43	45	47	49	51	......
25	27	29	31	33	36	38	40	42	44	47	49	51	53	(1)
26	28	30	32	35	37	39	42	44	46	49	51	53	55	(1)
27	29	31	34	36	38	41	43	46	48	50	53	55	58	(1)
28	30	32	35	37	40	42	44	47	50	52	55	57	60	(1)
29	31	34	36	39	41	44	46	49	52	54	57	59	62	(1)
30	32	35	37	40	43	45	48	51	53	56	59	61	64	(1)
31	33	36	39	41	44	47	50	52	55	58	61	63	66	(1)
32	34	37	40	43	46	48	51	54	57	60	62	65	68	(1)
33	35	38	41	44	47	50	53	56	59	62	64	67	70	(1)
34	36	39	42	45	48	51	54	57	60	63	66	69	73	(1)
35	37	40	44	47	50	53	56	59	62	65	68	72	75	(1)
36	38	42	45	48	51	54	58	61	64	67	70	74	77	(1)
Over 36	(1)	(1)	(1)	(1)	(1)	(1)	(1)	(1)	(1)	(1)	(1)	(1)	(1)	(1)

[1] Determine amount of kapok from formula (1) contained in § 160.048–4(c)(2).

TABLE 160.048–4(C)(1)(II)—WEIGHT OF FIBROUS GLASS (IN OUNCES) FOR FILLING RECTANGULAR BUOYANT CUSHION 2 INCHES THICK

Length (inches)	Width (inches)													
	12	13	14	15	16	17	18	19	20	21	22	23	24	Over 24
15	......	......	......	36	......	......	......	......	......	......	......	......	......	......
16	......	......	......	38	41	......	......	......	......	......	......	......	......	......
17	......	......	38	41	44	46	......	......	......	......	......	......	......	......
18	......	37	40	43	46	49	52	......	......	......	......	......	......	......
19	36	40	43	46	49	52	55	58	......	......	......	......	......	......
20	38	42	45	48	51	54	58	61	64	......	......	......	......	......
21	40	44	47	50	54	57	60	64	67	71	......	......	......	......
22	42	46	49	53	56	60	63	67	70	74	77	......	......	......
23	44	48	52	55	59	63	66	70	74	77	81	85	......	......
24	46	50	54	58	61	65	69	73	77	81	84	88	92	......
25	48	52	56	60	64	68	72	76	80	84	88	92	96	(1)
26	50	54	58	62	67	71	75	79	83	87	92	96	100	(1)
27	52	56	60	65	69	73	78	82	86	91	95	99	104	(1)
28	54	58	63	67	72	76	81	85	90	94	99	103	108	(1)
29	56	60	65	70	74	79	84	88	93	97	102	107	111	(1)
30	58	62	67	72	77	82	86	91	96	101	106	110	115	(1)
31	60	64	69	74	79	84	89	94	99	104	109	114	119	(1)
32	61	67	72	77	82	87	92	97	103	108	113	118	123	(1)
33	63	69	74	79	84	90	95	100	106	111	116	121	127	(1)
34	65	71	76	82	87	92	98	103	109	114	120	125	131	(1)
35	67	73	78	84	90	95	101	106	112	118	123	129	134	(1)
36	69	75	81	86	92	98	104	109	115	121	127	132	138	(1)
Over 36	(1)	(1)	(1)	(1)	(1)	(1)	(1)	(1)	(1)	(1)	(1)	(1)	(1)	(1)

[1] Determine amount of fibrous glass from formula (2) contained in § 160.048–4(c)(2).

(2) All buoyant cushions more than 2 inches thick, and all buoyant cushions 2 inches thick which are of shapes different from those covered by paragraph (c)(1) of this section, shall be filled with kapok or fibrous glass as determined in the following formulas:

Amount of kapok (ounces) = A × t + 22.5 (1)

Amount of fibrous glass (ounces) = A × t + 12.5 (2)

Where:

A = Top surface area of cushion in square inches as determined from measurements taken along finished edges.

t = Thickness of boxing or gusset of finished cushion in inches.

(d) *Pad covers for buoyant material.* Before being inserted in the outer cover the buoyant material shall be placed in waterproof vinyl film pad covers which shall be heat-sealed tight. The heat-sealed pad seams shall show an adhesion of not less than 8 pounds when one inch strips cut across and perpendicular to the seams are pulled apart at a rate of separation of the clamping jaws of the test machine of 12 inches per minute. Each cushion shall contain not less than four pads and all pads in a cushion shall contain approximately equal portions of the total amount of buoyant material in the cushion. The buoyant material may be inserted directly into the vinyl film pad covers, or may first be packed in bags made of print cloth or other suitable material and then inserted into the vinyl film pad covers. The pads shall be of such size as to adequately fill the outer cover, and prior to sealing, the pads shall be evacuated of air sufficiently that when sat on the pads will not "balloon" excessively because of the pressure in the pad covers. For 15″×15″×2″ cushions the four vinyl film pad covers shall each be cut approximately 12″ wide × 12″ long or approximately 8″ wide × 18″ long shall have a sealed area of approximately 125 square inches; shall contain not less than 5 ounces of kapok or 9 ounces of fibrous glass each; and the volume displacement of the individual heat-sealed pad inserts shall be 5½ pounds each, plus or minus ½ pound, when tested in accordance with the method set forth in § 160.048–5(e)(1), except that the pad

covers shall not be slit open, and the period of submergence shall be only long enough to determine the displacement of the pads.

(e) *Grab straps.* Grab straps shall be attached as shown on Dwg. No. 160.048–1 and shall finish 20 inches long and 1 inch wide at opposite ends. The grab straps, if formed from cover material shall be folded and stitched together so as to produce a double thickness with raw edges turned under. Other means will be given special consideration.

(f) *Seams and stitching.* Seams shall be constructed with not less than a ⅜ inch border between the seam and the edge of the cover materials. All stitching shall be a lock stitch, 7 to 9 stitches per inch, except as follows: Chain stitching 6 to 8 stitches per inch, with 20/4 thread on top and 40/3 thread on the bottom, will be acceptable in constructing straps.

(g) *Workmanship.* All cushions shall be of first class workmanship and shall be free from defects materially affecting their appearance or serviceability. Cushions classified as "seconds" or "irregular" will not be acceptable under this specification.

[CGFR 65–37, 30 FR 11583, Sept. 10, 1965]

§ 160.048–5 Inspections and tests.[1]

(a) *General.* Manufacturers of listed and labeled buoyant cushions shall maintain quality control of the materials used, manufacturing methods and the finished product so as to meet the applicable requirements, and shall make sufficient inspections and tests of representative samples and components produced to maintain the quality of the finished product. Records of tests conducted by the manufacturer and records of materials, including affidavits by suppliers that applicable requirements are met, entering into construction shall be made available to the recognized laboratory inspector or the Coast Guard inspector, or both, for review upon request. Any examinations, inspections and test which are required by the recognized laboratory

---

[1] The manufacturer of a personal flotation device must meet 33 CFR 181.701 through 33 CFR 181.705 which require an instruction pamphlet for each device that is sold or offered for sale for use on recreational boats.

127

for listed and labeled devices produced will be conducted by the laboratory inspector at the place of manufacture or other location at the option of the laboratory.

(b) *Lot size and sampling.* (1) A lot shall consist of not more than 1,000 buoyant cushions. A new lot shall be started with any change or modification in materials used or manufacturing methods employed. When a lot of buoyant cushions is ready for inspection, the manufacturer shall notify the recognized laboratory so that they may, at their discretion, assign an inspector to the plant for the purpose of making any tests and inspections deemed necessary. From each lot of buoyant cushions, the manufacturer or the recognized laboratory or U.S. Coast Guard inspector, when assigned, shall select samples in accordance with Table 160.048–5(b)(1) to be tested for buoyancy in accordance with paragraph (e) of this section.

TABLE 160.048–5(B)(1)—SAMPLING FOR BUOYANCY TESTS

Lot size	No. of cushions in sample
200 and under	1
201 to 400	2
401 to 600	3
601 to 1,000	4

(2) For a lot next succeeding one from which any sample cushion failed the buoyancy test, the sample shall consist of not less than 10 specimen cushions to be tested for buoyancy in accordance with paragraph (e) of this section.

(c) *Additional tests.* Unannounced examinations, tests and inspections of samples obtained either directly from the manufacturer or through commercial channels may be made to determine the suitability of a product for listing and labeling, or to determine conformance of a labeled product to the applicable requirements. These may be conducted by the recognized laboratory or the Coast Guard.

(d) *Test facilities.* The laboratory inspector, or the Coast Guard inspector, or both, shall be admitted to any place in the factory where work is being done on listed and labeled products, and either or both inspectors may take sam-

ples of parts or materials entering into construction of final assemblies, for further examinations, inspections, or tests. The manufacturer shall provide a suitable place and the apparatus necessary for the performance of the tests which are done at the place of manufacture.

(e) *Buoyancy*—(1) *Buoyancy test method.* Remove the buoyant pad inserts from the cushion and cut three slits in the vinyl film, each not less than 6 inches in length on both sides of each pad. Securely attach the spring scale in a position directly over the test tank. Suspend the weighted wire basket from the scale in such a manner that the basket is weighed while it is completely under water. In order to measure the actual buoyance provided by the pads, the underwater weight of the empty basket should exceed the buoyancy of the pads. To obtain the buoyancy of the pads, proceed as follows:

(i) Weigh the empty wire basket under water.

(ii) Place the pads inside the basket and submerge it so that the top of the basket is at least 2 inches below the surface of the water for 24 hours. The tank shall be locked or sealed during this 24-hour submergence period. It is important that after the pads have once been submerged that they shall remain submerged for the duration of the test, and at no time during the course of the test shall they be removed from the tank or otherwise exposed to air.

(iii) After the 24-hour submergence period unlock or unseal the tank and weigh the weighted wire basket with the pads inside while both are still under water.

(iv) The buoyancy is computed as (i) minus (iii).

(2) *Buoyancy required.* The buoyant pads from the cushion shall provide not less than 20 pounds total buoyancy.

[CGFR 65–37, 30 FR 11585, Sept. 10, 1965, as amended by CGFR 70–143, 35 FR 19963, Dec. 30, 1970; CGD 78–008, 43 FR 9772, Mar. 9, 1978]

§ 160.048–6   Marking.

(a) Each buoyant cushion must have the following information clearly marked in waterproof lettering:

(1) In letters that can be read at a distance of 2 feet:

Type IV Personal Flotation Device.
Inspected and tested in accordance with U.S. Coast Guard regulations.
Dry out thoroughly when wet.
(Kapok or Fibrous glass) buoyant material provides a minimum buoyant force of 20 lb.
Do not snag or puncture inner plastic cover.
If pads become waterlogged, replace device.
Approved for use on recreational boats only as a throwable device.
U.S. Coast Guard Approval No. 160.048/(assigned manufacturer's No.)/(Revision No.); (Model No.).
(Name and address of manufacturer or distributor.).
(Lot No.).
(Size; width, thickness, and length, including both top and bottom for trapezoidal cushions.).

(2) In letters that are distinctively set off or larger than all other marking, and are at least one-fourth of an inch in height:

WARNING: DO NOT WEAR ON BACK

(b) *Waterproofness of marking.* Marking for buoyant cushions shall be sufficiently waterproof so that after 72 hours submergence in water, it will withstand vigorous rubbing by hand while wet without the printed matter becoming illegible.

[CGFR 65–37, 30 FR 11585, Sept. 10, 1965, as amended by CGFR 70–143, 35 FR 19963, Dec. 30, 1970; CGD 72–163R, 38 FR 8119, Mar. 28, 1973; CGD 75–008, 43 FR 9771, Mar. 9, 1978; CGD 92–045, 58 FR 41608, Aug. 4, 1993; CGD 95–028, 62 FR 51213, Sept. 30, 1997]

EFFECTIVE DATE NOTE: At 62 FR 51213, Sept. 30, 1997, in §160.048–6, paragraph (a)(1) was amended and (c) was removed, effective Oct. 30, 1997.

§160.048–7 Procedure for approval.

(a) *Group approval.* A single group approval will be granted to each manufacturer to cover all buoyant cushions which have materials and construction strictly in conformance with this subpart, which are 2 inches thick, and which are filled with kapok or fibrous glass in accordance with §160.048–4(c)(1).

(b) *Special approvals.* Special approvals will be granted separately to each manufacturer for each kapok or fibrous glass buoyant cushion he proposes to manufacture which is not included under the group approval provided by paragraph (b) of this section, for example: A kapok or fibrous glass buoyant

cushion having cover material not specifically provided for by this subpart; or any buoyant cushion more than 2 inches thick; or any buoyant cushion having a different shape.

(c) A buoyant cushion is approved when it bears the compliance label of the recognized laboratory.

[CGFR 70–143, 35 FR 19963, Dec. 30, 1970, as amended by CGD 72–163R, 38 FR 8119, Mar. 28, 1973; CGD 93–055, 61 FR 13930, Mar. 28, 1996; 61 FR 15162, Apr. 4, 1996]

§160.048–8 Recognized laboratory.

(a) A manufacturer seeking Coast Guard approval of a product under this subpart shall follow the approval procedures of subpart 159.005 of this chapter, and shall apply for approval directly to a recognized independent laboratory. The following laboratories are recognized under §159.010–7 of this part, to perform testing and approval functions under this subpart:

Underwriters Laboratories, 12 Laboratory Drive, P.O. Box 13995, Research Triangle Park, NC 27709–3995, (919) 549–1400.

(b) Production oversight must be performed by the same laboratory that performs the approval tests unless, as determined by the Commandant, the employees of the laboratory performed production oversight receive training and support equal to that of the laboratory that performed the approval testing.

[CGD 93–055, 61 FR 13930, Mar. 28, 1996]

Subpart 160.049—Specification for a Buoyant Cushion Plastic Foam

§160.049–1 Incorporation by reference.

(a) *Specifications and Standards.* This subpart makes reference to the following documents:

(1) Federal Specifications:

CCC–C–700G–Cloth, Coated, Vinyl, Coated (Artificial Leather).
CCC–C–426D–Cloth, Cotton Drill.

(2) Federal standard:

No. 751—Stitches, Seams, and Stitchings.

(3) Coast Guard specifications:

160.055—Life Preservers, Unicellular Plastic Foam, Adult and Child.
164.015—Plastic Foam, Unicellular, Buoyant, Sheet and Molded Shapes.

(4) *Military specifications.* MIL-C-43006—Cloth, Laminated, Vinyl-Nylon, High Strength, Flexible.

(b) *Plan.* The following plan, of the issue in effect on the date unicellular plastic foam buoyant cushions are manufactured, form a part of this subpart:

(1) Coast Guard Dwg. No. 160.049-1.

(c) *Copies on file.* Copies of the specifications and plan referred to in this section shall be kept on file by the manufacturer, together with the approved plans and certificate of approval. The Coast Guard specifications and plan may be obtained upon request from the Commandant, U.S. Coast Guard, or recognized laboratory. The Federal Specifications and the Federal Standard may be purchased from the Business Service Center, General Services Administration, Washington, DC 20407.

[CGFR 65-37, 30 FR 11586, Sept. 10, 1965, as amended by CGFR 70-143, 35 FR 19964, Dec. 30, 1970; CGD 72-163R, 38 FR 8119, Mar. 28, 1973; CGD 78-012, 43 FR 27153, 27154, June 22, 1978; CGD 88-070, 53 FR 34535, Sept. 7, 1988]

§ 160.049-2 Types and sizes.

(a) *Type.* Buoyant cushions shall be of the box type, i.e., have top, bottom, and gusset. Pillow type cushions without a gusset are not acceptable.

(b) *Sizes.* Buoyant cushions shall have not less than 225 square inches of top surface area, shall contain not less than 630 cubic inches of buoyant material, shall not be less than 2 inches thick, and shall have widths and lengths which fall within the dimensions shown in Table 160.049-4(c)(1).

[CGFR 65-37, 30 FR 11586, Sept. 10, 1965]

§ 160.049-3 Materials.

(a) *General.* All components used in the construction of buoyant cushions must meet the applicable requirements of subpart 164.019.

(b) *Unicellular plastic foam.* The unicellular plastic foam shall be all new material complying with the requirements of Specification subpart 164.015 for Type A or B foam.

(c) *Cover.* Cotton fabrics and coated upholstery cloth meeting the minimum requirements set forth in paragraphs (c) (1) and (2) of this section, are acceptable for use as covers for buoyant cushions. Vinyl-dip coating meeting the requirements set forth in paragraph (c)(3) of this section will also be acceptable. Alternate materials will be given special consideration. Pro rata widths of like construction will be acceptable.

(1) *Cotton fabrics.* Cotton fabrics shall comply with the requirements of Federal Specification CCC-C-426 for Type I, Class 3 material.

(2) *Coated upholstery cloth.* Coated upholstery cloth shall comply with the requirements of Federal Specification CCC-A-700.

(3) *Vinyl-dip.* The vinyl-dip coating shall comply with the coating requirements of § 160.055-5(b)(2) except there are no color restrictions.

(4) *Adhesive.* The adhesive shall be an all-purpose waterproof vinyl type. Minnesota Mining and Manufacturing Co. EC-870 or EC-1070, United States Rubber Co. M6256, Herculite Protective Fabrics Corp. CVV, Pittsburgh Plate Glass Co. R.828, or equal, are acceptable.

(5) *Reinforcing fabric.* The reinforcing fabric shall be type II, class I, laminated vinyl-nylon high strength cloth in accordance with the requirements of Specification MIL-C-43006.

(d) *Grab Straps.* The grab straps shall be of materials permitted for the cover, or approved equivalent.

(e) *Thread.* Each thread must meet the requirements of subpart 164.023 of this chapter. Only one kind of thread may be used in each seam.

(f) *Welting.* The welting where used may be of any fiber or plastic material suitable for the purpose.

[CGFR 65-37, 30 FR 11586, Sept. 10, 1965, as amended by CGFR 70-143, 35 FR 19964, Dec. 30, 1970; CGD 78-012, 43 FR 27154, June 22, 1978; CGD 84-068, 58 FR 29493, May 20, 1993]

§ 160.049-4 Construction and workmanship.

(a) *General.* This specification covers buoyant cushions of the box type filled with unicellular plastic foam buoyant material. Such cushions consist essentially of a buoyant insert contained in an outer cover fitted with grab straps. The primary purpose of such cushions is to provide buoyancy to aid a person in keeping afloat in the water. Buoyant cushions providing less than 20 pounds buoyancy or less than 2 inches in thickness will not be acceptable.

(b) *Cover.* One piece of material each for the top and bottom shall be stitched together to form the cover except that piecing of the cover material will be allowed provided it is for decorative purposes only. Gusset or boxing materials shall be of not more than two pieces. If more than one piece of material is used for the top, bottom, boxing or gusset, they shall be attached by a double row of stitching of the type shown in Federal Standard No. 751, for Seam types SSw-2 or LSb-2. The top and bottom may be of any of the materials permitted for the cover, but the boxing or gusset shall be a cotton fabric as specified by § 160.049-3(b)(1) or other equivalent material of a porous nature. Nonporous materials will not be permitted for the boxing or gusset, but coated upholstery cloth specified by § 160.049-3(c)(2), perforated to permit adequate draining and drying will be acceptable.

(c) *Buoyant material.* A buoyant insert for a buoyant cushion must comply with the requirements in paragraph (c) (1) and (2) of this section and may be:

(1) Molded in one piece; or

(2) Built up from sheet material if it is formed from:

(i) Three pieces or less in each layer, cemented together with an all-purpose vinyl adhesive such as or equivalent to U.S. Rubber No. M-6256 or Minnesota Mining No. EC-870 and No. EC-1070;

(ii) Three layers or less that may be cemented; and

(iii) Staggered butts and seams of adjacent layers.

(d) *Grab Straps.* Grab straps shall be attached as shown on Dwg. No. 160,049-1 and shall finish 20 inches long and 1 inch wide at opposite ends. The grab straps, if formed from cover material shall be folded and stitched together so as to produce a double thickness with raw edges turned under. Other means will be given special consideration.

(e) *Seams and stitching.* Seams shall be constructed with not less than a ⅜-inch border between the seam and the edge of the cover materials. All stitching shall be a lock stitch, 7 to 9 stitches per inch, except as follows: Chain stitching 6 to 8 stitches per inch with

20/4 thread on top and 40/3 thread on the bottom, will be acceptable in constructing grab straps.

(f) *Workmanship.* All cushions shall be of first class workmanship and shall be free from defects materially affecting their appearance or serviceability. Cushions classified as "seconds" or "irregular" will not be acceptable under this specification.

[CGFR 65-37, 30 FR 11586, Sept. 10, 1965, as amended by CGD 72-163R, 38 FR 8119, Mar. 28, 1973]

§ 160.049-5 Inspections and tests.[1]

(a) *General.* Manufacturers of listed and labeled buoyant cushions shall maintain quality control of the materials used, manufacturing methods and the finished product so as to meet the applicable requirements, and shall make sufficient inspections and tests of representative samples and components produced to maintain the quality of the finished product. Records of tests conducted by the manufacturer and records of materials, including affidavits by suppliers that applicable requirements are met, entering into construction shall be made available to the recognized laboratory inspector or the Coast Guard inspector, or both, for review upon request. Any examinations, inspections and tests which are required by the recognized laboratory for listed and labeled devices produced will be conducted by the laboratory inspector at the place of manufacture or other location at the option of the laboratory.

(b) *Lot size and sampling.* (1) A lot shall consist of not more than 1,000 buoyant cushions. A new lot shall be started with any change or modification in materials used or manufacturing methods employed. When a lot of buoyant cushions is ready for inspection, the manufacturer shall notify the recognized laboratory so that they may, at their discretion, assign an inspector to the plant for the purpose of making any tests and inspections deemed necessary. From each lot of

---

[1] The manufacturer of a personal flotation device must meet 33 CFR 181.701 through 33 CFR 181.705 which require an instruction pamphlet for each device that is sold or offered for sale for use on recreational boats.

buoyant cushions, the manufacturer or the recognized laboratory or U.S. Coast Guard inspector, when assigned, shall select samples in accordance with table 160.049–5(b)(1) to be tested for buoyancy in accordance with paragraph (e) of this section.

TABLE 160.049–5(B)(1)—SAMPLING FOR BUOYANCY TESTS

Lot size	Number of cushions in sample
200 and under	1
201 to 400	2
401 to 600	3
601 to 1,000	4

(c) *Additional tests.* Unannounced examinations, tests and inspections of samples obtained either directly from the manufacturer or through commercial channels may be made to determine the suitability of a product for listing and labeling, or to determine conformance of a labeled product to the applicable requirements. These may be conducted by the recognized laboratory or the U.S. Coast Guard.

(d) *Test facilities.* The laboratory inspector, or the Coast Guard inspector, or both, shall be admitted to any place in the factory where work is being done on listed and labeled products, and either or both inspectors may take samples of parts or materials entering into construction of final assemblies, for further examinations, inspections, or tests. The manufacturer shall provide a suitable place and the apparatus necessary for the performance of the tests which are done at the place of manufacture.

(e) *Buoyancy*—(1) *Buoyancy test method.* Securely attach the spring scale in a position directly over the test tank. Suspend the weighted wire basket from the scale in such a manner that the basket is weighed while it is completely under water. In order to measure the actual buoyancy provided by the cushion, the underwater weight of the empty basket should exceed the buoyancy of the cushion. To obtain the buoyancy of the cushion, proceed as follows:

(i) Weigh the empty wire basket under water.

(ii) Place the cushion inside the basket and submerge it so that the top of the basket is at least 2 inches below the surface of the water for 24 hours. The tank shall be locked or sealed during this 24-hour submergence period. It is important that after the cushion has once been submerged that it shall remain submerged for the duration of the test, and at no time during the course of the test shall it be removed from the tank or otherwise exposed to air.

(iii) After the 24-hour submergence period unlock or unseal the tank and weigh the weighted wire basket with the cushion inside while both are still under water.

(iv) The buoyancy is computed as (i) minus (iii).

(2) *Buoyancy required.* Each cushion shall provide not less than 20 pounds buoyancy.

[CGFR 65–37, 30 FR 11587, Sept. 10, 1965, as amended by CGFR 70–143, 35 FR 19964, Dec. 30, 1970; CGD 75–008, 43 FR 9772, Mar. 9, 1978]

§ 160.049–6 **Marking.**

(a) Each buoyant cushion must have the following information clearly marked in waterproof lettering:

(1) In letters that can be read at a distance of 2 feet:

Type IV Personal Flotation Device.
Inspected and tested in accordance with U.S. Coast Guard regulations.
(Name of buoyant material) buoyant material provides a minimum buoyant force of 20 lb.
Dry out thoroughly when wet.
Approved for use on recreational boats only as a throwable device.
U.S. Coast Guard Approval No. 160.049/(assigned manufacturer's No.)/(Revision No.); (Model No.).
(Name and address of manufacturer or distributor.).
(Lot No.).
(Size; width, thickness, and length, including both top and bottom for trapezoidal cushions.).

(2) In letters that are distinctively set off or larger than all other marking, and are at least one-fourth of an inch in height:

WARNING: DO NOT WEAR ON BACK

(b) *Waterproofness of marking.* Marking for buoyant cushions shall be sufficiently waterproof so that after 72 hours submergence in water, it will withstand vigorous rubbing by hand while wet without the printed matter becoming illegible.

[CGFR 65–37, 30 FR 11588, Sept. 10, 1965, as amended by CGFR 70–143, 35 FR 19964, Dec. 30, 1970; CGD 72–163R, 38 FR 8119, Mar. 28, 1973; CGD 75–008, 43 FR 9771, Mar. 9, 1978; CGD 92–045, 58 FR 41608, Aug. 4, 1993; CGD 95–028, 62 FR 51213, Sept. 30, 1997]

EFFECTIVE DATE NOTE: At 62 FR 51213, Sept. 30, 1997, in §160.049–6, paragraph (a)(1) was amended and (c) was removed, effective Oct. 30, 1997.

§ 160.049–7 Procedure for approval.

(a) *Group approval.* A single group approval will be granted to each manufacturer to cover all buoyant cushions which have materials and construction strictly in conformance with this subpart, and which are in accordance with §160.049–4(c)(1).

(b) *Special approvals.* Special approvals will be granted separately to each manufacturer for each unicellular plastic foam buoyant cushion he proposes to manufacture which is not included under the group approval provided for by paragraph (b) of this section, for example: a buoyant cushion having cover material not specifically provided for by this subpart, or any buoyant cushion having a different shape.

(c) A buoyant cushion is approved when it bears the compliance label of the recognized laboratory.

[CGFR 70–143, 35 FR 19964, Dec. 30, 1970, as amended by CGD 72–163R, 38 FR 8119, Mar. 28, 1973; CGD 93–055, 61 FR 13930, Mar. 28, 1996]

§ 160.049–8 Recognized laboratory.

(a) A manufacturer seeking Coast Guard approval of a product under this subpart shall follow the approval procedures of subpart 159.005 of this chapter, and shall apply for approval directly to a recognized independent laboratory. The following laboratories are recognized under §159.010–7 of this part, to perform testing and approval functions under this subpart:

Underwriters Laboratories, 12 Laboratory Drive, P.O. Box 13995, Research Triangle Park, NC 27709–3995, (919) 549–1400.

(b) Production oversight must be performed by the same laboratory that performs the approval tests unless, as determined by the Commandant, the employees of the laboratory performing production oversight receive training and support equal to that of the laboratory that performed the approval testing.

[CGD 93–055, 61 FR 13930, Mar. 28, 1996]

Subpart 160.050—Specification for a Buoy, Life Ring, Unicellular Plastic

§ 160.050–1 Incorporation by reference.

(a) *Specifications and Standard.* This subpart makes reference to the following documents:

(1) Military specification:

MIL–R–16847—Ring buoy, lifesaving, unicellular plastic.

(2) Federal Specification:

V–T–295D–Thread, Nylon.

(3) Federal standard:

No. 595—Colors.

(4) Coast Guard specification:

164.015—Plastic foam, unicellular, buoyant, sheet and molded shape.

(b) *Copies on file.* Copies of the specifications referred to in this section shall be kept on file by the manufacturer, together with the certificate of approval. The Military Specification may be obtained from the Commanding Officer, Naval Supply Depot, 5801 Tabor Avenue, Philadelphia, Pa., 19120. The Federal Specifications and Federal Standard may be obtained from the Business Service Center, General Services Administration, Washington, DC 20407. The Coast Guard specification may be obtained from the Commandant, U.S. Coast Guard, Washington, DC 20593–0001.

[CGFR 66–64, 31 FR 562, Jan. 18, 1966, as amended CGD 72–163R, 38 FR 8120, Mar. 28, 1973; 38 FR 21784, Aug. 13, 1973; CGD 78–012, 43 FR 27153, 27154, June 22, 1978; CGD 88–070, 53 FR 34535, Sept. 7, 1988]

§ 160.050–2 Types and sizes.

(a) *Type.* Life buoys shall be of the annular ring type as described in this subpart, but alternate arrangements meeting the performance requirements set forth will be given special consideration.

(b) *Sizes.* Ring life buoys shall be of the sizes set forth in Table 160.050–2(b). A tolerance of a plus or minus 5 percent will be allowable on the dimensions indicated in Table 160.050–2(b).

TABLE 160.050–2(B)—SIZES AND DIMENSIONS OF RING LIFE BUOYS

Size	Dimensions (inches) Finished ring
30-inch	30
24-inch	24
20-inch	20

[CGFR 54–46, 19 FR 8707, Dec. 18, 1954, as amended by CGFR 62–17, 27 FR 9045, Sept. 11, 1962]

§ 160.050–3 Materials.

(a) *General.* All exposed materials must be resistant to oil or oil products, salt water and anticipated weather conditions encountered at sea. All components used in construction of buoys and life rings must meet the applicable requirements of subpart 164.019 of this chapter.

(b) *Unicellular plastic.* The unicellular plastic material used in fabrication of the buoy body shall meet the requirements of subpart 164.015 of this subchapter for Type C material. The buoy's body shall be finished with two coats of vinyl base paint. The ring life buoys shall be either international orange (Color No. 12197 of Federal Standard 595) or white in color and the colorfastness shall be rated "good" when tested in accordance with Federal Test Method Standard No. 191 Methods 5610, 5630, 5650, and 5660.

NOTE: On vessels on an international voyage, all ring life buoys shall be international orange in color.)

(c) *Grab line.* The grab line shall be ⅜-inch diameter polyethylene, polypropylene, or other suitable buoyant type synthetic material having a minimum breaking strength of 1,350 pounds.

(d) *Beckets.* The beckets for securing the grab line shall be 2-inch polyethylene, polypropylene, nylon, saran or other suitable synthetic material having a minimum breaking strength of 585 pounds. In addition, polyethylene and polypropylene shall be weather-resistant type which is stabilized as to heat, oxidation, and ultraviolet light degradation.

(e) *Thread.* Each thread must meet the requirements of subpart 164.023 of this chapter. Only one kind of thread may be used in each seam.

[CGFR 65–9, 30 FR 11477, Sept. 8, 1965, as amended by CGFR 65–64, 31 FR 562, Jan. 18, 1966; CGD 78–012, 43 FR 27154, June 22, 1978; CGD 84–068, 58 FR 29493, May 20, 1993]

§ 160.050–4 Construction and workmanship.

(a) *General.* This specification covers ring life buoys which provide buoyancy to aid in keeping persons afloat in the water. Each buoy consists of a body constructed in the shape of an annular ring, with an approximately elliptical body cross section and which is fitted with a grab line around the outside periphery. The outside and inside diameters of the ring and the length and width of the cross section of the body shall be uniform throughout.

(b) *Body.* The body shall be made in either one or two pieces. If of two pieces, the pieces shall be equal in size and shall be adhesive bonded along a center line through an axis passing through the flat area dimension of the body. The adhesive shall be a liquid cold setting, polymerizable, nonsolvent, containing material of the phenolepichlorhydrin type or equivalent having good strength retention under outdoor weathering conditions.

(c) *Grab line.* The finished length of the grab line shall be four times the outside diameter of the buoy. The ends of the grab line shall be securely and neatly spliced together, or shall be hand whipped with a needle and both ends securely and smoothly seized together. The grab line shall encircle the buoy and shall be held in place by the beckets. The spliced or seized ends of the grab line shall be placed in the center of the width of one of the beckets.

(d) *Beckets.* Each ring buoy shall be fitted with four beckets located at equidistant points about the body of the buoy. The beckets shall be passed around the body of the buoy with the free ends to the outside, and shall be securely cemented to the buoy with a suitable waterproof adhesive which is compatible with the unicellular plastic used in the buoy body. The ends of the beckets shall be turned under at least 1 inch, one end to go around the grab line, and the other to be laid flat against the first end. The beckets shall then be stitched to the grab line with not less than five hand stitches made with two parts of thread or machined stitched with not less than three stitches per inch. Alternate methods for rigging beckets and grab line will be given special consideration.

(e) *Weight.* The weight of the completely assembled buoy shall be not less than 2.5 pounds and not more than 4.25 pounds for the 20-inch size, not less than 3.0 pounds and not more than 5.5 pounds for the 24-inch size, and not less than 5.0 and not more than 7.5 pounds for the 30-inch size.

(f) *Workmanship.* Ring life buoys shall be of first class workmanship and free from any defects materially affecting their appearance or serviceability.

[CGFR 54–46, 19 FR 8707, Dec. 18, 1954, as amended by CGFR 62–17, 27 FR 9045, Sept. 11, 1962; CGFR 65–9, 30 FR 11477, Sept. 8, 1965]

§ 160.050–5 Sampling, tests, and inspection.

(a) *General.* Production tests and inspections must be conducted in accordance with this section, subpart 159.007 of this chapter, and if conducted by an independent laboratory, the independent laboratory's procedures for production inspections and tests as accepted by the Commandant. The Commandant may prescribe additional production tests and inspections necessary to maintain quality control and to monitor compliance with the requirements of this subchapter.

(b) *Oversight.* In addition to responsibilities set out in part 159 of this chapter and the accepted laboratory procedures for production inspections and tests, each manufacturer of a ring life buoy and each laboratory inspector shall comply with the following, as applicable:

(1) *Manufacturer.* Each manufacturer must—

(i) Perform all tests and examinations necessary to show compliance with this subpart and the subpart under which the ring life buoy is approved on each lot before any inspector's tests and inspection of the lot;

(ii) Follow established procedures for maintaining quality control of the materials used, manufacturing operations, and the finished product; and

(iii) Allow an inspector to take samples of completed units or of component materials for tests required by this subpart and for tests relating to the safety of the design.

(iv) Meet 33 CFR 181.701 through 33 CFR 181.705 which requires an instruction pamphlet for each device that is sold or offered for sale for use on recreational boats, and must make the pamphlet accessible prior to purchase.

(2) *Laboratory.* An inspector from the accepted laboratory shall oversee production in accordance with the laboratory's procedures for production inspections and tests accepted by the Commandant. During production oversight, the inspector shall not perform or supervise any production test or inspection unless—

(i) The manufacturer has a valid approval certificate; and

(ii) The inspector has first observed the manufacturer's production methods and any revisions to those methods.

(3) At least quarterly, the inspector shall check the manufacturer's compliance with the company's quality control procedures, examine the manufacturer's required records, and observe the manufacturer perform each of the required production tests.

(c) *Test facilities.* The manufacturer shall provide a suitable place and apparatus for conducting the tests and inspections necessary to determine compliance of ring life buoys with this subpart. The manufacturer shall provide means to secure any test that is not continuously observed, such as the 48 hour buoyancy test. The manufacturer must have the calibration of all test equipment checked in accordance with the test equipment manufacturer's recommendation and interval but not less than at least once every year.

(d) *Lots.* A lot may not consist of more than 1000 life buoys. A lot number must be assigned to each group of life buoys produced. Lots must be numbered serially. A new lot must be started whenever any change in materials or a revision to a production method is made, and whenever any substantial discontinuity in the production process occurs. The lot number assigned, along with the approval number, must enable

135

the ring life buoy manufacturer to determine the supplier's identifying information for the component lot.

(e) *Samples.* (1) From each lot of ring life buoys, manufacturers shall randomly select a number of samples from completed units at least equal to the applicable number required by table 160.050-5(e) for buoyancy testing. Additional samples must be selected for any tests, examinations, and inspections required by the laboratory's production inspections and tests procedures.

TABLE 160.050-5(e)—SAMPLING FOR
BUOYANCY TESTS

Lot size	Number of life buoys in sample
100 and under	1
101 to 200	2
201 to 300	3
301 to 500	4
501 to 750	6
751 to 1000	8

(2) For a lot next succeeding one from which any sample ring life buoy failed the buoyancy or strength test, the sample shall consist of not less than ten specimen ring life buoys to be tested for buoyancy in accordance with paragraph (f) of this section.

(f) *Tests—(1) Strength test.* The buoy body shall be suspended by a 2-inch-wide strap. A similar strap shall be passed around the opposite side of the buoy and a 200-pound weight suspended by it from the buoy. After 30 minutes, the buoy body shall be examined, and there shall be no breaks, cracks or permanent deformation.

(2) *Resistance to damage test.* The buoy body shall be dropped three times from a height of 6 feet onto concrete, and there shall be no breaks or cracks in the body.

(3) *Buoyancy test.* To obtain the buoyancy of the buoy, proceed as follows:

(i) Weigh iron or other weight under water. The weight shall be more than sufficient to submerge the buoy.

(ii) Attach the iron or other weight to the buoy and submerge with the top of the buoy at least 2 inches below the surface for 48 hours.

(iii) After the 48-hour submergence period, weigh the buoy with the weight attached while both are still under water.

(iv) The buoyancy is computed as paragraph (f)(3)(i) minus paragraph (f)(3)(iii) of this section.

(4) *Buoyancy required.* The buoys shall provide a buoyancy of not less than 16.5 pounds for the 20-and 24-inch sizes, and not less than 32 pounds for the 30-inch size.

(g) *Lot inspection.* On each lot, the laboratory inspector shall perform a final lot inspection to be satisfied that the ring life buoys meet this subpart. Each lot must demonstrate—

(1) First quality workmanship;

(2) That the general arrangement and attachment of all components are as specified in the approved plans and specifications; and

(3) Compliance with the marking requirements in the applicable approval subpart.

(h) *Lot acceptance.* When the independent laboratory has determined that the ring life buoys in the lot are of a type officially approved in the name of the company, and that such ring life buoys meet the requirements of this subpart, they shall be plainly marked in waterproof ink with the independent laboratory's name or identifying mark.

(i) *Lot rejection.* Each nonconforming unit must be rejected. If three or more nonconforming units are rejected for the same kind of defect, lot inspection must be discontinued and the lot rejected. The inspector must discontinue lot inspection and reject the lot if examination of individual units or the records for the lot shows noncompliance with either this subchapter or the laboratory's or the manufacturer's quality control procedures. A rejected unit or lot may be resubmitted for testing and inspection if the manufacturer first removes and destroys each defective unit or, if authorized by the laboratory, reworks the unit or lot to correct the defect. A rejected lot or rejected unit may not be sold or offered for sale under the representation that it meets this subpart or that it is Coast Guard-approved.

[CGFR 65-9, 30 FR 11478, Sept. 8, 1965, as amended by CGD 95-028, 62 FR 51213, Sept. 30, 1997]

EFFECTIVE DATE NOTE: At 62 FR 51213, Sept. 30, 1997, § 160.050-5 was revised, effective Oct. 30, 1997.

§ 160.050–6 Marking.

(a) Each ring buoy must have the following information in waterproof lettering:

Type IV Personal Flotation Device.
Inspected and tested in accordance with U.S. Coast Guard regulations.
(Name of buoyant material) buoyant material provides a minimum buoyant force of (32 lb. or 16½ lb.).
Approved for use on recreational boats only as a throwable device.
U.S. Coast Guard Approval No. 160.050/(assigned manufacturer's No.)/(Revision No.); (Model No.).
(Name and address of manufacturer or distributor).
(Size).
USCG (Marine Inspection Office identification letters).
(Lot No.).

(b) A method of marking that is different from the requirements of paragraph (a) of this section may be given consideration by the Coast Guard.

[CGD 72–163R, 38 FR 8120, Mar. 28, 1973, as amended by CGD 75–186, 41 FR 10437, Mar. 11, 1976; CGD 75–008, 43 FR 9771, Mar. 9, 1978; 43 FR 10913, Mar. 16, 1978; CGD 92–045, 58 FR 41608, Aug. 4, 1993; CGD 95–028, 62 FR 51214, Sept. 30, 1997]

EFFECTIVE DATE NOTE: At 62 FR 51214, Sept. 30, 1997, in § 160.050–6, paragraph (a)(1) was amended and (c) was removed, effective Oct. 30, 1997.

§ 160.050–7 Procedure for approval.

(a) *General.* Designs of ring life buoys are approved only by the Commandant, U.S. Coast Guard. Manufacturers seeking approval of a ring life buoy design shall follow the procedures of this section and subpart 159.005 of this chapter.

(b) Each application for approval of a ring life buoy must contain the information specified in § 159.005–5 of this chapter. The application and, except as provided in paragraphs (c) and (d)(2) of this section, a prototype ring life buoy must be submitted to the Commandant for preapproval review. If a similar design has already been approved, the Commandant may waive the preapproval review under §§ 159.005–5 and 159.005–7 of this chapter.

(c) If the ring life buoy is of a standard design, the application:

(1) Must include the following: A statement of any exceptions to the standard plans and specifications, including drawings, product description, construction specifications, and/or bill of materials.

(2) Need not include: The information specified in § 159.005–5(a)(2).

(d) If the ring life buoy is of a nonstandard design, the application must include the following:

(1) Plans and specifications containing the information required by § 159.005–12 of this chapter, including drawings, product description, construction specifications, and bill of materials.

(2) The information specified in § 159.005–5(a)(2) (i) through (iii) of this chapter, except that, if preapproval review has been waived, the manufacturer is not required to send a prototype ring life buoy sample to the Commandant.

(3) Performance testing results of the design performed by an independent laboratory that has a Memorandum of Understanding with the Coast Guard under § 159.010–7 of this subchapter covering the in-water testing of personal flotation devices showing equivalence to the standard design's performance in all material respects.

(4) Buoyancy and other relevant tolerances to be complied with during production.

(5) The text of any optional marking to be included on the ring life buoy in addition to the markings required by the applicable approval subpart.

(6) For any conditionally approved ring life buoy, the intended approval condition(s).

(e) The description of quality control procedures required by § 159.005–9 of this chapter may be omitted if the manufacturer's planned quality control procedures meet the requirements of those accepted by the Commandant for the independent laboratory performing production inspections and tests.

(f) *Waiver of tests.* A manufacturer may request that the Commandant waive any test prescribed for approval under the applicable subpart. To request a waiver, the manufacturer must submit to the Commandant and the laboratory described in § 159.010, one of the following:

(1) Satisfactory test results on a ring life buoy of sufficiently similar design as determined by the Commandant.

(2) Engineering analysis demonstrating that the test for which a waiver is requested is not appropriate for the particular design submitted for approval or that, because of its design or construction, it is not possible for the ring life buoy to fail that test.

[CGD 95–028, 62 FR 51214, Sept. 30, 1997]

EFFECTIVE DATE NOTE: At 62 FR 51214, Sept. 30, 1997, § 160.050–7 was revised, effective Oct. 30, 1997.

Subpart 160.051—Inflatable Liferafts for Domestic Service

SOURCE: CGD 85–205, 62 FR 25546, May 9, 1997, unless otherwise noted.

§ 160.051–1 Scope.

This subpart prescribes requirements for approval by the Coast Guard of A, B, and Coastal Service inflatable liferafts for use only in domestic service. These liferafts must comply with all of the requirements for SOLAS A and SOLAS B liferafts in subpart 160.151 except as specified in this subpart.

§ 160.051–3 Definitions.

In this subpart, the term:

A or B liferaft means an inflatable liferaft that meets the requirements prescribed in subpart 160.151 for a SOLAS A or SOLAS B liferaft, respectively, except that the capacity is less than 6 persons and the liferaft cannot contain SOLAS markings.

Coastal Service liferaft means a liferaft that does not meet the all of the requirements prescribed in subpart 160.151 for a SOLAS A or SOLAS B liferaft, but that instead meets the requirements of this subpart and is approved for use on certain uninspected vessels under subchapter C of this chapter.

§ 160.051–5 Design and performance of Coastal Service inflatable liferafts.

To obtain Coast Guard approval, each Coastal Service inflatable liferaft must comply with subpart 160.151, with the following exceptions:

(a) *Canopy requirements (Regulation III/38.1.5).* The canopy may—

(1) Be of a type that is furled when the liferaft inflates and that can be set in place by the occupants. A furled canopy must be secured to the buoyancy tubes over 50 percent or more of the liferaft's circumference;

(2) Be of an uninsulated, single-ply design; and

(3) Have an interior of any color.

(b) *Viewing port (Regulation III/38.1.5.5).* The liferaft need not have the viewing port described in Regulation III/38.1.5.5.

(c) *Rainwater collection (Regulation III/38.1.5.6).* The liferaft need not have the means of rainwater collection described in Regulation III/38.1.5.6.

(d) *Capacity (Regulation III/38.2.1).* The carrying capacity must be not less than four persons.

(e) *Floor insulation (Regulation III/39.2.2).* The floor may be uninsulated.

(f) *Boarding ramps (Regulation III/39.4.1).* The liferaft need be provided with boarding ramps only if the combined cross-section diameter of the buoyancy chambers is greater than 500 mm (19.5 in).

(g) *Stability (Regulation III/39.5.1).* Each Coastal Service inflatable liferaft must either meet the stability criteria in § 160.151–17(a) or be fitted with water-containing stability pockets meeting the following requirements:

(1) The total volume of the pockets must be not less than 25 percent of the minimum required volume of the principal buoyancy compartments of the liferaft.

(2) The pockets must be securely attached and evenly distributed around the periphery of the exterior bottom of the liferaft. They may be omitted at the locations of inflation cylinders.

(3) The pockets must be designed to deploy underwater when the liferaft inflates. If weights are used for this purpose, they must be of corrosion-resistant material.

(h) *Lamp (Regulation III/39.6.3).* The liferaft need not have the manually controlled interior lamp described in Regulation III/39.6.3.

(i) *Markings (Regulations III/39.7.3.4 and III/39.7.3.5).* The words "COASTAL SERVICE" must appear on the container, and the type of equipment pack must be identified as "Coastal Service". No "SOLAS" markings may appear on the container.

(j) *Drop test.* The drop test required under paragraph 1/5.1 of IMO Resolution A.689(17) and 160.151-27(a) may be from a lesser height, if that height is the maximum height of stowage marked on the container.

(k) *Loading and seating test.* For the loading and seating test required under paragraph 1/5.7 of IMO Resolution A.689(17) and §160.151-27(a), the loaded freeboard of the liferaft must be not less than 200 mm (8 in.).

(l) *Cold-inflation test.* The cold-inflation test required under paragraph 1/5.17.3.3.2 of IMO Resolution A.689(17) and §160.151-27(a) must be conducted at a test temperature of −18 °C (0 °F).

§160.051-7 Design and performance of A and B inflatable liferafts.

To obtain Coast Guard approval, each A and B inflatable liferaft must comply with the requirements in subpart 160.151, with the following exceptions:

(a) *Capacity (Regulation III/38.2.1).* The carrying capacity must be not less than four persons.

(b) *Markings (Regulations III/39.7.3.4 and III/39.7.3.5).* The type of equipment pack must be identified as "A" or "B", respectively, instead of "SOLAS A" or "SOLAS B". No "SOLAS" markings may appear on the container.

§160.051-9 Equipment required for Coastal Service inflatable liferafts.

In lieu of the equipment specified in §160.151-21, the following equipment must be provided with a Coastal Service inflatable liferaft:

(a) *Rescue quoit and heaving line.* One rescue quoit and a heaving line as described in §160.151-21(a).

(b) *Knife.* One knife, of a type designed to minimize the chance of damage to the inflatable liferaft and secured with a lanyard.

(c) *Bailer.* One bailer as described in §160.151-21(c).

(d) *Sponge.* One sponge as described in §160.151-21(d).

(e) *Sea anchor.* One sea anchor as described in §160.151-21(e).

(f) *Paddles.* Two paddles of the same size and type as used to pass the maneuverability test in paragraph 1/5.10 of IMO Resolution A.689(17).

(g) *Whistle.* One whistle as described in §160.151-21(i) of this part.

(h) *Flashlight.* One flashlight with spare batteries as described in §160.151-21(m).

(i) *Signalling mirror.* One signalling mirror as described in §160.151-21(o).

(j) *Survival instructions.* Instructions on how to survive as described in §160.151-21(v).

(k) *Instructions for immediate action.* Instructions for immediate action as described in §160.151-21(w).

(l) *Repair outfit.* One set of sealing clamps or plugs as described in §160.151-21(y)(1).

(m) *Pump or bellows.* One pump or bellows as described in §160.151-21(z).

(n) *Plugs for pressure-relief valves.* Plugs for pressure-relief valves as described in §160.151-21(aa).

Subpart 160.052—Specification for a Buoyant Vest, Unicellular Plastic Foam, Adult and Child

§160.052-1 Incorporation by reference.

(a) *Specifications and Standards.* This subpart makes reference to the following documents.

(1) [Reserved]

(2) Military specification:

MIL-W-530F—Webbing, Textile, Cotton, General Purpose, Natural and in Colors.

(3) Federal Standards:

No. 191—Textile Test Methods.
No. 751A—Stitches, Seams, and Stitching.

(4) Coast Guard specifications:

160.055—Life Preservers, Unicellular Plastic Foam, Adult and Child.
164.015—Plastic Foam, Unicellular, Buoyant Sheet and Molded Shapes.

(b) *Plans.* The following plans, of the issue in effect on the date buoyant vests are manufactured, form a part of this subpart:

Dwg. No. 160.052-1:
Sheet 1—Cutting Pattern and General Arrangement, Model AP.
Sheet 2—Cutting Pattern and General Arrangement, Model CPM.
Sheet 3—Cutting Pattern and General Arrangement, Model CPS.
Sheet 4—Insert Patterns.

(c) *Copies on file.* The manufacturer shall keep a copy of each specification and plan required by this section on file together with the certificate of approval. Plans and specifications may be obtained as follows:

(1) The Coast Guard plans and specifications may be obtained upon request from the Commandant (G–MSE), U.S. Coast Guard, Washington, DC 20593–0001, or a recognized laboratory listed in § 160.052–8b.

(2) The Federal Specifications and Standards may be purchased from the Business Service Center, General Services Administration, Washington, DC 20407.

(3) The military specification may be obtained from the Commanding Officer, Naval Supply Depot, 5801 Tabor Avenue, Philadelphia, PA 19120.

[CGFR 65–37, 30 FR 11588, Sept. 10, 1965, as amended by CGD 72–90R, 37 FR 10837, May 31, 1972; CGD 72–163R, 38 FR 8120, Mar. 28, 1973; CGD 78–012, 43 FR 27153, 27154, June 22, 1978; CGD 82–063b, 48 FR 4782, Feb. 3, 1983; CGD 88–070, 53 FR 34536, Sept. 7, 1988; CGD 95–072, 60 FR 50467, Sept. 29, 1995; CGD 96–041, 61 FR 50733, Sept. 27, 1996]

§ 160.052–2 Size and model.

(a) A standard buoyant vest is manufactured in accordance with a plan specified in § 160.052–1(b) and is a:

(1) Model AP, adult (for persons over 90 pounds);

(2) Model CPM, child, medium (for persons weighing from 50 to 90 pounds); or

(3) Model CPS, child, small (for persons weighing less than 50 pounds).

(b) A nonstandard buoyant vest is:

(1) Manufactured in accordance with the manufacturer's approved plan;

(2) Equivalent in performance to the standard buoyant vest; and

(3) Assigned a model designation by the manufacturer for the following sizes:

(i) Adult (for persons weighing over 90 pounds);

(ii) Child, medium (for persons weighing from 50 to 90 pounds);

(iii) Child, small (for persons weighing less than 50 pounds).

[CGD 72–163R, 38 FR 8120, Mar. 28, 1973]

§ 160.052–3 Materials—Standard vests.

(a) *General.* All components used in the construction of buoyant vests must meet the applicable requirements of subpart 164.019 of this chapter. The requirements for materials specified in this section are minimum requirements, and consideration will be given to the use of alternate materials in lieu of those specified. Detailed technical data and samples of all proposed alternate materials shall be submitted for approval before those materials are incorporated in the finished product.

(b) *Unicellular plastic foam.* The unicellular plastic foam shall be all new material complying with the requirements of specification Subpart 164.015 of this subchapter for Type A or B foam.

(c) *Envelope.* The buoyant vest envelope, or cover, shall be made from 39″, 2.85 cotton jeans cloth, with a thread count of approximately 96×64. The finished goods shall weigh not less than 4.2 ounces per square yard, shall have thread count of not less than 94×60, and shall have a breaking strength of not less than 85 pounds in the warp and 50 pounds in the filling. Other cotton fabrics having a weight and breaking strength not less than the above will be acceptable. There are no restrictions as to color, but the fastness of the color to laundering, water, crocking, and light shall be rated "good" when tested in accordance with Federal Test Method Standard No. 191, Methods 5610, 5630, 5650, and 5660.

(d) *Tie tapes and body strap loops.* The tie tapes and body strap loops for both adult and child sizes must be ¾-inch cotton webbing meeting the requirements of military specification MIL–T–43566 (Class I) for Type I webbing.

(d–1) *Body straps.* The complete body strap assembly, including hardware, must have a minimum breaking strength of 150 pounds for an adult size and 115 pounds for a child size. The specifications for the webbing are as follows:

(1) For an adult size vest, the webbing must be 1 inch;

(2) For a child size vest, the webbing must be three-quarter inch and meet the requirements of military specification MIL–W–530 for Type IIa webbing.

(e) [Reserved]

(f) *Thread.* Each thread must meet the requirements of subpart 164.023 of this chapter. Only one kind of thread may be used in each seam.

[CGFR 65–37, 30 FR 11588, Sept. 10, 1965, as amended by CGD 72–90R, 37 FR 10837, May 31, 1972; CGD 72–163R, 38 FR 8120, Mar. 28, 1973; CGD 73–130R, 39 FR 20684, June 13, 1974; CGD 78–012, 43 FR 27154, June 22, 1978; CGD 82–063b, 48 FR 4782, Feb. 3, 1983; CGD 84–068, 58 FR 29493, May 20, 1993]

§ 160.052–3a Materials—Dee ring and snap hook assemblies and other instruments of closure for buoyant vests.

(a) *Specifications.* Dee ring and snap hook assemblies and other instruments of closure for buoyant vests may have decorative platings in any thickness and must meet the following specifications:

(1) The device must be constructed of inherently corrosion resistant materials. As used in this section the term *inherently corrosion resistant materials* includes, but is not limited to brass, bronze, and stainless steel.

(2) The size of the opening of the device must be consistent with the webbing which will pass through the opening.

(b) *Testing requirements.* Dee ring and snap hook assemblies and other instruments of closure for buoyant vests must—

(1) Be tested for weathering. The Coast Guard will determine which one or more of the following tests will be used:

(i) Application of a 20 percent sodium-chloride solution spray at a temperature of 95 °F (35 °C) for a period of 240 hours in accordance with the procedures contained in method 811 of the Federal Test Method Standard No. 151.

(ii) Exposure to a carbon-arc weatherometer for a period of 100 hours.

(iii) Submergence for a period of 100 hours in each of the following:

(*a*) Leaded gasoline.

(*b*) Gum turpentine.

(iv) Exposure to a temperature of 0°±5 °F (17.6±2.775 °C) for 24 hours; and

(2) Within 5 minutes of completion of the weathering test required by paragraph (b)(1) of this section, the assembly must be attached to a support and bear 150 pounds for an adult size and 115 pounds for a child size for 10 minutes at ambient temperatures without breaking or distorting.

[CGD 73–130R, 39 FR 20684, June 13, 1974]

§ 160.052–4 Materials—nonstandard vests.

(a) *General.* All materials used in nonstandard buoyant vests must be equivalent to those specified in § 160.052–3 and be obtained from a supplier who furnishes an affidavit in accordance with the requirement in § 160.052–3(a).

(b) *Cover.* A vinyl-dip coating may be allowed for the covering of the vest instead of a fabric envelope if the coating meets the requirements in § 160.055–5(b)(2) of this chapter except there is no color restriction.

(c) *Reinforcing tape.* When used, the reinforcing tape around the neck shall be ¾″ cotton tape weighing not less than 0.18 ounces per linear yard having a minimum breaking strength of not less than 120 pounds.

[CGFR 65–37, 30 FR 11588, Sept. 10, 1965, as amended by CGD 72–90R, 37 FR 10837, May 31, 1972; 37 FR 11774, June 14, 1972, CGD 72–163R, 38 FR 8120, Mar. 28, 1973]

§ 160.052–5 Construction—standard vests.

(a) *General.* This specification covers buoyant vests which essentially consist of a fabric envelope in which are enclosed inserts of buoyant material arranged and distributed so as to provide the flotation characteristics and buoyancy required to hold the wearer in an upright or slightly backward position with head and face out of water. The buoyant vests are also fitted with straps and hardware to provide for proper adjustment and close and comfortable fit to the bodies of various size wearers.

(b) *Envelope.* The envelope or cover shall be made of three pieces. Two pieces of fabric shall be cut to the pattern shown on Dwg. No. 160.052–1, Sheet 1 for adult size, and Sheets 2 and 3 for child sizes, and joined together with a third piece which forms a 2″ finished gusset strip all around. Reinforcing strips of the same material as the envelope shall be stitched to the inside of the front piece of the envelope in way of the strap attachments as shown by the drawings.

(c) *Buoyant inserts.* The unicellular plastic foam buoyant inserts shall be cut and formed as shown on Dwg. 160.052–1, Sheet 4.

(d) *Tie tapes, body straps, and hardware.* The tie tapes, body straps, and hardware shall be arranged as shown on the drawings and attached to the envelope with the seams and stitching indicated.

(e) *Stitching.* All stitching shall be short lock stitch conforming to Stitch Type 301 of Federal Standard No. 751, and there shall be not less than 7 nor more than 9 stitches to the inch.

(f) *Workmanship.* Buoyant vests shall be of first-class workmanship and shall be free from any defects materially affecting their appearance or serviceability.

[CGFR 65–37, 30 FR 11588, Sept. 10, 1965, as amended by CGD, 72–163R, 38 FR 8120, Mar. 28, 1973]

§ 160.052–6 Construction—nonstandard vests.

(a) *General.* The construction methods used for nonstandard buoyant vests must be equivalent to those requirements in § 160.052–5 for a standard vest and also meet the requirements in this section.

(b) *Size.* Each nonstandard vest must contain the following volume of plastic foam buoyant material, determined by the displacement method:

(1) Five hundred cubic inches or more for an adult size;

(2) Three hundred and fifty cubic inches or more for a child, medium size;

(3) Two hundred and twenty-five cubic inches or more for a child, small size.

(c) *Arrangement of buoyant material.* The buoyant material in a nonstandard vest must:

(1) Be arranged to hold the wearer in an upright or backward position with head and face out of water;

(2) Have no tendency to turn a wearer face downward in the water; and

(3) Be arranged so that 70 to 75 percent of the total is located in the front of the vest.

(d) *Neck opening.* Each cloth-covered nonstandard vest must have at the neck opening:

(1) A gusset; or

(2) Reinforcing tape.

(e) *Adjustment, fit, and donning.* Each nonstandard vest must be made with adjustments to:

(1) Fit a range of wearers for the type designed; and

(2) Facilitate donning time for an uninitiated person.

[CGD 72–163R, 38 FR 8120, Mar. 28, 1973]

§ 160.052–7 Inspections and tests— standard and nonstandard vests.[1]

(a) *General.* Manufacturers of listed and labeled buoyant vests shall—

(1) Maintain quality control of the materials used, the manufacturing methods and workmanship, and the finished product to meet the requirements of this subpart by conducting sufficient inspections and tests of representative samples and components produced;

(2) Make available to the recognized laboratory inspector and the Coast Guard inspector, upon request, records of tests conducted by the manufacturer and records of materials used during production of the device, including affidavits by supplier; and

(3) Permit any examination, inspection, and test required by the recognized laboratory or the Coast Guard for a produced listed and labeled device, either at the place of manufacture or some other location.

(b) *Lot size and sampling.* (1) A lot consists of 500 buoyant vests or fewer.

(2) A new lot begins after any change or modification in materials used or manufacturing methods employed.

(3) The manufacturer of the buoyant vests shall notify the recognized laboratory when a lot is ready for inspection.

(4) The manufacturer shall select samples in accordance with the requirements in Table 160.052–7(b)(4) from each lot of buoyant vests to be tested for buoyancy in accordance with paragraph (e) of this section.

---

[1] The manufacturer of a personal flotation device must meet 33 CFR 181.701 through 33 CFR 181.705 which require an instruction pamphlet for each device that is sold or offered for sale for use on recreational boats.

TABLE 160.052–7(B)(4)—SAMPLE FOR BUOYANT VESTS

Lot size	Number of vests in sample
100 and under	1
101 to 200	2
201 to 300	3
301 to 500	4

(5) The manufacturer shall test—

(i) At least one vest from each lot for buoyancy in accordance with procedures contained in paragraph (e) of this section; and

(ii) At least one vest in each 10 lots for strength of the body strap assembly in accordance with the procedures contained in paragraph (f) of this section.

(6) If a vest fails the buoyancy test, the sample from the next succeeding lot must consist of 10 specimen vests or more to be tested for buoyancy in accordance with paragraph (e) of this section.

(7) The manufacturer shall keep on file and make available to the laboratory inspector and Coast Guard inspector the records of inspections and tests, together with affidavits concerning the material.

(c) *Additional compliance tests.* An inspector from the recognized laboratory or Coast Guard may conduct an examination, test and inspection of a buoyant device that is obtained from the manufacturer or through commercial channels to determine the suitability of the device for listing and labeling or to determine its conformance to applicable requirements.

(d) *Test facilities.* The manufacturer shall admit the laboratory inspector and the Coast Guard inspector to any part of the premises at the place of manufacture of a listed and labeled device to—

(1) Examine, inspect, or test a sample of a part or a material that is included in the construction of the device; and

(2) Conduct any necessary examination, inspection, or test in a suitable place and with appropriate apparatus provided by the manufacturer.

(e) *Buoyancy*—(1) *Buoyancy test method.* Remove the buoyant inserts from the vests. Securely attach the spring scale in a position directly over the test tank. Suspend the weighted wire basket from the scale in such a manner

that the basket can be weighed while it is completely under water. In order to measure the actual buoyancy provided by the inserts, the underwater weight of the empty basket should exceed the buoyancy of the inserts. To obtan the buoyancy of the inserts, proceed as follows:

(i) Weigh the empty wire basket under water.

(ii) Place the inserts inside the basket and submerge it so that the top of the basket is at least 2 inches below the surface of the water. Allow the inserts to remain submerged for 24 hours. The tank shall be locked or sealed during this 24-hour submergence period. It is important that after the inserts have once been submerged they shall remain submerged for the duration of the test, and at no time during the course of the test shall they be removed from the tank or otherwise exposed to air.

(iii) After the 24-hour submergence period, unlock or unseal the tank and weigh the wire basket with the inserts inside while both are still under water.

(iv) The buoyancy is computed as paragraph (e)(1)(i) of this section minus paragraph (e)(i)(iii) of this section.

(2) *Buoyancy required.* The buoyant inserts from adult size buoyant vests shall provide not less than 15½ pounds buoyancy in fresh water; the inserts from child medium size vests shall provide not less than 11 pounds buoyancy; and the inserts from child small size vests shall provide not less than 7 pounds buoyancy.

(f) *Body strap test.* The complete body strap assembly including hardware, shall be tested for strength by attaching the dee ring to a suitable support such that the assembly hangs vertically its full length. A weight as specified in § 160.052–3(d) shall be attached to the other end of the snap hook for 10 minutes. The specified weight shall not break or excessively distort the body strap assembly.

(g) *Additional approval tests for non-standard vests.* Tests in addition to those required by this section may be conducted by the inspector for nonstandard vests to determine performance equivalence to a standard vest. Such additional tests may include determining performance in water, suitability of materials, donning time, ease of adjustment, and similar equivalency tests. Costs of any additional tests must be assumed by the manufacturer.

[CGFR 65–37, 30 FR 11588, Sept. 10, 1965, as amended by CGD 72–90R, 37 FR 10837, May 31, 1972; CGD 72–163R, 38 FR 8120, Mar. 28, 1973; CGD 75–008, 43 FR 9772, Mar. 9, 1978]

§ 160.052–8 Marking.

(a) Each buoyant vest must have the following information clearly marked in waterproof lettering that can be read at a distance of 2 feet:

Type II—Personal flotation device.
Inspected and tested in accordance with U.S. Coast Guard regulations.
(Name of buoyant material) provides a minimum buoyant force of (15½ lb., 11 lb., or 7 lb.).
Dry out thoroughly when wet.
Approved for use on all recreational boats and on uninspected commercial vessels less than 40 feet in length not carrying passengers for hire by persons weighing (over 90 lb., 50 to 90 lb., or less than 50 lb.).
U.S. Coast Guard Approval No. 160.050/(assigned manufacturer's No.)/(Revision No.); (Model No.).
(Name and address of manufacturer or distributor).
(Lot No.)

(b) *Waterproof marking.* Marking for buoyant vests shall be sufficiently waterproof so that after 72 hours submergence in water it will withstand vigorous rubbing by hand while wet without the printed matter becoming illegible.

[CGD 72–163R, 38 FR 8120, Mar. 28, 1973, as amended by CGD 75–008, 43 FR 9771, Mar. 9, 1978]

§ 160.052–9 Recognized laboratory.

(a) A manufacturer seeking Coast Guard approval of a product under this subpart shall follow the approval procedures of subpart 159.005 of this chapter, and shall apply for approval directly to a recognized independent laboratory. The following laboratories are recognized under § 159.010–7 of this part, to perform testing and approval functions under this subpart:

Underwriters Laboratories, 12 Laboratory Drive, P.O. Box 13995, Research Triangle Park, NC 27709–3995, (919) 549–1400.

(b) Production oversight must be performed by the same laboratory that performs the approval tests unless, as determined by the Commandant, the employees of the laboratory perform-

ing production oversight receive training and support equal to that of the laboratory that performed the approval testing.

[CGD 93–055, 61 FR 13930, Mar. 28, 1996]

Subpart 160.053—Work Vests, Unicellular Plastic Foam

SOURCE: CGFR 59–22, 24 FR 4961, June 18, 1959, unless otherwise noted.

§ 160.053–1 Applicable specifications.

(a) *Specification.* The following specification of the issue in effect on the date unicellular plastic foam work vests are manufactured, form a part of this subpart:

(1) Military specification: MIL–L–17653A—Life Preserver, Vest, Work Type, Unicellular Plastic.

(2) [Reserved]

(b) *Copies on file.* Copies of the specification referred to in this section, as well as the various specifications forming a part thereof, shall be kept on file by the manufacturer, together with the certificate of approval. They shall be kept for a period consisting of the duration of approval and 6 months after termination of approval. Federal specifications may be purchased from the Business Service Center, General Services Administration, Washington, DC 20407. Military specifications may be obtained from the Commanding Officer, Naval Supply Depot, 5801 Tabor Avenue, Philadelphia, Pa. 19120.

[CGFR 59–22, 24 FR 4961, June 18, 1959, as amended by CGFR 65–16, 30 FR 10899 Aug. 21, 1965; CGD 72–163, 38 FR 8120, Mar. 28, 1973; CGD 78–012, 43 FR 27154, June 22, 1978; CGD 95–028, 62 FR 51215, Sept. 30, 1997]

EFFECTIVE DATE NOTE: At 62 FR 51215, Sept. 30, 1997, § 160.053–1 was amended by removing paragraph (c), effective Oct. 30, 1997.

§ 160.053–2 Type.

(a) Unicellular plastic foam work vests specified by this subpart shall be of the type described in Military Specification MIL–L–17653A, but alternate designs equivalent in materials, construction, performance, and workmanship will be given consideration.

(b) [Reserved]

§ 160.053–3 Materials, construction and workmanship.

(a) *General*. Except as otherwise specifically provided by this subpart and subparts 164.019 and 164.023 of this chapter, the materials, construction, and workmanship of unicellular plastic foam work vests specified by this subpart shall conform to the requirements of Military Specification MIL–L–17653A.

(b) *Color of envelope*. Indian Orange, Cable No. 70072, Standard Color Card of America, will be acceptable in lieu of the Scarlet-Munsell 7.5 red $6/10$ color specified for envelopes or covers by paragraph 3.1.1.1 of Specification MIL–L–17653A.

(c) *Color of webbing and thread*. The color of the webbing and thread need not match the color of the envelope as specified by paragraphs 3.1.3 and 3.2.8 of Specification MIL–L–17653A.

(d) *Materials; acceptance and quality*. All components used in the construction of work vests must meet the applicable requirements of subpart 164.019 of this chapter.

[CGFR 59–22, 24 FR 4961, June 18, 1959, as amended by CGD 84–068, 58 FR 29493, May 20, 1993]

§ 160.053–4 Inspections and tests.

(a) *General*. Work vests are not inspected at regularly scheduled factory inspections; however, the Commander of the Coast Guard District may detail a marine inspector at any time to visit any place where work vests are manufactured to observe production methods and to conduct any inspections or tests which may be deemed advisable. The marine inspector shall be admitted to any place in the factory where work is done on work vests or component materials, and samples of materials entering into construction may be taken by the marine inspector and tests made for compliance with the applicable requirements.

(b) *Manufacturer's inspections and tests*. Manufacturers of approved work vests shall maintain quality control of the materials used, manufacturing methods, workmanship, and the finished product so as to meet the requirements of this specification, and shall make full inspections and tests of representative samples from each lot to maintain the quality of their product.

(c) *Lot size*. A lot shall consist of not more than 500 work vests manufactured at the same time. Lots shall be numbered serially by the manufacturer, and if at any time during the manufacture of a lot, any change or modification in materials or production methods is made, a new lot shall be started.

(d) *Test facilities*. The manufacturer shall provide a suitable place and shall have on hand the necessary apparatus for conducting buoyancy tests in compliance with this specification. The apparatus shall include accurate spring scales of adequate capacity, weighted wire mesh baskets, and a test tank or tanks which can be locked or sealed in such a manner as to preclude disturbance of work vests undergoing tests or change in water level.

(e) *Buoyancy*—(1) *Buoyancy test method*. Remove the buoyant inserts from the vest. Securely attach the spring scale in a position directly over the test tank. Suspend the weighted wire basket from the scale in such a manner that the basket can be weighed while it is completely under water. In order to measure the actual buoyancy provided by the inserts, the underwater weight of the empty basket should exceed the buoyancy of the inserts. To obtain the buoyancy of the inserts, proceed as follows:

(i) Weigh the empty wire basket under water.

(ii) Place the inserts inside the basket and submerge it so that the top of the basket is at least 2 inches below the surface of the water. Allow the inserts to remain submerged for 24 hours. The tank shall be locked or sealed during this 24-hour submergence period.

(iii) After the 24-hour submergence period, unlock the tank and weigh the wire basket with the inserts inside while both are still under water.

(iv) The buoyancy is computed as paragraph (e)(1)(i) of this section minus paragraph (e)(1)(iii) of this section.

(2) *Buoyancy required*. The buoyant inserts from work vests shall provide not less than 17½ pounds buoyancy in fresh water.

§ 160.053–5 Marking.

(a) Each work vest must have the following information clearly printed in waterproof lettering that can be read at a distance of 2 feet:

Type V—Personal flotation device.
Inspected and tested in accordance with U.S. Coast Guard regulations.
(Name of buoyant material) buoyant material provides a minimum buoyant force of 17½ lbs.
Approved for use on Merchant Vessels as a work vest.
U.S. Coast Guard Approval No. 160.053/(assigned manufacturer's No.)/(Revision No.); (Model No.).
(Name and address of manufacturer or distributor.)
(Lot No.)
This vest is filled with (name of buoyant material), which will not be harmed by repeated wetting. Hang up and dry thoroughly when vest is wet.

(b) *Additional marking required.* In addition to the wording included on the marking tag, on a front compartment of each work vest there shall be stenciled in waterproof ink in letters not less than one inch in height, the words, "WORK VEST ONLY."

(c) *Waterproofness of marking tags.* Marking tags shall be sufficiently waterproof so that after 48 hours submergence in water, they will withstand rubbing by hand with moderate pressure while wet without the printed matter becoming illegible.

[CGFR 59–22, 24 FR 4961, June 18, 1959, as amended by CGD 72–163R, 38 FR 8121, Mar. 28, 1973; CGD 75–008, 43 FR 9771, Mar. 9, 1978]

§ 160.053–6 Procedure for approval.

(a) *General.* Work vests for use on merchant vessels are approved only by the Commandant, U.S. Coast Guard. Manufacturers seeking approval of a work vest shall follow the procedures of this section and subpart 159.005 of this chapter.

(b) If the work vest is of a standard design, as described by § 160.053–3, in order to be approved, the work vest must be tested in accordance with § 160.053–4 by an independent laboratory accepted by the Coast Guard under 46 CFR 159.010.

(c) If the work vest is of a non-standard design, the application must include the following:

(1) Plans and specifications containing the information required by § 159.005–12 of this chapter, including drawings, product description, construction specifications, and bill of materials.

(2) The information specified in § 159.005–5(a)(2) (i) through (iii) of this chapter, except that, if preapproval review has been waived, the manufacturer is not required to send a prototype work vest sample to the Commandant.

(3) Performance testing results of the design performed by an independent laboratory, that has a Memorandum of Understanding with the Coast Guard under § 159.010–7 of this subchapter covering the in-water testing of personal flotation devices, showing equivalence to the standard design's performance in all material respects.

(4) Any special purpose(s) for which the work vest is designed and the vessel(s) or vessel type(s) on which its use is intended.

(5) Buoyancy and other relevant tolerances to be complied with during production.

(6) The text of any optional marking to be included on the work vest in addition to the markings required by § 160.053.

[CGD 95–028, 62 FR 51215, Sept. 30, 1997]

EFFECTIVE DATE NOTE: At 62 FR 51215, Sept. 30, 1997, § 160.053–6 was revised, effective Oct. 30, 1997.

Subpart 160.054—Kits, First-Aid, for Inflatable Liferafts

SOURCE: CGFR 60–36, 25 FR 10637, Nov. 5, 1960, unless otherwise noted.

§ 160.054–1 Applicable specification.

(a) *Specification.* The following specification of the issue in effect on the date first aid kits are manufactured forms a part of this subpart:

(1) Coast Guard specification 160.041—Kits, First-Aid.

(2) [Reserved]

(b) *Copies on file.* Copies of the specification regulations referred to in this section shall be kept on file by the manufacturer, together with the approved plans and certificate of approval. They shall be kept for a period consisting of the duration of approval and 6 months after termination of approval. The Coast Guard specification may be obtained from the Commandant (G–MSE), U.S. Coast Guard, Washington, DC 20593–0001.

[CGFR 60–36, 25 FR 10637, Nov. 5, 1960, as amended by CGFR 65–16, 30 FR 10899, Aug. 21, 1965; CGD 88–070, 53 FR 34536, Sept. 7, 1988; CGD 95–072, 60 FR 50467, Sept. 29, 1995; CGD 96–041, 61 FR 50733, Sept. 27, 1996]

§ 160.054–2 Type and size.

(a) *Type.* First-aid kits covered by this specification shall be of the watertight type. Alternate arrangements of materials meeting the performance requirements of this specification will be given special consideration.

(b) *Size.* First-aid kits shall be of a size adequate for packing 12 standard single cartons of the kind indicated in specification subpart 160.041.

§ 160.054–3 Construction.

(a) *Construction.* The container shall be constructed of tough transparent material, not less than .008 inch nominal thickness, properly sealed around three edges, and having the fourth edge closed in such manner that it is capable of being opened and reclosed watertight. The re-openable closure may be a plastic zip seal closure without slider, or other means which meet the test requirements of § 160.054–5.

(b) [Reserved]

§ 160.054–4 Contents.

(a) *Individual cartons.* Cartons and their contents shall be the type indicated in Specification subpart 160.041.

(b) *Items.* The items contained in first-aid kit shall be as listed in Table 160.054–4(b).

TABLE 160.054–4(B)—ITEMS FOR FIRST-AID KIT

Item	No. per pkg.	Size of pkg.	No. of pkgs.
Bandage compress—4 inches	1	Single	1
Bandage compress—2 inches	4	Single	1
Waterproof adhesive compress—1 inch	16	Single	1
Eye dressing packet, ⅛ oz. Ophthalmic ointment, adhesive strips, cotton pads..	3	Single	1
Bandage, gauze, compressed, 2 inches × 6 yards	2	Single	1
Tourniquet, forceps, scissors, 12 safety pins	1, 1, 1, and 12, respectively	Double	1
Wire splint	1	Single	1
Ammonia inhalants	10	Single	1
Iodine applicators, (½ ml swab type)	10	Single	1
Aspirin, phenacetin and caffeine compound, 6½ Gr. tablets, vials of 20.	2	Single	1
Sterile petrolatum gauze, 3 inches by 18 inches	4	Single	1

(c) *Instructions.* Instructions for the use of the contents of the first-aid kit shall be printed in legible type and either shall be placed inside the container or printed on the container in waterproof ink. The instructions for the use of the contents are as indicated in Specification subpart 160.041, except that the triangular bandage is omitted.

§ 160.054–5 Inspections and tests.

(a) *Salt spray.* The container shall be exposed to a spray of 20 percent by weight of reagent grade sodium chloride at about 95 °F. for 100 hours. There shall be no disintegration of the material as a result of this test.

(b) *Container Watertightness.* With the required number of items inside, the closed container, with reclosable edge uppermost, shall be submerged under a head of one foot of water for a period of two hours. At the end of this period, the container shall be removed, surface dried, opened, and examined for the presence of moisture. No seepage shall be allowed.

[CGFR 60–36, 25 FR 10637, Nov. 5, 1960, as amended by CGD 95–028, 62 FR 51215, Sept. 30, 1997]

EFFECTIVE DATE NOTE: At 62 FR 51215, Sept. 30, 1997, § 160.054–5 was amended by removing paragraph (a) and redesignating paragraphs (b) and (c) as paragraphs (a) and (b), effective Oct. 30, 1997.

§ 160.054-6 Marking.

(a) Each approved first-aid kit shall be plainly and permanently marked with the following information: Name and address of the manufacturer, model number or other manufacturer's identification of the kit, the Coast Guard approval number, and the words "First-Aid Kit—For Inflatable Life Rafts". If the means for opening and re-closing are not self-evident, suitable directions shall be marked along the closure; such as, for the zip seal closure, an arrow, with the words "To Open, Lift by Thumb Nail", and "To Close, Press Together Full Length". The marking may be applied to the container by the silk screen process, using a suitable ink or paint, or may be applied by other means shown to be acceptable.

(b) [Reserved]

§ 160.054-7 Procedure for approval.

(a) *Manufacturer's plans.* In order to obtain approval, submit detailed plans showing fully the construction, material specification, arrangement, and list of contents to the Commander of the Coast Guard District in which the factory is located. Each drawing shall have an identifying number, and date, and shall indicate the manufacturer's symbol, trade name, or other identification for the first-aid kit. At the time of selection of the pre-approval sample, the manufacturer shall furnish the inspector four copies of all plans and specifications, corrected as may be required, for forwarding to the Commandant.

(b) *Pre-approval sample.* After the first drawings have been examined and found to appear satisfactory, a marine inspector will be detailed to the factory to observe the manufacturing facilities and methods and to obtain two samples, complete with contents which will be forwarded, prepaid by the manufacturer, to the Commandant for the necessary conditioning and tests in accordance with § 160.054-5 to determine the suitability of the first-aid kit for use in conjunction with lifesaving equipment on board merchant vessels.

The cost of the tests shall be borne by the manufacturer.

[CGFR 60-36, 25 FR 10637, Nov. 5, 1960, as amended by CGFR 65-16, 30 FR 10899, Aug. 21, 1965; CGD 88-070, 53 FR 34536, Sept. 7, 1988; CGD 95-028, 62 FR 51215, Sept. 30, 1997]

EFFECTIVE DATE NOTE: At 62 FR 51215, Sept. 30, 1997, § 160.054-7 was amended by removing paragraph (a) and redesignating paragraphs (b) and (c) as paragraphs (a) and (b), effective Oct. 30, 1997.

Subpart 160.055—Life Preservers, Unicellular Plastic Foam, Adult and Child, for Merchant Vessels

§ 160.055-1 Incorporation by reference.

(a) *Specifications and Standards.* This subpart makes reference to the following documents:

(1) *Military Specifications:*

MIL-W-530F—Webbing, Textile, Cotton, General Purpose, Natural or in Colors.
MIL-T-3530E—Thread and Twine; Mildew Resistant or Water Repellant Treated.
MIL-W-17337D—Webbing, Woven, Nylon.
MIL-C-43006D—Cloth and Strip Laminated, Vinyl-Nylon High Strength, Flexible.

(2) Federal Specifications:

CCC-C-700G—Cloth, Coated, Vinyl, Coated (Artificial Leather).
CCC-C-426D—Cloth, Drill, Cotton.

(3) Federal Standards:

No. 191—Textile Test Methods.
No. 595A—Color.
No. 751A—Stitches, Seams, and Stitchings.

(4) American Society for Testing and Materials (ASTM) Standards:

D413—Adhesion of Vulcanized Rubber (Friction Test).
D570—Water Absorption of Plastics.
D882—Tensile Properties of Thin Plastic Sheets and Films.
D1004—Tear Resistance of Plastic Film and Sheeting.

(5) Coast Guard specification:

164.015—Plastic Foam, Unicellular, Buoyant, Sheet and Molded Shape.

(b) *Plans.* The following plans, of the issue in effect on the date unicellular plastic foam life preservers are manufactured, form a part of this subpart:

Dwg. No. 160.055-IA:

Sheet 1—Construction and Arrangement, Vinyl Dip Coated, Model 62, Adult.

Sheet 2—Construction and Arrangement, Vinyl Dip Coated, Model 66, Child.

Dwg. No. 160.055–IB:

Sheet 1—Construction and Arrangement, Cloth Covered, Model 63, Adult.

Sheet 2—Buoyant Inserts, Model 63.

Sheet 3—Construction and Arrangement, Cloth Covered, Model 67, Child.

Sheet 4—Buoyant Inserts, Model 67.

(c) *Copies on file.* Copies of the specifications, standards, and plans referred to in this section shall be kept on file by the manufacturer, together with the approved plans and certificate of approval. The Coast Guard Specification and plans may be obtained upon request from the Commandant (G–MSE), U.S. Coast Guard, Washington, DC 20593–0001. The Federal Specifications and the Federal Standards may be purchased from the Business Service Center, General Services Administration, Washington, DC 20407. The Military Specifications may be obtained from the Commanding Officer, Naval Supply Depot, 5801 Tabor Avenue, Philadelphia, Pa. 19120. The ASTM Standards may be purchased from the American Society for Testing and Materials, 100 Barr Harbor Drive, West Conshohocken, PA 19428–2959.

[CGFR 66–73, 32 FR 5500, Apr. 4, 1967, as amended by CGD 72–163R, 38 FR 8121, Mar. 28, 1973; CGD 78–012, 43 FR 27153, 27154, June 22, 1978; CGD 88–070, 53 FR 34536, Sept. 7, 1988; CGD 95–072, 60 FR 50467, Sept. 29, 1995; CGD 96–041, 61 FR 50733, Sept. 27, 1996; CGD 97–057, 62 FR 51048, Sept. 30, 1997]

§ 160.055–2 Type and model.

Each life preserver specified in this subpart is a:

(a) Standard, bib type, vinyl dip coated:

(1) Model 62, adult (for persons weighing over 90 pounds); or

(2) Model 66, child (for persons weighing less than 90 pounds); or

(b) Standard, bib type, cloth covered;

(1) Model 63, adult (for persons weighing over 90 pounds); or

(2) Model 67, child (for persons weighing less than 90 pounds); or

(c) Nonstandard, shaped type:

(1) Model,[1] adult (for persons weighing over 90 pounds); or

(2) Model,[1] child (for persons weighless than 90 pounds).

[CGD 72–163R, 38 FR 8121, Mar. 28, 1973]

§ 160.055–3 Materials—standard life preservers.

(a) *General.* All components used in the construction of life preservers must meet the applicable requirements of subpart 164.019 of this chapter. The requirements for materials specified in this section are minimum requirements, and consideration will be given to the use of alternate materials in lieu of those specified. Detailed technical data and samples of all proposed alternate materials must be submitted for approval before those materials are incorporated in the finished product.

(b) *Unicellular plastic foam.* The unicellular plastic foam shall be all new material complying with the requirements of Subpart 164.015 of this chapter for Type A foam.

(c) *Envelope.* The life preserver envelope, or cover, shall be made of cotton drill. The color shall be Indian Orange, Cable No. 70072, Standard Color Card of America, issued by the Textile Color Association of the United States, Inc., 200 Madison Avenue, New York, N.Y., or Scarlet Munsell 7.5 Red 6/10. The drill shall be evenly dyed, and the fastness of the color to laundering, water, crocking, and light shall be rated "good" when tested in accordance with Federal Test Method Standard No. 191, Methods 5610, 5630, 5650, and 5660. After dyeing, the drill shall be treated with a mildew-inhibitor of the type specified in paragraph (e) of this section. The finished goods shall contain not more than 2 percent residual sizing or other nonfibrous material, shall weigh not less than 6.5 ounces per square yard, shall have a thread count of not less than 74 in the warp and 56 in the filling, and shall have a breaking strength (grab method) of not less than 105 pounds in the warp and 70 pounds in the filling. Properly mildew-inhibited drills meeting the physical requirements of Federal Specification CCC–C–

---

[1] A model designation for each nonstandard life preserver is to be assigned by the manufacturer. That designation must be different from any standard lifesaving device designation.

426 for Type I, Class 3 drill will be acceptable. If it is proposed to treat the fabric with a fire-retardant substance, full details shall be submitted to the Commandant for determination as to what samples will be needed for testing.

(d) *Thread.* Each thread must meet the requirements of subpart 164.023 of this chapter. Only one kind of thread may be used in each seam.

(e) *Mildew-inhibitor.* The mildew-inhibitor shall be dihydroxydichlorodiphenylmethane, known commercially as Compound G-4, applied by the aqueous method. The amount of inhibitor deposited shall be not more than 1.50 percent and not less than 1 percent of the dry weight of the finished goods.

(f) *Adhesive.* The adhesive shall be an all-purpose waterproof vinyl type. (Minnesota Mining and Manufacturing Co. EC-870 or EC-1070, United States Rubber Co. M-6256, Herculite Protective Fabrics Corp., CVV, Pittsburgh Plate Glass Co. R 828, or equal.)

(g) *Reinforcing fabric.* The reinforcing fabric shall be Type III, Class I, laminated vinyl-nylon high strength cloth in accordance with the requirements of Specification MIL-C-43006.

(h) *Webbing.* There are no restrictions as to color, but the fastness of the color to laundering, water, crocking, and light shall be rated "good" when tested in accordance with Federal Test Method Standard No. 191, Methods 5610, 5630, 5650, and 5660. The complete body strap assembly shall have a minimum breaking strength of 360 pounds.

(1) *Nylon webbing.* This webbing shall be 1-inch wide nylon webbing in accordance with the requirements of Specification MIL-W-17337.

(2) *Cotton webbing.* This webbing shall be 1-inch cotton webbing meeting the requirements of Specification MIL-W-530 for Type IIb webbing. This webbing shall be treated with a mildew-inhibitor of the type specified in paragraph (e) of this section.

(i) *Hardware.* All hardware shall be brass, bronze, or stainless steel, and of the approximate size indicated by the drawings. Steel hardware, protected against corrosion by plating, is not acceptable. Snap hook springs shall be phosphor bronze or other suitable corrosion-resistant material. Dee ring, o-ring, slide adjuster and snap hook ends shall be welded or brazed, or they may be a one-piece casting. The complete body strap assembly shall have a minimum breaking strength of 360 pounds.

(j) *Coating.* The coating for the plastic foam shall be a liquid elastomeric vinyl compound. The coating shall be International Orange in color (Color No. 12197 of Federal Standard 595) or Scarlet Munsel 7.5, Red 6/10 and shall meet the following requirements in Table 160.055-3(j):

TABLE 160.055-3(J)

Property	Test method	Requirement
Tensile strength	ASTM-D882, Method B, ½ in. dumbbell die	1,200 p.s.i., minimum.
Ultimate elongation	ASTM-D882, Method B, ½ in. dumbbell die	320 percent, minimum.
Tear resistance	ASTM-D1004, Constant Elongation Machine	90 pounds per inch, minimum.
Abrasion resistance	FS CCC-T-191, Method 5304, No. 8 cotton duck, 6 lb. tension, 2 lb. pressure.	100,000 double rubs.
Blocking	FS CCC-T-191, Method 5872, 30 minutes at 180 °F., ¼ p.s.i.	No blocking.
Accelerated weathering	FS CCC-T-191, Method 5670, 120 hours	Color change—very slight. Cracking—None. Flexibility—No change.
Plasticizer heat loss	FS CCC-A-700, paragraph 4.4.4, 48 hours at 221 °F.	8 percent, maximum.
Adhesion to foam—Tensile pull	ASTM-D413, machine method, 12 in. per minute, 1 in. strip.	
Film to foam skin		4 lb./in., minimum.
Film to foam (no skin)		2 lb./in., minimum.
Water absorption	ASTM-D570, 24 hours at 70 °F	0.5 percent, maximum.
Cold crack (unsupported film) 0 °F	Coast Guard, 164.015, paragraph 164.015-4(j)	No cracking.

[CGFR 66-73, 32 FR 5500, Apr. 4, 1967, as amended by CGD 72-163R, 38 FR 8121, Mar. 28, 1973; CGD 78-012, 43 FR 27153, 27154, June 22, 1978; CGD 84-068, 58 FR 29493, May 20, 1993]

§ 160.055-4 Materials—nonstandard life preservers.

All materials used in nonstandard life preservers must be equivalent to those specified in § 160.055-3 for standard life preservers.

[CGD 72-163R, 38 FR 8121, Mar. 28, 1973]

§ 160.055-5 Construction—Standard life preservers.

(a) *General.* This specification covers life preservers which essentially consist of plastic foam buoyant material arranged and distributed so as to provide the flotation characteristics and buoyancy required to hold the wearer in an upright or slightly backward position with head and face clear of the water. The life preservers are also arranged so as to be reversible and are fitted with straps and hardware to provide proper adjustment and fit to the bodies of various size wearers.

(b) *Construction—standard, vinyl dip coated life preserver.* This device is constructed from one piece of unicellular plastic foam with neck hole and the body slit in the front, vinyl dip coating, and fitted and adjustable body strap.

(1) *Buoyant material.* The buoyant material of the life preserver shall be a molded shape or made from one or two sheets of foam finished so as to have dimensions after coating in accordance with the pattern shown on Dwg. No. 160.055-1A, Sheet 1, for adult size and Sheet 2 for child size. The reinforcing fabric shall be cemented on the foam buoyant body before coating.

(2) *Coating.* After all cutting and shaping of the buoyant body and installation of the reinforcing fabric, the entire body of the life preserver shall be coated evenly and smoothly to a minimum thickness of 0.010″ with a liquid vinyl coating material of the type described in § 160.055-3(j).

(3) *Body strap.* After the coating on the buoyant body of the life preserver is fully cured, a nylon webbing body strap shall be attached as shown on Dwg. No. 160.055-1A.

(4) *Stitching.* All stitching shall be a short lock stitch, conforming to Stitch Type 301 of Federal Standard 751, with nylon thread, and there shall be not less than 9 nor more than 11 stitches to

the inch. Bar tacking with nylon thread is acceptable as noted on Dwg. No. 160-055-1A.

(c) *Construction—standard, cloth covered life preserver.* This device is constructed from three sections of unicellular plastic foam contained in a cloth envelope and has a neck hole, the body slit in the front, and a fitted and adjustable body strap.

(1) *Buoyant material.* The buoyant material of the life preserver shall be three sections of foam cut so as to have finished dimensions in accordance with the patterns shown on Dwg. No. 160.055-1B, Sheet 2, for adult size and Sheet 4, for child size. One or two layers of foam may be used to make up each section.

(2) *Envelope.* The envelope shall be cut to the pattern shown on Dwg. No. 160.055-1B, Sheet 1, for adult size, and Sheet 3, for child size, and joined by seams and stitching as shown on the drawing. Alternate finished envelopes are permitted as noted on Dwg. No. 160.055-1B.

(3) *Body strap.* The body strap may be cotton or nylon webbing and shall be attached by stitching as shown on the Dwg. No. 160.055-1B, Sheet 1, for adult size and Sheet 3, for child size.

(4) *Stitching.* All stitching shall be a short lock stitch conforming to Stitch Type 301 of Federal Standard No. 751, and there shall be not less than 7 nor more than 9 stitches to the inch if cotton thread is used, and not less than 9 nor more than 11 if nylon thread is used. Bar tacking is acceptable as noted on Dwg. No. 160.055-1B.

(d) *Workmanship.* Life preservers shall be of first-class workmanship and shall be free from any defects materially affecting their appearance or serviceability.

[CGFR 66-73, 32 FR 5500, Apr. 4, 1967, as amended by CGD 72-163R, 38 FR 8121, Mar. 28, 1973]

§ 160.055-6 Construction—nonstandard, life preservers.

(a) *General.* The construction methods used for a nonstandard life preserver must be equivalent to the requirements in § 160.055-5 for a standard life preserver and also meet the requirements in this section.

(b) *Size.* Each nonstandard life preserver must contain the following volume of plastic foam buoyant material, determined by the displacement method:

(1) 700 cubic inches or more for an adult size;

(2) 350 cubic inches or more for a child size.

(c) *Arrangement of buoyant materials.* The buoyant material in nonstandard life preservers must:

(1) Be arranged to hold the wearer in an upright or backward position with head and face out of water;

(2) Have no tendency to turn the wearer face downward in the water; and

(3) Be arranged so that 68 to 73 percent of the total is located in the front of the life preserver.

(d) *Adjustment, fit, and donning.* Each nonstandard life preserver must be capable of being:

(1) Worn reversed;

(2) Adjusted to fit a range of wearers for the type designed; and

(3) Donned in a time comparable to that of a standard life preserver.

[CGD 72–163R, 38 FR 8121, Mar. 28, 1973]

§ 160.055–7 Sampling, tests, and inspections.

(a) Production tests and inspections must be conducted by the manufacturer of a life preserver and the accepted laboratory inspector in accordance with this section and § 160.001–5.

(b) *Buoyancy test.* The buoyancy of the pad inserts from the life preserver shall be determined according to § 160.001–5(f) of this part with each compartment of the buoyant pad insert covers slit so as not to entrap air. The period of submersion must be at least 48 hours.

(c) *Buoyancy required.* The buoyant pad inserts from Model 3 adult life preservers shall provide not less than 25 pounds buoyancy in fresh water, and the pads from Model 5 child life preservers shall provide not less than 16.5 pounds buoyancy.

[CGD 95–028, 62 FR 51215, Sept. 30, 1997]

EFFECTIVE DATE NOTE: At 62 FR 51215, Sept. 30, 1997, § 160.055–7 was revised, effective Oct. 30, 1997.

§ 160.055–8 Marking.

Each life preserver must have the following information clearly marked in waterproof lettering:

(a) In letters three-fourths of an inch or more in height;

(1) Adult (for persons weighing over 90 pounds); or

(2) Child (for persons weighing less than 90 pounds).

(b) In letters that can be read at a distance of 2 feet:

Type I or Type V Personal Flotation Device. Inspected and tested in accordance with U.S. Coast Guard regulations.
(Name of buoyant material) buoyant material provides a minimum buoyant force of (22 lb. or 11 lb.).
Approved for use on all vessels by persons weighing (90 lb. or more, or less than 90 lb.).
U.S. Coast Guard Approval No. 160.055/(assigned manufacturer's No.)/(Revision No.); (Model No.).
(Name and address of manufacturer or distributor).
(Lot No.)

[CGD 72–163R, 38 FR 8121, Mar. 28, 1973, as amended by CGD 75–008, 43 FR 9771, Mar. 9, 1978; 43 FR 10913, Mar. 11, 1978]

§ 160.055–9 Procedure for approval—standard and nonstandard life preservers.

(a) *General.* Manufacturers seeking approval of a life preserver design shall follow the procedures of subpart 159.005 of this chapter, as explained in § 160.001–3 of this part.

(b) *Assignment of inspector; standard life preservers.* Upon receipt of an approval of a standard life preserver, a Coast Guard inspector is assigned to the factory to:

(1) Observe the production facilities and manufacturing methods;

(2) Select from a lot of 10 manufactured life preservers or more, three or more of each model for examination;

(3) Test the selected sample for compliance with the requirements of this subpart; and

(4) Forward to the Commandant a copy of his report of the tests and the production and manufacturing facilities, a specimen life preserver selected from those already manufactured but not tested, and one copy of an affidavit for each material used in the life preservers.

(b-1) *Approval number—standard life preserver.* An approval number is assigned to the manufacturer by the Coast Guard for a standard life preserver found to be in compliance with the requirements of this subpart.

(c) *Assignment of inspector—nonstandard life preserver.* Upon receipt of an application from a manufacturer for approval of nonstandard life preservers, an inspector is assigned to the factory to:

(1) Observe the production facilities and manufacturing methods;

(2) Select three samples of life preservers of each model for which approval is desired;

(3) Forward to the Commandant:

(i) Three samples of each model of life preserver;

(ii) A copy of the inspector's report of tests and the production and manufacturing facilities; and

(iii) Four copies each of fully dimensioned, full-scale drawings showing all details of construction of the sample life preservers submitted, material affidavits, and four copies of a bill of materials showing all materials used in construction of the life preservers submitted by the manufacturer.

(c-1) *Approval number—nonstandard life preserver.* An official approval number is assigned to the manufacturer by the Coast Guard for a nonstandard life preserver approved after tests.

(d) *Private brand labels.* Private brand labels are those bearing the name and address of a distributor in lieu of the manufacturer. In order for a manufacturer to apply for an approval number to be used on such a private brand label, he shall forward a letter of request to the Commander of the Coast Guard District in which the factory is located, setting forth the life preservers involved, together with a letter from his distributor also requesting that approval be issued. The manufacturer's request for approval together with that of his distributor, will be forwarded to the Commandant, and when deemed advisable, an approval number or numbers will be issued in the name of the distributor. Approvals issued to a distributor under such an arrangement shall apply only to life preservers made by the manufacturer named on the certificate of approval, and this manufacturer shall be responsible for compliance of the life preservers with the requirements of this subpart.

[CGFR 66–73, 32 FR 5500, Apr. 4, 1967, as amended by CGD 163R, 38 FR 8121, Mar. 28, 1973; CGD 78–012, 43 FR 27154, June 22, 1978; CGD 88–070, 53 FR 34536, Sept. 7, 1988; CGD 95–028, 62 FR 51215, Sept. 30, 1997]

EFFECTIVE DATE NOTE: At 62 FR 51215, Sept. 30, 1997, § 160.055–9 was amended by revising paragraph (a), effective Oct. 30, 1997.

Subpart 160.056—Rescue Boat

SOURCE: CGFR 61–15, 26 FR 9300, Sept. 30, 1961, unless otherwise noted.

§ 160.056–1 General requirements.

(a) Rescue boats accepted and in use prior to the effective date of this subpart may be continued in service if in satisfactory condition.

(b) All rescue boats must be properly constructed, of such form as to be readily maneuverable, and be of the open rowboat type. They shall be suitable for use of three persons.

(c) Rescue boats shall be constructed of materials acceptable to the Officer in Charge, Marine Inspection, having jurisdiction of construction.

§ 160.056–2 Construction.

(a) *General.* Rescue boats shall be square-sterned, of normal proportions, not less than 11 feet nor more than 14 feet in length. The length shall be the overall horizontal distance from bow to stern.

(b) *Construction.* The method of construction shall be such as is accepted as good engineering practice in the case of the specific material used. The hull shall be suitably stiffened to assure adequate strength.

(c) *Weight.* The weight of the rescue boat, fully equipped, shall not exceed 225 pounds.

(d) *Seats.* The rescue boat shall be fitted with three thwarts. The middle thwart shall be arranged as the rowing seat.

(e) *Internal buoyancy.* Buoyant material of suitable unicellular plastic foam shall be installed in the rescue boat. This material shall be protected from mechanical damage. It shall be distributed uniformly in the boat and such that at least one-quarter of the required volume is located at the sides of the boat. The minimum amount of buoyant material, in cubic feet, shall be determined by the following:

$$B = 2 + (W - W + d) + 62.4 - c \qquad (1)$$

Where:

B = Volume of buoyant material required in cubic feet.
W = Weight of equipped boat, in pounds.
d = Specific gravity of hull material.
c = Density of buoyant material, in pounds per cubic foot.

§ 160.056–3 Fittings and equipment.

(a) *Fittings.* (1) The rescue boat shall be fitted with one pair of rowlock sockets. Detachable rowlocks shall be permanently attached to the boat by chain or other suitable means.

(2) At least one eyebolt, ring, or other fitting suitable for attaching a painter shall be fitted to the bow and stern.

(b) *Equipment.* (1) The rescue boat shall be provided with one pair of oars of suitable size and material.

(2) A painter shall be attached to the bow and to the stern fittings. Each shall be of suitable material, at least ⅜-inch in diameter, and at least 30 feet long.

§ 160.056–4 Approval tests of prototype rescue boat.

(a) *Drop test.* The rescue boat, fully equipped, shall be dropped, in a free fall, from a ten-foot height into water. No damage which would render the rescue boat unserviceable shall result from this drop.

(b) *Stability and freeboard test.* The rescue boat shall have sufficient stability and freeboard so that the gunwale on the low side shall not be submerged with 350 pounds placed nine inches from the side in way of and about the level of the middle thwart.

(c) *Rescue boarding test.* With one man in the rowing position, a second kneeling on the stern thwart facing aft, and a third man balanced on the transom, the minimum freeboard of the transom shall be five inches. The men should average 165 pounds each. This test simulates the rescue of a person over the transom by a two-man boat crew.

(d) *Rowing test.* Three men, averaging 165 pounds each, shall be seated on the centerline of the boat, one on each thwart. One man, in the rowing position, using ordinary rowing technique, shall demonstrate the satisfactory course keeping and maneuvering characteristics of the boat in the ahead and astern directions.

§ 160.056–6 Name plate.

(a) Each rescue boat shall have permanently fitted at the transom a metal name plate, galvanically compatible with the hull material, and bearing information relating to the testing and approval of the prototype boat. Either raised or indented letters shall be used.

(b) The following information shall appear on the name plate:

RESCUE BOAT

U.S.C.G. Specification 160.056
Prototype approved ——————————
                                              (Date)
Approved by OCMI ——————————
                                              (Port)
Date of manufacture ——————————
                                              (Date)
Manufacturer's serial No. ——————
Manufacturer's name and address ————

§ 160.056–7 Procedure for approval.

(a) The manufacturer shall submit a request for approval to the Officer in Charge, Marine Inspection, having jurisdiction of the place of manufacture of the rescue boat.

(b) Formal plans will not be required. However, a combined general arrangement and construction plan is required, which includes principal dimensions, and descriptive data of hull material, buoyant material, and equipment.

(c) When plans and data are satisfactory, the Officer in Charge, Marine Inspection, will assign a marine inspector to conduct the tests required by § 160.056–4.

(d) Upon successful completion of the test, the inspector shall submit a written report to the Officer in Charge, Marine Inspection. A copy of this report, with plans and photographs, shall be forwarded to the Commandant for record purposes. The date of approval and the marine inspector's initials shall be indicated in this report.

(e) The Officer in Charge, Marine Inspection, shall issue a letter to the manufacturer indicating that approval of the rescue boat has been granted, and will include any conditions imposed. A copy of this approval letter shall be forwarded to the District Commander and to the Commandant.

(f) If a rescue boat is required on short notice, a boat may be approved on an individual basis: *Provided,* That the requirements in this subpart are met to the satisfaction of the Officer in Charge Marine Inspection. Sketches of the boat showing alterations may be submitted in lieu of the manufacturer's general arrangement and construction plan. Under these circumstances, the letter indicating that approval of the rescue boat has been granted shall be issued to the vessel using the boat.

[CGFR 61–15, 26 FR 9300, Sept. 30, 1961, as amended by CGFR 65–9, 30 FR 11480, Sept. 8, 1965]

Subpart 160.057—Floating Orange Smoke Distress Signals (15 Minutes)

SOURCE: CGD 76–048a and 76–048b, 44 FR 73091, Dec. 17, 1979, unless otherwise noted.

§ 160.057-1 Incorporations by reference.

(a) The following are incorporated by reference into this subpart:

(1) "The Color Names Dictionary" in *Color: Universal Language and Dictionary of Names,* National Bureau of Standards Special Publication 440, December 1976.

(2) "Development of a Laboratory Test for Evaluation of the Effectiveness of Smoke Signals," National Bureau of Standards Report 4792, July 1956.

(b) NBS Special Publication 440 may be obtained by ordering from the Superintendent of Documents, U.S. Government Printing Office, Washington, DC 20402 (Order by SD Catalog No. C13.10:440).

(c) NBS Report 4792 may be obtained from the Commandant (G–MSE), U.S. Coast Guard, Washington, DC 20593–0001.

(d) Approval to incorporate by reference the materials listed in this section was obtained from the Director of the Federal Register on November 1 and 29, 1979. The materials are on file in the Federal Register library.

[CGD 76–048a and 76–048b, 44 FR 73091, Dec. 17, 1979, as amended by CGD 82–063b, 48 FR 4782, Feb. 3, 1983; CGD 88–070, 53 FR 34536, Sept. 7, 1988; CGD 95–072, 60 FR 50467, Sept. 29, 1995; CGD 96–041, 61 FR 50733, Sept. 27, 1996]

§ 160.057-2 Type.

(a) Floating orange. smoke distress signals specified by this subpart shall be of one type which shall consist essentially of an outer container, ballast, an air chamber, an inner container, the smoke producing composition, and an igniter mechanism. Alternate arrangements which conform to the performance requirements of this specification will be given special consideration.

(b) [Reserved]

§ 160.057-3 Materials, workmanship, construction, and performance requirements.

(a) *Materials.* The materials shall conform strictly to the specifications and drawings submitted by the manufacturer and approved by the Commandant. Metal for containers shall be not less than 0.5 mm (0.020 in.) in thickness. Other dimensions or materials may be considered upon special request when presented with supporting data. Igniter systems shall be of corrosion-resistant metal. The combustible material shall be of such nature that it will not deteriorate during long storage, nor when subjected to frigid or tropical climates, or both.

(b) *Workmanship.* Floating orange smoke distress signals shall be of first class workmanship and shall be free from imperfections of manufacture affecting their appearance or that may affect their serviceability.

(c) *Construction.* The outer container shall be cylindrical and of a size suitable for intended use. All sheet metal seams should be hook jointed and soldered. The whole container shall be covered with two coats of waterproof paint or other equivalent protection system. The igniter mechanism shall operate and provide ignition of the signal automatically when the ring life buoy to which it is attached is thrown overboard.

(d) *Performance.* Signals shall meet all the inspection and test requirements contained in § 160.057-4.

§ 160.057-4 Approval and production tests.

(a) *Approval tests.* The manufacturer must produce a lot of at least 20 signals from which samples must be taken for testing for approval under § 160.057-7. The approval tests are the operational tests and technical tests in paragraphs (c) and (d) of this section. The approval tests must be conducted by an independent laboratory accepted by the Commandant under § 159.010 of this chapter.

(b) *Production inspections and tests.* Production inspections and tests of each lot of signals produced must be conducted under the procedures in § 159.007 of this chapter. Signals from a rejected lot must not be represented as meeting this subpart or as being approved by the Coast Guard. If the manufacturer identifies the cause of the rejection of a lot of signals, the signals in the lot may be reworked by the manufacturer to correct the problem. Samples from the rejected lot must be retested in order to be accepted. Records shall be kept of the reasons for rejection, the reworking performed on the rejected lot, and the results of the second test.

(1) *Lot size.* For the purposes of sampling the production of signals, a lot must consist of not more than 1,200 signals. Lots must be numbered serially by the manufacturer. A new lot must be started with: (i) Any change in construction details, (ii) any change in sources of raw materials, or (iii) the start of production on a new production line or on a previously discontinued production line.

(2) *Inspections and tests by the manufacturer.* The manufacturer's quality control procedures must include inspection of materials entering into construction of the signals and inspection of the finished signals, to determine that signals are being produced in accordance with the approved plans. Samples from each lot must be tested in accordance with the operational tests in paragraph (c) of this section.

(3) *Inspections and tests by an independent laboratory.* An independent laboratory accepted by the Commandant under § 159.010 of this chapter must perform or supervise the inspections and tests under paragraph (b)(2) of this section at least 4 times a year, unless the number of lots produced in a year is less than four. The inspections and tests must occur at least once during each quarterly period, unless no lots are produced during that period. If less than four lots are produced, the laboratory must perform or supervise the inspection and testing of each lot. In addition, the laboratory must perform or supervise the technical tests in paragraph (d) of this section at least once for every ten lots of signals produced, except that the number of technical tests must be at least one but not more than four per year. If a lot of signals tested by the independent laboratory is rejected, the laboratory must perform or supervise the inspections and tests of the reworked lot and the next lot of signals produced. The tests of each reworked lot and the next lot produced must not be counted for the purpose of meeting the requirement for the annual number of inspections and tests performed or supervised by the independent laboratory.

(c) *Operational tests.* Each lot of signals must be sampled and tested as follows:

(1) *Sampling procedure and accept/reject criteria.* A sample of signals must be selected at random from the lot. The size of the sample must be the individual sample size in Table 160.057-4(c)(1) corresponding to the lot size. Each signal in the sample is tested as prescribed in the test procedure in paragraph (c)(2) of this section. Each signal that has a defect listed in the table of defects (Table 160.057-4(c)(2)) is assigned a score (failure percent) in accordance with that table. In the case of multiple defects, only the score having the highest numerical value is assigned to that signal If the sum of all the failure percents (cumulative failure percent) for the number of units in the sample is less than or equal to the accept criterion, the lot is accepted. If this sum is equal to or more than the reject criterion the lot is rejected.

If the cumulative failure percent falls between the accept and reject criteria, another sample is selected from the production lot and the operational tests are repeated. The cumulative failure percent of each sample tested is added to that of the previous samples to obtain the cumulative failure percent for all the signals tested (cumulative sample size). Additional samples are tested and the tests repeated until either the accept or reject criterion for the cumulative sample size is met. If any signal in the sample explodes when fired, or ignites in a way that could burn or otherwise injure the person firing it, the lot is rejected without further testing. (This procedure is diagrammed in figure 160.057-4(c)).

(2) *Test procedure.* Each sample signal (specimen) must be tested as follows:

(i) *Conditioning of test specimens—water resistance.* Immerse specimen horizontally with uppermost portion of the signal approximately 25 mm (1 in.) below the surface of the water for a period of 24 hours.

(ii) *Smoke emitting time.* Ignite specimen according to the directions printed on the signal and place signal in tub or barrel of water. The smoke emitting time of a specimen shall be obtained by stop watch measurements from the time of distinct, sustained smoke emission until it ceases. There shall be no flame emission during the entire smoke emitting time of the signal. The smoke emitting time for a specimen shall not be less than 15 minutes. When the tests are performed or supervised by an independent laboratory, this test shall be conducted with approximately 6 mm (¼ in.) of gasoline covering the water in the tub or barrel. The gasoline vapors shall not ignite during the entire smoke emitting time of the signal.

(iii) *Ignition and smoke emitting characteristics.* Test specimens shall ignite and emit smoke properly when the directions on the signal are followed. Test specimens shall not ignite explosively in a manner that might be dangerous to the user or persons close by. Test specimens shall emit smoke at a uniform rate while floating in calm to rough water. Signals should be so constructed that water submerging the signal in moderately heavy seas will not cause it to become inoperable.

TABLE 160.057–4(C)(1)—ACCEPT AND REJECT CRITERIA FOR OPERATIONAL TEST LOTS

Lot size	Individual sample size	Sample	Cumulative sample size	Accept[1]	Reject[1]
150 or less.	2	First	2	([2])	200
		Second	4	([2])	200
		Third	6	0	200
		Fourth ..	8	0	300
		Fifth	10	100	300
		Sixth	12	100	300
		Seventh	14	299	300
151 to 500.	3	First	3	([2])	200
		Second	6	0	300
		Third	9	0	300
		Fourth ..	12	100	400
		Fifth	15	200	400
		Sixth	18	300	500
		Seventh	21	499	500
More than 501.	5	First	5	([2])	300
		Second	10	0	300
		Third	15	100	400
		Fourth ..	20	200	500
		Fifth	25	300	600
		Sixth	30	400	600
		Seventh	35	699	700

[1] Cumulative failure percent.
[2] Lot may not be accepted. Next sample must be tested.

TABLE 160.057–4(C)(2)

Kind of defects	Percentage of failures
a. Failure to ignite	100
b. Ignites or burns dangerously	100
c. Nonuniform smoke emitting rate	50
d. Smoke-emitting time less than 70 percent of specified time	100
e. Smoke-emitting time at least 70 percent but less than 80 percent of specified time	75
f. Smoke-emitting time at least 80 percent but less than 90 percent of specified time	50
g. Smoke-emitting time at least 90 percent but less than 100 percent of specified time	25

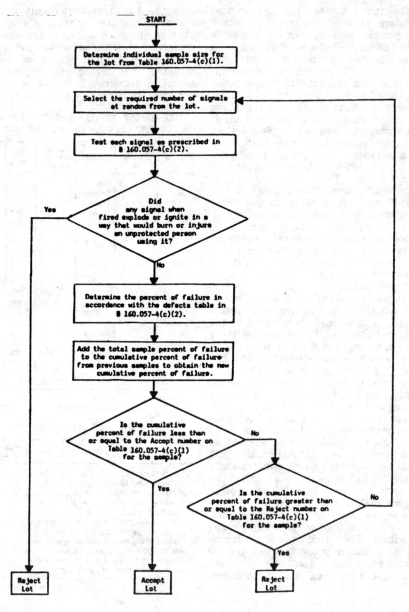

Figure 160.057-4(c). Operational test procedure.

(d) *Technical tests.* One signal must be subjected to each of the following tests. Each signal must pass the test in order for the lot of signals to be accepted.

(1) *Drop test.* One signal must be attached to a ring life buoy and arranged

to be ignited by the dropping buoy in the same manner as it would be when used on a vessel. The signal and buoy must be mounted at least 27 m (90 ft.) above the surface of a body of water. The buoy is released and must cause the signal to ignite and fall to the water with the buoy. The signal must remain afloat and emit smoke at least 15 minutes.

(2) *Wave test.* A signal shall be tested in a manner simulating its use at sea. The signal shall be ignited and thrown overboard under conditions where waves are at least 30 cm (1 ft.) high. The smoke emitting time must be for the full 15 minutes and the signal shall float in such a manner that it shall function properly during this test. The signal shall be attached to a ring life buoy in accordance with the manufacturer's instructions.

(3) *Underwater smoke emission.* Condition the signal in accordance with paragraph (c)(2)(i) of this section. Ignite specimen and let it burn about 15 seconds in air. Submerge the burning signal in water in a vertical position with head down. Obtain underwater smoke emission time by stop watch measurements from time of submersion until smoke emission ceases. The test specimen shall emit smoke under water not less than 30 seconds when subjected to this test.

(4) *Elevated Temperature, Humidity and Storage.* Place specimen in a thermostatically controlled even-temperature oven held at 75 °C. with not less than 90 percent relative humidity for 72 hours. Remove specimen and store at room temperature (20° to 25 °C.) with approximately 65 percent relative humidity for 10 days. If for any reason it is not possible to operate the oven continuously for the 72-hour period, it may be operated at the required temperature and humidity for 8 hours out of each 24 during the 72-hour conditioning period. (Total of 24 hours on and 48 hours off.) The signal shall not ignite or decompose during this conditioning. The signal shall ignite and operate satisfactorily following this conditioning.

(5) *Spontaneous ignition.* Place the specimen in a thermostatically controlled even-temperature oven held at 75 °C. with not more than 10% relative humidity for 48 consecutive hours. The signal must not ignite or undergo marked decomposition.

(6) *Susceptibility to explosion.* Remove smoke composition from signal and punch a small hole in the composition. Insert a No. 6 commercial blasting cap. Ignite the cap. The test specimen shall not explode or ignite.

(7) *Corrosion resistance.* Expose the complete specimen with cover secured hand-tight to a finely divided spray of 20 percent by weight sodium chloride solution at a temperature between 32 °C and 38 °C (90 °F and 100 °F) for 100 hours. The container and cap must not be corroded in any fashion that would impair their proper functioning.

(8) *Color of smoke.* Ignite specimen in the open air in daytime according to the directions printed on the signal, and determine the smoke color by direct visual comparison of the unshadowed portions of the smoke with a color chart held so as to receive the same daylight illumination as the unshadowed portions of the smoke. The color of the smoke must be orange as defined by sections 13 and 14 of the "Color Names Dictionary" (colors 34–39 and 48–54).

(9) *Volume and density of smoke.* The test specimen shall show less than 70 percent transmission for not less than 12 minutes when measured with apparatus having a light path of 19 cm (7½ in.), an optical system aperture of +3.7 degrees, and an entrance air flow of 18.4m^3 per minute (650 cu. ft. per minute), such apparatus to be as described in National Bureau of Standards Report No. 4792.

§160.057–5 **Marking.**

(a) *Directions for use.* Each floating orange smoke distress signal shall be plainly and indelibly marked in black lettering not less than 3 mm (⅛ in.) high "Approved for daytime use only", and in black lettering not less than 5 mm (³⁄₁₆ in.) high with the word "Directions". Immediately below shall be similarly marked in black lettering not less than 3 mm (⅛ in.) high in numbered paragraphs, and in simple and easily understood wording, instructions to be followed to make the device operative. Pasted-on labels are not acceptable.

(b) *Other markings.* (1) There shall be embossed or die-stamped, in the outer container in figures not less than 5 mm (³⁄₁₆ in.) high, numbers, indicating the month and year of manufacture, thus: "6-54" indicating June 1954. The outer container shall also be plainly and indelibly marked with the commercial designation of the signal, the words "Floating Orange Smoke Distress Signal (15 minutes)", name and address of the manufacturer, the Coast Guard Approval No., the service life expiration date (month and year to be entered by the manufacturer), the month and year of manufacture and the lot number.

(2) In addition to any other marking placed on the smallest packing carton or box containing floating orange smoke distress signals, such cartons or boxes shall be plainly and indelibly marked to show the service life expiration date, the month and year of manufacture, and the lot number.

(3) The largest carton or box in which the manufacturer ships signals must be marked with the following or equivalent words: "Keep under cover in a dry place."

(c) *Marking of expiration date.* The expiration date must be not more than 42 months from the date of manufacture.

NOTE: Compliance with the labeling requirements of this section does not relieve the manufacturer of the responsibility of complying with the label requirements of 15 U.S.C. 1263, the Federal Hazardous Substances Act.

§ 160.057-7 Procedure for approval.

(a) Signals are approved by the Coast Guard under the procedures in subpart 159.005 of this chapter.

(b) [Reserved]

Subpart 160.058—Desalter Kits, Sea Water, for Merchant Vessels

SOURCE: CGFR 65-9, 30 FR 11483, Sept. 8, 1965, unless otherwise noted.

§ 160.058-1 Applicable specification.

(a) *Specification.* The following specification, of the issue in effect on the date the desalter kits are manufactured, forms a part of this subpart:

(1) *Military specification.* MIL-D-5531D—Desalter Kit, Sea Water, Mark 2.

(2) [Reserved]

(b) *Copies on file.* A copy of the specification referred to in this section shall be kept on file by the manufacturer, together with the approved plans and certificate of approval. The Military Specification may be obtained from the Commanding Officer, Naval Supply Depot, 5801 Tabor Avenue, Philadelphia, Pa., 19120.

§ 160.058-2 Type.

(a) Desalter kits specified by this subpart shall be of the type described in the specification listed in §160.058-1(a)(1).

(b) [Reserved]

§ 160.058-3 Materials, workmanship, construction and performance requirements.

(a) The materials, construction, workmanship, general and detail requirements shall conform to the requirements of the specification listed in §160.058-1(a)(1), except as otherwise specifically provided by this subpart.

(b) [Reserved]

§ 160.058-4 Inspections.

(a) Desalter kits specified by this subpart are not inspected at regularly scheduled factory inspections; however, the Commander of the Coast Guard District in which the desalter kits are manufactured may detail a marine inspector at any time to visit places where desalter kits are manufactured to check materials and construction methods and to satisfy himself that the desalter kits are being manufactured in compliance with the requirements of the specification listed in §160.058-1(a)(1) as modified by this specification and are suitable for the intended purpose. The manufacturer shall admit the marine inspector to his plant and shall provide a suitable place and the necessary apparatus for the use of the marine inspector in conducting tests at the place of manufacture.

(b) [Reserved]

§ 160.058-5 Labeling and marking.

(a) In addition to the marking and instructions required by the specification listed in § 160.058-1(a)(1), the Coast Guard approval number shall be included. The contract number may be omitted.

(b) [Reserved]

Subpart 160.060—Specification for a Buoyant Vest, Unicellular Polyethylene Foam, Adult and Child

§ 160.060-1 Incorporation by reference.

(a) *Specifications and Standards.* This subpart makes reference to the following documents:

(1) [Reserved]

(2) Military Specification:

MIL-W-530F-Webbing, Textile, Cotton, General Purpose, Natural or in Colors.

(3) Federal Standards:

No. 191-Textile Test Methods.
No. 751A-Stitches, Seams, and Stitchings.

(4) Coast Guard Specification:

164.013-Foam, Unicellular Polyethylene (Buoyant, Slab, Slitted Trigonal Pattern)

(b) *Plans.* The following plans, of the issue in effect on the date buoyant vests are manufacture, form a part of this subpart:

Dwg. No. 160.060-1:

Sheet 1—Cutting Pattern and General Arrangement, Model AY.
Sheet 2—Cutting Pattern and General Arrangement, Model CYM.
Sheet 3—Cutting Pattern and General Arrangement, Model CYS.
Sheet 4—Insert Pattern, Model AY.
Sheet 5—Insert Pattern, Model CYM.
Sheet 6—Insert Pattern, Model CYS.

(c) *Copies on file.* Copies of the specifications and plans referred to in this section shall be kept on file by the manufacturer together with the Certificate of Approval.

(1) The Coast Guard plans and specifications may be obtained upon request from the Commandant (G–MSE), U.S. Coast Guard, Washington, DC 20593–0001 or a recognized laboratory listed in § 160.060-8b.

(2) The Federal Specifications and Standard may be purchased from the Business Service Center, General Services Administration, Washington, DC, 20407.

(3) The Military Specification may be obtained from the Commanding Offi-

cer, Naval Supply Depot, 5801 Tabor Avenue, Philadelphia, Pa., 19120.

[CGFR 65–37, 30 FR 11590, Sept. 10, 1965, as amended by CGD 72–90R, 37 FR 10839, May 31, 1972; CGD 78–012, 43 FR 27153, 27154, June 22, 1978; CGD 82–063b, 48 FR 4782, Feb. 3, 1983; CGD 88–070, 53 FR 34536, Sept. 7, 1988; CGD 95–072, 60 FR 50467, Sept. 29, 1995; CGD 96–041, 61 FR 50733, Sept. 27, 1996]

§ 160.060-2 Type and model.

Each buoyant vest specified in this subpart is a:

(a) Standard:

(1) Model AY, adult (for persons weighing over 90 pounds); or

(2) Model CYM, child, medium (for children weighing from 50 to 90 pounds); or

(3) Model CYS, child, small (for children weighing less than 50 pounds); or

(b) Nonstandard:

(1) Model,[1] adult (for persons weighing over 90 pounds);

(2) Model,[1] child, medium (for persons weighing from 50 to 90 pounds) or

(3) Model,[1] child, small (for persons weighing less than 50 pounds).

[CGD 72–163R, 38 FR 8122, Mar. 28, 1973]

§ 160.060-3 Materials—standard vests.

(a) *General.* All components used in the construction of buoyant vests must meet the applicable requirements of subpart 164.019 of this chapter. The requirements for materials specified in this section are minimum requirements, and consideration will be given to the use of alternate materials in lieu of those specified. Detailed technical data and samples of all proposed alternate materials must be submitted for approval before those materials are incorporated in the finished product.

(b) *Unicellular polyethylene foam.* The unicellular polyethylene foam shall be all new material complying with specification subpart 164.013 of this subchapter.

(c) *Envelope.* The buoyant vest envelope, or cover, shall be made from 39", 2.85 cotton jeans cloth, with a thread count of approximately 96 × 64. The finished goods shall weigh not less than

---

[1] A model designation for a nonstandard vest is to be assigned by the individual manufactured and must be different from any standard vest.

4.2 ounces per square yard, shall have thread count of not less than 94 × 60, and shall have a breaking strength of not less than 85 pounds in the warp and 50 pounds in the filling. Other cotton fabrics having a weight and breaking strength not less than the above will be acceptable. There are no restrictions as to color, but the fastness of the color to laundering, water, crocking, and light shall be rated "good" when tested in accordance with Federal Test Method Standard No. 191, Methods 5610, 5630, 5650, and 5660.

(d) *Tie tapes and body strap loops.* The tie tapes and body strap loops for both adult and child sizes must be ¾-inch cotton webbing meeting the requirements of military specification MIL-T-43566 (Class I) for Type I webbing.

(d-1) *Body straps.* The complete body strap assembly including hardware, must have a minimum breaking strength of 150 pounds for an adult size and 115 pounds for a child size. The specifications for the webbing are as follows:

(1) For an adult size vest, the webbing must be 1 inch.

(2) For a child size vest, the webbing must be three-quarter inch and meet military specification MIL-W-530 for Type IIa webbing.

(e) [Reserved]

(f) *Thread.* Each thread must meet the requirements of subpart 164.023 of this chapter. Only one kind of thread may be used in each seam.

[CGFR 65-37, 30 FR 11590, Sept. 10, 1965, as amended by CGD 72-90R, 37 FR 10839, May 31, 1972; CGD 72-163R, 38 FR 8122, Mar. 28, 1973; CGD 73-130R, 39 FR 20684, June 13, 1974; CGD 78-012, 43 FR 27154, June 22, 1978; CGD 82-063b, 48 FR 4782, Feb. 3, 1983; CGD 88-070, 53 FR 34536, Sept. 7, 1988; CGD 84-068, 58 FR 29494, May 20, 1993]

§ 160.060-3a Materials—Dee ring and snap hook assemblies and other instruments of closure for buoyant vests.

(a) *Specifications.* Dee ring and snap hook assemblies and other instruments of closure for buoyant vests may have decorative platings in any thickness and must meet the following specifications:

(1) The device must be constructed of inherently corrosion resistant materials. As used in this section the term *inherently corrosion resistant materials* includes, but is not limited to, brass, bronze, and stainless steel.

(2) The size of the opening of the device must be consistent with the webbing which will pass through the opening.

(b) *Testing requirements.* Dee ring and snap hook assemblies and other instruments of closure for buoyant vests must—

(1) Be tested for weathering. The Coast Guard will determine which one or more of the following tests will be used:

(i) Application of a 20 percent sodium-chloride solution spray at a temperature of 95 °F (35 °C) for a period of 240 hours in accordance with the procedures contained in method 811 of the Federal Test Method Standard No. 151.

(ii) Exposure to a carbon-arc weatherometer for a period of 100 hours.

(iii) Submergence for a period of 100 hours in each of the following:

(*a*) Leaded gasoline.

(*b*) Gum turpentine.

(iv) Exposure to a temperature of 0°±5 °F (17.6±2.775 °C) for 24 hours; and

(2) Within 5 minutes of completion of the weathering test required by paragraph (b)(1) of this section, the assembly must be attached to a support and bear 150 pounds for an adult size and 115 pounds for a child size for 10 minutes at ambient temperatures without breaking or distorting.

[CGD 73-130R, 39 FR 20684, June 13, 1974]

§ 160.060-4 Materials—nonstandard vests.

(a) *General.* All materials used in nonstandard buoyant vests must be equivalent to those specified in § 160.060-3 and be obtained from a supplier who furnishes an affidavit in accordance with the requirements in § 160.060-3(a).

(b) *Reinforcing tape.* When used, the reinforcing tape around the neck shall be ¾″ cotton tape weighing not less than 0.18 ounce per linear yard having a minimum breaking strength of not less than 120 pounds.

[CGFR 65-37, 30 FR 11590, Sept. 10, 1965, as amended by CGD 72-163R, 38 FR 8122, Mar. 28, 1973]

§ 160.060-5 Construction—standard vests.

(a) *General.* This specification covers buoyant vests which essentially consist of a fabric envelope in which are enclosed inserts of buoyant material arranged and distributed so as to provide the flotation characteristics and buoyancy required to hold the wearer in an upright or slightly backward position with head and face out of water. The buoyant vests are also fitted with straps and hardware to provide for proper adjustment and close and comfortable fit to the bodies of various size wearers.

(b) *Envelope.* The envelope or cover shall be made of three pieces. Two pieces of fabric shall be cut to the pattern shown on Dwg. No. 160.060-1, Sheet 1 for the adult size, and Sheets 2 and 3 for child sizes, and joined together with a third piece which forms a 2¼″ finished gusset strip all around. Reinforcing strips of the same material as the envelope shall be stitched to the inside of the front piece of the envelope in way of the strap attachments as shown by the drawings.

(c) *Buoyant inserts.* The unicellular plastic foam buoyant inserts shall be cut and formed as shown on Dwg. No. 160.060-1, Sheets 4, 5, and 6 for the adult, child medium, and child small sizes, respectively.

(d) *Tie tapes, body straps, and hardware.* The tie tapes, body straps, and hardware shall be arranged as shown on the drawings and attached to the envelope with the seams and stitching indicated.

(e) *Stitching.* All stitching shall be short lock stitch conforming to Stitch Type 301 of Federal Standard No. 751, and there shall be not less than 7 nor more than 9 stitches to the inch.

(f) *Workmanship.* Buoyant vests shall be of first-class workmanship and shall be free from any defects materially affecting their appearance or serviceability.

[CGFR 65-37, 30 FR 11590, Sept. 10, 1965, as amended by CGD 72-163R, 38 FR 8122, Mar. 28, 1973]

§ 160.060-6 Construction—nonstandard vests.

(a) *General.* The construction methods used for a nonstandard buoyant vest must be equivalent to the requirements in § 160.060-5 for standard vests and also meet the requirements specified in this section.

(b) *Sizes.* Each nonstandard vest must contain the following volume of unicellular polyethylene foam buoyant material, determined by the displacement method:

(1) Five hundred cubic inches or more for the adult size, for persons weighing over 90 pounds.

(2) Three hundred and fifty cubic inches or more for a child medium size, for children weighing from 50 to 90 pounds.

(3) Two hundred and twenty-five cubic inches or more for children weighing less than 50 pounds.

(c) *Arrangement of buoyant material.* The buoyant material in a nonstandard vest must:

(1) Be arranged to hold the wearer in an upright or backward position with head and face out of water;

(2) Have no tendency to turn the wearer face downward in the water; and

(3) Be arranged so that 70 to 75 percent of the total is located in the front of the vest.

(d) *Neck opening.* Each cloth covered nonstandard vest must have at the neck opening:

(1) A gusset; or

(2) Reinforcing tape.

(e) *Adjustment, fit, and donning.* Each nonstandard vest must be made with adjustments to:

(1) Fit a range of wearers for the type designed; and

(2) Facilitate donning time for an uninitiated person.

[CGD 72-163R, 38 FR 8122, Mar. 28, 1973]

§ 160.060-7 Inspections and tests— standard and nonstandard vests.[1]

(a) *General.* Manufacturers of listed and labeled buoyant vests shall—

(1) Maintain quality control of the materials used, the manufacturing methods, and the finished product to meet the applicable requirements of

_____

[1] The manufacturer of a personal flotation device must meet 33 CFR 181.701 through 33 CFR 181.705 which require an instruction pamphlet for each device that is sold or offered for sale for use on recreational boats.

this subpart by conducting sufficient inspections and tests of representative samples and components produced;

(2) Make available to the recognized laboratory inspector and the Coast Guard inspector, upon request, records of tests conducted by the manufacturer and records of materials used during production of the device, including affidavits by suppliers; and

(3) Permit any examination, inspection and test required by the recognized laboratory or the Coast Guard for a produced listed and labeled device, either at the place of manufacture or some other location.

(b) *Lot size and sampling.* (1) A lot shall consist of 500 buoyant vests or fewer;

(2) A new lot begins after any change or modification in materials used or manufacturing methods employed;

(3) The manufacturer of the buoyant vests shall notify the recognized laboratory when a lot is ready for inspection;

(4) The manufacturer shall select samples in accordance with the requirements in Table 160.060-7(b)(4) from each lot of buoyant vests to be tested for buoyancy in accordance with paragraph (e) of this section.

TABLE 160.060-7(B)(4)—SAMPLE FOR BUOYANCY TESTS

Lot size	Number of vests in sample
100 and under	1
101 to 200	2
201 to 300	3
301 to 500	4

(5) If a sample vest fails the buoyancy test, the sample from the next succeeding lot must consist of 10 specimen vests or more to be tested for buoyancy in accordance with paragraph (e) of this section.

(c) *Additional compliance tests.* An inspector from the recognized laboratory or Coast Guard may conduct an examination, test and inspection of a buoyant device that is obtained from the manufacturer or through commercial channels to determine the suitability of the device for listing and labeling, or to determine its conformance to applicable requirements.

(d) *Test facilities.* The manufacturer shall admit the laboratory inspector and the Coast Guard inspector to any part of the premises at the place of manufacture of a listed and labeled device to—

(1) Examine, inspect, or test a sample of a part or a material that is included in the construction of the device; and

(2) Conduct any examination, inspection, or test in a suitable place and with appropriate apparatus provided by the manufacturer.

(e) *Buoyancy*—(1) *Buoyancy test method.* Remove the buoyant inserts from the vests. Securely attach the spring scale in a position directly over the test tank. Suspend the weighted wire basket from the scale in such a manner that the basket can be weighed while it is completely under water. In order to measure the actual buoyancy provided by the inserts, the underwater weight of the empty basket should exceed the buoyancy of the inserts. To obtain the buoyancy of the inserts, proceed as follows:

(i) Weigh the empty wire basket under water.

(ii) Place the inserts inside the basket and submerge it so that the top of the basket is at least 2 inches below the surface of the water. Allow the inserts to remain submerged for 24 hours. The tank shall be locked or sealed during this 24-hour submergence period. It is important that after the inserts have once been submerged they shall remain submerged for the duration of the test, and at no time during the course of the test shall they be removed from the tank or otherwise exposed to air.

(iii) After the 24-hour submergence period, unlock or unseal the tank and weigh the wire basket with the inserts inside while both are still under water.

(iv) The buoyancy is computed as paragraph (e)(1)(i) of this section minus paragraph (e)(1)(iii) of this section.

(2) *Buoyancy required.* The buoyant inserts from adult size buoyant vests shall provide not less than 15½ pounds of buoyancy in fresh water; the inserts from the child medium size buoyant vests shall provide not less than 11 pounds buoyancy; and the inserts from the child small size buoyant vests shall provide not less than 7 pounds buoyancy.

(f) *Body strap test.* The complete body strap assembly, including hardware shall be tested for strength by attaching the dee ring to a suitable support such that the assembly hangs vertically its full length. A weight as specified in §160.060–3(d) shall be attached to the other end on the snap hook for 10 minutes. The specified weight shall not break or excessively distort the body strap assembly.

(g) *Additional approval tests for non-standard vests.* Tests in addition to those required by this section may be conducted by the inspector for a non-standard vest to determine performance equivalence to a standard vest. Such additional tests may include determining performance in water, suitability of materials, donning time, ease of adjustment, and similar equivalency tests. Costs for any additional tests must be assumed by the manufacturer.

[CGFR 65–37, 30 FR 11590, Sept. 10, 1965, as amended by CGD 72–90R, 37 FR 10839, May 31, 1972; CGD 72–163R, 38 FR 8122, Mar. 28, 1973; CGD 75–008, 43 FR 9772, Mar. 9, 1978]

§160.060–8 Marking.

(a) Each buoyant vest must have the following information clearly marked in waterproof lettering:

Type II Personal Flotation Device.
Inspected and tested in accordance with U.S. Coast Guard regulations.
Polyethylene foam buoyant material provides a minimum buoyant force of (15½ lb., 11 lb., or 7 lb.).
Dry out thoroughly when wet.
Approved for use on all recreational boats and on uninspected commercial vessels less than 40 feet in length not carrying passengers for hire by persons weighing (more than 90 lb., 50 to 90 lb., or less than 50 lb.).
U.S. Coast Guard Approval No. 160.060/(assigned manufacturer's No.)/(Revision No.); (Model No.).
(Name and address of manufacturer or distributor).
(Lot No.).

(b) *Waterproof marking.* Marking of buoyant vests shall be sufficiently waterproof so that after 72 hours submergence in water it will withstand vigorous rubbing by hand while wet without printed matter becoming illegible.

[CGD 72–163R, 38 FR 8122, Mar. 28, 1973, as amended by CGD 75–008, 43 FR 9771, Mar. 9, 1978]

§160.060–9 Recognized laboratory.

(a) A manufacturer seeking Coast Guard approval of a product under this subpart shall follow the approval procedures of subpart 159.005 of this chapter, and shall apply for approval directly to a recognized independent laboratory. The following laboratories are recognized under §159.010–7 of this part, to perform testing and approval functions under this subpart:

Underwriters Laboratories, 12 Laboratory Drive, P.O. Box 13995, Research Triangle Park, NC 27709–3995, (919) 549–1400.

(b) Production oversight must be performed by the same laboratory that performs the approval tests unless, as determined by the Commandant, the employees of the laboratory performing production oversight receive training and support equal to that of the laboratory that performed the approval testing.

[CGD 93–055, 61 FR 13930, Mar. 28, 1996]

Subpart 160.061—Fishing Tackle Kits, Emergency, for Merchant Vessels

SOURCE: CGFR 65–9, 30 FR 11483, Sept. 8, 1965, unless otherwise noted.

§160.061–1 Applicable specifications.

(a) The following specifications, of the issue in effect on the date emergency fishing tackle kits are manufactured, form a part of this subpart:

(1) Federal specifications:

QQ–I–706—Iron and steel; sheet, tinned (tin plate).
QQ–W–423—Wire, steel, corrosion-resisting
HH–P–91—Packing, fiber, hard sheet.
CCC–F–451—Flannel, canton.

(2) Military specifications:

MIL–H–2846—Hooks, fish, steel.
MIL–B–1418—Blades, razor, safety.
MIL–A–140—Adhesive, water-resistant, W.P. barrier-material.

(b) Copies of the specifications referred to in this section shall be kept on file by the manufacturer, together with the approved plans, if any, and the certificate of approval.

(1) The Federal Specifications may be purchased from the Business Service Center, General Services Administration, Washington, DC 20407.

(2) The Military Specifications may be obtained from the Commanding Officer, Naval Supply Depot, 5801 Tabor Avenue, Philadelphia, Pa. 19120.

§ 160.061–2 Requirements.

(a) *Material.* Material shall be as specified in this subpart.

(b) *Assembly.* Emergency fishing kits shall consist of fishing rigs, accessories, and instructions furnished in a hermetically sealed container.

(c) *Components.* Each fishing kit shall consist of the items listed in table 160.06–2(c).

TABLE 160.061–2(C)—FISHING KITS

Item No.	Description [1]	Quantity
1	Booklet, Fishing Instructions (Refer to § 160.061–3(i)).	1 ea.
2	Container, Fishing Kit (See Fig. 2)	1 ea.
3	Hooks, treble, size 1, short shank ..	2 ea.
4	Hooks, size 7/0, 5/0, 1/0, 2, 6, 8, O'Shaugnessy, straight shank, double strength.	2 ea.
5	Leader, wire, 0.011-inch diameter, 27-pound test (with No. 3 snap on one end and No. 7 swivel on the other end) 6-inch length.	2 ea.
6	Leader, wire, 0.016-inch diameter, 58-pound test (with No. 3 snap on one end and No. 4 swivel on the other end) 12-inch length.	2 ea.
7	Leader, monofilament, 0.021-inch diameter, 15-pound test, 4-foot length.	4 ea.
8	Line, monofilament, 18-pound test, 100-foot length.	1 ea.
9	Line, nylon or dacron, braided, 63-pound test, 150 feet length.	1 ea.
10	Pad, canton flannel, 2¾ inches square, specification CCC–F–451, color, bright yellow.	1 ea.
11	Pad, canton flannel, 2¾ inches square, specification CCC–F–451, color, bright red.	1 ea.
12	Lure, spoon, removable No. 6 hook, yellow feathers, blade length 1³⁄₃₂ inches, width ¹⁵⁄₃₂ inch, weight ¹⁄₂₀ ounce, polished copper finish.	1 ea.
13	Lure, spoon, removable No. 5/0 hook, yellow feathers, blade length 3 inches, width ⅞ inch, weight ²⁄₅ ounce, polished chrome finish.	1 ea.

TABLE 160.061–2(C)—FISHING KITS—Continued

Item No.	Description [1]	Quantity
14	Lure, spoon, free swinging No. 1 treble double strength, short shank, blade length 2³⁄₁₆ inches, width ¹³⁄₁₆ inch, weight ¼ ounce, stainless steel or chrome plated brass.	1 ea.
15	Sinkers, pinch on or equal, ¼ ounce, ⁵⁄₁₆ ounce, 1 ounce.	1 ea.
16	Foil, shiny, 4 inches square	1 ea.
17	Squid, tinned body, length 2 inches, weight ½ ounce.	1 ea.
18	Jig, painted lead head, bucktail feathered with 1/0 hook.	1 ea.
19	Jig, painted lead head, bucktail feathered with 3/0 hook.	1 ea.
20	Blades, razor, safety, single edge ...	1 ea.
21	Bait, pork rind, 4 inches long, ½ inch wide, with ends tapered to ⅛ inch wide and rounded.	4 ea.
22	Snap and swivels, No. 3	6 ea.
23	Card, leader knots and hitches (fig. 1).	1 ea.
24	Winder (see § 160.061–3(h))	2 ea.

[1] The tolerances of these items shall be plus or minus ¹⁄₃₂-inch on all dimensions.

§ 160.061–3 Design and construction.

(a) *Container.* The container shall be made of ethyl cellulose, clear, type EM—1, Specification MIL–P–3412 or better. The dimensions shall not exceed those specified in Figure 2. Other packaging arrangements acceptable to the Commandant will be considered.

(b) *Card.* A card showing leader knots and hitches shall be provided as per Figure 1. Size of card should not exceed 2¾ by 4¾ inches.

(c) *Hooks.* Unless otherwise specified, all hooks shall be of forged steel, hollow ground with filed out points. The hooks shall be of ringed type and shall be tinned. Hooks shall be tempered, tough, flexible, and resilient.

(d) *Leaders.* Wire leaders shall be of stainless steel, and shall be attached to snaps and swivels with not less than six turns of wire. Monofilament leaders shall be blue mist and shall be provided with a ⅝-inch inside diameter end loop on one end.

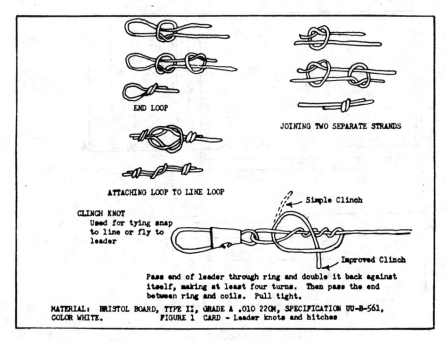

END LOOP

JOINING TWO SEPARATE STRANDS

ATTACHING LOOP TO LINE LOOP

CLINCH KNOT
Used for tying snap
to line or fly to
leader

Simple Clinch

Improved Clinch

Pass end of leader through ring and double it back against
itself, making at least four turns. Then pass the end
between ring and coils. Pull tight.

MATERIAL: BRISTOL BOARD, TYPE II, GRADE A .010 22OM, SPECIFICATION UU-B-561,
COLOR WHITE.   FIGURE 1 CARD - Leader knots and hitches

FIGURE 1

(e) *Snaps and swivels.* Swivels shall be either of brass or bronze. Snaps shall be stainless steel.

(f) *Lines.* Unless otherwise specified nylon lines shall be hard braided, waterproofed, and heat set to reduce "stretch". Lines may be either camouflage or mist in color.

(g) *Spoons.* Spoons shall be of the single-blade, egg-shaped dished type with either fixed or free-swinging hooks. The spoons shall be stainless steel or stamped from brass and plated to resist corrosion. Each spoon shall, on the forward end, be provided with an eye for attachment to the line. Spoons having free-swinging hooks shall have the hooks attached by means of a split ring through a hole in the rear of the blade. In fixed-hook spoons, the hook shall be attached to the spoon by a screw and shall be shaped to conform to the contour of the spoon. Feathers, if provided, shall be yellow hackle feathers attached to the hook by wrapping with thread, and the wrapping coated with red lacquer.

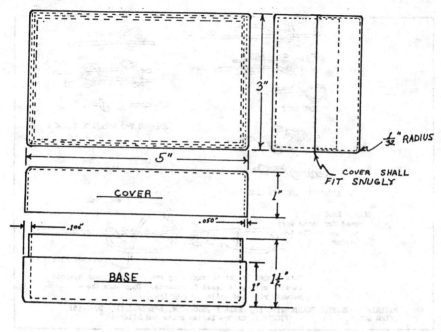

Figure 2

(h) *Winder.* Winders shall conform to Figure 3, or shall be of an equivalent commercial design suitable to contain required length of line.

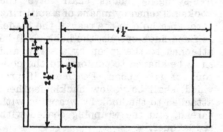

Figure 3—Winder. Material: Packing; fiber, hard sheet, Specification HH–P–91; dimensions in inches: Unless otherwise specified; tolerances: Fractions plus or minus ⅟₃₂-inch.

(i) *Booklet of instructions.* The fishing instructions shall be prepared in pamphlet form, approximately 2½ inches by 4½ inches on parchment paper, in waterproof ink, with printing on one side of the paper only. The booklet shall contain a complete description of

how and under what conditions each component should be used, and general suggestions for fishing. It shall be prepared in easy to read form in such a manner that a completely inexperienced person will know what equipment to use and how to use it. Both physical form and the contents of the booklet shall be specially approved by the Commandant, U.S. Coast Guard, prior to acceptance. A copy of approved contents for the instruction booklet will be furnished on request.

§ 160.061–4 Kit assembly.

(a) *Preparation of items.* The items shall be prepared for packing into the kit as indicated below. Each transparent envelope shall be closed by heat sealing.

Item No.	Preparation for assembly
1, 10, 11, 12, 13, 14, 15, 16, 17, 23, 24.	None.
3, 4, 5, 6, 7, 18, 19, 21, 22.	Insert in a transparent envelope.
8 and 9	Gather into a hank 4½ inches long and restrain with tape.

168

Item No.	Preparation for assembly
20	Wrap in paper envelope.

(b) *Packing of items.* The components of the kit, after being prepared as specified, shall be packed in the container in such manner that there is a minimum possibility of any item being bent or crushed. The marking label shall be placed on the bottom of the container with the wording facing out. The instruction booklet shall be packed, front cover up, under the lid. The container shall be sealed after the components have been packaged therein with an 18-inch length of ¾-inch wide adhesive tape conforming to Specification JAN-P-127. The tape shall be applied around the perimeter of the container with an equal amount on each side of the juncture of the two sections of the container. An alternate packaging arrangement acceptable to the Commandant will be acceptable.

§ 160.061-5 Marking.

(a) *General.* The containers shall be stenciled on the bottom in black with the manufacturer's name or trademark and type or model number in letters approximately ³⁄₁₆ inch high, together with the following legend in letters ³⁄₁₆ inch high:

UNITED STATES COAST GUARD

APPROVAL NO. 160.061/—

EMERGENCY FISHING TACKLE KIT

OPEN ONLY

FOR ACTUAL EMERGENCY USE

NOT FOR INSPECTION

(b) [Reserved]

Subpart 160.062—Releases. Life-saving Equipment, Hydraulic and Manual

SOURCE: CGFR 68-32, 33 FR 5721, Apr. 12, 1968, unless otherwise noted.

§ 160.062-1 Applicable specifications, and referenced material.

(a) *Specifications and standards.* The following specifications of the issue in effect on the date releases are manufactured or reconditioned shall form a part of the regulations of this subpart (see §§ 2.75-17 through 2.75-19 of subchapter A (Procedures Applicable to the Public) of this chapter):

(1) Military Specifications and Standards:

MIL-R-15041C—Releases, lifesaving equipment, hydraulic and manual.

MIL-STD-105—Sample procedures and tables for inspection by attributes.

(2) Federal Test Method Standards:

Standard No. 151—Metals, test methods.

(b) *Technical references.* For guidance purposes the technical reference may be used, which is entitled "Corrosion Handbook," 1948, by H. H. Uhlig, and published by John Wiley & Sons, Inc., 605 Third Avenue, New York, N.Y. 10016, and priced at $21 per copy.

(c) *Copies on file.* A copy of the specifications and standards listed in paragraph (a) of this section shall be kept on file by the manufacturer, together with the approved plans, specifications and certificate of approval. It is the manufacturer's responsibility to have the latest issue, including addenda and changes, of these specifications and standards on hand when manufacturing or reconditioning equipment under this specification subpart.

(1) The military specifications and standards may be obtained from the Commanding Officer, Naval Supply Depot, 5801 Tabor Avenue, Philadelphia, Pa. 19120.

(2) The Federal standards may be obtained from the Business Service Center, General Services Administration, Washington, DC 20407.

§ 160.062-2 Types.

(a) The hydraulic releases referred to under § 160.062-1(a)(1) are of the diaphram-spring plunger type, which releases a buoyant load under hydrostatic pressure.

(b) All hydraulic releases given an approval under this subpart shall be designed and tested to operate with spring-tensioned gripes. Such gripes shall be considered as a part of each approval.

(c) Alternate designs will be given special consideration, but the expense of their preliminary investigation at a laboratory accepted by the Commandant shall be borne by the manufacturer.

[CGFR 68-32, 33 FR 5721, Apr. 12, 1968, as amended by CGD 73-153R, 40 FR 4422, Jan. 30, 1975]

§ 160.062-3 Materials, construction, workmanship, and performance requirements.

(a) *General.* The materials, construction, workmanship, and performance requirements shall conform to the requirements of the specifications listed in § 160.062-1(a)(1) except as otherwise provided by this subpart. In addition, all metals and materials used in a hydraulic release must be compatible with each other so that the final assembly under conditions of use is not subject to such deleterious effects as galvanic corrosion, freezing, or buckling of moving parts, or loosening and tightening of joints due to differences in coefficients of thermal expansion. Galvanizing or other forms of metallic coating on the parts of a hydraulic release are not acceptable. The criteria for accepting any combination of materials shall be determined by testing or by the data stated in § 160.062-1(b).

(b) *Buoyant load capacity.* A hydraulic release working in conjunction with its spring-tensioned gripe must demonstrate that it can release buoyant loads between the limits of 200 pounds and 3,750 pounds and within the range of depths specified by paragraph (c) of this section.

(c) *Release depth.* A hydraulic release shall automatically release the buoyant loads described in paragraph (b) of this section at depths between 5 feet to 15 feet prior to being tested for either the temperature or the corrosion resistance tests of 160.062-4(c)(2). After exposure to these temperature and corrosion tests, a hydraulic release shall release the buoyant loads of paragraph (b) of this section between the depths of 5 feet to 25 feet.

§ 160.062-4 Inspections and tests.

(a) *General.* Marine inspectors shall be assigned to make factory inspections of hydraulic releases, as described in paragraph (d) of this section for sampling and testing. In addition, the Commander of the Coast Guard District may detail a marine inspector at any time to visit any place where approved hydraulic releases are manufactured or reconditioned to observe production methods and to conduct any inspections or tests which may be deemed advisable. The marine inspector shall be admitted to any place in the factory or place where work is done on hydraulic releases or their components. In addition, the marine inspector may take samples of assembled hydraulic releases or parts or materials used in their construction for further examination, inspection, or tests. The manufacturer shall provide a suitable place and the apparatus necessary for the performance of the tests which are conducted at the place of manufacture by the marine inspector.

(b) *Classification of tests.* The sampling, inspections, and tests conducted upon hydraulic releases shall fall within one of the following general classifications, as described hereafter:

(1) Preapproval tests.

(2) Factory inspections and tests.

(3) Spot check tests.

(4) Periodic servicing tests.

(c) *Preapproval testing.* The "Visual and dimensional examination" referred to in Table 160.062-4(c) shall be conducted by a marine inspector at the factory. The "Physical and operational tests" of that table shall be conducted at a laboratory accepted by the Commandant.

TABLE 160.062-4(C)—PREAPPROVAL TESTS [1]

Number of specimens	Name of tests	Reference
4	Visual and dimensional examination.	Para. 4.2.1, 4.2.2, and 4.3 of MIL-R-15041C.
4	Physical and operational tests.	Para. 4.2.1, 4.2.3, and 4.4 of MIL-R-15041C.

[1] These tests are called "Lot acceptance tests," in Military Specification MIL-R-15041C.

(1) *Visual and dimensional examination.* The marine inspector shall examine the 4 hydraulic release samples of the preapproval sample for their visual and dimensional characteristics. If all 4 of the devices are in agreement with the manufacturer's plans previously reviewed by the Commandant, the 4 devices will be accepted and are to be assembled for further testing under the

"Physical and operational tests" of paragraph (c)(2) of this section.

(2) *Physical and operational tests.* Each hydraulic release selected under Table 160.062–4(c) for the "Physical and operational tests" shall undergo each of the tests described in this paragraph without renewal of parts or repairs between the tests. The tests shall be conducted in the following sequence:

(i) *Submergence test.* A hydraulic release shall be tested by applying buoyant loads of its designed capacity to its spring-tensioned gripe as required under § 160.062–3(b) while the device is submerged in water or in a water-filled pressure testing tank. A hydraulic release shall show by its submergence test that it meets the buoyant capacity and release depth requirements of § 160.062–3 (b) and (c) by automatically tripping and releasing its load.

(ii) *Temperature test.* After its submergence test, a hydraulic release sample shall be placed in a cold box at minus 30 degrees F. for 4 hours. Upon completion of this conditioning, the sample device shall be opened for inspection and shall show no significant change in the position of the hydraulic or manual control as a result of the low temperature exposure.

(iii) *Corrosion resisting test.* After the completion of its temperature test, a hydraulic release sample shall be exposed to a 20 percent salt spray test for 160 continuous hours in accordance with Federal Test Method Standard No. 151. At the conclusion of this test, the sample device shall be entirely serviceable and shall show a minimal amount of corrosion.

(iv) *Second temperature test.* After its corrosion resisting test, a hydraulic release sample shall undergo a repeat of the temperature test, subdivision (ii) of this paragraph.

(v) *Second submergence test.* The final test of a hydraulic release sample shall be a repeat of the submergence test, paragraph (c)(2)(i) of this section.

(d) *Factory inspections and tests.* For purposes of sampling, a lot shall consist of not more than 500 hydraulic releases of the same model. Manufacturers of approved hydraulic releases shall maintain quality control of the materials used, manufacturing methods, workmanship, and the finished product

as to produce hydraulic releases in conformity with the approvals previously issued by the Commandant.

(1) *Visual and dimensional examination.* A random sample of hydraulic releases shall be selected by a marine inspector at the factory in accordance with Table 160.062–4(d)(1) from each assembled lot. After the samples have been selected, they will undergo an examination of visual and dimensional characteristics by referring to their approved drawings with their acceptance based on Table 160.062–4(d)(1) and MIL–STD–105, and checking for compliance with specific details as described therein.

TABLE 160.062–4(D)(1)—SAMPLING FOR VISUAL AND DIMENSIONAL EXAMINATION [1]

Number of release devices in inspection lot	Number of release devices in sample	Rejection number (defectives)
15 and under	All	
16 to 25	15	1
26 to 40	25	1
41 to 110	35	2
111 to 180	50	2
181 to 300	75	3
301 to 500	110	2

[1] This table is derived from Table I of Paragraph 4.2.2 of Military Specification MIL–R–15041C.

(2) *Physical and operational tests.* If the sampling and examination of paragraph (d)(1) of this section are satisfactory, the marine inspector shall select an additional random sample of hydraulic releases from the same assembled lot as described above. This second group of samples, of a number determined by Table 160.062–4(d)(2), shall be forwarded for testing at the manufacturer's expense to a laboratory accepted by the Commandant. Each hydraulic release shall undergo each of the tests described in this paragraph without renewal of parts or repairs between tests. The tests shall be conducted in the following sequence:

(i) *Submergence test.* Same test as described in paragraph (c)(2)(i) of this section.

(ii) *Temperature test.* Same test as described in paragraph (c)(2)(ii) of this section.

(iii) *Corrosion resisting test.* Same test as described in paragraph (c)(2)(iii) of this section.

(iv) *Second temperature test.* Same test as described in paragraph (c)(2)(iv) of this section.

(v) *Second submergence test.* Same test as described in paragraph (c)(2)(v) of this section.

TABLE 160.062–4(D)(2)—SAMPLING FOR PHYSICAL AND OPERATIONAL TESTS [1]

Number of release devices in inspection lot	Number release devices in sample	Rejection number (failures in the tests)
15 and under	4	1
16 to 25	5	1
26 to 40	7	1
41 to 110	10	1
111 to 180	12	1
181 to 300	16	1
301 to 500	20	1

[1] This table is derived from Table II of Paragraph 4.2.3 of Military Specification MIL–R–15041C.

(3) *Lot acceptance at a factory.* The submergence test of paragraph (c)(2)(i) shall be performed on each of the remaining hydraulic releases in a production lot after the selection of the lot samples required by paragraph (d)(2) of this section. Such individual submergence tests may be performed at the factory in a pressure tank apparatus which simulates the hydrostatic pressure and the various tension loads on the hydraulic release. Those hydraulic releases which do not pass this submergence test shall be removed from the production lot as unacceptable, but may be reworked and included in a subsequent lot. After the completion of these individual submergence tests and after receipt of the laboratory's test report showing that the tests on the lot samples were satisfactorily met, the Commander of the Coast Guard District in which the factory is located shall have the manufacturer notified that this production lot of hydraulic releases meets the requirements of this specification subpart. After being marked as required by § 160.062–5, the manufacturer may sell such hydraulic releases as approved equipment.

(i) Hydraulic releases which have been rejected may not, unless subsequently accepted, be sold or offered for sale under representation as being in compliance with this specification or as being approved for use on vessels subject to inspection under this chapter.

(4) *Records and test reports.* The manufacturer shall maintain records and copies of test reports for each production lot of hydraulic releases manufactured for a period of five (5) years from the date notified that a production lot meets the requirements in this subpart. These records and test reports, upon request, shall be made available to the marine inspector. The manufacturer will be provided with a copy of the laboratory's test report concerning each production lot of hydraulic releases submitted for testing.

(e) *Spot checks.* As one of the conditions in granting an approval for a hydraulic release under this subpart, the Coast Guard reserves the right to spot check at any time and at any place the product, parts, and complete assemblies of hydraulic releases covered by the approval. The spot check shall be by a marine inspector who shall be admitted to the place or places where work may be performed before, during, or after the manufacture of hydraulic releases or at any place where hydraulic releases may be assembled, reworked, repaired, or reconditioned by the manufacturer of any repair facility accepted by the Commandant in accordance with the procedure contained in § 160.062–7. A spot check includes having a marine inspector compare materials, parts, and workmanship and/or complete hydraulic releases with the manufacturer's approved plans, records and test reports to ascertain compliance with these requirements. The marine inspector may select samples of materials or parts used in the construction of hydraulic releases and complete hydraulic releases and may order or have performed any or all of the tests described in this section conducted on such devices or parts thereof. This work and any tests required shall be borne by the manufacturer without cost to the Coast Guard.

(f) *Periodic Servicing and Testing.* A hydraulic release is inspected as follows:

(1) *Inspection for devices not installed after manufacture.* A hydraulic release, that is not installed after manufacture and is stored for period of 24 months or less, is not required to be inspected or tested before installation but must be stamped by a marine inspector on the

inspection tag required in §160.062–5(b)(2) with—

(i) The word "Installed";

(ii) The installation date; and

(iii) The Marine Inspection Office identification letters.

(2) *Inspection for devices that have been installed.* A hydraulic release that is installed for a period of 12 months or more must pass the test contained in paragraph (f)(3) of this section and be marked as required in paragraph (f)(5) of this section. If, after passing the test, the device is stored for a period of 24 months or less, it must be stamped as required in paragraph (f)(1) of this paragraph by the marine inspector before reinstallation.

(3) *Devices stored longer than 24 months.* A hydraulic release that is stored for a period of more than 24 months must be inspected and tested by an employee of a repair or test facility, accepted in accordance with the requirement contained in §160.062–7 or §160.062–8, as follows:

(i) The device must be manually operated to determine if it releases.

(ii) If the device releases, it must pass the submergence test contained in paragraph (c)(2)(i) of this section, at a depth between 5 feet and 15 feet and be marked as required in paragraph (f)(5) of this section.

(iii) If the device fails to release or fails to pass the submergence test required in paragraph (f)(3)(ii) of this section, the device must be disassembled, repaired, and tested in accordance with the requirements contained in paragraph (f)(4) of this paragraph.

(4) *Disassembly and repair tests.* If a hydraulic release fails the test contained in paragraph (f)(3)(iii) of this section, it must be disassembled and repaired by the manufacturer or a repair facility accepted in accord with the requirements contained in §160.062–7 and be tested as follows:

(i) A production lot must be formed consisting of 12 or more but not exceeding 100 devices.

(ii) In the presence of a marine inspector, the device must pass the submergence test contained in paragraph (c)(2)(i) of this section at a depth between 5 feet and 15 feet.

(iii) Any device that fails must be—

(A) Repaired;

(B) Placed in a subsequent lot; and

(C) Submitted to the submergence test contained in paragraph (c)(2)(i) of this section at a depth between 5 feet and 15 feet.

(5) *Marking of devices.* If a hydraulic release passes the submergence test required in paragraph (c)(2)(i) of this section at a depth between 5 feet and 15 feet the marine inspector stamps the inspection tag with—

(i) The test date;

(ii) The Marine Inspection Office identification letters; and

(iii) The letters "USCG".

[CGFR 68–32, 33 FR 5721, Apr. 12, 1968, as amended by CGD 73–153R, 40 FR 4422, Jan. 30, 1975; CGD 75–186, 41 FR 10437, Mar. 11, 1976]

§160.062-5 Markings.

(a) Hydraulic releases manufactured prior to the granting of a certificate of approval to the manufacturer may be permitted in service only to July 1, 1969. However, such hydraulic releases meeting the type and design requirements covered by a current certificate of approval may be repaired and/or reconditioned as provided in §160.062–4(f) and be accepted as approved equipment when it bears the following markings:

(1) *Body marking.* The name of the manufacturer and the model designation are plainly visible.

(2) *Inspection tag markings.* Each hydraulic release repaired or reconditioned shall be provided with a 2" by 3½" stainless steel tag of a minimum thickness of 0.032 inches. This tag shall be permanently attached to a hydraulic release with a single stainless steel link made of wire ³⁄₁₆" in diameter. This link shall provide nonrigid attachment of the tag to the hydraulic release. The top of the inspection tag shall be stamped in block characters not less than ¹⁄₁₆" in height with the manufacturer's name, Coast Guard approval number, the limits of buoyant capacity in pounds, the Marine Inspection Office identification letters, and the letters "USCG." The remaining space on the tag will be used for the stamping of periodic servicing test dates and the marine inspector's initials as described in §160.062–4(f).

(b) Hydraulic release manufactured under a certificate of approval issued under this subpart shall be provided with 2 sets of markings as follows:

(1) *Body marking.* The metal body of a hydraulic release shall be stamped in block characters not less than ⅛″ in height on a plainly visible portion with the name of the manufacturer, the model designation, the limits of buoyant capacity in pounds, the method of manual release, the notation "DO NOT PAINT", Coast Guard approval number, the Marine Inspection Office identification letters, and the letters "USCG".

(2) *Inspection tag markings.* Each hydraulic release shall be provided at its time of manufacture with a 2″ by 3½″ stainless steel tag of a minimum thickness of 0.032 inch. This tag shall be permanently attached to a hydraulic release with a single stainless steel link made of wire 3/16″ in diameter. This link shall provide nonrigid attachment of the tag to the hydraulic release. The top of the inspection tag shall be stamped in block characters not less than ⅛″ in height with the original lot number of the hydraulic release, its date of manufacture, and its release depth range in feet. The remaining space on the tag will be used for the stamping of periodic servicing test dates and the Marine Inspection Office identification letters as described in § 160.062–4(f).

[CGFR 68–32, 33 FR 5721, Apr. 12, 1968, as amended by CGD75–186, 41 FR 10437, Mar. 11, 1976]

§ 160.062–6 Procedure for approval.

General. Hydraulic releases for use on lifesaving equipment for merchant vessels are approved only by the Commandant, U.S. Coast Guard. In order to be approved, the hydraulic releases must be tested in accordance with § 160.062–4(c) by an independent laboratory accepted by the Coast Guard under 46 CFR 159.010. The independent laboratory will forward the report to the Commandant for examination, and if satisfactory an official approval number will be assigned to the manufacturer for the model hydraulic release submitted.

[CGD 95–028, 62 FR 51215, Sept. 30, 1997]

EFFECTIVE DATE NOTE: At 62 FR 51215, Sept. 30, 1997, § 160.062–6 was revised, effective Oct. 30, 1997.

§ 160.062–7 Procedures for acceptance of repair facility.

(a) Before a repair facility is accepted by the Commandant to perform the services required in § 160.062–4(f), it must be inspected by the cognizant Officer in Charge, Marine Inspection, to determine if it has—

(1) The testing apparatus to perform all the tests required in § 160.062–4;

(2) A source of supply of replacement parts for a hydraulic release, evidenced by a signed agreement between the facility and his source of supply, or the parts for it; all replacement parts must be in compliance with applicable specifications and standards contained in § 160.062–1; and

(3) Employees competent to perform the services required in this paragraph. Each employee who is engaged in serving a hydraulic release must demonstrate his competence to the Officer in Charge, Marine Inspection by—

(i) Disassembling a hydraulic release;

(ii) Making all necessary repairs to the disassembled unit;

(iii) Reassembling the unit in conformance with the specifications and standards contained in § 160.062–1(a); and

(iv) Showing that the reassembled unit meets the buoyant capacity and release depth requirements contained in § 160.062–3 (b) and (c) after being inspected and tested in conformance with the requirements contained in § 160.062–4(f).

(b) Based on the report of the Officer in Charge, Marine Inspection, regarding the inspection required in paragraph (a) of this section, the Commandant notifies the facility that—

(1) It is an accepted repair facility for the reconditioning and testing of hydraulic releases; or

(2) It is not accepted as a repair facility, lists each discrepancy noted by the Officer in Charge, Marine Inspection, and describes the procedure for reinspection if applicable corrections are made.

[CGD 73–153R, 40 FR 4422, Jan. 30, 1975]

§ 160.062-8 Procedures for acceptance of testing facility.

(a) The Commandant may consider the acceptance of a facility that conducts only the submergence test contained in § 160.062–4(c)(2)(i). Before a facility is accepted by the Commandant to conduct this test, it must be inspected by the cognizant Officer in Charge, Marine Inspection, to determine if it has—

(1) The testing apparatus to perform the test required in § 160.062–4(c)(2)(i); and

(2) Employees competent to perform the test required in § 160.062–4(c)(2)(i). Each employee who is engaged in testing a device must demonstrate his competence to the Officer in Charge, Marine Inspection by conducting a submergence test.

(b) Based on the report of the Officer in Charge, Marine Inspection, regarding the inspection required in paragraph (a) of this section, the Commandant notifies each applicant, in accordance with the procedures described in § 160.062–7(b), whether or not it is an accepted testing facility.

[CGD 73–153R, 40 FR 4422, Jan. 30, 1975]

Subpart 160.064—Marine Buoyant Devices

§ 160.064–1 Applicable specifications.

(a) *Specifications.* There are no other Coast Guard specifications applicable to this subpart.

(b) [Reserved]

[CGFR 64–30, 29 FR 7388, June 6, 1964]

§ 160.064–2 Types and models.

(a) *Types.* Water safety buoyant devices covered by this subpart shall be of two general types, viz, those intended to be worn on the body and those intended to be thrown.

(b) *Models.* Water safety buoyant devices may be of different models which incorporate characteristics considered valuable for safety in various fields of water sports or boating activities.

(c) *Sizes.* Water safety buoyant devices designed to be worn shall be of sizes suitable for adults or children, as intended and marked on the device. Water safety buoyant devices intended to be thrown in water shall be of a minimum size intended for adults.

(d) *Dimensions.* A foam cushion designed to be thrown must be 2 inches or more in thickness and must have 225 or more square inches of top surface area.

[CGFR 64–30, 29 FR 7388, June 6, 1964, as amended by CGD 73–246R, 39 FR 36967, Oct. 16, 1974]

§ 160.064–3 Requirements.[1]

(a) *General.* Every water safety buoyant device shall conform to the requirements as accepted by the Commandant for listing and labeling by a recognized laboratory, and shall be of such design, materials, and construction as to meet the requirements specified in this section.

(b) *Designs and constructions.* Water safety buoyant devices shall be of designs suitable for the purposes intended. A design intended to be worn on the body shall be capable of being adjusted and secured to fit the range of wearers for which designed with as few fastenings or adjustments as are consistent with the purpose of the device. Designs may be varied, but shall not provide means intended for fastening or securing the device to a boat. The arrangement of the buoyancy of devices intended to be worn on the body shall provide for flotation of the wearer in an upright, slightly backward position in the water to as great a degree as is consistent with the special purpose intended, and in no case shall the device have a tendency to turn the wearer face downward in the water. Devices intended to be thrown shall not provide means for adjustment or close fitting to the body. Methods of construction shall provide strengths, with reinforcements where necessary, to be adequate for the intended use and purpose of the device.

(c) *Materials.* All materials used in any device covered by this subpart must meet the applicable requirements of subpart 164.019 of this chapter and shall be all new materials and shall be suitable for the purpose intended and

---

[1] The manufacturer of a personal flotation device must meet 33 CFR 181.701 through 33 CFR 181.705 which require an instruction pamphlet for each device that is sold or offered for sale for use on recreational boats.

shall be at least equivalent to corresponding materials specified for standard buoyant vests or buoyant cushions. Hardware or fastenings shall be of sufficient strength for the purpose of the device and shall be of inherently corrosion-resistant material, such as stainless steel, brass, bronze, certain plastics, etc. Decorative platings of any thickness are permissible. Fabrics, coated fabrics, tapes, and webbing shall be selected with a view to the purposes of the device and shall be either mildew resistant or treated for mildew resistance. Buoyancy shall be provided by inherently buoyant material and shall not be dependent upon loose, granulated material, gas compartments or inflation. So long as the minimum required buoyancy is provided by inherently buoyant material, the use of supplementary gas compartments, or inflation, will be permitted to supply additional buoyancy.

(d) *Buoyancy.* (1) Buoyancy for devices to be worn is as follows:

(i) Devices for persons weighing more than 90 pounds must have 15½ pounds or more of buoyancy.

(ii) Devices for persons weighing 50 to 90 pounds must have 11 pounds or more of buoyancy.

(iii) Devices for persons weighing less than 50 pounds must have 7 pounds or more of buoyancy.

(2) Buoyancy for devices to be thrown is as follows:

(i) Ring life buoys must have 16½ pounds or more of buoyancy.

(ii) Foam cushions must have 18 pounds or more of buoyancy.

(iii) A device other than those specified in paragraph (d)(2) (i) or (ii) of this section must have 20 pounds or more of buoyancy.

(3) The buoyancy values required in paragraphs (d) (1) and (2) of this section must be as follows:

(i) For each device containing foam buoyant materials, the required buoyancy value must remain after the device has been submerged in fresh water for 24 or more continuous hours.

(ii) For each device containing kapok, the required buoyancy value must remain after the device has been submerged in fresh water for 48 or more continuous hours.

(e) *Workmanship.* Water safety buoyant devices covered by this subpart shall be of first class workmanship and shall be free from any defects materially affecting their appearance or serviceability.

[CGFR 64-30, 29 FR 7388, June 6, 1964, as amended by CGD 73-246R, 39 FR 36967, Oct. 16, 1974; CGD 75-008, 43 FR 9772, Mar. 9, 1978; CGD 84-068, 58 FR 29494, May 20, 1993]

§ 160.064-4 Marking.

(a) Each water safety buoyant device must have the following information clearly marked in waterproof lettering:

(1) For devices to be worn:

(Type II or Type III) Personal Flotation Device.

Inspected and tested in accordance with U.S. Coast Guard regulations.

(Name of buoyant material) buoyant material provides a minimum buoyant force of (15½ lb., 11 lb., or 7 lb.).

(Special purpose intended.).

Approved for use on recreational boats only as a throwable device.

U.S. Coast Guard Approval No. 160.064/(assigned manufacturer's No.)/(Revision No.); (Model No.).

(Name and address of manufacturer or distributor).

(Lot No.).

(2) For devices to be thrown:

Type IV Personal Flotation Device.

Inspected and tested in accordance with U.S. Coast Guard regulations.

(Name of buoyant material) buoyant material provides a minimum buoyant force of (16½ lb., 18 lb., or 20 lb.).

(Special purpose intended).

Approved for use on all recreational boats less than 16 feet in length and all canoes and kayaks, and only as a throwable device on all other recreational boats.

U.S. Coast Guard Approval No. 160.064/(assigned manufacturer's No.)/(Revision No.); (Model No.).

(Name and address of manufacturer or distributor).

(Lot No.).

(b) *Durability of marking.* Marking shall be of a type which will be durable and legible for the expected life of the device.

[CGFR 64-30, 29 FR 7388, June 6, 1964, as amended by CGD 72-163R, 38 FR 8122, Mar. 28, 1973; CGD 73-246R, 39 FR 36967, Oct. 16, 1974; CGD 75-008, 43 FR 9772, Mar. 9, 1978; CGD 92-045, 58 FR 41609, Aug. 4, 1993; CGD 95-028, 62 FR 51215, Sept. 30, 1997]

EFFECTIVE DATE NOTE: At 62 FR 51215, Sept. 30, 1997, § 160.064-4 was amended by amending paragraph (a)(1) and removing paragraph (c), effective Oct. 30, 1997.

§ 160.064-6 **Examinations, tests and inspections.**

(a) *Manufacturer's inspection and tests.* Manufacturers of listed and labeled water safety buoyant devices shall maintain quality control of the materials used, manufacturing methods and the finished product so as to meet the applicable requirements, and shall make sufficient inspections and tests of representative samples and components produced to maintain the quality of the finished product. Records of tests conducted by the manufacturer and records of materials, including affidavits by suppliers that applicable requirements are met, entering into construction shall be made available to the recognized laboratory inspector or to the Coast Guard marine inspector, or both, for review upon request.

(b) *Laboratory inspections and tests.* Such examinations, inspections and tests as are required by the recognized laboratory for listed and labeled devices produced will be conducted by the laboratory inspector at the place of manufacture or other location at the option of the laboratory.

(c) *Test facilities.* The laboratory inspector, or the Coast Guard marine inspector assigned by the Commander of the District in which the factory is located, or both, shall be admitted to any place in the factory where work is being done on listed and labeled products, and either or both inspectors may take samples of parts or materials entering into construction or final assemblies, for further examinations, inspections, or tests. The manufacturer shall provide a suitable place and the apparatus necessary for the performance of the tests which are done at the place of manufacture.

(d) *Additional tests, etc.* Unannounced examinations, tests, and inspections of samples obtained either directly from the manufacturer or through commercial channels may be made to determine the suitability of a product for listing and labeling, or to determine conformance of a labeled product to the applicable requirements. These may be conducted by the recognized laboratory or the United States Coast Guard.

[CGFR 64-30, 29 FR 7388, June 6, 1964, as amended by CGD 73-246R, 39 FR 36967, Oct. 16, 1974]

§ 160.064-7 **Recognized laboratory.**

(a) A manufacturer seeking Coast Guard approval of a product under this subpart shall follow the approval procedures of subpart 159.005 of this chapter, and shall apply for approval directly to a recognized independent laboratory. The following laboratories are recognized under § 159.010-7 of this part, to perform testing and approval functions under this subpart:

Underwriters Laboratories, 12 Laboratory Drive, P.O. Box 13995, Research Triangle Park, NC 27709-3995, (919) 549-1400.

(b) Production oversight must be performed by the same laboratory that performs the approval tests unless, as determined by the Commandant, the employees of the laboratory performing production oversight receive training and support equal to that of the laboratory that performed the approval testing.

[CGD 93-055, 61 FR 13931, Mar. 28, 1996]

Subpart 160.066—Distress Signal for Boats, Red Aerial Pyrotechnic Flare

SOURCE: CGD 76-183a, 44 FR 73050, Dec. 17, 1979, unless otherwise noted.

§ 160.066-1 **Type.**

(a) Red aerial pyrotechnic distress signals specified by this subpart must be either self-contained or pistol launched, and either meteor or parachute assisted type.

(b) [Reserved]

§ 160.066-5 **Design, construction, and manufacturing requirements.**

(a) Each signal must be either:

(1) A self-contained unit with all necessary components for firing the signal, or

(2) A cartridge intended for firing from a signal pistol that is approved under Subpart 160.028 of this chapter.

(b) Each signal unit must have an interior chamber which contains the main propulsion charge and which is constructed so that it is capable of withstanding the forces generated by ignition without rupture, crack, or deformation of any kind.

(c) Signals must be constructed in lots numbered serially by the manufacturer. A new lot must be started when:

(1) Any change in construction details occurs;

(2) Any change in sources of raw materials occurs;

(3) Production is started on a new production line or on a previously discontinued production line; or

(4) A lot exceeds 30,000 units.

§ 160.066-7 Performance requirements

(a) Each signal must:

(1) Burn "vivid red" when tested as specified in §160.021-4(d)(7) for at least 5.5 seconds.

(2) Have a peak luminous intensity of at least 10,000 candela.

(3) Burn a total of not less than 1,000 candleminutes (Cm) using the formula $I \times T = Cm$

Where:

I = the luminous intensity measured as in subsection (c);

T = the total burn time of the device in minutes; and

Cm = the candle-minute rating of the device.

(4) Burn out completely before falling back to the level of launch.

(5) Function in a manner that would not cause burns or injury to an unprotected person firing the signal in accordance with the manufacturer's instructions.

(6) Not malfunction in a manner that would cause burns or injury to an unprotected person firing the signal in accordance with the manufacturer's instructions.

(b) Each signal must meet the requirements of paragraph (a) after:

(1) Submersion in water for 24 hours, or

(2) If protected by a sealed container, submersion in water for 24 hours inside the sealed container immediately followed by submersion for 10 minutes without the container, and

(3) Being exposed to the Elevated Temperature, Humidity, and Storage Test in §160.066-13(b).

(c) Testing for burn time and luminous intensity pursuant to paragraphs (a)(1) and (a)(2), respectively, shall be conducted in conformity with the following requirements and procedures:

(1) The chart speed of the light measuring equipment shall not be slower than 5 seconds per inch;

(2) The chart sweep of the light measuring equipment shall not be slower than .5 seconds for full scale;

(3) The first and last seconds of the burn shall be eliminated in measuring luminous intensity;

(4) The time during which the candle burns (excluding first and last seconds of burn) is to be used to determine the luminous intensity by averaging the readings taken during the burning; and

(5) Burn time is to be measured from first light of the signal to dark.

§ 160.066-9 Labeling.

(a) Each signal must be legibly and indelibly marked with the following information:

(1) The manufacturer's name,

(2) The designed burning time of the pyrotechnic candle(s),

(3) The specific signal pistol for which the signal is designed, if any,

(4) The lot number,

(5) The Coast Guard approval number,

(6) Operation and storage instructions,

(7) The month and year of expiration determined by §160.066-10, and

(8) The words:

"Aerial Flare. Acceptable as a Day and Night Visual Distress Signal for boats as required by 33 CFR 175.110. For Emergency Use Only".

(b) If the signal is too small to contain all of the information required by paragraph (a) and any labeling which may be required by paragraph (d), the information required by paragraphs (a) (2), (6), and (8) may be printed on a separate piece of paper packed with each signal or with the smallest container in which several signals are packed.

(c) The largest carton or box in which the manufacturer ships signals must be marked with the following or equivalent words: "Keep under cover in a dry place."

(d) Compliance with the labeling requirements of this section does not relieve the manufacturer of the responsibility of complying with the label requirements of the Federal Hazardous Substances Act, 15 U.S.C. 1263.

§ 160.066–10 Expiration date.

Each approved signal must have an expiration date marked on it. That date must not be more than forty-two months from date of manufacture.

§ 160.066–11 Approval procedures.

(a) Red aerial pyrotechnic flare distress signals are approved under the procedures of subpart 159.005 of this chapter.

(b) The manufacturer must produce a lot of at least 100 signals from which samples for approval testing must be drawn. Approval testing must be conducted in accordance with the operational tests in § 160.066–12 and the technical tests in § 160.066–13. In order for the signal to be approved, the samples must pass both the operational and the technical tests.

(c) The approval tests must be performed by an independent laboratory accepted by the Commandant under Subpart 159.010 of this chapter.

[CGD 76–183a, 44 FR 73050, Dec. 17, 1979, as amended by CGD 93–055, 61 FR 13931, Mar. 28, 1996]

§ 160.066–12 Operational tests.

(a) The procedure for conducting operational tests is described in figure (1).

(1) An "accept lot" decision must be reached in order to pass the operational tests.

(2) If a "reject lot" decision is reached, the entire lot is rejected.

(3) Signals from "reject lots" may be reworked by the manufacturer to correct the deficiency for which they were rejected and be resubmitted for inspection. Records shall be kept of the reasons for rejection, the reworking performed on the "reject lot", and the result of the second test. Signals from "reject lots" may not, unless subsequently accepted, be sold or offered for sale as being in compliance with this specification.

(b) Each signal selected for the operational tests must be conditioned by:

(1) Being submerged under at least 25 mm (1 in.) of water for 24 hours without any protection other than its waterproofing; or

(2) If waterproofing is provided by a sealed plastic bag or other waterproof packaging, submersion under 25 mm (1 in.) of water for 24 hours in the packaging, followed immediately by submersion under 25 mm (1 in.) of water for 10 minutes with the signal removed from the packaging.

(c) After each signal selected has undergone the conditioning required by paragraph (b) of this section it must be fired as described by the manufacturer's operating instructions. The following data as observed must be recorded for each signal:

(1) Burning time of the pyrotechnic candle;

(2) Color;

(3) Whether the pyrotechnic candle burns out above, at, or below the level of launch.

(d) A signal fails the operational tests if:

(1) It fails to fire,

(2) The pyrotechnic candle fails to ignite,

(3) The pyrotechnic candle continues to burn after it falls back to the level of launch,

(4) The observed color is other than vivid red, or

(5) The burning time is less than 5.5 seconds.

(e) A lot is rejected if a "reject lot" decision is reached using Figure (1) and Table 1 after completion of the operational tests.

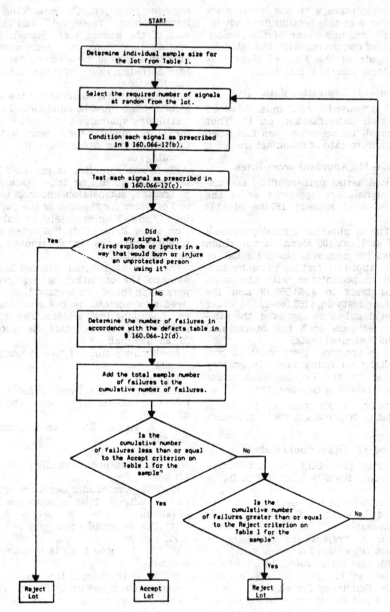

START

Determine individual sample size for
the lot from Table 1.

Select the required number of signals
at random from the lot.

Condition each signal as prescribed
in § 160.066–12(b).

Test each signal as prescribed in
§ 160.066–12(c).

Did
any signal when
fired explode or ignite in a
way that would burn or injure
an unprotected person
using it?

Yes

No

Determine the number of failures in
accordance with the defects table in
§ 160.066–12(d).

Add the total sample number
of failures to the
cumulative number of failures.

Is the
cumulative number
of failures less than or equal
to the Accept criterion on
Table 1 for the
sample?

No

Yes

Is the
cumulative number
of failures greater than or equal
to the Reject criterion on
Table 1 for the
sample?

No

Yes

Reject
Lot

Accept
Lot

Reject
Lot

Figure 1. Operational test procedure.

TABLE 1— ACCEPT AND REJECT CRITERIA FOR OPERATIONAL TEST LOTS

Lot size	Individual sample size	Sample	Cumulative sample size	Accept [1]	Reject [1]
280 or less.	8	First	8	[2]	4
		Second	16	1	5
		Third	24	2	6
		Fourth	32	3	7
		Fifth	40	5	8
		Sixth	48	7	9
		Seventh	56	9	10
281 to 500.	13	First	13	[2]	4
		Second	26	1	6
		Third	39	3	8
		Fourth	52	5	10
		Fifth	65	7	11
		Sixth	78	10	12
		Seventh	91	13	14
501 to 1,200.	20	First	20	[2]	5
		Second	40	3	8
		Third	60	6	10
		Fourth	80	8	13
		Fifth	100	11	15
		Sixth	120	14	17
		Seventh	140	18	19
1,201 to 3,200.	32	First	32	1	7
		Second	64	4	10
		Third	96	8	13
		Fourth	128	12	17
		Fifth	160	17	20
		Sixth	192	21	23
		Seventh	224	25	26
More than 3,200.	50	First	50	2	9
		Second	100	7	14
		Third	150	13	19
		Fourth	200	19	25
		Fifth	250	25	29
		Sixth	300	31	33
		Seventh	350	37	38

[1] Cumulative number of failures.
[2] Lot may not be accepted. Next sample must be tested.

§160.066–13 Technical tests.

(a) The following conditions apply to technical tests as described in this section:

(1) A total of nine signals must be selected at random from the lot being tested;

(2) If the signals are protected by sealed packaging, then the conditioning for the technical tests must be conducted with the signal in the sealed packaging;

(3) If signals in the test sample fail to pass one of the technical tests, the entire lot is rejected;

(4) Signals from "reject lots" may be reworked by the manufacturer to correct the deficiency for which they were rejected and be resubmitted for inspection. Records shall be kept of the reasons for rejection, the reworking performed on the "reject lot", and the result of the second test. Signals from "reject lots" may not, unless subsequently accepted, be sold or offered for sale as being in compliance with this specification.

(b) The Elevated Temperature, Humidity, and Storage Test must be conducted in the following manner:

(1) Select three signals from the nine;

(2) Place each signal in a thermostatically controlled even-temperature oven held at 55 Degrees C (131 Degrees F), and at not less than 90% relative humidity, for at least 72 hours (If for any reason it is not possbie to operate the oven continuously for the 72 hour period, it may be operated at the required temperature and humidity for 8 hours of each 24 during the 72 hour conditioning period.);

(3) After removal from the oven immediately place each signal in a chamber:

(i) At a temperature of at least 20 degrees C (68 degrees F) but not more than 25 degrees C (77 degrees F);

(ii) At not less than 65% relative humidity;

(iii) For ten days;

(4) Then remove each signal from any sealed packaging and fire it.

(5) The test sample fails the test if:

(i) Any signal ignites or decomposes before firing;

(ii) Any signal when fired malfunctions in a manner that would cause burns or injury to an unprotected person firing the signal, or;

(iii) Two or more of the signals fail to project and ignite the pyrotechnic candle.

(c) The Spontaneous Combustion Test must be performed in the following manner:

(1) Select three signals from the remaining six signals and place them in a thermostatically controlled even temperature over for 48 hours at a temperature of 75 degrees C (167 degrees F).

(2) The test sample fails the test if any signal ignites or decomposes during the test.

(d) The Luminous Intensity and Chromaticity Test must be performed in the following manner:

(1) Remove the pyrotechnic candle from the remaining three signals.

(2) Ignite, measure, and record the intensity of the burning candle with a visual photometer or equivalent photometric device or automatic recorder:

(i) While the specimen is supported in a horizontal position and the photometer is at right angles to the axis of the specimen,

(ii) At a distance of at least 3 m (10 ft.).

(3) Calculate the intensity of the candle as in § 160.066-7(c).

(4) Measure and record the chromaticity of the burning candle as specified in § 160.021-4(d)(4).

(5) The test sample fails the test if more than one signal has a luminous intensity of less than 10,000 candela, or more than one signal is not "vivid red".

§ 160.066-15 Production testing.

(a) Production tests must be performed under the procedures in Subpart 159.007 of this chapter.

(b) The operational tests in § 160.066-12 must be performed for every lot of signals produced.

(c) The technical tests in § 160.066-13 must be performed at least once every twelve months, or at least once every 10 lots, whichever occurs first.

(d) If a lot is rejected on the basis of the technical tests, then each subsequent lot produced must be tested according to the technical tests until samples from a lot pass these tests.

(e) An independent laboratory acceptable to the Commandant must perform or directly supervise:

(1) Each technical test, and

(2) All operational tests for at least four lots in a 12 month period, unless fewer than four lots are produced in a 12 month period. If less than four lots are produced in a 12 month period, each operational test must be performed or directly supervised by the independent laboratory.

(f) If a lot selected by the independent laboratory for an operational test is rejected, then the operational tests for the next lot produced, and the rejected lot, if reworked, must be performed or directly supervised by the independent laboratory. The tests required by this paragraph must not be counted for the purpose of meeting the requirements of paragraph (e).

(g) The independent laboratory selects the lots upon which technical tests are performed.

(h) If the manufacturer produces more than four lots within a 12 month period, the independent laboratory selects the lots for which it performs or directly supervises the operational tests.

(i) The operational test performed or directly supervised by the independent laboratory must occur at least once during each quarterly period, unless no lots are produced during that period.

(j) The independent laboratory, when it performs or directly supervises the technical tests required by paragraph (c) or (d) of this section, must inspect the signals selected for testing and compare them with the approved plans. Each signal inspected must conform to the plans.

Subpart 160.071   [Reserved]

Subpart 160.072—Distress Signals for Boats, Orange Flag

Source: CGD 76-183a, 44 FR 73054, Dec. 17, 1979, unless otherwise noted.

§ 160.072-1 Applicability.

(a) This subpart establishes standards for distress flags for boats.

(b) [Reserved]

§ 160.072-3 General performance requirements.

(a) Each flag must:

(1) Be a square or rectangle at least 90 cm (36 inches) wide and at least 90 cm (36 inches) long. If the flag is a rectangle, the shorter side cannot be less than ⅔ the length of the longer side;

(2) Have no less than 70% of the total area colored a bright red-orange color;

(3) Display a black disc and a black square on the red-orange background on both sides arranged as follows:

(i) The diameter of the disc and the length of one side of the square shall be equal, and shall each be ⅓ of the length of the longest side of the flag, or 30 cm (12 inches), whichever is greater.

(ii) The disc and square must be centered on one axis of the flag parallel to the longest side of the flag as shown in

Figure 160.072–3. If the flag is a square, the axis may be parallel to any side.

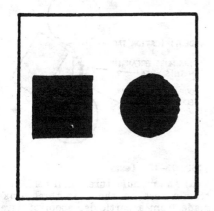

FIGURE 160.072–3

(iii) The disc and square shall be separated by a distance of ⅙ the length of the longest side of the flag or 15 cm (6 inches), whichever is greater.

(4) Be capable of passing the accelerated weathering test of §160.072–5;

(5) Have reinforced corners, each with a grommet; and,

(6) Be packaged with 4 pieces of line, with a tensile strength of at least 225 N (Newtons) (50 lbs) no less than 30 cm (12 inches) long, capable of passing through the grommets freely.

(b) [Reserved]

§160.072–5 Accelerated weathering test.

(a) Condition the flag, folded to 1/16th its size or as packaged, whichever is smaller, by submersion in 5% by weight sodium chloride solution for 2 hours followed immediately by storage at 95% (±5) related humidity and 40 °C (±3°) (100 °F ±5°) for at least 15 days.

(b) Unfold and suspend flag by the lines provided, secured through each grommet.

(c) Subject the flag to alternate 3 minute cycles of 5% by weight sodium chloride solution at 55 degrees (±5°) C and air blasts of 40 knots at 55 degrees (±5°) C, perpendicular to and over the entire surface of one side of the flag, without interruption for a period of not less than 24 hours.

(d) The flag fails the accelerated weathering test if

(1) After conditioning, the flag cannot be unfolded without damage,

(2) There is any tearing,

(3) The flag does not retain its bright red/orange color,

(4) The disc and square images no longer meet the requirements of §160.072–3(a)(3) or,

(5) There is any visible rot over more than 3% of the flag's surface.

§160.072–7 Manufacturer certification and labeling.

(a) Each distress flag intended as a Day Visual Distress Signal required by 33 CFR Part 175 must be certified by the manufacturer as complying with the requirements of this subpart.

(b) Each distress flag must be legibly and indelibly marked with:

(1) The manufacturer's name; and

(2) The following words—

"Day Visual Distress Signal for Boats. Complies with U.S. Coast Guard Requirements in 46 CFR 160.072. For Emergency Use Only".

§160.072–09 Manufacturer notification.

(a) Each manufacturer certifying flags in accordance with the specifications of this subpart must send written notice to the Commandant (G–MSE), U.S. Coast Guard, Washington, DC 20591—

(1) Within 30 days after first certifying a flag,

(2) Every five years as long as the manufacturer continues to produce flags, and

(3) Each time the design or construction material of the flag changes.

(b) [Reserved]

[CGD 76–183a, 44 FR 73054, Dec. 17, 1979, as amended by CGD 88–070, 53 FR 34536, Sept. 7, 1988; CGD 95–072, 60 FR 50467, Sept. 29, 1995; CGD 95–072, 60 FR 50467, Sept. 29, 1995; CGD 96–041, 61 FR 50733, Sept. 27, 1996]

Subpart 160.073—Float-Free Link or Life Floats and Buoyant Apparatus

SOURCE: CGD 79–167, 47 FR 41378, Sept. 20, 1982, unless otherwise noted.

§ 160.073-1 Scope.

(a) This subpart contains requirements for a float-free link used for connecting a life float or buoyant apparatus painter to a vessel. The float-free link is designed to be broken by the buoyant force of the life float or buoyant apparatus so that the float or apparatus breaks free of a vessel that sinks in water deeper than the length of the painter.

(b) [Reserved]

§ 160.073-5 Certification.

(a) The float-free link is not approved by the Coast Guard. The manufacturer of the link must certify that it meets all of the requirements of this subpart by application of the markings required in § 160.073-20.

(b) If the manufacturer wants the link to be listed in the Coast Guard publication COMDTINST M16714.3 (Series), "Equipment Lists," the manufacturer must send a letter requesting the listing to Commandant (G-MSE), U.S. Coast Guard, Washington, DC 20593-0001.

[CGD 79-167, 47 FR 41378, Sept. 20, 1982, as amended by CGD 88-070, 53 FR 34536, Sept. 7, 1988; CGD 95-072, 60 FR 50467, Sept. 29, 1995; CGD 96-041, 61 FR 50733, Sept. 27, 1996]

§ 160.073-10 Construction and performance.

(a) The link must be constructed essentially as shown in figure 160.073-10. The link must be formed from a single salt water corrosion-resistant wire. A loop at least 50 mm (2 in.) in diameter must be provided at each end of the wire. Each loop must be permanently secured.

(b) The breaking strength of each link must be between:

(1) 450 N (100 lb.) and 600 N (134 lb.) for links intended for life floats and buoyant apparatus of 10 persons and less capacity.

(2) 900 N (200 lb.) and 1200 N (268 lb.) for links intended for life floats and buoyant apparatus of 11 to 20 persons capacity.

(3) 1800 N (400 lb.) and 2400 N (536 lb.) for links intended for life floats and buoyant apparatus of 21 persons and more capacity.

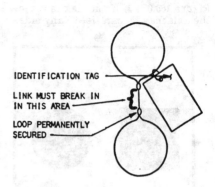

IDENTIFICATION TAG

LINK MUST BREAK IN IN THIS AREA

LOOP PERMANENTLY SECURED

§ 160.073-15 Tests.

(a) The manufacturer shall perform a tensile test on the first three links made from a particular spool of wire. The test must be done by slowly loading the link until it breaks. The link must break between the limits specified in § 160.073-10(b). The break must occur in the length of wire at or between the points where the loops are secured (see Figure 160.073-10).

(b) If each of the three links passes the test, each link constructed in the same manner from the same spool of wire may be certified by the manufacturer as meeting the requirements of this subpart.

(c) If one or more of the three links fails the test, no link manufactured in the same manner and from the same spool of wire as the test links may be certified as meeting the requirements of this subpart.

§ 160.073-20 Marking.

(a) Each link certified by the manufacturer to meet the requirements of this subpart must have a corrosion resistant, waterproof tag attached to it that has the following information on it (the manufacturer must make the appropriate entries in the indicated space):

FLOAT-FREE LINK FOR LIFE FLOATS AND BUOYANT APPARATUS
Of *(10 or less) (11 to 20) (21 or more)* persons capacity.
Normal breaking strength ____.
Meets U.S. coast guard
Requirements—46 CFR 160.073.
Made by: *(name and address)* ____
(Date) ____

(b) [Reserved]

Subpart 160.076—Inflatable Recreational Personal Flotation Devices

SOURCE: CGD 94–110, 60 FR 32848, June 23, 1995, unless otherwise noted.

§ 160.076–1 Scope.

(a) This subpart contains structural and performance standards for approval of inflatable recreational personal flotation devices (PFDs), as well as requirements for production follow-up inspections, associated manuals, information pamphlets, and markings.

(b) Inflatable PFDs approved under this subpart—

(1) Rely entirely upon inflation for buoyancy; and

(2) Are approved for use by adults only.

§ 160.076–3 Applicability.

Inflatable PFDs approved under this subpart may be used to meet the carriage requirements of 33 CFR 175.15 and 175.17 on the following types of vessels only:

(a) Recreational vessels.

(b) Uninspected recreational submersible vessels.

§ 160.076–5 Definitions.

As used in this part:

Commandant means the Chief of the Lifesaving and Fire Safety Division, Marine Safety and Environmental Protection. Address: Commandant (G–MSE–4), U.S. Coast Guard Headquarters, 2100 Second St. SW., Washington, DC 20593–0001; phone: 202–267–1444; facsimile: 202–267–1069; electronic mail: "mvi-3/G-M18@cgsmtp.uscg.mil".

Conditional approval means a category of PFD which has condition(s) on its approval with which the user must comply in order for the PFD to be counted toward meeting the carriage requirements of the vessel being used. All conditionally approved PFDs are designated Approval Type V.

First quality workmanship means construction which is free from any defect materially affecting appearance or serviceability.

Inflation medium means any solid, liquid, or gas that, when activated, provides inflation for buoyancy.

Inspector means a recognized laboratory representative assigned to perform, supervise or oversee the duties described in §§ 160.076–29 and 160.076–31 of this subpart or any Coast Guard representative performing duties related to the approval.

MOU means memorandum of understanding which describes the approval functions a recognized independent laboratory performs for the Coast Guard, and the recognized independent laboratory's working arrangements with the Coast Guard.

Performance type means the in-water performance classification of the PFD (I, II, or III).

PFD means personal flotation device as defined in 33 CFR 175.13.

PFD Approval Type means the Type designation assigned by the Commandant, as documented in the approval certificate for the PFD, based primarily on the in-water performance and serviceability of the PFD.

Plans and specifications means the drawings, product description, construction specifications, and bill of materials submitted in accordance with § 160.076–13 for approval of a PFD design.

[CGD 94–110, 60 FR 32848, June 23, 1995, as amended by CGD 95–072, 60 FR 50466, Sept. 29, 1995; CGD 94–110, 61 FR 13945, Mar. 28, 1996; CGD 96–041, 61 FR 50733, Sept. 27, 1996]

§ 160.076–7 PFD Approval Type.

(a) An inflatable PFD may be approved without conditions as a Type I, II, or III PFD for persons over 36 kg (80 lb) if it meets the requirements of this subpart.

(b) Each inflatable PFD that can be demonstrated to meet the in-water performance requirements of a type I, II or III PFD in UL 1180 during approval testing and the applicable requirements of this subpart provided that certain conditions are placed on its use, may be approved as a Type V PFD. Each such PFD has conditional approval.

[CGD 94–110, 60 FR 32848, June 23, 1995, as amended by CGD 94–110, 61 FR 13945, Mar. 28, 1996]

§ 160.076–9 Conditional approval.

(a) A conditionally approved inflatable PFD is categorized as a Type V

PFD and may be used to meet the Coast Guard PFD carriage requirements of 33 CFR part 175 only if the PFD is used in accordance with any requirements on the approval label. PFDs marked "Approved only when worn" must be worn whenever the vessel is underway and the intended wearer is not within an enclosed space if the PFD is intended to be used to satisfy the requirements of 33 CFR part 175. Note: Additional approved PFDs may be needed to satisfy the requirements of 33 CFR part 175 if "Approved only when worn" PFDs are not worn.

(b) PFDs not meeting the performance specifications for type I, II, or III PFDs in UL 1180 may be classified as Type V, conditionally approved PFDs, when the Commandant determines that the performance or design characteristics of the PFD make such classification appropriate.

[CGD 94–110, 60 FR 32848, June 23, 1995, as amended by CGD 94–110, 61 FR 13945, Mar. 28, 1996]

§ 160.076-11 Incorporation by reference.

(a) Certain materials are incorporated by reference into this subpart with the approval of the Director of the Federal Register in accordance with 5 U.S.C. 552(a) and 1 CFR part 51. To enforce any edition other than the one listed in paragraph (b) of this section, the Coast Guard must publish notice of the change in the FEDERAL REGISTER, and the material must be available to the public. All approved material is available for inspection at the Office of the Federal Register, 800 North Capitol Street NW., suite 700, Washington, DC and at the U.S. Coast Guard, Lifesaving and Fire Safety Division (G–MSE–4), 2100 Second Street, SW., Washington, DC 20593–0001, and is available from the sources indicated in paragraph (b) of this section.

(b) The materials approved for incorporation by reference in this subpart, and the sections affected are as follows:

AMERICAN SOCIETY FOR TESTING AND MATERIALS (ASTM)
100 Barr Harbor Drive, West Conshohocken, PA 19428–2959.
ASTM D 751–79 Standard Methods of Testing Coated Fabrics, 1979, 160.076–25;

ASTM D 1434–75 Gas Transmission Rate of Plastic Film and Sheeting, 1975, 160.076–25.
FEDERAL STANDARDS
Naval Publishing and Printing Center, Customer Service, 700 Robbins Avenue, Philadelphia, PA 19120.
In Federal Test Method Standard No. 191A (dated July 20, 1978) the following methods:
   (1) Method 5100, Strength and Elongation, Breaking of Woven Cloth; Grab Method, 160.076–25;
   (2) Method 5132, Strength of Cloth, Tearing; Falling-Pendulum Method, 160.076–25;
   (3) Method 5134, Strength of Cloth, Tearing; Tongue Method, 160.076–25.

UNDERWRITERS LABORATORIES (UL)
Underwriters Laboratories, Inc., 12 Laboratory Drive, Research Triangle Park, NC 27709–3995 (Phone (919) 549–1400; Facsimile: (919) 549–1842)
UL 1123, "Marine Buoyant Devices", February 17, 1995, 160.076–35;
UL 1180, "Fully Inflatable Recreational Personal Flotation Devices", May 15, 1995, 160.076–7; 160.076–21; 160.076–23; 160.076–25; 160.076–29; 160.076–31; 160.076–37; 160.076–39.
UL 1191, "Components for Personal Flotation Devices", May 16, 1995, 160.076–21; 160.076–25; 160.076–39.

[CGD 94–110, 60 FR 32848, June 23, 1995, as amended by CGD 95–072, 60 FR 50467, Sept. 29, 1995, CGD 94–110, 61 FR 13945, Mar. 28, 1996; CGD 96–041, 61 FR 50733, Sept. 27, 1996; CGD 97–057, 62 FR 51048, Sept. 30, 1997]

§ 160.076-13 Approval procedures for inflatable PFDs.

(a) Manufacturers seeking approval of an inflatable PFD design shall follow the procedures of this section and subpart 159.005 of this chapter.

(b) Each application for approval of an inflatable PFD must contain the information specified in § 159.005–5 of this chapter. The application must be submitted to a recognized laboratory. One copy of the application and, except as provided in paragraph (c)(2) of this section, a prototype PFD must be submitted to the Commandant for preapproval review. If a similar design has already been approved, the Commandant may authorize the recognized laboratory to waive the preapproval review under §§ 159.005–5 and 159.005–7 of this chapter.

(c) The application must include the following:
   (1) Plans and specifications containing the information required by § 159.005–12 of this chapter, including

drawings, product description, construction specifications, and bill of materials.

(2) The information specified in §159.005–5(a)(2) (i) through (iii) of this chapter must be included in the application, except that, if preapproval review has been waived, the manufacturer is not required to send a prototype PFD sample to the Commandant.

(3) The type of performance (Type I, II, or III) that the PFD is designed to provide along with the Approval Type sought (Type I, II, III, or V).

(4) Any special purpose(s) for which the PFD is designed and the vessel(s) or vessel type(s) on which its use is intended.

(5) Buoyancy, torque, and other relevant tolerances to be met during production.

(6) The text of any optional marking to be included on the PFD in addition to the markings required by §160.076–39.

(7) A draft of the information pamphlet required by §160.076–35.

(8) A draft of the owner's manual required by §160.076–37.

(9) For any conditionally approved PFD, the intended approval condition(s).

(d) The description required by §159.005–9 of this chapter of quality control procedures may be omitted if the manufacturer's planned quality control procedures meet the requirements of §§160.076–29 and 160.076–31.

(e) *Manual and pamphlet.* Before granting approval of a PFD design, the Commandant may require changes to the manual and information pamphlet submitted for review to ensure compliance with the requirements of §§160.076–35 and 160.076–37.

(f) *Waiver of tests.* A manufacturer may request that the Commandant waive any test prescribed for approval under this subpart. To request a waiver, the manufacturer must submit to the Commandant and the recognized laboratory, one of the following:

(1) Satisfactory test results on a PFD of sufficiently similar design as determined by the Commandant.

(2) Engineering analysis demonstrating that the test for which a waiver is requested is not appropriate for the particular design submitted for approval or that, because of its design or construction, it is not possible for the PFD to fail that test.

(g) *Alternative requirements.* A PFD that does not meet the requirements of this subpart may be approved by the Commandant if the device—

(1) Meets other requirements prescribed by the Commandant in place of or in addition to the requirements of this subpart; and

(2) As determined by the Commandant, provides at least the same degree of safety provided by other PFDs that meet the requirements of this subpart.

[CGD 94–110, 60 FR 32848, June 23, 1995, as amended by CGD 94–110, 61 FR 13946, Mar. 28, 1996]

§160.076–15 Suspension or termination of approval.

As provided in §159.005–15 of this chapter, the Commandant may suspend or terminate the approval of an inflatable PFD design if the manufacturer fails to comply with this subpart or the recognized laboratory's accepted procedures or requirements.

§160.076–17 Approval of design or material changes.

(a) The manufacturer must submit any proposed changes in design, material, or construction to the recognized laboratory and the Commandant for approval before changing PFD production methods.

(b) Determinations of equivalence of design, construction, and materials may be made only by the Commandant or a designated representative.

§160.076–19 Recognized laboratories.

(a) *PFDs.* The following laboratories are recognized under §159.010–9 of this chapter to perform the approval and production oversight functions required by this subpart:

Underwriters Laboratories, Inc., 12 Laboratory Drive, P.O. Box 13995, Research Triangle Park, NC 27709–3995, (919) 549–1400.

(b) *Components.* The following laboratories are recognized under subpart 159.010 of this chapter and may perform the component material acceptance, production oversight, and certification functions required by §160.076–21(a)(1):

Underwriters Laboratories, Inc., 12 Laboratory Drive, P.O. Box 13995, Research Triangle Park, NC 27709–3995, (919) 549–1400.

§ 160.076–21 Component materials.

(a) Each component material used in the manufacturer of an inflatable PFD must—

(1) Meet the applicable requirements of subpart 164.019 of this chapter, UL 1191, UL 1180, and this section; and

(2) Be of good quality and suitable for the purpose intended.

(b) The average permeability of inflation chamber material, determined in accordance with the procedures specified in § 160.076–25(d)(2)(iii) must not be more than 110% of the permeability of the materials determined in approval testing required by § 160.076–25(d)(2)(iii).

(c) The average grab breaking strength and tear strength of the inflation chamber material, determined in accordance with the procedures specified in §§ 160.076–25(d)(2)(i) and 160.076–25(d)(2)(ii), must be at least 90% of the grab breaking strength and tear strength determined from testing required by §§ 160.076–25(d)(2)(i) and 160.076–25(d)(2)(ii). No individual sample result for breaking strength or tear strength may be more than 20% below the results obtained in approval testing.

(d) Each manual, automatic, or manual-auto inflation mechanism must be marked in accordance with § 160.076–39(e).

[CGD 94–110, 60 FR 32848, June 23, 1995, as amended by CGD 94–110, 61 FR 13946, Mar. 28, 1996]

§ 160.076–23 Construction and performance requirements.

(a) Each inflatable PFD design must—

(1) Meet the requirements in UL 1180 applicable to the PFD performance type for which approval is sought; and

(2) Meet any additional requirements that the Commandant may prescribe to approve unique or novel designs.

(b) [Reserved]

[CGD 94–110, 60 FR 32848, June 23, 1995, as amended by CGD 94–110, 61 FR 13946, Mar. 28, 1996]

§ 160.076–25 Approval testing.

(a) To obtain approval of an inflatable PFD design, approval tests specified in UL 1180 and this section must be conducted or supervised by a recognized laboratory using PFDs that have been constructed in accordance with the plans and specifications submitted with the application for approval.

(b) Each PFD design must pass the tests required by UL 1180 and this section that are applicable to the PFD performance type for which approval is sought.

(c) Each test subject participating in the tests in UL 1180, section 6 shall in addition, demonstrate that the test subject can repack the PFD such that it can be used in the donning tests and manual activation tests required by—

(1) Section 6.2.3 of UL 1180; and

(2) Sections 6.4.1, and 6.4.2 of UL 1180, if the test engineer cannot verify that the manual and oral inflators are properly stowed.

(d) Each PFD design must pass the following tests and evaluations:

(1) *Visual examination.* The complete PFD must be visually examined for compliance with the construction and performance requirements of §§ 160.076–21 and 160.076–23 and UL 1180 and 1191.

(2) *Inflation chamber properties.* The following tests must be conducted after successful completion of all other approval tests. The test samples used in the following tests must come from one or more PFDs that were each used in all the Use Characteristics Tests required by UL 1180 section 6.

(i) *Grab breaking strength.* The grab breaking strength of chamber materials must be determined in accordance with Method No. 5100 of Federal Test Method Standard 191 or ASTM D 751.

(ii) *Tear strength.* The tear strength of chamber materials must be determined in accordance with Method No. 5132 or 5134 of Federal Test Method Standard 191 or ASTM D 751.

(iii) *Permeability.* The permeability of chamber materials must be determined in accordance with ASTM D 1434 using CO_2 as the test gas.

(iv) *Seam strength.* The seam strength of the seams in each inflation chamber of at least one PFD must be determined in accordance with ASTM D 751 except that 25 by 200 mm (1 by 8 in.)

samples may be used where insufficient length of straight seam is available.

(e) *Additional tests.* The Commandant may prescribe additional tests for approval of novel or unique designs.

[CGD 94–110, 60 FR 32848, June 23, 1995, as amended by CGD 94–110, 61 FR 13946, Mar. 28, 1996]

§ 160.076–27 [Reserved]

§ 160.076–29 Production oversight.

(a) Production tests and inspections must be conducted in accordance with this section and subpart 159.007 of this chapter unless the Commandant authorizes alternative tests and inspections. The Commandant may prescribe additional production tests and inspections necessary to maintain quality control and to monitor compliance with the requirements of this subpart.

(b) Production oversight must be performed by the same laboratory that performs the approval tests unless the Commandant determines that the employees of an alternative laboratory have received training and have access to the same information as the inspectors of the laboratory that conducted the approval testing.

(c) In addition to responsibilities set out in part 159 of this chapter and the accepted Laboratory Follow-up Procedures, each manufacturer of an inflatable PFD and each recognized laboratory inspector shall comply with the following, as applicable:

(1) *Manufacturer.* Each manufacturer must—

(i) Except as provided in paragraph (e)(2) of this section, perform all required tests and examinations on each PFD lot before any required inspector's tests and inspection of the lot;

(ii) Follow established procedures for maintaining quality control of the materials used, manufacturing operations, and the finished product;

(iii) Implement a continuing program of employee training and a program for maintaining production and test equipment;

(iv) Admit the inspector to any place in the factory where work is done on PFDs or component materials, and where parts or completed PFDs are stored;

(v) Have an inspector observe the production methods used in producing the first PFD lot and observe any revisions in production methods made thereafter; and

(vi) Allow the inspector to take samples of completed PFDs or of component materials for tests required by this subpart and for tests relating to the safety of the design.

(2) *Recognized laboratory oversight.* An inspector from a recognized laboratory shall oversee production in accordance with the MOU. During production oversight, the inspector shall not perform or supervise any production test or inspection unless—

(i) The manufacturer has a valid approval certificate; and

(ii) The inspector has first observed the manufacturer's production methods and any revisions to those methods.

(3) The inspector must perform or supervise testing and inspection of at least one in each five lots of PFDs produced.

(4) During each inspection, the inspector must check for compliance with the manufacturer's quality control procedures.

(5) Except as provided in paragraph (c)(6) of this section, at least once each calendar quarter, the inspector must examine the manufacturer's records required by § 160.076–33 and observe the manufacturer perform each of the tests required by § 160.076–31(c).

(6) If less than six lots are produced during a calendar year, only one lot inspection and one records' examination and test performance observation are required during that year. Each lot tested and inspected under paragraph (c)(3) of this section must be within seven lots of the previous lot inspected.

(d) *PFD lots.* A lot number must be assigned in accordance with UL 1180 to each group of PFDs produced. Lots must be numbered serially. A new lot must be started whenever any change in materials or a revision to a production method is made, and whenever any substantial discontinuity in the production process occurs. Changes in lots of component materials must be treated as changes in materials. The lot number assigned, along with the approval number, must enable the PFD manufacturer, by referring to the records required by this subpart, to determine the supplier of the components used in the PFD and the component supplier's identifying information for the component lot.

(e) *Samples.* For the tests, examinations, and inspections required by § 160.076–31, inspectors and manufacturers shall select samples as provided in this paragraph.

(1) Samples shall be selected at random from a lot in which all PFDs or materials in the lot are available for selection. Except as provided in § 160.076–31(c), samples must be selected from completed PFDs.

(2) Different samples must be selected for the manufacturer's and inspector's tests, except, if the total production for any five consecutive lots does not exceed 250 PFDs, the manufacturer's and inspector's tests may be run on the same sample(s) at the same time.

(3) The number of samples selected per lot must be at least equal to the applicable number required by Table 160.076–29A for manufacturers or Table 160.076–29B for inspectors.

(4) The following additional requirements apply as indicated in Table 160.076–29A to individual sample selections by manufacturers:

(i) Samples must be selected from each lot of incoming material. The

tests required under paragraphs 160.076–25(d)(2)(i) through 160.076–25(d)(2)(iv) prescribe the number of samples to select.

(ii) Samples selected for the indicated tests may not be used for more than one test.

(iii) If a sample fails the over-pressure test, the number of samples to be tested in the next lot produced must be at least two percent of the total number of PFDs in the lot or 10 PFDs, whichever is greater.

(iv) The indicated test must be conducted at least once each calendar quarter or whenever a new lot of material is used or a production process is revised.

(5) The following additional requirements apply as indicated in Table 160.076–29B to individual sample selections by inspectors:

(i) Samples selected for the indicated tests may not be used for more than one test.

(ii) The indicated test may be omitted if it was conducted by the manufacturer on the materials used and by the inspector on a previous lot within the past 12 months.

(iii) One sample of each means of marking on each type of fabric or finish used in PFD construction must be tested at least every six months or whenever a new lot of materials is used.

TABLE 160.076–29A—MANUFACTURER'S SAMPLING PLAN

	Number of Samples Per Lot					
Lot size:	1–100	101–200	201–300	301–500	501–750	751–1000
Tests:						
Inflation Chamber Materials			See Note (a)			
Seam Strength	1	1	2	2	3	4
Over-pressure (b)(c)	1	2	3	4	6	8
Air Retention			EVERY DEVICE IN THE LOT			
Buoyancy and Inflation Medium Retention	1	2	3	4	6	8
Tensile Strength			See Note (d)			
Detailed Product Examination	2	2	3	4	6	8
Retest Sample Size (b			13	13	20	20
Final Lot Inspection			EVERY DEVICE IN THE LOT			

Notes to Table: (a) See § 160.076–29(e)(4)(i). (b) See § 160.076–29(e)(4)(ii). (c) See § 160.076–29(e)(4)(iii). (d) See § 160.076–29(e)(4)(iv).

TABLE 160.076–29B—INSPECTOR'S SAMPLING PLAN

	Number of Samples Per Lot					
Lot size:	1–100	101–200	201–300	301–500	501–750	751–1000
Tests:						
Over-pressure (a	1	1	2	2	3	4
Air Retention	1	1	2	2	3	4
Buoyancy & Inflation Medium Retention	1	1	2	2	3	4

TABLE 160.076–29B—INSPECTOR'S SAMPLING PLAN—Continued

Lot size:	Number of Samples Per Lot					
	1–100	101–200	201–300	301–500	501–750	751–1000
Tensile Strength	See Note (b)					
Waterproof marking	See Note (c)					
Detailed Project Examination ....ª....	1	1	1	2	2	3
Retest Sample Size (ª	10	10	13	13	20	20
Final Lot Inspection	10	15	20	25	27	30

Notes to Table: (ª) See § 160.076–29(e)(5)(i). (b) See § 160.076–29(e)(5)(ii). (c) See § 160.076–29(e)(5)(iii).

(f) *Accept/reject criteria: manufacturer testing.* (1) A PFD lot passes production testing if each sample passes each test.

(2) In lots of 200 or less PFDs, the lot must be rejected if any sample fails one or more tests.

(3) In lots of more than 200 PFDs, the lot must be rejected if—

(i) One sample fails more than one test;

(ii) More than one sample fails any test or combination of tests; or

(iii) One sample fails one test and in redoing that test with the number of samples specified for retesting in Table 160.076–29A, one or more samples fail the retest.

(4) A rejected PFD lot may be retested only if allowed under § 160.076–31(e).

(g) *Accept/reject criteria: independent laboratory testing.* (1) A lot passes production testing if each sample passes each test.

(2) A lot must be rejected if—

(i) A sample fails more than one test;

(ii) More than one sample fails any test or combination of tests; or

(iii) One sample fails one test and in redoing that test with the number of samples specified for retesting in Table 160.076–29B, one or more samples fail the test.

(3) A rejected lot may be retested only if allowed under § 160.076–31(e).

(h) *Facilities and equipment.* (1) *General.* The manufacturer must provide the test equipment and facilities necessary for performing production tests, examinations, and inspections, unless Commandant has accepted testing at a location other than the manufacturer's facility.

(2) *Calibration.* The manufacturer must have the calibration of all test equipment checked at least every six months by a weights and measures agency or the equipment manufacturer, distributor, or dealer.

(3) *Facilities.* The manufacturer must provide a suitable place and the necessary equipment for the inspector to use in conducting or supervising tests. For the final lot inspection, the manufacturer must provide a suitable working environment and a smooth-top table for the inspector's use.

[CGD 94–110, 60 FR 32848, June 23, 1995, as amended by CGD 94–110, 61 FR 13946, Mar. 28, 1996; 61 FR 15868, 61 FR Apr. 9, 1996]

§ 160.076–31 **Production tests and examinations.**

(a) Samples used in testing must be selected in accordance with § 160.076–29(e).

(b) On each sample selected—

(1) The manufacturer must conduct the tests in paragraphs (c)(2) through (c)(8) of this section;

(2) The recognized laboratory inspector must conduct or supervise the tests in paragraphs (c)(4) through (c)(8) of this section; and

(3) In addition to meeting the requirements of this section, each test result must meet the requirements, if any, contained in the approved plans and specifications.

(c) When conducting the tests specified by this paragraph, the following conditions must be met:

(1) *Inflation chamber materials.* The average and individual results of testing the minimum number of samples prescribed by § 160.076–25(d)(2) must comply with the requirements in § 160.076–21 (b) and (c) for permeability, grab strength, and tear strength. Lots not

191

meeting this requirement must be rejected and, unless authorized by the Commandant, may not be subdivided and retested.

(2) *Seam strength.* The seams in each inflation chamber of each sample must be tested in accordance with § 160.076–25(d)(2)(iv). The results for each inflation chamber must be at least 90% of the results obtained in approval testing.

(3) *Over-pressure.* Each sample must be tested in accordance with and meet UL 1180 section 7.15. Prior to initiating the test at the specified values, samples may be prestressed by inflating them to a greater pressure than the required test pressure.

(4) *Air retention.* Each sample must be tested in accordance with and meet UL 1180 section 7.16. Prior to initiating the test at the specified values, test samples may be prestressed by inflating to a pressure greater than the design pressure, but not exceeding 50 percent of the required pressure for the tests in paragraph (c)(3) of this section. No alternate test method may be used that decreases the length of the test unless authorized by the Commandant. Such alternative test must require a proportionately lower allowable pressure loss and the same percentage sensitivity and accuracy as the standard allowable loss measured with the standard instrumentation.

(5) *Buoyancy and inflation medium retention.* Each sample must be tested in accordance with and meet UL 1180 section 7.2.2–7.2.10, except 7.2.5. Each buoyancy value must fall within the tolerances specified in the approved plans and specifications.

(6) *Tensile strength.* Each sample primary closure system must be tested in accordance with and meet UL 1180 section 7.4.1 and .2.

(7) *Detailed product examination.* Each sample PFD must be disassembled to the extent necessary to determine compliance with the following:

(i) All dimensions and seam allowances must be within tolerances prescribed in the approved plans and specifications.

(ii) The torque of each screw type mechanical fastener must be within its tolerance as prescribed in the approved plans and specifications.

(iii) The arrangement, markings, and workmanship must be as specified in the approved plans and specifications and this subpart.

(iv) The PFD must not contain any apparent defects.

(8) *Waterproof Marking Test.* Each sample must be completely submerged in fresh water for at least 30 minutes. The sample must then be removed, immediately placed on a hard surface, and the markings vigorously rubbed with the fingers for 15 seconds. If the printing becomes illegible, the sample must be rejected.

(d) *Final lot examination and inspection*—(1) *General.* On each PFD lot that passes production testing, the manufacturer shall perform a final lot examination and, on every fifth lot, a laboratory inspector shall perform a final lot inspection. Samples must be selected in accordance with paragraph § 160.076–29(e). Each final lot must demonstrate—

(i) First quality workmanship;

(ii) That the general arrangement and attachment of all components, such as body straps, closures, inflation mechanisms, tie tapes, and drawstrings, are as specified in the approved plans and specifications;

(iii) Compliance with the marking requirements in § 160.076–39; and

(iv) That the information pamphlet and owner's manual required by § 160.076–35 and 160.076–37, respectively, are securely attached to the device, with the pamphlet selection information visible and accessible prior to purchase.

(2) *Accept/reject criteria.* Each nonconforming PFD must be rejected. If three or more nonconforming PFDs are rejected for the same kind of defect, lot examination or inspection must be discontinued and the lot rejected.

(3) *Manufacturer examination.* This examination must be conducted by a manufacturer's representative who is familiar with the approved plans and specifications, the functioning of the PFD and its components, and the production testing procedures. This person must not be responsible for meeting production schedules or be supervised by someone who is. This person must prepare and sign the record required by

159.007–13(a) of this chapter and 160.076–33(b).

(4) *Independent laboratory inspection.* (i) The inspector must discontinue lot inspection and reject the lot if examination of individual PFDs or the records for the lot shows noncompliance with either this section or the laboratory's or the manufacturer's quality control procedures.

(ii) If the inspector rejects a lot, the inspector must advise the Commandant or the recognized laboratory within 15 days.

(iii) The inspector must prepare and sign the inspection record required by 159.007–13(a) of this chapter and 160.076–33(b). If the lot passes, the record must include the inspector's certification that the lot passed inspection and that no evidence of noncompliance with this section was observed.

(e) *Disposition of rejected PFD lot or PFD.* (1) A rejected PFD lot may be resubmitted for testing, examination or inspection if the manufacturer first removes and destroys each defective PFD or, if authorized by the Commandant, reworks the lot to correct the defect.

(2) Any PFD rejected in a final lot examination or inspection may be resubmitted for examination or inspection if all defects have been corrected and reexamination or reinspection is authorized by the Commandant.

(3) A rejected lot or rejected PFD may not be sold or offered for sale under the representation that it meets this subpart or that it is Coast Guard-approved.

[CGD 94–110, 60 FR 32848, June 23, 1995, as amended by CGD 94–110, 61 FR 13946, Mar. 28, 1996]

§ 160.076–33 Manufacturer records.

(a) Each manufacturer of inflatable PFDs shall keep the records of production inspections and tests as required by § 159.007–13 of this chapter, except that they must be retained for at least 120 months after the month in which the inspection or test was conducted.

(b) In addition to the information required by § 159.007–13 of this chapter, the manufacturer's records must also include the following information:

(1) For each test, the serial number of the test instrument used if more than one test instrument was available.

(2) For each test and inspection, the identification of the samples used, the lot number, the approval number, and the number of PFDs in the lot.

(3) For each lot rejected, the cause for rejection, any corrective action taken, and the final disposition of the lot.

(4) For all materials used in production the—

(i) Name and address of the supplier;

(ii) Date of purchase and receipt;

(iii) Lot number; and

(iv) Where required by § 164.019–5 of this chapter, the certification received with standard components.

(5) A copy of this subpart.

(6) Each document incorporated by reference in § 160.076–11.

(7) A copy of the approved plans and specifications.

(8) The approval certificate obtained in accordance with § 2.75–1 and 2.75–5 of this chapter.

(9) Certificates evidencing calibration of test equipment, including the identity of the agency performing the calibration, date of calibration, and results.

(c) A description or photographs of procedures and equipment used in testing required by § 159.007–13(a)(4) of this chapter, is not required if the manufacturer's procedures and equipment meet the requirements of this subpart.

(d) The records required by paragraph (b)(4) of this section must be kept for at least 120 months after preparation. All other records required by paragraph (b) of this section must be kept for at least 60 months after the PFD approval expires or is terminated.

§ 160.076–35 Information pamphlet.

A pamphlet that is consistent in format to that specified in UL 1123 must be attached to each inflatable PFD sold or offered for sale in such a way that a prospective purchaser can read the pamphlet prior to purchase. The pamphlet text and layout must be submitted to the Commandant for approval. The text must be printed in each pamphlet exactly as approved by the Commandant. Additional information, instructions, or illustrations must not be included within the approved text and layout. Sample pamphlet text and layout may be obtained by contacting the Commandant. This pamphlet may be combined with the manual required by § 160.076–37 if PFD selection and warning information is provided on the PFD packaging in such a way that it remains visible until purchase.

§ 160.076–37 Owner's manual.

(a) *General.* The manufacturer must provide an owner's manual with each inflatable PFD sold or offered for sale. A draft of the manual for each model must be submitted for approval in accordance with § 160.076–13.

(b) *Manual contents.* Each owner's manual must contain the information specified in section 11 of UL 1180, and, if the PFD is conditionally approved, an explanation of the meaning of, and reasons for, the approval conditions.

[CGD 94–110, 60 FR 32848, June 23, 1995, as amended by CGD 94–110, 61 FR 13947, Mar. 28, 1996]

§ 160.076–39 Marking.

(a) *General.* Each inflatable PFD must be marked as specified in UL 1180 section 10 and this section.

(b) PFD Type. Based on its approval certificate, each PFD must be marked as follows—

(1) "Type I PFD";

(2) "Type II PFD";

(3) "Type III PFD"; or

(4) "Type V [*insert exact text of description noted on the approval certificate, if any*] PFD—[*insert text required by paragraph (c) of this section*]. This PFD provides in-water performance equivalent to a Type [*insert performance type criteria noted on the approval certificate*] PFD."

(c) A Type V, conditionally approved, inflatable PFD must be marked with the approval conditions specified on the approval certificate.

(d) *Additional markings.* (1) Unless otherwise noted on the approval certificate, each inflatable PFD must be marked with the following:

(i) "NOT APPROVED TO MEET CARRIAGE REQUIREMENTS ON COMMERCIAL VESSELS."

(ii) The unique model, style, or part number of the inflation mechanism approved for use on the PFD.

(2) [Reserved]

(e) *Inflation mechanisms.* Each manual, automatic, or manual-auto inflation mechanism must be permanently marked with its unique model number.

[CGD 94–110, 60 FR 32848, June 23, 1995, as amended by CGD 94–110, 61 FR 13947, Mar. 28, 1996]

Subpart 160.077—Hybrid Inflatable Personal Flotation Devices

SOURCE: CGD 78–174, 50 FR 33928, Aug. 22, 1985, unless otherwise noted.

§ 160.077–1 Scope.

(a) This specification contains requirements for approving hybrid inflatable personal flotation devices (hybrid PFDs).

(b) Under this chapter and 33 CFR part 175, certain commercial vessels and recreational boats may carry Type I, II, or III hybrid PFDs to meet carriage requirements. Type V hybrid PFDs may be substituted for other required PFDs if they are worn under conditions prescribed in their manual as required by § 160.077–29 and on their marking as prescribed in § 160.077–31. For recreational boats or boaters involved in a special activity, hybrid PFD approval may also be limited to that activity.

(c) Unless approved as a Type I SOLAS Lifejacket, a hybrid PFD on an inspected commercial vessel will be approved only—

(1) As work vest; or

(2) For the special purpose stated on the approval certificate and PFD marking.

(d) A hybrid PFD may be approved for adults, weighing over 40 kg (90 lb); youths, weighing 23–40 kg (50–90 lb); small children, weighing 14–23 kg (30–50 lb); or for the size range of persons for which the design has been tested, as indicated on the PFD's label.

(e) This specification also contains requirements for—

(1) Manufacturers and sellers of recreational hybrid PFD's to provide an information pamphlet and owner's manual with each PFD; and

(2) Manufacturers of commercial hybrid PFD's to provide a user's manual.

[CGD 78–174, 50 FR 33928, Aug. 22, 1985, as amended by CGD 78–174, 60 FR 2486, Jan. 9, 1995]

§ 160.077–2 Definitions.

(a) *Commandant* means the Chief of the Lifesaving and Fire Safety Division, Marine Safety and Environmental Protection. Address: Commandant (G–MSE–4), U.S. Coast Guard Headquarters, 2100 Second Street SW., Washington, DC 20593–0001.

(b) *Commercial hybrid PFD* means a hybrid PFD approved for use on commercial vessels identified on the PFD label.

(c) *First quality workmanship* means construction which is free from any defect materially affecting appearance or serviceability.

(d) *Hybrid PFD* means a personal flotation device that has at least one inflation chamber in combination with inherently buoyant material.

(e) *Inflation medium* means any solid, liquid, or gas, that, when activated, provides inflation for buoyancy.

(f) *Inspector* means an independent laboratory representative assigned to perform duties described in § 160.077–23.

(g) *PFD* means a personal flotation device of a type approved under this subpart.

(h) *Recreational hybrid PFD* means a hybrid PFD approved for use on a recreational boat as defined in 33 CFR 175.3.

(i) [Reserved]

(j) *Reference vest* means a model AK–1, adult PFD; model CKM–1, child medium PFD; or model CKS–2, child small PFD, meeting the requirements of subpart 160.047 of this chapter, except that, in lieu of the weight and displacement values prescribed in Tables 160.047–4(c)(2) and 160.047–4(c)(4), each insert must have the minimum weight of kapok and displacement as shown in Table 160.077–2(j). To achieve the specified volume displacement, front and back insert pad coverings may be larger than the dimensions prescribed by § 160.047–1(b) and the width of the front fabric envelope and height of the back fabric envelope may be increased to accommodate a circumference no greater than 1/4″ larger than the filled insert circumference. As an alternative, unicellular plastic foam inserts of the specified displacement and of an equivalent shape, as accepted by the Commandant, may be substituted for kapok inserts.

TABLE 160.077–2(J)—REFERENCE VEST MINIMUM KAPOK WEIGHT AND VOLUME DISPLACEMENT

Reference PFD type	Front insert (2 each)		Back insert	
	Minimum kapok weight g (oz)	Volume displacement N (lb)	Minimum kapok weight g (oz)	Volume displacement N (lb)
Devices for adults, weighing over 40 kg (90 lb):				
Type II, III, and V Recreational	234 (8.25)	40±1 (9.0±0.25)	156 (5.5)	27±1 (6.0±0.25)
Devices for youths, weighing 23–40 kg (50–90 lb):				
Type I	184 (6.5)	31±1 (7.0±0.25)	170 (6.0)	30±1 (6.5±0.25)
Type II, III, and V [1]	156 (5.5)	26±1 (5.75±0.25)	149 (5.25)	24±1 (5.5±0.l25)
Devices for small children, weighing 14–23 kg (30–50 lb):				
Type I	128 (4.5)	21±1 (4.75±0.25)	156 (5.5)	30±1 (6.5±0.25)
Type II	100 (3.5)	17±1 (3.75±0.25)	135 (4.75)	22±1 (5.0±0.25)

[1] Both Recreational and Commercial.

(k) *Second stage donning* means adjustments or steps necessary to make a PFD provide its intended flotation characteristics after the device has been properly donned and then inflated.

(l) *SOLAS lifejacket*, in the case of a hybrid inflatable PFD, means a PFD approved as meeting the requirements for lifejackets in the 1983 Amendments to the International Convention for the Safety of Life at Sea, 1974 (SOLAS 74/

83), in addition to the requirements of this subpart.

[CGD 78-174, 50 FR 33928, Aug. 22, 1985, as amended by CGD 78-174A, 51 FR 4351, Feb. 4, 1986; CGD 88-070, 53 FR 34536, Sept. 7, 1988. Redesignated and amended by CGD 78-174, 60 FR 2486, Jan. 9, 1995; 60 FR 7131, Feb. 7, 1995; CGD 95-072, 60 FR 50466, Sept. 29, 1995; CGD 96-041, 61 FR 50733, Sept. 27, 1996]

§ 160.077-3 Required to be worn.

(a) A Type V hybrid PFD may be used to meet the Coast Guard PFD carriage requirements of subpart 25.25 of this chapter, and 33 CFR part 175, only if the PFD is used in accordance with any requirements on the approval label. PFDs marked "REQUIRED TO BE WORN" must be worn whenever the vessel is underway and the intended wearer is not within an enclosed space.

(b) If hybrid PFD's with the marking "REQUIRED TO BE WORN" are not worn under the conditions stated in paragraph (a) of this section, other approved PFD's will have to be provided to comply with the applicable carriage requirements in 33 CFR part 175 and subpart 25.25 of this chapter.

(c) The following PFD's must be marked "REQUIRED TO BE WORN" as specified in § 160.077-31:

(1) Each Type V recreational hybrid PFD.

(2) Each Type V commercial hybrid PFD.

[CGD 78-174, 50 FR 33928, Aug. 22, 1985. Redesignated and amended by CGD 78-174, 60 FR 2486, Jan. 9, 1995]

§ 160.077-4 Type.

(a) A hybrid PFD that successfully passes all applicable tests may be approved as a Type I, II, III, or V for various size ranges of persons weighing over 23 kg (50 lb), as Type I or II for persons weighing 14-23 kg (30-50 lb) or as Type I or II for other sizes. A Type V PFD has limitations on its approval.

(b) The approval tests in this subpart require each Type V hybrid PFD to have at least the same performance as a Type I, II, or III PFD for adult and youth sizes or Type I or II PFD for child sizes.

(c) A hybrid PFD may be approved for use on recreational boats, commer-

cial vessels or both if the applicable requirements are met.

[CGD 78-174, 60 FR 2486, Jan. 9, 1995]

§ 160.077-5 Incorporation by reference.

(a) Certain materials are incorporated by reference into this subpart with the approval of the Director of the Federal Register. The Office of the Federal Register publishes a table, "Material Approved for Incorporation by Reference," which appears in the Finding Aids section of this volume. In that table is found the date of the edition approved, citations to the particular sections of this part where the material is incorporated, addresses where the material is available, and the date of approval by the Director of the Federal Register. To enforce any edition other than the one listed in the table, notice of the change must be published in the FEDERAL REGISTER and the material made available to the public. All approved material is on file at the Office of the Federal Register, Washington, DC 20408, and at the U.S. Coast Guard, Lifesaving and Fire Safety Division (G-MSE-4), Washington, DC 20593.

(b) The materials approved for incorporation by reference in this subpart are:

AMERICAN SOCIETY FOR TESTING AND MATERIALS (ASTM)

ASTM B 117, Standard Method of Salt Spray (Fog) Testing.

ASTM D 471, Rubber Property—Effect of Liquids.

ASTM D 751, Standard Methods of Testing Coated Fabrics.

ASTM D 1434, Gas Transmission Rate of Plastic Film and Sheeting.

FEDERAL AVIATION ADMINISTRATION TECHNICAL STANDARD ORDER

TSO-C13, Federal Aviation Administration Standard for Life Preservers.

FEDERAL STANDARDS

In Federal Test Method Standard No. 191 the following test methods:

(1) Method 5100, Strength and Elongation, Breaking of Woven Cloth; Grab Method.

(2) Method 5132, Strength of Cloth, Tearing; Falling-Pendulum Method.

(3) Method 5134, Strength of Cloth, Tearing; Tongue Method.

(4) Method 5804.1, Weathering Resistance of Cloth; Accelerated Weathering Method.

(5) Method 5762, Mildew Resistance of Textile Materials; Soil Burial Method.

Federal Standard No. 751, Stitches, Seams, and Stitching.

MILITARY SPECIFICATIONS

MIL-L-24611(SH)—Life Preserver Support Package For Life Preserver, MK 4.

NATIONAL BUREAU OF STANDARDS (NBS)

"The Universal Color Language" and "The Color Names Dictionary" in *Color: Universal Language and Dictionary of Names*, National Bureau of Standards Special Publication 440.

UNDERWRITERS LABORATORIES (UL)

UL 1191, "Components for Personal Flotation Devices."

UL 1517, "Hybrid Personal Flotation Devices."

[CGD 78–174, 50 FR 33928, Aug. 22, 1985. Redesignated by CGD 78–174, 60 FR 2486, Jan. 9, 1995; CGD 95–072, 60 FR 50467, Sept. 29, 1995; CGD 96–041, 61 FR 50733, Sept. 27, 1996]

§ 160.077-6   Approval procedures.

(a) *General.* Subpart 159.005 of this chapter contains the approval procedures. Those procedures must be followed, excepted as modified in this paragraph.

(1) Preapproval review under §§ 159.005-5 and 159.005-7 may be omitted if a similar design has already been approved.

(2) The information required in all three subparagraphs of § 159.005-5(a)(2) must be included in the application.

(3) The application must also include the following:

(i) The type of performance (i.e. Donned Type I, Type II or Type III) that the PFD is designed to provide.

(ii) Any special purpose(s) for which the PFD is designed and the vessel(s) or type(s) of vessel on which its use is planned.

(iii) Buoyancy and torque tolerances to be allowed in production.

(iv) The text of any optional marking to be provided in addition to required text.

(v) The manual required by § 160.077-29 (UL 1517 text may be omitted in this submission).

(vi) The size range of wearers that the device is intended to fit.

(4) The description of quality control procedures required by § 159.005-9 of this chapter to be submitted with the test report may be omitted as long as the manufacturer's planned quality control procedures comply with § 160.077-23.

(b) *Waiver of tests.* If a manufacturer requests that any test in this subpart be waived, one of the following must be provided to the Commandant as justification for the waiver:

(1) Acceptable test results on a PFD of sufficiently similar design.

(2) Engineering analysis showing that the test is not applicable to the particular design or that by design or construction the PFD cannot fail the test.

(c) *Alternative Requirements.* A PFD that does not meet requirements in this subpart may still be approved if the device—

(1) Meets other requirements prescribed by the Commandant in place of or in addition to requirements in this subpart; and

(2) Provides at least the same degree of safety provided by other PFD's that do comply with this subpart.

[CGD 78–174, 50 FR 33928, Aug. 22, 1985, as amended by CGD 78–174A, 51 FR 4351, Feb. 4, 1986. Redesignated and amended by CGD 78–174, 60 FR 2491, Jan. 9, 1995]

§ 160.077-7   Procedure for approval of design or material revision.

(a) Each change in design, material, or construction of an approved PFD must be approved by the Commandant before being used in any production of PFDs.

(b) Determinations of equivalence of design, construction, and materials may be made only by the Commandant.

[CGD 78–174, 60 FR 2492, Jan. 9, 1995]

§ 160.077-9   Recognized laboratory.

(a) A manufacturer seeking Coast Guard approval of a product under this subpart shall follow the approval procedures of subpart 159.005 of this chapter, and shall apply for approval directly to a recognized independent laboratory. The following laboratories are recognized under § 159.010-7 of this part, to perform testing and approval functions under this subpart: Underwriters Laboratories, 12 Laboratory Drive, P.O. Box 13995, Research Triangle Park, NC 27709–3995, (919) 549–1400.

(b) Production oversight must be performed by the same laboratory that performs the approval tests unless, as determined by the Commandant, the employees of the laboratory performing production oversight receive training and support equal to that of the laboratory that performed the approval testing.

[CGD 93-055, 61 FR 13931, Mar. 28, 1996; 61 FR 15868, Apr. 9, 1996]

§ 160.077-11 Materials—Recreational Hybrid PFD's.

(a) *General*—(1) *Application.* This section contains requirements for materials used in recreational hybrid PFD's.

(2) *Condition of Materials.* All materials must be new.

(3) *Acceptance, certification, and quality.* All components used in the construction of hybrid PFDs must meet the applicable requirements of subpart 164.019 of this chapter.

(4) *Temperature range.* Unless otherwise specified in standards incorporated by reference in this section, all materials must be designed for use in all weather conditions throughout a temperature range of −30 °C to +65 °C (−22 °F to +150 °F).

(5) *Weathering Resistance.* Each nonmetallic component which is not suitably covered to shield against ultraviolet exposure must be designed to—

(i) Retain at least 40% of its strength after being subjected to 300 hours of sunshine carbon arc weathering as specified by Method 5804.1 of Federal Test Method Standard Number 191; or

(ii) Meet UL 1517, section 4.3.

(6) *Fungus Resistance.* Each non-metallic component must be designed to retain at least 90% of its strength after being subjected to the mildew resistance test specified by Method 5762 of Federal Test Method Standard 191 when untreated cotton is used as the control specimen. Also, the gas transmission rate of inflation chamber materials must not be increased by more than 10% after being subjected to this test. Materials that are covered when used in the PFD may be tested with that covering.

(7) *Corrosion resistance.* Each metal component must be—

(i) Galvanically compatible with each other metal part in contact with it; and

(ii) Unless it is expendable (such as an inflation medium cartridge), 410 stainless steel or have salt water and salt air corrosion characteristics equal or superior to 410 stainless steel or perform its intended function, and have no visible pitting or other damage on any surface, after 720 hours of salt spray testing according to ASTM B 117.

(8) *Materials not covered.* Materials not covered in this section must be of good quality and suitable for the purpose intended.

(b) *Flotation material.* Inherent buoyancy must be provided by—

(1) Plastic foam meeting—

(i) Subpart 164.013 of this chapter;

(ii) Subpart 164.015 of this chapter; or

(iii) UL 1191 and having a V factor of 89 except that foam with a lower V factor may be used if it provides buoyancy which, after a normal service life, is at least equal to that of a PFD made with material having a V factor of 89 and the required minimum inherent buoyancy when new; or

(2) Kapok meeting subpart 164.003 of this chapter.

(c) *Fabric*—(1) *All fabric.* All fabric, except inner envelope fabric, must—

(i) Be of a type accepted for use on Type I PFD's approved under subpart 160.002 of this chapter; or

(ii) Meet the Type V requirements for "Fabrics for Wearable Devices" in UL 1191, except that its breaking strength must be at least 400 N (90 lb.) in both the directions of greater and lesser thread count.

(2) *Rubber coated fabric.* Rubber coated fabric must be of a copper-inhibiting type.

(3) *Inner envelope fabric.* Inner envelope fabric must—

(i) Meet the requirements in paragraph (c)(i) of this section; or

(ii) Be of a type accepted for use on Type II PFD's approved under subpart 160.047 of this chapter.

(d) *Inflation chamber materials*—(1) *All materials.* The average permeability of inflation chamber material must not be more than 110% of the permeability of materials determined in approval testing prescribed in § 160.077-19(d). The average grab breaking strength and tear strength of the material must be at least 90% of the grab breaking strength and tear strength determined from testing prescribed in § 160.077-19(d). No individual sample result for breaking strength or tear strength may be more than 20% below the results obtained in approval testing.

(2) *Fabric covered chambers.* Each material used in the construction of inflation chambers that are covered with fabric must meet the requirements specified for—

(i) Bladder materials in section 3.2.6 of MIL-L-24611(SH) if the material is an unsupported film, except that any color or finish may be used; or

(ii) Coated fabric in section 3.1.1 of TSO-C13 if the material is a coated fabric.

(3) *Uncovered chambers.* Each material used in the construction of inflation chambers that are not covered with fabric must meet the requirements specified in paragraph (d)(2)(ii) and (a)(5)(i) of this section.

(e) *Thread.* Each thread must meet the requirements of subpart 164.023 of this chapter. Only one kind of thread may be used in each seam. Thread and fabric combinations must have similar elongation and durability characteristics.

(f) *Webbing.* Webbing used as a body strap, tie tape or drawstring, or reinforcing tape must meet §160.002-3(e), §160.002-3(f), and §160.002-3(h) of this chapter respectively. Webbing used for tie tape or drawstring must be capable of easily holding a knot and being easily tied and untied. Webbing used as reinforcing tape must be smooth enough to prevent chafing the wearer.

(g) *Closures*—(1) *Strength.* Each closure such as a buckle, snap hook and dee ring, or other type of fastening must comply with UL 1517, section 4.1. The width of each closure opening through which body strap webbing passes must be the same as the width of that webbing.

(2) *Means of Locking.* Each closure used to secure a PFD to the body, except a zipper, must have a quick and positive means of locking, such as a snap hook and dee ring.

(3) *Zipper.* If a zipper is used to secure a PFD to the wearer it must be—

(i) Easily initiated;

(ii) Non-jamming;

(iii) Right handed; and

(iv) Of a locking type.

(h) *Inflation medium.* If a hybrid PFD has an automatic or manual inflation mechanism—

(1) The inflation medium must not contain or produce compounds more toxic than CO_2 in sufficient quantity to cause an adverse reaction if inhaled through any of its oral inflation mechanisms; and

(2) Any chemical reaction during inflation must not leave a toxic residue.

(i) [Reserved]

(j) *Kapok pad covering.* If kapok flotation material is used, pad covering that meets §160.047-3(e) of this chapter must be provided to enclose the material in at least three separate pads.

[CGD 78-174, 50 FR 33928, Aug. 22, 1985, as amended by CGD 84-068, 58 FR 29494, May 20, 1993; CGD 78-174, 60 FR 2486, Jan. 9, 1995]

§160.077-13 Materials—Type I and Commercial Hybrid PFD.

(a) *General.* All commercial hybrid PFD materials must meet §160.077-11 and this section.

(b) *Closures.* Each closure other than a zipper must have a minimum breaking strength of 1000 N (225 lbs). If a zipper is used to secure the PFD to the body, it must be used in combination with another closure that has a quick and positive means of locking.

(c) *Retroreflective Material.* Each PFD must have at least 200 sq. cm. (31 sq. in.) of retroreflective material on its front side, at least 200 sq. cm. on its back side and at least 200 sq. cm. of material on each reversible side, if any. The material must be Type I material that is approved under Subpart 164.018 of this chapter. The material attached on each side must be divided equally between the upper quadrants of the side. The material, as attached, must not impair PFD performance.

[CGD 78-174, 50 FR 33928, Aug. 22, 1985, as amended by CGD 78-174, 60 FR 2487, Jan. 9, 1995]

§160.077-15 Construction and Performance—Recreational Hybrid PFD.

(a) *Performance.* (1) Each recreational hybrid PFD must be able to pass the tests in §160.077-19.

(2) Each recreational hybrid PFD must—

(i) If second stage donning is required, have an obvious method for doing it;

(ii) If it is to be marked as Type II or Type V providing Type I or II performance, not require second stage donning to achieve that performance;

(iii) Be capable of being worn while inflated at 60 N (13 lb.) of buoyancy without significantly changing its appearance from, or making it significantly less comfortable than, the uninflated condition;

(iv) Not cause significant discomfort to the wearer during and after inflation; and

(v) If it has a manual or automatic inflation mechanism and can be put on inside out, not restrict breathing when donned inside out, adjusted to fit, and inflated.

(b) *Construction; General.* Each recreational hybrid PFD must—

(1) Have one or more inflation chambers;

(2) Have at least one oral means of inflation on each inflation chamber;

(3) Have at least one automatic inflation mechanism that inflates at least one chamber, if marked as providing Type I or II performance;

(4) Be constructed so that the intended method of donning is obvious to an untrained wearer;

(5) Not have a channel that can direct water to the wearer's face to any greater extent than that of the reference vest defined in § 160.077–3(j).

(6) Have a retainer for each adjustable closure to prevent any part of the closure from being easily removed from the PFD;

(7) If marked as universally sized for wearers weighing over 40 kg (90 pounds), have a chest size range of at least 76 to 120 cm (30 to 52 in.);

(8) Not have means of access to any inherently buoyant inserts;

(9) Not have edges, projections, or corners, either external or internal, that are sufficiently sharp to damage the PFD or cause injury to anyone using or maintaining the PFD;

(10) Be of first quality workmanship;

(11) Unless otherwise allowed by the approval certificate—

(i) Not incorporate means obviously intended for attaching the PFD to the vessel; and

(ii) Not have any instructions indicating that attachment is intended;

(12) Except as otherwise required by this section, meet UL Standard 1517, sections 6.14, 6.20, 7.1, 7.3, 7.8, 8.4, and 9; and

(13) Provide the minimum buoyancies specified in Table 160.077–15(b)(13).

TABLE 160.077–15(B)(13)—BUOYANCY FOR RECREATIONAL HYBRID PFDS

	Adult	Youth	Small child
Inherent buoyancy (deflated condition):			
Type II	45 N (10 lb)	40 N (9 lb)	30 N (7 lb)
Type III	45 N (10 lb)	40 N (9 lb)	N/A
Type V	33 N (7.5 lb)	34 N (7.5 lb)	N/A
Total buoyancy (inflated condition):			
Type II	100 N (22 lb)	67 N (15 lb)	53 N (12 lb)
Type III	100 N (22 lb)	67 N (15 lb)	N/A
Type V	100 N (22 lb)	67 N (15 lb)	N/A

(14) Meet any additional requirements that the Commandant may prescribe, if necessary, to approve unique or novel designs.

(c) *Inflation mechanism.* (1) Each inflation mechanism on a recreational hybrid PFD must—

(i) Not require tools to activate it or replace its inflation medium cartridge or water sensitive element;

(ii) Have an intended method of operation that is obvious to an untrained wearer; and

(iii) Be located outside of its inflation chamber.

(2) Each oral inflation mechanism must—

(i) Be designed to operate without pulling on the mechanism;

(ii) Not be capable of locking in the open or closed position except that, a friction-fit dust cap that only locks in the closed position may be used; and

(iii) Have a non-toxic mouthpiece.

(3) Each automatic and manual inflation mechanism must—

(i) Have a simple method for replacing the inflation medium cartridge; and

(ii) Be in a ready-to-use condition or be conspicuously marked to indicate that the inflation mechanism is not in a ready-to-use condition and that the purchaser must assemble it.

(4) Each manual inflation mechanism must—

(i) Provide an easy means of inflation that requires only one deliberate action on the part of the wearer to actuate it; and

(ii) Be operated by pulling on an inflation handle that is marked "Jerk to Inflate" at two visible locations.

(5) Each automatic inflation mechanism must—

(i) Have an obvious method for indicating whether the mechanism has been activated; and

(ii) Be incapable of assembly without its water sensitive element.

(6) The marking required for the inflation handle of a manual inflation mechanism must be waterproof, permanent, and readable from a distance of 2.5 m (8 ft.).

(d) *Deflation mechanism.* (1) Each inflation chamber must have its own deflation mechanism.

(2) Each deflation mechanism must—

(i) Be readily accessible to either hand when the PFD is worn while inflated;

(ii) Not require tools to operate it;

(iii) Have an intended method of operation that is obvious to an untrained wearer, and

(iv) Not be able to be locked in the open or closed position.

(3) The deflation mechanism may be the oral inflation mechanism.

(e) *Sewn seams.* Stitching used in each structural seam of a PFD must provide performance equal to or better than a Class 300 Lockstitch meeting Federal Standard No. 751.

[CGD 78–174, 50 FR 33928, Aug. 22, 1985, as amended by CGD 78–174A, 51 FR 4351, Feb. 4, 1986; CGD 78–174, 60 FR 2487, Jan. 9, 1995]

§ 160.077–17 Construction and Performance—Type I and Commercial Hybrid PFD.

(a) *General.* Each commercial hybrid PFD must meet—

(1) Paragraph (b) of this section; and

(2) Section 160.077–15, except § 160.077–15(a)(2)(iii) and § 160.077–15(c)(1)(i).

(b) *Additional requirements.* Each commercial hybrid PFD must—

(1) Be able to pass the tests in § 160.077–21;

(2) Not present a snag hazard when properly worn;

(3) When worn inflated, have a visible external surface area of at least 1300 sq. cm (200 sq. in.) in front and 450 sq. cm (70 sq. in.) in back that are primarily vivid reddish orange as defined by sections 13 and 14 of the "Color Names Dictionary";

(4) Have at least one inflation chamber, except that a hybrid PFD approved as a SOLAS lifejacket must have at least two inflation chambers;

(5) Have at least one manual inflation mechanism.

(6) Have at least one automatic inflation mechanism that inflates at least one chamber; and

(7) Not require second stage donning after inflation.

(8) If approved for adults, be universally sized as specified in § 160.077–15(b)(7).

(9) Commercial hybrid PFDs employing closures with less than 1600 N (360 lb) strength, must have at least two closures that meet UL 1517, Section 22.1.

(10) Each commercial hybrid PFD must have an attachment for a PFD light securely fastened to the front shoulder area. The location should be such that if the light is attached it will not damage or impair the performance of the PFD.

(11) In the deflated and the inflated condition, provide buoyancies of at least the values in Table 160.077–17(b)(11).

TABLE 160.077–17(B)(11)—MINIMUM BUOYANCY OF TYPE I AND COMMERCIAL HYBRID PFDS

	Adult	Youth	Small child
Inherent buoyancy (deflated condition):			
Type I	70 N (15.5 lb)	50 N (11 lb)	40 N (9 lb)
Type V	60 N (13 lb)	34 N (7.5 lb)	N/A
Total buoyancy (inflated condition):			

TABLE 160.077-17(B)(11)—MINIMUM BUOYANCY OF TYPE I AND COMMERCIAL HYBRID PFDS—
Continued

	Adult	Youth	Small child
Type I	130 N (30 lb)	80 N (18 lb)	67 N (15 lb)
Type V	100 N (22 lb)	67 N (15 lb)	N/A

[CGD 78-174, 50 FR 33928, Aug. 22, 1985, as amended by CGD 78-174, 60 FR 2487, Jan. 9, 1995]

§ 160.077-19 Approval Testing—Recreational Hybrid PFD's.

(a) *General.* (1) This section contains approval tests and examinations for recreational hybrid PFD's. Each test and examination must be conducted or supervised by an independent laboratory. The tests must be done using PFD's that have been constructed in accordance with the plans and specifications in the application for approval. In each test only one PFD is required to be tested unless otherwise specified or needed to complete the tests in paragraph (d) of this section.

(2) All data relating to buoyancy and pressure must be taken at, or corrected to, standard atmospheric pressure of 760 mm (29.92 inches) of mercury and temperature of 20 ° C (68 ° F).

(3) The tests in paragraph (b) of this section must be completed before doing the tests in paragraph (d) of this section.

(4) In each test that specifies inflation by an automatic inflation mechanism and either or both of the other mechanisms, the automatic inflation mechanism must be tested first.

(5) Some tests in this section require PFD's to be tested while being worn. The number and characteristics of the test subjects must be as prescribed in section 11 of UL 1517.

(b) *Tests.* Each PFD design must be tested according to the procedures in the following tests and meet the requirements in those tests:

(1) *Donning and Operability,* UL 1517, section 12.

(2) *Jump Test,* UL 1517, section 13.

(3) *Flotation Stability and Inflation.*

(i) *Uninflated Flotation Stability,* UL 1517, section 14.

NOTE: If the freeboard of a test subject is close to zero, caution must be taken to prevent the subject from inhaling water. The subject may use lightweight breathing aids to avoid inhaling water.

(ii) *Inflation,* UL 1517, section 14.3 through 14.5 using a PFD with each automatic inflation mechanism disabled.

(iii) *Inflated flotation stability,* UL 1517, section 15, for Type II and Type III performance except comparisons are to be made to the appropriate size and Type reference vest as defined in § 160.077-2(j).

(4) *Water Emergence,* UL 1517, section 16.

(5) *Operation Force Test,* UL 1517, section 17.

(6) *Buoyancy, buoyancy distribution, and inflation medium retention test,* UL 1517, sections 18 and 19, except:

(i) Recreational hybrid inflatables must provide minimum buoyancy as specified in Table 160.077-15(b)(13):

(ii) The buoyancy and volume displacement of kapok buoyant inserts must be tested in accordance with the procedures prescribed in § 160.047-4(c)(4) and § 160.047-5(e)(1) in lieu of the procedures in UL 1517, section 18 and 19.

(7) *Inflation Chamber Tests.*

(i) *Over-pressure Test,* UL 1517, section 28.

(ii) *Air Retention Test,* UL 1517, section 29.

(8) *Temperature Cycling Tests,* UL 1517, section 23.

(9) *Solvent Exposure Test,* UL 1517, section 24.

(10) *Environmental Tests,* UL 1517, section 31.1.

(i) *Humidity Exposure,* UL 1517, section 31.4.

(ii) *Rain Exposure,* UL 1517, section 31.2 and 31.3.

(11) *Abrasion/Compression Test,* UL 1517, section 26.

(12) *Water Entrapment Test,* UL 1517, section 20.

(13) *Tensile Tests,* UL 1517, section 22.

(14) *Strength of Attachment of Inflation Mechanism,* UL 1517, section 30.

(15) *Flame Exposure Test*, UL 1517, section 25.

(16) *Impact Test*, UL 1517, section 21.

(17) *Seam Strength Test*, UL 1517, section 33.

(18) *Puncture Test*, UL 1517, section 27.

(c) *Visual Examination*. One complete PFD must be visually examined for compliance with the requirements of § 160.077-15.

(d) *Inflation Chamber Properties*—(1) *General*. The tests in this paragraph must be run if the tests in paragraph (b) of this section are successfully completed. The results of these tests will be used to check the quality of incoming PFD components and the production process. Test samples must come from one of more PFD's that were each used in all of the tests in paragraphs (b)(2), (b)(6), (b)(7), (b)(16), and (b)(18) of this section.

(2) *Grab breaking strength*. Grab breaking strength of chamber materials must be determined according to Method No. 5100 of Federal Test Method Standard 191, or ASTM D 751.

(3) *Tear strength*. Tear strength of chamber materials must be determined according to Method No. 5132 or 5134 of Federal Test Method Standard 191, or ASTM D 751.

(4) *Permeability*. The permeability of chamber materials must be determined according to ASTM D 1434 using CO_2 as the test gas.

(5) *Seam strength*. The seam strength of the seams in each inflation chamber of at least one PFD must be determined according to ASTM D 751, except that 25 mm by 200 mm (1 in. by 8 in.) samples may be used where insufficient length of straight seam is available.

(e) The Commandant may prescribe additional tests, if necessary, to approve unique or novel designs.

[CGD 78–174, 50 FR 33928, Aug. 22, 1985, as amended by CGD 78–174, 60 FR 2487, Jan. 9, 1995]

§ 160.077-21 Approval Testing—Type I and Commercial Hybrid PFD.

(a) *General*. This section contains commercial hybrid PFD approval tests. The provisions of § 160.077-19(a) apply to each test in this section.

(b) *Tests*. Each test prescribed in § 160.077-19(b), except the tests in paragraphs (b)(2), (b)(3)(i), (b)(3)(ii), and (b)(6), must be conducted and passed.

(c) *Additional tests*. Each PFD design must also be tested according to the procedures in the following tests and meet the requirements in these tests:

(1) *Jump test*, UL 1517, section S6 for Adult size. Youth and Small Child sizes are exempt from this test.

(2) *In-water removal*, UL 1517, section S9 for Adult and Youth sizes. The Small Child size is exempt from this test.

(3) *Buoyancy and inflation medium retention test*, UL 1517, Section S10, except the minimum buoyancies must be as specified in the Table 160.077-17(b)(11):

(4) *Flotation stability*.

(i) *Uninflated flotation stability*, UL 1517, section S7, except that for Type I devices the requirements of paragraph S7.1.A apply to all subjects regardless of their in-water weight. For Type V adult-size devices the requirements of paragraph S7.1.A apply to all adult subjects having an in-water weight of 13 lb or less, and the requirements of paragraph S7.1.B apply to all other adult subjects.

NOTE: —If the freeboard of a test subject is close to zero, caution must be taken to prevent the subject from inhaling water. The subject may use lightweight breathing aids to avoid inhaling water.

(ii) *Righting action test*, 46 CFR 160.176–13(d)(2) through (d)(5) for Type I hybrid PFDs. UL 1517, Section S8, for Type V hybrid PFDs.

(5) *Flotation stability—youths and small children*.

(i) *Uninflated flotation stability*, UL 1517, section S7, except that the requirements of paragraph S7.1.A apply to all subjects regardless of their in-water weight.

(ii) *Righting action test*, UL 1517, Section 15.3 through 15.13, for Youth and Small Child hybrid PFDs except comparisons are to be made to the appropriate size and type reference vest as defined in § 160.077-2(j).

(d) *Flotation Stability Criteria*. At the end of the righting action test—

(1) At least 75% of the PFD's retroreflective material on the outside of the PFD, and the PFD light, must be above the water when the subject is

floating in the stable flotation attitude; and

(2) The subject when floating in the stable flotation position and looking to the side, must be able to see—

(i) The water no more than 3 m (10 ft.) away; or

(ii) A mark on a vertical scale no higher than the lowest mark which can be viewed when floating in the same position in the reference vest defined in § 160.077–3(j).

(3) Each adult test subject must have a freeboard of at least:

(i) 100 mm (4 inches) if the PFD being tested is to be approved as a Type I hybrid PFD; or

(ii) 120 mm (4.75 inches) if the PFD being tested is to be approved as a SOLAS lifejacket.

(e) *Visual Examination.* One complete PFD must be visually examined for compliance with the requirements of § 160.077–15 and § 160.077–17.

(f) *Inflation Chamber Properties.* If the tests in paragraphs (b) and (c) of this section are completed successfully, the tests in § 160.077–19(d) must be run.

(g) The Commandant may prescribe additional tests, if necessary, to approve unique or novel designs.

[CGD 78–174, 50 FR 33928, Aug. 22, 1985, as amended by CGD 78–174, 60 FR 2488, Jan. 9, 1995; 60 FR 7131, Feb. 7, 1995; CGD 95–072, 60 FR 50466, Sept. 29, 1995]

§ 160.077–23   Production tests and inspections.

(a) *General.* (1) Production tests and inspections must be conducted in accordance with this section and subpart 159.007 of this chapter.

(2) The Commandant may prescribe additional production tests and inspections if needed to maintain quality control and check for compliance with the requirements of this subpart.

(b) *Test and Inspection Responsibilities.* In addition to responsibilities set out in part 159 of this chapter, each manufacturer of a hybrid PFD and each independent laboratory inspector must comply with the following, as applicable:

(1) *Manufacturer.* Each manufacturer must—(i) Perform all required tests and examinations on each PFD lot before the independent laboratory inspec-

tor tests and inspects the lot, except as provided in § 160.077–23(d)(5);

(ii) Perform required testing of each incoming lot of inflation chamber material before using that lot in production;

(iii) Have procedures for maintaining quality control of the materials used, manufacturing operations, and the finished product;

(iv) Have a continuing program of employee training and a program for maintaining production and test equipment;

(v) Have an inspector from the independent laboratory observe the production methods used in producing the first PFD lot produced and observe any revisions made thereafter in production methods;

(vi) Admit the inspector and any Coast Guard representative to any place in the factory where work is done on hybrid PFD's or component materials, and where completed PFD's are stored; and

(vii) Allow the inspector and any Coast Guard representative to take samples of completed PFD's or of component materials for tests prescribed in this subpart.

(2) *Independent Laboratory.*

(i) An inspector may not perform or supervise any production test or inspection unless—

(A) The manufacturer has a current approval certificate; and

(B) The inspector has first observed the manufacturer's production methods and any revisions to those methods.

(ii) Except as specified in paragraph (b)(2)(v) of this section, an inspector must perform or supervise testing and inspection of at least one PFD lot in each five lots produced.

(iii) During each inspection, the inspector must check for noncompliance with the manufacturer's quality control procedures.

(iv) Except as specified in paragraph (b)(2)(v) of this section, at least once each calendar quarter, the inspector must, as a check on the manufacturer's compliance with this section, examine the manufacturer's records required by § 160.077–25 and observe the manufacturer perform each of the tests required by paragraph (h) of this section.

(v) If less than six lots are produced during any calendar year, only one lot inspection in accordance with paragraph (b)(2)(ii) of this section, and one records examination and test performance observation in accordance with paragraph (b)(2)(iv) of this section is required during that year. Each lot tested and inspected must be within seven lots of the previous lot inspected.

(c) *PFD Lots.* A lot number must be assigned to each group of PFD's produced. No lot may exceed 1000 PFD's. A new lot must be started whenever any change in materials or a production method is made, or whenever any substantial discontinuity in the production process occurs. Changes in lots of component materials must be treated as changes in materials. Lots must be numbered serially. The lot number assigned, along with the approval number, must enable the PFD manufacturer, by referring to the records required by this subpart, to determine who produced the components used in the PFD.

(d) *Samples.* (1) Samples used in testing and inspections must be selected at random. Sampling must be done only when all PFD's or materials in the lot are available for selection.

(2) Each sample PFD selected must be complete, unless otherwise specified in paragraph (h) of this section.

(3) Each adult test subject must have a freeboard of at least:

(i) 100 mm (4 inches) if the PFD being tested is to be approved as a Type I hybrid PFD; or

(ii) 120 mm (4.75 inches) if the PFD being tested is to be approved as a SOLAS lifejacket.

(4) The number of samples selected per lot must be at least the number listed in Table 160.077–23A or Table 160.077–23B, as applicable, except as allowed in paragraph (d)(5) of this section.

(5) If the total production for any five consecutive lots does not exceed 250 devices, the manufacturer's and inspector's tests can be run on the same sample(s) at the same time.

TABLE 160.077–23A—MANUFACTURER'S SAMPLING

Tests:	Number of samples per lot					
	Lot size					
	1–100	101–200	201–300	301–500	501–750	751–1000
Inflation chamber materials.						
See note 1						
Seam strength	1	1	2	2	3	4
Over-pressure(2), (3)	1	2	3	4	6	8
Air retention.						
Every device in the lot						
Buoyancy and inflation media retention	1	2	3	4	6	8
Tensile strength(4)	1	1	1	1	1	1
Detailed product examination	2	2	3	4	6	8
Retest sample size(2)	....	....	13	13	20	20
Final lot examination.						
Every device in the lot						

NOTES TO TABLE:
(1) Samples must be selected from each lot of incoming material. The tests referenced in §160.077–19(d)(2) through §160.077–19(d)(4) prescribe the number of samples to select.
(2) Samples selected for this test may not be the same samples selected for other tests.
(3) If any sample fails this test, the number of samples to be tested in the next lot produced must be at least 2% of the total number of PFD's in the lot or 10 PFD's, whichever is greater.
(4) This test is required only when a new lot of materials is used and when a revised production process is used. However, the test must be run at least once every calendar quarter regardless of whether a new lot of materials or revised process is started in that quarter.

TABLE 160.077–23B—INSPECTOR'S SAMPLING

Tests:	Number of samples per lot					
	Lot size					
	1–100	101–200	201–300	301–500	501–750	751–1000
Over-pressure 1	1	1	2	2	3	4
Air retention	1	1	2	2	3	4

TABLE 160.077–23B—INSPECTOR'S SAMPLING—Continued

	Number of samples per lot					
	Lot size					
	1–100	101–200	201–300	301–500	501–750	751–1000
Buoyancy and inflation media retention	1	1	2	2	3	4
Tensile strength 2	1	1	1	1	1	1
Waterproof marking.						
Detailed product examination	See note 3 for sampling					
	1	1	1	2	2	3
Retest sample size 1	10	10	13	13	20	20
Final Lot Inspection	10	15	20	25	27	30

NOTES TO TABLE:
(1) Samples selected for this test may not be the same PFD's selected for other tests.
(2) This test may be omitted if the manufacturer has previously conducted it and the inspector has conducted the test on a previous lot within the past year.
(3) One sample of each means of marking on each type of fabric or finish used in PFD construction must be tested whenever a new lot of materials is used or at least every six months regardless of whether a new lot of materials was used within the past six months.

(e) *Accept/Reject Criteria: Manufacturer Testing.* (1) A PFD lot passes production testing if each sample passes each test.

(2) In lots of 200 or less PFD's the lot must be rejected if any sample fails one or more tests.

(3) In lots of more than 200 PFD's, the lost must be rejected if—

(i) One sample fails more than one test;

(ii) More than one sample fails; or

(iii) One sample fails one test and in redoing that test with the number of samples specified for retesting in Table 160.077–23A, one or more samples fail the test.

(4) A rejected PFD lot may be retested only if allowed under paragraph (k) of this section.

(5) In testing inflation chamber materials, a lot is accepted only if the average of the results of testing the minimum number of samples prescribed in the reference tests in §160.077–19(d) is within the tolerances specified in §160.077–11(d)(1). Any lot that is rejected may not be used in production.

(f) *Accept/Reject Criteria: Independent Laboratory Testing.* (1) A lot passes production testing if each sample passes each test.

(2) A lot must be rejected if—

(i) One sample fails more than one test;

(ii) More than one sample fails; or

(iii) One sample fails one test and in redoing that test with the number of samples specified for retesting in Table 160.077–23B, one or more samples fail the test.

(3) A rejected lot may be retested only if allowed under paragraph (k) of this section.

(g) *Facilities and Equipment*—(1) *General.* The manufacturer must provide the test equipment and facilities described in this section for performing production tests, examinations, and inspections.

(2) *Calibration.* The manufacturer must have the calibration of all test equipment checked at least annually by a weights and measures agency or the equipment manufacturer, distributor, or dealer.

(3) *Equipment.* The following equipment is required:

(i) *A Sample Basket* for buoyancy tests. It must be made of wire mesh and be of sufficient size and durability to hold a complete inflated PFD. The basket must be heavy enough or be sufficiently weighted to become submerged when holding a test sample.

(ii) *A Tank Filled with Fresh Water* for buoyancy tests. The height of the tank must be sufficient to allow a water depth of at least 5 cm (2 inches) from the water surface to the top of the basket when the basket is not touching the bottom. The length and width of the tank must be sufficient to prevent each submerged basket from contacting another basket or the tank sides and bottom. Means for locking or sealing the tank must be provided to prevent disturbance of any samples or a change in water level during testing.

(iii) *A Scale* that has sufficient capacity to weigh a submerged sample basket. The scale must be sensitive to 14 g (0.5 oz) and must not have an error exceeding ±14 g (0.5 oz).

(iv) *Tensile Test Equipment* that is suitable for applying pulling force in conducting body strap assembly strength subtests. The equipment assembly may be (A) a known weight and winch, (B) a scale, winch, and fixed anchor, or (C) a tensile test machine that is capable of holding a given tension. The assembly must provide accuracy to maintain a pulling force within ±2 percent of specified force. Additionally, if the closed loop test method is used, two cylinders of the type described in that method must be provided.

(v) *A Thermometer* that is sensitive to 0.5 ° C (1 ° F) and does not have an error exceeding ±0.25 ° C (0.5 ° F).

(vi) *A Barometer* that is capable of reading mm (inches) of mercury with a sensitivity of 1 mm (0.05 in.) Hg and an error not exceeding ±0.05 mm (0.02 in.) Hg.

(vii) *A Regulated Air Supply* that is capable of supplying the air necessary to conduct the tests specified in paragraphs (h)(4) and (h)(5) of this section.

(viii) *A Pressure Gauge* that is capable of measuring air pressure with a sensitivity of 1 kPa (0.1 psig) and an error not exceeding ±0.5 kPa (0.05 psig).

(ix) *A Torque Wrench* if any screw fasteners are used. The wrench must be sensitive to, and have an error of less than, one-half the specified tolerance for the torque values of the fasteners.

(x) *Inflation chamber materials test equipment.* If the required tests in paragraph (h)(2) of this section are performed by the PFD manufacturer, test equipment suitable for conducting Grab Breaking Strength, Tear Strength, Permeability, and Seam Strength tests must be available at the PFD manufacturer's facility.

(4) *Facilities.* The manufacturer must provide a suitable place and the necessary apparatus for the inspector to use in conducting or supervising tests. For the final lot inspection, the manufacturer must provide a suitable working environment and a smooth-top table for the inspector's use.

(h) *Production Tests and Examinations*—(1) *General.* (i) Samples used in testing must be selected according to paragraph (d) of this section.

(ii) On the samples selected for testing—

(A) The manufacturer must conduct the tests in paragraph (h)(2) through (h)(8) of this section; and

(B) The independent laboratory inspector must conduct or supervise the tests in paragraph (h)(4) through (h)(9) of this section.

(iii) Each individual test result must, in addition to meeting the requirements in this paragraph, comply with the requirements, if any, set out in the approved plans and specifications.

(2) *Inflation Chamber Materials.* Each sample must be tested according to § 160.077-19(d)(1) through § 160.077-19(d)(4). The average and individual results of testing the minimum number of samples prescribed in § 160.077-19(d) must comply with the requirements in § 160.077-11(d)(1).

(3) *Seam Strength.* The seams in each inflation chamber of each sample must be tested according to §§ 160.077-19(d)(1) and 160.077-19(d)(5). The results for each inflation chamber must be at least 90% of the results obtained in approval testing.

(4) *Over-pressure.* Each sample must be tested according to and meet UL 1517, section 28. Test samples may be prestressed by inflating them to a greater pressure than the required test pressure prior to initiating the test at the specified values.

(5) *Air Retention.* Each sample must be tested according to and meet UL 1517, section 36. Prior to initiating the test at the specified values, test samples may be prestressed by inflating to a pressure greater than the design pressure, but not exceeding 50 percent of the required pressure for the tests in paragraph (h)(4) of this section. Any alternate test method that decreases the length of the test must be accepted by the Commandant and must require a proportionately lower allowable pressure loss and the same percentage sensitivity and accuracy as the standard allowable loss measured with the standard instrumentation.

(6) *Buoyancy and Inflation Medium Retention.* Each sample must be tested according to and meet § 160.077-19(b)(6), except that the UL 1517 section 19 test

is not required unless specified on the approved plans and specifications. In addition to meeting the minimum values required by § 160.077–19(b)(6), each buoyancy value must fall within the tolerances specified in the approved plans and specifications.

(7) *Tensile Strength.* Each sample must be tested according to and meet UL 1517, section 22.

(8) *Detailed Product Examination.* Each sample must be disassembled to the extent necessary to determine compliance with the following:

(i) All dimensions and seam allowances must be within tolerances prescribed in the approved plans and specifications.

(ii) The torque of each screw type mechanical fastener must be within its tolerance as prescribed in the approved plans and specifications.

(iii) The arrangement, markings, and workmanship must be as specified on the approved plans and specifications and this subpart.

(iv) The PFD must not otherwise be defective.

(9) *Waterproof Marking Test.* Each sample is completely submerged in fresh water for at least 30 min. and then removed and immediately placed on a hard surface. The markings are vigorously rubbed with the fingers for 15 seconds. If the printing becomes illegible, the sample is rejected.

(i) [Reserved]

(j) *Final Lot Examination and Inspection.* (1) *General.* On each PFD lot that passes production testing, the manufacturer must perform a final lot examination and an independent laboratory inspector must perform a final lot inspection. Samples must be selected according to paragraph (d) of this section. Each final lot examination and inspection must show—

(i) First quality workmanship;

(ii) That the general arrangement and attachment of all components such as body straps, closures, inflation mechanisms, tie tapes, drawstrings, etc. are as specified in the approved plans and specifications; and

(iii) Compliance with the marking requirements in § 160.077–31.

(2) *Accept/Reject Criteria.* Each nonconforming PFD must be rejected. If three or more nonconforming PFD's are rejected for the same kind of defect, lot examination or inspection must be discontinued and the lot rejected.

(3) *Manufacturer Examination.* This examination must be done by a manufacturer's representative who is familiar with the approved plans and specifications, the functioning of the PFD and its components, and the production testing procedures. This person must not be responsible for meeting production schedules or be supervised by someone who is. This person must prepare and sign the inspection record required by § 159.077–13 of this chapter and § 160.077–25(b).

(4) *Independent Laboratory Inspection.* (i) The inspector must discontinue lot inspection and reject the lot if observation of the records for the lot or of individual PFD's shows noncompliance with this section or the manufacturer's quality control procedures.

(ii) An inspector may not perform a final lot inspection unless the manufacturer has a current approval certificate.

(iii) If the inspector rejects a lot, the inspector shall notify the Commandant immediately.

(iv) The inspector must prepare and sign the record required by § 159.077–13 of this chapter and § 160.077–25(b). If the lot passes, the record must also include the inspector's certification to that effect and a certification that no evidence of noncompliance with this section was observed.

(k) *Disposition of PFD's Rejected in Testing or Inspections.* (1) A rejected PFD lot may be resubmitted for testing, examination, or inspection if the manufacturer first removes and destroys each PFD having the same type of defect or, if authorized by the Commandant or an authorized representative of the Commandant, reworks the lot to correct the defect.

(2) Any PFD rejected in a final lot examination or inspection may be resubmitted for examination or inspection if all defects have been corrected and reexamination or reinspection is authorized by the Commandant or an authorized representative of the Commandant.

(3) A rejected lot or rejected PFD may not be sold or offered for sale with

the representation that it meets this subpart or that it is Coast Guard approved.

[CGD 78-174, 50 FR 33928, Aug. 22, 1985, as amended by CGD 78-174A, 51 FR 4351, Feb. 4, 1986; CGD 78-174, 60 FR 2488, Jan. 9, 1995]

§160.077-25 Manufacturer records.

(a) Each manufacturer of hybrid PFD's must keep the records required by §159.007-13 of this chapter, except that they must be retained at least 120 months after the month in which the inspection or test was conducted.

(b) Each record required by §159.007-13 of this chapter must also include the following information:

(1) For each test, the serial number of the test instrument used if there is more than one available.

(2) For each test and inspection, the identification of the samples used, the lot number, the approval number, and the number of PFD's in the lot.

(3) For each lot rejected, the cause for rejection, any corrective action taken, and the final disposition of the lot.

(c) The description or photographs of procedures and apparatus used in testing is not required for the records prescribed in §159.077-13 of this chapter as long as the manufacturer's procedures and apparatus meet the requirements of this subpart.

(d) Each manufacturer of hybrid PFD's must also keep the following records:

(1) Records for all materials used in production including the following:

(i) Name and address of the supplier.

(ii) Date of purchase and receipt.

(iii) Lot number.

(iv) Certification meeting §160.077-11(a)(4).

(2) A copy of this subpart.

(3) Each document incorporated by reference in §160.077-9.

(4) A copy of the approved plans and specifications.

(5) The approval certificate.

(6) Calibration of test equipment, including the identity of the agency performing the calibration, date of calibration, and results.

(e) The records required by paragraph (d)(1) of this section must be kept for at least 120 months after preparation. All other records required by paragraph (d) of this section must be kept for at least 60 months.

EFFECTIVE DATE NOTE: At 50 FR 33935, Aug. 22, 1985, §160.077-25 (a) and (e) were added. This amendment contains information collection requirements which will not be effective until approval has been obtained from the Office of Management and Budget. A notice will be published in the FEDERAL REGISTER.

§160.077-27 Pamphlet.

(a) Each recreational hybrid PFD sold or offered for sale must be provided with a pamphlet that a prospective purchaser can read prior to purchase. The required pamphlet text must be printed verbatim and in the sequence set out in paragraph (e) of this section. Additional information, instructions, or illustrations must not be included within the required text. The type size shall be no smaller than 8-point.

(b) Each pamphlet must be prominently marked "Seller, do not remove pamphlet."

(c) No person may sell or offer for sale any recreational hybrid PFD unless the pamphlet required by this section is provided with it.

(d) The text specified in paragraphs (e)(2) of this section must be accompanied by illustrations of the types of devices being described. The illustrations provided must be either photographs or drawings of the manufacturer's own products or illustrations of other Coast Guard-approved PFDs.

(e) For a Type I hybrid PFD intended for recreational use or a Type II, III, or V recreational hybrid PFD, the pamphlet contents must be as follows:

(1) The text in UL 1517, Section 39, item A;

(2) The following text and illustrations:

THERE ARE FIVE TYPES OF PERSONAL FLOTATION DEVICES

This is a Type [*insert approved Type*] Hybrid Inflatable PFD.

NOTE: The following types of PFDs are designed to perform as described in calm water and when the wearer is not wearing any other flotation material (such as a wetsuit).

Type I—A Type I PFD has the greatest required inherent buoyancy and turns most unconscious persons in the water from a face down position to a vertical and slightly backward position, therefore greatly increasing one's chances of survival. The Type I PFD is suitable for all waters, especially for cruising on waters where rescue may be slow coming, such as large bodies of water where it is not likely that boats will be nearby. This type PFD is the most effective of all types in rough water. It is reversible and available in only two sizes—Adult (over 40 kg (90 lb)) and child (less than 40 kg (90 lb)) which are universal sizes (designed for all persons in the appropriate category).

[Insert illustration of Type I PFD]

Type II—A Type II PFD turns most wearers to a vertical and slightly backward position in the water. The turning action of a Type II PFD is less noticeable than the turning action of a Type I PFD and the Type II PFD will not turn as many persons under the same conditions as the Type I. The Type II PFD is usually more comfortable to wear than the Type I. This type of PFD is designed to fit a wide range of people for easy emergency use, and is available in the following sizes: Adult (over 40 kg (90 lb)), Medium Child (23–40 kg (50–90 lb)), and two categories of Small Child (less than 23 kg (50 lb) or less than 14 kg (30 lb). Additionally, some models are sized by chest sizes. You may prefer to use the Type II where there is a good chance of fast rescue, such as areas where it is common for other persons to be engaged in boating, fishing and other water activities.

[Insert illustration of Type II PFD]

Type III—The Type III PFD allows the wearer to tilt backwards in the water, and the device will maintain the wearer in that position and will not turn the wearer face down. It is not designed to turn the wearer face up. A Type III is generally more comfortable than a Type II, comes in a variety of styles which should be matched to the individual use, and is often the best choice for water sports, such as skiing, hunting, fishing, canoeing, and kayaking. This type PFD normally comes in many chest sizes and weight ranges; however, some universal sizes are available. You may also prefer to use the Type III where there is a probability of quick rescue such as areas where it is common for other persons to be engaged in boating, fishing, and other water activities.

[Insert illustration of Type III PFD]

Hybrid Inflatable Type I, II, or III—A Type I, II, or III Hybrid PFD is an inflatable device which is the most comfortable PFD to wear and has a minimal amount of buoyancy when deflated and significantly increased buoyancy when inflated (See accompanying table for actual buoyancy for your Type of hybrid). When inflated it turns the wearer with the action of a Type I, II, or III PFD as indicated on its label. Boaters taking advantage of the extra comfort of hybrid inflatable

PFDs must take additional care in the use of these devices. Boaters should test their hybrid PFDs in the water, under safe, controlled conditions to know how well the devices float them with limited buoyancy. Approximately 90 percent of boaters will float while wearing a Type II or III hybrid inflatable PFD when it is not inflated. However, hybrid inflatable PFDs are not recommended for non-swimmers unless worn with enough additional inflation to float the wearer. Almost all boaters will float while wearing a Type I hybrid inflatable PFD that is not inflated. The PFD's 'performance type' indicates whether it should be used only where help is nearby, or if it also may be used where help may be slow coming. Type I hybrids are suitable where rescue may be slow coming, while Types II and III are good only when there is a chance of fast rescue. Type I hybrids are approved in three weight ranges, adult, for persons weighing over 40 kg (90 lb); youth, for persons weighing 23–40 kg (50–90 lb); and small child, for persons weighing 14–23 kg (30–50 lb). Type II hybrid PFDs are approved in the same size ranges as Type I hybrids but may be available in a number of chest sizes and in universal adult sizes. Type III hybrids are only approved in adult and youth sizes but may also be available in a number of chest sizes and in universal adult sizes.

[For a pamphlet provided with a Type I, II or III hybrid PFD, insert illustration of the Type Hybrid PFD being sold]

Type IV—A Type IV PFD is normally thrown or tossed to a person who has fallen overboard so that the person can grasp and hold the device until rescued. Until May 15, 1995 (or May 1, 1996 at commercial liveries), the Type IV is acceptable in place of a wearable device in certain instances. However, this type is suitable only where there is a good chance of quick rescue, such as areas where it is common for other persons to be nearby engaged in boating, fishing, and other water activities. It is not recommended for use by non-swimmers and children.

[Insert illustration of Type IV PFD]

Type V (General)—A Type V PFD is a PFD approved for restricted uses or activities such as boardsailing, or commercial white water rafting. These PFDs are not suitable for other boating activities. The label on the PFD indicates the kinds of activities for which the PFD may be used and whether there are limitations on how it may be used.

Type V Hybrid—A Type V Hybrid PFD is an inflatable device which can be the most comfortable and has very little buoyancy when it is not inflated, and considerably more buoyancy when it is inflated. In order for the device to count toward carriage requirements on recreational boats, it must be worn except when the boat is not underway or when the user is below deck. When inflated it turns the wearer similar to the action provided by a Type I, II, or III PFD (the type of performance is indicated on the label). This type of PFD is more comfortable because it is less bulky when it is not inflated. Boaters taking advantage of the extra comfort of hybrid inflatable PFDs must take additional care in the use of these devices. Boaters should test their hybrid PFDs in the water, under safe, controlled conditions to know how well the devices float them with limited buoyancy. Approximately 70 percent of boaters will float while wearing a Type V hybrid PFD when the device is not inflated. Therefore, it is not recommended for non-swimmers unless worn with enough additional inflation to float the wearer. The PFD's "performance type" indicates whether it should be used only where help is nearby, or if it may also be used where help may be slow coming. This type of PFD is approved in two sizes, adult, for persons weighing over 40 kg (90 lb); and youth, for persons weighing 23–40 kg (50–90 lb), and may be available in a number of chest sizes and in universal adult sizes.

[For a pamphlet provided with a Type V hybrid PFD, insert illustration of TYPE V Hybrid PFD]

(3) A table with the applicable PFD Type, size, and buoyancy values from Table 160.077–15(b)(13) or 160.077–17(b)(11), as applicable; and

(4) The text in UL 1517, Section 39, items D, E, and F.

[CGD 78–174, 50 FR 33928, Aug. 22, 1985, as amended by CGD 78–174, 60 FR 2489, Jan. 9, 1995]

§ 160.077-29 PFD Manuals.

(a) *Approval.* The text of each manual required by this section is reviewed with the application for approval. Changes may be required if needed to comply with this section.

(b) *Required Manuals.* An owner's manual must be provided with each recreational and commercial hybrid PFD sold or offered for sale as follows:

(1) The manual text for a recreational hybrid PFD must be printed verbatim and in the sequence set out in paragraph (c) or (d) of this section, as applicable.

(2) The manual for a commercial hybrid PFD must meet the requirements of paragraph (f) of this section except that the manual for a commercial Type I PFD which is also labeled for recreational use must meet the requirements of paragraph (c) of this section.

(3) Additional information, instructions, or illustrations may be included within the specified text of the manuals required by this section if there is no contradiction to the required information.

(c) *Type I, II or III Hybrid PFD.* For a Type I, II and III hybrid PFD the manual contents must be as follows:

(1) The following text:

HYBRID LIMITATIONS

This PFD has limited inherent buoyancy which means YOU MAY HAVE TO INFLATE THIS PFD TO FLOAT, and its inflatable portion requires maintenance. While these PFDs are not required to be worn, if you have an accident or fall overboard, you are much more likely to survive if you are already wearing a PFD.

There is only one way to find out if you will float while wearing the PFD when it is not inflated. That is to try this PFD in the water as explained in [insert reference to the section of the manual that discusses how to test the PFD]. If you have not tested this device in accordance with these guidelines, the Coast Guard does not recommend its use.

(2) Instructions on use including instructions on donning, inflation, replenishing inflation mechanisms, and recommended practice operation;

(3) Instructions on how to properly inspect and maintain the PFD, and recommendations concerning frequency of inspection;

(4) Instructions on how to get the PFD repaired;

(5) The text in UL 1517, Section 40, items B and D;

(6) The following text:

WHY DO YOU NEED A PFD?

A PFD provides buoyancy to help keep your head above water and to help you stay face up. The average in-water-weight of an adult is only about 5 to 10 pounds. The buoyancy provided by most PFDs will support that weight in water. However, the hybrid Type I, II, or III PFD may be an exception. The uninflated buoyancy provided by this PFD may only float 90 percent of the boating public. This is because the inherent buoyancy has been reduced to make it more comfortable to wear. So, you may not float adequately without inflating the device. Once the device is inflated you will have a minimum of 22 lb of buoyancy for adult sizes, which should be more than enough to float everyone. (See table above [below] for the actual minimum buoyancy for different Types of hybrids.) Your body weight alone does not determine your in-water-weight. Since there is no simple method of determining your weight in water, you should try the device in the water in both its deflated and inflated condition.

(7) The text in UL 1517, Section 40, item G;

(8) The following text:

WEAR YOUR PFD

Your PFD won't help you if you don't have it on. It is well-known that most boating accidents occur on calm water during a clear sunny day. It is also true that in approximately 80 percent of all boating accident fatalities, the victim did not use a PFD. Don't wait until it's too late. Non-swimmers and children especially should wear their PFD at all times when on or near the water. Hybrid Type I, II, III or V PFDs are not recommended for non-swimmers unless inflated enough to float the wearer.

(9) The text in UL 1517, Section 40, items I, J, K, and L; and

(10) A table with the applicable PFD Type, size, and buoyancy values from Table 160.077-15(b)(13) or 160.077-17(b)(11), as applicable, or provide a reference to appropriate pamphlet table, if the pamphlet is combined with the manual.

(d) *Type V Recreational Hybrid PFD.* For a Type V recreational hybrid PFD the manual contents must be as follows:

(1) The text in UL 1517, Section 40, item A;

(2) Instructions on use including instructions on donning, inflation, replenishing inflation mechanisms, and recommended practice operation;

(3) Instructions on how to properly inspect and maintain the PFD, and recommendations concerning frequency of inspection;

(4) Instructions on how to get the PFD repaired; and

(5) The text in UL 1517, section 40, that is not included under paragraph (d)(1) of this section.

(e) *Commercial Hybrid PFD.* (1) For a commercial hybrid PFD that is "REQUIRED TO BE WORN" the manual must meet the requirements of paragraph (d) of this section.

(2) For a commercial hybrid PFD approved as a "Work Vest Only" or Type I PFD the manual must meet the requirements of either paragraphs (e) (3) and (4) or of paragraph (c) of this sec-

tion. The manual for a commercial Type I hybrid PFD which is also labeled for use on recreational boats must meet the requirements of paragraph (c) of this section.

(3) Each commercial hybrid PFD approved with special purpose limitation must have a user's manual that—

(i) Explains in detail the proper care, maintenance, stowage, and use of the PFD; and

(ii) Includes any other safety information as prescribed by the approval certificate.

(4) If the manual required in paragraph (e)(3) of this section calls for inspection or service by vessel personnel, the manual must—

(i) Specify personnel training or qualifications needed;

(ii) Explain how to identify the PFDs that need to be inspected; and

(iii) Provide a log in which inspections and servicing may be recorded.

(5) If a PFD light approved under subpart 161.012 is not provided at time of sale, the manual must specify the recommended type of light to be used.

(6) Notwithstanding the requirements of paragraph (b) of this section, manufacturers that make shipments to purchasers that do not redistribute the PFDs, must provide at least one manual in each carton of PFDs shipped.

[CGD 78–174, 50 FR 33928, Aug. 22, 1985, as amended by CGD 78–174, 60 FR 2490, Jan. 9, 1995]

§ 160.077-30 Spare operating components and temporary marking.

(a) *Spare operating components.* Each recreational and commercial hybrid PFD must—

(1) If it has a manual or automatic inflation mechanism and is packaged and sold with one inflation medium cartridge loaded into the inflation mechanism, have at least two additional spare inflation cartridges packaged with it. If it is sold without an inflation medium cartridge loaded into the inflation mechanism, it must be packaged and sold with at least three cartridges; and

(2) If it has an automatic inflation mechanism and is packaged and sold with one water sensitive element loaded into the inflation mechanism, have

at least two additional spare water sensitive elements packaged with it. If it is sold without a water sensitive element loaded into the inflation mechanism, it must be packaged and sold with at least three water sensitive elements.

(b) *Temporary marking.* Each recreational and commercial hybrid PFD which is sold—

(1) In a ready-to-use condition but which has covers or restraints to inhibit tampering with the inflation mechanism prior to sale, must have any such covers or restraints conspicuously marked "REMOVE IMMEDIATELY AFTER PURCHASE."; or

(2) Without an inflation medium cartridge, a water sensitive element, or both pre-loaded into the inflation mechanism, must include the markings required in § 160.077–15(c)(3)(ii).

[CGD 78–174, 60 FR 2491, Jan. 9, 1995]

§ 160.077–31 PFD Marking.

(a) *General.* Each hybrid PFD must be marked with the applicable information required by this section. Each marking must be waterproof, clear, permanent, and readable from a distance of three feet.

(b) *Prominence.* Each marking, other than the text in paragraphs (c) and (d) of this section, must be significantly less prominent and in smaller print than paragraph (c) and (d) text.

(c) *Recreational Hybrid PFD.* Each recreational hybrid PFD must be marked with the following text using capital letters where shown and be presented in the exact order shown:

TYPE [*II, III, or V, as applicable*] PFD

[*See paragraph (k) of this section for exact text to be used here*]
Recreational hybrid inflatable—Approved for use only on recreational boats. [*For Type V only*] REQUIRED TO BE WORN to meet Coast Guard carriage requirements (except for persons in enclosed spaces as explained in owner's manual).
[*For Type V only*] When inflated this PFD provides performance equivalent to a [*see paragraph (h) of this section for exact test to be used here*].
A Pamphlet and Owner's Manual must be provided with this PFD.

WARNING—TO REDUCE THE RISK OF DEATH BY DROWNING

—YOU MAY HAVE TO INFLATE THIS PFD TO FLOAT.
—TRY THIS PFD IN THE WATER EACH SEASON TO SEE IF IT WILL FLOAT YOU WITHOUT INFLATION.
—CHOOSE THE RIGHT SIZE PFD AND WEAR IT—FASTEN ALL CLOSURES AND ADJUST FOR SNUG FIT.
—THIS PFD REQUIRES MAINTENANCE. FOLLOW MANUFACTURER'S USE AND CARE INSTRUCTIONS.
—REMOVE HEAVY OBJECTS FROM POCKETS IN AN EMERGENCY.
—[*Unless impact tested at high speed as noted on the approval certificate*] DO NOT USE IN HIGH-SPEED ACTIVITIES.
—DO NOT DRINK ALCOHOL WHILE BOATING.

(d) *Type I and Commercial Hybrid PFD.* Each Type I hybrid PFD intended for recreational use and each commercial hybrid PFD must be marked with the following text using capital letters where shown and be presented in the exact order shown:

TYPE [*"I", "V", or "V Work Vest Only"*, as applicable] PFD

[*See paragraph (k) of this section for exact text to be used here*]
Commercial hybrid inflatable—Approved for use on [*see paragraph (j) of this section for exact text to be used here*].
[*For Type V only*] When inflated this PFD provides performance equivalent to a [*see paragraph (h) of this section for exact test to be used here*].
[*For Type I devices intended for recreational use*] A Pamphlet and Owner's Manual must be provided with this PFD.

WARNING—TO REDUCE THE RISK OF DEATH BY DROWNING

—YOU MAY HAVE TO INFLATE THIS PFD TO FLOAT.
—TRY THIS PFD IN THE WATER EACH SEASON TO SEE IF IT WILL FLOAT YOU WITHOUT INFLATION.
—[*For Type I devices intended for recreational use*] CHOOSE THE RIGHT SIZE PFD AND WEAR IT.
—FASTEN ALL CLOSURES AND ADJUST FOR SNUG FIT.
—THIS PFD MUST BE MAINTAINED, STOWED, AND USED ONLY IN ACCORDANCE WITH THE OWNER'S MANUAL.
—REMOVE HEAVY OBJECTS FROM POCKETS IN AN EMERGENCY.
—[*Unless impact tested at high speed as noted on the approval certificate For Type I devices intended for recreational use*] DO NOT USE IN HIGH-SPEED ACTIVITIES.

—*[For Type I devices intended for recreational use]* DO NOT DRINK ALCOHOL WHILE BOATING.

(e) *All PFD's.* Each hybrid PFD must also be marked with the following information below the text required by paragraph (c) or (d) of this section:

(1) U.S. Coast Guard Approval Number (insert assigned approval number).

(2) Manufacturer's or private labeler's name and address.

(3) Lot Number.

(4) Date, or year and calendar quarter, of manufacture.

(5) Necessary vital care or use instructions, if any, such as the following:

(i) Warning against dry cleaning.

(ii) Size and type of inflation medium cartridges required.

(iii) Specific donning instructions.

(f) *Identification of User.* Each hybrid PFD must have adequate space within which to mark the name or other identification of the intended user.

(g) *Flotation material buoyancy loss.* When kapok flotation material is used, the statement "—REPLACE PFD IF PADS BECOME STIFF OR WATER-LOGGED." must follow the warning "—TRY THIS PFD IN THE WATER EACH SEASON TO SEE IF IT WILL FLOAT YOU WITHOUT INFLATION." required by paragraph (c) or (d) of this section.

(h) *Type equivalence.* The exact text to be inserted for Type V hybrid PFDs will be one of the following type equivalents as noted on the Approval Certificate.

(i) [Reserved]

(j) *Approved use.* Unless the Commandant has authorized omitting the display of approved use, the exact text to be inserted will be one or more of the following statements as noted on the approval certificate:

(1) "all recreational boats and on uninspected commercial vessels"

(2) "all recreational boats and on uninspected commercial vessels. REQUIRED TO BE WORN to meet Coast Guard carriage requirements (except for persons in enclosed spaces as explained in owner's manual)"

(3) "inspected commercial vessels as a WORK VEST only."

(4) "[*Insert exact text of special purpose or limitation and vessel(s) or vessel type(s), noted on approval certificate*]."

(k) *Size Ranges.* The exact text to be inserted will be one of the following statements as noted on the approval certificate:

(1) ADULT—For persons weighing more than 40 kg (90 lb).

(2) YOUTH—For persons weighing 23–40 kg (50–90 lb).

(3) CHILD SMALL—For persons weighing 14–23 kg (30–50 lb).

(4) "[*Other text noted on approval certificate*]."

[CGD 78–174, 50 FR 33928, Aug. 22, 1985, as amended by CGD 78–174A, 51 FR 4351, Feb. 4, 1986; CGD 78–174, 60 FR 2491, Jan. 9, 1995; 60 FR 7131, Feb. 7, 1995]

Subpart 160.151—Inflatable Liferafts (SOLAS)

SOURCE: CGD 85–205, 62 FR 25547, May 9, 1997, unless otherwise noted.

§ 160.151-1 Scope.

This subpart prescribes standards, tests, and procedures for approval by the Coast Guard of SOLAS A and SOLAS B inflatable liferafts, and for their periodic inspection and repair at approved facilities ("servicing"). Certain provisions of this subpart also apply to inflatable buoyant apparatus as specified in § 160.010–3 and to inflatable liferafts for domestic service as specified in subpart 160.051.

§ 160.151-3 Definitions.

In this subpart, the term:

Commandant means the Commandant (G–MSE), United States Coast Guard, 2100 Second Street, SW., Washington, DC 20593–0001.

Servicing means periodic inspection, necessary repair, and repacking by a servicing facility approved by the Coast Guard. Requirements for periodic inspection and repair of inflatable liferafts approved by the Coast Guard are described in §§ 160.151–35 through 160.151–57.

SOLAS means the International Convention for the Safety of Life at Sea, 1974, as amended by the International Maritime Organization through the

1988 (GMDSS) amendments, dated 9 November 1988.

SOLAS A Liferaft means a liferaft that meets the requirements of this subpart for an inflatable liferaft complying with SOLAS and equipped with a SOLAS A equipment pack.

SOLAS B Liferaft means a liferaft that meets the requirements of this subpart for an inflatable liferaft complying with SOLAS and equipped with a SOLAS B equipment pack.

§ 160.151-5 Incorporation by reference.

(a) Certain material is incorporated by reference into this subpart with the approval of the Director of the Federal Register in accordance with 5 U.S.C. 552(a) and 1 CFR part 51. To enforce any edition other than that specified in paragraph (b) of this section, the Coast Guard must publish notice of change in the FEDERAL REGISTER and make the material available to the public. All approved material is on file at the Office of the Federal Register, 800 North Capitol Street NW., Suite 700, Washington, DC, and at the U.S. Coast Guard, Office of Design and Engineering Standards (G–MSE), 2100 Second Street SW., Washington, DC 20593–0001, and is available from the sources indicated in paragraph (b) of this section.

(b) The material approved for incorporation by reference in this subpart and the sections affected are as follows:

AMERICAN SOCIETY FOR TESTING AND MATERIALS (ASTM)
1916 Race St., Philadelphia, PA 19103
ASTM F1014—Standard Specification for Flashlights on Vessels, 1986—160.151-21

INTERNATIONAL MARITIME ORGANIZATION (IMO)
Publications Section, 4 Albert Embankment, London SE1 7SR, England
Resolution A.689(17)—Recommendation on Testing of Life-saving Appliances, 27 November 1991, including amendments through Resolution MSC.54(66), adopted 30 May 1996—160.151-21; 160.151-27; 160.151-31; 160.151-57
Resolution A.657(16)—Instructions for Action in Survival Craft, 19 November 1989— 160.151-21
Resolution A.658(16)—Use and Fitting of Retro-reflective Materials on Life-saving Appliances, 20 November 1989—160.151-15; 160.151-57.

NATIONAL INSTITUTE OF STANDARDS AND TECHNOLOGY (FORMERLY NATIONAL BUREAU OF STANDARDS)

c/o National Technical Information Service, Springfield, VA 22161
NBS Special Publication 440 (Order No. PB265225) Color: Universal Language and Dictionary of Names, 1976—160.151-15

NAVAL FORMS AND PUBLICATIONS CENTER
Customer Service, Code 1052, 5801 Tabor Ave., Philadelphia, PA 19120
MIL-C-17415E—(Ships)—Cloth, Coated, and Webbing, Inflatable Boat and Miscellaneous Use—160.151-15

§ 160.151-7 Construction of inflatable liferafts.

Except as specified in this subpart, each SOLAS A and SOLAS B inflatable liferaft must meet the requirements of Chapter III of SOLAS. To be approved under this subpart, inflatable liferafts must be constructed in accordance with the following provisions of SOLAS:

(a) Chapter III, Regulation 30, paragraph 2 (III/30.2), General requirements for life-saving appliances.

(b) Chapter III, Regulation 38 (III/38) General requirements for liferafts.

(c) Chapter III, Regulation 39 (III/39) Inflatable liferafts.

(d) Chapter III, Regulation 51 (III/51) Training manual.

(e) Chapter III, Regulation 52 (III/52) Instructions for on-board maintenance.

§ 160.151-9 Independent laboratory.

Tests and inspections that this subpart requires to be conducted by an independent laboratory must be conducted by an independent laboratory accepted by the Coast Guard under subpart 159.010 of part 159 of this chapter to perform such tests and inspections. A list of accepted laboratories is available from the Commandant.

§ 160.151-11 Approval procedure.

(a) A manufacturer seeking approval of an inflatable liferaft must comply with the procedures in part 159, subpart 159.005, of this chapter and in this section.

(b) A manufacturer seeking approval of an inflatable liferaft must submit an application meeting the requirements of § 159.005-5 of this chapter for preapproval review. To meet the requirements of § 159.005-5(a)(2) of this chapter, the manufacturer shall submit—

215

(1) General-arrangement drawing including principal dimensions;

(2) Seating-arrangement plan;

(3) Plans for subassemblies;

(4) Plans for carriage and, in detail, stowage of equipment;

(5) Plans for the inflation system;

(6) Plans for the outer container;

(7) Plans for any lifting shackle or ring, including diameter in cross-section, used for connecting the suspension tackle of a davit-launched inflatable liferaft to the automatic disengaging device used for its hoisting and lowering;

(8) Other drawing(s) necessary to show that the inflatable liferaft complies with the requirements of this subpart;

(9) Description of methods of seam and joint construction;

(10) Samples and identification of each material used in the buoyancy chambers, floor, and canopy, including the identity of their manufacturers, and segments of each type of seam made from such materials; and

(11) Complete data pertinent to the installation and use of the proposed inflatable liferaft, including the maximum proposed height of its installation above the water, and the maximum length of the sea painter installed in the inflatable liferaft.

§ 160.151-13 Fabrication of prototype inflatable liferafts for approval.

If the manufacturer is notified that the information submitted in accordance with § 160.151-11 is satisfactory to the Commandant, fabrication of a prototype inflatable liferaft must proceed in the following sequence:

(a) The manufacturer shall arrange for an independent laboratory to inspect the liferaft during its fabrication and prepare an inspection report meeting the requirements of § 159.005-11 of this chapter. The independent laboratory shall conduct at least one inspection during layup of the buoyancy tubes of the liferaft, at least one inspection of the finished liferaft when fully inflated, and as many other inspections as are necessary to determine that the liferaft—

(1) Is constructed by the methods and with the materials specified in the plans;

(2) Passes the applicable inspections and tests required by § 160.151-31; and

(3) Conforms with the manufacturer's plans.

(b) The manufacturer shall submit the independent laboratory's inspection report to the Commandant for review.

(c) If, after review of the inspection report of the independent laboratory, the Commandant notifies the manufacturer that the liferaft is in compliance with the requirements of this subpart, the manufacturer may proceed with the approval tests required under §§ 160.151-27 and 160.151-29.

(d) The manufacturer shall notify the cognizant OCMI of where the approval tests required under §§ 160.151-27 and 160.151-29 will take place and arrange with the OCMI a testing schedule that allows for a Coast Guard inspector to travel to the site where the testing is to be performed.

(e) The manufacturer shall admit the Coast Guard inspector to any place where work or testing is performed on inflatable liferafts or their component parts and materials for the purpose of—

(1) Assuring that the quality-assurance program of the manufacturer is satisfactory;

(2) Witnessing tests; and

(3) Taking samples of parts or materials for additional inspections or tests.

(f) The manufacturer shall make available to the Coast Guard inspector the affidavits or invoices from the suppliers of all essential materials used in the production of inflatable liferafts, together with records identifying the lot numbers of the liferafts in which such materials were used.

(g) On conclusion of the approval testing, the manufacturer shall comply with the requirements of § 159.005-9(a)(5) of this chapter by submitting the following to the Commandant:

(1) The report of the prototype testing prepared by the manufacturer. The report must include a signed statement by the Coast Guard inspector who witnessed the testing, indicating that the report accurately describes the testing and its results.

(2) The final plans of the liferaft as built. The plans must include—

(i) The servicing manual described in §160.151–37;

(ii) The instructions for training and maintenance described in §§160.151–59 and 160.151–61, respectively;

(iii) The final version of the plans required under §160.151–11(b), including—

(A) Each correction, change, or addition made during the construction and approval testing of prototypes;

(B) Sufficient detail to determine that each requirement of this subpart is met;

(C) Fabrication details for the inflatable liferaft, including details of the method of making seams and joints; and

(D) Full details of the inflation system.

(3) A description of the quality-control procedures that will apply to the production of the inflatable liferaft. These must include—

(i) The system for checking material certifications received from suppliers;

(ii) The method for controlling the inventory of materials;

(iii) The method for checking quality of seams and joints; and

(iv) The inspection checklists used during various stages of fabrication to assure that the approved liferaft complies with the approved plans and the requirements of this subpart.

[CGD 85–205, 62 FR 25547, May 9, 1997; 62 FR 35392, July 1, 1997]

§160.151–15 Design and performance of inflatable liferafts.

To satisfy the requirements of the regulations of SOLAS indicated in §160.151–7, each inflatable liferaft must meet the following requirements of this section:

(a) *Workmanship and materials (Regulation III/30.2.1).* Each liferaft must be constructed of the following types of materials meeting MIL–C–17415E, or materials accepted by the Commandant as equivalent or superior—

(1) Type 2, Class B, for the canopy;

(2) Type 8 for seam tape;

(3) Type 11 for the inflatable floor; and

(4) Type 16, Class AA, for all other inflatable compartments and structural components.

(b) *Seams (Regulation III/30.2.1).* Each seam must be at least as strong as the weakest of the materials joined by the seam. Each seam must be covered with tape where necessary to prevent lifting of and damage to fabric edges.

(c) *Protection from cold inflation-gas (Regulation III/30.2.1).* Each inflatable compartment must be provided with a protective liner or baffling arrangement at the inflation-gas inlet, or other equally effective means to prevent damage from exposure to cold inflation-gas.

(d) *Compatibility of dissimilar materials (Regulation III/30.2.4).* Where dissimilar materials are combined in the construction of a liferaft, provisions must be made to prevent loosening or tightening due to differences in thermal expansion, freezing, buckling, galvanic corrosion, or other incompatibilities.

(e) *Color (Regulation III/30.2.6).* The primary color of the exterior of the canopy must be vivid reddish orange (color number 34 of NBS Special Publication 440), or a fluorescent color of a similar hue.

(f) *Retroreflective material (Regulation III/30.2.7).* Each inflatable liferaft must be marked with Type I retroreflective material approved under part 164, subpart 164.018, of this chapter as complying with SOLAS. The arrangement of the retroreflective material must comply with IMO Resolution A.658(16).

(g) *Towing attachments (Regulation III/38.1.4.)* Each towing attachment must be reinforced strongly enough to withstand the towing strain, and marked to indicate its function.

(h) *Weight (Regulation III/38.2.2).* The weight of the liferaft including its container and equipment may not exceed 185 kg (407.8 lb), unless the liferaft is intended for launching into the water directly from its stowed position using an inclined or hand-tilted rack, or is served by a launching appliance approved by the Commandant under approval series 160.163.

(i) *Lifelines (Regulation III/38.3.1).* Each lifeline must be made of nylon tubular webbing with a minimum diameter of 14 mm (9/16-inch), rope with a minimum diameter of 10 mm (⅜-inch), or equivalent. Each lifeline-attachment patch must have a minimum breaking strength of 1.5 kN (350 lb) pull exerted perpendicular to the base of the patch. Each bight of an exterior lifeline must be long enough to allow the lifeline to reach to the waterline of the liferaft when it is afloat.

(j) *Painter length (Regulation III/38.3.2).* On or before July 1, 1998, the length of the liferaft painter shall be not less than 10 meters (33 feet) plus the liferaft's maximum stowage height, or 15 meters (49 feet), whichever is greater.

(k) *Painter system (Regulation III/38.6.1).* The painter protruding from the liferaft container must be inherently resistant, or treated to be resistant, to deterioration from sunlight and salt spray, and resistant to absorption and wicking of water.

(l) *Inflation cylinders (Regulation III/39.2.3).* Each compressed-gas inflation cylinder within the liferaft must meet the requirements of § 147.60 of this chapter, and be installed so that—

(1) Slings and reinforcements of sufficient strength retain the inflation cylinders in place when the liferaft is dropped into the water from its stowage height and during inflation; and

(2) The painter and the inflation cylinders of the liferaft are linked to start inflation when the painter is pulled by one person exerting a force not exceeding 150 N (34 lb).

(m) *Boarding ladders (Regulation III/39.4.2).* The steps of each boarding ladder must provide a suitable foothold.

(n) *Canopy lamps (Regulation III/39.6.2).* The exterior liferaft canopy lamp must be approved by the Commandant under approval series 161.101.

(o) *Containers (Regulation III/39.7.1).* Each container for packing liferafts—

(1) Must include a telltale made with a seal-and-wire, or equivalent, method for indicating whether the liferaft has been tampered with or used since packing;

(2) Must be designed so that the liferaft breaks free of the container when inflation is initiated, without the need to manually open or remove any closing arrangement;

(3) Must have an interior surface smooth and free from splinters, barbs, or rough projections;

(4) Must be of rigid construction where the liferaft is intended for float-free launching or for exposed stowage on deck;

(5) If rigid, must be designed to facilitate securing the inflatable liferaft to a vessel to permit quick release for manual launching;

(6) If constructed of fibrous-glass-reinforced plastic, must be provided with a means to prevent abrasion of the liferaft fabric, such as by using a gel-coated interior finish of the container, enclosing the liferaft in an envelope of plastic film, or equivalent means; and

(7) Except as provided in paragraph (o)(4) of this section, may be of fabric construction. Each container of fabric construction must be made of coated cloth, include carrying handles and drain holes, and be adaptable to stowage and expeditious removal from lockers and deck-mounted enclosures adjacent to liferaft-launching stations. The weight of a liferaft in a fabric container including its container and equipment may not exceed 100 kg (220 lb).

§ 160.151–17 Additional requirements for design and performance of SOLAS A and SOLAS B inflatable liferafts.

To satisfy the requirements of the indicated regulations of SOLAS, each SOLAS A and SOLAS B inflatable liferaft must be manufactured in accordance with §§ 160.151–7 and 160.151–15, and must comply with the following additional requirements:

(a) *Stability (Regulation III/39.5.1).* (1) Each liferaft with a capacity of more than 8 persons must have a waterplane of circular or elliptical shape. A hexagonal, octagonal, or similar outline approximating a circular or elliptical shape is acceptable.

(2) Each liferaft manufactured under this subpart must have water-containing stability appendages on its underside to resist capsizing from wind and waves. On or before July 1, 1998, these appendages must meet the following requirements:

(i) The total volume of the appendages must not be less than 220 liters (7.77 ft³) for liferafts approved to accommodate up to 10 persons. The volume of an appendage is calculated using the bottom of the lowest opening in an appendage as the height of the appendage, and by deducting the volume of any objects inside the appendage. No opening designed to close as water is forced out of an appendage is an opening for the purpose of this calculation.

(ii) The total volume of the appendages for liferafts approved to accommodate more than 10 persons must be not less than 20 × N liters (0.706 × N ft³), where N = the number of persons for which the liferaft is approved.

(iii) The appendages must be securely attached and evenly distributed around the periphery of the exterior bottom of the liferaft. They may be omitted at the locations of inflation cylinders.

(iv) The appendages must consist of at least two separate parts so that damage to one part will permit at least half of the required total volume to remain intact.

(v) Openings in or between the appendages must be provided to limit the formation of air pockets under the inflatable liferaft.

(vi) The appendages must be designed to deploy underwater when the liferaft inflates, and to fill to at least 60 percent of their capacity within 25 seconds of deployment. If weights are used for this purpose, they must be of corrosion-resistant material.

(vii) The primary color of the appendages must be vivid reddish orange (color number 34 of NBS Special Publication 440), or a fluorescent color of a similar hue.

(b) *Boarding ramp (Regulation III/39.4.1)*. The boarding ramp must have sufficient size and buoyancy to support one person weighing 100 kg (220 lb), sitting or kneeling and not holding onto any other part of the liferaft.

(c) *Marking (Regulation III/39.8)*. On or before July 1, 1998, means must be provided for identifying the liferaft with the name and port of registry of the ship to which it is to be fitted, so that the identification can be changed without opening the liferaft container.

§160.151–21 Equipment required for SOLAS A and SOLAS B inflatable liferafts.

To obtain Coast Guard approval, the equipment in each SOLAS A and SOLAS B inflatable liferaft must meet the following specific requirements

when complying with the indicated regulations of SOLAS:

(a) *Heaving line (Regulation III/38.5.1.1)*. The buoyant heaving line described by Regulation III/38.5.1.1 must have a breaking strength of not less than 1.1 kN (250 lb), and must be attached to the inflatable liferaft near the entrance furthest from the painter attachment.

(b) *Jackknife (Regulation III/38.5.1.2)*. Each folding knife carried as permitted by Regulation III/38.5.1.2 must be a jackknife approved by the Commandant under approval series 160.043.

(c) *Bailer (Regulation III/38.5.1.3)*. Each bailer described by Regulation III/38.5.1.3 must have a volume of at least 2 L (125 in³).

(d) *Sponge (Regulation III/38.5.1.4)*. Each sponge described by Regulation III/38.5.1.4 must have a volume of at least 750 cm³ (48 in³) when saturated with water.

(e) *Sea anchors (Regulation III/38.5.1.5)*. Sea anchors without the swivels described by Regulation III/38.5.1.5 may be used if, during the towing test, a sea anchor of their design does not rotate when streamed. The sea anchors need not have the tripping lines described by Regulation III/38.5.1.5 if, during the towing test, a sea anchor of their design can be hauled in by one person.

(f) *Paddles (Regulation III/38.5.1.6)*. The paddles must be at least 1.2 m (4 ft) long and must be of the same size and type as used to pass the maneuverability test in paragraph 1/5.10 of IMO Resolution A.689(17).

(g) *Tin-opener (Regulation III/38.5.1.7)*. Each sharp part of a tin-opener described by Regulation III/38.5.1.7 must have a guard.

(h) *First-aid kit (Regulation III/38.5.1.8)*. Each first-aid kit described by Regulation III/38.5.1.8 must be approved by the Commandant under approval series 160.054.

(i) *Whistle (Regulation III/38.5.1.9)*. The whistle described by Regulation III/38.5.1.9 must be a ball-type or multi-tone whistle of corrosion-resistant construction.

(j) *Rocket parachute flare (Regulation III/38.5.1.10)*. Each rocket parachute flare described by Regulation III/38.5.1.10 must be approved by the Commandant under approval series 160.136.

(k) *Hand flare (Regulation III/ 38.5.1.11)*. Each hand flare described by Regulation III/38.5.1.11 must be approved by the Commandant under approval series 160.121.

(l) *Buoyant smoke signal (Regulation III/38.5.1.12)*. Each buoyant smoke signal described by Regulation III/38.5.1.12 must be of the floating type approved by the Commandant under approval series 160.122.

(m) *Electric torch (Regulation III/ 38.5.1.13)*. The waterproof electric torch described by Regulation III/38.5.1.13 must be a Type I or Type III flashlight constructed and marked in accordance with ASTM F1014. Three-cell-size flashlights bearing Coast Guard approval numbers in the 161.008 series may continue to be used as long as they are serviceable.

(n) *Radar reflector (Regulation III/ 38.5.1.14)*. The radar reflector may be omitted if the outside of the container of the inflatable liferaft includes a notice near the "SOLAS A" or "SOLAS B" marking indicating that no radar reflector is included.

(o) *Signalling mirror (Regulation III/ 38.5.1.15)*. Each signalling mirror described by Regulation III/38.5.1.15 must be approved by the Commandant under approval series 160.020.

(p) *Lifesaving signals (Regulation III/ 38.5.1.16)*. If not provided on a waterproof card or sealed in a transparent waterproof container as described in Regulation III/38.5.1.16, the table of lifesaving signals may be provided as part of the instruction manual.

(q) *Fishing tackle (Regulation III/ 38.5.1.17)*. The fishing tackle must be in a kit approved by the Commandant under approval series 160.061.

(r) *Food rations (Regulation III/ 38.5.1.18.)* The food rations must be approved by the Commandant under approval series 160.046.

(s) *Drinking water (Regulation III/ 38.5.1.19)*. The fresh water required by Regulation III/38.5.1.19 must be "emergency drinking water" approved by the Commandant under approval series 160.026. The desalting apparatus described in Regulation III/38.5.1.19 must be approved by the Commandant under approval series 160.058. After July 1, 1998, 1.0 liter/person of the required water may be replaced by an approved

manually powered reverse osmosis desalinator capable of producing an equal amount of water in two days.

(t) *Drinking cup (Regulation III/ 38.5.1.20)*. The drinking cup described in Regulation III/38.5.1.20 must be graduated in ounces or milliliters or both.

(u) *Anti-seasickness medicine (Regulation III/38.5.1.21)*. The anti-seasickness medicine required by Regulation III/ 38.5.1.21 must include instructions for use and be marked with an expiration date.

(v) *Survival instructions (Regulation III/38.5.1.22)*. The instructions required by Regulation III/38.5.1.22 on how to survive in a liferaft must—

(1) Be waterproof;

(2) Whatever other language or languages they may be in, be in English;

(3) Meet the guidelines in IMO Resolution A.657(16); and

(4) Be suspended in a clear film envelope from one of the arch tubes of the canopy.

(w) *Instructions for immediate action (Regulation III/38.5.1.23)*. The instructions for immediate action must—

(1) Be waterproof;

(2) Whatever other language or languages they may be in, be in English;

(3) Meet the guidelines in IMO Resolution A.657(16);

(4) Explain both the noise accompanying the operation of any provided pressure-relief valves, and the need to render them inoperable after they complete venting; and

(5) Be suspended from the inside canopy, so they are immediately visible by survivors on entering the inflatable liferaft. They may be contained in the same envelope with the instructions on how to survive if the instructions for immediate action are visible through both faces of the envelope.

(x) *Thermal protective aid (Regulation III/38.5.1.24)*.

Each thermal protective aid described by Regulation III/38.5.1.24 must be approved by the Commandant under approval series 160.174.

(y) *Repair outfit (Regulation III/ 39.10.1.1)*. The repair outfit required by Regulation III/39.10.1.1 must include—

(1) Six or more sealing clamps or serrated conical plugs, or a combination of the two;

(2) Five or more tube patches at least 50 mm (2 in) in diameter;

(3) A roughing tool, if necessary to apply the patches; and

(4) If the patches are not self-adhesive, a container of cement compatible with the liferaft fabric and the patches, marked with instructions for use and an expiration date.

(z) *Pump or bellows (Regulation III/ 39.10.1.2).* The pump or bellows required by Regulation III/39.10.1.2 must be manually operable and arranged to be capable of inflating any part of the inflatable structure of the liferaft.

(aa) *Plugs for pressure-relief valves.* Plugs for rendering pressure-relief valves inoperable must be provided in any liferaft fitted with such valves, unless the valves are of a type that can be rendered inoperable without separate plugs. If provided, plugs for pressure-relief valves must be usable with hands gloved in an immersion suit, and must either float or be secured to the liferaft by a lanyard.

§160.151–25 Additional equipment for inflatable liferafts.

The manufacturer may specify additional equipment to be carried in inflatable liferafts if the equipment is identified in the manufacturer's approved drawings and if the packing and inspection of the equipment is covered in the servicing manual. Any such additional equipment for which performance or approval standards are prescribed in this part or in 47 CFR part 80 must comply with those standards.

§160.151–27 Approval inspections and tests for inflatable liferafts.

(a) Except as provided in paragraph (b) of this section, to satisfy the testing requirements of: IMO Resolution A.689(17), part 1, paragraphs 5.1 through 5.15 inclusive; paragraph 5.16 for a davit-launched inflatable liferaft; and paragraph 5.17, a prototype inflatable liferaft of each design submitted for Coast Guard approval must meet the additional specific requirements and tests specified in paragraphs (c) and (d) of this section.

(b) The Commandant may waive certain tests for a liferaft identical in construction to a liferaft that has successfully completed the tests, if the liferafts differ only in size and are of essentially the same design.

(c) Tests must be conducted in accordance with the indicated paragraphs of IMO Resolution A.689(17), except:

(1) *Jump test (Paragraph 1/5.2).* One-half of the jumps must be with the canopy erect, and the remainder with the canopy furled or deflated. If a "suitable and equivalent mass" is used, it must be equipped with the shoes described in paragraph 1/5.2.1 of Resolution A.689(17), and arranged so the shoes strike the liferaft first.

(2) *Mooring-out test (Paragraph 1/5.5).* Initial inflation may be with compressed air.

(3) *Loading and seating test (Paragraph 1/5.7).* For a liferaft not intended for use with a launching or embarkation appliance, the persons used to determine seating capacity shall wear insulated buoyant immersion suits rather than lifejackets.

(4) *Boarding test (Paragraph 1/5.8).* This test must be performed using each boarding ramp or boarding ladder which is installed on the liferaft.

(5) *Canopy-closure test (Paragraph 1/5.12).* This test is required only for SOLAS A and SOLAS B inflatable liferafts. For a davit-launched liferaft, any opening near the lifting eye should be sealed during the test to prevent the ingress of water. The water accumulated within the liferaft at the end of the test must not exceed 4 liters (1 gallon).

(6) *Detailed inspection (Paragraph 1/5.14).* The independent laboratory's inspection of the prototype liferaft under §160.151–13(a) satisfies the requirements of paragraph 1/5.14.

(7) *Davit-launched liferafts—strength test (Paragraph 1/5.16.1).* The calculation of combined strength of the lifting components must be based on the lesser of—

(i) The lowest breaking strength obtained for each item; or

(ii) The component manufacturer's ultimate strength rating.

(d) The boarding ramp on each liferaft equipped with one must be demonstrated capable of supporting one person weighing 100 kg (220 lb), sitting or kneeling and not holding onto any other part of the liferaft.

§ 160.151-29 Additional approval tests for SOLAS A and SOLAS B inflatable liferafts.

To verify compliance with the requirements of Regulation III/39.5.1, on or before July 1, 1998, the following test must be conducted for SOLAS A and SOLAS B inflatable liferafts in addition to those required by § 160.151-27 and IMO Resolution A.689(17):

(a) *Test of filling time for stability appendages.* A representative sample of each type and size of stability appendage to be fitted to a liferaft must be tested as follows:

(1) The appendage must be attached to a testing jig similar in material and construction to the appendage's intended location on a liferaft. The method of attachment must be the same as used on a liferaft. The appendage and jig must be attached to a scale capable of recording peak readings, and suspended over a pool of calm water. The dry weight must be recorded.

(2) The appendage and jig must then be quickly lowered into the water until the appendage is completely submerged. When the appendage has been in the water for 25 seconds, it must be smoothly lifted completely out of the water, and the peak weight after the appendage is removed from the water recorded.

(3) The difference in weights measured according to paragraphs (a) (1) and (2) of this section must be at least 60 percent of the appendage's volume, calculated in accordance with § 160.151-17(a)(2)(i).

(b) [Reserved]

§ 160.151-31 Production inspections and tests of inflatable liferafts.

(a) Production inspections and tests of inflatable liferafts must be carried out in accordance with the procedures for independent laboratory inspection in part 159, subpart 159.007, of this chapter and with those of this section.

(b) Each liferaft approved by the Coast Guard must be identified with unique lot and serial numbers as follows:

(1) Each lot must consist of not more than 50 liferafts of the same design and carrying capacity.

(2) A new lot must begin whenever the liferafts undergo changes of design, material, production method, or source of supply for any essential component.

(3) The manufacturer may use a running-lot system, whereby the fabrication of the individual liferafts of a lot occurs over an extended interval under an irregular schedule. Each running lot must comprise not more than 10 liferafts of the same design and carrying capacity. Each running-lot system must be in accordance with a procedure proposed by the manufacturer and approved by the Commandant.

(4) Unless a lot is a running lot, each lot must consist of liferafts produced under a process of continuous production.

(c) Among the records required to be retained by the manufacturer under § 159.007-13 of this chapter, are affidavits or invoices from the suppliers identifying all essential materials used in the production of approved liferafts, together with the lot numbers of the liferafts constructed with those materials.

(d) Each approved liferaft must pass each of the inspections and tests described in IMO Resolution A.689(17), part 2, paragraphs 5.1.3 through 5.1.6 inclusive, and prescribed by paragraphs (e) through (g) of this section. For a davit-launched liferaft, these tests must be preceded by the test described in IMO Resolution A.689(17), part 2, paragraph 5.2.

(e) The test described in IMO Resolution A.689(17), Paragraph 2/5.1.5, must be conducted under the following conditions:

(1) The test must last 1 hour, with a maximum allowable pressure drop of 5 percent after compensation for changes in ambient temperature and barometric pressure.

(2) For each degree Celsius of rise in temperature, 0.385 kPa must be subtracted from the final pressure reading (0.031 psig per degree Fahrenheit). For each degree Celsius of drop in temperature, 0.385 kPa must be added to the final pressure reading (again, 0.031 psig per degree Fahrenheit).

(3) For each mm of mercury of rise in barometric pressure, 0.133 kPa must be added to the final temperature-corrected pressure reading (0.049 psig per 0.1 inch of mercury). For each mm of

mercury of drop in barometric pressure, 0.133 kPa must be subtracted from the final temperature-corrected pressure reading (again, 0.049 psig per 0.1 inch of mercury). Corrections for changes in ambient barometric pressure are necessary only if a measuring instrument open to the atmosphere, such as a manometer, is used.

(f) One liferaft from each lot of fewer than 30 liferafts, and two from each lot of 30 to 50 liferafts, must pass the test described in IMO Resolution A.689(17), part 2, paragraphs 5.1.1 and 5.1.2. If any liferaft fails this test—

(1) The reason for the failure must be determined;

(2) Each liferaft in the lot must be examined for the defect and repaired if reparable, or scrapped if irreparable; and

(3) The lot test must be repeated, including random selection of the liferaft or liferafts to be tested. If any liferafts from the lot have left the place of manufacture, they must be recalled for examination, repair, and testing as necessary; or else the required actions must take place at an approved servicing facility.

(g) On or before May 11, 1998, the manufacturer shall arrange for inspections by an accepted independent laboratory at least once in each calendar quarter in which production of liferafts approved by the Coast Guard takes place. The time and date of each inspection must be selected by the independent laboratory, to occur when completed liferafts are in the manufacturing facility and others are under construction. The manufacturer shall ensure that the inspector from the independent laboratory—

(1) Conducts the inspection and witnesses the tests required by paragraph (f) of this section, and further conducts a visual inspection to verify that the liferafts are being made in accordance with the approved plans and the requirements of this subpart;

(2) Examines the records of production inspections and tests for liferafts produced since the last inspection by an independent laboratory to verify that each required inspection and test has been carried out satisfactorily;

(3) Conducts a design audit on at least one liferaft approved by the Coast Guard each year. If possible, different models of liferafts must be examined in the design audit from year to year. To retain Coast Guard approval, the manufacturer shall demonstrate to the inspector during each design audit that—

(i) Each part used in the liferaft matches the part called for by the approved plans;

(ii) Each part and subassembly are of the materials and components indicated on the approved plans or their bills of materials; and

(iii) Each critical dimension is correct as shown either by measurement or by proper fit and function in the next-higher assembly.

(h) Until such time as the manufacturer has arranged for inspections by an accepted independent laboratory in accordance with paragraph (g) of this section, the manufacturer shall notify the cognizant OCMI whenever final production inspections and tests are to be performed so that the OCMI may, at his option, assign a marine inspector to the factory to witness the applicable tests and satisfy himself that the quality assurance program of the manufacturer is satisfactory.

§160.151-33 **Marking and labeling.**

(a) Whatever other languages they may be in, markings required on each inflatable liferaft and its container must be in English.

(b) The markings required on the liferaft container under Regulation III/39.7.3 of SOLAS must be on a plate or label sufficiently durable to withstand continuous exposure to environmental conditions at sea for the life of the liferaft. In addition, the container must be marked with the—

(1) Manufacturer's model identification; and

(2) U.S. Coast Guard approval number.

(c) In addition to the markings required on the inflatable liferaft under Regulation III/39.8 of SOLAS, the liferaft must be marked with the—

(1) Manufacturer's model identification;

(2) Lot number; and

(3) U.S. Coast Guard approval number.

§ 160.151-35 Servicing.

(a) *Inspection and repair.* Inflatable liferafts carried under the regulations in this chapter, and in chapter I of title 33 CFR, must be inspected periodically by a servicing facility approved by the Coast Guard, repaired as necessary, and repacked. Requirements for periodic inspection and repair of liferafts approved by the Coast Guard appear in §§ 160.151-37 through 160.151-57.

(b) *Manufacturer's requirements.* To retain Coast Guard approval of liferafts, the manufacturer must:

(1) Prepare a servicing manual or manuals complying with § 160.151-37 to cover each model and size of liferaft that the manufacturer produces. The manual or manuals must be submitted to the Commandant for approval.

(2) At least once each year, issue a list of revisions to the manual or manuals, and issue a list of bulletins affecting the manual or manuals, that are in effect.

(3) Make available to each servicing facility approved by the Coast Guard the manual or manuals, the revisions, the bulletins, the plans, and any unique parts and tools that may be necessary to service the liferaft. The plans may be either the manufacturing drawings, or special plans prepared especially for use by servicing technicians. They may be incorporated into the manual or manuals.

(4) Have a training program complying with § 160.151-39 for the certification of servicing technicians.

(5) Notify the OCMI for the zone in which the servicing facility is located whenever the manufacturer becomes aware of servicing at approved facilities that is not in accordance with the requirements of this subpart, or aware of falsification by an approved facility of records required by this subpart.

(c) A manufacturer of liferafts not approved by the Coast Guard may establish servicing facilities approved by the Coast Guard for such liferafts in the United States if the manufacturer meets the requirements of paragraph (b) of this section.

§ 160.151-37 Servicing manual.

(a) The servicing manual must provide instructions on performing the following tasks:

(1) Removing the inflatable liferaft from the container for testing without damaging the liferaft or its contents.

(2) Examining the liferaft and its container for damage and wear including deteriorated structural joints and seams.

(3) Determining the need for repairs.

(4) Performing each repair which can be made by a servicing facility.

(5) Identifying repairs that the manufacturer must perform.

(6) Determining when liferaft equipment must be replaced.

(7) Conducting tests required by § 160.151-57.

(8) Repacking the liferaft.

(9) Changing the maximum height of stowage of the liferaft by changing the length of the painter.

(10) Special equipment limitations or packing instructions, if any, necessary to qualify the liferaft for a particular height of stowage.

(11) Changing the service of the liferaft by changing the contents of the equipment pack.

(12) Proper marking of the liferaft container, including approval number, persons' capacity, maximum height of stowage, service (equipment pack), and expiration date of servicing.

(13) A list of parts for—

(i) Survival equipment;

(ii) Compressed-gas cylinders;

(iii) Inflation valves;

(iv) Relief valves; and

(v) Repair equipment.

(14) The necessary pressures for each size of approved liferaft for conducting the "Necessary Additional Pressure" test required by § 160.151-57(k).

(b) Each revision to a servicing manual, and each bulletin, that authorizes the modification of a liferaft, or that affects the compliance of a liferaft with any requirement under this subpart, must be submitted to and approved by the Commandant. Other revisions and bulletins need not be approved, but a copy of each must be submitted to the Commandant when issued.

(c) Each manual provided under this section must bear the original signature of a representative of the manufacturer attesting that it is a true copy of the manual approved by the Commandant.

§160.151–39 Training of servicing technicians.

(a) The training program for certification of servicing technicians must include—

(1) Training and practice in packing an inflatable liferaft, repairing buoyancy tubes, repairing inflation-system valves, and other inspections and operations described in the approved servicing manual;

(2) An evaluation at the end of the training to determine whether each trainee has successfully completed the training; and

(3) Issuance of a certificate of competence to each technician who successfully completes the training.

(b) The manufacturer shall maintain refresher training for recertification of previously trained servicing technicians. This training must include—

(1) Checking the performance of the technicians in the inspections and operations described in the manual;

(2) Retraining of the technicians in inspections and operations for which they are deficient;

(3) Training and practice in new inspections and operations;

(4) An evaluation at the end of the training to determine whether or not each trainee has successfully completed the training; and

(5) Issuance of a certificate of competence to each technician who successfully completes the training.

(c) Each time the manufacturer holds a course for servicing technicians who will perform servicing on liferafts approved by the Coast Guard, the manufacturer shall notify the cognizant OCMI sufficiently in advance to allow, at the option of the OCMI, for a Coast Guard inspector or inspectors to travel to the site where the training is to occur.

§160.151–41 Approval of servicing facilities.

(a) To obtain and maintain Coast Guard approval as an "approved servicing facility" for a particular manufacturer's inflatable liferafts, a facility must meet the requirements, and follow the procedures, of this section.

(b) The owner or operator of a servicing facility desiring Coast Guard approval shall apply to the cognizant OCMI. The application must include—

(1) The name and address of the facility;

(2) The name(s) of its competent servicing technician(s);

(3) Identification of the manufacturer(s) of the liferafts the facility will service; and

(4) Any limits or special conditions that should apply to the approval of the facility.

(c) The owner or operator of the servicing facility shall arrange for an inspection with the OCMI to whom the owner or operator applied under paragraph (b) of this section. A currently trained servicing technician shall successfully demonstrate the complete service to each make and type of liferaft for which approval as a servicing facility is sought, in the presence of a Coast Guard inspector or of a third-party inspector accepted by the OCMI, or such technician shall present evidence of having performed such service at the time of initial or refresher training. The service must include:

(1) Removing the liferaft from the container for testing without damaging the liferaft or its contents;

(2) Examining the liferaft and its container for damage and wear;

(3) Determining the need for repairs;

(4) Determining whether equipment must be replaced;

(5) Conducting the tests required by §160.151–57;

(6) Repacking the liferaft;

(7) Inflating the fully packed liferaft using its inflation mechanism; and

(8) Repairing a leak in a main buoyancy chamber, and subjecting the repaired chamber to the Necessary Additional Pressure test described in §160.151–57(k). This repair may be done on a liferaft that actually needs it, on one condemned, or on an inflatable chamber fabricated of liferaft material specifically for this purpose. (An otherwise serviceable liferaft should not be damaged for this purpose.)

(d) Whenever servicing of liferafts takes place, each servicing facility must allow Coast Guard inspectors or third-party inspectors accepted by the OCMI access to the place where the servicing occurs.

(e) Each servicing facility must employ at least one servicing technician who has successfully completed the manufacturer's training described in § 160.151–39 (a) or (b), including training in the servicing of davit-launched liferafts if the facility will service these. The training must have been completed within the preceding—

(1) 12 months for the facility to obtain its approval to service the liferafts of a particular manufacturer; or

(2) 36 months for the facility to retain approval to service the liferafts of a particular manufacturer.

§ 160.151–43 Conditions at servicing facilities.

(a) Each facility must maintain a room to service inflatable liferafts that—

(1) Is clean;

(2) Is fully enclosed;

(3) Has enough space to service the number of liferafts likely to be present for service at one time;

(4) Has a ceiling high enough to hold and allow overturning of a fully inflated liferaft of the largest size to be serviced, or is furnished with an equally efficient means to facilitate the inspection of bottom seams;

(5) Has a smooth floor that will not damage a liferaft, can be easily cleaned, and is kept clean and free from oil, grease, and abrasive material;

(6) Is well lit but free from direct sunlight;

(7) Is arranged to maintain an even temperature and low humidity in each area where liferafts are pressure tested, including by mechanical air-conditioning equipment in climates where it is necessary;

(8) Is arranged so that stored liferafts are not subjected to excessive loads and, if stacked one directly on top of another, does not have them stacked more than two liferafts high;

(9) Is efficiently ventilated but free of drafts; and

(10) Is a designated no-smoking area.

(b) In addition to the room required by paragraph (a) of this section, each facility must maintain areas or rooms for storage of liferafts awaiting servicing, repair, or delivery; for repair and painting of reinforced plastic containers; for storage of pyrotechnics and other materials, such as spare parts and required equipment; and for administrative purposes.

§ 160.151–45 Equipment required for servicing facilities.

Each servicing facility approved by the Coast Guard must maintain equipment to carry out the operations described in the manufacturer's servicing manual approved in accordance with § 160.151–35(b)(1), including—

(a) A set of plans, as specified in § 160.151–35(b)(3), for each inflatable liferaft to be serviced;

(b) A current copy of this subpart;

(c) A current copy of the manual approved in accordance with § 160.151–35(b)(1), including all revisions and bulletins in effect as indicated on the annual list issued in accordance with § 160.151–35(b)(2);

(d) Hot presses (if applicable);

(e) Safety-type glue pots or equivalents;

(f) Abrasive devices;

(g) A source of clean, dry, pressurized air; hoses; and attachments for inflating liferafts;

(h) A source of vacuum; hoses; and attachments for deflating liferafts;

(i) Mercury manometer, water manometer, or other pressure-measurement device or pressure gauge of equivalent accuracy and sensitivity;

(j) Thermometer;

(k) Barometer, aneroid or mercury;

(l) Calibrated torque-wrench for assembling the inflation system;

(m) Accurate weighing scale;

(n) Repair materials and equipment, and spare parts as specified in the applicable manual, except that items of limited "shelf life" need not be stocked if they are readily available;

(o) A complete stock of the survival equipment required to be stowed in the liferafts, except for items of equipment that are readily available;

(p) A means for load-testing davit-launched liferafts, unless the facility services only non-davit-launched liferafts;

(q) A supply of parts for all inflation components and valves specified in the applicable manual; and

(r) A tool board that clearly indicates where each small tool is stored, or has an equivalent means to make sure that no tools are left in the liferaft when re-packed.

§ 160.151-47 Requirements for owners or operators of servicing facilities.

To maintain Coast Guard approval, the owner or operator of each servicing facility approved by the Coast Guard must—

(a) Ensure that servicing technicians have received sufficient information and training to follow instructions for changes and for new techniques related to the inflatable liferafts serviced by the facility, and have available at least one copy of each manufacturer's approved servicing manual, revision, and bulletin;

(b) Calibrate each pressure gauge, mechanically-operated barometer, and weighing scale at intervals of not more than 1 year, or in accordance with the equipment manufacturer's requirements;

(c) Ensure that each liferaft serviced under the facility's Coast Guard approval is serviced by or under the direct supervision of a servicing technician who has completed the requirements of either § 160.151-39 (a) or (b);

(d) Ensure that each liferaft serviced under the facility's Coast Guard approval is serviced in accordance with the approved manual;

(e) Specify which makes of liferafts the facility is approved to service when representing that the facility is approved by the Coast Guard; and

(f) Ensure that the facility does not service any make of liferaft for an inspected vessel of the U.S. or any other U.S.-flag vessel required to carry approved liferafts, unless the facility is approved by the Coast Guard to service that make of liferafts.

§ 160.151-49 Approval of servicing facilities at remote sites.

A servicing facility may be approved for servicing liferafts at a remote site, provided that appropriate arrangements have been made to ensure that each such site meets the requirements of §§ 160.151-41(e), 160.151-43, and 160.151-45. The facility must have a portable assortment of test equipment, spare parts, and replacement survival equipment to accompany the technician doing the servicing. However, if repair

of liferafts will not be attempted at a remote site, equipment needed for repair does not need to be available at that site. A facility must be specifically authorized in its letter of approval to conduct servicing at a remote site.

§ 160.151-51 Notice of approval.

If the cognizant OCMI determines that the servicing facility meets the applicable requirements of §§ 160.151-39 through 160.151-47, the OCMI notifies the facility that it is approved and notifies the Commandant. The Commandant issues an approval letter to the servicing facility with copies to the OCMI and to the manufacturer(s) whose liferafts the facility is approved to service. The letter will specify any limits on the approval, and will assign the facility's approval code for use on the inspection sticker required by § 160.151-57(m)(3). The Commandant will maintain a current list of approved facilities.

§ 160.151-53 Notice to OCMI of servicing.

(a) Before servicing an inflatable liferaft under the servicing facility's Coast Guard approval, the owner or operator of the facility must tell the cognizant OCMI for each liferaft to be serviced—

(1) The make and size of the liferaft;

(2) The age of the liferaft; and

(3) Whether the liferaft is due for a five-year inflation test.

(b) The OCMI will inform the servicing facility whether the servicing of the liferaft must be witnessed by an inspector.

(c) If the OCMI requires the servicing of the liferaft to be witnessed by an inspector—

(1) The servicing facility must arrange a schedule with the OCMI that will allow a Coast Guard inspector to travel to the site where the servicing is to occur;

(2) The owner or operator of the servicing facility, by permission of the OCMI, may arrange for the servicing to be witnessed instead by a third-party inspector accepted by the OCMI if a Coast Guard marine inspector is not available in a timely manner; and

(3) The servicing facility must not begin servicing the liferaft until the inspector arrives at the site.

(d) No deviation from servicing-manual procedures may occur without the prior approval of the OCMI. To request the approval of a deviation, the owner or operator of the servicing facility shall notify the OCMI of the proposed deviation from the procedures, and must explain to the OCMI the need for the deviation.

§ 160.151–55 Withdrawal of approval.

(a) The OCMI may withdraw the approval of the servicing facility, or may suspend its approval pending correction of deficiencies, if the Coast Guard inspector or accepted third-party inspector finds that—

(1) The facility does not meet the requirements of §§ 160.151–41 through 160.151–47, or

(2) The servicing is not performed in accordance with § 160.151–57.

(b) A withdrawal of approval may be appealed in accordance with part 1, subpart 1.03, of this chapter.

(c) The OCMI may remove a suspension pending correction of deficiencies if the servicing facility demonstrates that the deficiencies have been corrected.

§ 160.151–57 Servicing procedure.

(a) Each inflatable liferaft serviced by a servicing facility approved by the Coast Guard must be inspected and tested in accordance with paragraphs (b) through (r) of this section, and the manufacturer's servicing manual approved in accordance with § 160.151–35(b)(1).

(b) The following procedures must be carried out at each servicing:

(1) The working-pressure leakage test described in IMO Resolution A.689(17), paragraph 2/5.1.5, must be conducted.

(2) Inflation hoses must be pressurized and checked for damage and leakage as part of the working-pressure leakage test, or in a separate test.

(3) An inflatable floor must be inflated until it is firm, and let stand for one hour. The inflatable floor must still be firm at the end of the hour.

(4) The seams connecting the floor to the buoyancy tube must be checked for slippage, rupture, and lifting of edges.

(5) Each item of survival equipment must be examined, and—

(i) Replaced if its expiration date has passed; and

(ii) Otherwise, repaired or replaced if it is damaged or unserviceable.

(6) Each battery must be replaced with a fresh one if—

(i) Its expiration date has passed;

(ii) It has no expiration date; or

(iii) It is to return to service in an item of survival equipment, but its measured voltage is less than its rated voltage.

(7) Each power cell for the top and inside canopy lights must be inspected and tested as prescribed in the servicing manual unless it is a battery serviced in accordance with paragraph (b)(6) of this section. Each cell that is tested and found satisfactory may be reinstalled. Each cell that is outdated, is not tested, or fails the test must be replaced.

(8) If the liferaft is equipped with an Emergency Position-Indicating Radio Beacon (EPIRB) or a Search and Rescue Transponder (SART), the EPIRB or SART must be inspected and tested in accordance with the manufacturer's instructions. An EPIRB must be tested using the integrated test circuit and output indicator to determine whether it is operative. Each EPIRB or SART not operative must be repaired or replaced.

(9) The manual inflation-pump must be tested for proper operation.

(10) Each damaged, faded, or incorrect instruction label or identification label on the liferaft or its container must be replaced.

(11) Each liferaft must be examined to ensure that it is properly marked with retroreflective material. The arrangement of the retroreflective material must meet the requirements of IMO Resolution A.658(16). Damaged or missing retroreflective material must be replaced with Type I material approved under part 164, subpart 164.018, of this subchapter as complying with SOLAS.

(12) Each inflation cylinder must be weighed. If its weight loss exceeds five percent of the weight of the charge, it must be recharged.

(c) When an inflation cylinder is recharged for any reason, the following inflation-head components must be renewed:

(1) The poppet-pin assembly, if any.

(2) Each plastic or elastomeric seal, and each other part that deteriorates with age.

(d) Each recharged inflation cylinder must stand for at least two weeks and be checked for leakage by weighing before being installed in a liferaft. An alternative mechanical or chemical test for fast detection of leakage may be used if the servicing manual approved by the Commandant in accordance with § 160.151–35(b)(1) provides for it.

(e) Each inflation cylinder that requires a hydrostatic test under 49 CFR 173.34 must be tested and marked in accordance with that section.

(f) At every second servicing of a davit-launched liferaft, the launching-load test in paragraph 2/5.2 of IMO Resolution A.689(17) must be conducted.

(g) At every fifth annual servicing, before the conduct of the tests and inspections required in paragraphs (b) through of this section, each liferaft must be removed from its container and, while still folded, inflated by the operation of its gas-inflation system.

(h) Each liferaft showing minor leaks during the gas inflation test conducted in accordance with paragraph (g) of this section, may be repaired.

(i) Each liferaft ten or more years past its date of manufacture must be condemned if it leaks extensively, or shows fabric damage other than minor porosity, during the gas inflation test conducted in accordance with paragraph (g) of this section.

(j) After the gas inflation test conducted in accordance with paragraph (g) of this section, the liferaft may be evacuated and refilled with air for the tests in paragraphs (b) through (f) of this section.

(k) At each annual servicing of a liferaft ten or more years past its date of manufacture during which the gas-inflation test in paragraph (g) of this section is not conducted, a "Necessary Additional Pressure" (NAP) test must be conducted. Before the tests and inspections required in paragraphs (b) through (f) of this section are conducted, the NAP test must be completed, using the following procedure:

(1) Plug or otherwise disable the pressure-relief valves.

(2) Gradually raise the pressure to the lesser of 2 times the design working pressure, or that specified in the manufacturer's servicing manual as sufficient to impose a tensile load on the tube fabric of 20 percent of its minimum required tensile strength.

(3) After 5 minutes, there should be no seam slippage, cracking, other defects, or pressure drop greater than 5 percent. If cracking in the buoyancy tubes is audible, accompanied by pressure loss, condemn the liferaft. If it is not, reduce the pressure in all buoyancy chambers simultaneously by enabling the pressure-relief valves.

(l) At each annual servicing of a liferaft 10 or more years past its date of manufacture, the integrity of the seams connecting the floor to the buoyancy tube must be checked by the following procedure, or an equivalent procedure specified in the manufacturer's approved servicing manual:

(1) With the buoyancy tube supported a sufficient distance above the floor of the servicing facility to maintain clearance during the test, a person weighing not less than 75 kg (165 lb) shall walk or crawl around the entire perimeter of the floor of the liferaft.

(2) The seams connecting the floor to the buoyancy tube must then be inspected for slippage, rupture, and lifting of edges.

(m) The servicing facility must complete the following for each liferaft that passes these inspections and tests:

(1) Permanently mark the liferaft on its outside canopy, or on a servicing-record panel on an interior portion of one of its buoyancy tubes near an entrance, with—

(i) The date of the servicing;

(ii) The identification and location of the servicing facility; and

(iii) If applicable, an indication that the special fifth-year servicing was performed.

(2) On or before July 1, 1998, permanently and legibly mark on the identification device provided in accordance with § 160.151–17(c), or on the outside canopy of the liferaft, the name, if known, of the vessel on which the raft will be installed or the name, if known, of the vessel owner.

(3) On or before November 10, 1997, affix an inspection sticker to the liferaft container or valise. The sticker must be of a type that will remain legible for at least 2 years when exposed to a marine environment, and that cannot be removed without being destroyed. The sticker must be about 100 mm x 150 mm (4 by 6 inches), with the last digit of the year of expiration superimposed over a background color that corresponds to the colors specified for the validation stickers for recreational-boat numbers in 33 CFR 174.15(c), and be marked with the Coast Guard identifying insignia in accordance with the requirements of 33 CFR 23.12. The sticker must also contain the following:

(i) The name of the manufacturer of the liferaft.

(ii) The year and month of expiration determined in accordance with paragraph (n) of this section.

(iii) Identification of the servicing facility, printed on the sticker or indicated on the sticker by punch using an approval code issued by the Commandant.

(n) The expiration date of the servicing sticker is 12 months after the date the liferaft was repacked, except that:

(1) For a new liferaft, the expiration date may be not more than two years after the date the liferaft was first packed, if—

(i) Dated survival equipment in the liferaft will not expire before the sticker expiration date; and

(ii) The liferaft will not be installed on a vessel certificated under SOLAS.

(2) For a liferaft stored indoors, under controlled temperatures (between 0 °C (32 °F) and 45 °C (113 °F)), for not more than 6 months from the date it was serviced or first packed, the expiration date may be extended up to the length of time the liferaft remained in storage.

(3) For a liferaft stored indoors, under controlled temperatures (between 0 °C (32 °F) and 45 °C (113 °F)), for not more than 12 months from the date it was serviced or first packed, the expiration date may be extended up to the length of time the liferaft remained in storage, if the liferaft is opened, inspected, and repacked in a servicing facility approved in accordance with §§ 160.151–49 and 160.151–51. When the liferaft is opened—

(i) The condition of the liferaft must be visually checked and found to be satisfactory;

(ii) The inflation cylinders must be checked and weighed in accordance with paragraph (b)(12) of this section;

(iii) All survival equipment whose expiration date has passed must be replaced; and

(iv) All undated batteries must be replaced.

(o) The servicing facility must remove and destroy the markings of Coast Guard approval on each liferaft condemned in the course of any servicing test or inspection.

(p) The servicing facility must issue a certificate to the liferaft owner or owner's agent for each liferaft it services. The certificate must include—

(1) The name of the manufacturer of the liferaft;

(2) The serial number of the liferaft;

(3) The date of servicing and repacking;

(4) A record of the fifth-year gas-inflation test required in paragraph (g) of this section, whenever that test is performed;

(5) A record of the hydrostatic test of each inflation cylinder required in paragraph (e) of this section, whenever that test is performed;

(6) A record of any deviation from the procedures of the manufacturer's servicing manual authorized by the OCMI in accordance with § 160.151–53(d);

(7) The identification of the servicing facility, including its name, address, and the approval code assigned by the Commandant in accordance with § 160.151–51;

(8) The name, if known, of the vessel or vessel owner receiving the liferaft; and

(9) The date the liferaft is returned to the owner or owner's agent.

(q) The servicing facility must keep a record of each liferaft approved by the Coast Guard that it services for at least five years, and must make those records available to the Coast Guard upon request. Those records must include—

(1) The serial number of the liferaft;

(2) The date of servicing and repacking;

(3) The identification of any Coast Guard or third-party inspector present;

(4) The name, if known, of the vessel or vessel owner receiving the liferaft; and

(5) The date the liferaft is returned to the owner or owner's agent.

(r) The servicing facility must prepare and transmit to the OCMI, at least annually, statistics showing the nature and extent of damage to and defects found in liferafts during servicing and repair. The facility must notify the OCMI immediately of any critical defects it finds that may affect other liferafts.

§ 160.151-59 Operating instructions and information for the ship's training manual.

(a) The liferaft manufacturer shall make operating instructions and information for the ship's training manual available in English to purchasers of inflatable liferafts approved by the Coast Guard, to enable vessel operators to meet regulations III/18.2, 19.3, 51, and 52 of SOLAS.

(b) The instructions and information required by paragraph (a) of this section may be combined with similar material for hydrostatic releases or launching equipment, and must explain—

(1) Release of the inflatable liferaft from its stowage position;

(2) Launching of the liferaft;

(3) Survival procedures, including instructions for use of survival equipment aboard; and

(4) Shipboard installations of the liferaft.

(c) The operating instructions required by paragraphs (a) and (b) of this section must also be made available in the form of an instruction placard. The placard must be not greater than 36 cm (14 in.) by 51 cm (20 in.), made of durable material and suitable for display near installations of liferafts on vessels, providing simple procedures and illustrations for launching, inflating, and boarding the liferaft.

§ 160.151-61 Maintenance instructions.

(a) The liferaft manufacturer shall make maintenance instructions available in English to purchasers of inflatable liferafts approved by the Coast

Guard, to enable vessel operators to meet regulations III/19.3 and III/52 of SOLAS.

(b) The maintenance instructions required by paragraph (a) of this section must include—

(1) A checklist for use in monthly, external, visual inspections of the packed liferaft;

(2) An explanation of the requirements for periodic servicing of the liferaft by an approved servicing facility; and

(3) A log for maintaining records of inspections and maintenance.

Subpart 160.171—Immersion Suits

SOURCE: CGD 84–069a, 52 FR 1188, Jan. 12, 1987, unless otherwise noted.

§ 160.171-1 Scope.

This subpart contains construction and performance requirements, and approval tests for adult and child insulated, buoyant immersion suits that are designed to prevent shock upon entering cold water and lessen the effect of hypothermia (extreme body heat loss due to immersion in cold water). Immersion suits approved under this subpart will meet the requirements of Regulation 33 of Chapter III of the International Convention for Safety of Life at Sea (SOLAS), 1974, under the Second Set of Amendments adopted 17 June 1983.

§ 160.171-3 Incorporations by reference.

(a) Certain materials are incorporated by reference into this subchapter with the approval of the Director of the Federal Register in accordance with 5 U.S.C. 552(a) and 1 CFR part 51. The Office of the Federal Register publishes a table, "Material Approved for Incorporation by Reference," which appears in the Finding Aids section of this volume. In that table is found citations to the particular sections of this part where the material is incorporated. To enforce any edition other than the one listed in paragraph (b) of this section, notice of change must be published in the FEDERAL REGISTER and the material made available. All approved material is on file at the Office of the Federal Register, Washington, DC 20408, and at the U.S. Coast Guard, Lifesaving and Fire Safety Division (G–MSE–4), Washington, DC 20593.

(b) The materials approved for incorporation by reference in this subpart are:

AMERICAN SOCIETY FOR TESTING AND MATERIALS
100 Barr Harbor Drive, West Conshohocken, PA 19428-2959.
ASTM B 117–73 (Reapproved 1979), Standard Method of Salt Spray (Fog) Testing.
ASTM C 177–76, Standard Test Method for Steady-State Thermal Transmission Properties by Means of the Guarded Hot Plate.
ASTM C 518–76, Standard Test Method for Steady-State Thermal Transmission Properties by Means of the Heat Flow Meter.
ASTM D 975–81, Standard Specification for Diesel Fuel Oils.
ASTM D 1004–66 (Reapproved 1976), Tear Resistance of Plastic Film and Sheeting.

FEDERAL STANDARDS SPECIFICATION UNIT (WFSIA)
Regional Office Building, Room 6039, 7th and D Streets SW, Washington, DC 20407.
National Bureau of Standards Special Publication 440—Color, Universal Language and Dictionary of Names; December 1976.
Federal Test Method Standard No. 191a dated July 20, 1978, Method 5304.1, Abrasion Resistance of Cloth, Oscillatory Cylinder (Wyzenbeek) Method, dated July 9, 1971.
Federal Standard No. 751a, Stitches, Seams, and Stitchings, dated January 25, 1965.

UNDERWRITERS LABORATORIES, INC.
12 Laboratory Drive, Research Triangle Park, NC 27709-3995.
UL 1191, First Edition (Standard for Components for Personal Flotation Devices), as revised March 29, 1977.

[CGD 84–069a, 52 FR 1188, Jan. 12, 1987, as amended by CGD 95–072, 60 FR 50467, Sept. 29, 1995; CGD 96–041, 61 FR 50733, Sept. 27, 1996; CGD 97–057, 62 FR 51048, Sept. 30, 1997]

§ 160.171-5 Independent laboratory.

The approval and production tests in this subpart must be conducted by an independent laboratory accepted by the Coast Guard under subpart 159.010 of this chapter.

§ 160.171-7 Approval procedures.

(a) *General.* An immersion suit is approved by the Coast Guard under the procedures in subpart 159.005 of this chapter.

(b) *Approval testing.* Each approval test must be conducted in accordance with § 160.171–17 or § 160.171–19.

(c) *Approval of child size and oversize adult suits.* No child size or oversize adult sized suit will be approved unless the adult size of the suit has been approved.

§ 160.171-9 Construction.

(a) *General.* Each immersion suit must be constructed primarily of a closed-cell flexible foam that meets the buoyancy and thermal insulation requirements in § 160.171–11 (a) and (c). Each suit must be designed to cover the wearer's entire body, except for the area of the nose and eyes. It must be capable of being worn inside-out or be clearly capable of being worn in only one way and, as far as possible, incapable of being donned incorrectly.

(b) *Impact resistance and body strength.* The body of each suit must be designed to allow the wearer to jump from a height of at least 4.5 m into the water without injury and without dislodging or damaging the suit.

(c) *Seams.* Stitching in each sewn structural seam of an immersion suit must be lock type stitching that meets the requirements in Federal Standard No. 751 for one of the following:

(1) Class 300 Lockstitch.

(2) Class 700 Single Thread Lockstitch.

Other stitches which are not true lock stitches may be used to reinforce a glued seam provided the adhesive alone has the required seam strength after the non-standard stitch has been removed.

(d) *Seam strength.* Each seam must have a strength of at least 225 Newtons (50 lb.).

(e) *Closures and seals.* Each closure and seal must be designed so that, following a jump from a height of not less than 4.5 m into the water, there is no undue ingress of water into the suit.

(f) *Hardware.* All hardware of an immersion suit must be of a size and design that allows ease of operation by the wearer. The hardware must be attached to the suit in a manner that allows the wearer to operate it easily and that prevents it from attaining a position in which it can be operated improperly.

(g) *Metal parts.* Each metal part of an immersion suit must be—

(1) 410 stainless steel or have salt water and salt air corrosion characteristics equal or superior to 410 stainless steel; and

(2) Galvanically compatable with each other metal part in contact with it.

(h) *Suit exterior.* The primary color of the exterior of each suit must be vivid reddish orange (color number 34 of National Bureau of Standards Publication 440). The exterior surface of the suit must resist tearing and abrasion when tested as prescribed in §160.171–17 (n) and (o).

(i) Buoyant materials and compartments. Buoyant materials used in a suit must not be loose or granular. The suit must not have an inflated or inflatable chamber, except as prescribed in §160.171–11(a)(2).

(j) *Hand and arm construction.* The hand of each suit must be a glove that allows sufficient dexterity for the wearer to pick up a 9.5 mm (3/8 in.) diameter wooden pencil from a table and write with it, after being immersed in water at 5° C for a period of one hour. The glove may not be removable unless it is attached to the arm and unless it can be secured to the arm or stowed in a pocket on the arm when not in use. A removable glove must be designed so that there is no undue ingress of water into the glove during use. Each arm with a removable glove must have a wristlet seal that meets paragraph (e) of this section.

(k) *Leg construction.* Each suit must be designed to minimize or reduce free air in its legs when the wearer enters the water headfirst.

(l) *Foot construction.* Each leg of a suit must have a foot that has a hard sole or enough room for a work shoe to be worn inside. The sole of each foot must be—

(1) Natural or synthetic rubber that is ribbed or bossed for skid resistance; and

(2) Designed to prevent the wearer from slipping when the suit is tested as prescribed in §160.171–17(c)(5).

(m) *Size.* Each adult suit must fit persons ranging in weight from 50 kg (110 lb.) to 150 kg (330 lb.) and in height from 1.5 m (59 in.) to 1.9 m (75 in.). Each child size suit must fit children or small adults ranging in weight from 20 kg (44 lb.) to 50 kg (110 lb.) and in height from 1.0 m (39 in.) to 1.5 m (59 in.). An oversize adult suit is intended for persons too large for the standard adult suit. Each suit must be capable of being worn comfortably over clothing and must not restrict the wearer's motion. The suit size and design must allow successful completion of the mobility tests prescribed in §160.171–17(c)(2) through (7).

(n) *Retroreflective material.* Each immersion suit must be fitted with Type I retroreflective material that meets subpart 164.018 of this chapter. When the wearer of an immersion suit is in any stable floating position, at least 200 cm^2 (31 sq. in.) of the material must be visible above water.

(o) *PFD Light.* Each immersion suit must be designed so that a light meeting the requirements of subpart 161.012 of this chapter can be attached to its front shoulder area and so that the light when attached does not damage the suit and cannot adversely affect its performance. If the manufacturer of the suit designates a specific location for the light, or designates a specific model light, this information must be clearly printed on the suit or in the instructions prescribed by §160.171–15(c).

(p) *Inflation tube.* If the suit has an inflatable auxiliary means of buoyancy, each joint in the oral inflation tube must be joined with a clamping device. A flange connection between the tube and the inflatable chamber must be reinforced so that the flange on the inflation tube is secured between the material of the inflatable section and the reinforcement.

§160.171–11 Performance.

(a) *Buoyancy.* Each suit must meet the following buoyancy requirements as measured in the test conducted under §160.171–17(h):

(1) The adjusted buoyancy of each adult and each oversize adult size suit must be at least 100 N (22 lb.). The adjusted buoyancy of each child size suit must be at least 50 N (11 lb.) The measured buoyancy must not be reduced by more than 5% after 24 hours submersion in fresh water.

(2) Each suit must have a stable floating position in which the wearer's head must be tilted to a position between 30° and 80° above the horizontal, with the mouth and nose at least 120 mm (4¾ in.) above the surface of the water. If necessary, this position may be obtained through the use of an auxiliary means of buoyancy such as an inflatable bladder behind the wearer's head.

(3) If an auxiliary means of buoyancy is necessary to meet paragraph (a)(2) of this section, the suit must have a stable floating position without the auxiliary means of buoyancy in which the mouth and nose of the wearer are at least 50 mm (2 in.) above the surface of the water.

(4) The buoyancy of any auxiliary means of buoyancy must not be counted when determining the buoyancy of the suit.

(b) *Righting.* The suit must be designed to turn the body of an unconscious person in the water from any position to one where the mouth is clear of the water in not more than five seconds, without assistance or the use of any means of auxiliary buoyancy which must be inflated by the wearer; or to allow the wearer to turn from a face down to a face up position in not more than 5 seconds, without assistance or the use of any means of auxiliary buoyancy. If an automatically inflated means of auxiliary buoyancy is used to meet this paragraph, the inflation mechanism must meet the requirements for commercial hybrid PFDs in § 160.077–15(c) of this chapter, and the tests required under § 160.077–21(c)(3) of this chapter. Auxiliary buoyancy, if fitted and/or inflated, must not interfere with righting.

(c) *Thermal protection.* The suit must be designed to protect against loss of body heat as follows:

(1) The thermal conductivity of the suit material when submerged 1 m (39 in.) in water must be less than or equal to that of a control sample of 4.75 mm (³⁄₁₆ in.) thick, closed-cell neoprene foam. The control sample of foam must have a thermal conductivity of not more than 0.055 watt/meter – ° K (0.38 Btu – in./hr. – sq.ft. – ° F).

(2) The suit must provide the wearer with sufficient thermal insulation, following one jump into the water from a height of 4.5 m, to ensure that the wearer's body core temperature does not fall more than 2° C (3.6° F) after a period of 6 hours immersion in calm circulating water at a temperature of between 0° C (32° F) and 2° C (35.6° F).

(d) *Donning time.* Each suit must be designed so that a person can don the suit correctly within two minutes after reading the donning and use instructions described in § 160.171–15(a).

(e) *Vision.* Each suit must be designed to allow unrestricted vision throughout an arc of 60° to either side of the wearer's straight-ahead line of sight when the wearer's head is turned to any angle between 30° to the right and 30° to the left. Each suit must be designed to allow a standing wearer to move head and eyes up and down far enough to see both feet and a spot directly overhead.

(f) *Water penetration.* An immersion suit must be designed to prevent undue ingress of water into the suit following a period of flotation in calm water of one hour.

(g) *Splash protection.* Each suit must have a means to prevent water spray from directly entering the wearer's mouth.

(h) *Storage temperature.* Each suit must be designed so that it will not be damaged by storage in its storage case at any temperature between – 30° C (– 22° F) and +65° C (149° F).

(i) *Flame exposure.* Each suit must be designed to prevent sustained burning or continued melting after it is totally enveloped in a fire for a period of 2 seconds.

(j) *Oil resistance.* Each immersion suit must be designed to be useable after a 24 hour exposure to diesel oil.

§ 160.171–13 Storage case.

(a) Each suit must have a storage case made of vinyl coated cloth or material that provides an equivalent measure of protection to the suit.

(b) Each storage case must be designed so that it is still useable after two seconds contact with a gasoline fire.

§160.171-15 Instructions.

(a) Each suit must have instructions for its donning and use in an emergency. The instructions must be in English and must not exceed 50 words. Illustrations must be used in addition to the words. These instructions must be on the exterior of the storage case or printed on a waterproof card attached to the storage case or to the suit.

(b) If the suit has an inflatable auxiliary means of buoyancy, separate instructions covering the use of the inflation valve must be provided on the suit near the valve or on a waterproof card attached near the valve.

(c) Instructions for donning and use of the suit in an emergency must also be available in a format suitable for mounting on a bulkhead of a vessel. This placard must be in English, must include illustrations, and must include a warning as to the risk of entrapment in a submerged compartment due to the buoyancy of the suit.

(d) Instructions for donning and use of the suit in an emergency, instructions for care and repair of the suit, and any additional necessary information concerning stowage and use of the suit on a vessel must be available in 8½×11 loose-leaf format suitable for inclusion in the vessel's training manual.

§160.171-17 Approval testing for adult size immersion suit.

Caution: During each of the in-water tests prescribed in this section, a person ready to render assistance when needed should be near each subject in the water.

(a) *General.* An adult size immersion suit must be tested as prescribed in this section. If the suit is also made in a child size, a child size suit must be tested as prescribed in §160.171-19. If the suit is also made in an oversize adult size, an oversize adult suit must be tested as prescribed in §160.171-17(g) to determine the measured buoyancy for the suit. No additional testing will be required if the oversize adult suit is of the same design as the adult suit except for extra material to provide for larger persons.

(b) *Test samples.* Each test prescribed in this section may be performed by using as many immersion suits as needed to make efficient use of the test subjects and test equipment, except that each subject in the impact test described in §160.171-17(c)(11) must not use more than one suit during the test, and the suits used in the impact test must also be used in the thermal protection test described in §160.171-17(d).

(c) *Mobility and flotation tests.* The mobility and flotation capabilities of each immersion suit must be tested under the following conditions and procedures:

(1) *Test subjects.* Seven males and three females must be used in the tests described in this paragraph. The subjects must represent each of the three physical types (ectomorphic, endomorphic, and mesomorphic). Each subject must be in good health. The heaviest subject, of either sex, must weigh at least 135 kg (298 lb.). The heaviest male subject must weigh at least 115 kg (254 lb.) and the lightest male subject must weigh not more than 55 kg (121 lb). The heaviest female subject must weigh at least 115 kg (254 lb.) and the lightest female subject must weigh not more than 55 kg (121 lb). Each subject must be unfamiliar with the specific suit under test. Each subject must wear a standard range of clothing consisting of:

(i) Underwear (short sleeved, short legged);

(ii) Shirt (long sleeved);

(iii) Trousers (not woolen);

(iv) Woolen or equivalent synthetic socks;

(v) Rubber soled work shoes.

(2) *Donning time.* Each subject is removed from the view of the other subjects and allowed one minute to examine a suit and the manufacturer's instructions for donning and use of the suit in an emergency. At the end of this period, the subject attempts to don the suit as rapidly as possible without the aid of a chair or any support to lean on. If the subject does not don the suit completely, including gloves and any other accessories, within two minutes, the subject removes the suit and is given a demonstration of correct donning, and again attempts to don the suit. At least nine of the ten subjects must be able to don the suit completely, including time to remove

shoes if necessary, in two minutes in at least one of the two attempts.

(3) *Field of vision.* The immersion suit's field of vision must be tested as follows:

(i) While wearing a suit, each subject sits upright and faces straight ahead. An observer is positioned to one side of the subject at an angle of 60° away from the subject's straight-ahead line of sight. The observer must be able to see the subject's closest eye at this position. The observer then walks past the front of the subject to a position on the subject's other side that is at an angle of 60° away from the subject's straight-ahead line of sight. The suit must not obstruct the observer's view of the subject's eyes at any point between the two positions.

(ii) While wearing the suit, each subject stands upright and faces straight ahead. An observer is positioned to one side of the subject at an angle of 90° away from the subject's straight-ahead line of sight. The subject then turns his or her head through an arc of 30° toward the position of the observer. This procedure is repeated with the observer positioned on the other side of the subject at an angle of 90° away from the subject's straight ahead line of sight. The suit must not obstruct the observer's view of the subject's eyes when the subject's head is turned 30° toward the observer.

(iii) While wearing the suit, each subject stands upright and faces straight ahead. Through a combination of head and eye movement, the subject looks first at a spot directly overhead, then looks at a spot on or between the feet. An observer must verify that the subject can make the necessary head and eye movements while wearing the suit.

(4) *Hand dexterity.* A physician must always be present during this test. While wearing a suit, including a removable glove if any, and after being immersed in water at 5° C (41° F) for a period of one hour, each subject must be able to pick up a 9.5 mm (⅜ in.) diameter wooden pencil from a flat hard surfaced table using only one hand. Still using only one hand, the subject must be able to position the pencil and write with it. At least eight of the ten test subjects must be able to complete this test. This test may be performed

in conjunction with the thermal protection test described in § 160.171–17(d), in which case five of the six test subjects specified in § 160.171–17(d)(1) must be able to complete the test.

(5) *Walking.* A 30 m (100 ft.) long walking course must be laid out on a smooth linoleum floor. The finish on the floor must allow water to lie on it in a sheet rather than in beads. The course may have gradual turns, but must not have any abrupt change in direction. Each subject is timed walking the course two times at a normal pace with the floor dry. Each subject then dons a suit and is timed again walking the course two times with the floor wet. The subject is given adequate rest between trials to avoid fatigue. The subject must not slip on the wet floor when wearing the suit. The average time for each subject to walk the course while wearing the suit must be not more than 1.25 times the subject's average time to walk the course without the suit.

(6) *Climbing.* A vertical ladder extending at least 5 meters (17 feet) above a level floor must be used for this test. Each subject is timed climbing the ladder twice to a rung at least 3 meters (10 feet) above the floor. The subject then dons a suit and is again timed climbing to the same rung twice. The subject is given adequate rest between trials to avoid fatigue. The average time for each subject to climb the ladder while wearing the suit must not be more than 1.25 times the subject's average time to climb the ladder without the suit.

(7) *Swimming and water emergence test.* A pool with an inflatable liferaft at one side must be used for this test. The liferaft must be of a type approved under Subpart 160.051 of this Chapter and must not have a boarding ramp. Each subject, wearing a life preserver but not the immersion suit, enters the water and swims 25 m. The subject must then be able to emerge from the pool onto the liferaft using only the hands placed on top of the liferaft as an aid and without pushing off of the bottom of the pool. Any subject unable to emerge onto the liferaft within 30 seconds is disqualified for this test. At least five subjects must qualify and be

used for this test. If less than five subjects of the original ten qualify, substitute subjects must be used. Each qualified subject, after sufficient rest to avoid fatigue, repeats this test wearing an immersion suit instead of the life preserver. At least two-thirds of the qualified subjects must be able to swim this distance, and emerge onto the liferaft within 30 seconds, wearing the immersion suit.

(8) *Stability and retroreflective material.* While wearing the suit in water without any auxiliary means of buoyancy, each subject assumes a face-up position and then allows his or her body to become limp. The distance from the water surface to the lowest part of the subject's mouth or nose is measured. This procedure is repeated using the auxiliary means of buoyancy, if one is provided. For each test subject, the stable position and the distance of the mouth and nose above the water must be prescribed in § 160.171–11(a)(2) and § 160.171–11(a)(3). During this test, each subject must be viewed by observers to determine whether the retroreflective material of the suit meets § 160.171–9(n).

(9) *Righting.* Each subject while wearing a suit in water, without the use of any auxiliary means of buoyancy, takes a deep breath, assumes a face-down position, allows his or her body to become limp, and slowly expels air. The suit must cause the subject to turn to a position where the face is clear of the water within 5 seconds; or if the suit does not turn the subject within 5 seconds, the subject must be able to turn face up under his or her own power within 5 seconds. If the suit is provided with any means of auxiliary buoyancy, the procedure is repeated under each of the following applicable conditions:

(i) With any means of auxiliary buoyancy attached but not inflated;

(ii) With any means of auxiliary buoyancy which must be inflated by the wearer inflated according to the instructions; or

(iii) With any means of auxiliary buoyancy which inflates automatically inflated by its automatic mechanism.

(10) *Water and air penetration.* Each subject is weighed while wearing a prewetted suit without any auxiliary means of buoyancy. The subject jumps into water from a height that will cause the subject to be completely immersed. The subject swims or treads water for approximately one minute, emerges from the water, and is weighed within 10 seconds after emerging. The procedure is repeated with the subject entering the water headfirst. If air accumulates in the legs as the subject enters the water head-first, it must be expelled automatically. At the end of this test, the weight of the subject in the suit must not exceed the weight of the subject in the suit at the beginning of the test by more than 500 grams. Each test subject then re-enters the water and floats for a period of one hour. The subject then emerges from the water and is weighed within 10 seconds. The weight of the subject in the suit at the end of this test must not exceed the weight of the subject in the suit at the beginning of the period of flotation by more than 200 grams.

(11) *Impact.* While wearing a suit without any auxiliary means of buoyancy, each subject jumps into water feet first six times from a height of 4.5 m (15 ft.) above the water surface. Each subject must be able to assume a face up stable position without assistance after each jump. The suit must not tear, separate at any seam, or exhibit any characteristic that could render it unsafe or unsuitable for use in water.

(d) *Thermal protection.* The thermal protection capability of a suit must be tested under the following conditions and procedures;

(1) *Test subjects.* Male subjects must be used for this test. Each subject must be familiarized with the test procedure before starting the test. Each subject must have the following ranges according to the Heath-Carter anthropometric method: endomorphy 3.5±1.0; mesomorphy 4.0±1.5; ectomorphy 3.5±1.0.

NOTE: The following publication, among others, contains guidance for use of the Heath-Carter anthropometric method: "Body Type and Performance," Hebbelinck and Ross; FITNESS, HEALTH AND WORK CAPACITY, INTERNATIONAL STANDARDS FOR ASSESSMENT; Larson, L. A. (Ed.); International Committee for the Standardization of Physical Fitness Tests; Macmillan; New York; 1974 (pp. 266–283).

Each subject must have had a normal night's sleep before the test, a well-balanced meal 1 to 5 hours before the test, and no alcoholic beverages for 24 hours before the test. In addition to the suit, each subject must wear:

(i) Underwear (short sleeved, short legged);

(ii) Shirt (long sleeved);

(ii) Trousers (not woolen);

(iv) Woolen or equivalent synthetic socks;

(v) Work shoes, if the suit is designed for shoes to be worn inside.

(2) *Test equipment.* The test must be conducted in calm water with a temperature between 0° C (32° F) and 2° C (35.6° F). The air temperature 300 mm (1 ft.) above the water surface must be between minus 10° C (14° F) and 20° C (68° F). Each subject must be instrumented with an electrocardiograph, a thermistor or thermocouple in the rectum placed 150 mm (6 in) beyond the anus, thermistor or thermocouple in the lumbar region, a thermistor or thermocouple on the tip of the index finger, and a thermistor or thermocouple on the tip of the great toe. Each thermistor or thermocouple must have an accuracy of 0.1° C (0.18° F). The suits used in this test must be the same ones previously subjected to the impact test described in § 160.171–17(c)(11).

(3) *Test procedure.* A physician must always be present during this test. Before donning the suit, each subject rests quietly in a room with a temperature between 10° C (50° F) and 25° C (77° F) for 15 minutes. The rectal temperature is then recorded as the initial rectal temperature. The subject dons a suit as rapidly as possible without damaging the instrumentation and immediately enters the water. The subject assumes a face-up, stable floating position. No auxiliary means of buoyancy may be used during this test. The subject remains in the water engaging in activity that maintains the heart rate between 50 and 140 per minute for the first hour, and between 50 and 120 per minute during the remainder of the test, except that no attempt is made to control heart rate if the subject is shivering. Each thermistor or thermocouple reading is recorded at least every 10 minutes.

(4) *Completion of testing.* Testing of a subject ends six hours after he first enters the water, unless terminated sooner.

(5) *Termination of test.* Testing of a subject must be terminated before completion if any of the following occurs:

(i) The physician determines that the subject should not continue.

(ii) The subject requests termination due to discomfort or illness.

(iii) The subject's rectal temperature drops more than 2° C (3.6° F) below the initial rectal temperature, unless the physician determines that the subject may continue.

(iv) The subject's lumbar, finger, or toe temperature drops below 10° C (50° F), unless the physician determines that the subject may continue.

(6) *Test results.* The test results must be prepared as follows:

(i) The total rectal temperature drop during the test period and the average lumbar, finger and toe temperature at the end of the test must be determined for each subject in the test, except subjects who did not complete testing for a reason stated in paragraph (d)(5)(i) or (d)(5)(ii) of this section. These temperatures and temperature drops must then be averaged. The average drop in rectal temperature must not be more than 2° C (3.6° F), and the average lumbar, toe and finger temperature must not be less than 5° C (41° F). Data from at least four subjects must be used in making these temperature calculations.

(ii) Rates of toe, finger, lumbar, and rectal temperature drop for each subject who did not complete testing for a reason stated in paragraph (d)(5)(iii) or (d)(5)(iv) of this section must be determined using the highest temperature measured and the temperature measured immediately before testing was terminated. These rates must be used to extrapolate to 6 hours the estimated rectal, finger, lumbar, and toe temperature at the end of that time. These estimated temperatures must be the temperatures used in computing the average temperatures described in paragraph (d)(6)(i) of this section.

(e) *Insulation.* Suit material must be tested under the following conditions and procedures, except that if the suit material meets the requirements for the control sample in paragraph (e)(1)(iii) of this section, the test procedure in paragraph (e)(2) of this section is not required.

(1) *Test equipment.* The following equipment is required for this test:

(i) A sealed copper or aluminum can that has at least two parallel flat surfaces and that contains at least two liters (two quarts) or water and no air. One possible configuration of the can shown in figure 160.171–17(e)(1)(i).

(ii) A thermistor or thermocouple that has an accuracy of ±0.1° C (±0.18° F) and that is arranged to measure the temperature of the water in the can.

(iii) A control sample of two flat pieces of 4.75 mm (3/16 in.) thick, closed cell neoprene foam of sufficient size to enclose the can between them. The control sample must have a thermal conductivity of not more than 0.055 watt/meter – ° K (0.38 Btu – in./hr. – sq.ft. – ° F). The thermal conductivity of the control sample must be determined in accordance with the procedures in ASTM C 177 or ASTM C 518.

(iv) Two flat pieces of suit material of sufficient size to enclose the can between them. The surface covering, surface treatment, and number of layers of the material tested must be the same as those of material used in the suit. If the material used in the suit varies in thickness or number of layers, the material tested must be representative of the portion of the suit having the least thickness or number of layers.

(v) A clamping arrangement to form a watertight seal around the edges of the material when the can is enclosed inside. A sealing compound may be used. Figure 160.171–17(e)(1)(v) shows one possible arrangement of the clamping arrangement.

(vi) A container of water deep enough to hold the entire assembly of the can, material, and clamp at least 1 meter (39 in.) below the surface of the water.

(vii) A means to control the temperature of the water in the container between 0° C (32° F) and 1° C (33.8° F).

(viii) A thermistor or thermocouple that has an accuracy of ±0.1° C (0.18° F) and that is arranged to measure the temperature of the water in the con-

tainer at the depth at which the can, material, and clamp are held.

(2) *Test procedure.* The can is held under water (which can be at room temperature) and clamped between the two pieces of the neoprene control sample so that the assembly formed conforms as closely as possible to the shape of the can, and so that water fills all void spaces between the can and the sample. When the water temperature in the can is at or above 45° C (113° F), the assembly is then placed in the container and submerged to a depth of 1 m (39 in.) at the highest point of the assembly. The water temperature in the container must be between 0° C (32° F) and 1° C (33.8° F) and must be maintained within this range for the remainder of the test. No part of the assembly may touch the bottom or sides of the container. Every two minutes the assembly is shaken and then inverted from its previous position. The time for the water inside the can to drop from 45° C (113° F) to 33° C (91° F) is recorded. This procedure is performed three times using the control sample and then repeated three times using the suit material instead of the control sample. The shortest time for the drop in water temperature when the suit material is used must be greater than or equal to the shortest time when the neoprene control sample is used.

(f) *Storage temperature.* Two samples of the immersion suits, in their storage cases, must be alternately subjected to surrounding temperatures of −30° C to +65° C. These alternating cycles need not follow immediately after each other and the following procedure, repeated for a total of ten cycles, is acceptable:

(1) 8 hours conditioning at 65° C to be completed in one day;

(2) The specimens removed from the warm chamber that same day and left exposed under ordinary room conditions until the next day;

(3) 8 hours conditioning at −30° C to be completed the next day; and

(4) The specimens removed from the cold chamber that same day and left exposed under ordinary room conditions until the next day. At the conclusion of the final cycle of cold storage, two test subjects who successfully

completed the donning test in paragraph (c)(2) of this section enter the cold chamber, unpack and don the immersion suits. Alternatively, the suits may be upacked in the chamber, then removed and immediately donned. Neither of the suits must show damage such as shrinking, cracking, swelling, dissolution or change of mechanical qualities.

(g) *Measured buoyancy.* The buoyancy of a suit must be measured under the following conditions and procedures:

(1) *Test equipment.* The following equipment is required for this test:

(i) A mesh basket that is large enough to hold a folded suit, and that is weighted sufficiently to overcome the buoyancy of the suit when placed in the basket.

(ii) A tank of water that is large enough to contain the basket submerged with its top edge 50 mm (2 in.) below the surface of the water.

(iii) A scale or load cell that has an accuracy of 0.15 Newtons (1/2 oz.) and that is arranged to support and weigh the basket in the tank.

(2) *Test procedure.* The basket is submerged so that its top edge is 50 mm (2 in.) below the surface of the water. The basket is then weighed. Thereafter, a suit is submerged in water and then filled with water, folded, and placed in the submerged basket. The basket is titled 45° from the vertical for five minutes in each of four different directions to allow all entrapped air to escape. The basket is then suspended with its top edge 50 mm (2 in.) below the surface of the water for 24 hours. At the beginning and end of this period, the basket and suit are weighed underwater. The measured buoyancy of the suit is the difference between this weight and the weight of the basket as determined at the beginning of the test. The measured buoyancy after 24 hours must not be more than 5% lower than the initial measured buoyancy. The measured buoyancy after 24 hours is used to determine adjusted buoyancy as described in paragraph (h) of this section.

(h) *Adjusted buoyancy.* The adjusted buoyancy of a suit is its measured buoyancy reduced by the percentage buoyancy loss factor of the buoyant suit material. The percentage buoyancy loss factor is part of the buoyancy

rating code determined in accordance with UL 1191, except that the minimum number of samples required to determine each property is 10 instead of 75.

(i) *Suit flame exposure.* The suit's resistance to flame must be tested under the following conditions and procedures:

(1) *Test equipment.* The following equipment is required for this test:

(i) A metal pan that is at least 300 mm (12 in.) wide, 450 mm (18 in.) long, and 60 mm (2½ in.) deep. The pan must have at least 12 mm (½ in.) of water on the bottom with approximately 40 mm (1½ in.) of gasoline floating on top of the water.

(ii) An arrangement to hold the suit over the gasoline.

(2) *Test procedure.* A suit is held from its top by the holding arrangement. The gasoline is ignited and allowed to burn for approximately 30 seconds in a draft-free location. The suit is then held with the lowest part of each foot 240 mm (9.5 in.) above the surface of the burning gasoline. After two seconds, measured from the moment the flame first contacts the suit, the suit is removed from the fire. The suit must not sustain burning or continue melting after removal from the flames. If the suit sustains any visible damage other than scorching, it must then be subjected to the stability test described in paragraph (c)(8) of this section, except that only one subject need be used; the impact test described in paragraph (c)(11) of this section, except that only one subject need be used; the thermal protection test described in paragraph (d) of this section, except that only one subject need be used; and the buoyancy test described in paragraph (g) of this section, except that the buoyancy test need be conducted for only 2 hours.

(j) *Storage case flame exposure.* The storage case must be tested using the same equipment required for the suit flame exposure test. The immersion suit must be inside the storage case for this test. The storage case is held from its top by the holding arrangement. The gasoline is ignited and allowed to burn for approximately 30 seconds in a draft-free location. The storage case is then held with its lowest part 240 mm

(9.5 in.) above the surface of the burning gasoline. After two seconds, measured from the moment the flames first contact the case, the case is removed from the fire. If the case is burning, it is allowed to continue to burn for six seconds before the flames are extinguished. The storage case material must not burn through at any point in this test and the immersion suit must not sustain any visible damage.

(k) *Corrosion resistance.* Each metal part of a suit that is not 410 stainless steel, or for which published evidence of salt-spray corrosion resistance equal to or greater than 410 stainless steel is not available, must be tested as described in ASTM B 117. A sample of each metal under test and a sample of 410 stainless steel must be tested for 720 hours. At the conclusion of the test, each sample of test metal must show corrosion resistance equal to or better than the sample of 410 stainless steel.

(l) *Body strength.* The body strength of a suit must be tested under the following conditions and procedures:

(1) *Test equipment.* The test apparatus shown in figure 160.171-17(1)(1) must be used for this test. This apparatus consists of—

(i) Two rigid cylinders each 125 mm (5 in.) in diameter, with an eye or ring at each end;

(ii) A weight of 135 kg (300 lb.); and

(iii) Ropes or cables of sufficient length to allow the suit to be suspended as shown in Figure 160.171-17(1)(1).

(2) *Test procedure.* The suit is cut at the waist and wrists, or holes are cut into it as necessary to accommodate the test apparatus. The suit is immersed in water for at least two minutes. The suit is then removed from the water and immediately arranged on the test apparatus, using each closure as it would be used by a person wearing the suit. The 135 kg (300 lb.) load is applied for 5 minutes. No part of the suit may tear or break during this test. The suit must not be damaged in any way that would allow water to enter or that would affect the performance of the suit.

(m) *Seam strength.* The strength of each different type of seam used in a suit must be tested under the following conditions and procedures:

(1) *Test equipment.* The following equipment must be used for this test.

(i) A chamber in which air temperature can be kept at 23° C (73.4° F) ±2° C (1.8° F) and in which relative humidity can be kept at 50% ±5%.

(ii) A device to apply tension to the seam by the means of a pair of top jaws and a pair of bottom jaws. Each set of jaws must grip the material on both sides so that it does not slip when the load is applied.

(2) *Test samples.* Each test sample must consist of two pieces of suit material, each of which is a 100 mm (4 in.) square. The two pieces are joined by a seam as shown in figure 160.171-17(m)(3). For each type of seam, 5 samples are required. Each sample may be cut from the suit or may be prepared specifically for this test. One type of seam is distinguished from another by the type and size of stitch or other joining method used and by the type and thickness of the materials joined at the seam.

(3) *Test procedure.* Each sample is conditioned for at least 40 hours at 23° C (73.4° F) ±2°(1.8° F) C and 50% ±5% relative humidity. Immediately after conditioning, each sample is mounted individually in the tension device as shown in figure 160.171-17(m)(3). The jaws are separated at a rate of 5 mm/second (12 in./minute). The force at rupture is recorded. The average force at rupture must be at least 225 Newtons (50 lb.).

(n) *Tear resistance.* The tear resistance of suit material must be determined by the method described in ASTM D 1004. If more than one material is used, each material must be tested. If varying thickness of a material are used in the suit, samples representing the thinnest portion of the material must be tested. If multiple layers of a material are used in the suit, samples representing the layer on the exterior of the suit must be tested. Any material which is a composite formed of two or more materials bonded together is considered to be a single material. The average tearing strength of each material must be at least 45 Newtons (10 lb.).

(o) *Abrasion resistance.* The abrasion resistance of each type of suit material on the exterior of the suit must be determined by the method described in

241

Federal Test Method Standard 191, Method 5304.1. If varying thicknesses of exterior suit material are used, samples representing the thinnest portion of the material must be tested. If exterior material has multiple layers, samples of the layer on the outside surface of the suit must be tested. Any exterior material which is a composite formed of two or more layers bonded together is considered to be a single material and the abradant must be applied to the surface that is on the exterior of the suit. The residual breaking strength of each material must be at least 225 Newtons (50 lb.).

(p) *Test for oil resistance.* After all its apertures have been sealed, an immersion suit is immersed under a 100 mm head of diesel oil, grade No. 2–D as defined in ASTM D–975, for 24 hours. The surface oil is then wiped off and the immersion suit subjected to the leak test prescribed in § 160.171-17(c)(10). The ingress of water must not be greater than 200 grams.

§ 160.171-19 **Approval testing for child size immersion suit.**

A child size suit must pass the following tests:

(a) The stability test prescribed in § 160.171-17(c)(8), except that only six children need be used as test subjects and they can be of either sex. The subjects must be within the ranges of weight and height prescribed in § 160.171-9(m). The heaviest subject must weigh at least 10 kg (22 lb.) more than the lightest subject. During this test the face seal, neck and chin fit are evaluated and must be comparable to the fit of the corresponding adult size suit on an adult.

(b) The buoyancy test prescribed in § 160.171-17(g).

(c) The body strength test prescribed in § 160.171-17(k) except that the cylinders must be 50 mm (2 in.) in diameter and the test weight must be 55 kg (120 lb.).

§ 160.171-23 **Marking.**

(a) Each immersion suit must be marked with the words "IMMERSION SUIT—COMPLIES WITH SOLAS 74/83," the name of the manufacturer, the date of manufacturer, the model, the size, and the Coast Guard approval number.

(b) Each storage case must be marked with the words "immersion suit" and the size.

(c) The markings for the child size immersion suits required under paragraphs (a) and (b) of this section must also include the following statements in print smaller than the word "child": "(Small Adult Under 50 kg. (110 lb.))", and "Children Require Adult Assistance for Donning and Use."

(d) If an auxiliary means of buoyancy is removable and is needed to meet § 160.171-11(a)(2), the marking on the suit must indicate that the suit is not Coast Guard approved unless the auxiliary means of buoyancy is attached.

§ 160.171-25 **Production testing.**

(a) Immersion suit production testing is conducted under the procedures in this section and subpart 159.007 of this chapter.

(b) One out of every 100 immersion suits produced must be tested as prescribed in § 160.171-17(g) and must be given a complete visual examination. The suit must be selected at random from a production lot of 100 suits and tested by or under the supervision of the independent laboratory. A suit fails this test if—

(1) The measured buoyancy of the suit differs by more than 10% from the measured buoyancy of the suit tested for approval,

(2) The adjusted buoyancy of the suit calculated using the buoyancy loss factor determined during approval testing is less than that required in § 160.171-11(a)(1), or

(3) The visual examination shows that the suit does not conform to the approved design.

(c) If the suit fails to pass the test as prescribed in paragraph (b)(1) or (b)(2) of this section, 10 additional suits from the same lot must be selected at random and subjected to the test. If a defect in the suit is detected upon visual examination, 10 additional suits from the same lot must be selected at random and examined for the defect.

(d) If one or more of the 10 suits fails to pass the test or examination, each suit in the lot must be tested or examined for the defect for which the lot was rejected. Only suits that pass the test or that are free of defects may be sold as Coast Guard approved.

(e) The manufacturer must ensure that the quality control procedure de-scribed in the test plans previously submitted for approval under § 159.005–9(a)(5)(iii) is followed.

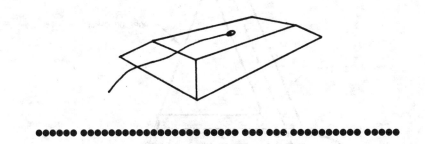

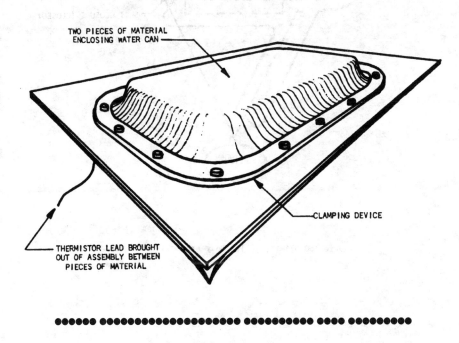

TWO PIECES OF MATERIAL
ENCLOSING WATER CAN

CLAMPING DEVICE

THERMISTOR LEAD BROUGHT
OUT OF ASSEMBLY BETWEEN
PIECES OF MATERIAL

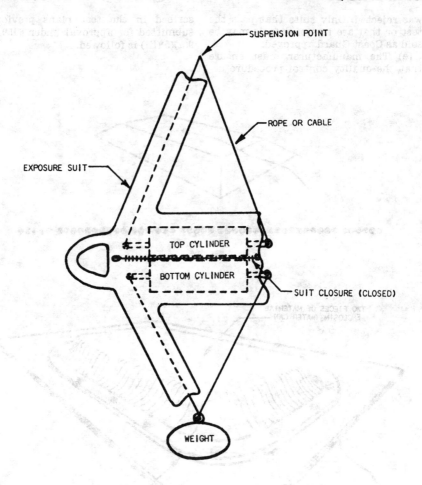

Figure 160.071-17(1)(1).   Body strength test apparatus.

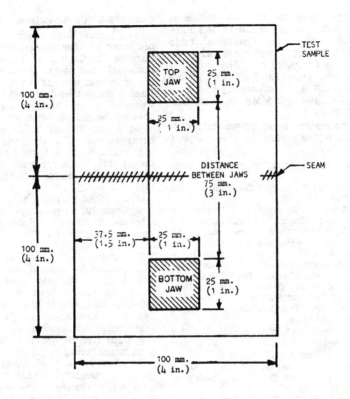

Figure 160.071-17(m)(3).

Method of mounting sample for seam strength test.

Subpart 160.174—Thermal Protective Aids

SOURCE: CGD 84–069b, 51 FR 19343, May 29, 1986, unless otherwise noted.

§160.174-1 Scope.

This subpart contains construction and performance requirements, and approval tests for thermal protective aids that are designed to minimize the occurrence of or aid in the recovery from hypothermia (lowered body temperature) during long periods in a survival craft.

§160.174-3 Incorporations by reference.

(a) Certain materials are incorporated by reference into this subchapter with the approval of the Director of the Federal Register. The Office of the Federal Register publishes a table, "Material Approved for Incorporation by Reference," which appears in the Finding Aids section of this volume. In that table is found citations to the particular sections of this part where the material is incorporated and the date of the approval by the Director of the Federal Register. To enforce any edition other than the one listed in

245

paragraph (b) of the section, notice of change must be published in the FEDERAL REGISTER and the material made available. All approved material is on file at the Office of the Federal Register, Washington, DC 20408, and at the U.S. Coast Guard, Lifesaving and Fire Safety Division (G–MMS–4), Washington, DC 20593.

(b) The materials approved for incorporation by reference in this subpart are:

AMERICAN SOCIETY FOR TESTING AND MATERIALS
100 Barr Harbor Drive, West Conshohocken, PA 19428–2959.
ASTM C 177–76, Standard Test Method for Steady-State Thermal Transmission Properties by Means of the Guarded Hot Plate.
ASTM C 518–76, Standard Test Method for Steady-State Thermal Transmission Properties by Means of the Heat Flow Meter.
ASTM D 1518–77, Thermal Transmittance of Textile Materials Between Guarded Hot-Plate and Cool Atmosphere.
ASTM D 1004–66, Tear Resistance of Plastic Film and Sheeting.
ASTM D 975–81, Standard Specification for Diesel Fuel Oils.
GENERAL SERVICES ADMINISTRATION
Specification Unit (WFSIA), Regional Office Building, Room 6039, 7th and D Streets SW., Washington, DC 20407
Federal Standard No. 751a—Stitches, Seams, and Stitchings.
National Bureau of Standards Special Publication 440—Color, Universal Language and Dictionary of Names.

[CGD 84–069b, 51 FR 19343, May 29, 1986, CGD 95–072, 60 FR 50467, Sept. 29, 1995; CGD 96–041, 61 FR 50733, Sept. 27, 1996; CGD 97–057, 62 FR 51049, Sept. 30, 1997]

§ 160.174–5 Independent laboratory.

(a) The approval and production tests and inspections in this subpart must be conducted by an independent laboratory accepted by the Coast Guard under subpart 159.010 of this chapter.

(b) [Reserved]

§ 160.174–7 Approval procedures.

(a) *General.* A thermal protective aid is approved by the Coast Guard under the procedures in subpart 159.005 of this chapter.

(b) *Approval testing.* Each approval test must be conducted in accordance with § 160.174–17.

§ 160.174–9 Construction.

(a) *General.* Each thermal protective aid must be constructed primarily of a durable insulating or heat reflecting material that meets the thermal insulation requirements in § 160.174–11(a). Each aid must be designed to cover the wearer's entire body, except for the area of the mouth, nose, and eyes.

(b) *Seams.* Stitching, if used in structural seams of a thermal protective aid, must be lock type stitching that meets the requirements in Federal Standard No. 751 for one of the following:

(1) Class 300 lockstitch.

(2) Class 700 single thread lock stitch.

(c) *Seam strength.* Each seam must have a strength of at least 225 Newtons (50 lb.).

(d) *Hardware.* All hardware of a thermal protective aid must be of a size and design that allows ease of operation by the wearer. The hardware must be attached to the aid in a manner that allows the wearer to operate it easily and that prevents it from attaining a position in which it can be operated improperly.

(e) *Metal parts.* Each metal part of a thermal protective aid must be—

(1) 410 stainless steel or have salt water and salt air corrosion characteristics equal to or superior to 410 stainless steel; and

(2) Galvanically compatible with each other metal part in contact with it.

(f) *Thermal protective aid exterior.* The primary color of the exterior surface of each thermal protective aid must be vivid reddish orange (color number 34 of National Bureau of Standards Publication 440). The exterior surface of the aid must resist tearing when tested as prescribed in § 160.174–17(i).

(g) *Hand and arm construction.* The hand of each thermal protective aid must be a glove that allows sufficient dexterity for the wearer to close and open the zipper or other hardware of the aid and to open and eat survival rations, unless the glove is removable. The glove may not be removable unless it is attached to the arm and unless it can be secured to the arm or stowed in a pocket on the arm when not in use.

(h) *Retroreflective material.* Each thermal protective aid must be fitted with at least 200 cm²(31 sq. in.) of Type I retroreflective material that meets subpart 164.018 of this chapter.

(i) *Size.* Each thermal protective aid must fit persons ranging in weight from 50 kg. (110 lbs.) to 150 kg. (330 lbs.) and in height from 1.5 m. (59 in.) to 1.9 m. (75 in.).

(j) *Lifejacket.* Each thermal protective aid must be designed so that any Type I Personal Flotation Device meeting the requirements of this chapter can be worn inside the aid and, when worn, will not damage the aid and will not adversely affect its performance.

§160.174–11 Performance.

(a) *Thermal protection.* The thermal protective aid must be designed to protect against loss of body heat as follows:

(1) The thermal conductivity of the material from which the thermal protective aid is constructed must be not more than 0.25 W/(m – °K).

(2) The thermal protective aid must prevent evaporative heat loss.

(3) The aid must function properly at an air temperature of – 30 °C (– 22 °F) to +20 °C (68 °F).

(b) *Donning Time.* Each thermal protective aid must be designed to enable a person to don the aid correctly within one minute after reading the donning and use instructions described in §160.174–15(a).

(c) *Storage Temperature.* A thermal protective aid must not be damaged by storage in its storage case at any temperature between – 30 °C (– 22 °F) and +65 C (149 °F).

(d) *In water performance.* The thermal protective aid must be designed to permit the wearer to remove it in the water within two minutes, if it impairs ability to swim.

(e) *Water penetration.* The fabric from which the thermal protective aid is constructed must maintain its watertight integrity when supporting a column of water 2 meters high.

(f) *Oil resistance.* Each thermal protective aid must be designed to be useable after 24 hours exposure to diesel oil.

§160.174–13 Storage case.

Each thermal protective aid must be provided with a ziplock bag or equivalent storage case.

§160.174–15 Instructions.

(a) Each thermal protective aid must have instructions for its donning and use in an emergency. The instructions must be in English and must not exceed 50 words. Illustrations must be used in addition to the words. The instructions must include advice as to whether to swim in the aid or discard it if the wearer is thrown into the water.

(b) The instructions required by paragraph (a) of this section must be on the exterior of the storage case, printed on a waterproof card attached to the storage case, or printed on the thermal protective aid and visible through a transparent storage case. The instructions must also be available in 8½×11 inch loose-leaf format for inclusion in the vessel's training manual.

§160.174–17 Approval testing.

(a) *General.* A thermal protective aid must be tested as prescribed in this section.

(b) *Mobility and swimming tests.* The mobility and swimming capabilities of each thermal protective aid must be tested under the following conditions and procedures:

(1) *Test subjects.* Seven males and three females must be used in the tests described in this paragraph. The subjects must represent each of the three physical types (ectomorphic, endomorphic, and mesomorphic). Each subject must be in good health. The heaviest male subject must weigh at least 25 kg (55 lb) more than the lightest male subject. The heaviest female subject must weigh at least 25 kg (55 lb) more than the lightest female subject. The heaviest subject must weigh 150±5 Kg (330±11 lbs.) and the lightest subject must weigh 50±5 Kg (110±11 lbs.). Each subject must be unfamiliar with the specific thermal protective aid under test. Each subject must wear a standard range of clothing consisting of:

(i) Underwear (short sleeved, short legged);

(ii) Shirt (long sleeved);

(iii) Trousers (not woolen);

247

(iv) Woolen socks;

(v) Rubber soled shoes; and

(vi) A life preserver.

(2) *Donning test.* Each subject is removed from the view of the other subjects and allowed one minute to examine the thermal protective aid and the manufacturer's instructions for donning and use of the aid in an emergency. At the end of this period, the subject attempts to don the thermal protective aid as rapidly as possible. If the subject does not don the thermal protective aid completely, including gloves and any other accessories, within 60 seconds, the subject removes the aid and is given a demonstration of correct donning, and again attempts to don the aid. At least nine out of ten subjects must be able to don the thermal protective aid completely in 60 seconds on at least one of the two attempts.

(3) *Discarding test.* If the thermal protective aid impairs the ability of the wearer to swim, it must be demonstrated that it can be discarded by the test subjects, when immersed in water, in not more than two minutes. Caution: During each of the in water tests prescribed in this section, a person ready to render assistance when needed should be near each subject in the water.

(i) Unless the manufacturer specifies in the instructions that the thermal protective aid does impair ability to swim and should always be discarded in the water, each subject, wearing a life preserver, enters the water and swims 25 meters. The subject, after sufficient rest to avoid fatigue, repeats this test wearing a thermal protective aid in addition to the life preserver. At least nine out of ten subjects must be able to swim this distance wearing the thermal protective aid in not more than 125% of the time taken to swim the distance wearing only a life preserver, or the aid will be determined to impair the ability to swim.

(ii) If the thermal protective aid is determined by the above test or specified by the manufacturer to impair the ability to swim, each subject, after entering the water from a height of one meter (three feet), attempts to remove the aid and discard it. At least nine out

of ten subjects must be able to discard the device within two minutes.

(c) [Reserved]

(d) *Storage temperature.* Two samples of the thermal protective aids, in their storage cases, are alternately subjected to surrounding temperatures of −30° C to +65° C. These alternating cycles need not follow immediately after each other and the following procedure, repeated for a total of ten cycles, is acceptable:

(1) 8 hours conditioning at 65° C to be completed in one day;

(2) The specimens removed from the warm chamber that same day and left exposed under ordinary room conditions until the next day;

(3) 8 hours conditioning at −30° C to be completed the next day; and

(4) The specimens removed from the cold chamber that same day and left exposed under ordinary room conditions until the next day. At the conclusion of step (3) of the final cycle of cold storage, two test subjects who successfully completed the donning test previously enter the cold chamber, unpack and don the thermal protective aids. The aids must not show any damage, such as shrinking, cracking, swelling, dissolution or change of mechanical qualities.

(e) *Water penetration.* A sample of the fabric from which the thermal protective aid is constructed is installed as a membrane at one end of a tube of at least 2.5 cm (one inch) diameter and 2 meters long. The tube is fixed in a vertical position with the membrane at the bottom, and filled with water. After one hour the membrane must continue to support the column of water with no leakage.

(f) *Insulation.* The material from which the thermal protective aid is constructed is tested in accordance with the procedures in ASTM C 177, ASTM C 518, or ASTM D 1518. The material must have a thermal conductivity of not more than 0.25 W/(m − °K).

(g) *Test for oil resistance.* After all its apertures have been sealed, a thermal protective aid is immersed under a 100 mm head of diesel oil, grade no. 2–D as defined in ASTM D–975, for 24 hours. The surface oil is then wiped off and a sample of the material from the aid is again tested in accordance with the procedures in ASTM C 177 or ASTM C 518. The material must still have a thermal conductivity of not more than 0.25 W/(m − ° K).

(h) *Seam strength.* The strength of each different type of seam used in a thermal protective aid must be tested under the following conditions and procedures.

(1) *Test equipment.* The following equipment must be used in this test:

(i) A chamber in which air temperature can be kept at 25° C (73.4° F) ±2° C (1.8° F) and in which relative humidity can be kept at 50% ±5%.

(ii) A device to apply tension to the seam by means of a pair of top jaws and a pair of bottom jaws. Each set of jaws must grip the material on both sides so that it does not slip when the load is applied. Each front jaw must be 25 mm (1 inch) wide by 25 mm (1 inch) long. The distance between the jaws before the load is applied must be 75mm (3 inches).

(2) *Test samples.* Each test sample consists of two pieces of the material from which the thermal protective aid is constructed, each of which is 100 mm (4 inches) square. The two pieces are joined by a seam as shown in figure 160.171–17(m)(3). For each type of seam, 5 samples are required. Each sample may be cut from a thermal protective aid or may be prepared specifically for this test. One type of seam is distinguished from another by the type and size of stitch or other joining method used (including orientation of warp and fill, if any) and by the type and thickness of the materials joined at the seam.

(3) *Test procedure.* Each sample is conditioned for at least 40 hours at 23° C±2° C and 50% ±5% relative humidity. Immediately after conditioning, each sample is mounted individually in the tension device as shown in figure 160.171–17(m)(3). The jaws are separated at a rate of 5 mm/second (12 in/minute). The maximum force to achieve rupture is recorded. The average force at rupture must be at least 225 Newtons (50 lb).

(i) *Tear resistance.* The tear resistance of the material from which a thermal protective aid is constructed must be determined by the method described in ASTM D 1004. If more than one mate-

rial is used, each material must be tested. If varying thicknesses of a material are used in the aid, samples representing the thinnest portion of the material must be tested. If multiple layers of a material are used in the aid, samples representing the layer on the exterior of the aid must be tested. Any material that is a composite formed of two or more materials bonded together is considered to be a single material. The average tearing strength of each material must be at least 45 Newtons (10 lb).

[CGD 84–069b, 51 FR 19343, May 29, 1986, as amended by CGD 84–069a, 52 FR 1197, Jan. 12, 1987]

§160.174–23 Marking.

(a) Each thermal protective aid must be marked with the words "Thermal Protective Aid," the name of the manufacturer, the model, the date of manufacture or a lot number from which the date of manufacture may be determined, and the Coast Guard approval number.

(b) Each storage case must be marked with the words "Thermal Protective Aid" or the thermal protective aid must have a similar marking which is visible through a transparent storage case.

§160.174–25 Production testing.

(a) Thermal protective aid production testing is conducted under the procedures in this section and subpart 159.007 of this chapter.

(b) One out of every 100 thermal protective aids produced must be given a complete visual examination. The sample must be selected at random from a production lot of 100 thermal protective aids and examined by or under the supervision of the independent laboratory. The sample fails if the visual examination shows that the aid does not conform to the approved design.

(c) If a defect in the thermal protective aid is detected upon visual examination, 10 additional samples from the same lot must be selected at random and examined for the defect.

(d) If one or more of the 10 samples fails the examination, each thermal protective aid in the lot must be examined for the defect for which the lot was rejected. Only thermal protective aids that are free of defects may be sold as Coast Guard approved.

[CGD 84–069b, 51 FR 19343, May 29, 1986; 51 FR 20650, June 6, 1986]

Subpart 160.176—Inflatable Lifejackets

SOURCE: CGD 78–174b, 54 FR 50320, Dec. 5, 1989, unless otherwise noted.

§ 160.176–1 Scope.

(a) This subpart contains structural and performance standards and procedures for approval of inflatable lifejackets, as well as requirements for associated manuals, servicing programs, and shore-side service facilities.

(b) Other regulations in this chapter provide that inflatable lifejackets must be:

(1) Serviced annually at designated servicing facilities; and

(2) Maintained in accordance with their user manuals.

(c) Inflatable lifejackets approved under this subpart—

(1) Rely entirely upon inflation for buoyancy;

(2) Meet the requirements for lifejackets in the 1983 Amendments to the International Convention for the Safety of Life at Sea, 1974 (SOLAS 74/83);

(3) Have performance equivalent to Type I Personal Flotation Devices (PFD's) with any one chamber deflated; and

(4) Are designed to be worn by adults.

§ 160.176–2 Application.

(a) Inflatable lifejackets approved under this subpart may be used to meet carriage requirements for Type I PFD's only on:

(1) Uninspected submersible vessels; and

(2) Inspected vessels for which a servicing program has been approved by the Commandant.

(b) [Reserved]

§ 160.176–3 Definitions.

(a) *Commandant* means the Chief of the Lifesaving and Fire Safety Division, Marine Safety and Environmental Protection. Address: Commandant (G–MSE–4), U.S. Coast Guard Head-

quarters, 2100 Second St. SW., Washington, DC 20593–0001.

(b) *First quality workmanship* means construction which is free from any defect materially affecting appearance or serviceability.

(c) *Functional deterioration* means—

(1) Damage such as deformation in hardware or a rip, tear, or loose stitches;

(2) Decline in any performance characteristic; or

(3) Any other change making the lifejacket unfit for use.

(d) *Functional residual capacity* (FRC) means the amount of lung volume a person has remaining at the bottom of the normal breathing cycle when at rest.

(e) *Inflation medium* means any solid, liquid, or gas, that, when activated, provides inflation for buoyancy.

(f) *Inspector* means an independent laboratory representative assigned to perform the duties described in § 160.176–15 of this subpart.

(g) *PFD* means personal flotation device as defined in 33 CFR 175.13.

(h) *Reference vest* means a model AK–1 PFD meeting subpart 160.047 of this part, except that, in lieu of the weight and displacement values prescribed in Tables 160.047–4(c)(2) and § 160.047–(4)(c)(4), each front insert must have a weight of kapok of at least 8.25 oz. and a volume displacement of 9.0 ± 0.25 lb., and the back insert must have a weight of kapok of at least 5.5 oz. and a volume displacement of 6.0 ± 0.25 lb. To achieve the specified volume displacement, front insert envelopes may be larger than the dimensions prescribed by § 160.047–1(b).

(i) [Reserved]

(j) *Second stage donning* means adjustments or steps necessary to make a lifejacket provide its intended flotation characteristics after the device has been properly donned and then inflated.

[CGD 78–174b, 54 FR 50320, Dec. 5, 1989, as amended by CGD 95–072, 60 FR 50466, Sept. 29, 1995; CGD 96–041, 61 FR 50733, Sept. 27, 1996]

§ 160.176–4 Incorporation by reference.

(a) Certain materials are incorporated by reference into this subpart with the approval of the Director of the Federal Register in accordance with 5

U.S.C. 552(a). To enforce any edition other than the one listed in paragraph (b) of this section, notice of the change must be published in the FEDERAL REGISTER and the material made available to the public. All approved material is on file at the Office of the Federal Register, 800 North Capitol Street, NW., suite 700, Washington, DC and at the U.S. Coast Guard, Lifesaving and Fire Safety Division (G-MSE-4), 2100 Second Street, SW., Washington, DC 20593-0001, and is available from the sources indicated in paragraph (b) of this section.

(b) The materials approved for incorporation by reference in this subpart, and the sections affected are:

AMERICAN SOCIETY FOR TESTING AND MATERIALS (ASTM)
100 Barr Harbor Drive, West Conshohocken, PA 19428-2959.
ASTM B 177-73/79 Standard Method of Salt Spray (Fog) Testing, 1973—160.176-8; 160.176-13
ASTM D 751-79 Standard Methods of Testing Coated Fabrics, 1979—160.176-13
ASTM D 975-81 Standard Specification for Diesel Fuel Oils, 1981—160.176-13
ASTM D 1434-75 Gas Transmission Rate of Plastic Film and Sheeting, 1975—160.176-13
FEDERAL AVIATION ADMINISTRATION TECHNICAL STANDARD ORDER
Policy and Procedure Br., AWS-110, Aircraft Engineering Division, Office of Airworthiness, 800 Independence Ave., SW., Washington, DC 20591
TSO-C13d, Federal Aviation Administration Standard for Life Preservers, January 3, 1983—160.176-8
FEDERAL STANDARDS
Naval Publications and Forms Center, Customer Service, Code 1052, 5801 Tabor Ave., Philadelphia, PA 19120
In Federal Test Method Standard No. 191A (dated July 20, 1978) the following methods:
(1) Method 5100, Strength and Elongation, Breaking of Woven Cloth; Grab Method—160.176-13
(2) Method 5132, Strength of Cloth, Tearing; Falling-Pendulum Method—160.176-13
(3) Method 5134, Strength of Cloth, Tearing; Tongue Method—160.176-13
(4) Method 5804.1, Weathering Resistance of Cloth; Accelerated Weathering Method—160.176-8
(5) Method 5762, Mildew Resistance of Textile Materials; Soil Burial Method—160.176-8
Federal Standard No. 751a, Stitches, Seams, and Stitching, January 25, 1965—160.176-9
MILITARY SPECIFICATIONS

Naval Publications and Forms Center, Customer Service, Code 1052, 5801 Tabor Ave., Philadelphia, PA 19120
MIL-L-24611—Life Preserver Support Package For Life Preserver, MK 4, dated May 18, 1982—160.176-8
NATIONAL INSTITUTE OF STANDARDS AND TECHNOLOGY (NIST) (FORMERLY NATIONAL BUREAU OF STANDARDS)
C/O Superintendent of Documents, U.S. Government Printing Office, Washington, DC 20402
Special Pub. 440, *Color: Universal Language and Dictionary of Names;* "The Universal Color Language" and "The Color Names Dictionary", 1976—160.176-9
UNDERWRITERS LABORATORIES (UL)
Underwriters Laboratories, Inc., 12 Laboratory Drive, Research Triangle Park, NC 27709-3995.P.O. Box 13995, Research Triangle Park, NC 27709-3995
UL 1191, "Components for Personal Flotation Devices", November 11, 1984—160.176-8; 160.176-13

[CGD 78-174b, 54 FR 50320, Dec. 5, 1989, as amended by CGD 95-072, 60 FR 50467, Sept. 29, 1995; CGD 96-041, 61 FR 50733, Sept. 27, 1996; CGD 97-057, 62 FR 51049, Sept. 30, 1997]

§160.176-5 Approval procedures.

(a) *Modifications to general procedures.* Subpart 159.005 of this chapter contains the approval procedures. Those procedures must be followed, except as modified in this paragraph.

(1) Preapproval review under §§159.005-5 and 159.005-7 may be omitted if a similar design has already been approved.

(2) The information required under §159.005-5(a)(2) (i) through (iii) of this chapter must be included in the application.

(3) The application must also include the following:

(i) The Type of performance (i.e. Type I or Type V) that the lifejacket is designed to provide.

(ii) Any special purpose(s) for which the lifejacket is designed and the vessel(s) or vessel type(s) on which its use is planned.

(iii) Buoyancy and torque values along with tolerances to be allowed in production. The Coast Guard normally will approve tolerances of up to ±10% unless prototypes are tested at greater extremes or greater tolerances are otherwise justified.

(iv) The text of any optional marking to be provided in addition to required text.

(v) The service manual and written guidelines required by §§ 160.176–19(c) and 160.176–19(d) of the part and the user's manual required by § 160.176–21 of this part.

(vi) A list of proposed servicing facilities.

(4) The description of quality control procedures required by § 159.005–9 of this chapter to be submitted with the test report may be omitted as long as the manufacturer's planned quality control procedures comply with § 160.176–15 of this part.

(5) The test report must include, in addition to information required by § 159.005–9 of this chapter, a report of inspection of each proposed servicing facility. The report must include the time, date, place, and name of the person doing the inspection and observations that show whether the facility meets §§ 160.176–19(b)(2), 160–176–19(b)(4), and 160.176–19(d) of this part.

(6) The certificate of approval, when issued, is accompanied by a letter to the manufacturer listing the servicing facilities that have been approved. Copies of the letter are also provided for each facility.

(7) An approval will be suspended or terminated under § 159.005–15 of this chapter if the manufacturer fails to maintain approved servicing facilities that meet § 160.176–19 of this part.

(b) *Manuals and guidelines*. The manuals and servicing facility guidelines required by this subpart are reviewed with the application for lifejacket approval. Changes will be required if needed to comply with §§ 160.176–19 and 160.176–21 of this part.

(c) *Approval of servicing facilities*. (1) Approval of servicing facilities initially proposed for use is considered during and as a part of the lifejacket approval process described in paragraph (a) of this section.

(2) Other servicing facilities may subsequently be considered for approval, upon submission of a letter of application to Commandant containing each of the applicable items required of manufacturers and laboratories under § 159.005–5 of this chapter and the following:

(i) A copy of guidelines meeting § 160.176–19(d) of this part, if different

from those originally approved with the lifejacket;

(ii) A list of the sources the servicing facility proposes to use for parts and manuals for the servicing of the make and model of lifejacket applied for; and

(iii) A report of inspection prepared by an independent laboratory which includes the time, date, and place of the inspection, the name of the inspector, and observations that show whether the facility meets §§ 160.176–19(b)(2) through 160.176–19(b)(4) and 160.176–19(d) of this part.

(3) To conduct servicing at a remote or mobile site, the servicing facility must be authorized in its letter of approval to conduct this type of servicing. Approval for servicing at these sites is obtained according to paragraph (c)(2) of this section except that portable or mobile equipment must be available when evaluating the compliance with § 160.176–19(b)(3) of this part.

(4) Each change to equipment, procedure, or qualification and training of personnel of an approved servicing facility must be also approved.

(d) *Waiver of tests*. If a manufacturer requests that any test in this subpart be waived, one of the following must be provided to the Commandant as justification for the waiver:

(1) Acceptable test results on a lifejacket of sufficiently similar design.

(2) Engineering analysis showing that the test is not applicable to the particular design or that by design or construction the lifejacket can not fail the test.

(e) *Alternative requirements*. A lifejacket that does not meet requirements in this subpart may still be approved if the device—

(1) Meets other requirements prescribed by the Commandant in place of or in addition to requirements in this subpart; and

(2) Provides at least the same degree of safety provided by other lifejackets that do comply with this subpart.

[CGD 78–174b, 54 FR 50320, Dec. 5, 1989, as amended by CGD 78–174b, 56 FR 29441, June 27, 1991]

§ 160.176–6 Procedure for approval of design or material revision.

(a) Each change in design, material, or construction must be approved by the Commandant before being used in lifejacket production.

(b) Determinations of equivalence of design, construction, and materials may only be made by the Commandant.

§ 160.176-7 Independent laboratories.

A list of independent laboratories which have been accepted by the Commandant for conducting or supervising the following tests and inspections required by this subpart, may be obtained from the Commandant:

(a) Approval tests.

(b) Production tests and inspections.

(c) Inspection of approved servicing facilities.

(d) Testing of materials for the purpose of making the certification required by § 160.176-8(a)(3) of this part.

§ 160.176-8 Materials.

(a) *General*—(1) *Acceptance, certification, and quality.* All components used in the construction of lifejackets must meet the requirements of subpart 164.019 of this chapter.

(2) *Condition of materials.* All materials must be new.

(3) *Temperature range.* Unless otherwise specified in standards incorporated by reference in this section, all materials must be usable in all weather conditions throughout a temperature range of $-30\,^\circ$ C to $+65\,^\circ$ C($-22\,^\circ$ F to $+150\,^\circ$ F).

(4) *Weathering resistance.* Each non-metallic component which is not suitably covered to shield against ultraviolet exposure must retain at least 40% of its strength after being subjected to 300 hours of sunshine carbon arc weathering as specified by Method 5804.1 of Federal Test Method Standard Number 191A.

(5) *Fungus resistance.* Each non-metallic component must retain at least 90% of its strength after being subjected to the mildew resistance test specified by Method 5762 of Federal Test Method Standard No. 191A when untreated cotton is used as the control specimen. Also, the gas transmission rate of inflation chamber materials must not be increased by more than 10% after being subjected to this test. Materials that are covered when used in the lifejacket may be tested with the covering material.

(6) *Corrosion resistance.* Each metal component must—

(i) Be galvanically compatible with each other metal part in contact with it; and

(ii) Unless it is expendable (such as an inflation medium cartridge), be 410 stainless steel, have salt water and salt air corrosion characteristics equal or superior to 410 stainless steel, or perform its intended function and have no visible pitting or other damage on any surface after 720 hours of salt spray testing according to ASTM B 117.

(7) *Materials not covered.* Materials having no additional specific requirements in this section must be of good quality and suitable for the purpose intended.

(b) *Fabric*—(1) *All fabric.* All fabric must—

(i) Be of a type accepted for use on Type I life preservers approved under subpart 160.002 of this part; or

(ii) Meet the Type V requirements for "Fabrics for Wearable Devices" in UL 1191 except that breaking strength must be at least 400 N (90 lb.) in both directions of greater and lesser thread count.

(2) *Rubber coated fabric.* Rubber coated fabric must be of a copper-inhibiting type.

(c) *Inflation chamber materials*—(1) *All materials.* (i) The average permeability of inflation chamber material, determined according to the procedures specified in § 160.176-13(y)(3) of this part, must not be more than 110% of the permeability of the materials determined in approval testing prescribed in § 160.176-13(y)(3) of this part.

(ii) The average grab breaking strength and tear strength of the material, determined according to the procedures specified in §§ 160.176-13(y)(1) and 160.176-13(y)(2) of this part, must be at least 90% of the grab breaking strength and tear strength determined from testing prescribed in §§ 160.176-13(y)(1) and 160.176-13(y)(2) of this part. No individual sample result for breaking strength or tear strength may be more than 20% below the results obtained in approval testing.

(2) *Fabric covered chambers.* Each material used in the construction of inflation chambers that are covered with

fabric must meet the requirements specified for—

(i) "Bladder" materials in section 3.2.6 of MIL–L–24611(SH) if the material is an unsupported film; or

(ii) Coated fabric in section 3.1.1 of TSO–C13d if the material is a coated fabric.

(3) *Uncovered chambers.* Each material used in the construction of inflation chambers that are not covered with fabric must meet the requirements specified in paragraph (c)(2)(ii) of this section.

(d) *Thread.* Each thread must meet the requirements of subpart 164.023 of this chapter. Only one kind of thread may be used in each seam. Thread and fabric combinations must have similar elongation and durability characteristics.

(e) *Webbing.* Webbing used as a body strap, tie tape or drawstring, or reinforcing tape must meet § 160.002–3(e), § 160.002–3(f), § 160.002–3(h) of this part respectively. Webbing used for tie tape or drawstring must easily hold a knot and be easily tied and untied. Webbing used as reinforcing tape must not chafe the wearer.

(f) *Closures*—(1) *Strength.* Each buckle, snap hook, dee ring or other type of fastening must have a minimum breaking strength of 1600 N (360 lbs). The width of each opening in a closure, through which body strap webbing passes, must be the same as the width of that webbing.

(2) *Means of Locking.* Each closure used to secure a lifejacket to the body, except a zipper, must have a quick and positive locking mechanism, such as a snap hook and dee ring.

(3) *Zipper.* If a zipper is used to secure the lifejacket to the body, it must be—

(i) Easily initiated;

(ii) Non-jamming;

(iii) Right handed;

(iv) Of a locking type; and

(v) Used in combination with another type of closure that has a quick and positive means of locking.

(g) *Inflation medium.* (1) No inflation medium may contain any compound that is more toxic than CO_2 if inhaled through any of the oral inflation mechanisms.

(2) Any chemical reaction of inflation medium during inflation must not produce a toxic residue.

(h) *Adhesives.* Adhesives must be waterproof and acceptable for use with the materials being bonded.

(i) [Reserved]

(j) *Retroreflective Material.* Each lifejacket must have at least 200 sq. cm. (31 sq. in.) of retroreflective material on its front side, at least 200 sq. cm. on its back side, and at least 200 sq. cm. of material on each reversible side. The retroreflective material must be Type I material that is approved under subpart 164.018 of this chapter. The retroreflective material attached on each side must be divided equally between the upper quadrants of the side. Attachment of retroreflective material must not impair lifejacket performance or durability.

(k) *PFD light.* Each lifejacket must have a PFD light that is approved under subpart 161.012 of this chapter and that meets the requirements of Regulations III/30.2 and III/32.3 of the 1983 Amendments to the International Convention for the Safety of Life at Sea, 1974 (SOLAS 74/83). The light must be securely attached to the front shoulder area of the lifejacket. Attachment of the light must not impair lifejacket performance.

(l) [Reserved]

(m) *Whistle.* Each lifejacket must have a whistle of the ball type or multi-tone type and of corrosion-resistant construction. The whistle must be securely attached to the lifejacket by a lanyard. The lanyard must be long enough to permit the whistle to reach the mouth of the wearer. If the lanyard would normally allow the whistle to hang below the waist of the average size wearer, the whistle must be stowed in a pocket on the lifejacket. The attachment of the whistle must not impair lifejacket performance.

[CGD 78–1746, 54 FR 50320, Dec. 5, 1989, as amended by CGD 78–174b, 56 FR 29441, June 27, 1991; CGD 84–068, 58 FR 29494, May 20, 1993]

§ 160.176–9 Construction.

(a) *General Features.* Each inflatable lifejacket must—

(1) Have at least two inflation chambers;

(2) Be constructed so that the intended method of donning is obvious to an untrained wearer;

(3) If approved for use on a passenger vessel, be inside a sealed, non-reusable package that can be easily opened;

(4) Have a retainer for each adjustable closure to prevent any part of the closure from being easily removed from the lifejacket;

(5) Be universally sized for wearers weighing over 40 kg. (90 pounds) and have a chest size range of at least 76 to 120 cm. (30 to 52 in.);

(6) Unless the lifejacket is designed so that it can only be donned in one way, be constructed to be donned with either the inner or outer surface of the lifejacket next to the wearer (be reversible);

(7) Not have a channel that can direct water to the wearer's face to any greater extent than that of the reference vest defined in §160.176–3(h) of this part;

(8) Not have edges, projections, or corners, either external or internal, that are sharp enough to damage the lifejacket or to cause injury to anyone using or maintaining the lifejacket;

(9) Have a means for drainage of entrapped water;

(10) Be primarily vivid reddish orange, as defined by sections 13 and 14 of the "Color Names Dictionary," on its external surfaces;

(11) Be of first quality workmanship;

(12) Unless otherwise allowed by the approval certificate—

(i) Not incorporate means obviously intended for attaching the lifejacket to the vessel; and

(ii) Not have any instructions indicating attachment to a vessel is intended; and

(13) Meet any additional requirements that the Commandant may prescribe, if necessary, to approve unique or novel designs.

(b) Inflation mechanisms. (1) Each inflatable lifejacket must have

(i) At least one automatic inflation mechanism;

(ii) At least two manual inflation mechanisms on separate chambers;

(iii) At least one oral inflation mechanism on each chamber; and

(iv) At least one manual inflation mechanism or one automatic inflation mechanism on each inflation chamber.

(2) Each inflation mechanism must

(i) Have an intended method of operation that is obvious to an untrained wearer;

(ii) Not require tools to activate the mechanism;

(iii) Be located outside its inflation chamber; and

(iv) Be in a ready to use condition.

(3) Each oral inflation mechanism must

(i) Be easily accessible after inflation for the wearer to "top off" each chamber by mouth;

(ii) Operate without pulling on the mechanism;

(iii) Not be able to be locked in the open or closed position; and

(iv) Have a non-toxic mouthpiece.

(4) Each manual inflation mechanism must

(i) Provide an easy means of inflation that requires only one deliberate action on the part of the wearer to actuate it;

(ii) Have a simple method for replacing its inflation medium cartridge; and

(iii) Be operated by pulling on an inflation handle that is marked "Jerk to Inflate" at two visible locations.

(5) Each automatic inflation mechanism must

(i) Have a simple method for replacing its inflation medium cartridge and water sensitive element;

(ii) Have an obvious method of indicating whether the mechanism has been activated; and

(iii) Be incapable of assembly without its water sensitive element.

(6) The marking required for the inflation handle of a manual inflation mechanism must be waterproof, permanent, and readable from a distance of 2.5 m (8 feet).

(c) Deflation mechanism. (1) Each chamber must have its own deflation mechanism.

(2) Each deflation mechanism must

(i) Be readily accessible to either hand when the lifejacket is worn while inflated;

(ii) Not require tools to operate it;

(iii) Not be able to be locked in the open or closed position; and

(iv) Have an intended method of operation which is obvious to an untrained wearer.

(3) The deflation mechanism may also be the oral inflation mechanism.

(d) *Sewn seams.* Stitching used in each structural seam of a lifejacket must provide performance equal to or better than a Class 300 Lockstitch meeting Federal Standard No. 751a.

(e) *Textiles.* All cut edges of textile materials must be treated or sewn to minimize raveling.

(f) *Body strap attachment.* Each body strap assembly must be securely attached to the lifejacket.

§ 160.176–11 Performance.

(a) *General.* Each inflatable lifejacket must be able to pass the tests in § 160.176–13 of this part.

(b) *Snag Hazard.* The lifejacket must not present a snag hazard when properly worn.

(c) *Chamber Attachment.* Each inflation chamber on or inside an inflatable lifejacket must not be able to be moved to a position that-

(1) Prevents full inflation; or

(2) Allows inflation in a location other than in its intended location.

(d) *Comfort.* The lifejacket must not cause significant discomfort to the wearer during and after inflation.

§ 160.176–13 Approval Tests.

(a) *General.* (1) This section contains requirements for approval tests and examinations of inflatable lifejackets. Each test or examination must be conducted or supervised by an independent laboratory. The tests must be done using lifejackets that have been constructed in accordance with the plans and specifications in the application for approval. Unless otherwise specified, only one lifejacket, which may or may not have been subjected to other tests, is required to be tested in each test. One or more lifejackets that have been tested as prescribed in paragraph (h) of this section must be used for the tests prescribed in paragraphs (j), (n), (q), and (r) of this section. The tests prescribed in paragraph (y) of this section require one or more lifejackets as specified in that paragraph.

(2) All data relating to buoyancy and pressure must be taken at, or corrected to, an atmospheric pressure of 760 mm (29.92 inches) of mercury and a temperature of 20 °C (68 °F).

(3) The tests in this section are not required to be run in the order listed, except where a particular order is specified.

(4) Some tests in this section require a lifejacket to be tested while being worn. In each of these tests the test subjects must represent a range of small, medium, and large heights and weights. Unless otherwise specified, a minimum of 18 test subjects, including both males and females, must be used. The test subjects must not be practiced in the use of the lifejacket being tested. However, they must be familiar with the use of other Coast Guard approved lifejackets. Unless specified otherwise, test subjects must wear only swim suits. Each test subject must be able to swim and relax in the water.

NOTE: Some tests have inherent hazards for which adequate safeguards must be taken to protect personnel and property in conducting the tests.

(b) *Donning.* (1) No second stage donning is allowed in the tests in this paragraph. Test subjects may read the donning instructions to be provided with the device, if any. An uninflated lifejacket with size adjustment at its mid-range is given to each test subject with the instruction: "Please don as quickly as possible, adjust to fit snugly, and inflate." Each subject must, within one minute, don the uninflated lifejacket, adjust it to fit snugly, and then activate the manual inflation mechanism.

NOTE: For this test the manual inflation mechanism may be disabled.

(2) The average time of all subjects to complete the test in paragraph (b)(1) of this section must not exceed 30 seconds. The criteria in this paragraph do not apply to the tests in paragraphs (b)(3) and (b)(4) of this section.

(3) The test in paragraph (b)(1) of this section is repeated with each subject wearing an insulated, hooded parka and gloves made from heavy, cotton-jersey (knit) fabric.

(4) The test in paragraph (b)(1) of this section is then repeated twice more with a fully inflated lifejacket. In the

§160.176–13

first test the subjects must wear swim suits and in the second test, parka and gloves.

(c) *Inflation Testing.* No second stage donning is allowed in the tests in this paragraph. A lifejacket with each automatic inflation mechanism disabled must be used for the tests prescribed in paragraphs (c)(1) and (c)(2) of this section. For the tests prescribed in paragraph (c)(4) of this section, remove any non-reusable cover or packaging from the lifejacket, but do not open any cover or closure which is intended to be closed when the lifejacket is worn in the uninflated condition.

(1) Each test subject dons an uninflated lifejacket and is instructed to enter the water and swim for approximately 30 seconds and then, on command, inflate the lifejacket using only oral inflation mechanisms. Within 30 seconds after the command is given, the lifejacket must be sufficiently inflated to float each subject with respiration unimpeded.

(2) Each test subject dons an uninflated lifejacket and is instructed to enter the water and swim for approximately 30 seconds, bring both hands to the surface, and then, on command, inflate the lifejacket using each manual inflation mechanism. Each test subject must find and operate all the manual inflation mechanisms within 5 seconds after the command is given. The manual inflation mechanisms must inflate the lifejacket sufficiently to float the wearers within 5 seconds after the mechanisms are operated. Within 20 seconds after activation each subject must be floating in the position described in paragraph (d)(3) of this section.

(3) One small and one large test subject don uninflated lifejackets and jump feet first from a height of 1 meter into the water. The automatic inflation mechanisms must inflate the lifejackets sufficiently to float the wearers within 10 seconds after the subjects enter the water. Within 20 seconds after entering the water each subject must be floating in the position described in paragraph (d)(3) of this section.

(4) Air at a pressure of 4.2 kPa (0.6 psig) is applied separately to each oral inflation mechanism of the lifejacket.

In each application the chamber must fully inflate within 1 minute.

(5) Each oral inflation mechanism of an unpacked lifejacket is connected to a regulated air source constantly supplying air at a pressure of 7 kPa (1 psig). Each mechanism must pass at least 100,000 cc of air per minute.

(d) *Flotation stability*—(1) *Uninflated flotation stability.* Lifejackets with their automatic inflation mechanisms disabled must be used for this test. Each subject dons an uninflated lifejacket, enters the water, and assumes an upright, slightly back of vertical, position. Each subject then relaxes. For each subject that floats, the uninflated lifejacket must not tend to turn the wearer face-down when the head is allowed to fall back.

(2) *Righting action.* (i) Each test subject dons an uninflated lifejacket, enters the water, allows the automatic inflation mechanism to inflate the lifejacket, and swims for 30 seconds. While swimming, freedom of movement and comfort are observed and noted by the person conducting the test. Freedom of movement and comfort must comply with §160.176–11(d). Also, each subject must demonstrate that the lifejacket can be adjusted while the subject is in the water.

(ii) Each subject then takes three gentle breast strokes and while still face-down in the water, relaxes completely while slowly exhaling to FRC. Each subject remains in this limp position long enough to determine if the lifejacket will turn the subject from the face-down position to a position in which the subject's breathing is not impaired. The time from the last breast stroke until breathing is not impaired is recorded. Each subject repeats these steps two additional times, and the average time for the three righting actions is calculated. This average time must not exceed 5 seconds.

(iii) If the lifejacket does not have automatic inflation mechanisms for all chambers, the tests in paragraphs (d)(2)(i) and (d)(2)(ii) of this section are repeated with each lifejacket fully inflated.

(iv) Each subject then performs the test in paragraph (d)(2)(ii) of this section with one chamber of the lifejacket deflated. This test is then repeated as many times as necessary to test the lifejacket with a different chamber deflated until each chamber has been tested in this manner.

(v) Each subject then performs the test in paragraph (d)(2)(ii) of this section but exhales to FRC at the end of the third breast stroke and holds the breath prior to relaxing.

(3) *Static measurements.* At the end of each test with each subject in § 160.176-13(d)(2)(ii), through § 160.176-13(d)(2)(v)—

(i) The freeboard (the distance from the water surface to the bottom of the mouth) must be at least 100 mm (4.0 in.) without repositioning of any part of the body and at least 120 mm (4.75 in.) after the head is positioned on the lifejacket for maximum freeboard and then relaxed;

(ii) The distance from water surface to the lower portion of the ear canal must be at least 50 mm (2 in.);

(iii) The torso angle (the angle between a vertical line and a line passing through the shoulder and hip) must be between 20° and 65° (back of vertical);

(iv) The face-plane angle (the angle between a vertical line and a line passing through the most forward part of the forehead and chin) must be between 15° and 60° (back of vertical);

(v) The lowest mark on a vertical scale 6 m (20 ft.) from and in front of the subject which the subject can see without moving the head must be no higher than 0.3 m (12 in.) from the water level.

(vi) The subject when looking to the side, must be able to see the water within 3 m (10 ft.) away; and

(vii) At least 75% of the retroreflective material on the outside of the lifejacket, and the PFD light, must be above the water.

(4) *Average requirements.* The test results for all subjects must be averaged for the following static measurements and must comply with the following:

(i) The average freeboard prior to positioning the head for maximum freeboard must be at least 120 mm (4.75 in.);

(ii) The average torso angle must be between 30° and 50° (back of vertical); and

(iii) The average face-plane angle must be between 20° and 50° (back of vertical).

(5) *"HELP" Position.* Starting in a relaxed, face-up position of static balance, each subject brings the legs and arms in towards the body so as to attain the "HELP" position (a fetal position, but holding the head back). The lifejacket must not turn the subject face down in the water.

(e) *Jump test.* (1) Each test subject dons an uninflated lifejacket and with hands above head, jumps feet first, into the water from a height of 4.5 m (15 ft.). No second stage donning is allowed during this test and the lifejacket must—

(i) Inflate automatically, float the subject to the surface, and stabilize the body with the mouth out of the water;

(ii) Maintain its intended position on the wearer;

(iii) Not be damaged; and

(iv) Not cause injury to the wearer.

(2) The jump test in paragraph (e)(1) of this section is repeated using a lifejacket which has been fully inflated manually.

(3) The jump test in paragraph (e)(2) of this section is then conducted with one chamber deflated. This test is then repeated as many times as necessary to test the lifejacket with a different chamber deflated until each chamber has been tested in this manner.

NOTE: Before conducting these tests at the 4.5 m height, subjects should first do the test from heights of 1 m and 3 m to lessen the possibility of injury. It is suggested that subjects wear a long-sleeve cotton shirt to prevent abrasions when testing the device in the inflated condition and that the teeth should be tightly clenched together when jumping.

(f) *Water emergence*—(1) *Equipment.* A pool with a wooden platform at one side must be used for this test. The platform must be 300 mm (12 in.) above the water surface and must not float on the water. The platform must have a smooth painted surface. Alternatively, a Coast Guard approved inflatable liferaft may be used in lieu of a platform.

(2) *Qualifying.* Each test subject enters the water wearing only a bathing suit and swims 25 m. The subject must then be able to emerge from the pool onto the platform using only his or her

hands on the top of the platform as an aid and without pushing off of the bottom of the pool. Any subject unable to emerge onto the platform within 30 seconds is disqualified for this test. If less than 2/3 of the test subjects qualify, substitute subjects must be used.

(3) *Test.* Each qualified subject dons an inflated lifejacket, enters the water and swims 25 m. Afterward, at least 2/3 of the qualified subjects must then be able to climb out of the pool in the manner prescribed in paragraph (f)(2) of this section within 45 seconds while wearing the lifejacket. If marking on the lifejacket so indicates, and if the wearer can read the marking while the lifejacket is being worn, the subjects may deflate the device during the 45 second attempt.

(g) *Lanyard pull test and strength.* (1) An uninflated lifejacket is placed on a rigid metal test form built according to Figure 160.176–13(n)(2) and suspended vertically.

(2) The inflation handle of each manual inflation mechanism is attached to a force indicator. The force indicator is then used to activate each manual inflation mechanism separately. The force required to activate each mechanism is recorded. In each test the force must be between 25 and 70 N (5 and 15 lb.).

(3) A weight of 225 N (50 lb.) is in turn attached to the inflation handle of each manual inflation mechanism. The weight is then allowed to hang freely for 5 minutes from each manual inflation mechanism. The handle must not separate from the mechanism.

(h) *Temperature cycling tests.* (1) Three uninflated lifejackets, 2 packed and 1 unpacked, are maintained at room temperature (20 ± 3 °C (68 + 6 °F)) for 4 hours and then at a temperature of 65 ± 2 °C (150 ± 5 °F) for 20 hours. The lifejackets are then maintained at room temperature for at least 4 hours, after which they are maintained at a temperature of minus 30 ± 2 °C (−22 ± 5 °F) for 20 hours. This cycle is then repeated once.

(2) Upon the completion of the conditioning in paragraph (h)(1) of this section all sealed or non-reusable packaging is removed from the two packed units. The lifejackets must show no functional deterioration after being inflated immediately after removal from the conditioning. The lifejackets must be inflated as follows:

(i) One unit which was packed during conditioning must fully inflate within 2 minutes using only oral inflation.

(ii) The other unit which was packed during conditioning must fully inflate within 45 seconds of submersion in water at 2 ± 2 °C (37 ± 5 °F) as a result of automatic inflation.

(iii) The unit which was unpacked during conditioning must fully inflate within 30 seconds of activation of the manual inflation mechanisms.

(3) The same 3 lifejackets used for the test in paragraph (h)(1) of this section are deflated and, with 2 repacked and 1 unpacked, are maintained at room temperature for 4 hours and then at a temperature of minus 30 ± 2 °C (−22 ± 5 °F) for 20 hours. The lifejackets are then stored at room temperature for at least 4 hours, after which they are maintained at a temperature of 65 ± 2 °C (150 ± 5 °F) for 20 hours. This cycle is then repeated once. The steps in paragraph (h)(2) of this section are then repeated, and the lifejackets must meet the criteria in that paragraph.

(i) [Reserved]

(j) *Buoyancy and inflation medium retention test.* A lifejacket which has been used in the tests in paragraph (h) of this section must be used for this test.

(1) *Equipment.* The following equipment is required for this test:

(i) A wire mesh basket that is large enough to hold the inflated lifejacket without compressing it, is designed not to allow the lifejacket to float free, and is heavy enough to overcome the buoyancy of the lifejacket.

(ii) A scale that is sensitive to 14 g (0.5 oz.) and that has an error of less than ±14 g (0.5 oz.).

(iii) A test tank, filled with fresh water, that is large enough to hold the basket with its top 50 mm (2 in.) below the surface without the basket touching the tank.

(2) *Method.* One inflation chamber is inflated using its automatic inflation mechanism. The lifejacket is placed in the basket. The basket is then suspended from the scale and submerged in the test tank with the lifejacket and basket completely below the water surface. An initial reading of the scale is

taken after 30 minutes and again after 24 hours. The buoyancy of the lifejacket is the submerged weight of the basket minus the submerged weight of the basket with the lifejacket inside. This test is repeated as many times as necessary until each chamber has been tested. On each chamber that does not have an automatic inflation mechanism the manual or oral inflation mechanism may be used.

(3) *Requirement.* The buoyancy of each inflation chamber must be within the tolerances specified in the plans and specifications for the lifejacket required by § 160.176–5(a)(2) of this part. Each inflation chamber must retain at least 95% of its initial buoyancy after being submerged for 24 hours.

(k) *Uninflated floatation test.* A packed lifejacket, with all automatic inflation mechanisms disabled, is dropped from a height of 1 m (3 ft.) into fresh water. The lifejacket must remain floating on the surface of the water for at least 30 minutes. This test is repeated with an unpacked, uninflated lifejacket, with all automatic inflation mechanisms disabled.

(1) [Reserved]

(m) *Environmental tests*—(1) *Salt spray exposure.* An uninflated lifejacket is subjected to 720 hours of salt spray as specified by ASTM B 117. The automatic inflation mechanism(s) must not be activated by the salt spray. The lifejacket is then inflated first using the automatic inflation mechanism(s) and then twice more using first the manual mechanisms and then the oral mechanisms. The lifejacket must show no functional deterioration.

(2) *Rain exposure.* An uninflated lifejacket is mounted on a rigid metal test form built according to Figure 160.176–13(n)(2). The test form must be vertical. Spray nozzles that deliver 0.05 mm of water per second (0.7 inch/hour) over the area of the lifejacket at a tempera-ture between 2 and 16 °C (35 and 60 °F) and at a 45° angle below horizontal toward the lifejacket are mounted 1.5 m (4.5 ft.) above the base of the test form. There must be at least 4 nozzles evenly spaced around the lifejacket at a horizontal distance of 1 m from the center of the lifejacket and each nozzle must deliver water at the same rate. Water is then sprayed on the lifejacket for 1 hour. The lifejacket must not inflate during the test.

(n) *Tensile tests.* Two lifejackets that have been subjected to the tests in paragraph (h) of this section must be used for these tests.

(1) *Body tensile test.* (i) In this test one lifejacket must be fully inflated and the other deflated.

(ii) Two unconnected rigid cylinders are passed through the body portion of each lifejacket, or through the encircling body strap for yoke style devices, with one closure fastened and adjusted to its mid range, as shown in Figure 160.176–13(n)(1). Each cylinder must be 125 mm (5 inches) in diameter. The top cylinder is connected to a winch or pulley system. The bottom cylinder is connected to a test load which when combined with the weight of the lower cylinder and the linkage equals 325 kg (720 lb.). The winch or pulley system lifts the top cylinder so the test load is raised off of its support. The test load is left suspended for 30 minutes.

(iii) There must be no functional deterioration of any component of either lifejacket during the test. Each friction type closure must not permit slippage of more than 25 mm (1 in.).

(iv) If a lifejacket has friction type closures, the test must be repeated immediately after the lifejacket has been immersed in water for a least 2 minutes.

(v) The test is repeated until each different type of closure is tested separately.

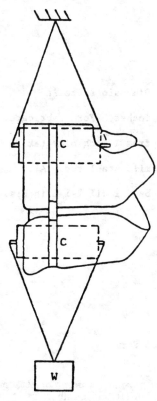
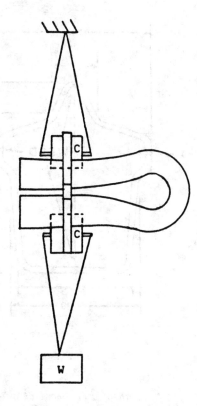

Vest style lifejacket   Yoke style lifejacket

C - Cylinder (5 inches in diameter)

W - Test Weight

Figure 160.176-13(n)(1) Body Tensile Test Arrangement

(2) *Shoulder tensile test.* Each shoulder section of a lifejacket is subjected to this test separately. A fully inflated lifejacket, with all closures fastened, must be secured to a rigid metal test form built according to Figure 160.176-13(n)(2). A 2 ±¼ in. wide web is passed through the shoulder section of the lifejacket and is connected to a winch or pulley system. The bottom portion of the form is connected to a dead weight load which when combined with the weight of the form and the linkage equals 90 kg. (200 lb.). The winch or pulley system is operated to raise the weight off of its support. The weight is left suspended for 30 minutes. There must be no functional deterioration of any component of the lifejacket during the test.

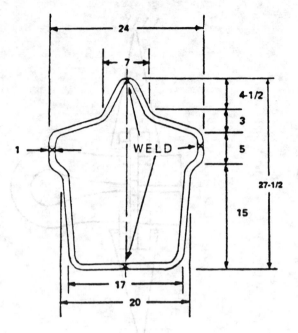

Dimensions are in inches. Form fabricated from 1 inch diameter mild steel rod. All bend radii 1-1/2 inches.

Figure 160.176-13(n)(2)　Test Form

(3) *Strength of attachment of inflation mechanism.* (i) A fully inflated lifejacket is secured to a rigid metal test form as in Figure 160.176–13(n)(2), and the pressure of each inflated chamber is measured. The top portion of the form is then connnected to a winch or pulley system. A 35 kg (75 lb.) weight is attached by a line to one of the inflation mechanisms as close as possible to the point of attachment on the lifejacket. The winch or pulley system is operated to raise the weight off of its support. The weight is left suspended for 5 minutes and then released. The inflation chamber to which the inflation mechanism is attached must not lose more than 3 kPa (0.4 psig) or 20% of its original pressure.

(ii) The test is paragraph (n)(3)(i) of this section is repeated until each type of inflation mechanism has been tested separately.

(iii) The test is then repeated as many additional times as necessary to test each joint in each type of inflation

mechanism beyond its point of attachment to an inflation chamber. In each test the point of attachment must be as close as possible to the joint being tested.

(o) [Reserved]

(p) *Impact test.* (1) an uninflated lifejacket is secured to the test form shown in Figure 160.176–13(n)(2). The lifejacket, with the automatic inflation mechanism disabled, is secured to the form as it is intended to be worn. The lifejacket is accelerated to 25 m/s (50 mph) horizontally and is then dropped from a height of not more than 0.5 m (1.5 ft.) into the water in the following positions:

(i) Face down, shoulder forward.
(ii) Face down, shoulder back.
(iii) Back down, shoulder forward.
(iv) Back down, shoulder back.
(v) Left side down, shoulder forward.
(vi) Right side down, shoulder back.

(2) Following each impact, there must be no sign of functional deterioration, and the lifejacket must not come off of the test form. After each

impact the closures may be readjusted as necessary.

(3) Following the six impacts, the lifejacket must fully inflate using only its oral inflation mechanisms.

(4) The test in this paragraph is repeated on the same lifejacket after inflating, with manual inflation mechanisms, all chambers that have those mechanism.

(q) *Flame exposure test.* A lifejacket that has been subjected to the tests in paragraph (h) of this section must be used for this test.

(1) *Equipment.* The following equipment is required for this test:

(i) A test pan 300 mm by 450 mm by 60 mm (12 in. by 18 in. by 2½ in.) containing 12 mm (½ in.) of water under 25 mm (1 in.) of N-heptane.

(ii) an arrangement to hold the lifejacket over the N-heptane.

(2) *Method.* The test is only conducted when there is no significant air movement other than that caused by the fire. The N-heptane is ignited and allowed to burn for 30 seconds. A lifejacket which has been fully inflated with air is then passed through the flames in an upright, forward, vertical, free-hanging position with the bottom of the lifejacket 240 mm C 9½ in.) above the top edge of the test pan. The lifejacket is exposed to the flames for 2 seconds.

(3) *Requirement.* The lifejacket must not burn or melt for more than 6 seconds after being removed from the flames. The lifejacket must remain inflated throughout the test. If the lifejacket sustains any visible damage other than discoloration after being exposed to the flames, the lifejacket must—

(i) pass the test in paragraph (e)(2) of this section, except that only one subject is used and the test is done six times; and

(ii) pass the tensile test in paragraph (n)(1) of this section, except that a weight of 245 kg (540 lb.) is used in lieu of the 325 kg (720 lb.) weight.

(r) *Solvent exposure test.* Lifejackets with their automatic inflation mechanisms disabled must be used for this test. Two uninflated lifejackets that have been subjected to the tests in paragraph (h) of this section are totally submerged in diesel fuel, grade

No. 2–D as defined in ASTM D 975, for 24 hours. The lifejackets are then removed and the excess fuel removed. One lifejacket must fully inflate using only its manual inflation mechanisms and the other using only its oral inflation mechanisms. The lifejackets must show no functional deterioration as a result of the test.

(s) *Puncture test.* A fully inflated lifejacket is placed on a flat, level surface. A test point 4 mm (⁵⁄₃₂ in.) in diameter tapering to a rounded point, 1 mm (³⁄₆₄ in.) in diameter, is pressed against an inflation chamber of the lifejacket perpendicular to the surface of the chamber at a rate of 300 mm/minute (12 in./minute). The test point is applied until the inflation chamber is punctured or the chamber walls are touching each other. The force required to puncture the inflation chamber or make the chamber walls touch each other is recorded. The force required must exceed 30 N (7 lb.).

(t) *Inflation chamber tests—*(1) *Overpressure test.* One lifejacket is used in this test. Before pressurizing the lifejacket, each over-pressure valve, if any, must be blocked. One inflation chamber is then pressurized with air to 70 kPa (10 psig) and held for 5 minutes. After the 5 minute period, there must be no sign of permanent deformation, damage, or pressure loss of more than 3.5 kPa (0.5 psig). This test is then repeated as many times as necessary to test a different chamber until each chamber has been tested in this manner.

(2) *Air retention test.* One inflation chamber of a lifejacket is filled with air until air escapes from the over-pressure valve or, if the lifejacket does not have an over-pressure valve, until its design pressure, as stated in the plans and specifications, is reached. After 12 hours the lifejacket must still be firm with an internal pressure of at least 14 kPa (2.0 psig). This test is then repeated as many times as necessary to test a different chamber until each chamber has been tested in this manner.

(u) *Seam strength test.* Samples of each type of structural sewn seam must be subjected to and pass the "Seam Strength (Sewability) Test" specified in Underwriters Laboratories

Standard UL 1191 except that the breaking strength of each seam in the directions of both greater and lesser thread count must be at least 400 N (90 lb.).

(v) [Reserved]

(w) *Visual examination.* One complete lifejacket must be visually examined for compliance with the requirements of §§ 160.176-9 and 160.176-11 of this part

(x) [Reserved]

(y) *Inflation chamber properties.* The tests in this paragraph must be run after successful completion of all other approval tests. The results of these tests will be used to check the quality of incoming lifejacket components and the production process. Test samples must come from one or more lifejackets that were each used in all of the tests in paragraphs (e), (j), (p), (s), and (t) of this section.

(1) *Grab breaking strength.* The grab breaking strength of chamber materials must be determined according to Method No. 5100 of Federal Test Method Standard 191A or ASTM D 751.

(2) *Tear strength.* The tear strength of chamber materials must be determined according to Method No. 5132 or 5134 of Federal Test Method Standard 191A or ASTM D 751.

(3) *Permeability.* The permeability of chamber materials must be determined according to ASTM D 1434 using CO_2 as the test gas.

(4) *Seam strength.* The seam strength of the seams in each inflation chamber of at least one lifejacket must be determined according to ASTM D 751 except that 25 by 200 mm (1 by 8 in.) samples may be used where insufficient length of straight seam is available.

(z) *Additional tests.* The Commandant may prescribe additional tests, if necessary, to approve novel or unique designs.

[CGD 78-174b, 54 FR 50320, Dec. 5, 1989, as amended by CGD 78-174b, 56 FR 29441, June 27, 1991]

§ 160.176-15 Production tests and inspections.

(a) *General.* (1) Production tests and inspections must be conducted in accordance with this section and subpart 159.007 of this chapter.

(2) The Commandant may prescribe additional production tests and inspec-

tions if needed to maintain quality control and check for compliance with the requirements in this subpart.

(b) *Test and inspection responsibilities.* In addition to responsibilities set out in part 159 of this chapter, each manufacturer of an inflatable lifejacket and each independent laboratory inspector must comply with the following, as applicable:

(1) *Manufacturer.* Each manufacturer must—

(i) Perform all required tests and examinations on each lifejacket lot before the independent laboratory inspector tests and inspects the lot;

(ii) Perform required testing of each incoming lot of inflation chamber material before using that lot in production;

(iii) Have procedures for maintaining quality control of the materials used, manufacturing operations, and the finished product;

(iv) Have a continuing program of employee training and a program for maintaining production and test equipment;

(v) Have an inspector from the independent laboratory observe the production methods used in producing the first lifejacket lot produced and observe any revisions made thereafter in production methods;

(vi) Admit the inspector and any Coast Guard representative to any place in the factory where work is done on lifejackets or component materials, and where completed lifejackets are stored; and

(vii) Allow the inspector and any Coast Guard representative to take samples of completed lifejackets or of components materials for tests prescribed in this subpart.

(2) *Independent laboratory.* (i) An inspector may not perform or supervise any production test or inspection unless—

(A) The manufacturer has a current approval certificate; and

(B) The inspector has first observed the manufacturer's production methods and any revisions to those methods.

(ii) An inspector must perform or supervise all required tests and inspections of each lifejacket lot produced.

(iii) During each inspection, the inspector must check for noncompliance with the manufacturer's quality control procedures.

(iv) At least once each calendar quarter, the inspector must, as a check on manufacturer compliance with this section, examine the manufacturer's records required by § 160.176-17 of this part and observe the manufacturer in performing each of the tests required by paragraph (h) of this section.

(c) *Lifejacket lots.* A lot number must be assigned to each group of lifejackets produced. No lot may exceed 1000 lifejackets. A new lot must be started whenever any change in materials or a revision to a production method is made, and whenever any substantial discontinuity in the production process occurs. Changes in lots of component materials must be treated as changes in materials. Lots must be numbered

serially. The lot number assigned, along with the approval number, must enable the lifejacket manufacturer, by referring to the records required by this subpart, to determine who produced the components used in the lifejacket.

(d) *Samples.* (1) Samples used in testing and inspections must be selected at random. Sampling must be done only when all lifejackets or materials in the lot are available for selection.

(2) Each sample lifejacket selected must be complete, unless otherwise specified in paragraph (h) of this section.

(3) The inspector may not select the same samples tested by the manufacturer.

(4) The number of samples selected per lot must be at least the applicable number listed in Table 160.176-15A or Table 160.176-15B.

TABLE 160.176-15A—MANUFACTURER'S SAMPLING PLAN

	Number of Samples Per Lot					
	Lot Size					
	1–100	101–200	201–300	301–500	501–750	751–1000
Tests:						
Inflation Chamber Materials.						
SEE NOTE (1)						
Seam Strength	1	1	2	2	3	4
Over-pressure [2][3]	1	2	3	4	6	8
Air Retention.						
EVERY DEVICE IN THE LOT						
Buoyancy & Inflation Media Retention	1	2	3	4	6	8
Tensile Strength [4]	1	1	1	1	1	1
Detailed Product Examination	2	2	3	4	6	8
Retest Sample Size [2]	—	—	13	13	20	20
Final Lot Inspection:.						
EVERY DEVICE IN THE LOT						

[1] Samples must be selected from each lot of incoming material. The tests referenced in §§ 160.176-13(y)(1) through 160.176-13(y)(4) of this part prescribe the number of samples to select.
[2] Samples selected for this test may not be the same samples selected for other tests.
[3] If any sample fails the over-pressure test, the number of samples to be tested in the next lot produced must be at least 2% of the total number of lifejackets in the lot or 10 lifejackets, whichever is greater.
[4] This test is required only when a new lot of materials is used and when a revised production process is used. However, the test must be run at least once every calendar quarter regardless of whether a new lot of materials or a revised process is started in that quarter.

TABLE 160.176-15B—INSPECTOR'S SAMPLING PLAN

	Number of samples per lot					
	Lot size					
	1–100	101–200	201–300	301–500	501–750	751–1000
Tests:						
Over-pressure [1]	1	2	3	4	6	8
Air Retention	1	2	3	4	6	8
Buoyancy & Inflation Media Retention	1	2	3	4	6	8
Tensile Strength [2]	1	1	1	1	1	1
Waterproof marking.						
SEE NOTE (3) FOR SAMPLING						
Detailed Product Examination	2	2	2	3	3	3
Retest Sample Size [1]	10	10	13	13	20	20

TABLE 160.176–15B—INSPECTOR'S SAMPLING PLAN—Continued

	Number of samples per lot					
	Lot size					
	1–100	101–200	201–300	301–500	501–750	751–1000
Final Lot Inspection:	20	32	50	60	70	80

[1] Samples selected for this test may not be the same lifejackets selected for other tests.
[2] This test may be omitted if the manufacturer has previously conducted it on the lot and the inspector has conducted the test on a previous lot during the same calendar quarter.
[3] One sample of each means of marking on each type of fabric or finish used in lifejacket construction must be tested. This test is only required when a new lot of materials is used. However, the test must be run at least once every calendar quarter regardless of whether a new lot of materials is started in that quarter.

(e) *Accept/reject criteria: manufacturer testing.* (1) A lifejacket lot passes production testing if each sample passes each test.

(2) In lots of 200 or fewer lifejackets, the lot must be rejected if any sample fails one or more tests.

(3) In lots of more than 200 lifejackets, the lot must be rejected if—

(i) One sample fails more than one test;

(ii) More than one sample fails any test or combination of tests; or

(iii) One sample fails one test and in redoing that test with the number of samples specified for retesting in Table 160.176–15A, one or more samples fail the test.

(4) A rejected lifejacket lot may be retested only if allowed under paragraph (k) of this section.

(5) In testing inflation chamber materials, a lot is accepted only if the average of the results of testing the minimum number of samples prescribed in the reference tests in §160.176–13(y) of this part is within the tolerances specified in §160.176–8(c)(1) of this part. A rejected lot may not be used in production.

(f) *Accept/reject criteria: independent laboratory testing.* (1) A lot passes production testing if each sample passes each test.

(2) A lot must be rejected if—

(i) One sample fails more than one test;

(ii) More than one sample fails any test or combination of tests; or

(iii) One sample fails one test and in redoing that test with the number of samples specified for retesting in Table 160.176–15B, one or more samples fail the test.

(3) A rejected lot may be retested only if allowed under paragraph (k) of this section.

(g) *Facilities and equipment*—(1) *General.* The manufacturer must provide the test equipment and facilities described in this section for performing production tests, examinations, and inspections.

(2) *Calibration.* The manufacturer must have the calibration of all test equipment checked at least every six months by a weights and measures agency or the equipment manufacturer, distributor, or dealer.

(3) *Equipment.* The following equipment is required:

(i) *A sample basket* for buoyancy tests. It must be made of wire mesh and be of sufficient size and durability to securely hold a completely inflated lifejacket under water without compressing it. The basket must be heavy enough or be sufficiently weighted to submerge when holding an inflated test sample.

(ii) *A tank filled with fresh water* for buoyancy tests. The height of the tank must be sufficient to allow a water depth of 5 cm (2 inches) minimum between the top of the basket and water surface when the basket is not touching the bottom. The length and width of the tank must be sufficient to prevent each submerged basket from contacting another basket or the tank sides and bottom. Means for locking or sealing the tank must be provided to prevent disturbance of any samples or a change in water level during testing.

(iii) *A scale* that has sufficient capacity to weigh a submerged basket for buoyancy tests. The scale must be sensitive to 14 g (0.5 oz.) and must not have an error exceeding ±14 g (0.5 oz.).

(iv) *Tensile test equipment* that is suitable for applying pulling force in conducting body strap assembly strength subtests. The equipment assembly may be (A) a known weight and winch, (B) a scale, winch, and fixed anchor, or (C) a tensile test machine that is capable of holding a given tension. The assembly must provide accuracy to maintain a pulling force within ±2 percent of specified force. Additionally, if the closed loop test method in § 160.176–13(h)(1) of this Part is used, two cylinders of the type described in that method must be provided.

(v) *A thermometer* that is sensitive to 0.5 °C (1 °F) and does not have an error exceeding ±0.25 °C (0.5 °F).

(vi) *A barometer* that is capable of reading mm (inches) of mercury with a sensitivity of 1 mm (0.05 in.) Hg and an error not exceeding ±5 mm (0.02 in.) Hg.

(vii) *A regulated air supply* that is capable of supplying the air necessary to conduct the tests specified in paragraphs (h)(4) and (h)(5) of this section.

(viii) *A pressure gauge* that is capable of measuring air pressure with a sensitivity of 1 kPa (0.1 psig) and an error not exceeding ±0.5 kPa (0.05 psig).

(ix) *A torque wrench* if any screw fasteners are used. The wrench must be sensitive to, and have an error of less than, one half the specified tolerance for the torque values of the fasteners.

(4) *Facilities:* The manufacturer must provide a suitable place and the necessary apparatus for the inspector to use in conducting or supervising tests. For the final lot inspection, the manufacturer must provide a suitable working environment and a smooth-top table for the inspector's use.

(h) *Production tests and examinations—* (1) *General.* (i) Samples used in testing must be selected according to paragraph (d) of this section.

(ii) On each sample selected—

(A) The manufacturer must conduct the tests in paragraphs (h)(2) through (h)(8) of this section; and

(B) The independent laboratory inspector must conduct or supervise the tests in paragraphs (h)(4) through (h)(9) of this section.

(iii) Each individual test result must, in addition to meeting the requirements in this paragraph, meet the requirements, if any, set out in the approved plans and specifications required by § 160.176–5(a)(2) of this part.

(2) *Inflation chamber materials.* Each sample must be tested according to §§ 160.176–13(y)(1) through 160.176–13(y)(3) of this part. The average and individual results of testing the minimum number of samples prescribed by § 160.176–13(y) of this part must comply with the requirements in § 160.176–8(c)(1) of this part.

(3) *Seam strength.* The seams in each inflation chamber of each sample must be tested according to § 160.176–13(y)(4) of this part. The results for each inflation chamber must be at least 90% of the results obtained in approval testing.

(4) *Over-pressure.* Each sample must be tested according to and meet § 160.176–13(t)(1) of this part.

(5) *Air retention.* Each sample must be tested according to and meet § 160.176–13(t)(2) of this part.

(6) *Buoyancy and inflation medium retention.* Each sample must be tested according to and meet § 160.176–13(j) of this part. Each buoyancy value must fall within the tolerances specified in the approved plans and specifications.

(7) *Tensile strength.* Each sample must be tested according to and meet § 160.176–13(n) of this part.

(8) *Detailed product examination.* Each sample lifejacket must be disassembled to the extent necessary to determine compliance with the following:

(i) All dimensions and seam allowances must be within tolerances prescribed in the approved plans and specifications required by § 160.176–5(a)(2) of this part.

(ii) The torque of each screw type mechanical fastener must be within its tolerance as prescribed in the approved plans and specifications.

(iii) The arrangement, markings, and workmanship must be as specified in the approved plans and specifications and this subpart.

(iv) The lifejacket must not otherwise be defective.

(9) *Waterproof marking test.* Each sample is completely submerged in fresh water for a minimum of 30 minutes, and them removed and immediately placed on a hard surface. The markings are vigorously rubbed with the fingers

for 15 seconds. If the printing becomes illegible, the sample is rejected.

(i) [Reserved]

(j) *Final lot examination and inspection*—(1) *General.* On each lifejacket lot that passes production testing, the manufacturer must perform a final lot examination and an independent laboratory inspector must perform a final lot inspection. Samples must be selected according to paragraph (d) of this section. Each final lot examination and inspectin must show—

(i) First quality workmanship;

(ii) That the general arrangement and attachment of all components such as body straps, closures, inflation mechanisms, tie tapes, drawstrings, etc. are as specified in the approved plans and specifications; and

(iii) Compliance with the marking requirements in § 160.176-23 of this Part.

(2) *Accept/reject criteria.* Each nonconforming lifejacket must be rejected. If three or more nonconforming lifejackets are rejected for the same kind of defect, lot examination or inspection must be discontinued and the lot rejected.

(3) *Manufacturer examination.* This examination must be done by a manufacturer's representative who is familiar with the approved plans and specifications required by § 160.176-5(a)(2) of this part, the functioning of the lifejacket and its components, and the production testing procedures. This person must not be responsible for meeting production schedules or be supervised by someone who is. This person must prepare and sign the record required by § 159.007-13(a) of this chapter and § 160.176-17(b) of this part.

(4) *Independent laboratory inspection.* (i) The inspector must discontinue lot inspection and reject the lot if observation of the records for the lot or of individual lifejackets shows noncompliance with this section or the manufacturer's quality control procedures.

(ii) An inspector may not perform a final lot inspection unless the manufacturer has a current approval certificate.

(iii) If the inspector rejects a lot, the Commandant must be advised immediately.

(iv) The inspector must prepare and sign the inspection record required by § 159.007-13(a) of this chapter and § 160.176-17(b) of this part. If the lot passes, the record must also include the inspector's certification to that effect and a certification that no evidence of noncompliance with this section was observed.

(v) If the lot passes, each lifejacket in the lot must be plainly marked with the words, "Inspected and Passed, (Date), (Inspection Laboratory ID)." This marking must be done in the presence of the inspector. The marking must be permanent and waterproof. The stamp which contains the marking must be kept in the independent laboratory's custody at all times.

(k) *Disposition of rejected lifejacket lot or lifejacket.* (1) A rejected lifejacket lot may be resubmitted for testing, examination or inspection if the manufacturer first removes and destroys each defective lifejacket or, if authorized by the Commandant, reworks the lot to correct the defect.

(2) Any lifejacket rejected in a final lot examination or inspection may be resubmitted for examination or inspection if all defects have been corrected and reexamination or reinspection is authorized by the Commandant.

(3) A rejected lot or rejected lifejacket may not be sold or offered for sale under representation that it meets this subpart or that it is Coast Guard approved.

[CGD 78-1746, 54 FR 50320, Dec. 5, 1989, as amended by CGD 78-174b, 56 FR 29442, June 27, 1991]

§ 160.176-17 Manufacturer records.

(a) Each manufacturer of inflatable lifejackets must keep the records required by § 159.007-13 of this chapter except that they must be retained for at least 120 months after the month in which the inspection or test was conducted.

(b) Each record required by § 159.007-13 of this chapter must also include the following information:

(1) For each test, the serial number of the test instrument used if there is more than one available.

(2) For each test and inspection, the identification of the samples used, the lot number, the approval number, and the number of lifejackets in the lot.

(3) For each lot rejected, the cause for rejection, any corrective action taken, and the final disposition of the lot.

(c) The description or photographs of procedures and apparatus used in testing is not required for the records prescribed in § 159.007–13 of this chapter as long as the manufacturer's procedures and apparatus meet the requirements of this subpart.

(d) Each manufacturer of inflatable lifejackets must also keep the following records:

(1) Records for all materials used in production including the following:

(i) Name and address of the supplier.

(ii) Date of purchase and receipt.

(iii) Lot number.

(iv) Certification meeting § 160.176–8(a)(3) of this part.

(2) A copy of this subpart.

(3) Each document incorporated by reference in § 160.176–4 of this part.

(4) A copy of the approved plans and specifications required by § 160.176–5(a)(2) of this part.

(5) The approval certificate.

(6) Calibration of test equipment, including the identity of the agency performing the calibration, date of calibration, and results.

(7) A listing of current and formerly approved servicing facilities.

(e) The records required by paragraph (d)(1) of this section must be kept for at least 120 months after preparation. All other records required by paragraph (d) of this section must be kept for at least 60 months after the lifejacket approval expires or is terminated.

§ 160.176–19 Servicing.

(a) *General.* This section contains requirements for servicing facilities, manuals, training, guidelines, and records. Other regulations in this chapter require inflatable lifejackets to be serviced at approved facilities at 12 month intervals.

(1) Each manufacturer of an approved inflatable lifejacket must provide one or more Coast Guard approved facilities for servicing those lifejackets. The manufacturer must notify the Commandant whenever an approved facility under its organization no longer provides servicing of a lifejacket make

and model listed in the guidelines required by paragraph (d) of this section.

(2) Each manufacturer of an approved inflatable lifejacket must make replacement parts available to Coast Guard approved independent servicing facilities.

(b) *Servicing facilities.* Each Coast Guard approved servicing facility must meet the requirements of this paragraph and paragraph (d) of this section in order to receive and keep its approval for each make and model of lifejacket. Approval is obtained according to § 160.176–5(c) of this part.

(1) Each servicing facility must conduct lifejacket servicing according to its servicing guidelines and follow the procedures in the service manual required by this section.

(2) Each servicing facility must have a suitable site for servicing which must be clean, well lit, free from excessive dust, drafts, and strong sunlight, and have appropriate temperature and humidity control as specified in the service manual.

(3) Each servicing facility must have the appropriate service, repair, and test equipment and spare parts for performing required tests and repairs.

(4) Each servicing facility must have a current manufacturer's service manual for each make and model of lifejacket serviced.

(5) A servicing facility may have more than one servicing site provided that each site meets the requirements of paragraph (b)(2) of this section.

(6) Each servicing facility must be inspected at intervals not exceeding six months by an accepted independent laboratory, and a report of the inspections must be submitted to the Commandant at least annually. The report must contain enough information to show compliance with paragraphs (b) (1) through (4) of this section and paragraph (d) of this section. Where a facility uses more than one site the report must show compliance at each site at least biennially.

(c) *Service manual.* (1) Each manufacturer of an approved inflatable lifejacket must prepare a service manual for the lifejacket. The service manual must be approved by the Commandant according to § 160.176–5(b) of this part.

(2) The manufacturer must make the service manual, service manual revisions, and service bulletins available to each approved servicing facility.

(3) Each service manual must contain the following:

(i) Detailed procedures for inspecting, servicing, and repackaging the lifejacket.

(ii) A list of approved replacement parts and materials to be used for servicing and repairs, if any.

(iii) A requirement to mark the date and servicing facility name on each lifejacket serviced.

(iv) Frequency of servicing.

(v) Any specific restrictions or special procedures prescribed by the Coast Guard or manufacturer.

(4) Each service manual revision and service bulletin which authorizes the modification of a lifejacket, or which affects a requirement under this subpart, must be approved by the Commandant. Other revisions and service bulletins are not required to be approved, but a copy of each must be sent to the Commandant when it is issued. At least once each year, the manufacturer must provide to the Commandant and to each servicing facility approved to service its lifejackets a bulletin listing each service manual revision and bulletin in effect.

(d) *Servicing facilities guidelines.* Each servicing facility must have written guidelines that include the following:

(1) Identification of each make and model of lifejacket which may be serviced by the facility as well as the manual and revision to be used for servicing.

(2) Identification of the person, by title or position, who is responsible for the servicing program.

(3) Training and qualifications of servicing technicians.

(4) Provisions for the facility to retain a copy of its current letter of approval from the Coast Guard at each site.

(5) Requirements to—

(i) Ensure each inflatable lifejacket serviced under its Coast Guard approval is serviced in accordance with the manufacturer's service manual;

(ii) Keep servicing technicians informed of each approved servicing manual revision and bulletin and en-

sure servicing technicians understand each change and new technique related to the lifejackets serviced by the facility;

(iii) Calibrate each pressure gauge, weighing scale, and mechanically-operated barometer at intervals of not more than one year;

(iv) Ensure each inflatable lifejacket serviced under the facility's Coast Guard approval is serviced by or under the supervision of a servicing technician who meets the requirements of item (3) of this paragraph;

(v) Specify each make and model of lifejacket it is approved to service when it represents itself as approved by the U.S. Coast Guard; and

(vi) Not service any lifejacket for a U.S. registered commercial vessel, unless it is approved by the U.S. Coast Guard to service the make and model of lifejacket.

(e) *Servicing records.* Each servicing facility must maintain records of all completed servicing. These records must be retained for at least 5 years after they are made, be made available to any Coast Guard representative and independent laboratory inspector upon request, and include at least the following:

(1) Date of servicing, number of lifejackets serviced, lot identification, approval number, and test results data for the lifejackets serviced.

(2) Identification of the person conducting the servicing.

(3) Identity of the vessel receiving the serviced lifejackets.

(4) Date of return to the vessel.

§ 160.176–21 User manuals.

(a) The manufacturer must develop a user's manual for each model of inflatable lifejacket. The content of the manual must be provided for approval according to §§ 160.176–5(a)(3)(v) and 160.176–5(b) of this part.

(b) A user's manual must be provided with each lifejacket except that only five manuals need be provided to a single user vessel if more than five lifejackets are carried on board.

(c) Each user's manual must contain in detail the following:

(1) Instructions on use of the lifejacket and replacement of expendable parts.

(2) Procedures for examining serviceability of lifejackets and the frequency of examination.

(3) Pages for logging on board examinations.

(4) Frequency of required servicing at approved servicing facilities.

(5) Instructions, if any, on proper stowage.

(6) Procedures for getting the lifejackets repaired by a servicing facility or the manufacturer.

(7) Procedures for making emergency repairs on board.

(8) Any specific restrictions or special instructions.

§ 160.176–23 Marking.

(a) *General.* Each inflatable lifejacket must be marked with the information required by this section. Each marking must be waterproof, clear, and permanent. Except as provided elsewhere in this subpart, each marking must be readable from a distance of three feet.

(b) *Prominence.* Each marking required in paragraph (d) of this section, except vital care and use instructions, if any, must be less prominent and in smaller print than markings required in paragraph (c) of this section. Each optional marking must be significantly less prominent and smaller than required markings. The marking "ADULT" must be in at least 18 mm (¾ inch) high bold capital lettering. If a lifejacket is stored in a package, the package must also have the marking "ADULT" or this marking must be easily visible through the package.

(c) *Text.* Each inflatable lifejacket must be marked with the following text in the exact order shown:

ADULT—For a person weighing more than 90 pounds.

Type V PFD—Approved for use on (*see paragraph (e) of this section for exact text to be used here*) in lieu of (*see paragraph (f) of this section for exact text to be used here*).

This lifejacket must be serviced, stowed, and used in accordance with (*insert description of service manual and user's manual*).

When fully inflated this lifejacket provides a minimum buoyant force of (*insert the design buoyancy in lb.*).

(d) *Other Information.* Each lifejacket must also be marked with the following information below the text required by paragraph (c) of this section:

(1) U.S. Coast Guard Approval No. (*insert assigned approval number*).

(2) Manufacturer's or private labeler's name and address.

(3) Lot Number.

(4) Date, or year and calendar quarter, of manufacture.

(5) Necessary vital care or use instructions, if any, such as the following:

(i) Warning against dry cleaning.

(ii) Size and type of inflation medium cartridges required.

(iii) Specific donning instructions.

(e) *Approved applications.* The text to be inserted in paragraph (c) of this section as the approved use will be one or more of the following as identified by the Commandant on the approval certificate issued according to § 159.005–13(a)(2) of this chapter:

(1) The name of the vessel.

(2) The type of vessel.

(3) Specific purpose or limitation approved by the Coast Guard.

(f) *Type equivalence.* The exact text to be inserted in paragraph (c) of this section as the approved performance type will be one of the following as identified by the Commandant on the approval certificate:

(1) Type I PFD.

(2) Type V PFD—(*insert exact text of additional description noted on the approval certificate*).

[CGD 78–1746, 54 FR 50320, Dec. 5, 1989, as amended by CGD 78–174b, 56 FR 29442, June 27, 1991]

PART 161—ELECTRICAL EQUIPMENT

Subpart 161.001 [Reserved]

Subpart 161.002—Fire-Protective Systems

AUTHORITY: 46 U.S.C. 3306, 3703, 4302; E.O. 12234, 45 FR 58801, 3 CFR, 1980 Comp., p. 277; 49 CFR 1.46.

Subpart 161.001   [Reserved]

Subpart 161.002—Fire-Protective Systems

SOURCE: 21 FR 9032, Nov. 21, 1956, unless otherwise noted.

§ 161.002-1   Incorporation by reference.

(a) Certain material is incorporated by reference into this subpart with the approval of the Director of the Federal Register under 5 U.S.C. 552(a) and 1 CFR part 51. To enforce any edition other than that specified in paragraph (b) of this section, the Coast Guard must publish notice of change in the FEDERAL REGISTER; and the material must be available to the public. All approved material is available for inspection at the Office of the Federal Register, 800 North Capitol Street NW., suite 700, Washington, DC, and at the U.S. Coast Guard, (G–MSE), 2100 Second Street SW., Washington, DC 20593–0001, and is available from the sources indicated in paragraph (b) of this section.

(b) The material approved for incorporation by reference in this subpart and the sections affected are as follows:

AMERICAN BUREAU OF SHIPPING (ABS)
American Bureau of Shipping, Two World Trade Center, 106th Floor, New York, NY 10048.
Rules for Building and Classing Steel Vessels, 1996—161.002–4(b).

AMERICAN SOCIETY FOR TESTING AND MATERIALS (ASTM)
American Society for Testing and Materials, 100 Barr Harbor Drive, West Conshohocken, PA 19428–2959.
ASTM B 117–95, Standard Practice for Operating Salt Spray (Fog) Apparatus, 1996—161.002–4(b).

FACTORY MUTUAL ENGINEERING AND RESEARCH (FMER)
Factory Mutual Engineering and Research, ATTN: Librarian, 1151 Boston-Providence Turnpike, Norwood, MA 02062.
Class Number 3150: Audible Signal Devices, December, 1974—161.002–4(b).
Class Number 3210: Thermostats for Automatic Fire Detection, July, 1978—161.002–4(b).
Class Number 3230–3250: Smoke Actuated Detectors for Automatic Fire Alarm Signaling, February, 1976—161.002–4(b).

Class Number 3260: Flame Radiation Detectors for Automatic Fire Alarm Signaling, September, 1994—161.002-4(b).

Class Number 3820: Electrical Utilization Equipment, September, 1979—161.002-4(b).

INTERNATIONAL ELECTROTECHNICAL COMMISSION (IEC)

International Electrotechnical Commission, 1, Rue de Varembe, Geneva, Switzerland.

IEC 533, Electromagnetic Compatibility of Electrical and Electronic Installations in Ships, 1977—161.002-4(b).

INTERNATIONAL MARITIME ORGANIZATION (IMO)

International Maritime Organization, Publications Section 4 Albert Embankment, London SE1 7SR, United Kingdom.

International Convention for the Safety of Life at Sea, 1974 (SOLAS 74) Consolidated Edition (Including 1992 Amendments to SOLAS 74, and 1994 Amendments to SOLAS 74), 1992—161.002-4(b).

NATIONAL FIRE PROTECTION ASSOCIATION (NFPA)

National Fire Protection Association, 1 Batterymarch Park, Quincy, MA 02269.

NFPA 72, National Fire Alarm Code, 1993—161.002-4(b).

LLOYD'S REGISTER OF SHIPPING (LR)

Lloyd's Register of Shipping, ATTN: Publications, 17 Battery Place, New York, NY 10004-1195.

LR Type Approval System; Test Specification Number 1, 1990—161.002-4(b).

UNDERWRITERS LABORATORIES, INC. (UL)

Underwriters Laboratories, Inc., 12 Laboratory Drive, Research Triangle Park, NC 27709-3995.

UL 38, Standard for Manually Actuated Signaling Boxes for Use with Fire-Protective Signaling Systems, 1994—161.002-4(b).

UL 268, Standard for Smoke Detectors for Fire Protective Signaling Systems, 1989 (including revisions through June 1994)—161.002-4(b).

UL 521, Standard for Heat Detectors for Fire Protective Signaling Systems, 1993 (including revisions through October 1994)—161.002-4(b).

UL 864, Standard for Control Units for Fire-Protective Signaling Systems, 1991 (including revisions through May 1994)—161.002-4(b).

[CGD 94–108, 61 FR 28291, June 4, 1996; 61 FR 36787, July 12, 1996; 62 FR 23910, May 1, 1997; CGD 97–057, 62 FR 51049, Sept. 30, 1997]]

§161.002-2 Types of fire-protective systems.

(a) *General.* Fire-protective systems covered by this subpart shall include, but not be limited to, automatic fire and smoke detecting systems, manual fire alarm systems, sample extraction smoke detection systems, watchman's supervisory systems, and combinations of these systems.

(b) *Automatic fire detecting systems.* For the purpose of this subpart, automatic fire and smoke detecting systems will be considered to consist of normal and emergency power supplies, a fire detecting control unit, fire detectors, smoke detectors, and audible and visual alarms distinct in both respects from the alarms of any other system not indicating fire.

(c) *Manual fire alarm systems.* For the purpose of this subpart, manual fire alarm systems will be considered to consist of normal and emergency power supplies, a fire alarm control unit, manual fire alarm boxes, and audible and visual alarms distinct in both respects from the alarms of any other system not indicating fire. Manual fire alarm systems are usually combined with automatic fire detecting systems.

(d) *Sample extraction smoke detection systems.* For the purpose of this subpart, Sample extraction smoke detection systems will be considered to consist of a control unit, a blower box, and a piping system to conduct air samples from the protected spaces to the control unit.

(e) *Watchman's supervisory systems.* For the purpose of this subpart, a watchman's supervisory equipment will be considered to be apparatus, either electrical or mechanical, used to verify the presence of watchmen and the regular performance of their assigned duties.

[CGFR 56–39, 21 FR 9032, Nov. 21, 1956, as amended by CGFR 70–143, 35 FR 19966, Dec. 30, 1970; CGD 94–108, 61 FR 28292, June 4, 1996]

§161.002-3 Materials and workmanship.

(a) *Suitability.* All materials used in the construction of fire-protective equipment shall be of the quality best suited for the purpose intended.

(b) *Materials covered by reference specifications.* Where specifications are referred to for a given material, it is intended to require that the quality of material used shall be at least equal to that covered in the reference specifications.

[21 FR 9032, Nov. 21, 1956, as amended by CGD 94–108, 61 FR 28292, June 4, 1996]

§ 161.002–4 General requirements.

(a) *Introduction.* The purpose of fire-protective systems is to give warning of the presence of fire in the protected spaces. To meet this end, the basic requirements of the fire-protective systems are reliability, sturdiness, simplicity of design, ease of servicing, and the ability to withstand shipboard shock and vibration and the adverse effects of sea humidity.

(b) *Standards.* (1) All fire-protective systems must be designed, constructed, tested, marked, and installed according to the applicable standards under § 161.002–1 and subchapter J (Electrical Engineering) of this chapter.

(2) All systems must be listed or certified as meeting these standards by an independent laboratory that is accepted by the Commandant under part 159 of this chapter for the testing and listing or certification of fire detection equipment and systems.

(3) All parts of the system must pass the environmental tests for control and monitoring equipment in either ABS Rules for Building and Classing Steel Vessels Table 4/11.1 or pass the Category ENV3 tests of Lloyd's Register Type Approval System, Test Specification Number 1, as appropriate.

(4) Those parts of the system that are to be installed in locations requiring exceptional degrees of protection must also pass the salt spray (mist) test in either ABS Rules for Building and Classing Steel Vessels Table 4/11.1; Category ENV3 of Lloyd's Register Type Approval System, Test Specification No. 1; or ASTM B–117 with results as described in corrosion-resistant finish in § 110.15–1 of this chapter.

[21 FR 9032, Nov. 21, 1956, as amended by CGD 94–108, 61 FR 28292, June 4, 1996; 62 FR 23910, May 1, 1997]

§ 161.002–8 Automatic fire detecting systems, general requirements.

(a) *General.* An automatic fire detecting system shall consist of a power supply; a control unit on which are located visible and audible fire and trouble signalling devices; and fire detector circuits, as required, originating from the control unit. Power failure alarm devices may be separately housed from the control unit and may be combined with other power failure alarm systems when specifically approved.

(b) [Reserved]

[21 FR 9032, Nov. 21, 1956, as amended by CGD 94–108, 61 FR 28292, June 4, 1996]

§ 161.002–9 Automatic fire detecting system, power supply.

The power supply for an automatic fire detecting system must meet the requirements of § 113.10–9 of subchapter J (Electrical Engineering Regulations) of this chapter.

[CGD 74 FR 125a, 47 FR 15279, Apr. 8, 1982]

§ 161.002–10 Automatic fire detecting system control unit.

(a) *General.* The fire detecting system control unit shall consist of a dripproof enclosed panel containing visible and audible fire alarm signalling devices, visible and audible trouble alarm signalling devices, visible and audible power failure alarm devices, power supply transfer switch, charging equipment when employed, and overcurrent protection for power supplies.

(b) *Fire alarms*—(1) *General.* The operation of a fire detecting and alarm system must cause automatically—

(i) The sounding of a vibrating type fire bell with a gong diameter not smaller than 15 cm (6 inches) or other audible alarm that has an equivalent sound level and that is mounted at the control unit and at the remote annunciator panel, when provided;

(ii) The sounding of a vibrating type fire bell with a gong diameter not smaller than 20 cm (8 inches) or other audible alarm that has an equivalent sound level and that is located in the engine room; and

(iii) an indication of the fire detecting zone from which the signal originated, visible at the control unit and at the remote annunciator panel, when provided;

(2) *Maintaining alarm.* The audible and visible alarms resulting from the operation of a fire detector having self-restoring contacts shall be maintained automatically by the control unit until a resetting device is operated manually.

(3) *Silencing audible alarm.* Manual means shall be provided at the control unit to silence the audible fire alarms,

but operation of the audible fire alarm device shall permit the visible fire alarm to remain until manually reset as described in paragraph (b)(2) of this section.

(4) *Non-interference.* The control unit shall be so arranged as to permit one or any number of fire alarms simultaneously, and an alarm on one circuit shall not interfere with the normal operation of any other circuit, except that the audible fire alarms, when silenced by the means provided by paragraph (b)(3) of this section, need not sound upon receipt of succeeding sensor signals.

(5) *Source of energy.* The source of energy for the alarms referred to in this paragraph shall be the "normal source". On a system supplied by duplicate storage batteries, the "normal source" shall be construed to mean that part of the supply circuit on the load side of the battery transfer switch and fuses. On a system supplied by a branch circuit the "normal source" shall be construed to mean the load side of any transformer or rectifier employed to modify the nature or magnitude of the supply potential.

(c) *Electrical supervision*—(1) *Circuits.* The circuits formed by conductors extending from the control unit to the fire detectors of each zone shall be electrically supervised.

(2) *Normal source.* The normal source of energy to the control unit shall be electrically supervised.

(3) *Audible fire alarms.* The engine room audible fire alarm shall be electrically supervised.

(d) *Power failure alarms*—(1) *Loss of potential.* The loss of potential from a supervised normal source of energy automatically shall be indicated at the control unit by the sounding of an audible power failure alarm. The source of energy for the alarm shall be the emergency power source. The source of energy for the alarm of a system supplied by duplicate storage batteries shall be the storage battery being charged.

(2) *Silencing audible alarm.* Means shall be provided at the control unit to silence the audible power failure alarm by transferring the signal to a visible indicator which shall remain until the

silencing means is restored to its normal position.

(e) *Trouble alarms*—(1) *Open Circuit.* An open circuit occurring in either supervised circuit covered by paragraph (c) (1) or (3) of this section shall automatically be indicated at the control unit by the sounding of an audible trouble alarm and by a visual indicator showing the circuit or zone from which the signal originated except that on systems employing closed-circuit series connected detectors, an open circuit in the zone wiring may cause a fire alarm.

(2) *Silencing audible alarm.* Manual means shall be provided at the control unit to silence the audible alarm. Operation of the silencing means shall permit the visible alarm to remain until the trouble has been corrected.

(3) *Non-interference.* The control unit shall be so arranged as to permit one or any number of trouble alarms simultaneously, and an alarm on one circuit shall not interfere with the normal operation of any other circuit, except that the audible trouble alarm, when silenced by the means provided by paragraph (e)(2) of this section, need not sound on receipt of succeeding trouble signals.

(4) *Source of energy.* The source of energy for the trouble alarms required by this paragraph shall be the normal source as defined in paragraph (b)(5) of this section.

(f) *Circuit testing*—(1) *Fire alarm and trouble alarm test.* Means shall be provided at the control unit for individually testing each fire detecting zone circuit. The testing means shall be capable of simulating a fire condition and a trouble condition.

(2) *Ground test.* Means shall be provided at the control unit for manual testing of each individual fire detecting zone circuit for the presence of grounds. Systems whose normal source of supply is derived from a circuit from the ship's alternating-current temporary emergency bus shall be provided with a two-winding transformer in the supply circuit and located in the control unit to isolate electrically the fire detecting system from the ship's electrical system.

(g) *Power supply transfer switch.* An automatic transfer switch with no "off" position shall be provided in the control unit for selecting the source of power, except that systems employing duplicate storage batteries may be provided with a manual transfer switch.

(1) *Automatic transfer switch.* Upon reduction of potential from the normal power source of 15 to 20 percent, the automatic fire detection system shall automatically be disconnected from the normal source and connected to the emergency source. Upon restoration of potential from the normal source of 85 to 95 percent of normal valves, the automatic fire detection system shall automatically be transferred back to normal source.

(2) *Manual transfer switch.* Automatic fire detecting systems employing duplicate storage batteries as the power supplies shall be provided with a manual transfer switch with no "off" position to select the battery to supply the system and the battery to be charged.

(h) *Automatic fire detecting system, battery charging and control*—(1) *General.* Automatic fire detecting systems employing duplicate storage batteries as the power supply shall be provided with battery charging and control facilities as specified by this paragraph.

(2) *Transfer switch.* A manual transfer switch shall be provided in accordance with paragraph (g)(2) of this section.

(3) *Voltmeter and voltmeter switch.* A voltmeter and a voltmeter switch shall be provided at the control unit and connected to read (i) voltage of battery supplying system and (ii) voltage of battery on charge.

(4) *Ammeter.* An ammeter shall be provided to indicate the charging current to the battery on charge.

(5) *Reverse current protection.* An undervoltage or reverse current relay shall be provided to disconnect the battery on charge from the charging source in the event of loss of potential from the charging source unless reverse current flow is effectively blocked by a rectifier.

(6) *Resistors.* Fixed and variable resistors shall be provided to regulate the charging rate, together with a two-position switch to select between a normal charging rate and a high charging rate.

(7) *Overcurrent protection.* The batteries shall be protected against overcurrent by fuses rated at not less than 150 percent and not more than 200 percent of the maximum normal battery load.

(8) *Location.* The equipment required by this paragraph shall be located in or adjacent to the control unit.

[CGFR 56–39, 21 FR 9035, Nov. 21, 1956, as amended by CGFR 70–143, 35 FR 19666, Dec. 30, 1970; CGD 94–108, 61 FR 49691, Sept. 23, 1996]

§ 161.002–12 Manual fire alarm systems.

(a) *General.* A manual fire alarm system shall consist of a power supply, a control unit on which are located visible and audible fire and trouble alarms, and fire alarm circuits as required originating from the control unit and terminating at manual fire alarm boxes. Power failure alarm devices may be separately housed from the control unit and may be combined with other power failure alarm systems when specifically approved.

(b) *Types.* Manual fire alarm systems shall be one of the following types, or a combination of several types:

(1) Manual fire alarm stations superimposed on and connected as an integral part of the fire detector circuit wiring of an automatic fire detection system.

(2) Electrical system using manually operated fire alarm boxes.

(3) Other types as may be developed.

(c) *Power supply.* The power supply shall be as specified for automatic fire detecting system by § 161.002–9.

(d) *Manual fire alarm system control unit.* The manual fire alarm system control unit shall be as specified for automatic fire detecting systems by § 161.002–10.

[21 FR 9032, Nov. 21, 1956, as amended by CGD 94–108, 61 FR 28292, June 4, 1996]

§ 161.002–14 Watchman's supervisory systems.

(a) *General.* The watchman's supervisory system shall consist of apparatus to verify the presence of watchmen and the regular performance of their assigned duties.

(b) *Types.* The watchman's supervisory systems shall be one of the following types, or a combination of several types:

(1) A mechanical system consisting of portable spring-motor-driven recording clocks in conjunction with key stations located along the prescribed routes of the watchmen to operate the clock recording mechanism.

(2) An electrical system employing a recorder located at a central station in conjunction with key stations along the prescribed route of the watchmen.

(3) Other types that may be developed.

(c) *Portable spring-motor-driven recording clocks.* (1) Each clock shall run for at least one week without rewinding and shall be substantially mounted and strongly encased. It shall be made so that the recordings cannot be seen without opening the case and so that the case cannot be opened without indicating, by a distinctive recording, the time of opening and closing.

(2) The records of the recording watch clock shall be legible and permanent.

(d) *Key stations for use with portable recording watch clocks.* (1) The key station shall be of substantial construction and provided with a hinged cover. The key shall be attached to the station by means of a strong link chain. The key stations shall be mounted in such a manner that they cannot be removed without giving evidence of removal.

(2) Keys shall be made so that they are difficult to duplicate, and shall be of a pattern susceptible of variations tending to reduce the probability that a set of keys for one clock will operate other clocks.

[21 FR 9032, Nov. 21, 1956, as amended by CGFR 59-7, 24 FR 3241, Apr. 25, 1959]

§ 161.002-15 Sample extraction smoke detection systems.

The smoke detecting system must consist of a means for continuously exhausting an air sample from the protected spaces and testing the air for contamination with smoke, together with visual and audible alarms for indicating the presence of smoke.

[CGD 94-108, 61 FR 28292, June 4, 1996]

§ 161.002-17 Equivalents.

The Commandant may approve any arrangement, fitting, appliance, apparatus, equipment, calculation, information, or test that provides a level of safety equivalent to that established by specific provisions of this subpart. Requests for approval must be submitted to Commandant (G-MSE). If necessary, the Commandant may require engineering evaluations and tests to demonstrate the equivalence of the substitute.

[CGD 94-108, 61 FR 28292, June 4, 1996]

§ 161.002-18 Method of application for type approval.

(a) The manufacturer must submit the following material to Commandant (G-MSE), U.S. Coast Guard Headquarters, 2100 Second Street SW., Washington, DC 20593-0001:

(1) A formal written request that the system be reviewed for approval.

(2) Three copies of the system's instruction manual, including information concerning installation, programming, operation, and troubleshooting.

(3) One copy of the complete test report generated by an independent laboratory accepted by the Commandant under part 159 of this chapter for the testing and listing or certification of fire-protective systems. A current list of these facilities may be obtained from the address in this section.

(4) Three copies of a list prepared by the manufacturer that contains the name, model number, and function of each major component and accessory, such as the main control cabinet, remote annunicator cabinet, detector, zone card, isolator, central processing unit, zener barrier, special purpose module, or power supply. This list must be identified by the following information assigned by the manufacturer:

(i) A document number.

(ii) A revision number (the original submission being revision number 0).

(iii) The date that the manufacturer created or revised the list.

(b) The Coast Guard distributes a copy of the approved instruction manual to the manufacturer and to the Coast Guard Marine Safety Center (MSC).

(c) The manufacturer shall maintain an account of the equipment offered for approval. The list identification information in paragraphs (a)(4)(i) through (a)(4)(iii) of this section appears on the Certificate of Approval and indicates the official compilation of components for the approved system. If the manufacturer seeks to apply subsequently for the approval of a revision (because of, for example, additional accessories becoming available, replacements to obsolete components, or a change in materials or standards of safety), changes to the approved list must be submitted for review and approval.

(d) To apply for a revision, the manufacturer must submit—

(1) A written request under paragraph (a) of this section;

(2) An updated list under paragraph (b) of this section; and

(3) A report by an independent laboratory accepted by the Commandant under part 159 of this chapter for the testing and listing or certification of fire-protective systems indicating compliance with the standards and compatibility with the system.

(e) If the Coast Guard approves the system or a revision to a system, it issues a certificate, normally valid for a 5-year term, containing the information in paragraphs (a)(4)(i) through (a)(4)(iii) of this section.

[CGD 94-108, 61 FR 28292, June 4, 1996]

Subpart 161.006—Searchlights, Motor Lifeboat, for Merchant Vessels

SOURCE: CGFR 49-43, 15 FR 127, Jan. 11, 1950, unless otherwise noted.

§ 161.006-1 Applicable specifications.

(a) The following specifications, of the issue in effect on the date motor lifeboat searchlights are manufactured, form a part of this subpart:

(1) Navy Department specifications:

42S5—Screws, machine, cap and set, and nuts.

43B11—Bolts, nuts, studs, and tap-rivets (and materials for same).

(2) Federal specification:

QQ-B-611—Brass, Commercial; bars, plates, rods, shapes, sheets, and strip.

(3) A.S.T.M. standards:

B117-44T—Method of salt spray (fog), testing (tentative).

B141-45—Specification for electrodeposited coatings of nickel and chromium on copper, and copper-base alloys.

(4) Underwriters' Laboratories, Inc.:

Standard for flexible cord and fixture wire, third edition, October, 1935.

(b) Copies of the above specifications shall be kept on file by the manufacturer, together with the approved plans and certificate of approval.

§ 161.006-2 Type.

(a) The motor lifeboat searchlight shall be of the incandescent type equipped with a lamp of approximately 90 watts of proper voltage for use with the electric power installation of the lifeboat, usually a 12-volt radio storage battery.

(b) [Reserved]

§ 161.006-3 Materials and workmanship.

(a) *Materials.* The materials shall be of best quality and suitable in every respect for the purpose intended. All materials shall be corrosion resistant. The use of acid flux in making joints shall not be permitted.

(b) *Workmanship.* The workmanship shall be first class in every respect.

§ 161.006-4 Requirements.

(a) *Corrosion-resisting materials.* Silver, corrosion-resisting steel, copper, brass, bronze and copper-nickel alloys are considered satisfactory corrosion-resistant materials within the intent of this subpart.

(b) *Searchlight parts.* The motor lifeboat searchlight shall, in general consist of the following parts:

Yoke and pedestal.
Housing.
Front door.
Reflector.
Lamp socket.
Supply cable.

(c) *Weight and dimensions.* The height of the motor lifeboat searchlight shall not exceed 19 inches and the weight shall not exceed 16 pounds, unless otherwise approved.

(d) *Wiring.* The motor lifeboat searchlight shall be wired with a five-foot length of rubber-jacketed hard service flexible cord, Underwriters' Laboratories, Inc., Type S, or equivalent, of a size not less than No. 16 AWG. At the point where the cable enters the searchlight, a waterproof entrance bushing with packing gland and cord grip shall be provided.

(e) *Lamp and socket.* The motor lifeboat searchlight shall be provided with a lamp of not less than 80 watts nor more than 100 watts, and a suitable lamp socket. Means shall be provided for adjusting and securing the lamp socket at any position between the focal point and a point not less than ¼ inch away from the focal point in either direction in the axis of the beam.

(f) *Housing.* The housing shall be constructed of brass, Federal Specification QQ–B–611, Composition E, copper alloy, or other suitable corrosion-resistant material as approved, of a thickness not less than No. 20 AWG. The housing shall be capable of free movement of at least 60 degrees above and 20 degrees below the horizontal, and of a free movement of 360 degrees in a horizontal plane. It shall be possible to lock the barrel in any desired position, vertically or horizontally, without the use of tools. A sturdy metal hand grip shall be provided at the back of the housing for housing-adjusting purposes.

(g) *Front door.* A front door shall be attached to the housing in such a manner that it can be readily opened or removed, without the use of tools, for the purpose of relamping. The door, when closed, shall be waterproof. Clear front door glass shall be used.

(h) *Reflector.* The reflector shall be paraboloidal. It shall be constructed of brass, Federal Specification QQ–B–611 Composition E, finished and with electroplated coatings of nickel and chromium in accordance with A.S.T.M. Specification B141–45, Type K. C., or as otherwise approved. The reflector shall furnish a minimum average illumination of 100 foot candles, when measured as specified in §161.006–5 (b) (2).

(i) *Yoke and pedestal.* The yoke and pedestal shall be of rugged construction. The pedestal shall be suitable for bolting to a flat surface with not less than four ⅜-inch diameter bolts.

(j) *Beam spread.* The beam shall be at least 60 feet in diameter at 200 yards. The edge of the beam shall be defined as a point at which the intensity of the light is 10 percent of the maximum intensity.

(k) *Bolts, nuts, and screws.* Bolts and nuts shall conform to the requirements of Navy Department Specification 43B11. Screws shall conform to the requirements of Navy Department Specification 42S5.

(l) *Name plate.* The motor lifeboat searchlight shall be provided with a permanent metallic name plate giving the name of manufacturer, type designation, and drawing number.

§161.006–5 Sampling, inspections and tests.

(a) *General.* Motor lifeboat searchlights specified by this subpart are not inspected at regularly scheduled factory inspections of production lots, but the Commander of the Coast Guard District may detail an inspector at any time to visit any place where such searchlights are manufactured to check materials and construction methods and to conduct such tests and examinations as may be required to satisfy himself that the searchlights are being manufactured in compliance with the requirements of this specification and with the manufacturer's plans and specifications approved by the Commandant.

(b) *Methods of test*—(1) *Waterproof test.* The searchlight shall be subjected for 5 minutes to a stream of water under a head of approximately 35 feet from a hose not less than 1 inch in diameter from a distance of approximately 10 feet. The hose nozzle shall be adjusted to give a solid stream at the enclosure. No leakage shall occur in this test.

(2) *Beam candlepower.* All light except that produced from the searchlight under test shall be excluded from the room in which measurements are made. The searchlight shall be operated at rated voltage with a seasoned lamp as specified in §161.006–4(e). Measurements of beam candlepower shall be made at the corners of a 6-inch square located in the center of the beam at a distance of 32 feet immediately in front of the searchlight.

(3) *Corrosion resistance.* The searchlight shall be subjected to a 200-hour salt spray test in accordance with A. S. T. M. Standard B117–44T. There shall be no evidence of corrosion that will be

279

detrimental to the operation of the searchlight.

(4) *Heat run.* The searchlight, completely assembled, shall be operated continuously for 2 hours at rated voltage following which the waterproof test shall be conducted. This cycle shall be repeated 3 times. The ambient temperature shall be approximately 25 °C. The water stream shall be from an ordinary cold water tap.

§ 161.006–6 Procedure for approval.

(a) *General.* Motor lifeboat searchlights are approved only by the Commandant, United States Coast Guard, Washington, DC, 20226. Correspondence relating to the subject matter of this specification shall be addressed to the Commander of the Coast Guard District in which the factory is located.

(b) *Manufacturer's plans and specifications.* In order to obtain approval of motor lifeboat searchlights, submit detailed plans and specifications, including a complete bill of material, assembly drawings, and parts drawings descriptive of the arrangement and construction of the device, to the Commander of the Coast Guard District in which the factory is located. Each drawing shall have an identifying drawing number, date, and an identification of the device; and the general arrangement for assembly drawing shall include a list of all drawings applicable, together with drawing numbers and alteration numbers. The manufacturer will be advised whether or not the drawings and specifications appear satisfactory or what corrections appear necessary and then he may proceed with the construction of the pre-approval sample in accordance therewith. The pre-approval sample, together with four copies of the plans and specifications corrected as may be required, shall be forwarded to the Commandant via the Commander of the Coast Guard District in which the factory is located for inspection and tests. The cost of the tests is to be borne by the manufacturer.

Subpart 161.008 [Reserved]

Subpart 161.010—Floating Electric Waterlight

SOURCE: CGD 85–208, 54 FR 27020, June 27, 1989, unless otherwise noted.

§ 161.010–1 Incorporation by reference.

(a) Certain materials are incorporated by reference into this part with the approval of the Director of the Federal Register in accordance with 5 U.S.C. 552(a). To enforce any edition other than the one listed in paragraph (b) of this section, notice of change must be published in the FEDERAL REGISTER and the material made available to the public. All approved material is on file at the Office of the Federal Register, 800 North Capitol Street, NW., suite 700, Washington, DC, and at the U.S. Coast Guard, Office of Design and Engineering Standards (G–MSE), 2100 Second Street SW., Washington, DC 20593–0001, and is available from the sources indicated in paragraph (b) of this section.

(b) The material approved for incorporation by reference in this part, and the sections affected are:

UNDERWRITERS LABORATORIES, INC.
12 Laboratory Drive, Research Triangle Park, NC 27709–3995
ANSI/UL 1196, Standard for Floating Waterlights, Second Edition March 23, 1987. 161.010–2; 161.010–4

[CGD 85–208, 54 FR 27020, June 27, 1989, as amended by CGD 95–072, 60 FR 50467, Sept. 29, 1995; CGD 96–041, 61 FR 50733, Sept. 27, 1996; CGD 97ndash;057, 62 FR 51049, Sept. 30, 1997]]

§ 161.010–2 Design, Construction, and Test Requirements.

Each floating electric waterlight shall meet the requirements of ANSI/UL 1196.

§ 161.010–3 Inspections and methods of test.

(a) Each inspection and test report required by this subpart shall comply with § 159.005–11 of this chapter.

(b) The U.S. Coast Guard reserves the right to make any inspection or test it deems necessary to determine the conformance of the materials and equipment to this subpart.

(c) The facilities, materials, and labor for all tests shall be furnished at no cost to the U.S. Coast Guard.

§161.010–4 Procedure for approval.

(a) A request for approval of an automatic floating electric waterlight must be submitted to the Commandant (G–MSE), U.S. Coast Guard, 2100 Second Street SW., Washington, DC 20593–0001.

(b) All inspections and tests must be performed by an independent laboratory which meets the requirements of §159.010–3 of this chapter. A list of independent laboratories accepted by the Coast Guard as meeting §159.010–3 of this chapter may be obtained by contacting the Commandant (G–MSE).

(c) Each request for approval must contain;

(1) The name and address of the applicant,

(2) One copy of all plans and specifications that meet the requirements of §159.005–12 of this chapter,

(3) A pre-approval sample of the waterlight,

(4) An inspection and test report verifying compliance with the construction and test requirements of ANSI/UL 1196, and

(5) A statement by the manufacturer certifying that the waterlight complies with the requirements of this subpart.

[CGD 85–208, 54 FR 27020, June 27, 1989, as amended by CGD 95–072, 60 FR 50467, Sept. 29, 1995; CGD 96–041, 61 FR 50734, Sept. 27, 1996]

Subpart 161.011—Emergency Position Indicating Radiobeacons

§161.011–1 Purpose.

This subpart prescribes approval requirements for emergency position indicating radiobeacons (EPIRB).

[39 FR 10139, Mar. 18, 1974]

§161.011–5 Classes.

EPIRB's are classed as follows:

(a) Class A—an EPIRB that has been type approved or type accepted by the FCC as a Class A EPIRB. These EPIRB's are capable of floating free of a vessel and activating automatically if the vessel sinks.

(b) Class C—An EPIRB that has been type approved or type accepted by the FCC as a Class C EPIRB. These EPIRB's are manually activated and are not required to be Coast Guard approved.

[39 FR 10139, Mar. 18, 1974, as amended by CGD 80–024, 49 FR 40409, Oct. 16, 1984]

§161.011–10 EPIRB approval.

(a) The Coast Guard approves the class of EPIRB's listed in §161.011–5(a) of this subpart.

(b) An application for type approval or type acceptance of an EPIRB should be submitted to the FCC in accordance with Title 47 of the Code of Federal Regulations, Part 2. When requested by the FCC, the Coast Guard reviews the test results in the application that concern installation and automatic operation (if required) of the EPIRB. The Coast Guard provides the results of the review to the manufacturer, and to the FCC for its use in acting upon the application.

(c) Upon notification of the FCC type acceptance or type approval, the Commandant (G–MSE) issues a certificate of approval for the EPIRB.

[CGD 80–024, 49 FR 40409, Oct. 16, 1984, as amended by CGD 95–072, 60 FR 50467, Sept. 29, 1995; CGD 96–041, 61 FR 50734, Sept. 27, 1996]

Subpart 161.012—Personal Flotation Device Lights

SOURCE: CGD 76–028, 44 FR 38785, July 2, 1979, unless otherwise noted.

§161.012–1 Scope.

(a) This subpart prescribes construction and performance requirements, approval and production tests, and procedures for approving personal flotation device lights fitted on Coast Guard approved life preservers, buoyant vests, and other personal flotation devices.

(b) [Reserved]

§161.012–3 Definitions.

(a) As used in this subpart, *PFD* means Coast Guard approved personal flotation device.

(b) For the purpose of §161.012–7, *storage life* means the amount of time after the date of manufacture of the power source of a light that the power source can be stored under typical marine environmental conditions on a vessel and still have sufficient power for the light to meet the requirements of § 161.012–9.

§ 161.012–5   Approval procedures.

(a) An application for approval of a PFD light under this subpart must be sent to the Commandant (G–MSE), U.S. Coast Guard, Washington, DC 20593–0001.

(b) Each application for approval must contain—(1) The name and address of the applicant;

(2) Two copies of plans showing the construction details of the light;

(3) A detailed description of the applicant's production testing program; and

(4) A laboratory test report containing the observations and results of approval testing.

(c) The Commandant advises the applicant whether the light is approved. If the light is approved, an approval certificate is sent to the applicant.

[CGD 76–028, 44 FR 38785, July 2, 1979, as amended by CGD 88–070, 53 FR 34536, Sept. 7, 1988; CGD 95–072, 60 FR 50467, Sept. 29, 1995; CGD 96–041, 61 FR 50734, Sept. 27, 1996]

§ 161.012–7   Construction.

(a) Each light must be designed to be attached to a PFD without damaging the PFD or interfering with its performance.

(b) Each light and its power source must be designed to be removed and replaced without causing damage to the PFD.

(c) The storage life of the power source of a light must be twice as long as the period between the date of manufacture and the expiration date of the power source.

(d) Each light, prior to activation, must be capable of preventing leakage from its container of any chemicals it contains or produces.

(e) Each component of a light must be designed to remain serviceable in a marine environment for at least as long as the storage life of the light's power source.

(f) No light may have a water pressure switch.

(g) Each light must be designed so that when attached to a PFD, its light beam, at a minimum, is visible in an arc of 180 degrees above or in front of the wearer.

(h) Each light, including its power source, must fit into a cylindrical space that is 150 mm (6 in.) long and 75 mm (3 in.) in diameter.

(i) Each light, including its power source, must not weigh more than 225g (8 oz.).

(j) Each light that is designed to operate while detached from a PFD must have a lanyard that can be used to connect it to the PFD. The lanyard must be at least 750 mm (30 in.) long.

(k) Each light designed to operate while detached from a PFD must be capable of floating in water with its light source at or above the surface of the water.

§ 161.012–9   Performance.

(a) If a light is a flashing light, its flash rate when first activated, or within five minutes thereafter, must be between 50 and 70 flashes per minute.

(b) Each light must—(1) Begin to shine within 2 minutes after activation; and

(2) Within 5 minutes after activation be capable of being seen from a distance of at least one nautical mile on a dark clear night.

(c) Each light must be designed to operate underwater continuously for at least 8 hours at a water temperature of 15°±5 °C (59°±9 °F). However, if the light needs air to operate, underwater operation is required only for 50 or more seconds during each minute of the eight hour period.

(d) Each light must be designed to operate both in sea water and in fresh water.

(e) A light that concentrates its light beam by means of a lens or curved reflector must not be a flashing light.

(f) Each light must be designed to operate in accordance with this section after storage for 24 hours at a temperature of 65°±2 °C (149°±44 °F), and after storage for 24 hours at −30°±2 °C (−22°±4 °F).

§ 161.012–11   Approval tests.

(a) The approval tests described in this section must be conducted for each light submitted for Coast Guard approval. The tests must be conducted by a laboratory that has the equipment, personnel, and procedures necessary to conduct the approval tests required by this subpart, and that is free of influence and control of the applicant and other manufacturers, suppliers, and vendors of PFD lights.

(b) A sample light must be activated at night under clear atmospheric conditions. However, two lights must be used if the power source is water activated, and one light must be activated in fresh water and the other in salt water having the approximate salinity of sea water. The light, or lights, must begin to shine within 2 minutes after activation and, within 5 minutes after activation, must be seen from a distance of at least one nautical mile against a dark background.

(c) At least ten sample lights must be selected at random from a group of at least 25. Each sample light must be kept at a constant temperature of 65°±2 °C (149°±4 °F) for 24 hours. Each sample light must then be kept at a constant temperature of minus 30°±2 °C (minus 22°±4 °F) for 24 hours. Five samples must then be submerged in salt water having the approximate salinity of sea water and the five other samples must be submerged in fresh water. The temperature of the water must be 15°±5 °C (59°±9 °F). The lights must then be activated and left submerged for eight hours. However, if their power sources need a supply of air to operate, the lights may be brought to their normal operating positions at the surface of the water for up to 10 seconds per minute during the eight hour period. At least nine of the ten lights must operate continuously over the eight hour period. If the lights are flashing lights, at least nine of ten must have a flash rate of between 50 and 70 flashes per minute when first activated or within five minutes thereafter.

(d) Individual tests must be conducted on a sample light to determine whether the light meets the requirements of §161.012–7, except that technical data showing compliance with §160.012–7(c) may be submitted with the application for approval in lieu of performing an individual test.

§161.012–13 Production tests and inspections.

(a) The manufacturer of approved lights must randomly select a sample of ten lights from each lot of lights produced. Each lot must not exceed 1,000 lights. At least nine of the ten lights, when tested in accordance with the test described in §161.012–11(c), must meet the test criteria prescribed by that section. If less than nine lights meet the test criteria, another random sample of ten lights must be taken and tested. If less than nine of these lights meet the test criteria, none of the lights in the lot may be sold as Coast Guard approved equipment.

(b) The Coast Guard does not inspect lights approved under this subpart on a regular schedule. However, the Commandant may select samples and conduct tests and examinations whenever necessary to determine whether the lights are being manufactured in compliance with the requirements in this subpart.

§161.012–15 Markings.

(a) Each light manufactured under Coast Guard approval must be permanently and legibly marked with:

(1) The manufacturer's name or trade mark that clearly identifies the model designation;

(2) The Coast Guard approval number asssigned to light; and

(3) Instructions on how to activate the light.

(b) The power source of each light must be permanently and legibly marked with its date of manufacture and expiration date. Each date must include the month and year.

§161.012–17 Instructions.

(a) Each light must have instructions on how to attach it to a PFD in a manner that complies with §161.012–7(a). However, in the case of lights that are to be attached by a PFD manufacturer, only one set of instructions need be provided for each shipment of lights.

(b) If a light is designed to be attached to a finished PFD, any attachment materials that are not supplied with the light must be clearly identified in the instructions. If a light is to

283

be attached to a finished PFD by a PFD purchaser, any attachment materials not supplied with the light must be generally available for purchase.

(c) Each set of instructions must—(1) Clearly identify the kind of PFD construction (for example fabric covered or vinyl dipped) to which the light can be attached; and

(2) Not require penetration of the bouyant material of the PFD.

Subpart 161.013—Electric Distress Light for Boats

SOURCE: CGD 76-183a, 44 FR 73054, Dec. 17, 1979, unless otherwise noted.

§ 161.013-1 Applicability.

(a) This subpart establishes standards for electric distress lights for boats.

(b) [Reserved]

§ 161.013-3 General performance requirements.

(a) Each electric light must:

(1) Emit a white light which meets the intensity requirements of § 161.013-5;

(2) Be capable of automatic signaling in a manner which meets the requirements of § 161.013-7;

(3) Contain an independent power source which meets the requirements of § 161.013-9;

(4) Float in fresh water with the lens surface at or above the surface of the water;

(5) Be equipped with a waterproof switch; and

(6) Meet the requirement of paragraphs (a) (1) through (4) of this section after floating for at least 72 hours followed by submersion in 5% by weight sodium chloride solution for at least 2 hours.

(b) The electric light may not be equipped with a switch mechanism which permits continuous display of a beam of light except that the light may be equipped with a switch which returns to the off position when pressure is released.

§ 161.013-5 Intensity requirements.

(a) If an electric light emits light over an arc of the horizon of 360 degrees, the light must:

(1) When level, have a peak intensity within 0.1 degrees of the horizontal plane;

(2) Have a peak Equivalent Fixed Intensity of at least 75 cd; and,

(3) Have a minimum Equivalent Fixed Intensity within a vertical divergence of ±3 degrees of at least 15 cd.

(b) If an electric light emits a directional beam of light, the light must:

(1) Have an Equivalent Fixed Intensity of no less than 25 cd within ±4 degrees vertical and ±4 degrees horizontal divergence centered about the peak intensity; and,

(2) Have a minimum peak Equivalent Fixed Intensity of 2,500 cd.

(c) The Equivalent Fixed Intensity (EFI) is the intensity of the light corrected for the length of the flash and is determined by the formula:

$$EFI = I \times (t_c - t_1) / 0.2 + (t_c - t_1)$$

Where:

I is the measured intensity of the fixed beam,

t_c is the contact closure time in seconds, (0.33 for this S-O-S signal), and

t_1 is the incandescence time of the lamp in seconds.

(d) An electric light which meets the requirements of either paragraph (a) or (b) of this section need not, if capable of operating in both manners, meet the requirements of the other paragraph.

§ 161.013-7 Signal requirements.

(a) An electric light must have a flash characteristic of the International Morse Code for S-O-S and, under design conditions,

(1) Each short flash must have a duration of ⅓ second;

(2) Each long flash must have a duration of 1 second;

(3) The dark period between each short flash must have a duration of ⅓ second;

(4) The dark period between each long flash must have a duration of ⅓ second;

(5) The dark period between each letter must have a duration of 2 seconds;

(6) The dark period between each

S-O-S signal must have a duration of 3 seconds.

(b) The flash characteristics described in paragraph (a) must be produced automatically when the signal is activated.

§ 161.013–9 Independent power source.

(a) Each independent power source must be capable of powering the light so that it meets the requirements of § 161.013–3(a)(1) and emits a recognizable flash characteristic of the International Morse Code for S-O-S at a rate of between 3 and 5 times per minute after six hours of continuous display of the signal.

(b) If the independent power source is rechargeable, it must have a waterproof recharger designed for marine use.

(c) If the independent power source requires external water to form an electrolyte, it must operate in sea water and fresh water.

§ 161.013–11 Prototype test.

(a) Each manufacturer must test a prototype light identical to the lights to be certified prior to the labeling required by § 161.013–13.

(b) If the prototype light fails to meet any of the general performance requirements of § 161.013–3 the lights must not be certified under this subpart.

(c) Each manufacturer must:

(1) Forward the test results within 30 days to the Commandant (G–MSE), U. S. Coast Guard, Washington, DC 20593–0001; and

(2) Retain records of the test results for at least 5 years, or as long as the light is manufactured and certified, whichever is longer.

[CGD 76–183a, 44 FR 73054, Dec. 17, 1979, as amended by CGD 88–070, 53 FR 34536, Sept. 7, 1988; CGD 95–072, 60 FR 50467, Sept. 29, 1995; CGD 96–041, 61 FR 50734, Sept. 27, 1996]

§ 161.013–13 Manufacturer certification and labeling.

(a) Each electric light intended as a Night Visual Distress Signal required by 33 CFR part 175 must be certified by the manufacturer as complying with the requirements of this subpart.

(b) Each electric light must be legibly and indelibly marked with:

(1) Manufacturer's name;

(2) Replacement battery type;

(3) Lamp size; and

(4) The following words—

"Night Visual Distress Signal for Boats Complies with U. S. Coast Guard Requirements in 46 CFR 161.013. For Emergency Use Only."

(c) If an electric light is designed for use with dry cell batteries the label must advise the consumer on the battery replacement schedule which under normal conditions would maintain performance requirements of § 161.013–3.

§ 161.013–17 Manufacturer notification.

Each manufacturer certifying lights in accordance with the specifications of this subpart must send written notice to the Commandant (G–MSE), U. S. Coast Guard, Washington, DC 20593–0001 within 30 days after first certifying them, and send a new notice every five years thereafter as long as it certifies lights.

[CGD 76–183a, 44 FR 73054, Dec. 17, 1979, as amended by CGD 88–070, 53 FR 34536, Sept. 7, 1988; CGD 95–072, 60 FR 50467, Sept. 29, 1995; CGD 96–041, 61 FR 50733, Sept. 27, 1996]

PART 162—ENGINEERING EQUIPMENT

Subpart 162.017—Valves, Pressure-Vacuum Relief, for Tank Vessels

Sec.
162.017–1 Applicable specifications.
162.017–2 Type.
162.017–3 Materials, construction, and workmanship.
162.017–4 Inspections and testing.
162.017–5 Marking.
162.017–6 Procedure for approval.

Subpart 162.018—Safety Relief Valves, Liquefied Compressed Gas

162.018–1 Applicable specifications, and referenced material.
162.018–2 Scope.
162.018–3 Materials.
162.018–4 Construction and workmanship.
162.018–5 Blow-down adjustment and popping tolerance.
162.018–6 Marking.
162.018–7 Flow rating tests.
162.018–8 Procedure for approval.

Subpart 172.027—Combination Solid Stream and Water Spray Firehose Nozzles

162.027–1 Incorporation by reference.
162.027–2 Design, construction, testing and marking requirements.

162.027-3 Approval procedures.

Subpart 162.028—Extinguishers, Fire, Portable, Marine Type

162.028-1 Applicable specifications.
162.028-2 Classification.
162.028-3 Requirements.
162.028-4 Marine type label.
162.028-5 Independent laboratories: Listing.
162.028-6 Examinations, tests, and inspections.
162.028-7 Procedure for listing and labeling.
162.028-8 Termination of listing or labeling.

Subpart 162.039—Extinguishers, Fire, Semiportable, Marine Type

162.039-1 Applicable specifications.
162.039-2 Classification.
162.039-3 Requirements.
162.039-4 Marine type label.
162.039-5 Recognized laboratory.
162.039-6 Examinations, tests, and inspections.
162.039-7 Procedure for listing and labeling.
162.039-8 Termination of listing or labeling.

Subpart 162.050—Pollution Prevention Equipment

162.050-1 Scope.
162.050-3 Definitions.
162.050-4 Documents incorporated by reference.
162.050-5 Contents of application.
162.050-7 Approval procedures.
162.050-9 Test report.
162.050-11 Marking.
162.050-13 Factory production and inspection.
162.050-14 Sample collection and preservation.
162.050-15 Designation of facilities.
162.050-17 Separator test rig.
162.050-19 Monitor and bilge alarm test rig.
162.050-21 Separator: Design specification.
162.050-23 Separator: Approval tests.
162.050-25 Cargo monitor: Design specification.
162.050-27 Cargo monitor: Approval tests.
162.050-29 Bilge monitor: Design specification.
162.050-31 Bilge monitor: Approval tests.
162.050-33 Bilge alarm: Design specification.
162.050-35 Bilge alarm: Approval tests.
162.050-37 Vibration test.
162.050-39 Measurement of oil content.

AUTHORITY: 33 U.S.C. 1321(j) 1903; 46 U.S.C. 3306, 3703, 4104, 4302; E.O. 12234, 45 FR 58801, 3 CFR, 1980 Comp., p. 277; E.O. 11735, 38 FR 21243, 3 CFR, 1971–1975 Comp., p. 793; 49 CFR 1.46.

Subpart 162.017—Valves, Pressure-Vacuum Relief, for Tank Vessels

SOURCE: CGFR 50–9, 15 FR 1680, Mar. 25, 1950, unless otherwise noted.

§ 162.017-1 Applicable specifications.

(a) There are no other specifications applicable to this subpart.

(b) [Reserved]

§ 162.017-2 Type.

This specification covers the design and construction of pressure-vacuum relief valves intended for use in venting systems on all tank vessels transporting inflammable or combustible liquids.

[56 FR 35827, July 29, 1991]

§ 162.017-3 Materials, construction, and workmanship.

(a) The valves shall be of substantial construction and first class workmanship and shall be free from imperfections which may affect its serviceability.

(b) Bodies of pressure-vacuum relief valves must be made of bronze or such corrosion-resistant material as may be approved by the Commandant (G-MSE).

(c) Valve discs, spindles, and seats shall be made of bronze or such corrosion-resistant material as may be approved by the Commandant.

(d) Where springs are employed to actuate the valve discs, the springs shall be made of corrosion-resistant material. Springs plated with corrosion-resistant material are not acceptable.

(e) Flame screens shall be made of corrosion-resistant wire.

(f) Nonmetallic materials will not be permitted in the construction of the valves, except bushings used in way of moving parts and gaskets may be made of nonmetallic material resistant to attack by the product carried. Nonmetallic diaphragms will be allowed where diaphragm failure will not result in unrestricted flow of cargo vapors to the atmosphere nor in an increase in the pressure or vacuum at which the valve normally releases.

(g) The design and construction of the valves shall permit overhauling and repairs without removal from the line.

(h) Valve discs shall be guided by a ribbed cage or other suitable means to prevent binding, and to insure proper seating. Where valve stems are guided by bushings suitably designed to prevent binding and to insure proper seating, the valves need not be fitted with ribbed cages.

(i) The disc shall close tight against the valve seat by metal to metal contact, however, resilient seating seals may be provided if the design is such that the disc closes tight against the seat in case the seals are destroyed or in case they carry away.

(j) Pressure-vacuum relief valves for venting cargo tanks shall be of not less than 2½ inches nominal pipe size.

(k) Bodies of valves shall be designed to withstand a hydrostatic pressure of at least 125 pounds per square inch without rupturing or showing permanent distortion.

(l) The valve discs may be solid or made hollow so that weight material may be added to vary the lifting pressure. If hollow discs are employed, a watertight bolted cover shall be fitted to encase the weight material. The pressure at which the discs open shall not exceed 120 percent of the set pressure.

(m) The free area through the valve seats at maximum lift shall not be less than the cross-sectional area of the valve inlet connection.

(n) Double flame screens of 20×20 corrosion-resistant wire mesh with a ½-inch corrosion-resistant separator on a single screen of 30×30 corrosion-resistant wire mesh shall be fitted on all openings to atmosphere. The net free area through the flame screens shall not be less than 1½ times the cross-sectional area of the vent inlet from the cargo tanks.

(o) Valve bodies may have screwed or flanged pipe connections, or such types of connections as may be approved by the Commandant. If flanged, the thickness and drilling shall comply with USA standards for 150-pound bronze flanged fittings.

(p) Where design of valve does not permit complete drainage of condensate to attached cargo tank or vent line, the valve body shall be fitted with a plugged drain opening on the side of the atmospheric outlet of not less than ½ inch pipe size.

(q) Relief pressure adjusting mechanisms shall be permanently secured by means of lockwires, locknuts, or other acceptable means.

[CGFR 50-9, 15 FR 1680, Mar. 25, 1950, as amended by CGFR 68-82, 33 FR 18907, Dec. 18, 1968; CGD 88-032, 56 FR 35827, July 29, 1991; CGD 95-072, 60 FR 50467, Sept. 29, 1995; CGD 96-041, 61 FR 50734, Sept. 27, 1996]

§162.017-4 Inspections and testing.

Pressure-vacuum relief valves may be inspected and tested at the plant of the manufacturer. An inspector may conduct such tests and examinations as may be necessary to determine compliance with this specification.

[56 FR 35827, July 29, 1991]

§162.017-5 Marking.

(a) Each valve shall be legibly marked with the style, type or other designation of the manufacturer, the size, pressure and vacuum setting and name or registered trademark of the manufacturer and Coast Guard approval number. The minimum wording for showing the approval number shall be "USCG/162.017/* *" or "USCG 162.017-* *".

(b) [Reserved]

[CGFR 68-82, 33 FR 18908, Dec. 18, 1968]

§162.017-6 Procedure for approval.

(a) General. Pressure-vacuum relief valves intended for use on tank vessels must be approved for such use by the Commandant (G-MSE), U.S. Coast Guard, Washington, DC 20593-0001.

(b) Drawings and specifications. Manufacturers desiring approval of a new design or type of pressure-vacuum relief valve shall submit drawings in quadruplicate showing the design of the valve, the sizes for which approval is requested, method of operation, thickness and material specification of component parts, diameter of seat opening and lift of discs, mesh and size of wire of flame screens.

(c) Pre-approval tests. Before approval is granted, the manufacturer shall have

* *Number to be assigned by the Commandant.

287

tests conducted, or submit evidence that such tests have been conducted, by the Underwriters' Laboratories, the Factory Mutual Laboratories, or by a properly supervised and inspected test laboratory acceptable to the Commandant (G-MSE), relative to determining the lift, relieving pressure and vacuum, and flow capacity of a representative sample of the pressure-vacuum relief valve in each size for which approval is desired. Test reports including flow capacity curves must be submitted to the Commandant (G-MSE).

[56 FR 35827, July 29, 1991, as amended by CGD 95-072, 60 FR 50467, Sept. 29, 1995; CGD 96-041, 61 FR 50734, Sept. 27, 1996]

Subpart 162.018—Safety Relief Valves, Liquefied Compressed Gas

§ 162.018-1 Applicable specifications, and referenced material.

(a) There are no other specifications applicable to this subpart except as noted in this subpart.

(b) The following referenced material from industry standards of the issue in effect on the date safety relief valves are manufactured shall form a part of the regulations of this subpart (see §§ 2.-75-17 through 2.75-19 of Subchapter A (Procedures Applicable to the Public) and Subpart 50.15 of Subchapter F (Marine Engineering) of this chapter):

(1) ASME (American Society of Mechanical Engineers) Code (see § 50.-15-5 of subchapter F (Marine Engineering) of this chapter): The following paragraph from section VIII of the ASME Code:

(i) UG-131, flow rating of valves, see § 162.018-7(a).

(2) CGA (Compressed Gas Association) standard: The following standard of the Compressed Gas Association (see § 50.15-20(a) of Subchapter F (Marine Engineering) of this chapter):

(i) S-1.2.5.2, Flow test data for safety and relief valves for use on pressure vessels, see § 162.018-7(a).

(c) A copy of this specification and the referenced material listed in this section, if used, shall be kept on file by the manufacturer, together with the approved plans, specifications, and cer-

tificate of approval. It is the manufacturer's responsibility to have the latest issue, including addenda and changes, of the referenced material on hand when manufacturing equipment under this subpart.

(1) The ASME Code may be obtained from the American Society of Mechanical Engineers, United Engineering Center, 345 East 47th Street, New York, N.Y. 10017.

(2) The CGA standard may be obtained from the Compressed Gas Association, 500 Fifth Avenue, New York, N.Y. 10036.

[CGFR 68-82, 33 FR 18908, Dec. 18, 1968]

§ 162.018-2 Scope.

(a) This specification covers requirements for the design, construction and testing of safety relief valves intended for use on unfired pressure vessels containing liquefied compressed gases installed on merchant vessels subject to inspection by the Coast Guard.

(b) [Reserved]

[CGFR 52-43, 17 FR 9540, Oct. 18, 1952]

§ 162.018-3 Materials.

(a) The materials used in the manufacture of safety relief valves shall conform to the applicable requirements of subchapter F (Marine Engineering) of this chapter, except as otherwise specified in this subpart, and shall be resistant to the corrosive or other action of the liquefied compressed gas in the liquid or gas phase.

(b) All pressure containing external parts of valves must be constructed of materials melting above 1700 °F. for liquefied flammable gas service. Consideration of lower melting materials for internal pressure-containing parts will be given if their use provides significant improvement to the general operation of the valve. Flange gaskets shall be metal or spiral wound asbestos.

(c) Nonferrous materials shall not be used in the construction of valves for anhydrous ammonia or other service where susceptible to attack by the lading.

(d) The seats and disks shall be of suitable corrosion resistant material. Seats and disks of cast iron or malleable iron shall not be used. Springs shall be of best quality spring steel consistent with the design of the valve and the service requirement.

[CGFR 52–43, 17 FR 9540, Oct. 18, 1952, as amended by CGFR 68–82, 33 FR 18908, Dec. 18, 1968; CGD 72–206R, 38 FR 17230, June 29, 1973]

§ 162.018–4 Construction and workmanship.

(a) Safety relief valves shall be of either the internal or external spring-loaded type, suitable for the intended service.

(b) Safety relief valve body, base, bonnet and internals shall be designed for a pressure of not less than the set-pressure of the valve.

(c) All safety relief valves shall be so constructed that the failure of any part cannot obstruct the free and full discharge of vapors from the valve.

(d) The nominal size of a safety relief valve shall be the inside diameter of the inlet opening to the individual valve disk. No safety relief valve shall be smaller than ¾ inch nor larger than 6 inches. Safety relief valves shall have flanged or welded end inlet connections and either flanged or screwed outlet connections, except outlets exceeding 4 inches in diameter shall be flanged.

(e) Safety relief valves shall be of the angle or straight-through type, fitted with side or top outlet discharge connections.

(f)(1) Springs shall not show a permanent set exceeding 1 percent of their free length 10 minutes after being released from a cold compression test closing the spring solid.

(2) Springs may not be re-set for any pressure more than 10 percent above or 10 percent below that for which the valve is marked.

(3) If the operating conditions of a valve are changed so as to require a new spring under paragraph (f)(2) of this section for a different pressure, the valve shall be adjusted by the manufacturer or his authorized representative.

(g) The design and construction of safety relief valves shall permit easy access for inspection and repair.

(h) Safety relief valves shall be tapped for not less than ¼ inch pipe size drain at the lowest practicable point where liquid can collect.

[CGFR 52–43, 17 FR 9540, Oct. 18, 1952]

§ 162.018–5 Blow-down adjustment and popping tolerance.

(a) Safety relief valves shall be so constructed that no shocks detrimental to the valve or pressure vessel are produced when lifting or closing. Safety relief valves shall be designed to open sharply and reach full lift and capacity at the maximum accumulation. Valve closure after popping shall be clean and sharp. Safety relief valves shall operate satisfactorily without wiredrawing and chattering at any stage of operation.

(b) Safety relief valves having adjustible blow-down construction shall be adjusted to close after blowing down not more than 5 percent of the set pressure. Valves shall be adjusted to pop within a tolerance of plus or minus 3 percent of the set pressure, except that for pressures of 70 p.s.i. and below, the tolerance in popping pressure shall not vary more than plus or minus 2 p.s.i.

[CGFR 52–43, 17 FR 9541, Oct. 18, 1952]

§ 162.018–6 Marking.

(a) Each safety relief valve shall be plainly marked by the manufacturer with the required data in such a way that the marking will not be obliterated in service. The marking may be stamped on the valve or stamped or cast on a plate securely fastened to the valve. The marking shall include the following data:

(1) The name or identifying trademark of the manufacturer.

(2) Manufacturer's design or type number.

(3) Size ____ inches. (The pipe size of the valve inlet).

(4) Set pressure ____ p.s.i.

(5) Rated capacity ____ cubic feet per minute of the gas or vapor (at 60 °F. and 14.7 p.s.i.a.).

(6) Coast Guard approval number. The minimum wording for showing approval shall be "USCG 162.018/* *" or "USCG 162.018–* *".

(b) [Reserved]

[CGFR 68–82, 33 FR 18908, Dec. 18, 1968]

---

* *Number to be assigned by the Commandant.

§ 162.018-7 Flow rating tests.

(a) Flow rating of valves shall be conducted in accordance with UG-131 of section VIII of the ASME Code, S-1.2.5.2 of the Compressed Gas Association Standards, or other procedure approved by the Commandant.

(b) [Reserved]

[CGFR 68-82, 33 FR 18908, Dec. 18, 1968]

§ 162.018-8 Procedure for approval.

(a) *General.* Safety relief valves for use on pressure vessels containing liquefied compressed gases shall be approved by the Commandant (G-MSE), U.S. Coast Guard, Washington, DC 20593-0001.

(b) *Plan submittal.* Manufacturers desiring to secure approval of a new design or type of safety relief valve shall submit in quadruplicate detail drawings showing the valve construction, and material specifications of the component parts. In the event the design is changed, amended drawings shall be submitted to the Commandant for reapproval.

(c) *Pre-approval tests.* (1) Prior to approval of safety relief valves by the Commandant, manufacturers shall have capacity certification tests conducted, in accordance with § 162.018-7 or submit satisfactory evidence that such tests have been conducted and approved by The National Board of Boiler and Pressure Vessel Inspectors or by a properly supervised and inspected test laboratory acceptable to the Commandant.

(2) Reports of conducted tests on designs of safety relief valves different from those previously approved shall be submitted by the manufacturer when requesting approval for different designs.

[CGFR 52-43, 17 FR 9540, Oct. 18, 1952, as amended by CGFR 68-82, 33 FR 18908, Dec. 18, 1968; CGD 88-070, 53 FR 34536, Sept. 7, 1982; CGD 96-041, 61 FR 50734, Sept. 27, 1996]

Subpart 162.027—Combination Solid Stream and Water Spray Firehose Nozzles

Source: CGD 95-027, 61 FR 26009, May 23, 1996, unless otherwise noted.

§ 162.027-1 Incorporation by reference.

(a) Certain material is incorporated by reference into this part with the approval of the Director of the Federal Register under 5 U.S.C. 552(a) and 1 CFR part 51. To enforce any edition other than that specified in paragraph (b) of this section, the Coast Guard must publish a notice of change in the FEDERAL REGISTER and the material must be available to the public. All approved material is available for inspection at the Office of the Federal Register, 800 North Capitol Street NW., Suite 700, Washington, DC and at the U.S. Coast Guard, Office of Design and Engineering Standards (G-MSE), 2100 Second Street SW, Washington, DC and is available from the sources indicated in paragraph (b) of this section.

(b) The material approved for incorporation by reference in this part and the sections affected are as follows:

American Society for Testing and Materials (ASTM)
100 Barr Harbor Drive, West Conshohocken, PA 19428-2959.
ASTM F 1546-94, Standard Specification for Firehose Nozzles—162.027-2; 162.027-3

[CGD 95-027, 61 FR 26009, May 23, 1996, as amended by CGD 96-041, 61 FR 50734, Sept. 27, 1996; CGD 97-057, 62 FR 51049, Sept. 30, 1997]

§ 162.027-2 Design, construction, testing and marking requirements.

(a) Each combination solid stream and water spray firehose nozzle required to be approved under the provisions of this subpart must be designed, constructed, tested, and marked in accordance with the requirements of ASTM F 1546-94.

(b) All inspections and tests required by ASTM F 1546-94 must be performed by an independent laboratory accepted by the Coast Guard under subpart 159.010 of this chapter. A list of independent Laboratories accepted by the Coast Guard as meeting subpart 159.010 of this chapter may be obtained by contacting the Commandant (G-MSE).

(c) The independent laboratory shall prepare a report on the results of the testing and shall furnish the manufacturer with a copy of the test report upon completion of the testing required by ASTM F 1546–94.

[CGD 95–027, 61 FR 26009, May 23, 1996, as amended by CGD 96–041, 61 FR 50734, Sept. 27, 1996]

§ 162.027–3 Approval procedures.

(a) Firehose nozzles designed, constructed, tested, and marked in accordance with ASTM F 1546–94 are considered to be approved under the provisions of this chapter.

(b) Firehose nozzles designed, constructed, tested and marked in accordance with the provisions of this subpart in effect prior to June 24, 1996, are considered to be approved under the provisions of this chapter.

Subpart 162.028—Extinguishers, Fire, Portable, Marine Type

SOURCE: CGFR 60–36, 25 FR 10640, Nov. 5, 1960, unless otherwise noted.

§ 162.028–1 Applicable specifications.

(a) There are no other Coast Guard specifications applicable to this subpart.

(b) [Reserved]

§ 162.028–2 Classification.

(a) Every portable fire extinguisher shall be classified as to type and size as specified in § 76.50–5 (Subchapter H—Passenger Vessels) of this chapter.

(b) [Reserved]

§ 162.028–3 Requirements.

(a) *General.* Every portable fire extinguisher shall conform to the requirements for listing and labeling by a recognized laboratory, and shall be of such design, materials, and construction as to meet the requirements specified in this section.

(b) *Design and weight.* Every portable fire extinguisher shall be self-contained, i.e., when charged it shall not require any additional source of extinguishing agent or expellant energy for its operation during the time it is being discharged, and it shall weigh not more than 55 pounds, maximum, when fully charged.

(c) *Materials.* Materials used for exposed working parts shall be corrosion-resistant to salt water and spray. Materials used for other exposed parts shall be either corrosion-resistant or shall be protected by a suitable corrosion-resistant coating.

(1) *Corrosion-resistant materials.* The materials which are considered to be corrosion-resistant are copper, brass, bronze, certain copper-nickel alloys, certain alloys of aluminum, certain plastics, and certain stainless steels.

(2) *Corrosion-resistant coatings.* (i) The following systems of organic or metallic coatings for exposed non-working ferrous parts, when applied on properly prepared surfaces after all cutting, forming, and bending operations are completed, are considered to provide suitable corrosion resistance:

(*a*) Bonderizing, followed by the application of zinc chromate primer, followed by one or more applications of enamel; or,

(*b*) Hot-dipped or electrodeposited zinc in thicknesses not less than 0.002 inch; or,

(*c*) Electrodeposited cadmium in thicknesses not less than 0.001 inch; or,

(*d*) Hot-dipped or sprayed aluminum in thicknesses not less than 0.002 inch; or,

(*e*) Copper plus nickel in total thicknesses not less than 0.003 inch, of which the nickel is not less than 0.002 inch, plus any thickness of chrome.

(ii) The metallic platings of less than the thicknesses specified in this paragraph are not acceptable for the protection against corrosion of ferrous parts.

(3) *Decorative platings.* Decorative platings in any thicknesses applied over corrosion-resistant materials and corrosion-resistant coatings are acceptable for either working or non-working parts.

(4) *Dissimilar metals.* The use of dissimilar metals in combination shall be avoided wherever possible, but when such contacts are necessary, provisions (such as bushings, gaskets, or o-rings) shall be employed to prevent such deleterious effects as galvanic corrosion, freezing or buckling of parts, and loosening or tightening of joints due to differences in thermal expansion.

(5) *Suitability of materials.* All extinguishers submitted for approval shall

undergo the salt spray test in accordance with paragraph (c)(6) of this section.

(6) *Salt spray tests.* Expose the complete fully charged specimen extinguisher to a 20 percent sodium chloride solution spray at a temperature of 95 °F. (35 °C.) for a period of 240 hours. The procedures and apparatus described in Method 811 of Federal Test Method Standard No. 151 are suitable. Alternate methods may be found satisfactory if the results are comparable. Following the test, allow the specimen extinguisher to air dry for a period of 48 hours. Following the air drying—

(i) The extinguisher must be capable of being operated and recharged in a normal fashion;

(ii) Any coating required in this section to be corrosion resistant must remain intact and must not be removable (when such removal exposes a material subject to corrosion) by such action as washing or rubbing with a thumb or fingernail;

(iii) No galvanic corrosion may appear at the points of contact or close proximity of dissimilar metals;

(iv) The extinguisher and its bracket, if any, must not show any corrosion, except corrosion that can be easily wiped off after rinsing with tap water, on surfaces having no protective coating or paint; and,

(v) The gauge on a stored pressure extinguisher must remain watertight throughout the test.

(d) *Bursting pressure.* For all extinguishers except the carbon dioxide type, the hydrostatic bursting pressure of the extinguisher and component parts which are subjected to pressure, exclusive of the hose, shall be at least five times the maximum working pressure during discharge of the extinguisher at approximately 70 °F. During this test, a pressure gauge if fitted will usually be removed to avoid breaking the indicating mechanism, but the gauge shall be capable of withstanding the same test without leaking.

(e) *Vibration resistance.* The complete, fully charged specimen extinguisher, secured in its bracket which is mounted to the test machine, shall be tested in accordance with sections 3.1 through 3.1.4.4 of Military Standard MIL–STD–167. Following this test, there shall be

no obvious failures of parts or assemblies, and the specimen shall be capable of being operated satisfactorily without undue effort or special procedures on the part of the operator, and the specimen shall be capable of being recharged satisfactorily in accordance with the directions on the name plate without the use of extraordinary tools or procedures.

(f) *Additional marking.* (1) As part of the usual name plate marking, there shall be included the rated capacity of the extinguisher in gallons, quarts, or pounds, and complete instructions for recharging, including the identification of the recharge materials and of the pressure cartridge or separate container if one is used.

(2) For extinguishers which are not ordinarily discharged or opened during the regular maintenance inspections and tests, the weight of the fully charged extinguisher shall be diestamped, embossed, or cast in a conspicuous location on the name plate, valve body, or shell of the extinguisher.

(3) Pasted-on type paper or decalcomania labels are not acceptable for any of the required extinguisher markings.

(4) For stored pressure type or cartridge operated type water or antifreeze portable fire extinguishers, each extinguisher name plate shall be marked to indicate whether the extinguisher is to be filled with plain water or with anti-freeze solution. Combination type name plates showing the charge may be either plain water or antifreeze solution will not be permitted.

(5) Recharge packages shall be legibly marked with the name of the recharge and the capacity of contents in gallons, quarts, or pounds, in addition to the usual recharge package marking. Recharge pressure cartridges shall, in addition to the usual marking, also be plainly marked to show the distinctive identifying designation of the cartridge.

(g) *Mounting bracket.* Every portable fire extinguisher shall be supplied with a suitable bracket which will hold the extinguisher securely in its stowage location on vessels or boats, and which is arranged to provide quick and positive release of the extinguisher for immediate use.

(h) *Carbon dioxide type.* Every carbon dioxide type extinguisher shall be fitted with a valve which will withstand a minimum bursting pressure of 6,000 p.s.i., and a discharge hose or tube which will withstand a minimum bursting pressure of 5,000 p.s.i. The hose shall be constructed with either a wire braid or other conducting material for conducting static charges occurring at the discharge nozzle back to the body of the extinguisher.

(i) [Reserved]

(j) *Dry chemical type.* (1) [Reserved]

(2) Every dry chemical stored pressure type portable fire extinguisher, i.e., one which employs a single chamber for both the dry chemical and expellant gas, shall be fitted with a pressure gauge or device to show visual indication of whether or not the pressure in the chamber is in the operating range.

(k) *Toxic extinguishing agents.* Every portable fire extinguisher shall contain only agents which qualify for the Underwriters' Laboratories, Inc., toxicity rating of Group 5 or Group 6, and which in normal fire extinguishing use do not generate decomposition products in concentrations hazardous to life.

(l) *Gauge.* Every pressure gauge used on a portable fire extinguisher shall have an accuracy of at least 2 percent of the scale range for the middle half of the scale conforming to ASME Grade B commercial accuracy. The gauge when new shall be watertight, i.e., with the connection capped or plugged, no water shall penetrate to the interior of the case during submergence one foot below the surface of water for a period of two hours. The gauge shall be constructed of corrosion-resistant materials, so that the pointer or face lettering will not be obliterated by the action of salt water if some leakage should occur after rough handling or extended periods of service. The gauge, when attached to the fire extinguisher, shall pass the salt spray and vibration tests prescribed by §162.028–3 (c)(1) and (e).

(m) *Fire tests.* In addition to the usual fire tests conducted to determine the suitability and adequacy of portable fire extinguishers, additional fire tests, such as those described in National Bureau of Standards Building Materials and Structures Report 150, issued June 14, 1957, may be employed in determining the suitability for "marine type" listing and labeling.

(n) *Additional tests.* Every portable extinguisher may be additionally examined and tested to establish its reliability and effectiveness in accordance with the intent of this specification for a "marine type" portable fire extinguisher when considered necessary by the Coast Guard or by the recognized laboratory.

[CGFR 60–36, 25 FR 10640, Nov. 5, 1960, as amended by CGFR 62–17, 27 FR 9046, Sept. 11, 1962; CGFR 56–28, 29 FR 12726, Sept. 9, 1964; CGFR 64–67, 29 FR 14742, Oct. 29, 1964; CGD 72–214R, 38 FR 6880, Mar. 14, 1973; CGD 73–73R, 38 FR 27354, Oct. 3, 1973]

§ 162.028–4 Marine type label.

(a) In addition to all other marking, every portable extinguisher shall bear a label containing the "marine type" listing manifest issued by a recognized laboratory. This label will include the classification of the extinguisher in accordance with the Coast Guard classification system, and the Coast Guard approval number, thus: "Marine Type USCG Type _____, Size _____, Approval No. 162.028/_____." All such labels are to be obtained from the recognized laboratory and will remain under its control until attached to product found acceptable under its listing and labeling program.

(b) All such labels are to be obtained only from the recognized laboratory and will remain under its control until attached to product found acceptable under its inspection and labeling program.

[CGFR 60–36, 25 FR 10640, Nov. 5, 1960, as amended by CGFR 64–19, 29 FR 7360, June 5, 1964]

§ 162.028–5 Independent laboratories: Listing.

The following have met the standards under §159.101–7 for listing as an independent laboratory to perform or supervise approval or productions inspections or tests of portable fire extinguishers:

(a) For dry chemical, CO₂, water and foam type portable fire extinguishers:

(1) Underwriters Laboratories, Inc., mailing address: P.O. Box 247, Northbrook, Illinois 60062.

(2) Underwriters' Laboratories of Canada, mailing address: 7 Crouse Rd, Scarborough, Ontario, MIR 3A9, Canada.

(b) For halon type fire extinguishers:

(1) Underwriters Laboratories, Inc., mailing address: P.O. Box 247, Northbrook, Illinois 60062.

(2) Underwriters' Laboratories of Canada, mailing address: 7 Crouse Rd, Scarborough, Ontario, MIR 3A9, Canada.

(3) Factory Mutual Research Corporation, mailing address: 1151 Boston-Providence Turnpike, P.O. Box 688, Norwood, MA 02062.

[CGD 83–050, 49 FR 7566, Mar. 1, 1984]

§ 162.028–6 Examinations, tests, and inspections.

(a) Full examinations, tests, and inspections to determine the suitability of a product for listing and labeling, and to determine conformance of labeled product to the applicable requirements are conducted by the recognized laboratory. Whenever any work is being done on components or the assembly of such product, the manufacturer shall notify the recognized laboratory in order that an inspector may be assigned to the factory to conduct such examinations, inspections, and tests as to satisfy himself that the quality assurance program of the manufacturer is satisfactory, and that the labeled product is in conformance with the applicable requirements.

(b) Manufacturers of listed or labeled marine type portable fire extinguishers shall maintain quality control of the materials used, manufacturing methods, and the finished product so as to meet the applicable requirements, and shall make sufficient inspections and tests of representative samples of the extinguishers and various components produced to maintain the quality of the finished product. Records of tests conducted by the manufacturer shall be made available to the laboratory inspector or to the merchant marine inspector, or both, for review upon request.

(c) Follow-up check tests, examinations, and inspections of product listed and labeled as a "marine type" portable fire extinguisher acceptable to the Commandant as approved for use on merchant vessels and motorboats may be conducted by the Coast Guard, as well as by the recognized laboratory.

(d) The laboratory inspector, or the Coast Guard marine inspector assigned by the Commander of the District in which the factory is located, or both, shall be admitted to any place in the factory where work is being done on listed or labeled product, and either or both inspectors may take samples of parts or materials entering into construction, or final assemblies, for further examinations, inspections or tests. The manufacturer shall provide a suitable place and the apparatus necessary for the performance of the tests which are done at the place of manufacture.

§ 162.028–7 Procedure for listing and labeling.

(a) Manufacturers having a marine-type portable fire extinguisher which they consider has characteristics suitable for general use on merchant vessels and motorboats may make application for listing and labeling as a marine-type portable fire extinguisher by addressing a request directly to a recognized laboratory. The laboratory will inform the submitter as to the requirements for inspection, examinations, and testing necessary for such listing and labeling. The request shall include permission for the laboratory to furnish a complete test report together with a description of the quality control procedures to the Commandant.

(b) The U.S. Coast Guard will review the test report and quality control procedures to determine if the requirements in § 162.028–3 have been met. If this is the case, the Commandant will notify the laboratory that the extinguisher is approved and that when the extinguisher is listed and labeled, it may be marked as being U.S. Coast Guard approved.

(c) If disagreements concerning procedural, technical, or inspection questions arise over U.S. Coast Guard approval requirements between the manufacturer and the laboratory, the opinion of the Commandant shall be requested by the laboratory.

(d) The manufacturer or the laboratory may at any time request clarification or advice from the Commandant on any question which may arise regarding manufacturing and approval of approved devices.

[CGD 72–214R, 38 FR 6880, Mar. 14, 1973]

§ 162.028–8 Termination of listing or labeling.

(a) Listing or labeling as a marine type portable fire extinguisher acceptable to the Commandant as approved for use on inspected vessels and motorboats, may be terminated, withdrawn, cancelled, or suspended by written notice to the recognized laboratory from the Commandant, or by written notice to the manufacturer from the recognized laboratory or from the Commandant, under the following conditions:

(1) When the manufacturer does not desire to retain the service.

(2) When the listed product is no longer being manufactured.

(3) When the manufacturer's own program does not provide suitable assurance of the quality of the listed or labeled product being manufactured.

(4) When the product manufactured no longer conforms to the current applicable requirements.

(5) When service experience or laboratory or U.S. Coast Guard reports indicate a product is unsatisfactory.

(b) [Reserved]

[CGFR 60–36, 25 FR 10640, Nov. 5, 1960, as amended by CGD 72–214R, 38 FR 6880, Mar. 14, 1973]

Subpart 162.039—Extinguishers, Fire, Semiportable, Marine Type

SOURCE: CGFR 65–9, 30 FR 11487, Sept. 8, 1965, unless otherwise noted.

§ 162.039–1 Applicable specifications.

(a) There are no other Coast Guard specifications applicable to this subpart.

(b) [Reserved]

§ 162.039–2 Classification.

(a) Every semiportable fire extinguisher shall be classified as to type and size as specified in § 76.50–5 (Subchapter H—Passenger Vessels) of this chapter.

(b) [Reserved]

§ 162.039–3 Requirements.

(a) *General.* Every semiportable fire extinguisher shall conform to the requirements for listing and labeling by a recognized laboratory and shall be of such design, materials, and construction as to meet the requirements specified in this section.

(b) *Design.* Every semiportable extinguisher shall be fitted with hose of sufficient length to a nozzle or nozzles to provide for suitable application of the extinguishing agent to any part of the space protected (a length of pipe may connect the outlet of the supply to the hose connection); shall weigh more than 55 pounds when fully charged; shall be self-contained, i.e., when charged, it shall not require any additional source of extinguishing agent or expellent energy for its operation; and shall provide simple means for immediate operation by a single operator. The design, materials and construction shall provide reliability of operation and performance after non-use for long periods under conditions encountered in marine service.

(c) *Materials.* Materials used for exposed working parts, except those used for inversion mechanism or similar purposes, shall be corrosion-resistant to salt water and spray. Materials used for other exposed parts shall be either corrsion-resistant or shall be protected by a suitable corrosion-resistant coating.

(1) *Corrosion-resistant materials.* The materials which are considered to be corrosion-resistant are copper, brass, bronze, certain copper-nickel alloys, certain alloys of aluminum, certain plastics, and certain stainless steels.

(2) *Corrosion-resistant coatings.* (i) The following systems of organic or metallic coatings for exposed nonworking ferrous parts except for ICC cylinders, when applied on properly prepared surfaces after all cutting, forming, and bending operations are completed, are considered to provide suitable corrosion resistance:

(a) Bonderizing, followed by the application of zinc chromate primer, followed by one or more applications of enamel; or,

(b) Inorganic zinc coatings; or,

(c) Hot-dipped or electrodeposited zinc in thicknesses not less than 0.002 inch; or,

(d) Electrodeposited Cadmium in thicknesses not less than 0.001 inch; or,

(e) Hot-dipped or sprayed aluminum in thicknesses not less than 0.002 inch; or,

(f) Copper plus nickel in total thicknesses not less than 0.003 inch, or which the nickel is not less than 0.002 inch, plus any thickness of chrome.

(ii) The metallic platings of less than the thicknesses specified in this paragraph are not acceptable for the protection against corrosion of ferrous parts.

(3) *Decorative platings.* Decorative platings in any thicknesses applied over corrosion-resistant materials and corrosion-resistant coatings are acceptable for either working or nonworking parts.

(4) *Dissimilar metals.* The use of dissimilar metals in combination shall be avoided wherever possible, but when such contacts are necessary, provisions (such as bushings, gaskets, or o-rings) shall be employed to prevent such deleterious effects as galvanic corrosion, freezing or buckling of parts, and loosening or tightening of joints due to differences in thermal expansion.

(5) *Suitability of materials.* In event of question as to the suitability of the materials (including coatings) used, the salt spray test described in paragraph (c)(6) of this section shall be conducted.

(6) *Salt spray test.* Expose either component parts, subassemblies, or the complete fully charged specimen extinguisher to a 20 percent sodium-chloride solution spray at a temperature of 95 °F. (35 °C.) for a period of 240 hours. The procedures and apparatus described in Method 811 of Federal Test Method Standard No. 151 are suitable. Alternate methods may be found satisfactory if the results are comparable. Following the test, allow the specimen extinguisher to air dry for a period of 48 hours. Following the air drying, the specimen extinguisher shall be capable of being operated satisfactorily without undue effort or special procedures on the part of the operator, and it shall be capable of being recharged satisfactorily in accordance with the directions on the nameplate without the use of extraordinary tools or procedures.

(d) *Gauges.* Every pressure gauge used on a semiportable fire extinguisher shall have an accuracy of at least 2 percent of the scale range for the middle half of the scale conforming to ASME Grade B commercial accuracy. The gauge when new shall be watertight, i.e., with the connection capped or plugged, no water shall penetrate to the interior of the case during submergence 1 foot below the surface of water for a period of 2 hours. The gauge shall be constructed of corrosion-resistant materials, so that the pointer or face lettering will not be obliterated by the action of salt water if some leakage should occur after rough handling or extended periods of service. The gage, when attached to the extinguisher, shall pass the salt spray and vibration tests prescribed by paragraphs (c)(6) and (e) of this section.

(e) *Vibration resistance.* Either component parts, subassemblies, or the complete, fully charged specimen extinguisher, shall be tested in accordance with sections 3.1 through 3.1.4.4 of Military Standard MIL-STD-167. Following this test, there shall be no obvious failures of parts or assemblies, and they shall be capable of being operated satisfactorily without undue effort or special procedures on the part of the operator, and the extinguisher shall be capable of being recharged satisfactorily in accordance with the directions on the name plate without the use of extraordinary tools or procedures.

(f) *Carbon dioxide type.* Every carbon dioxide type extinguisher shall be fitted with a valve which will withstand a minimum bursting pressure of 6,000 p.s.i., and a discharge hose or tube which will withstand a minimum bursting pressure of 5,000 p.s.i. The hose shall be constructed with either a wire braid or other conducting material for conducting static charges occurring at the discharge nozzle back to the body of the extinguisher.

(g) *Chemical-foam type.* Every chemical foam type semiportable fire extinguisher shall have a nozzle which will provide operating characteristics such that when it is held about 3 feet above the ground at an elevation of approximately 30°, and with the extinguisher and contents both at approximately 70 °F. and 120 °F., the range of the stream shall not exceed 40 feet, and the major portion of the discharge shall fall between 20 and 40 feet, measured horizontally, from the nozzle. The duration of the effective discharge shall be between 2.5 and 4.0 minutes, effective discharge being considered as occurring while the major portion of the discharge falls beyond 10 feet, measured horizontally, from the nozzle.

(h) [Reserved]

(i) *Toxic extinguishing agents.* Every semiportable fire extinguisher shall contain only agents which qualify for the Underwriters' Laboratories, Inc., toxicity rating of Group 5 or Group 6, and which in normal fire extinguishing use do not generate decomposition products in concentrations hazardous to life. Acceptance of extinguishing agents under these requirements will be determined by the Coast Guard.

(j) *Fire tests.* Fire tests may be employed in determining the suitability for "marine type" listing and labeling.

(k) *Additional tests.* Every semiportable extinguisher may be additionally examined and tested to establish its reliability and effectiveness in accordance with the intent of this specification for a "marine type" semiportable fire extinguisher when considered necessary by the Coast Guard or by the recognized laboratory.

(1) *Additional marking.* (1) As part of the usual nameplate marking, there shall be included the rated capacity of the extinguisher in gallons, quarts, or pounds, and complete instructions for recharging, including the identification of the recharge materials and of the pressure containing cylinder or separate container if one is used.

(2) Pasted-on type paper or decalcomania labels are not acceptable for any of the required extinguisher marking.

(3) Recharge packages shall be legibly marked with the name of the recharge and the capacity of contents in gallons, quarts, or pounds in addition to the usual recharge package marking. Recharge pressure containing cylinders shall, in addition to the usual marking, also be plainly marked to show the distinctive identifying designation of the cylinder.

(m) *Securing means.* Every semi-portable fire extinguisher shall be supplied with a suitable means for holding the extinguisher securely in its stowage location on vessels or boats. The materials shall be sufficiently corrosion-resistant or protected against corrosion to withstand the test prescribed by paragraph (c)(6) of this section without showing more than traces of slight corrosion, which may be easily wiped off after rinsing with tapwater.

[CGFR 65-9, 30 FR 11487, Sept. 8, 1965, as amended by CGFR 65-64, 31 FR 563, Jan. 15, 1966; CGD 73-73R, 38 FR 27354, Oct. 3, 1973; CGD 77-039, 44 FR 34133, June 14, 1979]

§ 162.039-4 Marine type label.

(a) In addition to all other marking, every semiportable extinguisher shall bear a label containing the "marine type" listing manifest issued by a recognized laboratory. This label will include the classification of the extinguisher in accordance with the Coast Guard classification system, and the Coast Guard approval number, thus: "Marine Type USCG Type ___, Size ___, Approval No. 162.039/Ex__." All such labels are to be obtained from the recognized laboratory and will remain under its control until attached to product found acceptable under its listing and labeling program.

(b) [Reserved]

§ 162.039-5 Recognized laboratory.

(a) A recognized laboratory is one which is regularly engaged in the examination, testing, and evaluation of semi-portable fire extinguishers; which has an established factory inspection, listing, and labeling program; and which has special standards for listing and labeling as a "marine type" semiportable fire extinguisher acceptable to the Commandant as approved for use on merchant vessels and motorboats. The following laboratories are recognized, and the semiportable fire extinguishers bearing their "marine type" labels are approved for use on merchant vessels and motorboats:

(1) Underwriters' Laboratories, Inc., mailing address: Post Office Box 247, Northbrook, Ill., 60062.

(2) [Reserved]

(b) [Reserved]

§ 162.039–6 Examinations, tests, and inspections.

(a) Full examinations, tests, and inspections to determine the suitability of a product for listing and labeling, and to determine conformance of labeled product to the applicable requirements are conducted by the recognized laboratory. Whenever any work is being done on components or the assembly of such product, the manufacturer shall notify the recognized laboratory in order that an inspector may be assigned to the factory to conduct such examinations, inspections, and tests as to satisfy himself that the quality assurance program of the manufacturer is satisfactory, and that the labeled product is in conformance with the applicable requirements.

(b) Manufacturers of listed or labeled marine type semiportable fire extinguishers shall maintain quality control of the materials used, manufacturing methods, and the finished product so as to meet the applicable requirements, and shall make sufficient inspections and tests of representative samples of the extinguishers and various components produced to maintain the quality of the finished product. Records of tests conducted by the manufacturer shall be made available to the laboratory inspector or to the Coast Guard marine inspector, or both, for review upon request.

(c) Followup check tests, examinations, and inspections of product listed and labeled as a "marine type" semiportable fire extinguisher acceptable to the Commandant as approved for use on merchant vessels and motorboats may be conducted by the Coast Guard, as well as by the recognized laboratory.

(d) The laboratory inspector, or the Coast Guard merchant marine inspector assigned by the Commander of the District in which the factory is located, or both, shall be admitted to any place in the factory where work is being done on listed or labeled product, and either or both inspectors may take samples of parts or materials entering into construction, of final assemblies, for further examinations, inspections, or tests. The manufacturer shall provide a suitable place and the apparatus necessary for the performance of the tests which are done at the place of manufacture.

§ 162.039–7 Procedure for listing and labeling.

(a) Manufacturers having models of extinguishers which they believe are suitable for marine service may make application for listing and labeling of such product as a "marine type" semiportable fire extinguisher which will be acceptable to the Commandant as approved for use on merchant vessels, by addressing a request directly to a recognized laboratory. The laboratory will inform the submitter as to the requirements for inspections, examinations, and testing necessary for such listing and labeling. All costs in connection with the examinations, tests, and inspections, listings and labelings are payable by the manufacturer.

(b) [Reserved]

§ 162.039–8 Termination of listing or labeling.

(a) Listing or labeling as a marine type semiportable fire extinguisher acceptable to the Commandant as approved for use on inspected vessels or motorboats may be terminated, withdrawn, canceled, or suspended by written notice to the recognized laboratory from the Commandant, or by written notice to the manufacturer from the recognized laboratory or from the Commandant under the following conditions:

(1) When the manufacturer does not desire to retain the service.

(2) When the listed product is no longer being manufactured.

(3) When the manufacturer's own program does not provide suitable assurance of the quality of the listed or labeled product being manufactured.

(4) When the product manufactured no longer conforms to the current applicable requirements.

(b) [Reserved]

Subpart 162.050—Pollution Prevention Equipment

SOURCE: 44 FR 53359, Sept. 13, 1979, unless otherwise noted.

§162.050-1 Scope.

(a) This subpart contains—

(1) Procedures for approval of 100 p.p.m. separators, 15 p.p.m. separators, cargo monitors, bilge monitors, and bilge alarms;

(2) Design specifications for this equipment;

(3) Tests required for approval;

(4) Procedures for obtaining designation as a facility authorized to conduct approval tests;

(5) Marking requirements; and

(6) Factory inspection procedures.

(b) [Reserved]

§162.050-3 Definitions.

(a) *p.p.m.* means parts per million by volume of oil in water;

(b) *100 p.p.m. separator* means a separator that is designed to remove enough oil from an oil-water mixture to provide a resulting mixture that has an oil concentration of 100 p.p.m. or less;

(c) *15 p.p.m. separator* means a separator that is designed to remove enough oil from an oil-water mixture to provide a resulting mixture that has an oil concentration of 15 p.p.m. or less;

(d) *Cargo monitor* means an instrument that is designed to measure and record the oil content of cargo residues from cargo tanks and oily mixtures combined with these residues;

(e) *Bilge monitor* means an instrument that is designed to measure and record the oil content of oily mixtures from machinery space bilges and fuel oil tanks that carry ballast;

(f) *Bilge alarm* means an instrument that is designed to measure the oil content of oily mixtures from machinery space bilges and fuel oil tanks that carry ballast and activate an alarm at a set concentration limit; and

(g) *Independent laboratory* means a laboratory that—

(1) Has the equipment and procedures necessary to approve the electrical components described in §§162.050-21(b)

and 162.050-25(c), or to conduct the test described in §162.050-37(a); and

(2) Is not owned or controlled by a manufacturer, supplier, or vendor of separators, monitors, or bilge alarms.

§162.050-4 Documents incorporated by reference.

(a) The following documents are incorporated by reference into this subpart:

(1) Underwriters Laboratories Standard 913 (as revised April 8, 1976).

(2) "Experimental Statistics", National Bureau of Standards Handbook No. 91 (October 1966).

(3) "Standard Practice for Determination of Precision and Bias of Methods of Committee D-19 on Water, D-2777-77", American Society for Testing and Materials.

(b) The documents listed in this section may be obtained as follows:

(1) The UL standard may be obtained from Underwriters Laboratories, Inc., Publications Stock, 333 Pfingsten Road, Northbrook, Illinois 60062.

(2) The ASTM standard may be obtained from the American Society for Testing and Materials, 1916 Race Street, Philadelphia, Pa. 19103.

(3) The NBS handbook may be obtained from the Superintendent of Documents, U.S. Government Printing Office, Washington, DC 20402.

(c) The documents listed in this section are also on file in the Federal Register library.

(d) Approval to incorporate by reference the materials listed in this section was obtained from the Director of the Federal Register on August 21, 1979.

§162.050-5 Contents of application.

(a) An application for approval of a 15 p.p.m. or 100 p.p.m. separator, a cargo or bilge monitor, or a bilge alarm must contain the following information:

(1) A brief description of the item submitted for approval.

(2) The name and address of the applicant and its manufacturing facility.

(3) A detailed description of quality control procedures, in-process and final inspections and tests followed in manufacturing the item, and construction and sales record keeping systems maintained.

(4) Arrangement drawings and piping diagrams of the item that give the information prescribed by § 56.01–10(d) of this chapter.

(5) Detailed electrical plans of the type described in § 111.05–5(d) of this chapter.

(6) An instructions manual containing detailed instructions on installation, operation, calibration and zeroing, and maintenance of the item.

(7) For each monitor and bilge alarm and each control on a separator, the vibration test report described in § 162.050–37.

(8) For each cargo monitor, a statement of whether it is to be used with crude oils, refined products, or both.

(9) A list of the substances used in operating the item that require certification under part 147 of this chapter as articles of ships' stores and supplies.

(10) The name of the facility to conduct approval testing.

(11) If the applicant intends to use a test rig other than a test rig of the facility, a detailed description of the rig.

(b) An applicant may incorporate by reference in his application information that he has submitted in a previous application.

§ 162.050-7 Approval procedures.

(a) An application for approval of equipment under this subpart must be sent to the Commandant (G–MSE), U.S. Coast Guard, Washington, DC 20593–0001.

(b) The application is examined by the Coast Guard to determine whether the item complies with the design requirements and vibration standard prescribed in this subpart and to determine what probability the item has of passing the approval tests. The applicant is notified of the results of the examination.

(c) If examination of the application reveals that it is incomplete, it is returned to the applicant with a statement of reasons why it is incomplete.

(d) The applicant must make arrangements for approval testing directly with a testing facility and must provide the facility with a copy of the instructions manual for the equipment to be tested.

(e) If applications for approval of a separator have been made for more

than one size, the applicant, in lieu of submitting each size for approval testing, may submit each size that has a capacity exceeding fifty (50) cubic meters per hour throughput, if any, and two additional sizes that have a capacity of fifty (50) cubic meters per hour throughput or less. One of the additional sizes must have a capacity that is in the highest quartile of capacities manufactured in the 0–50 cubic meters per hour throughput range and the other must be from the lowest quartile.

(f) Each approval test must be performed by a facility designated under § 162.050–15. The facility must perform each test in accordance with the test conditions prescribed in this subpart for the test, prepare a test report for the item if it completes all of the tests, and send the report with four copies to the Commandant (G–MSE). The applicant may observe the tests. (If an item does not complete testing, a new application must be made before retesting.)

(g) The Commandant (G–MSE), sends a copy of the test report to the applicant and advises him whether the item is approved. If the item is approved, an approval certificate is sent to the applicant. The approval certificate lists conditions of approval applicable to the item.

(h) A separator is approved under this subpart if—

(1) It meets the design requirements in § 162.050–21 and is tested in accordance with this subpart;

(2) In the case of a 100 p.p.m. separator, the oil content of each sample of separated water effluent taken during approval testing is 100 p.p.m. or less;

(3) In the case of a 15 p.p.m. separator, the oil content of each sample of separated water effluent taken during approval testing is 15 p.p.m. or less;

(4) During Test No. 3S an oily mixture is not observed at the separated water outlet of the separator;

(5) During Test No. 5S its operation is continuous; and

(6) Any substance used in operating the separator that requires certification under part 147 of this chapter as an article of ships' stores or supplies has been certified.

(i) A cargo monitor is approved under this subpart if—

(1) It meets the design requirements in § 162.050–25 and is tested in accordance with this subpart;

(2) Each oil content reading recorded during approval testing is within ±10 p.p.m. or ±20 percent of the oil content of the sample of influent mixture taken at the time of the reading;

(3) Its response time is twenty (20) seconds or less in Test No. 3CM;

(4) The time intervals between successive readings recorded in Test No. 4CM are twenty (20) seconds or less; and

(5) Any substance used in operating the monitor that requires certification under part 147 of this chapter as an article of ships' stores or supplies has been certified.

(j) A bilge monitor is approved under this subpart if—

(1) It meets the design requirements in § 162.050–29 and is tested in accordance with this subpart;

(2) Except as provided in paragraph (j)(5) of this section, each oil content reading recorded during approval testing is within ±10 p.p.m. or ±20 percent of the oil content of the sample of influent mixture taken at the time of the reading;

(3) The time intervals between successive readings recorded in Test No. 3BM are twenty (20) seconds or less;

(4) The time intervals between successive readings recorded in Test No. 4BM are twenty (20) seconds or less;

(5) The oil content of the sample taken each time the device required by § 162.050–29(c)(1) actuates is 15 p.p.m. ±5 p.p.m.;

(6) The oil content of the sample taken each time the device required by § 162.050–29(c)(2) actuates is 100 p.p.m. ±20 p.p.m.; and

(7) Any substance used in operating the monitor that requires certification under part 147 of this chapter as an article of ships' stores or supplies has been certified.

(k) A bilge alarm is approved under this subpart if—

(1) It meets the design requirements in § 162.050–33 and is tested in accordance with this subpart;

(2) The oil content of each sample taken during approval testing is 15 p.p.m. ±5 p.p.m.;

(3) Its response time is twenty seconds or less in Test No. 2A; and

(4) Any substance used in operating the alarm that requires certification under part 147 of this chapter as an article of ships' stores or supplies has been certified.

[44 FR 53359, Sept. 13, 1979, as amended by CGD 82–063b, 48 FR 4783, Feb. 3, 1983; 48 FR 45114, Oct. 3, 1983; CGD 88–070, 53 FR 34537, Sept. 7, 1988; CGD 95–072, 60 FR 50467, Sept. 29, 1995; CGD 96–041, 61 FR 50734, Sept. 27, 1996]

§ 162.050–9 Test report.

(a) A report of approval testing must contain the following:

(1) Name of the testing facility.

(2) Name of the applicant.

(3) Date of receiving the item for testing and the dates of the tests conducted.

(4) Trade name and brief description of the item.

(5) A listing of the following properties of the test oils used:

(i) Relative density at 15 °C.

(ii) Viscosity in centistokes at 37.8 °C.

(iii) Flashpoint.

(iv) Weight of ash content.

(v) Weight of water content.

(vi) Relative density at 15 °C. the of water used during testing and the weight of solid content in the water.

(vii) The data recorded during each test.

(b) [Reserved]

§ 162.050–11 Marking.

(a) Each separator, monitor, and bilge alarm manufactured under Coast Guard approval must be plainly marked by the manufacturer with the information listed in paragraph (b) of this section. The marking must be securely fastened to the item.

(b) Each marking must include the following information:

(1) Name of the manufacturer.

(2) Name or model number of the item.

(3) If the item is a separator, the maximum throughput and the maximum influent pressure at which the separator is designed to operate.

(4) The month and year of completion of manufacture.

(5) The manufacturer's serial number for the item.

(6) The Coast Guard approval number assigned to the item in the certificate of approval.

(7) A list of bilge cleaners, solvents, and other chemical compounds that do not impair operation of the item.

(8) If the item is a cargo monitor, the oils for which use has been approved.

(9) If the item is a separator that uses replaceable filter or coalescer elements, the part numbers of the elements.

§ 162.050-13 Factory production and inspection.

(a) Equipment manufactured under Coast Guard approval must be of the type described in the current certificate of approval issued for the equipment.

(b) Equipment manufactured under Coast Guard approval is not inspected on a regular schedule at the place of manufacture. However, the Commandant may detail Coast Guard personnel at any time to visit a factory where the equipment is manufactured to conduct an inspection of the manufacturing process.

§ 162.050-14 Sample collection and preservation.

(a) Each sample obtained in approval testing must be approximately one (1) liter in volume and must be collected in a narrow-necked glass bottle that has a pressure sealing cap. The cap must be lined with a material that will not affect the oil content of the sample.

(b) Each sample must be preserved by the addition of 5 ml. of hydrochloric acid at the time of collection. The hydrochloric acid must consist of equal amounts of concentrated reagent grade hydrochloric acid and distilled water.

(c) Each sample must be refrigerated at or below 4 °C. until analyzed. However, refrigeration is not necessary if there is no time delay between sample collection and analysis.

§ 162.050-15 Designation of facilities.

(a) Each request for designation as a facility authorized to perform approval tests must be submitted to the Com-

mandant (G-MSE), U.S. Coast Guard, Washington, DC 20593-0001.

(b) Each request must include the following:

(1) Name and address of the facility.

(2) Each type of equipment the facility proposes to test.

(3) A description of the facility's capability to perform approval tests including detailed information on the following:

(i) Management organization including personnel qualifications.

(ii) Equipment available for conducting sample analysis.

(iii) Materials available for approval testing.

(iv) Each of the facility's test rigs, if any.

(c) The Coast Guard reviews each request submitted to determine whether the facility meets the requirements of paragraphs (g)(1) through (g)(4) of this section.

(d) If the facility meets the requirements in paragraphs (g)(1) through (g)(4) of this section, it is then supplied with twelve samples containing mixtures of oil in water that are within a 10 to 30 p.p.m. range.

(e) The facility must measure the oil content of each sample using the method described in §162.050-39 and report the value of each of the 12 measurements to the Commandant (G-MSE), U.S. Coast Guard, Washington, DC 20593.

(f) The measurements must meet the following criteria:

(1) Except as provided in paragraph (f)(2) of this section, the absolute value of Tn for each measurement, as determined by the method described in paragraph 10.3.2 of the American Society for Testing and Materials, "Standard Practice for Determination of Precision and Bias of Methods of Committee D-19 on Water", D-2777-77, must be less than or equal to 2.29 at a confidence level of 0.05.

(2) The absolute value of Tn for one measurement may exceed 2.29 if the Tn values for the other eleven measurements are less than or equal to 2.23 at a confidence level of 0.05. If the Tn value for one measurement exceeds 2.29, that measurement is not used in the method described in paragraph (f)(3) of this section.

(3) The value of $\bar{X}\leq$ for the 12 measurements described in paragraph (e) of this section, or for 11 measurements if paragraph (f)(2) of this section applies, must be within the range of -1 $\bar{X}\leq$d $+1$ at a minimum confidence level of 0.01 when $\bar{X}\leq$d is determined by the method described in paragraph 3–3.1.4 of "Experimental Statistics", National Bureau of Standards Handbook No. 91 (October 1966).

(g) To obtain authorization to conduct approval tests—

(1) A facility must have the management organization, equipment for conducting sample analysis, and the materials necessary to perform the tests;

(2) Each facility test rig must be of a type described in §162.050–17 or §162.050–19;

(3) The loss or award of a specific contract to test equipment must not be a substantial factor in the facility's financial well being;

(4) The facility must be free of influence and control of the manufacturers, suppliers, and vendors of the equipment; and

(5) The oil content measurements submitted to the Commandant must meet the criteria in paragraph (f) of this section.

(h) A facility may not subcontract for approval testing unless previously authorized by the Coast Guard. A request for authorization to subcontract must be sent to the Commandant (G–MSE), U.S. Coast Guard, Washington, DC 20593–0001.

[44 FR 53359, Sept. 13, 1979, as amended by CGD 82–063b, 48 FR 45114, Oct. 3, 1983; CGD 88–070, 53 FR 34537, Sept. 7, 1988; CGD 95–072, 60 FR 50467, Sept. 29, 1995; CGD 96–041, 61 FR 50734, Sept. 27, 1996]

§162.050–17 Separator test rig.

(a) This section contains requirements for test rigs used in approval testing of separators. A diagram of a typical test rig is shown in Figure 162.050–17(a).

(b) Each mixture pump on a test rig must—

(1) Be a centrifugal pump capable of operating at one thousand (1,000) revolutions per minute or more;

(2) Have a delivery capacity of at least one and one half (1.5) times the maximum throughput at which the separator being tested is designed to operate;

(3) Have a maximum delivery pressure that is equal to or greater than the maximum influent pressure at which the separator is designed to operate; and

(4) Have either bypass piping to its suction side or a throttle valve or orifice on its discharge side.

(c) The inlet piping of the test rig must be sized so that—

(1) Influent water flows at a Reynolds Number of at least ten thousand;

(2) The influent flow rate is between one and three meters per second; and

(3) Its length is at least twenty (20) times its inside diameter.

(d) Each sample point on a test rig must meet the design requirements described in Figure 162.050–17(e) and must be in a vertical portion of the test rig piping.

§162.050–19 Monitor and bilge alarm test rig.

(a) This section contains requirements for test rigs used in approval testing of monitors and bilge alarms. A typical test rig is described in Figure 162.050–19. The mixture pipe shown in Figure 162.050–19 is the portion of test rig piping between the oil injection point and the monitor or bilge alarm piping.

(b) Each sample point on a test rig must be of the type described in Figure 162.050–17(e) and must be in a vertical portion of the test rig piping.

(c) Each test rig must have a centrifugal pump that is designed to operate at one thousand (1,000) revolutions per minute or more.

(d) The mixture pipe on a test rig must have a uniform inside diameter.

FIGURE 162,050—17(a) - SEPARATOR TEST RIG

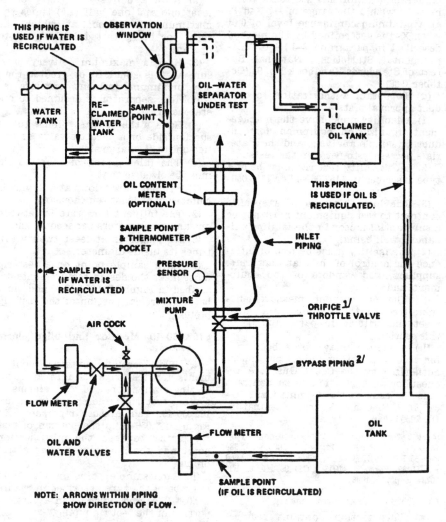

THIS PIPING IS
USED IF WATER IS
RECIRCULATED

OBSERVATION
WINDOW

WATER
TANK

RE-
CLAIMED
WATER
TANK

SAMPLE
POINT

OIL—WATER
SEPARATOR
UNDER TEST

RECLAIMED
OIL TANK

OIL CONTENT
METER
(OPTIONAL)

THIS PIPING
IS USED IF OIL IS
RECIRCULATED.

SAMPLE POINT
& THERMOMETER
POCKET

INLET
PIPING

SAMPLE POINT
(IF WATER IS
RECIRCULATED)

PRESSURE
SENSOR

MIXTURE
PUMP 3/

ORIFICE 1/
THROTTLE VALVE

AIR COCK

BYPASS PIPING 2/

FLOW METER

OIL AND
WATER VALVES

FLOW METER

OIL
TANK

SAMPLE POINT
(IF OIL IS RECIRCULATED)

NOTE: ARROWS WITHIN PIPING
       SHOW DIRECTION OF FLOW.

1/ NOT REQUIRED IF MIXTURE PUMP HAS BYPASS PIPING. SEE § 162.050—17(b) (4)

2/ NOT REQUIRED IF MIXTURE PUMP PIPING HAS ORIFICE. SEE § 162.050—17(b)(4)

3/ NOT REQUIRED IF SEPARATOR HAS SUPPLY PUMP. SEE § 162.050—17(b)

FIGURE 162.050—17(e) · SAMPLE POINT

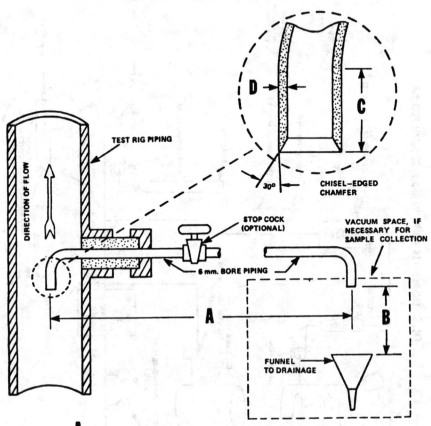

A dimension A is not greater than 400 mm.

B height B is large enough to insert a sample bottle.

C distance C is a straight line of not less than 60 mm.

D width D is not greater than 2 mm.

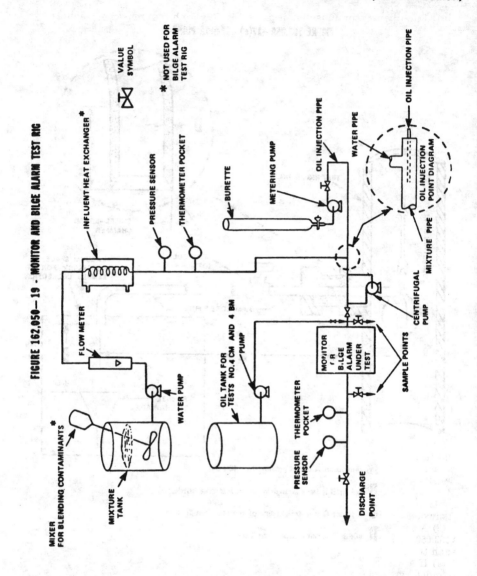

FIGURE 162.050—19 · MONITOR AND BILGE ALARM TEST RIG

§ 162.050-21 Separator: Design specification.

(a) A separator must be designed to operate in each plane that forms an angle of 22.5° with the plane of its normal operating position.

(b) The electrical components of a separator that are to be installed in an explosive atmosphere must be approved by an independent laboratory as components that Underwriters Laboratories Standard 913 (dated April 8, 1976) defines as intrinsically safe for use in a Class I, Group D hazardous location.

(c) Each separator component that is a moving part must be designed so that its movement during operation of the separator does not cause formation of static electricity.

(d) Each separator must be designed in accordance with the applicable requirements in subchapters F and J of this chapter.

(e) Each separator must be designed to be operated both automatically and manually. Each separator to be installed in an unattended machinery space must be capable of operating automatically for at least twenty-four (24) hours.

(f) Each separator must be designed so that adjustments to valves or other equipment are not necessary to start it.

(g) Each part of a separator that is susceptible to wear and tear must be readily accessible for maintenance in its installed position.

(h) A separator must be designed so that it does not rely in whole or in part on dilution of influent mixtures as a means of performing its function.

§ 162.050-23 Separator: Approval tests.

(a) *Test Conditions.* (1) Each test described in this section must be performed at a throughput and influent pressure equal to the maximum throughput and pressure at which the separator being tested is designed to operate. The tests and each of the steps in the tests must be carried out in the order described in this section. Each test must be performed without time delay between steps in the test.

(2) Except as provided in Test No. 6S, the influent oil used in each test must be a heavy fuel oil that has a relative density of approximately 0.94 at 15 °C and a viscosity of at least 220 centistokes (approximately 900 seconds Redwood No. 1) at 37.8 °C.

(3) A test rig of the type described in § 162.050-17 must be used in performing each test.

(4) If a separator has a supply pump, it must be tested using that pump. If a separator does not have a supply pump, it must be tested using the mixture pump on the test rig.

(5) The influent water used in each test must be clean fresh water or clean fresh water in solution with sodium chloride. The water or solution must have a relative density at 15 °C that is equal to or less than 0.085 plus the relative density of the heavy fuel oil used in the tests.

(6) Each test must be conducted at an ambient temperature of between 10 °C and 30 °C.

(7) The oil content of each sample must be measured using the method described in § 162.050-39.

(8) Influent oil content must be determined during testing by measuring the flow rates of the oil and water that are mixed to form the influent or by use of an oil content meter on the inlet piping of the test rig. If an oil content meter is used, a sample of influent and a meter reading must be taken at the beginning of each test. If the meter reading is not within ±10 percent of the oil content of the sample, the meter readings subsequently taken during the test are unacceptable test results.

(9) When collecting a sample at a sample point that has a stop cock, the first minute of fluid flow through the stop cock must not be included in the sample collected.

(10) In each test, the separator must be operated in accordance with the procedures described in its instruction manual.

(11) No maintenance, including replacement of parts, may be performed on a separator during or between the tests described in this section.

(12) A one (1) liter sample of each oil to be used in testing must be taken and provided for use in the sample analysis required by § 162.050-39 .

(13) The separator may not be operated manually in Test No. 5S.

(b) *Test No. 1S.* The separator is filled with water and started. It is fed with oil for at least five (5) minutes and then with an oil-water influent containing an oil content of between 5,000 and 10,000 p.p.m. until a steady flow rate occurs. After the flow rate is steady, the influent is fed to the separator for thirty (30) minutes. Samples of separated water effluent are taken after the first ten (10) and twenty (20) minutes. At the end of the thirty (30) minute period, the air cock on the test rig is opened and, if necessary, the oil and water supply valves are closed to stop the flow of influent. A sample is then taken of the separated water effluent as the effluent flow ceases.

(c) *Test No. 2S*. Test No. 1S is repeated using an influent containing approximately 25 percent oil and 75 percent water.

(d) *Test No. 3S*. The separator is fed with oil until oil is discharged at the oil discharge outlet of the separator at essentially the same rate that oil is being fed to the separator. The separator is then fed with oil for five (5) additional minutes. If any oily mixture is discharged from the separated water outlet on the separator during the test, that observation is recorded.

(e) *Test No. 4S*. The separator is fed with water for fifteen (15) minutes. Samples of the separated water effluent are taken at the beginning of the test and after the first ten (10) minutes.

(f) *Test No. 5S*. The separator is operated automatically for three (3) hours. During the test, the separator is continuously fed with an influent varying from water to a mixture of 25 percent oil in water and back to water every fifteen (15) minutes. The oil concentration in the influent is varied in at least five (5) equal increments during each fifteen (15) minute period and the time intervals between the incremental changes are equal. During the last hour, the separator must be inclined at an angle of 22.5° with the plane of its normal operating position. During the last time increment in which the unit is fed a 25 percent oil mixture, a sample of the separated water effluent is taken. If the separator stops at any time during this test, that observation is recorded.

(g) *Test No. 6S*. Tests No. 1S and No. 2S are repeated using, in lieu of a heavy fuel oil in the influent, a light distillate fuel oil having a relative density of approximately 0.83 at 15 °C.

§ 162.050–25 Cargo monitor: Design specification.

(a) This section contains requirements that apply to cargo monitors.

(b) Each monitor must be designed so that it is calibrated by a means that does not involve manually mixing a known quantity of oil and a known quantity of water to form a mixture and manually feeding the mixture into the monitor.

(c) The electrical components of a monitor that are to be installed in an explosive atmosphere must be approved by an independent laboratory as components that Underwriters Laboratories Standard 913 (dated April 8, 1976) defines as intrinsically safe for use in a Class I, Group D hazardous location.

(d) Each monitor component that is a moving part must be designed so that its movement during operation of the monitor does not cause formation of static electricity.

(e) A monitor must be designed to operate in each plane that forms an angle of 22.5° with the plane of its normal operating position.

(f) Each monitor must be designed in accordance with the applicable requirements contained in subchapters F and J of this chapter.

(g) Each monitor must be designed so that it records each change in oil content of the mixture it is measuring within twenty (20) seconds after the change occurs.

(h) Each monitor must have a device that produces a warning signal and a signal that can be used to actuate valves in a vessel's fixed piping system, when—

(1) The oil content of the mixture being measured exceeds the concentration limit set by the operator of the monitor; and

(2) Malfunction, breakdown, or other failure of the monitor occurs.

(i) Each monitor must have a means to determine whether it is accurately calibrated.

[44 FR 53359, Sept. 13. 1079, as amended by CGD 76–088c, 48 FR 45727, Oct. 6, 1983]

§ 162.050–27 Cargo monitor: Approval tests.

(a) This section contains requirements that apply to cargo monitors.

(b) *Test conditions*. (1) The tests and each step in the tests must be carried out in the order described in this section. Each test must be performed without time delay between steps in the test.

(2) A test rig of the type described in § 162.050–19 must be used in performing each test.

(3) Each mixture used during the tests must be prepared by combining oil supplied from the oil injection pipe

308

of the test rig and water supplied from the mixture tank of the test rig. However, if the flow of oil through the oil injection pipe becomes intermittent, oil and water may be combined in the mixture tank to form the mixture.

(4) A mixture may be circulated through a monitor only once during testing.

(5) Unless otherwise provided in a specific test, the water used in each test must be clean, fresh water.

(6) The oil used in each test, except Test No. 2CM, must be Arabian light crude oil.

(7) Each test must be performed at an ambient temperature of between 10 °C and 30 °C.

(8) Unless otherwise provided in a specific test, each test must be performed at the maximum mixture pressure, the maximum flow rate, and the power supply ratings at which the monitor is designed to operate.

(9) The particulate contaminant described in Table 162.050–27(g) must be of a type that does not lose more than three (3) percent of its weight after ignition and must be insoluble in a 500 p.p.m. mixture.

(10) In each test the monitor must be operated in accordance with the procedures described in its instructions manual.

(11) Unless otherwise provided in a specific test, the centrifugal pump shown in Figure 162.050–19 must be operated at one thousand (1,000) revolutions per minute or more in each test.

(12) Whenever the oil content of a mixture is recorded, a sample of the mixture must also be taken. The oil content of the sample must be measured using the method described in § 162.050–39.

(13) A one (1) liter sample of each oil to be used in testing must be taken and provided for use in the sample analysis required by § 162.050–39.

(c) *Test No. 1CM.* The cargo monitor is calibrated and zeroed. It is then fed with water for 15 minutes and then with mixtures in the following concentrations: 15 p.p.m., 50 p.p.m., 100 p.p.m., and each additional concentration, in increments of 50 p.p.m. up to the highest oil concentration that can be read on the monitor. Each mixture is fed to the monitor in the order listed

for fifteen (15) minutes. Water is fed to the monitor for a (15) minute period between each mixture. At the end of each (15) minute period, an oil content reading is obtained and recorded.

(d) *Test No. 2CM.* (1) If the cargo monitor is designed for use with crude oils, it is fed with a mixture of water and the first oil listed in Table 162.050–27(d) at the following concentrations: 15 p.p.m., 100 p.p.m., and a concentration that is ninety (90) percent of the highest oil concentration in water that can be read on the monitor. Each concentration is fed to the monitor in the order listed until a steady reading occurs and is recorded. After each steady reading is recorded, the monitor is fed with water for fifteen (15) minutes. At the end of each fifteen (15) minute period of feeding the monitor with water, an oil content reading is again obtained and recorded.

(2) The steps described in paragraph (d)(1) of this section are repeating using each of the other oils listed in Table 162.050–27(d).

TABLE 162.050–27(D)—OIL TYPE AND CHARACTERISTICS

Oil type	Characteristics
1. Sahara blend crude oil	Density—low. Viscosity—low. Pour point—very low. Producing country—Algeria. General description—mixed base.
2. Arabian light crude oil	Density—medium. Viscosity—medium. Pour point—low. Producing country—Saudi Arabia. General description—mixed base.
3. Nigerian medium crude oil.	Density—high. Viscosity—medium. Pour point—low. Producing country—Nigeria. General description—naphthenic base.
4. Bachaquero 17 crude oil	Density—very high. Viscosity—very high. Pour point—low. Producing country—Venezuela. General description—asphaltic base.
5. Minas crude oil	Density—medium. Viscosity—high. Pour point—very high. Producing country—Indonesia. General description—paraffinic base.
6. Residual fuel oil	Bunker C or No. 6 Fuel Oil.

(3) If any oil listed in Table 162.050–27(d) is unavailable, an oil with similar properties may be substituted in testing.

(4) If the monitor is to be used with refined oil products, the steps described in paragraph (d)(1) of this section are performed using each of the following:

(i) Leaded regular grade automotive gasoline.

(ii) Unleaded automotive gasoline.

(iii) Kerosene.

(iv) Light diesel or No. 2 fuel oil.

(e) *Test No. 3CM.* (1) The cargo monitor is fed with water, zeroed, and then fed with a 100 p.p.m. mixture. The time at which the monitor first detects oil in the mixture, the times of reading 63 p.p.m. and 90 p.p.m., and the time of reaching the highest steady reading of oil content are recorded. The oil content of the mixture at the highest steady reading is also recorded.

(2) The metering pump is turned off and the time at which the highest reading starts to decrease, the times of reading 37 p.p.m. and 10 p.p.m., and the time of returning to the lowest steady oil content reading are recorded. The oil content of the mixture at the lowest steady reading is also recorded.

(3) The time interval between first detecting oil in the mixture and reading 63 p.p.m., and the time interval between the first decrease in the highest reading and reading 37 p.p.m., are averaged and recorded as the response time for the monitor.

(f) *Test No. 4CM.* (1) The cargo monitor is fed with water, zeroed, and then fed with a mixture containing ten (10) percent oil for one (1) minute. The following times occurring during this procedure are recorded:

(i) Time at which the monitor first detects oil.

(ii) Time of reading 100 p.p.m.

(iii) Time of exceeding the highest oil concentration that can be read on the monitor.

(iv) Time of returning to the highest oil concentration that can be read on the monitor.

(v) Time of returning to a reading of 100 p.p.m.

(vi) Time of returning to the lowest steady oil content reading.

(2) The oil content of the mixture at the lowest steady reading described in paragraph (f)(1)(vi) of this section is recorded.

(3) The monitor is fed with water, zeroed, and then fed with oil for one (1) minute after which the flow of water is resumed. The times described in paragraph (f)(1) of this section are recorded.

(4) The monitor is fed with a 100 p.p.m. mixutre until a steady oil content reading is obtained and recorded.

(g) *Test No. 5CM.* (1) The cargo monitor is fed with a 500 p.p.m. mixture until a steady reading is obtained and recorded.

(2) The monitor is fed with a 500 p.p.m. mixture to which enough sodium chloride has been added to provide a concentration of 60,000 parts per million of sodium chloride in water. The oil content reading, when steady, is recorded.

(3) The monitor is fed with a 500 p.p.m. mixture to which enough of the contaminant described in Table 162.050–27(g) has been added to provide a concentration of 100 parts per million of particulate contaminant in water. The oil content reading, when steady, is recorded.

TABLE 162.050–27(G)—INSOLUBLE PARTICULATE CONTAMINANT; PHYSICAL DESCRIPTION,p0,6/7

Particle sizes, microns: Percentage [1]	
0–5	39±2
5–10	18±3
10–20	16±3
20–40	18±3
40–80	9±3

[1] By weight of particle size in contaminant.

(h) *Test No. 6CM.* (1) The cargo monitor is fed with a 100 p.p.m. mixture until a steady oil content reading is obtained and recorded.

(2) The monitor is fed with a 100 p.p.m. mixture that has first passed through the centrifugal pump of the test rig. The pump is run at one fourth (¼) of its design speed. The oil content reading, when steady, is recorded.

(3) The steps described in paragraph (h)(2) of this section are repeated with the pump running at one-half (½) of its design speed and then repeated at its design speed.

(i) *Test No. 7CM.* (1) The steps described in paragraph (h)(1) of this section are repeated.

(2) The temperature of the mixture is adjusted to 10 °C and the flow continued until a steady oil content reading is obtained and recorded.

(3) The steps described in paragraph (i)(2) of this section are repeated with the temperature of the mixture at 65 °C or the highest mixture temperature at which the cargo monitor is designed to operate, whichever is lower.

(j) *Test No. 8CM.* (1) The steps described in paragraph (h)(1) of this section are repeated.

(2) If the monitor has a positive displacement mixture pump, the mixture pressure is lowered to one half of the monitor's maximum design pressure. If the monitor has a centrifugal mixture pump, or is not equipped with a mixture pump, the mixture flow rate is reduced to one-half of the monitor's design flow rate. The reduced flow rate or mixture pressure is maintained until a steady oil content reading is obtained and recorded.

(3) If the monitor has a positive displacement mixture pump, the mixture pressure is increased to twice the monitor's design pressure. If the monitor has a centrifugal mixture pump or does not have a mixture pump, the mixture flow rate is increased to twice the monitor's maximum design flow rate. The increased flow rate or mixture pressure is maintained until a steady oil content reading is obtained and recorded.

(k) *Test No. 9CM.* (1) The steps described in paragraph (h)(1) of this section are repeated.

(2) The water and metering pumps on the test rig are stopped for eight (8) hours after which the steps described in paragraph (h)(1) of this section are repeated.

(l) *Test No. 10CM.* (1) The supply voltage to the cargo monitor is increased to one hundred and ten (110) percent of its design supply voltage. The monitor is then fed a 100 p.p.m. mixture for one (1) hour. At the end of the one (1) hour period, an oil content reading is obtained and recorded.

(2) The steps described in paragraph (l)(1) of this section are repeated with the supply voltage to the monitor lowered to ninety (90) percent of its design supply voltage.

(3) Upon completing the steps described in paragraph (l)(2) of this sec-

tion, the supply voltage to the monitor is returned to the design rating.

(4) The steps described in paragraphs (l)(1), (l)(2), and (l)(3) of this section are repeated varying each other power supply to the monitor in the manner prescribed in those steps for supply voltage.

(m) *Test No. 11CM.* (1) The monitor is calibrated and zeroed.

(2) The steps described in paragraph (h)(1) of this section are repeated.

(3) A 100 p.p.m. mixture is fed to the monitor for eight (8) hours. At the end of the eight (8) hour period, an oil content reading is obtained and recorded.

(4) The monitor is fed with water until a steady oil content reading is obtained and recorded.

(n) *Test No. 12CM.* (1) All power to the monitor is shut off for one (1) week. After one week the monitor is started, zeroed, and calibrated.

(2) The monitor is fed with a 100 p.p.m. mixture for one (1) hour. An oil content reading is then obtained and recorded.

(3) The monitor is fed with water for one (1) hour. An oil content reading is then obtained and recorded.

(4) The steps described in paragraphs (n)(2) and (n)(3) of this section are repeated three (3) additional times. During the last hour in which the monitor is fed with a 100 p.p.m. mixture, the monitor is inclined at an angle of 22.5° with the plane of its normal operating position.

§ 162.050–29 Bilge monitor: Design specification.

(a) This section contains requirements that apply to bilge monitors.

(b) Each bilge monitor must be designed to meet the requirements of this section and the requirements for a cargo monitor in §§ 162.050–25 (b) through (g) and § 162.050–25(i).

(c) Each bilge monitor must have—

(1) A device that produces a warning signal, and a signal that can be used to actuate stop valves in a vessel's fixed piping system, when the oil content of the mixture being measured exceeds 15 p.p.m. ±5 p.p.m.;

(2) A device that produces a warning signal, and a signal that can be used to actuate stop valves in a vessel's fixed piping system, when the oil content of

311

the mixture being measured exceeds 100 p.p.m. ±20 p.p.m.; and

(3) A device that produces a warning signal, and a signal that can be used to actuate stop valves in a vessel's fixed piping system, when malfunction, breakdown, or other failure of the bilge monitor occurs.

(d) Each bilge monitor must have a device that is designed to record continuously the concentration of oil in p.p.m. that the monitor measures and to record the date and time of the measurements. The record must be durable enough to be kept for three (3) years. If the device has more than one scale, it must have a means to show on the record the scale in use at the time of the reading.

§ 162.050-31 Bilge monitor: Approval tests.

(a) This section contains requirements that apply to bilge monitors.

(b) *Test conditions.* (1) Each test must be conducted under the conditions prescribed in this section and under the conditions prescribed for cargo monitors in §§ 162.050-27 (b)(1) through (b)(4) and §§ 162.050-27 (b)(7) through (b)(13).

(2) Except as provided in Test No. 2BM, the oil used in each test must be a heavy fuel oil that has a relative density of approximately 0.94 at 15 °C. and a viscosity of at least 220 centistokes (approximately 900 seconds Redwood No. 1) at 37.8 °C.

(3) The water used in each test must be clean fresh water or clean fresh water in solution with sodium chloride. The water must have a relative density at 15 °C. that is equal to or less than 0.085 plus the relative density of the heavy fuel oil used in the tests.

(c) *Test No. 1BM.* (1) The bilge monitor is calibrated and zeroed. It is then fed with water for 15 minutes and then with mixtures in the following concentrations: 15 p.p.m., 50 p.p.m., 75 p.p.m., 100 p.p.m., and each additional concentration, in increments of 25 p.p.m. up to the highest oil concentration that can be read on the monitor. Each concentration is fed to the monitor in the order listed for fifteen (15) minutes. Water is fed to the monitor for fifteen (15) minutes between each mixture. At the end of each fifteen (15)

minute period an oil content reading is obtained and recorded.

(2) The metering and water pumps of the test rig are started and the oil content of the mixture is increased until the device required by § 162.050-29(c)(1) actuates. The oil content of the mixture causing actuation is recorded.

(3) The oil content of the mixture is then increased until the device required by § 162.050-29(c)(2) actuates. The oil content of the mixture causing actuation is recorded.

(d) *Test No. 2BM.* Test No. 1BM is repeated using, in lieu of a heavy fuel oil in the mixture, a light distillate fuel oil having a relative density of approximately 0.83 at 15 °C.

(e) *Test No. 3BM.* (1) The bilge monitor is fed with water, zeroed, and then fed with a 15 p.p.m. mixture until a steady reading is obtained and recorded. The time of first detecting oil in the mixture and the time of reaching the highest steady reading of oil content are also recorded. The metering pump is turned off after the highest steady reading is obtained. The time at which the highest steady reading starts to decrease and the time of returning to the lowest steady oil content reading are recorded. The oil content of the lowest steady reading is also recorded.

(2) The steps in paragraph (1) of this section are repeated using a 100 p.p.m. mixture.

(f) *Test No. 4BM.* (1) The bilge monitor is fed with water, zeroed, and then fed with a mixture containing (10) percent oil for one (1) minute. The following times occurring during this procedure are recorded:

(i) Time at which the monitor first detects oil.

(ii) Time of actuation of the device required by § 162.050-29(c)(1).

(iii) Time of actuation of the device required by § 162.050-29(c)(2).

(iv) Time of exceeding the highest oil concentration that can be read on the monitor.

(v) Time of returning to the highest oil concentration that can be read on the monitor.

(vi) Time of returning to the lowest steady oil content reading.

(2) The oil content of the mixture at the lowest steady reading described in

paragraph (f)(1)(vi) of this section is recorded.

(3) The monitor is fed with water, zeroed, and then fed with oil for one (1) minute after which the flow of water is resumed. The times described in paragraph (f)(1) of this section are recorded.

(4) The monitor is fed with a 15 p.p.m. mixture until a steady oil content reading is obtained and recorded.

(5) The monitor is fed with a 100 p.p.m. mixture until a steady oil content reading is obtained and recorded.

(g) *Test No. 5BM.* (1) The bilge monitor is fed with an 80 p.p.m. mixture until a steady reading is obtained and recorded.

(2) The monitor is fed with an 80 p.p.m. mixture to which enough sodium chloride has been added to provide a concentration of 60,000 parts per million of sodium chloride in water. The oil content reading, when steady, is recorded.

(3) The monitor is fed with an 80 p.p.m. mixture to which enough of the contaminant described in Table 162.050-27(g) has been added to provide a concentration of 20 parts per million of particulate contaiminant in water. The oil content reading, when steady, is recorded.

(h) *Test No. 6BM.* (1) The bilge monitor is fed with a 5–10 p.p.m. mixture until a steady reading is obtained and recorded.

(2) If the monitor has a positive displacement mixture pump, the mixture pressure is lowered to one half of the monitor's maximum design pressure. If the monitor has a centrifugal mixture pump or is not equipped with a mixture pump, the mixture flow rate is reduced to one half of the monitor's maximum design flow rate. After reduction of the pressure or flow rate, the oil content of the mixture is increased until the device required by §162.050-29(c)(1) actuates. The oil content causing actuation is recorded.

(3) The monitor is fed with an 80 p.p.m. mixture until a steady reading is obtained and recorded. The oil content of the mixture is then increased until the device required by §162.050-29(c)(2) actuates. The oil content causing actuation is recorded.

(4) If the monitor has a positive displacement mixture pump, the mixture

pressure is increased to twice the monitor's maximum design pressure. If the monitor has a centrifugal mixture pump or if the monitor is not equipped with a mixture pump, the mixture flow rate is increased to twice the monitor's maximum design flow rate. After increasing the pressure or flow rate, the oil content of the mixture is increased until the device required by §162.050-29(c)(1) actuates. The oil content causing actuation is recorded.

(5) The steps described in paragraph (h)(3) of this section are repeated.

(i) *Test No. 7BM.* (1) The steps described in paragraphs (c)(2) and (c)(3) of this section are repeated.

(2) The water and metering pumps on the test rig are stopped for eight (8) hours after which the steps described in paragraphs (c)(2) and (c)(3) of this section are repeated.

(j) *Test No. 8BM.* (1) The supply voltage to the bilge monitor is increased to one hundred and ten (110) percent of its design supply voltage. The monitor is then fed a 10 p.p.m. mixture for one (1) hour. At the end of the one (1) hour period, the oil content reading is recorded.

(2) The oil content of the mixture is increased until the device required by §162.050-29(c)(1) actuates. The oil content causing actuation is recorded.

(3) The bilge monitor is fed with an 80 p.p.m. mixture for one (1) hour. At the end of the one (1) hour period, an oil content reading is obtained and recorded.

(4) The oil content of the mixture is increased until the device required by §162.050-29(c)(2) actuates. The oil content causing actuation is recorded.

(5) The steps described in paragraphs (j)(1) through (j)(4) of this section are repeated with the supply voltage to the bilge monitor lowered to ninety (90) percent of its design voltage.

(6) Upon completing the steps described in paragraph (j)(5) of this section, the supply voltage to the monitor is returned to the design rating.

(7) The steps described in paragraphs (j)(1) through (j)(4) of this section are repeated varying each other power supply to the monitor in the manner prescribed in those steps for supply voltage.

313

(k) *Test No. 9BM.* (1) The steps described in paragraphs (c)(2) and (c)(3) of this section are repeated.

(2) An 80 p.p.m. mixture is fed to the bilge monitor for eight (8) hours. At the end of the eight (8) hour period, an oil content reading is obtained and recorded.

(3) The steps described in paragraphs (c)(2) and (c)(3) of this section are repeated.

(4) The monitor is fed with water until a steady reading is obtained and recorded.

(l) *Test No. 10BM.* (1) All power to the bilge monitor is shut off for one (1) week. After one week the monitor is started, zeroed, and calibrated.

(2) The monitor is fed with an 80 p.p.m. mixture for one (1) hour. An oil content reading is then obtained and recorded.

(3) The steps described in paragraphs (c)(2) and (c)(3) of this section are repeated.

(4) The monitor is fed with water for one (1) hour. An oil content reading is then obtained and recorded.

(5) The steps described in paragraphs (l)(2), (l)(3), and (l)(4) of this section are repeated three (3) additional times. During the last time that the step described in paragraph (i)(2) of this section is repeated, the monitor is inclined at an angle of 22.5° with the plane of its normal operating position.

§ 162.050–33 Bilge alarm: Design specification.

(a) This section contains requirements that apply to bilge alarms.

(b) Each bilge alarm must be designed to meet the requirements for a cargo monitor in §§ 162.050–25(b) through (g), § 162.050–25(i), and the requirements in this section.

(c) Each bilge alarm must have a device that produces a warning signal, and a signal that can be used to actuate stop valves in a vessel's fixed piping system, when—

(1) the oil content of the mixture being measured by the bilge alarm exceeds 15 p.p.m. ±5 p.p.m., and

(2) malfunction, breakdown, or other failure of the bilge alarm occurs.

§ 162.050–35 Bilge alarm: Approval tests.

(a) This section contains requirements that apply to bilge alarms.

(b) *Test Conditions.* (1) Each test must be conducted under the conditions prescribed for cargo monitors in §§ 162.050–27 (b)(1) through (b)(5), §§ 162.050–27 (b)(7), (b)(8), (b)(10), (b)(11), and (b)(13).

(2) Each test must be performed using a light distillate fuel oil having a relative density of approximately 0.83 at 15 °C.

(3) The oil content of each sample must be measured using the method described in § 162.050–39.

(c) *Test No. 1A.* The bilge alarm is calibrated and zeroed. The metering and water pumps of the test rig are started and the oil content of the mixture is increased until the alarm actuates. A sample of the mixture causing actuation of the alarm is taken. The alarm is then fed with water for fifteen (15) minutes.

(d) *Test No. 2A.* (1) The bilge alarm is fed with a 40 p.p.m mixture until the bilge alarm actuates. The time of turning on the metering pump of the test rig and the time of alarm actuation are recorded. The flow rate on the flow meter of the test rig is also recorded.

(2) The response time of the alarm is calculated as follows:

$$\text{response time} = T_2 - \left[T_1 + \frac{(\pi)\left(D^2\right)(L)}{4Q} \right]$$

T_2=time of alarm actuation
T_1=time of turning on the metering pump of the test rig
D=inside diameter of the mixture pipe (cm)
L=length of the mixture pipe (cm)
Q=flow rate (cm³/sec)

(e) *Test No. 3A.* (1) The metering and water pumps of the test rig are started and the oil content of the mixture is increased until the bilge alarm actuates. A sample of the mixture causing actuation of the alarm is taken.

(2) If the alarm has a positive displacement mixture pump, the mixture pressure is reduced to one-half (½) of the alarm's maximum design pressure. If the alarm has a centrifugal mixture pump or is not equipped with a mixture

pump, the mixture flow rate is reduced to one-half (½) of the alarm's maximum design flow rate. After reduction of pressure or flow rate, the oil content in the mixture is increased until the alarm actuates. A sample of the mixture causing actuation of the alarm is taken.

(3) If the alarm has a positive displacement mixture pump, the influent pressure is increased to twice the alarm's minimum design pressure. If the alarm has a centrifugal mixture pump or if the alarm is not equipped with a mixture pump, the influent flow rate is increased to twice the alarm's maximum design flow rate. After increasing the pressure or flow rate, the oil content in the mixture is increased until the alarm actuates. A sample of the mixture causing actuation is taken.

(f) *Test No. 4A.* (1) The steps described in paragraph (e)(1) of this section are repeated.

(2) The metering and water pumps of the test rig are stopped for eight (8) hours.

(3) The metering and water pumps are started and the oil content of the mixture is increased until the bilge alarm actuates. A sample of the mixture causing actuation is taken.

(g) *Test No. 5A.* (1) The supply voltage to the bilge alarm is raised to one-hundred ten (110) percent of its design supply voltage. The oil content of the mixture is then increased until the alarm actuates. A sample of the mixture causing actuation is taken.

(2) The supply voltage to the alarm is lowered to ninety (90) percent of its design suppy voltage. The oil content of the mixture is then increased until the alarm actuates. A sample of the mixture causing actuation is taken.

(3) Upon completion of the steps described in paragraph (g)(2) of this section, the supply voltage to the alarm is returned to its design value.

(4) The steps described in paragraphs (g)(1), (g)(2), and (g)(3) of this section are repeated varying each other power supply to the alarm in the manner prescribed in those steps for supply voltage.

(h) *Test No. 6A.* (1) The steps described in paragraph (e)(1) of this section are repeated.

(2) The bilge alarm is fed with a 5 to 10 p.p.m. mixture for eight (8) hours. After eight (8) hours the oil content of the mixture is then increased until the alarm actuates. A sample of the mixture causing actuation is taken.

(i) *Test No. 7A.* (1) All power to the bilge alarm is shut off for one (1) week. After one (1) week the alarm is then started, zeroed, and calibrated.

(2) The steps described in paragraph (e)(1) of this section are repeated. Water is then fed to the monitor for one (1) hour.

(3) The steps described in paragraph (i)(2) are repeated seven (7) additional times. During the last hour, the alarm must be inclined at an angle of 22.5° with the plane of its normal operating position.

§162.050–37 Vibration test.

(a) Equipment submitted for Coast Guard approval must first be tested under the conditions prescribed in paragraph (b) of this section. The test must be performed at an independent laboratory that has the equipment to subject the item under test to the vibrating frequencies and amplitudes prescribed in paragraph (b) of this section. The test report submitted with the application for Coast Guard approval must be prepared by the laboratory and must contain the test results.

(b) Each monitor and bilge alarm and each control of a separator must be subjected to continuous sinusoidal vibration in each of the following directions for a 4 hour period in each direction:

(1) Vertically up and down.

(2) Horizontally from side to side.

(3) Horizontally from end to end.
The vibrating frequency must be 80Hz, except that the vibrating frequency of equipment that has a resonant frequency between 2Hz and 80Hz must be the resonant frequency. If the vibrating frequency is between 2Hz and 13.2Hz, the displacement amplitude must be ±1mm. If the vibrating frequency is between 13.2Hz and 80 Hz, the acceleration amplitude must be ± [(.7)(gravity)].

§ 162.050–39 Measurement of oil content.

(a) *Scope.* This section describes the method and apparatus to be used in measuring the oil content of a sample taken in approval testing of each separator, monitor, or alarm. Light oil fractions in the sample, with the exception of volatile components lost during extractions, are included in each measurement.

(b) *Summary of method.* Each sample is acidified to a low pH and extracted with two volumes of solvent. The oil content of the sample is determined by comparison of the infrared absorbance of the sample extract against the absorbance of known concentrations of a reference oil in solvent.

(c) *Apparatus.* The following apparatus is used in each measurement:

(1) Separatory funnel that is 1000 ml. or more in volume and that has a Teflon stopcock.

(2) Infrared spectrophotometer.

(3) A cell of 5 mm. pathlength that has sodium chloride or infrared grade quartz with a minimum of 80 percent transmittance at 2930 cm^{-1}. (This cell should be used if the oil content of the sample to be measured is expected to have a concentration of between 2 p.p.m. and 80 p.p.m.)

(4) A cell of pathlength longer than 5 mm. that has sodium chloride or infrared grade quartz with a minimum of 80 percent transmittance at 2930 cm^{-1}. (This cell should be used if the oil content of the sample to be measured is expected to have a concentration of between 0.1 p.p.m. and 2 p.p.m.)

(5) Medium grade filter paper.

(6) 100 ml. glass stoppered volumetric flasks.

(d) *Reagents.* The following regaents are used in each measurement:

(1) Hydrochloric acid prepared by mixing equal amounts of concentrated, reagent grade hydrochloric acid and distilled water.

(2) Reagent grade sodium chloride.

(3) One of the following solvents:

(i) Spectrographic grade carbon tetrachloride.

(ii) Reagent grade Freon 113, except that this solvent may not be used to analyze samples in approval testing of cargo monitors. (Ucon 113, Genatron 113, or an equivalent fluorocarbon solvent are also acceptable.)

(4) Reference oil, which is the oil used in the portion of the test during which the sample is collected.

(5) Stock reference standard prepared by weighing 0.30 g. of reference oil in a tared 100 ml. volumetric flask and diluting to 100 ml. volume with solvent.

(e) *Preparation of. calibration standards.* A series of dilutions is prepared by pipetting volumes of stock reference standard into 100 ml. volumetric flasks and diluting to volume with solvent. A convenient series of volumes of the stock reference standard is 5, 10, 15, 20, and 25 ml. The exact concentrations of the dilutions in milligrams of oil per 100 milliliters of diluted stock reference standard are calculated. The calibration standards are the dilutions.

(f) *Extraction.* (1) A reagent blank is carried through each step described in this paragraph and paragraph (g) of this section.

(2) The pH of each sample is checked by dipping a glass rod into the sample and touching the rod with pH-sensitive paper to ensure that the pH is 2 or lower. More acid is added if necessary until the pH is 2 or lower. The glass rod is then rinsed in the sample bottle with solvent.

(3) The sample is poured into a separatory funnel and 5 g. of sodium chloride are added.

(4) Fifty (50) ml. of solvent are added to the sample bottle. The bottle is capped tightly and shaken thoroughly to rinse its inside. The contents of the bottle are then transferred to the separatory funnel containing the sample and extracted by shaking vigorously for 2 minutes. The layers are allowed to separate.

(5) The solvent layer is drained through a funnel containing solvent moistened filter paper into a 100 ml. volumetric flask.

(6) Fifty (50) ml. of solvent are added to the sample bottle. The bottle is capped tightly and shaken thoroughly to rinse its inside surface. The contents of the bottle are then transferred to the separatory funnel containing the water layer of the sample. The contents of the separatory funnel are then extracted by shaking vigorously for 2

minutes. The layers are allowed to separate. The solvent layer is then drained through a funnel containing solvent moistened filter paper into the volumetric flask containing the solvent layer of the sample.

(7) The tips of the separatory funnel, filter paper, and funnel are rinsed with small portions of solvent and the rinsings are collected in the volumetric flask containing the solvent layer of the sample. The volume is adjusted with solvent up to 100 ml. The flask is then stoppered and its contents are thoroughly mixed.

(8) The water layer remaining in the separatory funnel is drained into a 1000 ml. graduated cylinder and the water volume estimated to the nearest 5 ml.

(g) *Infrared spectroscopy.* (1) The infrared spectrophotometer is prepared according to manufacturer instructions.

(2) A cell is rinsed with two volumes of the solvent layer contained in the volumetric flask. The cell is then completely filled with the solvent layer. A matched cell containing solvent is placed in the reference beam.

(3) If a scanning spectrophotometer is used, the solvent layer in the cell and the calibration standards are scanned from 3200 cm^{-1} to 2700 cm-1. If a single beam spectrophotometer is used, the manufacturer's instructions are followed and the absorbance is measured at or near 2930 cm-1.

(4) If the scan is recorded on absorbance paper, a straight baseline of the type described in Figure 162.050–39(g) is constructed. To obtain the net absorbance, the absorbance of the baseline at 2930 cm^{-1} is subtracted from the absorbance of the maximum peak on the curve at 2930 cm-1.

(5) If the scan is recorded on transmittance paper, a straight baseline is constructed on the hydrocarbon band plotted on the paper. The net absorbance is:

$$\log_{10} \frac{\%T(\text{baseline})}{\%T(\text{peak maximum})}$$

(6) A plot is prepared for net absorbance vs. oil content of the calibration standards or of the percentages of stock reference standard contained in the calibration standards.

FIGURE 162,050—39(g) - SPECTRUM ILLUSTRATING BASELINE CONSTRUCTION

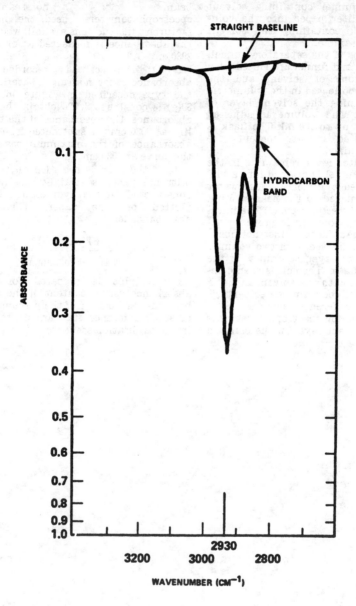

(7) If the net absorbance of a sample determined by the calibration plot exceeds 0.8 or the linear range of the spectrophotometer, a dilution of the solvent layer contained in the volumetric flask after completing the step

described in paragraph (f)(7) of this section is prepared by the pipetting an appropriate volume of the solvent layer into a second volumetric flask and diluting to volume with solvent. If the net absorbance is less than 0.1 when determined in accordance with the procedures in this paragraph, it is recalculated using a longer pathlength cell.

(h) *Calculations.* (1) The plot described in paragraph (g)(6) of this section is used to determine the milligrams of oil in each 100 ml. of solvent layer contained in the volumetric flask after completing the steps described in paragraph (f) or paragraph (g)(7) of this section.

(2) The oil content of the sample is calculated using the following formula:

oil content of sample=$R{\times}D{\times}1000/V$

R = mg. of oil in 100 ml. of solvent layer determined from plot.

D = 1 or, if the step described in paragraph (g)(7) of this section is performed, the ratio of the volume of the second volumetric flask described in that paragraph to the volume of solvent layer pipetted into the second volumetric flask.

V = The volume of water in milliliters drained into the graduated cylinder at the step described in paragraph (f)(8) of this section.

(3) The results are reported to two significant figures for oil contents below 100 mg/l and to three significant figures for oil contents above 100 mg/l. The results are converted to p.p.m.

PART 163—CONSTRUCTION

Subpart 163.001 [Reserved]

Subpart 163.002—Pilot Hoist

AUTHORITY: 46 U.S.C. 3306, 3703, 5115; E.O. 12234, 45 FR 58801, 3 CFR, 1980 Comp., p. 277; 49 CFR 1.46.

SOURCE: CGFR 50–30, 16 FR 1086, Feb. 6, 1951, unless otherwise noted.

Subpart 163.001 [Reserved]

Subpart 163.002—Pilot Hoist

SOURCE: CGD 74–140, 46 FR 63287, Dec. 31, 1981, unless otherwise noted.

§ 163.002–1 Scope.

(a) This subpart contains standards and approval and production tests for pilot hoists used on merchant vessels.

(b) The requirements in this subpart apply to a pilot hoist designed for use along a vertical portion of a vessel's hull.

§ 163.002–3 Applicable technical regulations.

(a) This subpart makes reference to the following Coast Guard regulations in this chapter:

(1) Subpart 58.30 (Fluid Power and Control Systems).

(2) Section 94.33–10 (Description of Fleet Angle).

(3) Part 111 (Electrical System, General Requirements).

(4) Subpart 163.003 (Pilot Ladder).

(b) [Reserved]

§ 163.002–5 Definitions.

(a) *Maximum persons capacity* means—

(1) If the hoist has a rigid ladder, one person; or

(2) If the hoist has a platform, one person per square meter (10.75 sq. ft.) or fraction thereof of platform area (including hatch area);

(b) *Working load* means the sum of the weights of—

(1) The rigid ladder or lift platform, the suspension cables (if any) and the pilot ladder on a pilot hoist; and

(2) 150 kilograms (330 pounds) times the maximum persons capacity of the hoist;

(c) *Lift height* means the distance from the lowest step of the pilot ladder on a pilot hoist to the deck of a vessel on which the hoist is designed for installation when—

(1) The suspension cables of the hoist are run out until only three turns of cable remain on each drum; or

(2) If the hoist does not have suspension cables, the ladder or lift platform is in its lowest position.

§ 163.002-7 Independent laboratory.

(a) The approval and production tests in this subpart must be conducted by, or under the supervision of, an independent laboratory accepted by the Coast Guard under subpart 159.010 of this chapter.

(b) [Reserved]

§ 163.002-9 Approval procedure.

(a) *General.* A pilot hoist is approved by the Coast Guard under the procedures in subpart 159.005 of this chapter.

(b) *Approval testing.* Each approval test must be conducted in accordance with § 163.002-21.

(c) *Approval of alternative designs.* A pilot hoist that does not meet the materials, construction, or performance requirements of this subpart may be approved if the application and any approval tests prescribed by the Commandant in place of or in addition to the approval tests required by this subpart, show that the alternative materials, construction, or performance is at least as effective as that specified by the requirements of this subpart.

§ 163.002-11 Materials.

(a) *Gears.* Each gear in a pilot hoist must be made of machine cut steel or machine cut bronze, or must be of a design of equivalent strength, durability, reliability and accuracy.

(b) *Suspension cables.* Each suspension cable on a pilot hoist must be a corrosion-resistant wire rope other than galvanized wire rope.

(c) *Corrosion-resistant materials.* Materials of a pilot hoist that are not in watertight enclosures must be—

(1) Corrosion-resistant or must be treated to be corrosion-resistant; and

(2) Galvanically compatible with each other adjoining material.

(d) *Aluminum alloys.* Any aluminum alloy which is not resistant to stress corrosion in marine atmospheres (i.e., contains more than 0.6 percent copper), must not be used in a structural component or in any other hoist component subject to stress.

§ 163.002-13 Construction.

(a) *General.* Each hoist must have a rigid ladder or a lift platform on which a person being raised or lowered may stand.

(b) *Spreader.* Each hoist must have a spreader or other device to prevent twisting of its ladder or lift platform. If a spreader is provided, it must be at least 1800 millimeters (5 feet, 10 inches) long.

(c) *Rollers.* The rigid ladder or lift platform on a pilot hoist and the ends of its spreader (if a spreader is provided) must have rollers at each point of contact with the vessel that allow the ladder or platform to move smoothly over the side of the vessel.

(d) *Load carrying parts.* Each load carrying part of a pilot hoist must be designed to have a minimum breaking strength of at least six times the load imposed on the part by the working load during operation of the hoist.

(e) *Exposed moving parts.* Each exposed moving part of a pilot hoist that poses a hazard to personnel must have a screen or guard.

(f) *Nonfunctional sharp edges and projections of excessive length.* A pilot hoist must not have nonfunctional sharp edges and must not have fastening devices or other projections of excessive length.

(g) *Installation requirements.* Each pilot hoist must be designed to allow—

(1) Its installation along the edge of a deck at a vertical portion of the hull;

(2) Its installation on the deck in a manner that does not require use of the vessel's side rails for support; and

(3) Unobstructed passage between the ladder or lift platform of the hoist and the deck of a vessel.

(h) *Deck interlock for portable hoist.* A pilot hoist, if portable, must have a deck interlock that prevents movement of the ladder or lift platform when the hoist is not installed.

(i) *Power source.* Each hoist must be designed to operate on electric, pneumatic, or hydraulic power or a combination of these.

(j) *Electrical equipment.* Electrical equipment of a pilot hoist must meet the electrical engineering regulations in part 111 of this chapter. The operating voltage of electrical equipment on the ladder or lift platform of a pilot hoist must not exceed 25 volts.

(k) *Pneumatic and hydraulic equipment.* Pneumatic and hydraulic equipment of a pilot hoist must comply with the marine engineering regulations of subpart 58.30 of this chapter. Each pneumatically powered hoist must have a water trap, air filter, air regulator, pressure gauge, and oil lubricator in the air line between the vessel's compressed air source and the pneumatic motor.

(l) *Hoist control lever.* Each pilot hoist must have a control lever for raising and lowering its ladder or lift platform. Movement of the lever upward or toward the operator must result in upward movement of the ladder or lift platform. Movement of the control in the opposite direction must result in downward movement of the ladder or lift platform. The control must be designed so that when released by the operator the ladder or lift platform stops immediately.

(m) *Emergency disconnect device.* Each pilot hoist must have a switch or valve for disconnecting the main power source in an emergency.

(n) *Power indicator.* Each pilot hoist must have an indicator to show the operator when power is being supplied to the hoist.

(o) *Arrangement of controls and power indicator.* The hoist control lever, the emergency disconnect device, and the power indicator on a pilot hoist must be arranged so that the hoist operator, when standing, can view all movement of the ladder or lift platform while using this equipment.

(p) *Hand-operated device and interlock.* Each pilot hoist must have a hand-operated device for raising and lowering its ladder or lift platform. The device must be operable from a standing position. The hoist must have an interlock that prevents simultaneous operation of its hand-operated device and its power source. Any removable hand gear, crank, or wheel of the hand-operated device must be securely stowed on the hoist.

(q) *Upper position step.* Unless a hoist has a pneumatic motor that stalls at the end of cable travel without jarring, jerking, or damaging the hoist, it must have one or more limit switches or valves that stop the ladder or lift platform at its upper end of travel without jarring, jerking, or damaging the hoist.

(r) *Means of lubrication.* Each hoist must have a means to lubricate its bearings. Sliding-contact gearing, such as worm gears, must operate in an oil bath, or have another means of lubricating the gear teeth on each revolution. Each lubricant enclosure must be designed so that it can be readily filled, drained, and checked for lubricant level.

(s) *Machinery housing.* Each machinery housing on a pilot hoist except gear boxes and other enclosures that retain lubricants, must have means that permit examination of all internal moving parts using common tools or without tools. Each machinery housing, except gear boxes and other enclosures that retain lubricants, must be designed to prevent moisture accumulation.

(t) *Suspension cable.* If a hoist has suspension cables, at least 2 cables must be provided and they must be arranged so that the ladder or lift platform remains level and stationary if one of the cables breaks. Each cable must be arranged to lead fair in a 15 degree vessel list toward the side of the vessel on which the hoist is installed. The devices for attaching the cables to their winch drums must be capable of supporting 2.2 times the workig load with the cables run all the way out.

(u) *Sheaves and drums.* Each sheave and each winch drum for a suspension cable on a pilot hoist must be of a size recommended by the cable supplier for the diameter and construction of the cable. Each sheave must have a device that prevents the cable from jumping out of the sheave groove. Each drum must be designed to accept one level wind of wrap. The fleet angle of a grooved drum must not exceed 8 degrees, and the fleet angle of a non-grooved drum must not exceed 4 degrees.

NOTE: The term *fleet angle* is defined in § 94.33-10 of this chapter.

(v) *Rigid ladder.* A rigid ladder on a pilot hoist must have thermally insulated handholds and a padded backrest so that the person being raised or lowered may firmly brace himself or herself between the ladder and the backrest. The ladder must be at least 2.5 m (100 in.) long from the bottom rung to the top of the handholds.

(w) *Ladder rungs.* Each rigid ladder must have at least six rungs, each with a non-skid surface that does not retain water. Adhesive non-skid sheets may not be used. (For example, a suitable surface for a wooden rung is one that has grooves at least 3 mm (⅛ in.) deep cut in a diamond pattern so that water runs off the edge of the step. Non-skid grit is applied directly to the step surface.) The stepping surface of each rung must be not less than 115 mm (4½ in.) wide and not less than 400 mm (16 in.) long. The distance from the top of one rung to the top of the next must be uniform, between 300 mm (12 in.) and 350 mm (13¾ in.).

(x) *Platform railing.* A lift platform on a pilot hoist must be enclosed by a guardrail that has a diameter of between 30 millimeters (1¼ inches) and 75 millimeters (3 inches). The center of the guardrail must be at least 900 millimeters (3 feet) above the platform. At least one intermediate rail must be provided between the guardrail and the platform. Each rail must be set back from the edge of the platform at least 50 millimeters (2 inches). Each gate in the rails must have a latch that can keep the gate securely closed.

(y) *Platform floor.* The platform floor of a pilot hoist must have a non-skid surface and must be at least 750 millimeters (30 inches) by 750 millimeters, exclusive of the surface area of any hatch. Each hatch in the platform floor must be at least 750 millimeters (30 inches) by 750 millimeters. Each hatch must have a means to keep it securely positioned both when opened and closed.

(z) *Pilot ladder fittings.* The bottom of the rigid ladder or lift platform on a pilot hoist must have fittings to attach a pilot ladder of the type that meets the requirements of subpart 163.003 of this chapter. The fittings must be arranged so that—

(1) The distance between the top of the highest step on the pilot ladder and the surface of the lift platform or top of the bottom rung on the rigid ladder is between 300 and 350 millimeters (12 and 13¾ inches);

(2) The steps of the pilot ladder are directly below and in line with the steps of the rigid ladder or edge of the lift platform; and

(3) The pilot ladder can bear on the side of the vessel when in use.

(aa) *Emergency stop switch.* Each pilot hoist must have an emergency stop switch that can be operated by a person on the ladder or lift platform.

(bb) *Fasteners.* Each fastening device securing a part of a pilot hoist must have a means to prevent the device from loosening.

(cc) *Gears.* Each gear must be keyed to its shaft.

(dd) *Welding.* Each weld must be made using automatic welding equipment or be made by a welder who is qualified by the U.S. Coast Guard, U.S. Navy, American Bureau of Shipping, American Welding Society, American Society of Mechanical Engineers, or other organization that has similar procedures for welder qualifications that are acceptable to the Commandant.

§ 163.002-15 Performance.

(a) Each pilot hoist must have sufficient performance capability to pass the approval tests in § 163.002-21.

(b) [Reserved]

§ 163.002-17 Instructions and markings.

(a) *Instruction plates or placards.* Each pilot hoist must have instructions that show its method of operation and lubrication of its working parts. The instructions must be on one or more corrosion-resistant plates, or must be weatherproof placards. The instructions must be attached to the hoist. Each instruction must be in English or must have understandable symbols or pictograms. The operator of the hoist must be able to see and read the operating instructions when operating the hoist control lever. The lubricating instructions must state the recommended lubricants for the temperature range in which the hoist is designed to operate. The temperature range must be stated in both degrees Celsius and Fahrenheit.

(b) *Marking of controls.* Each control on a pilot hoist and each position of the control must be identified by a marking on the hoist.

(c) *Marking of gauges.* Each gauge on a pilot hoist must be marked with its normal operating range.

(d) *Manual.* Each pilot hoist must have a manual of installation instructions, operating instructions, maintenance and repair instructions, a lubrication chart, a parts list, a list of sources of repair parts, and a log for keeping maintenance records. Each manual must be in English.

§ 163.002–21 Approval tests.

(a) *General.* If a pilot hoist fails one of the tests in this section the cause of the failure must be identified and any needed design changes made. After a test failure and any design change, the failed test, and any other previously completed tests affected by the change, must be rerun.

(b) *Visual examination.* Before starting the tests described in this section an assembled pilot hoist is examined for evidence of noncompliance with the requirements in §§ 163.002–11 and 163.002–13.

(c) The following approval tests must be conducted:

(1) *Rung strength.* If the pilot hoist has a rigid ladder a static load of 900 kilograms (2000 pounds) is applied to the center of a ladder rung for one minute. The load must be uniformly distributed over a 100 millimeter (4 inch) wide contact surface. The test must be repeated using a second ladder rung. The rungs must not break or crack during these tests.

(2) *Platform strength.* If the pilot hoist has a lift platform, the platform is lifted to a level where it is supported only by its suspension components. A static load of 900 kilograms (2000 pounds) is then applied to the center of the plat-

form for one minute. The load must be uniformly distributed over a 100 millimeter (4 inch) square contact surface. The test must be repeated enough additional times so that the load is placed in the center of each hatch cover when in its closed position, and in the center of each area of the platform located between floor supports. The platform must not break or crack during these tests.

(3) *Deck interlock.* If the pilot hoist is portable, it is placed in an uninstalled position. Its hoist control lever is then activated. The deck interlock must prevent movement of the ladder or lift platform when the lever is activated.

(4) *Lifting and lowering speed and level wind.* The hoist is installed in a level operating position and a weight equal to the weight of the pilot ladder plus 150 kg (330 lb.) times the maximum persons capacity of the hoist is placed on its ladder or lift platform. The ladder or lift platform is repeatedly raised and lowered under power operation until a total distance of at least 150 meters (500 feet) has been traversed. The ladder or lift platform is raised and lowered each time through a distance of at least 5 meters (16 feet). The average speed of raising the ladder or lift platform and the average lowering speed during this test must both be between 15 and 21 meters per minute (50 and 70 feet per minute). During the test, each suspension cable must have one level wind of wrap each time it is rewound onto its drum.

(5) *Upper position stop.* The hoist is installed in a level operating position and a weight equal to the weight of the pilot ladder plus 150 kg (330 lb.) times the maximum persons capacity is attached to the hoist. The hoist must be able to raise the weight to the upper limit of travel of the ladder or lift platform and must be able to stop at the upper limit without jarring, jerking, or damage. The test is repeated with no weight on the ladder or lift platform.

(6) *Cable securing device.* If the hoist has suspension cables, it is installed in a level operating position and the cables are run all the way out. A weight equal to 2.2 times the working load is then attached to the cables. The cables must remain securely attached to the

drums for at least one minute after the weight has been attached.

(7) *Controls and power indicator.* The hoist is installed in a level operating position and a weight equal to the working load is attached to the hoist. The hoist control lever is then operated with the power both on and off. The lever, when operated, must meet the requirements in § 163.002–13(1). The power indicator must meet the requirements in § 163.002–13(n) during the test. When the power is turned off, the ladder or lift platform must stop immediately and remain stationary until power is turned on. The emergency stop switch on the ladder or lift platform is activated at some point when the ladder or lift platform is being raised or lowered. Upon activation, the ladder or lift platform must stop and remain stationary.

(8) *Hand operation and interlock.* The hoist is installed in a level operating position and a weight equal to the working load is attached to the hoist. The hand operated device is then engaged. One person, when using the hand operated device, must be able to raise and lower the weight through a distance of at least 5 meters (16 ft.) in each direction and must be able to raise and lower it at a speed of at least 1.5 meters per minute (5 ft. per minute). When raising or lowering the hoist with the hand operated device, the power source for the hoist is turned on, or an attempt is made to turn it on. Then, with power source turned off, hand operated device is disengaged. The power source is then turned on and an attempt made to engage the hand operated device. The interlock must prevent simultaneous operation of the power source and the hand operated device.

(9) *2.2x overload.* The hoist is installed in a level operating position. Each roller on the ladder or lift platform is placed in contact with a vertical surface. A weight equal to the difference between 2.2 times the working load and the weight of the ladder or lift platform is placed on the ladder or lift platform. The ladder or lift platform is raised through a distance of at least 5 meters (16 feet) and the hoist control lever is then released. The ladder or lift platform must stop without jarring or

damage and must hold the weight for at least one minute. The weight is then lowered through a distance of not less than 5 meters (16 feet) and the control lever is then released. The ladder or lift platform must stop within 600 millimeters (2 ft.) of where the hoist was when the lever was released and the ladder or lift platform must remain stationary for at least one minute thereafter. Each roller must move smoothly over the vertical surface without jamming or sliding during the test.

(10) *6x overload.* The hoist is installed in a level operating position. A load of six times the working load is attached to the hoist. (If the hoist has suspension cables, the cables must be run out at least one meter (3 ft.) before adding the load to the hoist.) The weight must remain stationary for at least one minute without damage to any part of the hoist. The test is repeated simulating a vessel list of 15 degrees toward the side on which the hoist is installed.

(11) *Level wind suspension cable.* If the hoist has suspension cables, it is installed in a level operating position with the cables wound onto the drums. A weight equal to the working load is attached to the hoist. The cables are run all the way out and then rewound back onto the drums at least ten times. Each drum and cable is observed for level winding as the cable is wound onto the drum. The test must be repeated with a weight equal to the weight of the rigid ladder or lift platform. In each test, each cable must always rewind onto the drum in one level wind of wrap.

(12) *Rung friction test.* One rung of each type used on a rigid ladder must be subjected to this test. This test compares the dry and wet surface friction characteristics of ladder rungs with those of a standard oak step.

(i) The standard step must have a surface of clean oak that meets § 163.003–11(b) of this chapter and that is 115 mm (4½ in.) wide by 400 mm (16 in.) long. The stepping surface must have grooves that are 3 mm (⅛ in.) deep and 3 mm wide. The grooves must run in two different directions at right angles to each other, and at 45 degree angles with each edge of the stepping surface, so that the grooves form a diamond pattern covering the stepping surface.

The centers of all parallel grooves must be 13 mm (½ in.) apart.

(ii) The standard step must be set in a level position. A metal block must be placed on one end of the step so that the block is in contact with the stepping surface. The metal block must weigh between 1.5 kg (3.3 lb.) and 3.0 kg (6.6 lb.) and must not be more than 100 mm (4 in.) wide by 135 mm (5⅜ in.) long. The surface of the block in contact with the step must have leather or composition shoe sole material attached to it.

(iii) The end of the step that has the metal block on it must be slowly raised until the block starts to slide. The angle of the step in this position must be measured and recorded. The step and block must then be placed under water and the procedure repeated.

(iv) The procedure in paragraph (c)(12)(iii) of this section must be repeated using a rigid ladder rung in place of the standard step.

(v) The ladder rung must then be secured in a horizontal position with a block resting on its stepping surface. The block must be of a size similar to the one used in the previous tests and have the same shoe sole surface used in the previous tests. The block must be arranged to apply a vertical load of 40 kg (88 lb.) to the rung. The block must be then moved back and forth in the same line from one end of the stepping surface to the other. This must be done for a total of 1,500 cycles.

(vi) The rung must again be tested as described in paragraph (c)(12)(iii) of this section, except that the initial position of the block must be on a part of the stepping surface that was subjected to the 1,500 cycles of rubbing.

(vii) The angles at which the block starts to slide on a wet and dry ladder rung when tested under paragraphs (c)(12)(iv) and (c)(12)(vi) of this section must be equal to or greater than the corresponding angles measured for the standard step when tested under paragraph (c)(12)(iii) of this section.

§163.002–25 Marking.

(a) Each pilot hoist manufactured under Coast Guard approval must have a corrosion-resistant nameplate. The nameplate must contain the—

(1) Name of the manufacturer;

(2) Manufacturer's brand or model designation;

(3) Working load;

(4) Lift height;

(5) Maximum persons capacity;

(6) Hoist serial number;

(7) Date of manufacture; and

(8) Coast Guard approval number.

(b) The hoist must be permanently and legibly marked with the name of the laboratory that conducted the production tests.

§163.002–27 Production tests and examination.

Each pilot hoist manufactured under Coast Guard approval must be tested as prescribed in §163.002–21(c)(9) and subpart 159.007 of this chapter. The tests must be conducted by an independent laboratory. If the hoist fails the tests its defects must be corrected and retested until it passes. The laboratory must also conduct the visual examination described in §163.002–21(b). The hoist may not be sold as Coast Guard approved unless it passes testing and unless each defect discovered in the visual examination is corrected

Subpart 163.003—Pilot Ladder

SOURCE: CGD 74–140, 46 FR 63291, Dec. 31, 1981, unless otherwise noted.

§163.003–1 Scope.

(a) This subpart contains standards and approval and production tests for a pilot ladder used on a merchant vessel to embark and disembark pilots and other persons when away from the dock.

(b) The requirements in this subpart apply to a pilot ladder designed for use along a vertical portion of a vessel's hull.

§163.003–3 ASTM standard.

The following standard of the American Society of Testing and Materials is incorporated by reference into this subpart: ASTM D 1435 entitled "Standard Recommended Practice for Outdoor Weathering of Plastics."

§163.003–7 Independent laboratory.

The approval and production tests in this subpart must be conducted by or under the supervision of an independent laboratory accepted by the Coast Guard under subpart 159.010 of this chapter.

§ 163.003-9 Approval procedure.

(a) *General.* A pilot ladder is approved by the Coast Guard under the procedures in subpart 159.005 of this chapter.

(b) *Approval testing.* Each approval test must be conducted in accordance with § 163.003-21.

(c) *Approval of alternatives.* A pilot ladder that does not meet the materials, construction, or performance requirements of this subpart may be approved if the application and any approval tests prescribed by the Commandant in place of or in addition to the approval tests required by this subpart, show that the alternative materials, construction, or performance is at least as effective as that specified by the requirements of this subpart. The Commandant may also prescribe different production tests if the tests required by this subpart are not appropriate for the alternative ladder configuration.

§ 163.003-11 Materials.

(a) *Suspension members.* Each suspension member must be mildew-resistant manila rope or a dacron polyester rope with a polypropylene core of a color that contrasts with the dacron. Each suspension member must have a breaking strength of not less than 24 kN (5,400 lb.) and a nominal circumference of not less than 60 mm (2¼ in.).

(b) *Wooden parts.* Each wooden part of a pilot ladder must be hardwood that is free from knots and any other defects affecting its strength or durability.

(c) *Wood preservative.* After each wooden part is formed and finished, it must be treated with water-repellant wood preservative that is properly applied.

(d) *Molded steps.* Each step made of molded construction must be rubber or resilient plastic.

(e) *Metal parts.* Each metal fastener must be made of a corrosion resistant metal. Each other metal part must be made of corrosion-resistant metal or of steel galvanized by the hot dip process after the part is formed.

(f) *Plastics.* Each plastic material must be of a type that retains at least 30 percent of its original tensile strength and at least 80 percent of its original impact strength when subjected to the one year outdoor weathering test described in ASTM D 1435.

§ 163.003-13 Construction.

(a) *General.* Each pilot ladder must have two suspension members on each side. Each step in the ladder must be supported by each suspension member.

(b) *Suspension member.* The suspension members of a pilot ladder must meet the following requirements:

(1) Each suspension member must be continuous from the top of the ladder to the bottom and must not be painted or otherwise coated or covered.

(2) Except as provided in paragraph (g) of this section—

(i) The top end of one suspension member on each side of the ladder must extend at least 3 m (10 ft.) beyond the top ladder step; and

(ii) The top ends of the other suspension members must be just above the top step and must have an eye splice or thimble large enough to fit two passes of a suspension member.

(3) The top end of each suspension member that does not have an eye splice or thimble must be served or treated to prevent fraying.

(4) Each pair of suspension members must be clamped together both above and below each step. Marline seizing may not be used.

(5) The clear space between the suspension members on one side of a ladder and those on the other side must be at least 400 mm (16 in.), but not more than 480 mm (19 in.).

(6) The suspension members must not have fittings at the bottom of the ladder that can be used for attaching additional ladder sections.

(c) *Steps.* Pilot ladder steps must meet the following requirements:

(1) The four lowest steps must be molded steps and the rest of the steps must be either wooden or molded steps.

(2) The top face of each step must have a rectangular surface that is at least 115 mm (4½ in.) wide with a non-skid surface that does not retain water. Adhesive non-skid sheets may not be used. (For example, a suitable surface

for a step is one that has grooves at least 3 mm (⅛ in.) deep cut in a diamond pattern so that water runs off the edge of the step. Non-skid grit is applied directly to the step surface extending to almost the full width of the step.)

(3) Each step at its thinnest point must be at least 25 mm (1 in.) thick and in determining this thickness, the depth of the grooves in the non-skid surface and the diameter of any hole extending from one side of the step to the other must not be counted.

(4) Each step must be at least 480 mm (19 in.) long.

(5) Each step must be designed so that it can be removed and replaced without unstringing the ladder. If special replacement steps are made to meet this requirement, the replacement steps must meet the requirements of this section.

(6) If a step has grooves for its suspension members, the grooves must be in the sides of the steps.

(7) The spacing from the top of one step to the top of the next step must be uniform and this spacing must be between 300 mm (12 in.) and 350 mm (13¾ in.).

(8) Each step must be a bright orange color, except that this color is not required for the non-skid surface. If a step is painted, it must be painted with a two-part epoxy paint intended for marine use, or a paint of equivalent durability.

(9) The height of each device attached to the step for securing the suspension members must not be more than one-half the width of the step so that the step is not prevented from rolling if the ladder is caught between a pilot boat and the hull of the vessel.

(10) Each replacement step must be either white or yellow instead of the orange color required under paragraph (c)(8) of this section, and must have the special marking required in §163.003–25(b).

(d) *Spreaders.* Each pilot ladder with 5 or more steps must have one or more spreaders that meet the following requirements:

(1) Each spreader must be at least 1.8 m (70 in.) long.

(2) The spreaders must be positioned at intervals of not more than 9 steps.

(3) The lowest spreader on a ladder must be on the fifth step from the bottom.

(e) *Fasteners.* Each fastening device securing a part of a pilot ladder must have a means to prevent the device from loosening.

(f) *Workmanship.* A pilot ladder must not have splinters, burrs, sharp edges, corners, projections, or other defects that could injure a person using the ladder.

(g) *Special arrangements for pilot hoists.* Each pilot ladder produced for use with an approved pilot hoist must have at least 8 steps. The top ends of its suspension members need not have an eye splice or thimble or be arranged as required in paragraph (b) of this section if necessary to permit attaching the ladder to fittings of a particular pilot hoist. The spreader required in paragraph (d) of this section may be omitted from an 8 step ladder for a pilot hoist.

[CGD 74–140, 46 FR 63291, Dec. 31, 1981, as amended by CGD 79–032, 49 FR 25456, June 21, 1984]

§163.003–15 Performance.

(a) Each pilot ladder must be capable of being rolled up for storage.

(b) Each ladder when rolled up must be able to unroll freely and hang vertically.

(c) Each suspension member must be arranged so that, when the ladder is in use on a vessel, the suspension member cannot come in contact with the vessel's side.

(d) Each step must be arranged so that it can bear on the side of the vessel when the ladder is in use.

§163.003–17 Strength.

(a) Each pilot ladder must be designed to pass the approval tests in §163.003–21.

(b) [Reserved]

§163.003–21 Approval tests.

(a) *General.* Each approval test must be conducted on a ladder of the longest length for which approval has been requested. If the ladder fails one of the tests, the cause of the failure must be identified and any needed design changes made. After a test failure and any design change, the failed test, and any other previously completed tests affected by the change, must be rerun. Any ladder step that has a residual deflection after testing under this section may not be used thereafter in any ladder represented as Coast Guard approved.

(b) *Visual examination.* Before starting the approval tests, an assembled pilot ladder is examined for evidence of noncompliance with the requirements in §§ 163.003–11, 163.003–13, and 163.003–15.

(c) The following approval tests must be conducted:

(1) *Step flexibility test.* This test is performed on six different steps, one of which must be a molded step and one of which must be a replacement step if special replacement steps are made by the manufacturer. Each step is placed on a pair of supports located at the points where the step would ordinarily be attached to the suspension members. A static load must be applied uniformly for a period of at least one minute over a contact surface that is at the center of the step and is approximately 100 mm (4 in.) wide. The load must be 150 kg (330 lb.) for each molded step that is used only as one of the four bottom steps in the ladder. The load must be 320 kg (700 lb.) for each other step. The deflection of the step is measured while the step is under load and after the load is removed. The step must not deflect more than 20 mm (¾ in.) under the load, and there must be no residual deflection after the load is removed.

(2) *Strength test #1.* An assembled ladder is supported so that a static load, if placed on any of its steps, would exert a force on both the step and each suspension member. A static load of 900 kg (2,000 lb.) is then placed on one step for at least one minute. The load must be uniformly distributed over a contact surface that is approximately 100 mm (4 in.) wide. The center of the contact surface must be at the center of the step. This test is performed on six different steps, one of which must be a molded step. None of the steps may break or crack. No attachment between any step and a suspension member may loosen or break during this test.

(3) *Strength test #2.* An assembled ladder is suspended vertically to its full length. A static load of 900 kg (2,000 lb.) is then applied to the bottom step of the ladder so that it is distributed equally between the suspension members. The suspension members, and inserts must not break, incur any elongation or deformation that remains after the test load is removed, or be damaged in any other way during this test.

(4) *Strength test #3.* A rolled up ladder is attached to anchoring fixtures in a location away from any wall or structure that would prevent it from falling freely, and where it can hang to its full length vertically. The ladder when dropped must unroll freely. When unrolling the ladder, its steps and attachments must not become cracked, broken, or loosened. Other similar damage making the ladder unsafe to use must likewise not occur.

(5) *Step friction test.* One step of each type used on a pilot ladder must be subjected to this test. This test compares the dry and wet surface friction characteristics of ladder steps with those of a standard oak step.

(i) The standard step must have a surface of clean oak that meets S/163.003–11(b) and that is 115 mm (4½ in.) wide by 400 mm (16 in.) long. The stepping surface must have grooves that are 3 mm (⅛ in.) deep and 3 mm wide. The grooves must run in two different directions at right angles to each other, and at 45 degree angles with each edge of the stepping surface, so that the grooves form a diamond pattern covering the stepping surface. The centers of all parallel grooves must be 13 mm (½ in.) apart.

(ii) The standard step must be set in a level position. A metal block must be placed on one end of the step so that the block is in contact with the stepping surface. The metal block must weigh between 1.5 kg (3.3 lb.) and 3.0 kg (6.6 lb.) and must not be more than 100 mm (4 in.) wide by 135 mm (5⅜ in.) long. The surface of the block in contact with the step must have leather or composition shoe sole material attached to it.

(iii) The end of the step that has the metal block on it must be slowly raised until the block starts to slide. The angle of the step in this position must be measured and recorded. The step and block must then be placed under water and the procedure repeated.

(iv) The procedure in paragraph (c)(6)(iii) of this section must be repeated using a pilot ladder step in place of the standard step.

(v) The ladder step must then be secured in a horizontal position with a block resting on its stepping surface. The block must be of a size similar to the one used in the previous tests and have the same shoe sole surface used in the previous tests. The block must be arranged to apply a vertical load of 40 kg (88 lb.) to the step. The block must be then moved back and forth in the same line from one end of the stepping surface to the other. This must be done for a total of 1,500 cycles.

(vi) The step must again be tested as described in paragraph (c)(6)(iii) of this section, except that the initial position of the block must be on a part of the stepping surface that was subjected to the 1,500 cycles of rubbing.

(vii) The angles at which the block starts to slide on a wet and dry ladder step when tested under paragraphs (c)(6)(iv) and (c)(6)(vi) of this section must be equal to or greater than the corresponding angles measured for the standard step when tested under paragraph (c)(6)(iii) of this section.

§ 163.003–25 Marking.

(a) Each pilot ladder step manufactured under Coast Guard approval must be branded or otherwise permanently and legibly marked on the bottom with—

(1) The name of the manufacturer;

(2) The manufacturer's brand or model designation;

(3) The lot number or date of manufacture; and

(4) The Coast Guard approval number.

(b) In addition to the markings required under paragraph (a) of this section each step sold as a replacement step must be branded or otherwise permanently and legibly marked with the words "REPLACEMENT STEP ONLY."

[CGD 74–140, 46 FR 63291, Dec. 31, 1981, as amended by CGD 79–032, 49 FR 25456, June 21, 1984]

§ 163.003–27 Production tests and examination.

(a) *General.* Each ladder produced under Coast Guard approval must be tested in accordance with this section and subpart 159.007 of this chapter. Steps that fail testing may not be marked with the Coast Guard approval number and each assembled ladder that fails testing may not be sold as Coast Guard approved.

(b) *Test No. 1: Steps.* Steps must be separated into lots of 100 steps or less. Steps of different types must be placed in separate lots. One step from each lot must be selected at random and tested as described in § 163.003–21(c)(2) except that supports are placed under the step at the points where it would be attached to suspension members in an assembled ladder. If the step fails the test, ten more steps must be selected at random from the lot and tested. If one or more of the ten steps fails the test, each step in the lot must be tested. No step that has any residual deflection after the test may be used in a ladder represented by the manufacturer as Coast Guard approved.

(c) *Test No. 2: Ladders.* Assembled ladders must be separated into lots of 20 ladders or less. One ladder must be selected at random from the ladders in each lot. The ladder selected must be at least 3 m (10 ft.) long or, if each ladder in the lot is less then 3 m long, a ladder of the longest length in the lot must be selected. The ladder must be tested as prescribed in § 163.003–21(c)(3) except that only a 3 m section of the ladder need be subjected to the static load. If the ladder fails the test, each other ladder in the lot must be tested.

(d) *Independent laboratory.* Each production test must be conducted or supervised by an independent laboratory. However, if a test is performed more than 4 different times per year, laboratory participation is required only 4 times per year. If the laboratory does not participate in all tests, the times of laboratory participation must be as selected by the laboratory. The times selected must provide for effective monitoring throughout the production schedule.

(e) *Visual examination.* The visual examination described in § 163.003–21(b)

329

must be conducted as a part of each production test.

§ 163.003–29 Effective date and status of prior approval.

(a) Approval certificates for pilot ladders issued under subpart 160.017 terminate on March 31, 1982.

(b) Applications for approval of pilot ladders under this subpart will be accepted on and after December 31, 1982.

(c) In previous regulations, pilot ladders were referred to as Type I—Rope Suspension Ladders.

PART 164—MATERIALS

Subpart 164.003—Kapok, Processed

Subpart 164.006—Deck Coverings for Merchant Vessels

Subpart 164.007—Structural Insulations

Subpart 164.008—Bulkhead Panels

Subpart 164.009—Noncombustible Materials for Merchant Vessels

Subpart 164.012—Interior Finishes for Merchant Vessels

Subpart 164.013—Foam, Unicellular Polyethylene (Buoyant, Slab, Slitted Trigonal Pattern)

Subpart 164.015—Plastic Foam, Unicellular, Buoyant, Sheet and Molded Shape

Subpart 164.018—Retroreflective Material for Lifesaving Equipment

Subpart 164.019—Personal Flotation Device Components

Subpart 164.023—Thread for Personal Flotation Devices

AUTHORITY: 46 U.S.C. 3306, 3703, 4302; E.O. 12234, 45 FR 58801, 3 CFR, 1980 Comp., p. 277; 49 CFR 1.46.

Subpart 164.003—Kapok, Processed

SOURCE: 11 FR 188, Jan. 3, 1946, unless otherwise noted.

§ 164.003–1 Applicable specifications.

(a) There are no other specifications applicable to this subpart.

(b) [Reserved]

§ 164.003–2 Grades.

(a) Processed kapok shall be of but one grade as in this subpart.

(b) [Reserved]

§ 164.003–3 Material and workmanship.

(a) The raw kapok fiber shall be long, clean, creamy white in color, lustrous, free from discoloration and adulteration with other fiber, and of a quality equal to that grown in Java.

(b) Kapok shall be processed by teasing in a machine using the air-blow method. Mechanical separation of fiber masses is permitted, but machines using violent beating which breaks down the fibers or causes undue pow-

dering or pulverizing are not permitted. Provision shall be made for trapping seeds and heavy objects in gravity traps and the dust or powder in an efficient dust collector.

(c) Processed kapok shall have a buoyancy in fresh water of at least 48 pounds per cubic foot when tested in accordance with § 164.003–4(d). Rejected kapok shall not be used in lifesaving products inspected by the Coast Guard.

(d) The processed kapok shall contain not more than 5 percent by weight of sticks, seeds, dirt or other foreign material and shall be free from objectionable odor and adulteration with other fibers.

§ 164.003–4 Inspections and tests.

(a) Kapok fibers to be used in a finished product subject to inspection by the Coast Guard shall be subject to inspection and tests at the plant of the manufacturer of such product, who shall furnish the necessary testing tank, test cages, and scales.

(b) Acceptance of kapok prior to being incorporated into finished products, or during the course of manufacture, shall in no case be construed as a guarantee of the acceptance of the finished product.

(c) Not less than a one-pound sample from each 1,000 pounds of kapok shall be tested for buoyancy by the inspector. At his discretion, the inspector may select additional samples for tests if deemed advisable.

(d) The buoyancy test shall be made with 16 ounces of processed kapok uniformly packed in a rigid wire box or cage with metal reinforced edges, and submerged by weights in a tank of fresh water to a depth of 12 inches below the surface of the water, measurement made to the top of box, for 48 hours. The test box shall be cylindrical in shape, and as nearly as practicable ⅓ cubic foot in volume, 4 inches deep, 13.54 inches diameter, all inside measurements; constructed of about 0.065 inch galvanized iron wire with about ¼ inch mesh, and lined with about 0.007 inch copper wire screen about 18 meshes to the inch, to prevent the kapok from pushing out through the larger wire meshes. At the end of forty-eight hours submergence, the buoyancy shall be determined by subtracting the submerged weight of the box, accessory weights and kapok from the submerged weight of the box and weights without the kapok, and dividing the remainder by the volume of the kapok expressed in cubic feet.

(e) Kapok fiber shall, at the option of the inspector, be subjected to a microscopic examination to detect adulteration with other fiber.

(f) Processed kapok shall, at the option of the inspector, be subjected to separation of kapok fibers from foreign matter by hand, the portions of each weighed, and percentage of foreign matter computed for compliance with § 164.003–3(d).

§ 164.003–5 Procedure for approval.

(a) Processed kapok is not subject to formal approval, but will be accepted by the inspector on the basis of this subpart for use in the manufacture of lifesaving equipment utilizing it.

(b) [Reserved]

Subpart 164.006—Deck Coverings for Merchant Vessels

SOURCE: CGFR 53–25, 18 FR 7874, Dec. 5, 1953, unless otherwise noted.

§ 164.006–1 Applicable specifications.

(a) There are no other specifications applicable to this subpart.

(b) [Reserved]

§ 164.006–2 Grades.

(a) Deck coverings shall be of but one grade as specified in this subpart, and shall be known as "an approved deck covering."

(b) [Reserved]

§ 164.006–3 Construction, materials, and workmanship.

(a) It is the intent of this specification to obtain a deck covering made largely of incombustible materials with low heat transmission qualities which will produce a minimum of smoke when exposed to high temperatures.

(b) Deck coverings shall be of such a quality as to successfully pass all of the tests set forth in § 164.006–4.

§ 164.006–4 Inspection and testing.

(a) All tests shall be conducted at the National Bureau of Standards or other laboratories designated by the Coast Guard.

(b) *Smoke tests.* (1) A sample of each thickness submitted shall be tested for smoke emission. Each sample shall be laid on a ¼″×12″×27″ steel plate. Normal protective coatings and deck attachments shall be incorporated in the samples. Each sample shall be heated in a furnace whose temperature is limited to the standard decking curve reaching 1,325 degrees F. at the end of one hour. Smoke observations shall be made at intervals not greater than five minutes during the one-hour period of test.

(2) Instantaneous values of the percent of light transmission shall be calculated from the observations noted in paragraph (b)(1) of this section. A plot of light transmission values shall be made using straight lines between instantaneous values.

(3) Any instantaneous value of 10 percent light transmission or less shall be considered sufficient cause for rejection of a deck covering.

(4) Average values of light transmission shall be calculated for 15, 30, and 60 minutes. Averages shall be an arithmetic mean with values taken at one minute intervals from the plotted curve noted in paragraph (b)(2) of this section. If any of the three average values of light transmission is less than the values set forth below, it will be considered sufficient cause for rejection of a deck covering:

15 minutes—90 percent light transmission.
30 minutes—60 percent light transmission.
60 minutes—50 percent light transmission.

(c) *Fire resistance and integrity tests.* (1) A sample of each thickness submitted shall be tested for fire resistance and integrity. Each sample shall be laid on a ¼″×12″×27″ steel plate. Normal protective coatings and deck attachments shall be incorporated in the samples. Each sample shall be heated in a furnace whose temperature is controlled according to the standard fire exposure curve reaching 1,700 degrees F. at the end of one hour. Temperature of the unexposed side as indicated by a thermocouple under a 0.40 inch asbestos pad shall be observed at intervals not greater than 5 minutes during the one-hour period of test.

(2) Data from these tests shall be analyzed to determine the thicknesses necessary to limit the average temperature rise on the unexposed surface to 250 degrees F. above the original temperature at the end of 15, 30, and 60 minutes.

(3) Excessive cracking, buckling, or disintegration may be considered cause for rejection.

(d) *Organic carbon content test.* (1) The organic carbon content shall be determined and shall not exceed 0.12 gram per cubic centimeter of the molded deck covering.

(e) *Spot check tests.* (1) Deck coverings are not inspected at regularly scheduled factory inspections; however, the cognizant Officer in Charge, Marine Inspection, may detail a marine inspector at any time to visit any place where deck coverings are manufactured to conduct any inspections or examinations deemed advisable and to select representative samples for further examination, inspection or tests. The marine inspector shall be admitted to any place where work is done on deck coverings or component materials.

(2) Manufacturers of approved deck coverings shall maintain quality control of materials used, manufacturing methods, and the finished product so as to meet the requirements of this specification, and any other conditions outlined on the certificate of approval, but the Coast Guard also reserves the right to make spot-check tests of approved deck coverings at any time on samples selected by a marine inspector at the place of manufacture or samples obtained from other sources in the field. The manufacturer will incur no expense for such tests, but the results shall be binding upon the approval of his product. The manufacturer will be advised in advance of the time of testing of the samples selected and may witness the tests if he so desires.

[CGFR 53–25, 18 FR 7874, Dec. 5, 1953, as amended by CGFR 61–15, 26 FR 9302, Sept. 30, 1961]

§ 164.006–5 **Procedure for approval.**

(a) If a manufacturer desires to have a deck covering approved, a request shall be presented to the Commandant of the Coast Guard, together with the following information:

(1) The trade name and designation of the deck covering.

(2) The range of thicknesses in which it is proposed to lay the deck covering together with any information the manufacturer may have as to maximum or minimum thicknesses.

(3) Description of method of attachment to or protection of the steel deck together with the trade name and designation of adhesive or protective coating if used.

(4) A sample of the molded deck covering at least 6 inches square and ¼ inch thick. This may or may not be attached to a backing material at the manufacturer's option.

(b) The material submitted will be examined and the manufacturer advised as to the number and thicknesses of samples to be submitted together with the estimated cost of the tests.

(c) If the deck covering is indicated as being suitable, the manufacturer shall then submit the following:

(1) Two samples of each thickness to be tested laid in the manner designated on a ¼″×12″×27″ steel plate for the purpose of the smoke test and fire resistance and integrity test noted in §164.006–4 (b) and (c).

(2) Sufficient bulk material (unmixed) to lay a sample one inch thick on an area of 12″×27″. If an adhesive or protective coating is used, a liberal sample shall be supplied.

(3) If the manufacturer desires to witness the tests, he should so indicate at this time.

(4) A commitment that he will reimburse the National Bureau of Standards for the cost of the tests when billed by them.

(d) The above material will be submitted to the National Bureau of Standards by the Coast Guard for testing. The tests noted in §164.006–4 will be conducted and a report submitted to the Coast Guard.

(e) A copy of the test report will be forwarded to the manufacturer and he will be advised if his material is approved under this specification, and if approved, in what thicknesses it may be laid, and in what thicknesses it must be laid to meet the requirements for Class A–60 decks without the use of any other insulating material. If approved, this information will be published in the FEDERAL REGISTER.

[CGFR 53–25, 18 FR 7874, Dec. 5, 1953, as amended by CGFR 61–62, 27 FR 180, Jan. 6, 1962]

Subpart 164.007—Structural Insulations

SOURCE: CGFR 69–72, 34 FR 17498, Oct. 29, 1969, unless otherwise noted.

§ 164.007-1 Applicable specification and referenced material.

(a) *Specification.* The following specification of the issue in effect on the date of manufacture of the structural insulation shall form a part of the regulations of this subpart (see §§ 2.75–17 through 2.75–19 of subchapter A (Procedures Applicable to the Public) of this chapter:

(1) Coast Guard specification:

Subpart 164.009 of this part, Incombustible Materials for Merchant Vessels.

(b) *Technical reference.* For guidance purposes the technical reference may be used, which is entitled American Society for Testing Materials Standard E–119. "Fire Tests of Building Construction and Materials", ASTM, 1916 Race Street, Philadelphia, Pa. 19103.

(c) *Copies on file.* A copy of the specification listed in paragraph (a) of this section shall be kept on file by the manufacturer, together with the certificate of approval and this specification. It is the manufacturer's responsibility to have the latest issue of the specification on hand together with the certificate of approval and approved plans when manufacturing under this specification subpart.

(1) The Coast Guard specification may be obtained from the Commandant (G–MSE), U.S. Coast Guard, Washington, DC 20593–0001.

[CGFR 69–72, 34 FR 17498, Oct. 29, 1969, as amended by CGD 82–063b, 48 FR 4783, Feb. 3, 1983; CGD 88–070, 53 FR 34537, Sept. 7, 1988; CGD 95–072, 60 FR 50467, Sept. 29, 1995; CGD 96–041, 61 FR 50734, Sept. 27, 1996]

§ 164.007-2 Purpose.

The purpose of this specification is to set forth tests necessary to measure the insulation value of structural insulation specimens under fire exposure conditions. The tests are not intended to measure the integrity of structural components of an assembly Insulation meeting this specification is adequate to limit the average temperature rise of a steel bulkhead to 139 °C. (250 °F.) at the end of a 60-minute standard fire test.

§ 164.007-3 Conditions of approval.

(a) Structural insulation shall be of such quality as to successfully meet the requirements for an incombustible material as set forth in subpart 164.009 of this part.

(b) Structural insulation shall be of such quality and thickness as to successfully pass all of the tests set forth in § 164.007–4, and the retests required by § 164.007–8.

(c) The product shall be so marked as to be readily identifiable to an inspector in the field. The marking shall include the Coast Guard approval number.

§ 164.007-4 Testing procedure.

(a) *Tests.* All tests, including the retests, shall be conducted at the National Bureau of Standards or other laboratories designated by the Coast Guard.

(b) *Test of physical properties.* (1) Density measurement: The smallest sample for density measurements of solid materials shall be 30 cm × 30 cm (12″×12″) by the submitted thickness. Length and width measurements shall be made to the nearest 1 mm. (¹⁄₃₂″), thickness to the nearest 0.25 mm. (0.01″), allowance being made of any nonflatness of the major surfaces of the specimen. Measurements of dimensions of fibrous insulations shall be made to the nearest 1.5 mm. (¹⁄₁₆″) on a nominal 30 cm. (12″) cube assembled from sheets of thickness as received. The average of at least four measurements of each dimension shall be reported. The weight shall be determined with a scale or balance sensitive and accurate to 0.5 percent or less of the total weight. The dimensional and weight measurements shall not be made until the sample has been conditioned 1 week, or longer if required to reach constant weight, in an atmosphere at 23° ±1 °C. (73 °F.±2°) and 50 percent relative humidity.

(2) Transfer to a previously dried and weighed wide-mouth weighing bottle provided with a glass stopper. Remove the stopper and heat the bottle and sample at 105°±5 °C. (221°±9 °F.) for 4 hours, insert the stopper, cool and weigh. Calculate the content of moisture and other volatiles as percent of the final dry weight of the sample.

(c) *Preparation of fire test specimens.* (1) The fire test specimens shall be conditioned to approximately constant weight with air being maintained at a relative humidity of 40 to 70 percent and a temperature of 15° to 25 °C. (50° to 77 °F.). After conditioning, but before testing, the temperature of the specimens shall not exceed 40 °C. (104 °F.).

(2) Representative samples of the structural insulation, of a thickness or thicknesses and density as specified in § 164.007-9(a)(5), shall be tested as part of an assembly which forms a portion of a vertical wall of a furnace. The assembly shall be at least 100 cm. × 150 cm. (40″×60″) in size. More than one sample may be tested, see § 164.007-7.

(3) The specimens shall be attached to a 5±0.3 mm. (³⁄₁₆″) thick steel plate and mounted in the furnace with the steel plate forming the exterior wall of the furnace. Any stiffening members on the steel plate shall be installed on the face not adjacent to the insulation. Spacer strips of asbestos cement board or similar material, up to 5 cm. (2″) in width, shall be installed around the periphery of the panel. For fibrous insulations, the attachment to the steel plate shall be made by means of 5 mm. (0.19″) diameter steel pins on 30 cm. (12″) centers covered by 18-gage, 4 cm. (1½″) mesh expanded metal. Alternate methods will be given consideration. For other materials, typical installation practice shall be used.

(d) *Furnace control.* (1) The furnace temperature shall be determined by at least four mineral insulated thermocouples having rapid response, and distributed so as to represent fairly the furnace temperature and to insure as uniform heating as possible. The thermocouples shall be arranged so that the hot junction is approximately

10 cm. from the nearest point of the specimen.

(2) The furnace temperature shall be continuously controlled so as to follow the standard time-temperature curve within the accuracy specified in paragraph (d)(4) of this section.

(3) The standard time-temperature curve is defined by a smooth curve drawn through the following points:

At the beginning of the test, 20 °C. (68 °F.)
At the end of the first 5 minutes, 538 °C. (1,000 °F.).
At the end of the first 10 minutes, 704 °C. (1,300 °F.).
At the end of the first 30 minutes, 843 °C. (1,550 °F.).
At the end of the first 60 minutes, 927 °C. (1,700 °F.).

For a further definition of the time-temperature curve, see Appendix I of the ASTM Standard E–119, "Fire Tests of Building Construction and Materials".

(4) The accuracy of the furnace control shall be such that the area under the mean time-temperature curve is within 15 percent of the area under the standard time-temperature curve during the first 10 minutes of the test, within 10 percent during the first one-half hour, and within 5 percent for any period after the first one-half hour. At any time after the first 10 minutes of the test the mean furnace temperature shall not differ from the standard curve by more than 100 °C. (180 °F.). Consideration will be given to adjusting the results for variation of the furnace exposure from that prescribed. If corrections are made, they shall be in accordance with the procedures set forth in the ASTM E–119.

(e) *Temperature of unexposed surface.* For the unexposed surface temperature measurement a thermocouple of 0.5 mm. (0.020″) diameter wires shall be soldered centrally with high temperature solder to one surface of a disc of copper 12 mm. in diameter and 0.2 mm. thick. The discs shall be covered with an oven-dry asbestos pad 50 mm. × 50 mm, and 4 mm. thick. The disc and the pad may be fixed to the surface of the steel plate by pins, tape, or a suitable adhesive. The asbestos pad shall have a density of approximately 1,000 kg./m.³ and thermal conductivity of 0.11 kcal/ m/hr. × °C. at 100 °C. (212 °F.).

(f) *Temperature observations.* (1) All observations shall be taken at intervals not exceeding 5 minutes. The surface temperature on the exterior side of the steel plate shall be measured by thermocouples located as follows:

(i) One thermocouple located approximately in the center of each quadrant of the steel plate (four thermocouples total).

(ii) One thermocouple close to the center of the steel plate.

(iii) One thermocouple in way of or as close as possible to one of the pins or other through metallic connections (if any) used for holding the insulation in place.

(iv) Further thermocouples at the discretion of the testing laboratory or Coast Guard for the purpose of determining the temperature at points deemed likely to give a greater temperature rise than any of the above-mentioned thermocouples.

(2) The average temperature rise on the unexposed surface shall be obtained by averaging the readings of the thermocouples mentioned in paragraphs (f)(1) (i) and (ii) of this section.

(g) *Other observations.* Throughout the test observations shall be made of all changes and occurrences, which are not criteria of performance, but which may create hazard in case of a fire; for example the emission of appreciable volumes of smoke or noxious vapors from the unexposed side of the test specimen. The specimen shall be examined after the test for changes that have taken place and the information shall be noted in the test report.

(h) *Duration of testing.* The test shall be continued for at least one hour or until the maximum surface temperature rise values noted in § 164.007-5(a) have been reached, whichever occurs later.

§ 164.007-5　Test requirements.

The insulation value of the specimens for the full scale test shall be such that the average temperature of the thermocouples on the unexposed surface described in § 164.007-4(f)(2) will not rise more than 139 °C. (250 °F.) above the initial temperature, nor will the temperature at any one point on the surface, including any through metallic connection, rise more than 181 °C. (325 °F.) above the original temperature at the end of 60 minutes. The results obtained on the small scale test 2′×2′ (60 cm. × 60 cm.) shall be recorded.

§ 164.007-6　Test report.

(a) The test report required shall contain at least the following:

(1) Name of manufacturer.

(2) Purpose of test.

(3) Test conditions and date of test.

(4) Description of the panel tested giving the details of the assembly comprising a steel plate, insulation (thickness and density) spacer strips and fastening and the method of mounting the panel assembly in the test furnace.

(5) Complete time-temperature data, including initial temperature, for each thermocouple together with curves of average temperature for the unexposed surface of the insulation and the thermocouple recording the highest temperature. In addition, for § 164.007-9(g)(2), complete time-temperature data consisting of a numerical time-temperature table for each furnace and each surface of insulation thermocouple together with the initial temperature of each thermocouple.

(6) A log maintained by the owner relative to deflections, cracking or loosening of the insulation, smoke or gas emission, glow, flame emission, and any other important data. The time of each observation should be noted.

(7) Photographs of both sides of the panel before and after testing.

(8) Summary of test results.

(b) [Reserved]

§ 164.007-7　Analysis of results.

(a) When only one sample is tested, the results of the test shall be binding and no analysis by the Coast Guard will be undertaken.

(b) When more than one sample of the same density material is tested simultaneously and the results are not exact, the Coast Guard may analyze the results. Data from the tests may be analyzed to determine the minimum thickness to meet the requirements of § 164.007-5(a).

(c) Consideration will be given to correction for inaccurate furnace control in accordance with §164.007-4(d)(4).

[CGFR 69-72, 34 FR 17498, Oct. 29, 1969; 34 FR 19030, Nov. 29, 1969]

§164.007-8 Retests.

(a) Manufacturers of approved structural insulation shall maintain quality control of materials used, manufacturing methods, and the finished product utilizing appropriate quality control testing so as to meet the requirements of this specification, and any other conditions outlined on the certificate of approval. Structural insulation materials are not inspected at regularly scheduled factory inspections; however, approved materials are subject to retest for continued compliance with the requirements of this subpart on the following basis:

(1) The Coast Guard may detail a marine inspector or other Coast Guard designated inspector at any time to visit any place where structural insulation is manufactured to conduct any inspections or examinations deemed advisable and to select representative samples for further examination, inspection, or tests. The inspector shall be admitted to any place where work is done on structural insulation or component materials.

(2) At a frequency of not less than once every 5 years following issuance of approval, samples of an approved material selected from production stock shall be forwarded by the inspector to the Commandant for testing in accordance with the requirements of this subpart. Where the plant is outside the jurisdiction of a Coast Guard District Commander, the frequency of such testing shall be once every 2 years. The cost of such testing shall be borne by the manufacturer. The nature of the product or its production may dictate a differing retest frequency.

(3) The Coast Guard reserves the right to make spot-check tests of approved structural insulation at any time on samples selected by a marine inspector obtained during installation on a vessel. The manufacturer will incur no expense for such tests, but the results, shall be binding upon the approval of his product.

(b) A small scale furnace test (2′×2′ furnace test 60 cm. × 60 cm.) shall be conducted. The time of failure shall not vary from the original small scale test values by more than 10 percent. In addition tests shall be conducted to determine incombustibility (§164.009), density and thickness. Values of retesting for density and thickness shall not vary from the original test values by more than 10 percent.

§164.007-9 Procedure for approval.

The following items shall be accomplished in sequential order.

(a) *Test request information.* If a manufacturer desires to have a structural insulation approved, a written request shall be submitted to the Commandant of the Coast Guard together with the following:

(1) If the material has already been approved as an incombustible material under subpart 164.009 of this part, the approval number of the material shall be indicated. If not, the procedure set forth in subpart 164.009 of this part shall be followed; and such approval shall be obtained prior to submittal under this specification.

(2) A description and trade name of the structural insulation.

(3) A statement of the composition of the material and the percentage of each component.

(4) A sample of the material at least 1 foot square in the thickness and density proposed by the manufacturer to be tested. When more than one thickness of a material of the same density is to be tested, only a sample of a single thickness need be submitted.

(5) The range of thicknesses and densities in which it is proposed to manufacture or use the material together with any information or recommendations that the manufacturer may have as to maximum or minimum thickness or density.

(6) The location of the place or places where the material will be manufactured.

(7) Description of attachment to or protection of the bulkhead or deck. If an adhesive is used, a liberal sample shall be supplied.

(8) A sketch showing typical installation methods and indicating limitations if any.

(9) A general statement describing manufacturing procedures indicating the degree of quality control exercised and the degree of inspection performed by outside organizations.

(10) A statement indicating proposed methods for field identification of the products as being approved. Identification shall include the Coast Guard approval numbers.

(b) *Test suitability.* The above information will be examined by the Coast Guard, and if it is indicated that the material is in all respects suitable for testing, the manufacturer will be so advised. Coast Guard comments on the manufacturer's recommended thickness and density of the sample or samples for the fire resistance test will be given at this time, together with the estimated cost of the required test.

(c) *Samples to be submitted.* If the material is indicated as being suitable for testing, the manufacturer shall submit a 100 cm. × 150 cm. (40″×60″) sample, a 30 cm. × 30 cm. (12″×12″) sample and a 60 cm. × 60cm. (24″×24″) sample for each thickness and density proposed to the Fire Research section of the National Bureau of Standards, Washington, DC 20234, and shall advise the Coast Guard of the shipment. A separate test will be made for each density of the material for which approval is desired.

(d) *Pretest information.* At this time the manufacturer shall submit to the Coast Guard the following:

(1) A statement that the material is offered for testing as described pursuant to paragraph (a)(3) of this section is completely representative of the product which will be manufactured and sold under U.S. Coast Guard approval if such approval is granted and that the shipbuilder will be advised of the proper installation methods and the limitations of the approval.

(2) A commitment that he will reimburse the National Bureau of Standards for the cost or review of the tests when billed by them.

(3) If the manufacturer desires to witness the test, he should so indicate at this time.

(e) *Test authorization.* The National Bureau of Standards will then be authorized to conduct the tests noted in § 164.007–4 and, upon completion of all testing, the manufacturer will be billed directly by the National Bureau of Standards. Four copies of the test report containing the information required by § 164.007–6 will be submitted to the Coast Guard.

(f) *Notification of results.* A copy of the report will be forwarded to the manufacturer and he will be advised if his material is approved under this subpart. If approved, any stipulations of the approval will be specified. This information will be published in the FEDERAL REGISTER, and a certificate of approval will be issued to the manufacturer.

(g) *Other laboratories.* (1) If the manufacturer desires to have the test conducted at some laboratory other than the National Bureau of Standards, this information shall be supplied at the time of initial contact with the Coast Guard. If the proposed laboratory is acceptable to the Coast Guard, the manufacturer will be so advised, and any special testing requirements together with any estimated cost of expenses incurred by the National Bureau of Standards for their review will be specified at this time. The Coast Guard shall be notified in advance of the date of the test so that a representative may be present.

(2) The laboratory shall submit four copies of a detailed test report to the Coast Guard together with representative samples of the material taken before and after testing. The test report and samples will be examined by the National Bureau of Standards for compliance with this subpart. The test report shall include the information required by § 164.007–6 together with any other pertinent data.

Subpart 164.008—Bulkhead Panels

SOURCE: CGFR 69–72, 34 FR 17500, Oct. 29, 1969, unless otherwise noted.

§ 164.008–1 Applicable specification and reference material.

(a) *Specification.* The following specification of the issue in effect on the date of manufacture of the bulkhead panel shall form a part of the regulations of this subpart (see §§ 2.75–17 through 2.75–19 of subchapter A, Procedures Applicable to the Public, of this chapter):

(1) Coast Guard specification:

Subpart 164.009 of this part, Incombustible Materials for Merchant Vessels.

(b) *Technical reference.* For guidance purposes this technical reference may be used, which is entitled American Society for Testing Materials Standard E-119, "Fire Tests of Building Construction and Materials", ASTM, 1916 Race Street, Philadelphia, Pa. 19103.

(c) *Copies on file.* A copy of the specification listed in paragraph (a) of this section shall be kept on file by the manufacturer, together with the certificate of approval and this specification. It is the manufacturer's responsibility to have the latest issue of the specification on hand together with the certificate of approval and approved plans when manufacturing under this specification subpart.

(1) The Coast Guard specification may be obtained from the Commandant (G–MSE), U.S. Coast Guard, Washington, DC 20593–0001.

[CGFR 69–72, 34 FR 17500, Oct. 29, 1969, as amended by CGD 82–063b, 48 FR 4783, Feb. 3, 1983; CGD 88–070, 53 FR 34537, Sept. 7, 1988; CGD 95–072, 60 FR 50467, Sept. 29, 1995; CGD 96–041, 61 FR 50734, Sept. 27, 1996]

§ 164.008–2 Conditions of approval.

(a) Bulkhead panel material shall be of such quality as to successfully meet the requirements for an incombustible material as set forth in subpart 164.009 of this part.

(b) Bulkhead panels used in Class B–15 construction and as a component in Class A–30 or Class A–15 construction shall meet the thermal insulation requirements of § 164.008–4(a) for at least 15 minutes, and the integrity requirements of § 164.008–4(b) for at least 30 minutes.

(c) Bulkhead panels for use as a component in Class A–60 construction shall meet the thermal insulation requirements of § 164.008–4(a) for at least 15 minutes and the integrity requirements of § 164.008–4(b) for at least 60 minutes.

(d) The product shall be so marked as to be readily identifiable to an inspector in the field. The marking shall include the Coast Guard approval number.

(e) The specimen to be tested shall be representative of the typical installation on board a vessel and any limitations shall be shown on the sketch required by § 164.008–7(a)(7).

(f) The bulkhead panel shall successfully pass the retests required by § 164.008–6.

§ 164.008–3 Testing procedure.

(a) *Tests.* All tests, including the retests, shall be conducted at the National Bureau of Standards or other laboratories designated by the Coast Guard.

(b) *Preparation of test specimen.* (1) The test specimens shall be conditioned to approximately constant weight with the air being maintained at a relative humidity of 40 to 70 percent and a temperature of 15° to 25 °C. (59° to 77 °F.). After conditioning, but before testing, the temperature of the specimen should not exceed 40 °C. (104 °F.).

(2) The specimens shall be mounted in the furnace in a vertical position in such a way as to give an exposed surface of at least 4.65 square meters (50 square feet) and a height of at least 2.44 meters (8 feet).

(3) The specimen shall be supported at the top and secured on the vertical sides and at the bottom in a manner representative of conditions in service. If provision for movement at the edges of a bulkhead panel is made for a particular construction in service, the specimen should stimulate these conditions.

(4) The method of securing shall be such that there is no possibility of misinterpretation of test results due to the passage of flame at the edges of the specimen when the method of fixing is not the subject of the test.

(c) *Furnace control.* (1) The furnace temperature shall be determined by at least four mineral insulated thermocouples having rapid response and distributed so as to represent fairly the furnace temperature and to insure as uniform heating as possible. The thermocouples shall be arranged so that the hot junction is approximately 10 cm. (4″) from the nearest point of the specimen.

(2) The furnace temperature shall be continuously controlled so as to follow

the standard time-temperature curve within the accuracy specified in paragraph (c)(4) of this section.

(3) The standard time-temperature curve is defined by a smooth curve drawn through the following points:

At the beginning of the test, 20 °C. (68 °F.).
At the end of the first 5 minutes, 538 °C. (1,000 °F.).
At the end of the first 10 minutes, 704 °C. (1,300 °F.).
At the end of the first 30 minutes, 843 °C. (1,550 °F.).
At the end of the first 60 minutes, 927 °C. (1,700 °F.).

For a further definition of the time-temperature curve, see Appendix I of the ASTM Standard E119, "Fire Tests of Building Construction and Materials".

(4) The accuracy of the furnace control shall be such that the area under the mean time-temperature curve is within 15 percent of the area under the standard curve during the first 10 minutes of the test, within 10 percent during the first one-half hour, and within 5 percent for any period after the first one-half hour. At any time after the first 10 minutes of the test the mean furnace temperature shall not differ from the standard curve by more than 100 °C. (180 °F.). Consideration will be given to adjusting the results for variation of the furnace exposure from that prescribed. If corrections are made, they shall be in accordance with the procedures set forth in ASTM E-119.

(5) The pressure in the furnace shall be equal to that in the laboratory at about one-third of the height of the specimen.

(d) *Temperature of unexposed surface.* For the unexposed surface temperature measurement, a thermocouple of 0.5 mm. (0.020″) diameter wires shall be soldered centrally with high temperature solder to one surface of a disc of copper 12 mm. diameter and 0.2 mm. thick. The discs shall be covered with an oven-dry asbestos pad 50 mm. × 50 mm. and 4 mm. thick. The disc and the pad may be fixed to the surface of the specimen by pins, tape or a suitable adhesive, depending on the nature of the specimen material. The asbestos pad shall have a density of approximately 1,000 kg./m.^{3} and thermal conductivity

of 0.11 kcal./m./hr. × C. at 100 °C. (212 °F.).

(e) *Flame penetration.* (1) Where cracks or openings are formed during the test, an ignition test as prescribed in §164.008-4(b) shall take place immediately after the appearance of cracks or damage, followed by similar tests at frequent intervals. The purpose of the test is to indicate whether cracks and openings formed during the test are such that they would lead to passage of flame.

(2) The cotton wool used for the tests prescribed in §164.008-4(b) shall consist of new undyed soft fibers without any admixture of artificial fibers, and shall be free from thread, leaf, and shell fiber dust. A suitable material for this purpose is sold in the form of rolls for surgical use. A pad shall be cut measuring 10 cm. × 10 cm. approximately 2 cm. thick and weighing between 3 and 4 grams. It shall be oven-dried prior to the test. The pad shall be attached by means of wire clips to a 10 cm. × 10 cm. frame of 1 mm. diameter. A wire handle approximately 75 cm. long attached to the frame would facilitate its use on the specimen.

(3) When testing for cracks or openings during the test, the pad shall be held in a vertical position facing the crack or opening with the aperture located in a central part of the cotton wool. The pad may be reused if it has not absorbed any moisture or become charred during the previous application.

(f) *Temperature observations.* (1) All observations shall be taken at intervals not exceeding 5 minutes. The surface temperatures on the unexposed side of the test specimen shall be measured by thermocouples located as follows:

(i) One thermocouple located approximately in the center of each quadrant of the steel plate (four thermocouples total).

(ii) One thermocouple close to the center of the test specimen, but away from the joint, if any.

(iii) At least one thermocouple at the vertical joint of the test specimen.

(iv) Further thermocouples at the discretion of the testing laboratory or Coast Guard for the purpose of determining the temperature at points deemed likely to give a greater temperature rise than any of the above mentioned thermocouples.

(2) The average temperature rise on the unexposed surface shall be obtained by averaging the readings of the thermocouples mentioned in paragraphs (f)(1) (i) and (ii) of this section.

(g) *Other observations.* Throughout the test, observations shall be made of all changes and occurrences, which are not criteria of performance but which may create hazard in case of a fire; for example the emission of appreciable volumes of smoke or noxious vapors from the unexposed side of the test specimen. The specimen shall be examined after the test for changes that have taken place and the information shall be noted in the test report.

(h) *Duration of testing.* The test shall be continued for at least 30 minutes to meet the requirements of §164.008-2(b) or at least 60 minutes to meet the requirements of §164.008-2(c). In either case, the test shall be continued until the maximum surface temperature rise values noted in §164.008-4(a) have been reached, or until cracks which lead to flaming as specified in §164.008-4(b) are formed.

§164.008-4 Test requirements.

(a) Thermal insulation: The insulation value of the specimens for the full scale test shall be such that the average temperature of thermocouples on the unexposed surface described in §164.008-3(f)(2) will not rise more than 139 °C. (250 °F.) above the initial temperature, nor will the temperature at any point on the surface, including any joint, rise more than 225 °C. (405 °F.) above the initial temperature at the end of 15 minutes. When failure is due to excessive temperature rise on the joint, consideration will be given to alternate joint construction. The results obtained on the small scale test (2′×2′) (60 cm. × 60 cm.) shall be recorded.

(b) The test shall determine the length of time, up to one hour, that the bulkhead panel, including the joint can withstand the passage of flame. Cracks and openings shall not be such as to lead to flaming of a cotton wool test pad as prescribed in §164.008-3(e)(3) held facing the aperture at about 25 mm. for a period of 30 seconds. If no flaming oc-

curs, the pad shall be removed and reapplied after a suitable interval.

§164.008-5 Test report.

(a) The test report required by §164.008-7 (e) and (g) shall include at least the following:

(1) Name of manufacturer.

(2) Purpose of test.

(3) Test conditions and date of test.

(4) Description of the panel tested giving size, thickness, density, detail of joint and method of assembling in test furnace.

(5) Complete time-temperature data, including initial temperature, for each thermocouple together with curves of average temperature for the unexposed surface of the insulation and the thermocouple recording the highest temperature. In addition, for §164.008-7(g)(2) complete time-temperature data consisting of a numerical time-temperature table for each furnace and each surface of insulation thermocouple together with the initial temperature of each thermocouple.

(6) A log setting forth the observer's notes relative to deflections, smoke or gas emission, glow, flame emission, and any other important data. The time of each observation should be noted.

(7) Complete observations on the appearance of cracks and data on the testing of the cracks as specified in §164.008-4(b).

(8) Photographs of both sides of the panel before and after testing.

(9) Summary of test results.

(b) [Reserved]

[CGFR 69–72, 34 FR 17500, Oct. 29, 1969; 34 FR 19030, Nov. 29, 1969]

§164.008-6 Retests.

(a) Manufacturers of approved bulkhead panels shall maintain quality control of materials used, manufacturing methods, and the finished product utilizing appropriate quality control testing so as to meet the requirements of this specification, and any other conditions outlined on the certificate of approval. Bulkhead panels are not inspected at regularly scheduled factory inspections; however, approved bulkhead panels are subject to retest for continued compliance with the requirements of this subpart on the following basis:

(1) The Coast Guard may detail a marine inspector or other Coast Guard designated inspector at any time to visit any place where bulkhead panels are manufactured to conduct any inspections or examinations deemed advisable and to select representative samples for further examination, inspection, or tests. The inspector shall be admitted to any place where work is done on bulkhead panels or component materials.

(2) At a frequency of not less than once every 5 years following issuance of approval, samples of an approved bulkhead panel selected from production stock shall be forwarded by the inspector to the Commandant for testing in accordance with the requirements of this subpart. Where the plant is outside the jurisdiction of a Coast Guard District Commander, the frequency of such selection and testing shall be every 2 years. The cost of such testing shall be borne by the manufacturer. The nature of the product or its production may dictate a differing retest frequency.

(3) The Coast Guard reserves the right to make spot-check tests of approved bulkhead panels at any time on samples selected by a marine inspector obtained during installation on a vessel. The manufacturer will incur no expense for such tests, but the results shall be binding upon the approval of his product.

(b) A small scale furnace test (2′x 2′ furnace test) shall be conducted. The time of failure shall not vary from the original (2′x2′ furnace) test values by more than 10 percent. In addition, tests shall be conducted to determine incombustibility (§ 164.009), density and thickness. Values on retesting for density and thickness shall not vary from the original test values by more than 10 percent.

§ 164.008–7 Procedure for approval.

The following items shall be accomplished in sequential order.

(a) *Test request information.* If a manufacturer desires to have a bulkhead panel approved, a written request shall be submitted to the Commandant of the Coast Guard, together with the following:

(1) If the material has already been approved as an "Incombustible Material" under subpart 164.009 of this part, the approval number of the material shall be indicated. If not, the procedure set forth in subpart 164.009 of this part shall be followed; and such approval shall be obtained prior to submittal under this specification.

(2) The description and trade name of the bulkhead panel.

(3) A statement of the composition of the material and the percentage of each component.

(4) A sample of the material at least 1 foot square in each thickness and density of the material as manufactured.

(5) The range of thicknesses and/or densities in which it is proposed to manufacture or use the material, together with any information or recommendations the manufacturer may have as maximum or minimum thickness or density.

(6) The location of the place or places where the material will be manufactured.

(7) A sketch showing typical installation methods and indicating limtations, if any.

(8) A general statement describing manufacturing procedures indicating the degree of quality control exercised and the degree of inspection performed by outside organizations.

(9) A statement indicating proposed methods for field identification of the products as being approved. Identification shall include the Coast Guard approval number.

(b) *Test suitability.* The above information will be examined by the Coast Guard and if it is indicated that the material is in all other respects suitable for testing, the manufacturer will be so advised. Coast Guard comments on the manufacturer's recommended thickness and density of the panel for the fire resistance and integrity test will be given at this time together with the estimated cost of the tests.

(c) *Samples to be submitted.* If the material is indicated as being suitable for testing, the manufacturer shall submit the samples required by paragraph (c)(1) of this section to the Fire Research Section of the National Bureau of Standards, Washington, DC 20234, and shall advise the Coast Guard of the shipment.

(1) One representative panel of the material having a surface approximately 4.65 square meters (50 square feet) and a height of 2.44 meters (8 feet) containing at least one vertical joint, located at approximately one-third panel width from one edge (20–24 inches), and one representative panel of the material having 60 cm. × 60 cm. (2′×2′) dimensions. If the manufacturer desires to submit the panel in thickness or size other than that recommended, prior approval shall be obtained from the Commandant. The manufacturer shall supply any labor required for fabrication of the panel and for attaching the panel to the frame for testing.

(d) *Pretest information.* At this time the manufacturer shall submit to the Coast Guard the following:

(1) A statement that the material as offered for testing and as described pursuant to §164.008–6(a)(3) is completely representative of the product which will be manufactured and sold under U.S. Coast Guard approval if such approval is granted and that the shipbuilder will be advised of the proper installation methods and the limitations of the conditions of approval.

(2) A commitment from the manufacturer that he will reimburse the National Bureau of Standards for the cost of the tests or review when billed by them.

(3) If the manufacturer desires to witness the test, he should so indicate at this time.

(e) *Test authorization.* The National Bureau of Standards will then be authorized to conduct the test noted in §164.008–4(a) and, upon completion of all testing, the manufacturer will be billed directly by the National Bureau of Standards, four copies of the report containing the information required by §164.008–5 shall be submitted to the Coast Guard.

(f) *Notification of results.* A copy of the report will be forwarded to the manufacturer, and he will be advised if his material is approved under this subpart. If approved, any stipulations of the approval will be specified. This information will be published in the FEDERAL REGISTER, and a certificate of approval will be issued to the manufacturer.

(g) *Other laboratories.* (1) If the manufacturer desires to have the tests conducted at some laboratory other than the National Bureau of Standards, this information shall be supplied at the time of initial contact with the Coast Guard. If the proposed laboratory is acceptable to the Coast Guard, the manufacturer will be so advised and any special testing requirements together with an estimated cost of expenses incurred by the National Bureau of Standards for their review will be specified at this time. Payment will be made as noted in paragraph (d)(2) of this section. The Coast Guard shall be notified in advance of the date of the test so that a representative may be present.

(2) The laboratory shall submit four copies of a detailed test report to the Coast Guard, together with representative samples of the material being taken before and after testing. The test report and samples will be examined by the National Bureau of Standards for compliance with this subpart. The test report shall include the information required by §164.008–5 together with any other pertinent data.

Subpart 164.009—Noncombustible Materials for Merchant Vessels

SOURCE: CGD 74–129, 41 FR 41701, Sept. 23, 1976, unless otherwise noted.

§ 164.009-1 General.

(a) This subpart contains—

(1) Procedures for approval of noncombustible materials used in merchant vessel construction;

(2) The test and measurements required for approval of materials; and

(3) A list of noncombustible materials for which specific approval under this subpart is not required.

(b) The test and measurements described in this subpart are conducted by a laboratory designated by the Commandant. The following laboratories are so designated:

Underwriters Laboratories, Inc., 333 Pfingsten Road, Northbrook, IL 60062

Dantest, National Institute for Testing and Verification, Amager Boulevard 115, DK 2300 Copenhagen S., Denmark

[CGD 74–129, 41 FR 41701, Sept. 23, 1976, as amended by CGD 86–035, 54 FR 36316, Sept. 1, 1989]

§ 164.009-3 Noncombustible materials not requiring specific approval.

The following noncombustible materials may be used in merchant vessel construction though not specifically approved under this subpart:

(a) Sheet glass, block glass, clay, ceramics, and uncoated fibers.

(b) All metals, except magnesium and magnesium alloys.

(c) Portland cement, gypsum, and magnesite concretes having aggregates of only sand, gravel, expanded vermiculite, expanded or vesicular slags, diatomaceous silica, perlite, or pumice.

(d) Woven, knitted or needle punched glass fabric containing no additives other than lubricants not exceeding 2.5 percent.

[CGD 86–035, 54 FR 36316, Sept. 1, 1989]

§ 164.009-7 Contents of application.

An application for approval of a material under this subpart must contain the following:

(a) The trade name of the material.

(b) The thickness or density, or both, of the material, or the range of thicknesses or densities, or both, of the material as manufactured.

(c) The composition of the material.

(d) The density and percentage of moisture and volatile matter of each component of the material.

(e) The address of the factory manufacturing the material.

(f) A sample representative of the material that is 305 mm long and 305 mm wide and that has a height equal to the largest thickness of the material as manufactured.

(g) If the applicant intends to observe the test and measurements of the sample, a statement to that effect.

(h) A commitment by the applicant to pay for the cost of the test and measurements when billed by the designated laboratory.

§ 164.009-9 Procedure for approval.

(a) An application for approval of a material under this subpart must be sent to the Commandant (G–MSE), U.S. Coast Guard, Washington, DC 20593–0001.

(b) The application is examined by the Coast Guard to determine the probability that the material meets the requirements for approval. The Coast Guard notifies the applicant of the results of the examination and of the sample size necessary for submission to the designated laboratory.

(c) The designated laboratory notifies the applicant of the time and place for submission and testing of the sample.

(d) The designated laboratory conducts the tests and measurements of the sample in accordance with the procedures in this subpart, prepares a test report, and sends four copies of the report to the Commandant (G–MSE). The applicant may observe the test and measurements.

(e) The Commandant sends a copy of the test report to the applicant and advises him whether the material is approved. If the material is approved, an approval certificate is sent to the applicant.

[CGD 74–129, 41 FR 41701, Sept. 23, 1976, as amended by CGD 82–063b, 48 FR 4783, Feb. 3, 1983; CGD 88–070, 53 FR 34537, Sept. 7, 1988; CGD 95–072, 60 FR 50467, Sept. 29, 1995; CGD 96–041, 61 FR 50734, Sept. 27, 1996]

§ 164.009-11 Furnace apparatus.

(a) The test furnace apparatus consists of a furnace tube, stabilizer, draft shield, furnace stand, temperature coil controls with a voltage stabilizer, specimen holder, specimen insertion device, and three thermocouples (a furnace thermocouple to measure furnace temperature, a surface thermocouple to measure temperature at the surface of a specimen, and a specimen thermocouple to measure temperature at the center of a specimen). A detailed plan of the construction and arrangement of the furnace apparatus may be obtained from the Commandant (G–MSE).

(b) Temperatures measured by the thermocouples are recorded by an instrument having a measuring range that corresponds to the temperature changes that occur during a furnace calibration or test. The temperature recording equipment is accurate to within at least 0.5 percent of temperatures recorded during a test.

[CGD 74-129, 41 FR 41701, Sept. 23, 1976, as amended by CGD 82-063b, 48 FR 4783, Feb. 3, 1983; CGD 95-072, 60 FR 50467, Sept. 29, 1995; CGD 96-041, 61 FR 50734, Sept. 27, 1996]

§164.009-13 Furnace calibration.

A calibration is performed on each new furnace and on each existing furnace as often as necessary to ensure that the furnace is in good working order. In each calibration the energy input to the furnace is adjusted so that the furnace thermocouple gives a steady reading of 750±10 °C. The wall temperature of the furnace tube is then measured by an optical micro-pyrometer at intervals of 10mm on 3 equally spaced vertical axes. The furnace is correctly calibrated if the temperature of the furnace tube wall is between 825 and 875 °C. 50 mm above and below the midline of the wall and if the average wall temperature is approximately 850 °C.

§164.009-15 Test procedure.

(a) *General.* Paragraphs (b) through (k) of this section contain the test procedures for each material submitted for approval, except fiberglass and other materials that melt at 750°±10 °C. Paragraph (l) of this section contains test procedures for fiberglass and other materials that melt at 750°±10 °C.

(b) *Preparation of specimens.* (1) The designated laboratory prepares 5 cylindrical specimens representative of the properties of the sample submitted for testing. The dimensions of each specimen are as follows:

diameter: 45(+2/-0) mm
height: 50±3 mm
volume: 80±5 cm^3

(2) If the height of the sample, except a composite material, is less than 47 mm, the specimens prepared consist of layers of the sample.

(3) If the sample is a composite material and has a height that is not 50±3mm, the layers of the specimen prepared are proportional in thickness to the layers of the sample.

(4) The top and bottom faces of each specimen prepared are the faces of the material as manufactured.

(5) If it is not practicable to prepare a specimen by the procedures described in paragraphs (b)(2) through (b)(4) of this section, the test is performed on five specimens of each component of the sample made to the dimensions prescribed in paragraph (b)(1) of this section.

(c) *Conditioning of specimen.* Each specimen is conditioned for at least 20 hours in a ventilated oven maintained at 60±5 °C. and is then cooled to room temperature in a desiccator.

(d) *Weight of specimen.* The weight of each conditioned specimen after cooling is determined before it is tested.

(e) *Placement of specimen in holder.* After a specimen is conditioned and weighed, it is placed in the specimen holder. A specimen that is made of layers of a composite material is held firmly together in the specimen holder.

(f) *Attachment of thermocouples.* After the specimen is placed in the specimen holder, the thermocouples are attached to the specimen as follows: A vertical hole with a diameter of 2 mm and a depth that is half the height of the specimen is made in the center of the top of the specimen. The specimen thermocouple is then inserted into the hole so that its hot junction is at the center of the specimen. The surface thermocouple is put in contact with the surface of the specimen at its midheight.

(g) *Preparation of the apparatus.* The apparatus is examined to determine whether it is in good working order and to ensure that the equipment is protected against drafts and is not exposed to direct sunlight or artificial illumination. The furnace temperature is stabilized at 750 °C.±10 °C. and kept at that temperature for the duration of the test. The furnace temperature is stabilized when no adjustments are needed in the energy input to the furnace to keep the temperature constant.

(h) *Insertion of specimen.* After the furnace temperature is stabilized for at least 10 minutes, the specimen is inserted into the furnace. The insertion is completed within 5 seconds. The specimen is positioned so that the hot junction of the surface thermocouple is diametrically opposite the hot junction of the furnace thermocouple.

(i) *Heating period.* The heating period begins upon insertion of the specimen into the furnace and continues for 20 minutes, or until peak temperatures have passed.

(j) *Test observations.* Temperature measurements at each thermocouple are made at intervals of not more than 10 seconds during the heating period, and note is taken of the occurrence and duration of any flaming. At the end of the heating period, the specimen is removed from the furnace and weighed while still hot.

(k) *Test results.* Material is approved under this subpart if the test results of the sample submitted are within the following limits:

(1) The highest temperature recorded for each specimen during the test by the furnace thermocouple, when averaged with the highest temperatures recorded for the other specimens, is not more than 50 °C. above the stabilized furnace temperature.

(2) The highest temperature recorded for each specimen during the test by the surface thermocouple, when averaged with the highest temperatures recorded for the other specimens, is not more than 50 °C. above the stabilized furnace temperature.

(3) The duration of flaming of each specimen during the test, when averaged with duration of flaming recorded for the other specimens, is not more than 10 seconds.

(4) The average weight loss of the specimens after heating is not more than 50 percent of their average weight after conditioning.

(1) *Fiberglass and other materials that melt at 750 °C.±10 °C.* If the material submitted for approval is fiberglass or other material that melts at 750°±10 °C., it is tested as described in paragraphs (b) through (k) of this section, except the average weight loss of the sample is determined as follows:

(1) Five cylindrical specimens in addition to the five cylindrical specimens required in paragraph (b) of this section are prepared as described in paragraph (b) of this section.

(2) Each of the additional specimens is placed on a weighing dish and both the specimen and the weighing dish are conditioned as described in paragraph (c) of this section.

(3) The weight of each specimen and its weighing dish is determined as described in paragraph (d) of this section.

(4) After a specimen and weighing dish are conditioned and weighed, they are placed in the specimen holder with the specimen supported by weighing dish. No specimen thermocouple or surface thermocouple is attached to the specimen.

(5) The apparatus is prepared as described in paragraph (g) of this section, and after the furnace temperature has stabilized for at least 10 minutes, the specimen and weighing dish are inserted into the furnace. The specimen and weighing dish are then heated for 20 minutes or until peak temperatures have passed. At the end of the heating period, the specimen and weighing dish are removed from the furnace and weighed while still hot.

(6) The average weight loss of the specimens after heating may not be more than 50 percent of their average weight before heating.

§ 164.009-17 Density measurement.

(a) The measurements described in this section are made to determine the density of a sample.

(b) If the sample is a solid material, a specimen that has a length of 305 mm, a width of 305 mm, and thickness equal to that of the sample is prepared. The length and width are measured to the nearest 0.80 mm and the thickness to the nearest 0.25 mm. Allowance is made for any irregularity in the surfaces of the specimen. The average of at least four measurements of each dimension is determined.

(c) If the sample is fibrous insulation, a specimen is prepared from sheets of the sample submitted. The sample is a cube and each dimension is 305 mm±1.60 mm. The average of at least four measurements of each dimension is determined.

(d) The weight of a specimen is determined with a sensitive balance scale accurate to at least 0.5 percent of the weight of the specimen.

(e) The dimension and weight measurements of a specimen are made after it has been conditioned for at least one week, and for any additional time needed for the specimen to reach a constant weight, in an atmosphere that is

22.8 °C.±2 °C. and 50 percent ±5 percent relative humidity.

§ 164.009-19 Measurement of moisture and volatile matter content.

(a) The measurements described in this section are made to determine the moisture and volatile matter content of a sample.

(b) A specimen cut from the density specimen of a sample is conditioned for at least one week, and for any additional time needed for the specimen to reach a constant weight, in an atmosphere that is 22.8 °C.±2 °C., and 50 percent ±5 percent relative humidity. The conditioned specimen is then weighed and transferred to a previously weighed wide mouth weighing bottle that has a glass stopper. With the stopper removed, the bottle, stopper, and specimen are heated at 105 °C.±5 °C. for four hours. After four hours, the stopper is inserted in the bottle and the bottle and sample are cooled and weighed.

(c) The content of moisture and volatile matter is the difference between the two weighings and is reported as a percentage of the weight of the conditioned specimen.

§ 164.009-21 Laboratory report.

The laboratory report of the test and measurements of a material contains the following:

(a) Name of the designated laboratory.

(b) Name of manufacturer of the material.

(c) Date of receipt of the material and dates of the test and measurements.

(d) Trade name of the material.

(e) Description of the material.

(f) Density of the sample.

(g) Percentage of moisture and volatile matter in the sample.

(h) Description of the specimens tested if the specimens are prepared from composite material.

(i) If the test was done on individual components of the sample, a description of the components.

(j) Test results including the following:

(1) Complete time and temperature data for each thermocouple.

(2) Each observation of flame emission and the time and duration of each emission.

§ 164.009-23 Factory inspection.

The Coast Guard does not inspect noncombustible materials approved under this subpart on a regular schedule. However, the Commander of the Coast Guard District in which a factory is located may detail a marine inspector at any time to visit a factory where a noncombustible material is manufactured to conduct an inspection of the manufacturing and quality control procedures and to select representative samples of the material for examination or tests to verify that the material is as stated in the original application for approval. The manufacturer is advised in advance of the time of testing samples selected and may witness the tests upon request.

§ 164.009-25 Marking.

The manufacturer must mark each shipping container for an approved noncombustible material with the approval number and date of approval of the material.

Subpart 164.012—Interior Finishes for Merchant Vessels

§ 164.012-1 Applicable specifications.

(a) The following specifications, of the issue in effect on the contract date for the particular installation on any vessel, form a part of this subpart:

(1) American Society for Testing Materials' standard: E 84-50T—Tentative Method of Fire Hazard Classification for Building Materials.

(2) National Fire Protection Association's standard: NFPA No. 255—Method of Test of Surface Burning Characteristics of Building Materials.

(3) Coast Guard specifications: 164.008—Bulkhead Panels for Merchant Vessels. 164.009—Incombustible Materials for Merchant Vessels.

(b) A copy of this subpart, together with copies of the specifications referred to in this section, shall be kept on file by the manufacturer of any Interior Finish except those qualifying under § 164.012-5(c). It should be noted that the standards listed in paragraphs

(a) (1) and (2) of this section are identical and, therefore, only one need to be kept on file. The Coast Guard specifications may be obtained upon request from the Commandant (G–MSE), U.S. Coast Guard, Washington, DC 20593–0001. The American Society for Testing Materials Standards may be purchased from that society at 1916 Race Street, Philadelphia, Pa., 19103. The National Fire Protection Association Standard may be purchased from that association at 1 Batterymarch Park, Quincy, MA 02269.

[CGFR 61–15, 26 FR 9303, Sept. 30, 1961, as amended by CGFR 65–16, 30 FR 10903, Aug. 21, 1965; CGD 88–070, 53 FR 34537, Sept. 7, 1988; CGD 95–072, 60 FR 50467, Sept. 29, 1995; CGD 96–041, 61 FR 50734, Sept. 27, 1996]

§ 164.012–5 Scope.

(a) The purpose of this specification is to set forth the fire protection standards for "Interior Finishes" applied to "Bulkhead Panels" or "Incombustible Materials" approved under subpart 164.008 or 164.009 of this subchapter. The term "Interior Finish" means any coating, overlay, or veneer except standard paint which is applied for decorative or other purpose. It includes not only the visible finish, but all material used in its composition and in its application to the approved "Bulkhead Panel" or "Incombustible Material." When finishes are applied to both sides of a panel, each must comply with this specification.

(b) "Interior Finishes" of not more than 0.075″ thickness qualifying under § 164.012–10 and those materials which are described in paragraph (c) of this section, may be used without restriction on all merchant vessels, including those locations where combustible veneers, trim, moldings, and decorations are specifically prohibited by subpart 72.05 of subchapter H (Rules and Regulations for Passenger Vessels) of this chapter.

(c) With the exception of nitrocellulose or other highly inflammable or noxious fume-producing paints or lacquers (which are prohibited), a limited number of coats of any standard paint, or any "Incombustible Material" approved under subpart 164.009 of this subchapter in any thickness, or a combination thereof, are considered as automatically satisfying the intent of this specification and no test or proof of compliance will be required. Paint may be applied to one or both sides of "Bulkhead Panels" or "Incombustible Materials," but it shall never be applied as an internal layer in sandwich or laminar construction.

[CGFR 61–15, 26 FR 9303, Sept. 30, 1961]

§ 164.012–10 Requirements.

(a) For an "Interior Finish" to qualify under this specification it shall not be more than 0.075 inch thick (including adhesive and any underlayment) and shall be subjected to the test described in either standard listed in § 164.012–1(a) (1) or (2). The "Interior Finish" shall be applied to a ¼-inch asbestos cement board, "Bulkhead Panel" or "Incombustible Material" approved under subparts 164.008 and 164.009, in the same manner as will be employed for the shipboard installation. The classification ratings determined by this test shall not exceed the following values:

Flame spread classification 20
Smoke classification 10

(b) [Reserved]

[CGFR 70–143, 35 FR 19967, Dec. 30, 1970]

§ 164.012–11 Marking.

In addition to that information required by the recognized laboratory, the following information and special markings shall be included:

Complies with USCG subpart 164.012. Approval No. 164.012/—.

[CGFR 70–143, 35 FR 19967, Dec. 30, 1970]

§ 164.012–12 Recognized laboratory.

A recognized laboratory is one which is operated as a nonprofit public service and is regularly engaged in the examination, testing, and evaluation as to the safety of insulation and surfacing materials; which has an established factory inspection, listing, and labeling program; and which has standards for evaluating listing and labeling which are acceptable to the Commandant.

The following laboratories are recognized:

Underwriters' Laboratories, Inc.
207 East Ohio Street
Chicago, IL 60611

[CGFR 70-143, 35 FR 19967, Dec. 30, 1970]

§ 164.012-13 Examinations, tests, and inspections.

(a) *Manufacturer's inspection and tests.* Manufacturers of listed and labeled Interior Finishes shall maintain quality control of the materials used, manufacturing methods and the finished product so as to meet the applicable requirements, and shall make sufficient inspections and tests of representative samples and components produced to maintain the quality of the finished product. Records of tests conducted by the manufacturer and records of materials, including affidavits by suppliers that applicable requirements are met, entering into manufacture shall be made available to the recognized laboratory inspector or the Coast Guard marine inspector, or both, for review upon request.

(b) *Laboratory inspection and tests.* Such examinations, inspections and tests as are required by the recognized laboratory for listed and labeled material produced will be conducted by the laboratory inspector at the place of manufacture or other location at the option of the laboratory.

(c) *Test facilities.* The laboratory inspector, or the Coast Guard marine inspector assigned by the Commander of the District in which the factory is located, or both, shall be admitted to any place in the factory where work is being done on listed and labeled products, and either or both inspectors may take samples of parts or materials entering into construction of final assemblies, for further examinations, inspections, or tests. The manufacturer shall provide a suitable place and the apparatus necessary for the performance of the tests which are done at the place of manufacture.

(d) *Additional tests, etc.* Unannounced examinations, tests, and inspections of samples obtained either directly from the manufacturer or through commercial channels may be made to determine the suitability of a product for listing and labeling, or to determine conformance of a labeled product to the applicable requirements. These may be conducted by the recognized laboratory or the U.S. Coast Guard.

[CGFR 70-143, 35 FR 19967, Dec. 30, 1970]

§ 164.012-14 Procedure for listing and labeling.

(a) Manufacturers having a surfacing material which they consider has characteristics suitable for general use on merchant vessels may make application for listing and labeling as an interior finish by addressing a request directly to a recognized laboratory. The laboratory will inform the submitter as to the requirements for inspection, examinations, and testing necessary for such listing and labeling. The request shall include a permission for the laboratory to furnish a complete test report together with a description of the quality control procedures to the Commandant, U.S. Coast Guard.

(b) The U.S. Coast Guard will review the test report and quality control procedures to determine if the approval requirements have been met. If this is the case, the Commandant will notify the laboratory that the material is approved and that when the material is listed and labeled it may be marked as being U.S. Coast Guard approved. Notice of U.S. Coast Guard approval will be published in CG-190.

(c) If disagreements concerning procedural, technical or inspection questions arise over U.S. Coast Guard approval requirements the opinion of the Commandant shall be requested by the laboratory.

(d) The manufacturer may at any time request clarification or advice from the Commandant on any question which may arise regarding manufacturing and approval of approved devices.

[CGFR 70-143, 35 FR 19967, Dec. 30, 1970]

§ 164.012-15 Termination of listing and labeling.

(a) Listing and labeling as an interior finish acceptable to the Commandant as approved may be terminated, withdrawn, canceled, or suspended by written notice to the recognized laboratory from the Commandant, or by written notice to the manufacturer from the recognized laboratory or from the Commandant.

(b) The condition which may be the cause for termination of listing and labeling may be any of the following:

(1) When the manufacturer does not desire to retain the service.

(2) When the listed product is no longer being manufactured.

(3) When manufacturer's own program does not provide suitable assurance of the quality of the listed and labeled product being manufactured.

(4) When the product manufactured no longer conforms to the current applicable requirements of the U.S. Coast Guard and the recognized laboratory.

(5) When service experience or laboratory or U.S. Coast Guard reports indicate a product is unsatisfactory.

[CGFR 70–143, 35 FR 19967, Dec. 30, 1970]

Subpart 164.013—Foam, Unicellular Polyethylene (Buoyant, Slab, Slitted Trigonal Pattern)

SOURCE: CGD 95–028, 62 FR 51216, Sept. 30, 1997, unless otherwise noted.

EDITORIAL NOTE: At 62 FR 51216, Sept. 30, 1997, subpart 164.013 was revised, effective Oct. 30, 1997. The superseded text of the revised subpart remaining in effect until Oct. 30, 1997, appears in the October 1, 1996, revision of title 46 parts 156–165.

§ 164.013–1 Scope.

(a) This subpart contains performance requirements, acceptance tests, and production testing and inspection requirements for polyethylene foam used in the construction of personal flotation devices (PFDs) approved under part 160 of this subchapter. Manufacturers shall also comply with the requirements of subpart 164.019 of this chapter.

(b) All polyethylene foams accepted under this subpart are non-standard components. Acceptance of polyethylene foam prior to being incorporated into finished PFDs, or during the course of manufacture, shall in no case be construed as a guarantee of the acceptance of the finished PFD.

§ 164.013–2 Incorporation by reference.

(a) Certain materials are incorporated by reference into this subpart with the approval of the Director of the Federal Register in accordance with 5 U.S.C. 552(a) and 1 CFR part 51. To enforce any edition other than the one listed in paragraph (b) of this section, notice of change must be published in the FEDERAL REGISTER and the material made available to the public. All approved material incorporated by reference may be inspected at the Office of the FEDERAL REGISTER, 800 North Capitol Street, NW., suite 700, Washington, DC 20002, and at the U.S. Coast Guard, Lifesaving and Fire Safety Division (G-MSE-4), Washington, DC 20593–0001, and is available from the source indicated in paragraph (b) of this section.

(b) The materials approved for incorporation by reference in this subpart, and the sections affected are as follows:

UNDERWRITERS LABORATORIES (UL)

Underwriters Laboratories, Inc., P.O. Box 13995, Research Triangle Park, NC 27709–3995 (Phone (919) 549–1400; Facsimile: (919) 549–1842).

UL 1191, Standards for Components for Personal Flotation Devices, May 16, 1995—164.013–3; 160.013–5.

1(c) *Copies on file.* Copies of the specifications and letter of acceptance shall be kept on file by the manufacturer.

§ 164.013–3 Material properties and workmanship.

(a) *General.* The unicellular polyethylene foam shall be all new material complying with the requirements outlined in this specification. Unicellular polyethylene foam must comply with the requirements of UL 1191, sections 24, 25, and 26 and its assigned Use Code. Thickness tolerances of the foam must permit the manufacture of PFDs complying with their required buoyancy tolerances.

(b) *Use Codes 4BC, 4H.* Each foam which has a C-factor of at least 94 according to UL 1191 may be assigned Use Codes 4BC and 4H.

(c) *Use Codes 2, 3, 5R.* Each foam which has a V-factor of at least 85 according to UL 1191 may be assigned Use Codes 2, 3, 5R (recreational use applications).

§164.013-4 Samples submitted for acceptance.

Application samples. A product sample submitted for acceptance as required by §164.019-7(c)(4) must consist of at least one square foot by the thickness of foam produced.

§164.013-5 Acceptance tests.

Manufacturers shall ensure that the performance and identification tests described in UL 1191, as appropriate, are performed on a minimum of five samples in each of the lightest and darkest colors submitted for acceptance by a recognized laboratory accepted under §164.019.

§164.013-6 Production tests, inspections, and marking.

Manufacturers shall provide in-plant quality control of polyethylene foam in accordance with the requirements of §164.019-13 and any requirements of the recognized laboratory. The manufacturer of the foam has primary responsibility for quality control over the production of the foam.

§164.013-7 Marking.

(a) *General.* The manufacturer must ensure that each shipping label, and each unit of put-up, is permanently and clearly marked in a color which contrasts with the color of the surface on which the marking is applied. Each label must be marked with —

(1) The manufacturer's or supplier's name, trade name, or symbol;

(2) The unique style, part, or model number of the material;

(3) The thickness of the material;

(4) The lot number of the material; and

(5) The product Use Code or Codes.

(b) Each unit of put-up must be marked with the appropriate recognized laboratory's certification marking(s).

Subpart 164.015—Plastic Foam, Unicellular, Buoyant, Sheet and Molded Shape

Source: CGFR 65–37, 30 FR 11593, Sept. 10, 1965 unless otherwise noted.

§164.015-1 Applicable specifications and standards.

(a) *Specifications.* The following specification and standard, of the issue in effect on the date the plastic foam material is manufactured, form a part of this subpart:

(1) Military specification:

MIL–F–859—Fuel Oil, Boiler.

(2) Federal specification:

C–C–91—Candle illuminating.

(3) Federal standard:

Standard 601—Rubber: Sampling and Testing.

(4) A.S.T.M. standard:

D1692T—Flammability of Plastic Foam and Sheeting.

(b) *Copies on file.* Copies of the specifications and standards referred to in this section shall be kept on file by the plastic foam manufacturer with this subpart.

(1) The Federal Specification and the Federal Standard may be purchased from the Business Service Center, General Services Administration, Washington, DC, 20407.

(2) The Military Specification may be obtained from the Commanding Officer, Naval Supply Depot, 5801 Tabor Avenue, Philadelphia, Pa. 19120.

(3) The A.S.T.M. Standard may be purchased from the American Society for Testing Materials, 1916 Race Street, Philadelphia, Pa. 19103.

[CGFR 65–37, 30 FR 11593, Sept. 10, 1965, as amended by CGFR 65–64, 31 FR 563 Jan. 18, 1966]

§164.015-2 Types.

(a) Unicellular expanded polyvinyl chloride-acetate copolymer or synthetic rubber modified polyvinyl chloride, polymer or copolymer plastic foam shall be of three types as follows:

Type A—for life preservers, buoyant vests or buoyant cushions.

Type B—for buoyant vests or buoyant cushions.

Type C—for ring life buoys.

(b) [Reserved]

§164.015-3 Material and workmanship.

(a) The unicellular plastic foam shall be all new material complying with the requirements of this specification. The results of the tests described in

§ 164.015-4 shall yield property values within the limits shown in Table 164.015-4(a).

(b) The unicellular plastic foam shall be produced in sheet stock or molded shapes.

§ 164.015-4 **Inspections and tests.**

(a) *General.* Unicellular plastic foam to be used in a finished product subject to inspection by the Coast Guard also shall be subject to inspection at the plant where the foam is manufactured. The manufacturer of the foam has primary responsibility for quality control over the production of the foam. A marine inspector shall be admitted to any place in the factory where production or partial processing of the foam takes place, and he may take samples of the foam or other materials for further inspections or tests. The manufacturer shall provide a suitable place and the apparatus necessary for the performance of certain tests to be witnessed by the marine inspector, the results of which shall comply with Table 164.015-4(a). Unless otherwise specified, all tests shall be conducted at a temperature of 21°±3 °C. (70°±5 °F.) The properties listed in Table 164.015-4(a) shall be determined on specimens of sheet foam or molded shapes.

TABLE 164.015-4(A)

Properties	Test method	Units	Type A	Type B	Type C
Density (maximum)	164.015-4(b)	Pounds/feet^3	5.0	5.0	8.5
Buoyancy in fresh water (minimum)	164.015-4(c)	Pounds/feet^3	54.0	54.0	52.0
Volume loss on heat aging (maximum).	164.015-4(d)	Percent	5.0	5.0	4.0
Compression deflection at 25 percent.	164.015-4(e)	P.s.i.	3.0 max.	3.0 max.	7.0 min.
Compression set (maximum)	164.015-4(f)	Percent	24	24	20
Fire retardance (maximum)	164.015-4(g)(1)	Seconds	2	....	30
		Inches	1	....	3
	164.015-4(g)(2)	Inches per minute	....	4	....
Tensile strength (minimum)	164.015-4(h)	P.s.i.	30	20	60
Ultimate elongation (minimum)	164.015-4(h)	Percent	75	75	....
Water absorption (maximum)	164.015-4(i)	Pounds/feet^2	.06	.06	.06
Flexibility at 0±2F 164.015-4(j) No cracking No cracking					
Oil resistance	164.015-4(k)		(¹)	(¹)	(¹)
Odor	164.015-4(l)		(²)	(²)	(²)

¹ No softening or swelling.
² Not objectionable.

(b) *Density.* The density of the material shall be determined by dividing the weight of the material by its volume and shall be expressed in pounds per cubic foot. The volume shall be determined by measuring the volume of water displaced by the material or by direct measurement of the specimen using vernier calipers reading to 0.001 inch A sheet specimen 4"x4"xthickness furnished shall be used unless the foam is molded shape, then the largest single piece so molded shall be used.

(c) *Buoyancy in fresh water—*(1) *Specimens.* The buoyancy test shall be made with a sample of the sheet material measuring 12"×12"×thickness of material furnished or with the largest molded shape furnished.

(2) *Procedure.* Securely attach a spring scale in a position directly over a test tank. Suspend a weighted wire basket from the scale in such a manner that the basket can be weighed while completely submerged in water. Proceed as follows:

(i) Weigh the empty basket under water.

(ii) Place the sample inside the basket and submerge it so that the top of the basket is at least 2 inches below the surface of the water. Allow the samples to remain submerged for 24 hours.

(iii) After 24 hours submergence period, weigh the wire basket with the sample inside while both are still under water.

(iv) The buoyancy is computed as paragraph (c)(2)(i) of this section minus (c)(2)(iii) of this section. The resulting value is divided by the volume of the polyvinyl chloride foam expressed in cubic feet. The final result is in lbs./cu. ft.

(d) *Volume loss on heat aging*—(1) *Specimen.* Test specimens shall consist of pieces 4"×4"×the thickness of the material furnished. Where the foam is an object of molded shape, the largest single piece so molded shall be used for this test.

(2) *Procedure.* Volume before and after the heat aging test shall be determined by measuring the volume of water displaced by the material. The specimens shall be placed in an oven maintained at 140°±2 °F., for a period of one week. At the end of that period the specimens shall be removed from the oven and allowed to recover in the open for 5 hours at 70°±2 °F. before the measurement of final volume is made. The test shall be run in triplicate, the results averaged and the percentage of volume loss calculated.

(e) *Compression deflection.* Compression deflection shall be determined in accordance with method 12151 of Federal Standard 601, except that the deflection shall be maintained at 25 percent with automatic or manual control, and the load observed and recorded 60 seconds after the 25 percent deflection is reached.

(f) *Compression set*—(1) *Specimens.* The specimens shall have parallel top and bottom surfaces which shall be at right angles to the side surfaces. The specimen may be cylindrical or rectangular. The minimum dimension across the top shall be at least 1.0 times the thickness and the top a minimum of 1 square inch in area, and a maximum of 16 square inches in area.

(2) *Apparatus.* The apparatus shall consist of a compression device with two parallel plates, between which the test specimen shall be compressed by means of four studs and nuts. The plates may be steel, aluminum or any rigid smooth metal of sufficient thickness to withstand the required compression stresses without bending. The surfaces against which the test specimens are held shall be smooth and shall be thoroughly cleaned and wiped dry before each test. Metal shims inserted between the plates shall be used to limit the compression of the specimen.

(3) *Procedure.* Thickness, before and after the compression set test shall be measured as specified in paragraph (h)(1) of this section. The test specimens shall be compressed 25% of the original thickness for 22 hours. At the end of that period, the test specimens shall be removed from the set apparatus and allowed to rest for 24 hours before measurement of final thickness is made. The compression set shall be calculated by means of the following formula:

Compression set (percent) = $[(h_o - h_i) + (h_o - h_e)] \times 100$ (1)

where:

h_o=the original thickness.
h_i=the thickness 24 hours after removal from apparatus.
h_e=the test compression thickness.

(g) *Fire retardance*—(1) *Types A and C foams.* The test specimens shall be ¼ inch in thickness, 1 inch in width and approximately 6 inches in length. The specimens shall be clamped at one end in a position such that the long dimension forms a 45° angle with the horizontal and with the widths in a vertical position. A bunsen burner with a 1 inch yellow flame shall be applied to the lower or free end of the specimen for 15 seconds. The burner shall then be removed and the time that the specimen continues to burn after removal of the burner shall be recorded as burning time. The length of char shall also be recorded. The test shall be performed in a location free from drafts. The average results of three determinations shall be reported. A plain wax candle equivalent to those meeting Federal Specification C–C 91 may be substituted for the bunsen burner.

(2) *Type B foam.* The test specimens shall be ½ inch in thickness, 2 inches in width and approximately 6 inches in length. The specimens shall be tested in accordance with American Society for Testing Materials Designation D–1692T specification standard.

(h) *Tensile strength and the ultimate elongation*—(1) *Specimens.* The test specimens shall be dumbbell shaped, conforming in shape to die I of method 4111 of Standard FED–STD–601. The thickness of the specimen shall be ¼ inch. Two specimens shall be taken from the center of the sample piece and two from one side, keeping the skin surface intact. The thickness shall be measured to the nearest 0.001 inch by a suitable measurement device such as a vernier caliper with a sliding vernier to read 0.001 inch. Care shall be taken not to compress or distort the specimen when measuring. The specimens taken from the center will be skinless; the others will have skin on one side. One-inch bench marks shall be placed midway on the constricted portion of the tensile specimen.

(2) *Procedure.* (i) The tensile strength of the specimens shall be determined in a standard tensile testing machine with a rate of separation of jaws set at 2 inches per minute. The bench marks shall be followed with a suitable pair of dividers until the specimen ruptures. A minimum of 4 specimens shall be tested and if any specimen breaks at the clamp or any specimen exhibits any obvious defects, the results obtained therewith shall be discarded. A new similar specimen shall then be prepared and tested. The tensile strength shall be calculated by dividing the breaking load (to the nearest 0.1 pound) by the original area of the cross section of the specimen in square inches and the result shall be expressed in pounds per square inch. The percent ul-

timate elongation shall be calculated as follows:

$$D_1 - D + D \times 100 \qquad (2)$$

where:

D = distance between knife edges of bench marker.

D_1 = distance between bench marks at moment of rupture to the nearest ⅟₃₂ inch.

(3) *Averaging determinations.* The tensile strength in pounds per square inch and percent ultimate elongation of four determinations shall be averaged for each sample.

(i) *Water absorption*—(1) *Specimens.* Test specimens shall be 4″×4″ square and approximately 1″ in thickness. The specimen may have the natural skin on the top and bottom surfaces.

(2) *Procedure.* The specimens shall be weighed and submerged in water under a 10-foot head of water (equal to 4.35 psi) at room temperature (65°–95 °F.) for 48 hours. The specimens shall then be placed in a stream of air for the minimum time required to remove visible water from the surface, and re-weighed. The results shall be calculated in terms of pounds of water gain per square foot of total exposed surface.

(j) *Flexibility*—(1) The size of the specimen shall be approximately 1′×8′ with a thickness of ¼′±⅟₁₆″. The test specimens and equipment shall be conditioned for at least 4 hours at 0 °F. ±2 °F., and bent 180° around a ½″ diameter steel mandril within 5 seconds at the test temperature. Care shall be taken to avoid warming the test specimens, particularly at or near the bend point, in performing the test.

(k) *Oil resistance*—(1) *Specimens.* The test specimens shall be a disk approximately 1″ in diameter and 1″ (approximately) in thickness.

(2) *Procedure.* The specimen shall be immersed in fuel oil conforming to Navy special grade of Specification MIL–F–859 for 70 hours. The specimen shall then be removed, dipped in alcohol and blotted with filter paper. The specimen shall then be compared to an untreated specimen of similar size for apparent softness and visible swelling.

(1) *Odor.* The odor of unicellular polyvinyl chloride foam shall be determined by sniffing.

[CGFR 65–37, 30 FR 11593, Sept. 10, 1965, as amended by CGFR 65–64, 31 FR 563, Jan. 18, 1966]

§ 164.015–5 Procedure for acceptance.

(a) Unicellular plastic foam is not subject to formal approval, but will be accepted by the Coast Guard on the basis of this subpart for use in the manufacture of lifesaving equipment utilizing it.

(b) Upon receipt of an application requesting acceptance, the Commander of the Coast Guard District will detail a marine inspector to the factory to observe the production facilities and manufacturing methods and to select from foam already manufactured sufficient sample material for testing for compliance with the requirements of this specification. A copy of the marine inspector's report, together with the sample material and one copy of an independent laboratory test report will be forwarded to the Commandant and if satisfactory notice of acceptance will be given to the manufacturer.

(c) Acceptance of unicellular plastic foam prior to being incorporated into finished products, or during the course of manufacture, shall in no case be construed as a guarantee of the acceptance of the finished products.

(d) The manufacturer of the foam shall provide the manufacturer of the lifesaving equipment with an affidavit certifying that the foam conforms to all of the requirements of this subpart.

Subpart 164.018—Retroreflective Material for Lifesaving Equipment

SOURCE: CGD 76–028, 44 FR 38786, July 2, 1979, unless otherwise noted.

§ 164.018–1 Scope.

This subpart prescribes design requirements, approval tests, and procedures for approving retroreflective material used on lifesaving equipment.

§ 164.018–3 Classification.

The following types of retroreflective material are approved under this specification:

(a) Type I—Material used on flexible surfaces and rigid surfaces, except rigid surfaces that are continuously exposed.

(b) Type II—Weather resistant material used on continuously exposed rigid surfaces.

§ 164.018–5 Specifications and standards incorporated by reference.

(a) The following federal and military specifications and standards are incorporated by reference into this subpart:

(1) Federal Specification L–P–375 C (April 23, 1970), entitled "Plastic Film, Flexible, Vinyl Chloride", as amended by Amendment 2 of December 2, 1976.

(2) Federal Specification L–S–300 B (July 12, 1974), entitled "Sheeting and Tape, Reflective: Nonexposed Lens, Adhesive Backing."

(3) Federal Specification CCC–C–426 D (August 12, 1970), entitled "Cloth, Drill, Cotton."

(4) Federal Specification CCC–C–443 E (December 2, 1974), entitled "Cloth, Duck, Cotton (Single and Plied Filling Yarns, Flat)."

(5) Federal Test Method Standard 141a (September 1, 1965), entitled "Paint, Varnish, Lacquer and Related Materials; Methods of Inspection, Sampling and Testing." (Method 6141 "Washability of Paints", and Method 6142 "Scrub Resistance" as amended May 1, 1974).

(6) Federal Test Method Standard 370 (March 1, 1977), entitled "Instrumental Photometric Measurements of Retroreflective Materials and Retroreflective Devices."

(7) Military Specification MIL–C–17415 E (April 16, 1964), entitled "Cloth, Coated, and Webbing, Inflatable Boat and Miscellaneous Use", as amended by Amendment 5 of April 26, 1976.

(8) Military Specification MIL–R–21607 D (August 5, 1976), entitled "Resins, Polyester, Low Pressure Laminating, Fire-retardant."

(9) Military Specification MIL–C–43006 E (March 24, 1978), entitled "Cloth and Strip Laminated, Vinyl Nylon High Strength, Flexible."

(b) Federal and military specifications and standards may be obtained from Customer Service, Naval Publications, Forms Center, 5801 Tabor Ave.,

Philadelphia, Pa. 19120. These materials are also on file in the Federal Register library.

(c) Approval to incorporate by reference the materials listed in this section was obtained from the Director of the Federal Register on June 14, 1979.

(d) When changes are made to a specification or standard incorporated by reference into this subpart, the effective date for its use will be the effective date set by the issuing authority unless otherwise determined by the Coast Guard.

§ 164.018–7   Approval procedures.

(a) An application for approval of retroreflective material must be sent to the Commandant (G–MSE), U.S. Coast Guard, Washington, DC 20593–0001.

(b) Each application for approval must contain—(1) The name and address of the applicant;

(2) Two copies of plans or specifications of the material;

(3) A detailed description of the quality control procedures used in manufacturing the material; and

(4) A test report containing observations and results of approval testing conducted.

(c) The Commandant advises the applicant whether the retroreflective material is approved. If the material is approved, an approval certificate is sent to the applicant.

[CGD 76–028, 44 FR 38786, July 2, 1979, as amended by CGD 82–063b, 48 FR 4783, Feb. 3, 1983; CGD 88–070, 53 FR 34537, Sept. 7, 1988; CGD 95–072, 60 FR 50467, Sept. 29, 1995; CGD 96–041, 61 FR 50734, Sept. 27, 1996]

§ 164.018–9   Design requirements.

(a) Type I retroreflective material must be capable of being attached to lifesaving equipment either by sewing it to the equipment or by means of an adhesive. Type II material must be capable of being attached to lifesaving equipment either by mechanical fasteners or by an adhesive.

(b) The following information must be stated on retroreflective material or on the package in which it is supplied to a user:

(1) Each surface to which the retroreflective material is designed to be attached.

(2) The instructions for attaching the material to each surface described in paragraph (b)(1) of this section.

(c) When retroreflective material designed for use with an adhesive is tested in accordance with the "adhesion" test method listed in § 164.018–11, the material must not peel for a distance of more than 5 cm (2 in.).

(d) When dry material is tested in accordance with the "reflective intensity" test method listed in § 164.018–11, the reflective intensity of the material must be equal to or greater than the values for reflective intensity listed in Table 164.018–9.

(e) When wet material is tested in accordance with the "reflective intensity during rainfall" test method listed in § 164.018–11, the reflective intensity of the material must be at least 90 percent of the values listed in Table 164.018–9.

(f) The reflective intensity of material after testing in accordance with the "resistance to accelerated weathering" test method listed in § 164.018–11 must be at least 50 percent of the values listed in Table 164.018–9.

(g) After testing in accordance with the "fungus resistance" test method listed in § 164.018–11, retroreflective material must not support fungus growth, and the reflective intensity of the material must be equal to or greater than the values for reflective intensity listed in Table 164.018–9.

(h) The reflective intensity of materials after testing in accordance with the "resistance to water immersion" test method described in § 164.018–11, must be equal to or greater than the values listed in Table 164.018–9, except that retroreflectivity is not required in the area extending outward 5 mm (0.2 inches) from each side of the cuts made in the material.

(i) The reflective intensity of material after testing in accordance with the "abrasion resistance" test method described in § 164.018–11(b)(2), must be at least 50 percent of the values listed in Table 164.018–9

(j) After retroreflective material is tested in accordance with the "soil resistance and cleanability" test method described in § 164.018–11(b)(3) the material must not have any visible damage or permanent soiling.

(k) Except as provided in paragraphs (c) through (j) of this section, retroreflective material when tested in accordance with the test methods listed in §164.018-11 must meet the requirements prescribed for those test methods in Federal Specification L-S-300.

TABLE 164.018-9—REFLECTIVE INTENSITY

Divergence angle [1] (Observation angle) [2]	Incidence angle [1] (Entrance angle) [2]	Reflective intensity [1] (Specific intensity per unit area) [2]
0.2°	-4°	150
.2°	+30°	75
.2°	+45°	50
.5	-4°	57
.5	+30°	33
.5	+45°	25
2.0°	-4°	2.5
2.0°	+30°	2.0
2.0°	+45°	1.0

[1] These terms are described in Federal Specification L-S-300.
[2] These terms are described in Federal Test Method Standard 370.

§164.018-11 Approval tests.

(a) Retroreflective material submitted for Coast Guard approval must be tested in accordance with the following test methods described in Federal Specification L-S-300:

(1) Test conditions.

(2) Test panels.

(3) Adhesion test method using a 0.79 kg (1.75 lb.) test weight, except that one test panel must be immersed in distilled water in a covered container for 16 hours before the weight is applied and the other test panel must be immersed in salt water (4% NaCl by weight) in a covered container for 16 hours before the weight is applied. (This test method is required only for retroreflective material that is designed for use with an adhesive. If a particular test panel used in testing results in a test failure, the retroreflective material will not be approved for attachment to material of the type used as the test panel. The retroreflective material may nevertheless be approved for use with other types of material depending on the results of testing with the other panels. See paragraph (d) of this section for a listing of tests panels used.)

(4) Flexibility at standard conditions test method, except that when testing Type I material—

(i) The material must be unmounted;

(ii) A 1.5 mm (⅟₁₆-inch) mandrel must be used in place of the mandrel described in the test method; and

(iii) After testing at standard conditions, the material must be placed in a chamber at a temperature of -18 °C. (0 °F.) for at least 1 hour and then retested in the chamber at that temperature.

(5) Reflective intensity.

(6) Resistance to accelerated weathering test method and subtest methods "reflective intensity after accelerated weathering," "reflective intensity during rainfall," and "adhesion after accelerated weathering." (The "adhesion after accelerated weathering" test method is required only for materials designed for use with an adhesive. The "resistance to accelerated weathering" test method must be performed for 250 hours, if testing Type I material, and for 1,000 hours if testing Type II material.)

(7) Resistance to heat, cold, and humidity.

(8) Fungus resistance.

(b) Retroreflective material submitted for approval must also be tested as follows:

(1) *Resistance to water immersion.* Two test panels are used. The test panels and test conditions must meet paragraphs (a)(1) and (a)(2) of this section. The retroreflective material on each test panel is cut with a sharp knife from each corner to the corner diagonally opposite so that an "X" is formed. The cuts must be made completely through the material to the metal panel. One panel is immersed in distilled water in a covered container. The other panel is immersed in salt water (4% NaCl by weight) in a covered container. After 16 hours in water, the panels are removed from the containers, rinsed of deposits, and dried. Reflective intensity values at the angles listed in Table 164.018-9 must be measured within 2 hours after removal of the panels from the water. When measuring the reflective intensity values, the area within 5 mm (0.2 in.) of either side of the "X" cuts, and within 5 mm of the cut edges of the material, must not be counted.

(2) *Abrasion resistance.* One test panel is used. The panel and test conditions must meet paragraphs (a)(1) and (a)(2)

357

of this section. The test apparatus must meet Federal Test Method Standard 141, Method 6142, except that the brush must be dry. One thousand brush strokes are applied to the material. The test panel is then wiped with a clean soft cloth. Thereafter, the reflective intensity of the area of the material in contact with the brush is measured at the angles listed in Table 164.018–9.

(3) *Soil resistance and cleanability.* One panel is used. The test panel and test conditions must meet paragraphs (a)(1) and (a)(2) of this section. A soiling medium is applied to the material as described in Federal Test Method Standard 141, Method 6141. The soiled area is then covered with a laboratory watch glass or similar device. After 24 hours, the material is uncovered and the soil medium wiped off with a clean, dry, soft cloth. The material is then wetted with mineral spirits and wiped with a cloth soaked in mineral spirits. Thereafter, it is washed with a 1 percent (by weight) solution of detergent in warm water and rinsed and dried with a clean, dry, soft cloth.

(c) Each measurement of reflective intensity required in paragraphs (a), (b)(1), and (b)(2) of this section must be made using either—

(1) The L–S–300 procedure for measuring reflective intensity; or

(2) The procedure for measuring specific intensity per unit area in Federal Test Method Standard 370, except that the test apparatus arrangement required in L–S–300 must be used.

(d) If material is designed for use with an adhesive, the "adhesion" test method required by paragraph (a)(3) of this section must be repeated using a 0.79 kg. (1.75 lb.) test weight and using each of the following materials as test panels in place of the aluminum test panels required by this test method:

(1) Smooth panel of cured polyester laminating resin meeting MIL–R–21607 (Types I and II material).

(2) Cotton drill (Type I material only) meeting CCC–C–426, or cotton duck meeting CCC–C–443 (Type I material only).

(3) Vinyl-nylon laminated cloth meeting MIL–C–43006 (Type I material only).

(4) Vinyl film meeting L–P–375 (Type I material only).

(5) Rubber coated cloth meeting MIL–C–17415 (Type I material only).

(e) Each flexible material listed in paragraph (d) of this section when used as a test panel must be bonded to a rigid backing.

(f) Test panel material listed in paragraph (d) of this section must—

(1) Be taken from an item of Coast Guard approved lifesaving equipment; or

(2) Be certified by the manufacturer of the material that it meets the applicable specification in paragraph (d) of this section.

§ 164.018–13 Production inspections.

The Coast Guard does not inspect retroreflective material approved under this subpart on a regular schedule. However, the Commandant may select samples and conduct tests and examinations whenever necessary to determine whether retroreflective material is being manufactured in compliance with the requirements of this subpart.

Subpart 164.019—Personal Flotation Device Components

SOURCE: CGD 84–068, 58 FR 29494, May 20, 1993, unless otherwise noted.

§ 164.019–1 Scope.

(a) This subpart contains general requirements for standard personal flotation device (PFD) components, procedures for acceptance of non-standard PFD components, and production quality control requirements for all PFD components, used in the construction of PFDs approved under part 160 of this subchapter.

(b) Other subparts of this part contain specific requirements applicable to particular PFD components used in the construction of Coast Guard-approved PFDs.

(c) Part 160 of this chapter contains specific requirements and limitations concerning the use of PFD components in the construction of particular Coast Guard-approved PFDs.

§ 164.019-3 Definitions.

Acceptance means certification by the Coast Guard that a component is suitable for use in the manufacture of Coast Guard-approved PFDs.

Commandant means the Chief of the Lifesaving and Fire Safety Division, Marine Safety and Environmental Protection, U.S. Coast Guard. Address: Commandant (G-MSE), U.S. Coast Guard Headquarters, 2100 Second St. SW., Washington, DC 20593-0001. Telephone: 202-267-1444.

Component manufacturer means either a component manufacturer or supplier seeking acceptance of a component, or a component manufacturer or supplier who has obtained acceptance of a component.

Inspector means a Coast Guard marine inspector, authorized representative of the Coast Guard, or a recognized laboratory representative.

Non-standard component means a PFD component which is equivalent in performance to a standard component.

PFD Type means the performance type designation as indicated in 33 CFR part 175 and this subchapter.

Standard component means a PFD component which complies in all respects with the material, construction, and performance requirements of a subpart of this part or part 160 of this chapter.

Use Code means an alphanumeric code assigned by the Commandant (G-MSE) to a PFD component to designate the PFD Type(s) in which it may be used. Assigned Use Codes are listed in table 164.019-3.

TABLE 164.019-3

Use code	PFD type acceptable for use
1	I, II, and III.
2	II and III.
3	III.
4B	IV (all Ring Buoys).
4BC	IV (Buoyant Cushions).
4RB	IV (Recreational Ring Buoys only).
5	Wearable Type V (intended use must be specified).
5H	V (Hybrid).
5R	V (Recreational Style).
5SB	V (Sailboard vests).
5WV	V (Work vests).
6	Special, limited, or restricted use.
Suffix A	Adult only.
Suffix C	Child only.

[CGD 84-068, 58 FR 29494, May 20, 1993, as amended by CGD 95-072, 60 FR 50467, Sept. 29, 1995; CGD 96-041, 61 FR 50734, Sept. 27, 1996]

§ 164.019-4 Component requirements.

(a) PFDs may be constructed only with Coast Guard-accepted PFD components meeting the requirements of this subchapter.

(b) PFD components may be used in the construction of PFDs only in accordance with their Use Codes.

§ 164.019-5 Standard components; acceptance criteria and procedures.

(a) *General.* Standard components used in the construction of PFDs must meet the applicable requirements of this part or part 160 and the documentation requirements of this section.

(b) *Use Codes.* Each standard component is assigned a Use Code as indicated in table 164.019-3. Additional Use Codes may be assigned by the Commandant.

(c) *Method and documentation of acceptance.* Except as provided in paragraph (d) of this section, the following requirements pertaining to the shipment of standard components must be met in order for the standard components to be considered Coast Guard-accepted standard components:

(1) Each shipment of standard components must be accompanied by an affidavit complying with § 164.019-11.

(2) A sample affidavit, or a copy of the affidavit, provided with the first shipment of standard components to a PFD manufacturer, must be provided to the Commandant.

(3) A revised sample affidavit, or a copy of the revised affidavit, must be provided to the Coast Guard any time the information on the affidavit accompanying a shipment of standard components materially changes.

(d) *Exception.* Affidavits are not required to be provided for standard components that are under the quality control oversight program of a recognized laboratory meeting the requirements of § 164.019-17.

(e) *Suspension or termination of acceptance.* The procedures in §§ 2.75-40 and 2.75-50 of this chapter for suspension and termination of approvals also apply to Coast Guard acceptances of PFD components.

§ 164.019-7 Non-standard components; acceptance criteria and procedures.

(a) *General.* Non-standard components may be used in the construction of PFDs only if they have been accepted by the Coast Guard in accordance with the requirements of this section.

(b) *Use Codes.* Each non-standard component is assigned a Use Code as indicated in table 164.019-3. Additional Use Codes may be assigned by the Commandant.

(c) *Request for acceptance.* The component manufacturer or the recognized laboratory that performs the acceptance testing required by the applicable subpart of this part or part 160 of this chapter must submit, in writing, to the Commandant, a request for acceptance of any non-standard component. The request must include the information, supporting documentation, and samples required by this section.

(1) The request must include a statement of the intended use of the component by the PFD manufacturer, and the Use Code(s) for which acceptance is requested. Intended uses must be for one or more of the following—

(i) Outer Envelope Fabric (exterior fabrics on wearable PFDs);

(ii) Cover Fabric (for throwable PFDs);

(iii) Inner Envelope Fabric;

(iv) Closure (including zippers) or Adjustment Hardware;

(v) Body Strap;

(vi) Grab Strap (applies to buoyant cushions only);

(vii) Tie Tape;

(viii) Reinforcing Tape;

(ix) Thread;

(x) Flotation Foam; or

(xi) Other (specify).

(2) The request must include a statement identifying the component in detail and including the unique style, part, or model number, the identification data required by the applicable subpart of this part, and any other manufacturer's identifying data. No two components which differ in any way, e.g., size, material composition, construction, may utilize the same identification number.

(3) The report of a recognized laboratory's test data in accordance with the "acceptance tests" required by the applicable subpart of this part or part 160 must be submitted with the request. Each report must include the name of the laboratory and a description of the test equipment and test methods used, and must be signed and dated by an authorized laboratory official.

(4) A sample of each component that is being considered must be submitted with the request. Where the lightest and darkest colors are being tested, samples of both colors must be submitted. A one linear yard sample is required in the case of textiles.

(5) The request must include a list of all materials used in the construction of the particular component. The list must contain specific identification and quantity of all materials used.

(6) For hardware and other mechanical components, the request must include scaled drawings showing details and dimensions of the mechanism.

(7) A statement of dimensional and performance tolerances, as appropriate, that will be maintained in production must be submitted with request.

(8) The request must include a description of the quality control procedures that will be in effect during production.

(9) The request must include a detailed description of the recognized laboratory's procedures for oversight of the manufacturer's program of production quality control, including a description of the laboratory's certification marking(s).

(10) The request must include any appropriate installation or use guidelines for the component.

(d) *Documentation of acceptance.* When an acceptance is granted, the Commandant provides written notice to the applicant.

(e) *Alternate requirements.* A component that does not meet the requirements of this subchapter is eligible for acceptance if it—

(1) Meets other requirements prescribed by the Commandant in lieu of or in addition to the requirements of this subpart; and

(2) Provides at least the same degree of safety as provided by a component that does comply with this subpart.

(f) *Additional tests and documentation.* The Commandant may prescribe additional tests or request additional documentation, if necessary, to determine the acceptability or suitability of a particular product.

(g) *Suspension or termination of acceptance.* The producers in §§ 2.75–40 and 2.75–50 of this chapter for suspension and termination of approvals also apply to Coast Guard acceptances of PFD components.

[CGD 84–068, 58 FR 29494, May 20, 1993; 58 FR 32416, June 9, 1993]

§ 164.019–9 Procedure for acceptance of revisions of design, process, or materials.

(a) The manufacturer shall not change the design, material, manufacturing process, or construction of a non-standard component unless it has been previously approved by the Commandant, in accordance with paragraph (b) of this section.

(b) The manufacturer or the recognized laboratory that performs the acceptance testing required by the applicable subpart of this part or part 160 of this chapter shall submit requests for acceptance of revisions in design, material, manufacturing process, or construction of a non-standard component in writing and describe the revision in detail similar to the original request for acceptance.

§ 164.019–11 Certification (affidavits).

General. Affidavits required by § 164.019–5(c) must be notarized, and certify that a component complies in all respects with the material and construction requirements of a subpart of this part or part 160 of this chapter. Each affidavit must contain the following information:

(a) Name and address of company.

(b) Name and title of signing company official.

(c) Description of the component by use of the unique style, part, or model number and other applicable distinctive characteristics such as weight, size, denier, treatments or coatings, etc.

(d) Production data (to include lot, batch number, and quantity shipped) in sufficient detail to enable the manufacturer or purchaser to trace a shipment of components back to the lots of raw materials used in its manufacture.

(e) The intended use of the component, from the list in § 164.019–7(c)(1).

(f) The PFD Type(s) for which the component is a standard component, as determined by—

(1) The standard material component requirements of part 160 of this chapter with which the component complies; or

(2) The Use Code(s) of the component.

(g) A statement indicating the specific provision(s) of this subchapter with which the component complies.

(h) A copy of the records of all required production tests performed on the component lots that are covered by the affidavit.

§ 164.019–13 Production quality control requirements.

(a) *General.* Each component manufacturer shall establish procedures for maintaining quality control of the materials used in production, manufacturing operations, and the finished product.

(b) *Recognized laboratory oversight.* Each manufacturer of non-standard components shall supplement its procedures for assuring production quality control with a program of oversight by a recognized laboratory, as described in the oversight procedures submitted to the Coast Guard in accordance with § 164.019–7(c)(9). The laboratory's oversight program must be performed at the place of manufacture unless alternate procedures have been accepted by the Commandant.

(c) *Production tests and inspections.* Production tests and inspections must be conducted in accordance with this section and subpart 159.007 of this chapter.

(d) *Responsibilities; component manufacturers.* Each component manufacturer shall—

(1) Perform all production tests and inspections required by the applicable subpart of this part;

(2) Adhere to the accepted quality control procedures for the component as submitted to the Coast Guard in accordance with § 164.019–7(c)(8); and

(3) Establish a continuing program of employee training and a program for maintaining production and test equipment.

(e) *Responsibilities; recognized laboratories.* The same recognized laboratory that performed the acceptance testing shall, at least quarterly, or more frequently if required by the applicable subpart of this part or by the oversight procedures submitted in accordance with § 164.019–7(c)(9)—

(1) Audit the component manufacturer's records required by § 164.019–15;

(2) Perform, or supervise the performance of, the tests required by this section, the applicable subpart of this part, and the accepted quality control and oversight procedures; and

(3) Verify, during each inspection, compliance by the manufacturer with the manufacturer's established quality control program and provide a summary report of any noncompliance to the Commandant at least annually.

(f) *Component lots.*

(1) *Lot numbers.* The manufacturer shall assign a lot number to each group of components manufactured. A new lot must be started whenever any change is made in materials, design, or production method, and whenever any substantial discontinuity in the manufacturing process (such as a change in shift) occurs. Changes in lots of incoming materials must be treated as changes in materials. Lots must be numbered serially. The lot number assigned, in combination with the unique product name or identification, must enable the component manufacturer (or supplier), by referring to the records required by this subpart, to determine the source(s) of all raw materials used in that lot.

(2) *Lot size.* The maximum lot size for any particular component must be as defined in the applicable subpart of this part.

(g) *Samples.* (1) Procedures for selection of test samples, and required sample sizes, must be in accordance with the applicable subpart of this part.

(2) The inspector shall select different samples than were tested by the manufacturer.

(h) *Detailed product examination*—(1) *General.* In addition to the tests and inspections required by the applicable subpart of this part, the manufacturer or the inspector shall examine each sample component to determine that—

(i) The construction, markings, and workmanship conform to the information submitted in the request for acceptance; and

(ii) The component is not otherwise defective.

(2) *Inspection responsibility.* The manufacturer shall ensure that the inspection required by paragraph (h)(1) of this section is performed by a manufacturer's representative familiar with the performance requirements for the component, and all of the production quality control requirements. The manufacturer's representative must not be responsible for meeting production schedules, or be subject to supervision by someone responsible for meeting production schedules.

(i) [Reserved]

(j) *Accept/reject criteria.* (1) A component lot passes production testing and is therefore accepted if each sample tested passes each test.

(2) A lot having a production test failure may be accepted if it meets the following additional test requirements.

(i) When the basis of acceptability is an average result, a second sampling with an identical number of samples is taken. The results of this second sampling must be averaged with the initial results. If the average result passes the test, then the lot may be accepted.

(ii) When the basis of acceptability is individual sample results, a second sampling is taken. The size of the second sampling must be as specified in the subpart of this part which covers the component. If each sample in this sampling passes the test, the lot may be accepted.

(3) A rejected lot of components may be resubmitted for testing, examination, or inspection if—

(i) The manufacturer first removes each component having the same type of defect or;

(ii) After obtaining authorization from the Commandant or the recognized laboratory, the manufacturer reworks the lot to correct the defect.

(4) A rejected lot or rejected component may not be sold or offered for sale with the representation that it meets the requirements of this subpart or is

accepted by the Coast Guard, and may not be used in the construction of Coast Guard-approved PFDs.

(k) *Facilities and equipment*—(1) *General.* The manufacturer shall provide the test equipment and facilities for performing production tests, examinations, and inspections described in the applicable subpart of this part and in the quality control and oversight procedures submitted in accordance with § 164.019-7(c) (8) and (9).

(2) *Calibration.* The manufacturer shall have the calibration of all test equipment checked at least every 6 months by a weights and measures agency or by the equipment manufacturer, distributor, or dealer.

(3) *Facilities for inspector's use.* The manufacturer shall provide a suitable place and the necessary apparatus for the inspector to use in conducting or supervising tests. For the detailed product examination, the manufacturer shall provide a suitable working environment and a smooth-top table for the inspector's use.

(4) *Access to facilities.* The manufacturer shall permit the inspector to have access to any place in the factory where work is being done on PFD components or where components are stored. The inspector may take samples of parts or materials entering into production or completed components, for further examinations, inspections, or tests.

(l) [Reserved]

(m) *Alternate procedures for standard components.* In lieu of the quality control procedures specified in this section, manufacturers of standard components may follow the quality control procedures in a Federal or military specification with which the component is required to comply by this subchapter, or equivalent procedures accepted by the Commandant.

(n) *Additional tests.* The Commandant may prescribe additional production tests and inspections to maintain quality control. A representative of the Commandant may conduct inspections for compliance with the requirements of this subpart.

[CGD 84–068, 58 FR 29494, May 20, 1993; 58 FR 32416, June 9, 1993]

§ 164.019-15 Component manufacturer records.

(a) Each component manufacturer shall retain records as required by § 159.007-13 of this chapter.

(b) The records required by paragraph (a) of this section must include the following information:

(1) For each test, the serial number of the test instrument used if there is more than one available.

(2) For each test and inspection, the identification of the samples used, the lot number, the unique component identification, and the quantity of the component in the lot.

(3) The cause for rejection, any corrective action taken, and the final disposition of each lot rejected.

(c) Manufacturers utilizing procedures and apparatus meeting the requirements of the applicable subpart of this part or the independent laboratory's accepted follow-up inspection procedures are not required to include the description of procedures or photographs or apparatus required by § 159.007-13 of this chapter in the manufacturers' records.

(d) In addition to the records required by paragraphs (a) and (b) of this section, each component manufacturer shall retain the following:

(1) Records for all materials used in production, including name and address of the supplier, date of purchase and receipt, and lot number.

(2) A copy of this subpart, and other subparts applicable to the component manufactured.

(3) Each document incorporated by reference in the applicable subpart(s) of this part.

(4) A copy of the accepted component specifications and identifying data.

(5) Records of calibration of all test equipment, including the identity of the agency performing the calibration, date of calibration, and results.

(e) Manufacturers shall retain the records required by paragraph (d)(1) of this section for at least 60 months.

(f) Upon request, manufacturers shall make available to the inspector or to the Commandant records of tests conducted by the manufacturer and records of materials entering into construction, including affidavits by suppliers certifying that applicable requirements are met.

§ 164.019-17 Recognized laboratory.

(a) *General.* A laboratory may be designated as a recognized laboratory under this subpart if it is—

(1) Accepted by the Coast Guard as an independent laboratory under subpart 159.010 of this subchapter; and

(2) Established in the inspection of factory production, listing, and labeling, by having an existing program and standards for evaluation, listing, and marking components, that are acceptable to the Commandant.

(b) *Designated recognized laboratories.* A current listing of recognized laboratories is available from the Commandant upon request.

Subpart 164.023—Thread for Personal Flotation Devices

SOURCE: CGD 84-068, 58 FR 29497, May 20, 1993, unless otherwise noted.

§ 164.023-1 Scope.

This subpart contains performance requirements, acceptance tests, and production testing and inspection requirements for thread used in the construction of personal flotation devices (PFDs) approved under part 160 of this subchapter. Manufacturers must also comply with the requirements of subpart 164.019 of this chapter.

§ 164.023-3 Specifications and standards incorporated by reference.

(a) Certain materials are incorporated by reference into this subpart with the approval of the Director of the Federal Register in accordance with 5 U.S.C. 552(a) and 1 CFR part 51. To enforce any edition other than the one listed in paragraph (b) of this section, notice of change must be published in the FEDERAL REGISTER and the material made available to the public. All approved material may be inspected at the Office of the Federal Register, 800 North Capitol Street, NW., suite 700, Washington, DC and at the U.S. Coast Guard, Lifesaving and Fire Safety Division (G–MSE–4), Washington, DC 20593–0001, and is available from the source indicated in paragraph (c) of this section.

(b) The materials approved for incorporation by reference in this subpart, and the sections affected are:

FEDERAL STANDARDS AND TEST METHOD STANDARDS

The following test methods in Federal Test Method Standard No. 191A, Textile Test Methods, July 20, 1978:

(1) Method 4010, Length-Weight Relation; Thread; Yards Per Pound (m/kg)—164.023-11.

(2) Method 4100, Strength and Elongation, Breaking; and Tenacity; of Thread and Yarn; Single Strand—164.023-7.

(3) Method 5804, Weathering Resistance of Cloth; Accelerated Weathering Method—164.023-7.

FEDERAL SPECIFICATIONS

(4) V–T–285E—Thread, Polyester, August 21, 1986—164.023-5.

(5) V–T–295E—Thread, Nylon, August 1, 1985—164.023-5.

MILITARY SPECIFICATIONS

(6) MIL–T–43548C—Thread, Polyester Core: Cotton-, Rayon-, or Polyester-Covered, September 30, 1986—164.023-5.

(7) MIL–T –43624A—Thread, Polyester, Spun, January 22, 1982—164.023-5.

(c) All reference materials are available from the Naval Publications and Forms Center, Customer Service, Code 1052, 5801 Tabor Ave., Philadelphia, PA 19120.

[CGD 84-068, 58 FR 29497, May 20, 1993, as amended by CGD 95-072, 60 FR 50467, Sept. 29, 1995; CGD 96-041, 61 FR 50734, Sept. 27, 1996]

§ 164.023-5 Performance; standard thread.

(a) *Use Codes 1, 2, 3, 4BC, 4RB, 5 (any).* Each thread which complies with all of the requirements of a specification listed in table 164.023-5(a) is assigned Use Codes 1, 2, 3, 4BC, 4RB, and 5 (any).

TABLE 164.023–5(A)

[Use codes 1, 2, 3, 4BC, 4RB, 5(any)]

Federal or military specification	Material	Type	Class	Ticket No. or size range
V–T–285E	Polyester	I or II	1	E, F, FF.

TABLE 164.023–5(A)—Continued

[Use codes 1, 2, 3, 4BC, 4RB, 5(any)]

Federal or military specification	Material	Type	Class	Ticket No. or size range
V–T–295E	Nylon	I or II	A	E, F, FF.
MIL–T–43624A	Polyester			24 through 12.
MIL–T–43548C	Polyester covered only			24 through 12.

(b) *Use Code 4B.* Each thread which meets the requirements of Federal Specifications V–T–295, Type II, Class A, number size 4, is assigned Use Code 4B.

§ 164.023–7 Performance; non-standard thread.

(a) *Use Codes 1, 2, 3, 4BC, 4RB, 5 (any).* Each non-standard thread which meets all of the requirements of paragraphs (a)(1) through (a)(3) of this section is assigned Use Codes 1, 2, 3, 4BC, 4RB, and 5 (any).

(1) *Single strand breaking strength.* The thread, as received, must have a single strand breaking strength of not less than 25 N (5.7 lb.), when tested in accordance with Test Method 4100 in Federal Test Method Standard No. 191A using a Constant-Rate-of-Traverse (CRT) testing machine.

(2) *Single strand breaking strength (after weathering).* After exposure in a sunshine carbon-arc weatherometer in accordance with Test Method 5804 in Federal Test Method Standard No. 191A for a period of 100 hours, the thread must retain at least 60 percent of its single strand breaking strength as received, and have a breaking strength of at least 21 N (4.7 lb.).

(3) *Loop breaking strength.* The thread, as received, must have a loop breaking strength of not less than 45 N (10.0 lb.), when tested in accordance with Test Method 4100 in Federal Test Method Standard No. 191A using a CRT testing machine, except that—

(i) Each specimen must consist of two 35 cm (14 in.) pieces of thread; and

(ii) Both ends of one piece of thread must be secured without twisting in one clamp of the testing machine so that the length of the loop formed equals one half the distance between the clamps. One end of the second piece must then be passed without twisting through the loop formed by the first,

and both ends must be secured in the other clamp of the machine. The breaking strength must then be determined under the single strand test.

(b) *Use Code 4B.* Each non-standard thread which meets all of the requirements of paragraphs (b)(1) and (b)(2) of this section is assigned Use Code 4B.

(1) *Single strand breaking strength.* The thread as received must have a single strand breaking strength of not less than 160 N (36.0 lb.) when tested in accordance with Test Method 4100 in Federal Test Method Standard No. 191A using a CRT testing machine.

(2) *Single strand breaking strength (after weathering).* After exposure in a sunshine carbon-arc weatherometer in accordance with Test Method 5804 in Federal Test Method Standard No. 191A for a period of 100 hours, the thread must retain at least 60 percent of its single strand breaking strength.

(c) *Prohibited threads.* Cotton thread, and monofilament thread of any composition, will not be accepted for use in structural applications unless demonstrated to the Commandant to be equivalent to standard thread in durability in all foreseeable conditions of use and stowage.

§ 164.023–9 Samples submitted for acceptance.

Application samples. A product sample submitted for acceptance as required by § 164.019–7(c)(4) must consist of at least one unit of put-up of thread.

§ 164.023–11 Acceptance tests.

(a) *Performance testing.* Manufacturers shall ensure that the performance tests described in § 164.023–7 (a) or (b), as appropriate, are performed on a minimum of five samples in each of the lightest and darkest colors submitted for acceptance.

(b) *Identification testing.* Manufacturers shall ensure that the following identification tests are conducted:

(1) The average length/weight ratio of the thread in meters per kilogram (yards per pound) must be determined in accordance with Test Method 4010 in Federal Test Method Standard 191A.

(2) The generic chemical composition of the thread must be determined by qualitative infrared analysis, thermogravimetric analysis, differential scanning calorimeter, or other equivalent means adequate to conclusively identify the composition of the product tested.

(3) Elongation at break must be determined on the same samples tested for single strand breaking test in accordance with § 164.023–7(a)(1) or (b)(1), as appropriate.

§ 164.023–13 Production tests and inspections.

(a) *Manufacturer's test equipment and facilities.* The manufacturer shall provide the following test equipment and facilities for use in production tests and inspections:

(1) A Constant Rate of Traverse tensile testing machine, capable of initial clamp separation of ten inches and a rate of separation of 30 cm (12 in.) per minute.

(2) Fletcher, Callaway, U.S. Rubber clamps, or equivalent cam-actuated clamps to prevent slippage and twist of the samples.

(3) An analytical balance or grain-yarn scale, accurate to within 0.25 percent of the measured value.

(b) *Lot size.* Lot size must not exceed 460,000 meters (500,000 yds.) or 45 kg (100 lb.) of any color.

(c) *Sample selection.* Samples must be selected at random by the manufacturer (or inspector, as applicable) after the entire lot of thread has been completed.

(d) *Second sampling.* A second sampling, where required, must consist of five times the original sample size.

(e) *Manufacturer's production tests.* The component manufacturer shall perform the following tests on the samples indicated (each sample to include at least 5 specimens unless otherwise specified in the referenced test procedure) on each lot of thread:

(1) *Breaking strength.* One sample must be tested in accordance with § 164.023–7(a)(1) or § 164.023–7(b)(1), as applicable.

(2) *Length/weight ratio.* One sample must be tested in accordance with § 164.023–11(b)(1).

(f) *Recognized laboratory production tests.* Manufacturers shall ensure that the following tests and inspections are performed on non-standard components by a recognized laboratory:

(1) *Composition.* At least annually, one sample of each accepted thread must be tested in accordance with § 164.023–11(b)(2).

(2) *Breaking strength.* At least quarterly, one sample in each of the lightest and darkest colors accepted must be tested in accordance with § 164.023–7(a)(1) or § 164.023–7(b)(1), as applicable. This test may be performed by a recognized laboratory, or witnessed by a recognized laboratory inspector at the manufacturer's plant, at the laboratory's discretion.

(3) *Elongation.* At least annually, one sample of each accepted thread in each of the lightest and darkest colors accepted must be tested in accordance with § 164.023–11(b)(3). This test may be performed by a recognized laboratory, or witnessed by a recognized laboratory inspector at the manufacturer's plant, at the laboratory's discretion.

(g) *Accept/reject criteria.* Unless the alternate procedures as permitted by § 164.019–013(m) are followed, the results of required production testing on a lot must meet the following criteria for the lot to be shipped as Coast Guard-accepted thread:

(1) Breaking strength test results must be within 10 percent below and 20 percent above the acceptance testing values but not less than the performance minimums.

(2) Length/weight values must be within 5 percent of the acceptance testing values but not less than the performance minimums.

(3) Elongation values must be within 20 percent of the acceptance testing values but not less than the performance minimums.

(4) Composition testing must indicate that the sample tested is of identical composition to the sample tested for

acceptance or in accordance with the performance specification.

§ 164.023–15 Marking.

(a) *General*. The manufacturer must ensure that each shipping label, and each spool or individual unit of put-up, is permanently and clearly marked in a color which contrasts with the color of the surface on which the marking is applied. Each label must be marked with—

(1) The manufacturer's or supplier's name, trade name, or symbol;

(2) The unique style, part, or model number of the thread;

(3) The size of the thread;

(4) The composition of the thread; and

(5) The lot number of the thread.

(b) *Non-standard thread*. In addition to the markings specified in paragraph (a) of this section, each unit of put-up of non-standard thread must be marked with the appropriate recognized laboratory's certification marking(s).

PART 165   [RESERVED]

FINDING AIDS

A list of CFR titles, subtitles, chapters, subchapters and parts and an alphabetical list of agencies publishing in the CFR are included in the CFR Index and Finding Aids volume to the Code of Federal Regulations which is published separately and revised annually.

Material Approved for Incorporation by Reference
Table of CFR Titles and Chapters
Alphabetical List of Agencies Appearing in the CFR
List of CFR Sections Affected

Material Approved for Incorporation by Reference

(Revised as of October 1, 1997)

The Director of the Federal Register has approved under 5 U.S.C. 552(a) and 1 CFR Part 51 the incorporation by reference of the following publications. This list contains only those incorporations by reference effective as of the revision date of this volume. Incorporations by reference found within a regulation are effective upon the effective date of that regulation. For more information on incorporation by reference, see the preliminary pages of this volume.

46 CFR (PARTS 159–165)
COAST GUARD, DEPARTMENT OF TRANSPORTATION
American Bureau of Shipping
Publications Dept., Two World Trade Center, New York, NY 10048

Rules for Building and Classing Steel Vessels, 1995	161.002–1; 161.002–4(b)
Rules for Building and Classing Steel Vessels, 1996	161.002–1; 161.002–4(b)

American Society for Mechanical Engineers
Service Center, 22 Law Drive, P.O. Box 2900, Fairfield, NJ 07007, Telephone (610) 832-9585, FAX (610) 832-9555
Boiler and Pressure Vessel Code:
Boiler and Pressure Vessel Code:

Section I—par. PG–67 to 72 Design and Construction, and Tests 1977–1979.	162.001–1
Par. PG–69—Testing 1977–1979	162.001–1
Par. PG–71—Mounting 1977–1979	162.001–1
Par. PG–110—Stamping of Safety Valves 1977–1979	162.001–1
Section IV—par. HG–402 Discharge Capacities of Safety and Safety Relief Valves, 1980.	162.012–1; 162.013–1
Section VIII—Par. UG–131 Certification of Capacity for Pressure Relief Valves, 1980.	162.018–1

American Society for Testing and Materials
100 Barr Harbor Drive, West Conshohocken, PA, 19428-2959, Telephone (610) 832-9585, FAX (610) 832-9555

ASTM A 27–80 Mild to Medium Strength Carbon Steel Castings	160.032–1
ASTM A 36–77 Structural Steel	160.035–1
ASTM A 216–77 Carbon-Steel Casting Suitable for Fusion Welding for High Temperature Service.	160.032–1
ASTM A 525–80 Steel Sheets, Zinc-Coated (Galvanized) by the Hot Dip Process.	160.035–1
ASTM B 61–80 Steam or Valve Bronze Castings	162.014–1
ASTM B 117–73 Method of Salt Spray (Fog) Testing	160.171–3; 161.004–1; 161.006–1
ASTM B 117–73 (reapproved 1979) Standard Method of Salt Spray (Fog) Testing.	160.176–8; 160.176–13
ASTM B 117–95 Standard Practice for Operating Salt Spray (Fog) Apparatus.	161.002–1; 161.002–4(b)
ASTM C 177–76 Standard Test Method for Steady State Thermal Transmission Properties by Means of the Guarded Hot Plate.	160.171–3; 160.174–3

371

46 CFR (PARTS 159–165)—Continued
COAST GUARD, DEPARTMENT OF TRANSPORTATION—Continued

ASTM C 518–76 Standard Test Method for Steady State Thermal Transmission Properties by Means of the Heat Flow Meter.	160.171–3; 160.174–3
ASTM D 413–76 Adhesion of Vulcanized Rubber (Friction Test)	160.055–1
ASTM D 570–77 Water Absorbtion of Plastics	160.055–1
ASTM D 751–79 Standard Methods of Testing Coated Fabrics	160.076–25
ASTM D 882–75 Tensile Properties of Thin Plastic Sheeting	160.055–1; 160.071–3
ASTM D 975–81 Standard Specification for Diesel Fuel Oils	160.171–3; 160.174–3
ASTM D 1004–66 Tear Resistance of Plastic Film and Sheeting	160.055–1; 160.171–3; 160.174–3
ASTM D 1434–75 Gas Transmission Rate of Plastic Film and Sheeting	160.076–25
ASTM D 1435–75 Standard Recommended Practice for Outdoor Weathering of Plastics.	163.003–1
ASTM D 1518–77 Thermal Transmittance of Textile Materials Between Guarded Hot-Plate and Cool Atmosphere.	160.174–3
ASTM D 1571–77 Cloth Woven Asbestos	164.009–3
ASTM D 3574–77 Flexible Cellular Materials—Slab Bonded and Molded Urethane Foam, Testing.	164.031–1
ASTM E 84–80 Standard Test Method for Surface Burning Characteristics of Building Materials.	164.012–1
ASTM E 119–80 Fire Testing of Building Construction and Materials	164.007–1; 164.008–1
ASTM F 1014–86 Standard Specification for Flashlights on Vessels	160.051–7(c)(4), (d)(4); 160.151–21
ASTM F 1546–94 Standard Specification for Fire Hose Nozzles	162.027–1; 162.027–2

Coast Guard
Commandant [G–MVI], 2100 Second St. SW, Washington, DC 20593

DWG No. F–49–6–1 Life Preserver, Kapok, Adult	160.002–1
DWG No. F–49–6–5 Life Preserver, Kapok, Child	160.002–1
DWG No. 160.005–1 Life Preserver, Fibrous Glass, Adult and Child (Jacket Type).	160.005–1
DWG No. 160.009 Cork and Balsa Wood Ring Life Buoy; arrangement and construction details.	160.009–1
DWG No. 160.013–1 Hatchet (Lifeboat and Liferaft)	160.013–1
DWG No. 160.027–4 Rectangular Balsa Wood Life Float with Platform, Net and Rigging.	160.027–1
DWG No. 160.043–1(b) Jackknife (with Can Opener)	160.043–1
DWG No. 160.047–1 Buoyant Vest, Kapok or Fibrous Glass, Adult and Child.	160.047–1
DWG No. 160.048–1 Buoyant Cushion, Fibrous Glass	160.048–1
DWG No. 160.049–1 Buoyant Cushion, Plastic Foam	160.049–1
DWG No. 160.052–1 Buoyant Vest, Unicellular Plastic Foam, Adult and Child.	160.052–1
DWG No. 160–055–1A Life Preservers, Unicellular Plastic Foam, Adult.	160.055–1
DWG No. 160.055–1B Life Preservers, Unicellular Foam, Child	160.055–1
DWG No. 160.060–1 Buoyant Vest, Unicellular Polyethylene Foam, Adult and Child.	160.060–1
DWG No. 164.013–1 Pattern, Trigonal Slit, for Polyethylene Foam Slab Material.	164.013–1

Material Approved for Incorporation by Reference

46 CFR (PARTS 159–165)—Continued
COAST GUARD, DEPARTMENT OF TRANSPORTATION—Continued
Compressed Gas Association
1725 Jefferson Davis Highway, Suite 1004, Arlington, VA 22202
S–1.2.5.2—Flow Tests of Safety Relief Valves (Pamphlet 1.2, para.   162.018–1
5.2), 1979.

Factory Mutual Engineering and Research (FMER)
ATTN: Librarian, 1151 Boston-Providence Turnpike, Norwood, MA
02062

Class Number 3150, Audible Signal Devices, December 1974	161.002–1; 161.002–4(b)
Class Number 3210, Thermostats for Automatic Fire Detection, July 1978.	161.002–1; 161.002–4(b)
Class Number 3230–3250, Smoke Actuated Detectors for Automatic Fire Alarm Signaling, February 1976.	161.002–1; 161.002–4(b)
Class Number 3260, Flame Radiation Detectors for Automatic Fire Alarm Signaling, September 1994.	161.002–1; 161.002–4(b)
Class Number 3820, Electrical Utilization Equipment, September 1979	161.002–1; 161.002–4(b)

Federal Aviation Administration, Technical Standard Order
Policy and Procedure Br., AWS–110, Aircraft Engineering Division,
Office of Airworthiness, 800 Independence Ave., S.W., Washington,
DC 20591
TSO–C13d, Federal Aviation Administration Standard for Life Pre-   160.176–8
servers, January 3, 1983.

International Electrotechnical Commission (IEC)
1 Rue de Varembe, Geneva, Switzerland
IEC 533 Electromagnetic Compatibility of Electrical and Electronic   161.002–1; 161.002–
Installations in Ships. 1977.   4(b)

International Maritime Organization (IMO)
4 Albert Embankment, London SE1 7SR, England

International Convention for the Safety of Life at Sea, 1974 (SOLAS 74) Consolidated Edition, (including 1992 Amendment to SOLAS 74, 1994 Amendments to SOLAS 74), 1992.	161.002–1; 161.002–4(b)
IMO Resolution A.657(16), Instructions for Action in Survival Craft, dated October 1989.	160.151–21
IMO Resolution A.658(16), Use and Fitting of Retro-Reflective Materials on Life-Saving Appliances, dated November 1989.	160.151–15; 160.151–57
IMO Resolution A.689(17), Recommendation on Testing of Life-Saving Appliances, dated November, 1991 with amendments.	160.151–21; 160.151–27; 160.151–31; 160.151–57

Lloyd's Register of Shipping
ATTN: Publication, 17 Battery Place, New York, NY 10004–1195
LR Type Approval System; Test Specification Number 1, 1990 ....   161.002–1; 161.002–
                                                       4(b)

National Fire Protection Agency
1 Batterymarch Park, Quincy, MA 02269-9101, FAX (617) 770-
3500

NFPA 72 National Fire Alarm Code, 1993	161.002–1; 161.002–4(b)
NFPA 255 Method of Test of Surface Burning Characteristics of Building Materials, 1972.	164.012–1

Title 46–Shipping

COAST GUARD, DEPARTMENT OF TRANSPORTATION—Continued

National Institute of Standards and Technology (formerly National Bureau of Standards)

C/O Superintendent of Documents, U.S. Government Printing Office, Washington, DC 20402, Telephone 202–512-1800

Special Pub. 440 (SD Cat. No. C13.10:440) Color: Universal Language and Dictionary of Names, 1976. ..... 160.010–1; 160.021–1; 160.022–1; 160.024–1; 160.036–1; 160.037–1; 160.057–1; 160.151–15; 160.171–3; 160.174–3; 160.176–9

Department of Defense

DODSSP Standardization Document Order Desk, 700 Robbins Ave., Bldg. 4D, Philadelphia, PA 19111-5098

Federal Specifications:

C–C–91 Candle, Illuminating, D 164.015–1

CCC–C–426 Cloth, Cotton Drill, D 160.048–1; 160.049–1; 160.055–1; 164.018–5

CCC–C–443 Cloth, Cotton, Duck, Plied Filling Yarns, Flat, E, and Amdt. 1. ..... 160.009–1, 164.018–5

CCC–C–700 Cloth, Coated, Vinyl (Artificial Leather), G 160.048–1; 160.049–1; 160.055–1

GG–K–391 Kits (Empty), First Aid, Burn Treatment and Snakebite; and kit contents, A, and Amdt. 4. ..... 160.041–1

GGG–A–926 Axes, C, and Amdt. 2 ..... 160.013–1

HH–M–351 Millboard, Asbestos, E, and Amdt. 2 ..... 164.009–3

L–P–375 Plastic Film, Flexible, Vinyl Chloride, C, and Amdt. 3 ..... 160.002–1; 160.005–1; 160.047–1; 160.048–1; 164.018–1

L–P–390 Plastic Molding and Extrusion Materials, Polyethylene and Copolymers (Low, Medium, and High Density), C, and Amdt. 1. ..... 161.010–1

L–P–393 Plastic Molding Material Polycarbonate, Injection and Extrusion, A, and Amdt. 2. ..... 161.010–1

L–S–300 Sheeting and Tape, Reflective: Non-exposed Lens, Adhesive Backing, B. 164.018–5

QQ–B–611 Brass, Commercial; Bars, plates, rods shapes, Sheets and Strip, A. 161.006–1

QQ–I–706 Iron and Steel; Sheet, tinned (Tinplate), A, and Amdt. 1. ..... 160.061–1

QQ–W–423 Wire, Steel, Corrosion-resisting, B 160.061–1

T–R–605 Rope, Manila and Sisal, B, and Amdt. 3 ..... 160.009–1; 160.028–1; 160.031–1

TT–E–489 Enamel, Alkyd, Gloss (for Exterior and Interior Surfaces), G. 161.001–1; 161.010–1

TT–P–59 Paint, Ready-mixed, International Orange (not for Residential Use), E, and Amdt. 1. ..... 160.035–1

V–T–285 Thread, Polyester, D 160.001–1

V–T–285E, Thread, Polyester, August 21, 1986 ..... 164.023–5

Material Approved for Incorporation by Reference

46 CFR (PARTS 159–165)—Continued
COAST GUARD, DEPARTMENT OF TRANSPORTATION—Continued

V–T–295 Thread, Nylon, D	160.001–1
V–T–295E, Thread, Nylon, August 1, 1985	164.023–5
VV–G–671 Grease; Lubricating, Graphite, E	161.001–1
W–B–101 Batteries and Cells; Dry, H	161.008–1; 161.010–1
WW–C–621 Couplings; Hose, Cotton (Rubberlined) and Linen (Unlined), E, and Amdt. 1.	162.027–1

Federal Standards and Test Method Standards:

No. 141 Paint, Varnish, Lacquer, and Related Materials; Methods of Inspection, Sampling, and Testing, A.	164.018–5
No. 151 Metals, Test Methods, B, and Notice 2	160.062–1
No. 191 Textiles, Test Methods, A	160.002–1; 160.005–1; 160.047–1; 160.052–1; 160.055–1; 160.060–1; 160.171–3
No. 191A (dated July 20, 1978) the following methods:	?????
(1) Method 5100, Strength and Elongation, Breaking of Woven Cloth; Grab Method.	160.076–25; 160.176–13
(2) Method 5132, Strength of Cloth, Tearing; Falling-Pendulum Method.	160.076–25; 160.176–13
(3) Method 5134, Strength of Cloth, Tearing; Tongue Method	160.076–25; 160.176–13
(4) Method 5804.1, Weathering Resistance of Cloth; Accelerated Weathering Method.	160.176–8
(5) Method 5762, Mildew Resistance of Textile Materials; Soil Burial Method.	160.176–8
(6) Method 4010, Length-Weight Relation; Thread; Yards Per Pound (m/kg).	164.023–11
(7) Method 4100, Strength and Elongation, Breaking; and Tenacity; of Thread and Yarn; Single Strand.	164.023–7
(8) Method 5804, Weathering Resistance of Cloth; Accelerated Weathering Method.	164.023–7
No. 370 Instrumental Photometric Measurements of Retroflective Materials and Retroflective Devices, 1977.	164.018–1
No. 595 Colors, A, and Notice 5	160.050–1; 160.055–1
No. 751a, Stitches, Seams, and Stitchings (January 25, 1965)	160.002–1; 160.005–1; 160.009–1; 160.047–1; 160.048–1; 160.048–1; 160.052–1; 160.055–1; 160.060–1; 160.171–3; 160.176–9
No 751a, Stitches, Seams, and Stitchings, Class 300 Lockstitch and Class 700 Single Lockstitch.	160.174–3(b)

Military Specifications:

MIL–B–18 Batteries, Dry, D, and Amdt. 2	161.001–1; 161.010–1

46 CFR (PARTS 159–165)—Continued
COAST GUARD, DEPARTMENT OF TRANSPORTATION—Continued

MIL–B–2766 Batt, Fibrous Glass, Lifesaving Equipment, B, and Interim Amdt. 1.	160.005–1; 160.047–1; 160.048–1
MIL–B–16444 Bronze, Hydraulic (ounce metal): castings, A, and Notice 1.	160.027–1
MIL–C–17415 Cloth, Coated and Webbing, Inflatable Boat and Miscellaneous Use, E, and Amdt. 1.	160.051–1; 164.018–1; 160.151–15
MIL–C–43006 Cloth Laminated, Vinyl-Nylon, High Strength, Flexible, E.	160.049–1; 160.055–1; 164.018–5
MIL–D–3716 Dessicants (Activated) for Dynamic Dehumidification, A, and Amdt. 2.	161.001–1
MIL–D–5531 Desalter Kit Sea water Mark Q, E	160.058–1
MIL–E–15090 Enamel, equipment, light gray (Formula No. 111), B, and Amdt. 2.	160.026–1
MIL–F–859 Fuel Oil, Boiler, E and Amdt. 2	164.015–1; 164.016–1
MIL–I–16923 Insulating Compound, Electrical Embedding, G, and Amdt. 1.	161.010–1
MIL–L–1204 Lamp, Safety, Flame, B	160.016–1
MIL–L–2648 Light, Marker, Distress, Floating Automatic Non-magnetic, D, and Amdt. 2.	161.001–1
MIL–L–7178 Lacquer, Cellulose Nitrate, Glass for Aircraft Use, A, and Amdt. 1.	160.026–1
MIL–L–17653A Life Preserver, Vest, Work Type, Unicellular Plastic, B, and Amdt. 3.	160.053–1
MIL–L–19496 (ships) Lifeboat, CO_2 Inflatable Mark 5, Mod 1, 15-person Capacity, D, and Amdt. 1.	160.051–1
MIL–L–24611 Life Preserver Support Package For Life Preserver, MK 4, dated May 18, 1982.	160.176–8
MIL–L–45505 Line-throwing Apparatuses, Rocket and Projectile Units, A.	160.040–1
MIL–M–15617 Mats, Fibrous Glass for Reinforcing Plastics, A, and Amdt. 1.	160.035–1
MIL–P–79 Plastic Rods and Tubes, Thermosetting, Laminated, C, and Amdt. 2.	160.001–1; 161.010–1
MIL–P–17549 Plastic Laminates, Fibrous Glass Reinforced, Marine Structural, C, and Amdt. 2.	160.035–1
MIL–P–18066 Plywood, Ship and Boat Construction, B	160.035–1
MIL–P–19644 Plastic Foam, Molded Polystyrene (Expanded Bead Type), C.	160.010–1; 160.035–1
MIL–P–21929 Plastic Materials, Cellular Polyurethane, Foam-in-Place, Rigid (2 and 4 Pounds Per Cubic Foot), B, and Amdt. 1.	160.010–1; 160.035–1
MIL–P–40619 Plastic Material, Cellular, Polystyrene (for Buoyancy Applications), A.	160.010–1; 160.035.1; 164.013–1
MIL–R–900 Rubber Gasket Material, 45 Durometer Hardness, F	161.001–1
MIL–R–2765 Rubber Sheet, Strip, Extruded, and Molded Shapes, Synthetic, Oil Resistant, C.	161.001–1
MIL–R–7575 Resin, Polyester, Low-Pressure Laminating, C, and Amdt. 2.	160.035–1
MIL–R–16847 Ring Buoys, Lifesaving, Unicellular Plastic, E, and Amdt. 2.	160.050–1
MIL–R–21607 Resins, Polyester, Low-Pressure Laminating, Fire-retardant, D.	160.010–1; 160.035–1; 164.018–5

Material Approved for Incorporation by Reference

46 CFR (PARTS 159–165)—Continued
COAST GUARD, DEPARTMENT OF TRANSPORTATION—Continued

MIL–R–23139 Rocket Motors, Surfaced Launched, Development and Qualification Requirements for, B.	160.040–1
MIL–S–18655 Signal, Smoke and Illumination, Marine, C	160.023–1
MIL–T–43548C, Thread, Polyester Core: Cotton-, Rayon-, or Polyester-Covered, September 30, 1986.	164.023–5
MIL–T–43624A, Thread, Polyester, Spun, January 22, 1982	164.023–5
MIL–W–530 Webbing, Textile, Cotton, General Purpose, Natural or in Colors, F, and Amdt. 2.	160.002–1; 160.005–1; 160.047–1; 160.052–1; 160.055–1

Underwriters Laboratories, Inc.

Available from: Global Engineering Documents, 15 Inverness Way East, Englewood, CO 80112, Telephone (800) 854–7179 or

Global Engineering Documents, 7730 Carondelet Ave., Suite 470, Clayton, MO 63105, Telephone (800) 854–7179

UL 38 Standard for Manually Actuated Signaling Boxes For Use With Fire-Protective Signaling Systems, 1994.	161.002–1; 161.002–4(b)
UL 62–80 Flexible Cord and Fixture Wire	161.006–1
UL 198B–81 Class H Fuses	161.004–1
UL 268 Standard for Smoke Detectors for Fire Protective Signaling Systems, 1989 (revisions through June, 1994).	161.002–1; 161.002–4(b)
UL 521 Standard for Heat Detectors for Fire Protective Signaling Systems, 1993 (revisions through October, 1994).	161.002–1; 161.002–4(b)
UL 864 Standard for Control Units for Fire Protective Signaling Systems, 1991 (revisions through May, 1994).	161.002–1; 161.002–4(b)
UL 1123, Marine Buoyant Devices, February 17, 1995	159.001–4; 159.001–3; 160.076–35
UL 1180, Fully Inflatable Recreational Personal Flotation Devices, May 15, 1995.	160.076–7; 160.076–21; 160.076–23; 160.076–25; 160.076–27; 160.076–29; 160.076–31; 160.076–37; 160.076–39
UL 1191, Components for Personal Flotation Devices, Third Edition, May 16, 1995.	160.076–21; 160.076–25; 160.076–39; 164.013–2; 164.013–3; 164.013–5
UL 1196 Standard for Floating Waterlights, Second Edition, March 23, 1987.	161.010–1; 161.010–2; 161.010–4

Table of CFR Titles and Chapters
(Revised as of September 30, 1997)

Title 1—General Provisions

I Administrative Committee of the Federal Register (Parts 1—49)
II Office of the Federal Register (Parts 50—299)
IV Miscellaneous Agencies (Parts 400—500)

Title 2—[Reserved]

Title 3—The President

I Executive Office of the President (Parts 100—199)

Title 4—Accounts

I General Accounting Office (Parts 1—99)
II Federal Claims Collection Standards (General Accounting Office—Department of Justice) (Parts 100—299)

Title 5—Administrative Personnel

I Office of Personnel Management (Parts 1—1199)
II Merit Systems Protection Board (Parts 1200—1299)
III Office of Management and Budget (Parts 1300—1399)
IV Advisory Committee on Federal Pay (Parts 1400—1499)
V The International Organizations Employees Loyalty Board (Parts 1500—1599)
VI Federal Retirement Thrift Investment Board (Parts 1600—1699)
VII Advisory Commission on Intergovernmental Relations (Parts 1700—1799)
VIII Office of Special Counsel (Parts 1800—1899)
IX Appalachian Regional Commission (Parts 1900—1999)
XI Armed Forces Retirement Home (Part 2100)
XIV Federal Labor Relations Authority, General Counsel of the Federal Labor Relations Authority and Federal Service Impasses Panel (Parts 2400—2499)
XV Office of Administration, Executive Office of the President (Parts 2500—2599)
XVI Office of Government Ethics (Parts 2600—2699)
XXI Department of the Treasury (Parts 3100—3199)
XXII Federal Deposit Insurance Corporation (Part 3201)
XXIII Department of Energy (Part 3301)

Title 6—[Reserved]

Title 7—Agriculture

Title 7—Agriculture—Continued

Title 8—Aliens and Nationality

Title 9—Animals and Animal Products

Title 10—Energy

Title 11—Federal Elections

Title 12—Banks and Banking

Title 12—Banks and Banking—Continued

Title 13—Business Credit and Assistance

Title 14—Aeronautics and Space

Title 15—Commerce and Foreign Trade

383

Title 15—Commerce and Foreign Trade—Continued

Title 16—Commercial Practices

Title 17—Commodity and Securities Exchanges

Title 18—Conservation of Power and Water Resources

Title 19—Customs Duties

Title 20—Employees' Benefits

384

Title 24—Housing and Urban Development

Title 25—Indians

387

Title 30—Mineral Resources

Title 31—Money and Finance: Treasury

Title 32—National Defense

389

Title 45—Public Welfare—Continued

Title 46—Shipping

Title 47—Telecommunication

Title 48—Federal Acquisition Regulations System

Title 49—Transportation

Title 49—Transportation—Continued

Title 50—Wildlife and Fisheries

CFR Index and Finding Aids

Alphabetical List of Agencies Appearing in the CFR
(Revised as of September 30, 1997)

Agency	CFR Title, Subtitle or Chapter
ACTION	45, XII
Administrative Committee of the Federal Register	1, I
Advanced Research Projects Agency	32, I
Advisory Commission on Intergovernmental Relations	5, VII
Advisory Committee on Federal Pay	5, IV
Advisory Council on Historic Preservation	36, VIII
African Development Foundation	22, XV
Federal Acquisition Regulation	48, 57
Agency for International Development, United States	22, II
Federal Acquisition Regulation	48, 7
Agricultural Marketing Service	7, I, IX, X, XI
Agricultural Research Service	7, V
Agriculture Department	
Agricultural Marketing Service	7, I, IX, X, XI
Agricultural Research Service	7, V
Animal and Plant Health Inspection Service	7, III; 9, I
Chief Financial Officer, Office of	7, XXX
Commodity Credit Corporation	7, XIV
Cooperative State Research, Education, and Extension Service	7, XXXIV
Economic Research Service	7, XXXVII
Energy, Office of	7, XXIX
Environmental Quality, Office of	7, XXXI
Farm Service Agency	7, VII, XVIII
Federal Acquisition Regulation	48, 4
Federal Crop Insurance Corporation	7, IV
Food and Consumer Service	7, II
Food Safety and Inspection Service	9, III
Foreign Agricultural Service	7, XV
Forest Service	36, II
Grain Inspection, Packers and Stockyards Administration	7, VIII; 9, II
Information Resources Management, Office of	7, XXVII
Inspector General, Office of	7, XXVI
National Agricultural Library	7, XLI
National Agricultural Statistics Service	7, XXXVI
Natural Resources Conservation Service	7, VI
Operations, Office of	7, XXVIII
Rural Business-Cooperative Service	7, XVIII, XLII
Rural Development Administration	7, XLII
Rural Housing Service	7, XVIII, XXXV
Rural Telephone Bank	7, XVI
Rural Utilities Service	7, XVII, XVIII, XLII
Secretary of Agriculture, Office of	7, Subtitle A
Transportation, Office of	7, XXXIII
World Agricultural Outlook Board	7, XXXVIII
Air Force Department	32, VII
Federal Acquisition Regulation Supplement	48, 53
Alaska Natural Gas Transportation System, Office of the Federal Inspector	10, XV
Alcohol, Tobacco and Firearms, Bureau of	27, I
AMTRAK	49, VII
American Battle Monuments Commission	36, IV
American Indians, Office of the Special Trustee	25, VII

Agency	CFR Title, Subtitle or Chapter
Animal and Plant Health Inspection Service	7, III; 9, I
Appalachian Regional Commission	5, IX
Architectural and Transportation Barriers Compliance Board	36, XI
Arctic Research Commission	45, XXIII
Armed Forces Retirement Home	5, XI
Arms Control and Disarmament Agency, United States	22, VI
Army Department	32, V
Engineers, Corps of	33, II; 36, III
Federal Acquisition Regulation	48, 51
Assassination Records Review Board	36, XIV
Benefits Review Board	20, VII
Bilingual Education and Minority Languages Affairs, Office of	34, V
Blind or Severely Disabled, Committee for Purchase From People Who Are	41, 51
Board for International Broadcasting	22, XIII
Census Bureau	15, I
Central Intelligence Agency	32, XIX
Chief Financial Officer, Office of	7, XXX
Child Support Enforcement, Office of	45, III
Children and Families, Administration for	45, II, III, IV, X
Christopher Columbus Quincentenary Jubilee Commission	45, XXII
Civil Rights, Commission on	45, VII
Civil Rights, Office for	34, I
Coast Guard	33, I; 46, I; 49, IV
Commerce Department	44, IV
Census Bureau	15, I'
Economic Affairs, Under Secretary	37, V
Economic Analysis, Bureau of	15, VIII
Economic Development Administration	13, III
Emergency Management and Assistance	44, IV
Export Administration, Bureau of	15, VII
Federal Acquisition Regulation	48, 13
Fishery Conservation and Management	50, VI
Foreign-Trade Zones Board	15, IV
International Trade Administration	15, III; 19, III
National Institute of Standards and Technology	15, II
National Marine Fisheries Service	50, II, IV
National Oceanic and Atmospheric Administration	15, IX; 50, II, III, IV, VI
National Telecommunications and Information Administration	15, XXIII; 47, III
National Weather Service	15, IX
Patent and Trademark Office	37, I
Productivity, Technology and Innovation, Assistant Secretary for	37, IV
Secretary of Commerce, Office of	15, Subtitle A
Technology, Under Secretary for	37, V
Technology Administration	15, XI
Technology Policy, Assistant Secretary for	37, IV
Commercial Space Transportation	14, III
Commodity Credit Corporation	7, XIV
Commodity Futures Trading Commission	5, XLI; 17, I
Community Planning and Development, Office of Assistant Secretary for	24, V, VI
Community Services, Office of	45, X
Comptroller of the Currency	12, I
Construction Industry Collective Bargaining Commission	29, IX
Consumer Product Safety Commission	5, LXXI; 16, II
Cooperative State Research, Education, and Extension Service	7, XXXIV
Copyright Office	37, II
Cost Accounting Standards Board	48, 99
Council on Environmental Quality	40, V
Customs Service, United States	19, I
Defense Contract Audit Agency	32, I
Defense Department	5, XXVI; 32, Subtitle A
Advanced Research Projects Agency	32, I
Air Force Department	32, VII

397

399

400

401

Agency	CFR Title, Subtitle or Chapter
Federal Employees Health Benefits Acquisition Regulation	48, 16
Postal Rate Commission	5, XLVI; 39, III
Postal Service, United States	5, LX; 39, I
Postsecondary Education, Office of	34, VI
President's Commission on White House Fellowships	1, IV
Presidential Commission on the Assignment of Women in the Armed Forces	32, XXIX
Presidential Documents	3
Prisons, Bureau of	28, V
Productivity, Technology and Innovation, Assistant Secretary	37, IV
Public Contracts, Department of Labor	41, 50
Public and Indian Housing, Office of Assistant Secretary for	24, IX
Public Health Service	42, I
Railroad Retirement Board	20, II
Reclamation, Bureau of	43, I
Refugee Resettlement, Office of	45, IV
Regional Action Planning Commissions	13, V
Relocation Allowances	41, 302
Research and Special Programs Administration	49, I
Rural Business-Cooperative Service	7, XVIII, XLII
Rural Development Administration	7, XLII
Rural Housing Service	7, XVIII, XXXV
Rural Telephone Bank	7, XVI
Rural Utilities Service	7, XVII, XVIII, XLII
Saint Lawrence Seaway Development Corporation	33, IV
Science and Technology Policy, Office of	32, XXIV
Science and Technology Policy, Office of, and National Security Council	47, II
Secret Service	31, IV
Securities and Exchange Commission	17, II
Selective Service System	32, XVI
Small Business Administration	13, I
Smithsonian Institution	36, V
Social Security Administration	20, III; 48, 23
Soldiers' and Airmen's Home, United States	5, XI
Special Counsel, Office of	5, VIII
Special Education and Rehabilitative Services, Office of	34, III
State Department	22, I
Federal Acquisition Regulation	48, 6
Surface Mining and Reclamation Appeals, Board of	30, III
Surface Mining Reclamation and Enforcement, Office of	30, VII
Surface Transportation Board	49, X
Susquehanna River Basin Commission	18, VIII
Technology Administration	15, XI
Technology Policy, Assistant Secretary for	37, IV
Technology, Under Secretary for	37, V
Tennessee Valley Authority	5, LXIX; 18, XIII
Thrift Depositor Protection Oversight Board	12, XV
Thrift Supervision Office, Department of the Treasury	12, V
Trade Representative, United States, Office of	15, XX
Transportation, Department of	5, L
Coast Guard	33, I; 46, I; 49, IV
Commercial Space Transportation	14, III
Contract Appeals, Board of	48, 63
Emergency Management and Assistance	44, IV
Federal Acquisition Regulation	48, 12
Federal Aviation Administration	14, I
Federal Highway Administration	23, I, II; 49, III
Federal Railroad Administration	49, II
Federal Transit Administration	49, VI
Maritime Administration	46, II
National Highway Traffic Safety Administration	23, II, III; 49, V
Research and Special Programs Administration	49, I
Saint Lawrence Seaway Development Corporation	33, IV
Secretary of Transportation, Office of	14, II; 49, Subtitle A
Surface Transportation Board	49, X

Agency	CFR Title, Subtitle or Chapter
Transportation, Office of	7, XXXIII
Travel Allowances	41, 301
Treasury Department	5, XXI; 17, IV
Alcohol, Tobacco and Firearms, Bureau of	27, I
Community Development Financial Institutions Fund	12, XVIII
Comptroller of the Currency	12, I
Customs Service, United States	19, I
Engraving and Printing, Bureau of	31, VI
Federal Acquisition Regulation	48, 10
Federal Law Enforcement Training Center	31, VII
Fiscal Service	31, II
Foreign Assets Control, Office of	31, V
Internal Revenue Service	26, I
International Investment, Office of	31, VIII
Monetary Offices	31, I
Secret Service	31, IV
Secretary of the Treasury, Office of	31, Subtitle A
Thrift Supervision, Office of	12, V
Truman, Harry S. Scholarship Foundation	45, XVIII
United States and Canada, International Joint Commission	22, IV
United States and Mexico, International Boundary and Water Commission, United States Section	22, XI
United States Enrichment Corporation	10, XI
Utah Reclamation Mitigation and Conservation Commission	43, III
Veterans Affairs Department	38, I
Federal Acquisition Regulation	48, 8
Veterans' Employment and Training, Office of the Assistant Secretary for	41, 61; 20, IX
Vice President of the United States, Office of	32, XXVIII
Vocational and Adult Education, Office of	34, IV
Wage and Hour Division	29, V
Water Resources Council	18, VI
Workers' Compensation Programs, Office of	20, I
World Agricultural Outlook Board	7, XXXVIII

List of CFR Sections Affected

All changes in this volume of the Code of Federal Regulations which were made by documents published in the FEDERAL REGISTER since January 1, 1986, are enumerated in the following list. Entries indicate the nature of the changes effected. Page numbers refer to FEDERAL REGISTER pages. The user should consult the entries for chapters and parts as well as sections for revisions.

For the period before January 1, 1986, see the "List of CFR Sections Affected, 1949–1963, 1964–1972, and 1973–1985" published in seven separate volumes.

46 CFR—Continued

46 CFR—Continued

1989

46 CFR

1990

(No regulations were published from
January 1, 1990 through December 31,
1990)

1991

46 CFR

46 CFR—Continued

1992

46 CFR

1993

46 CFR

46 CFR—Continued

1994

(No regulations were published from January 1, 1994 through December 31, 1994)

1995

46 CFR

○